The Stuart Editions

THE COMPLETE ENGLISH POETRY
OF
JOHN MILTON

The Stuart Editions

J. Max Patrick, *series editor*

ALREADY PUBLISHED

An Anthology of Jacobean Drama, VOLUME I

EDITED WITH AN INTRODUCTION, NOTES, AND VARIANTS
BY RICHARD C. HARRIER

The Complete Poetry of Ben Jonson

EDITED WITH AN INTRODUCTION, NOTES, AND VARIANTS
BY WILLIAM B. HUNTER, JR.

Short Fiction of the Seventeenth Century

SELECTED AND EDITED BY CHARLES C. MISH

The Complete Poetry of Robert Herrick

EDITED WITH AN INTRODUCTION AND NOTES
BY J. MAX PATRICK

The Complete English Poetry of John Milton

ARRANGED IN CHRONOLOGICAL ORDER WITH AN
INTRODUCTION, NOTES, AND VARIANTS
BY JOHN T. SHAWCROSS

The Stuart Editions

The Complete English Poetry

of

JOHN MILTON

(EXCLUDING HIS TRANSLATIONS OF PSALMS 80–88)

ARRANGED IN CHRONOLOGICAL ORDER
WITH AN INTRODUCTION, NOTES, VARIANTS,
AND LITERAL TRANSLATIONS OF THE FOREIGN LANGUAGE POEMS
BY
JOHN T. SHAWCROSS

New York University Press
1963

INTRODUCTION

Arranged according to probable date of composition of the verse, this edition brings together all original poems and poetic paraphrases written by Milton exclusive of two sets of psalm translations. Included therefore are nine poems not published in either of the two collected editions of the minor poems appearing in Milton's lifetime: two verses found with his Commonplace Book, a third poem on Hobson the university carrier possibly by Milton, four sonnets, and two Latin epigrams from two prose works.

Because of the exigencies of space, it has been necessary to omit all foreign language versions of the poems, including Horace's Latin, and *Psalms 80–88*. However, the poems originally written in Latin, Greek, or Italian are given complete in new translations, which attempt insofar as possible to follow the original lines. The editor alone is responsible for these translations. The two sets of psalms are important to Milton's prosodic development, but since additional pages had to be found to bring this edition into one volume, the deletion of these psalms best afforded the retention of all other poems and materials for study of Milton's accomplishments. Given in chronological order for these psalms are notes indicating their importance and date. Textual notes are retained for all foreign language poems and for both these sets of psalms. I have attempted to narrow the dates of composition as much as is presently possible; when apparent proof of date is missing a question mark is added. But the reader should bear in mind that such dating is open to question and that it may be in dispute by scholars. Full discussion of dating will be found in the textual notes.

Milton frequently altered poems after he had recorded them in the earliest versions which have survived, but perhaps only *Arcades, A Mask, Samson Agonistes, Paradise Regain'd,* and *Paradise Lost* underwent extensive revisions. Accordingly, I place these poems, except for *Paradise Regain'd,* under the date of what I believe their first complete (though not finally revised) composition; *Paradise Regain'd* has been excepted because the received text seems to me to be an extensive transformation of what may have been an early version. The dating of the three major poems—*Samson Agonistes*, *Paradise Re-gain'd*, and *Paradise Lost*—is particularly uncertain and has been frequently challenged.

Textual principles are explained in the introduction to the textual notes. Generally, the basic text is that which seems to be closest to Milton—holograph copy, then scribal copy, and so forth. Alterations from the basic text are few; and all verbal variants in known significant texts are recorded in the textual notes. All dates for years are given in new style. Milton's prose works are cited from first editions, the paging of which is indicated in the Yale edition of the prose.

The advice and knowledge of Professors J. Max Patrick and William B. Hunter, Jr., have been so pervasively instructive to me that I feel their influence throughout this edition in both great matters and small. But the decisions underlying the texts and commentary—and thus any faults—are my own.

BIOGRAPHICAL TABLE

1608
Born (Dec. 9), Bread St., Cheapside, London.

1618 ?–1620 ?
Tutored by Thomas Young.

1620 ?–1624
At St. Paul's School, London, under Alexander Gill. C. 1623 or 1624 family moved to home in St. Martin's-in-the-Fields, Westminster(?).

1625–1632 July
At Christ's College, Cambridge, ostensibly to enter clerical life. C. 1631 family moved to home in Hammersmith.

1625
Admitted to Christ's College (Feb. 12), at which he matriculated on Apr. 9.

1626
Period of rustication (Lent term through spring vacation).

1629
Bachelor's degree conferred (Mar. 26).

1632
Master's degree conferred (July 3).

1632 July–1635 ?
At Hammersmith with family. "A Mask" ("Comus") performed, Sept. 29, 1634.

1635 ?–1638
At Horton, Bucks, with family. Frequently in London after death of mother, Apr. 3, 1637. Publications: *A Mask* (1637/8 ?); "Lycidas" in *Justa Edovardo King naufrago* (1638).

1638 Apr. ?–1639 Aug. ?
Continental tour to France and Italy.

1639 autumn–1648
Tutoring until c. 1647. Studies continued; prose and poetic

writings, some published and others begun. Residence: St. Bride's Churchyard (a few months) and Aldersgate St., London (1639–Sept. ? 1645).

1641

Publications: "Postscript" (?) in Smectymnuus, *An Answer to a Booke entituled, An Humble Remonstrance* (Mar.); *Of Reformation* (May ?); *Of Prelatical Episcopacy* (July ?); *Animadversions upon the Remonstrants Defence, against Smectymnuus* (July).

1642

Publications: *The Reason of Church Government* (Feb. ?); *An Apology against a Pamphlet call'd A Modest Confutation* (Apr.). Married to Mary Powell (May ?), who soon returned to her family's home in Forest Hill (July ?).

1643

Father came to live with Milton (Apr.). Publication: *The Doctrine and Discipline of Divorce* (Ed. 1, c. Aug.).

1644

Publications: *Doctrine and Discipline* (Ed. 2, enlarged, Feb.); *Of Education* (June); *The Judgement of Martin Bucer* (Aug.); *Areopagitica* (Nov.). Sight began noticeably to fail (autumn ?).

1645

Publications: *Tetrachordon* and *Colasterion* (Mar.); *Poems* (Ed. 1, autumn ?). Wife Mary returned home (summer ?). Residence: Barbican (Sept. ?–autumn 1647).

1646

Daughter Anne born (July 29).

1647

Father died (Mar. 13 ?). Residence: High Holborn (autumn–c. Mar. 1649).

1648

Daughter Mary born (Oct. 25).

1649–1660 ?

Period of public service as Secretary for Foreign Tongues to Council of State: appointed Mar. 15, 1649; continued in position until at least Oct. 22, 1659.

1649

Publications: *The Tenure of Kings and Magistrates* (Ed. 1, Feb.); *Observations upon the Articles of Peace* (May); *Eikonoklastes* (Ed. 1, Oct., in answer to *Eikon Basilike,* c. Feb.). Residence: Charing Cross (c. Mar.–Nov.) and Scotland Yard, Whitehall (Nov.–Dec. 1651).

1650

Publications: *Tenure* (Ed. 2, enlarged, Feb.); *Eikonoklastes* (Ed. 2, enlarged). Probably lost sight of left eye.

1651

Publication: *Joannis MiltonI Angli Pro Populo Anglicano Defensio* (Feb., in answer to Salmasius' *Defensio regia pro Carolo I,* which appeared in England by May 1649; revision of so-called "Defensio prima" was published in Oct. 1658. Also *Joannis Philippi Angli Responsio Ad Apologiam Anonymi,* by the younger surviving son of Milton's sister Anne, published toward end of year in answer to John Rowland's *Pro Rege et Populo Anglicano Apologia* written against "Defensio prima.") Son John born (Mar. 16). Became totally blind before Feb. 1652, and granted assistance in secretaryship. Residence: Petty France, Westminster (Dec.–Sept. ? 1660).

1652

Daughter Deborah born (May 2); wife Mary died (May 5 ?); and son John died (June 16 ?). Work on poetry and prose (?) through 1658.

1654

Publication: *Joannis MiltonI Angli Pro Populo Anglicano Defensio Secunda* (May, in answer to Pierre du Moulin's *Regii Sanguinis Clamor,* Aug. ? 1652, which attacked the Commonwealth).

1655

Publication: *Joannis MiltonI Angli pro se Defensio* (Aug., in answer to Alexander More's *Fides Publica,* Oct. ? 1654).

1656

Married to Katherine Woodcock (Nov. 12).

1657

Daughter Katherine born (Oct. 19).

1658

Second wife, Katherine, died (Feb. 3); daughter Katherine
died (Mar. 17). Publication: edited Sir Walter Raleigh's
The Cabinet-Council (May ?).

1659

Publications and other writings: *A Treatise of Civil Power*
(Feb.); *Considerations Touching the likeliest means to
remove Hirelings* (Aug.); *A Letter to a Friend, Concerning the Ruptures of the Commonwealth* (written
Oct. 20, first published by John Toland in 1698); possible work, "Proposalls of certaine expedients for the preventing of a civill war now feard, & the settling of a
firme government" (autumn ?, first published in Columbia Milton).

1660

Period of transition between governments, loss of office, and
governmental harassment and imprisonment. Publica-
tions and other writings: *The Readie & Easie Way to
Establish A Free Commonwealth* (Mar.; Ed. 2, revised,
c. Apr.); *The Present Means, and brief Delineation of a
Free Commonwealth* ("Letter to General Monk," written
after Mar. 3, first published by John Toland in 1698);
Brief Notes Upon a Late Sermon (Apr.). Residence:
Holborn near Red Lyon Fields (Sept. ?–early 1661).
Escaped death penalty under Act of Oblivion of Aug.
29; in prison, after burning of books written by him
(Oct. ?–Dec. 15).

1661–1674

Period of general retirement; work on poetry and prose.

1661

Residence: Jewin St. (early 1661–Mar. ? 1663).

1663

Married to third wife, Elizabeth Minshull (Feb. 24). Residence: Artillery Walk, Bunhill Fields (Mar. ?–1674).

1665

Stayed at Chalfont St. Giles, Bucks, to escape plague (June ?–
Feb. ? 1666).

1667

Publication: *Paradise Lost* (Ed. 1; Aug. ?; further issues,
1668, 1669).

1669
Publication: *Accedence Commenc't Grammar* (June ?).

1670
Publication: *The History of Britain* (Nov. ?).

1671
Publication: *Paradise Regain'd* and *Samson Agonistes* (early in year).

1672
Publication: *Joannis Miltoni Angli, Artis Logicæ Plenior Institutio* (May ?).

1673
Publications: *Of True Religion, Hæresie, Schism, Toleration* (May ?); *Poems* (Ed. 2, enlarged, together with *Of Education,* Ed. 2, Nov. ?).

1674
Publications: *Joannis Miltoni Angli, Epistolarum Familiarium Liber Unis* (with college prolusions, May); *Paradise Lost* (Ed. 2, revised, July); *A Declaration, or Letters Patent* (July ?). Died, apparently of gout (Nov. 8 ?); buried in St. Giles, Cripplegate (Nov. 12).

Posthumous publications: *Literæ Pseudo-Senatûs Anglicani* (Oct. ? 1676; a free and inaccurate English version appeared in 1682); *Mr. John Miltons Character of the Long Parliament* (Apr. ? 1681); *A Brief History of Moscovia* (Feb. ? 1682); *Letters of State* (translated by Edward Phillips, with four sonnets and a biographical memoir, 1694); *Joannis Miltoni Angli De Doctrina Christiana* (1825; translated and published in same year by Charles R. Sumner).

CONTENTS

ABBREVIATIONS

The following abbreviations, in addition to those which are commonplace, those which are standard for books of the Bible, and those which are easily recognizable short forms, will be found in this edition:

Aen.	*Aeneid*	*PQ*	*Philological Quarterly*
Ec.	Virgil, *Eclogues*	*PR*	*Paradise Regain'd*
El.	*Elegy*	*Ps.*	*Psalm*
FQ	*Faerie Queene*	*Rep.*	Plato, *Republic*
HLQ	*Huntington Library Quarterly*	*RES*	*Review of English Studies*
Meta.	Ovid, *Metamorphoses*	*SA*	*Samson Agonistes*
MLN	*Modern Language Notes*	*Son.*	*Sonnet*
MLR	*Modern Language Review*	*SP*	*Studies in Philology*
NQ	*Notes and Queries*	*TLS*	*Times Literary Supplement*
Od.	*Odyssey*	*TM*	Trinity Manuscript
PL	*Paradise Lost*	*UTQ*	*University of Toronto Quarterly*
PMLA	*Publications of the Modern Language Association*		

A PARAPHRASE ON PSALM 114[1]

When the blest seed of *Terah*'s faithfull Son,[2]
After long toil their liberty had won,
And past from *Pharian*[3] fields to *Canaan* Land,
Led by the strength of the Almighties hand,
Jehovah's wonders were in *Israel* shown,   5
His praise and glory was in *Israel* known.
That[4] saw the troubl'd Sea, and shivering fled,
And sought to hide his froth-becurled head
Low in the earth, *Jordans* clear streams recoil,
As a faint host that hath receiv'd the foil.[5]   10
The high, huge-bellied Mountains skip like Rams
Amongst their Ews, the little Hills like Lambs.
Why fled the Ocean? And why skipt the Mountains?
Why turned *Jordan* toward his Crystall Fountains?
Shake earth, and at the presence be agast   15
Of him that ever was, and ay shall last,
That glassy flouds from rugged rocks can crush,
And make soft rills from fiery flint-stones gush.

(1624)

[1] Harris Fletcher, analyzing the grammar school lesson of paraphrasing from one language to another, points out that "Milton's
effort was cast into eighteen lines, or two more than the original
verse divisions called for, and was more or less done in this fashion: lines 2, 4, 8, 10 were really added lines; but in lines 13–14
Milton compressed the four lines of verses 5 and 6 . . ." (*Intellectual Development*, I, 191). Compare the translation of Milton's
rendition of this same psalm in Greek.
[2] Abraham; the original cites only Jacob, the blest seed of
Abraham.
[3] Egyptian.
[4] "the strength of the Almighties hand," object of "saw."
[5] the sword; therefore, "hath been driven back."

PSALM 136[1]

Let us with a gladsom mind
Praise the Lord, for he is kind.
   For his mercies ay endure,
   Ever faithfull, ever sure.

Let us blaze his Name abroad,   5
For of gods he is the God.
   For, &c.

O let us his praises tell,
That doth the wrathfull tyrants quell.   10
   For, &c.

That with his miracles doth make
Amazed Heav'n and Earth to shake.
   For, &c.   15

That by his wisdom did create
The painted Heav'ns so full of state.
   For, &c.   20

That did the solid Earth ordain
To rise above the watry plain.
   For, &c.

That by his all-commanding might   25
Did fill the new-made world with light.
   For, &c.

And caus'd the Golden-tressed Sun
All the day long his cours to run.   30
   For, &c.

The horned Moon to shine by night
Amongst her spangled sisters bright.
   For, &c.   35

[1] Though this paraphrase elaborates upon the Hebrew, its result, unlike that in *Ps.* 114, is relative simplicity of language and image. Phrases have been traced to George Buchanan (in his Latin paraphrases of the psalms) and to Joshua Sylvester (in his translation of DuBartas' *Divine Weeks and Works*). Milton omitted verses 12, 18, and 22 of the original.

He with his thunder-clasping hand
Smote the first-born of *Egypt* Land.
   For, &c.   40

And in despight of *Pharao* fell,
He brought from thence his *Israel.*
   For, &c.

The ruddy waves he cleft in twain,   45
Of the *Erythræan* main.[2]
   For, &c.

The floods stood still like Walls of Glass,
While the Hebrew Bands did pass.   50
   For, &c.

But full soon they did devour
The Tawny[3] King with all his power.
   For, &c.   55

His chosen people he did bless
In the wastfull Wildernes.
   For, &c.   60

In bloody battail he brought down
Kings of prowess and renown.
   For, &c.

He foild bold *Seon* and his host,   65
That rul'd the *Amorrean* coast.
   For, &c.

And large-limb'd *Og* he did subdue,
With all his over-hardy crew.   70
   For, &c.

And to his servant *Israel*
He gave their Land therin to dwell.
   For, &c.   75

He hath with a piteous eye
Beheld us in our misery.
   For, &c.   80

And freed us from the slavery
Of the invading enemy.
   For, &c.

[2] the Red Sea.
[3] dark-complexioned.

All living creatures he doth feed,   85
And with full hand supplies their need.
   For, *&c.*

Let us therfore warble forth
His mighty Majesty and worth.   90
   For, *&c.*

That his mansion hath on high
Above the reach of mortall eye.
   For his mercies ay endure,   95
   Ever faithfull, ever sure.

(1624)

APOLOGUS DE RUSTICO ET HERO
(The Fable of the Peasant and the Overlord)[1]

Every year a peasant gathered from an appletree the most
savory fruit / and gave the choice apples to his overlord who
lived in the city. / He, pleased with the unbelievable sweetness of the fruit, / transferred the apple tree itself to his own
gardens. / The tree, fruitful up to this time but weak from
old age, [5] / when moved from its accustomed soil, instantly
withered to inactivity. / When at last it was evident to the
overlord that he had been deceived / by a vain hope, he
cursed the hands so swift in bringing loss. / And he cried,
"Alas, how much more satisfactory it was to receive / with
a grateful heart these gifts, although small, from my ten-
ant. [10] / Would I could curb my greed and my voracious
gullet: / now both the fruit and its parent are lost to me."

(1624–25)

CARMINA ELEGIACA
(Elegiac Verses)[1]

Arise, up, arise. Now that it is time, shake off slumbers; /
light is appearing; leave the props of your languid bed. / Now

[1] A version of a popular fable by Aesop, Milton's twelve elegiac
lines were derived from ten by Mantuan (*Sylvarum*, Bk. 4).

---

[1] These and the following verses were written on a loose sheet
found in Milton's Commonplace Book with only this title given for
the first. Grammar school exercises, they versify a prose theme on
early rising found on the reverse of the sheet: "Mane citus lectum
fuge" ("Quick, hasten from your bed in the morning").

sings the sentinel cock, the harbinger bird / of the sun, and, watchful, calls everyone to his own affairs. / The flaming Titan[2] thrusts his head from the Eastern waves [5] / and scatters his glittering splendor through the joyful fields. / The Daulian[3] modulates her melodious song from the oak / and the gentle lark pours forth her perfect notes. / Now the wild rose breathes forth its fragrant perfumes; / now the violets diffuse their scent and the grain grows rapidly. [10] / Behold, the fruitful consort of Zephyr[4] clothes the fields with new growth, / and the soil becomes moist with glassy dew. / Lazy one, you are not likely to find such things in your soft bed, / when tranquil sleep weighs down your wearied eyes. / There dreams interrupt dull slumbers [15] / and many griefs disturb your mind. / There the seeds of a wasting malady are generated. / What strength can a listless man be capable of? / Arise, up, arise. Now that it is time, shake off slumbers; / light is appearing; leave the props of your languid bed. [20]

(1624–25)

"IGNAVUS SATRAPAM DEDECET . . ."
("Slothful sleep . . .")[1]

Slothful sleep is unbecoming to a famous governor / who presides over people divided into many sections of the land. / While the warlike son of old Daunas[2] / lay prone on his purple couch, / bold Euryalus and quick Nisus [5] / cunningly attacked in the frightening night / the sleeping Rutilians and the Volscian camp: / hence slaughter arose and discordant shout. . . .

(Incomplete; 1624–25)

2 Hyperion, here identified with the Sun.
3 the swallow.
4 Chloris, wife of the West Wind.

---

1 The meter is the lesser Aesclepiad (an irregular verse form used by Horace) with a spondee for the first foot.

2 Turnus, king of the Rutili and leader of the Volscians and other Italian tribes who resisted Aeneas' invasion. When in a drunken sleep, his army was attacked by Euryalus and Nisus (Aen., IX, 314–66).

ELEGIA PRIMA
(Elegy 1)

To Charles Diodati[1]

At last, dear friend, your letter has reached me / and its news-filled paper conveyed your words, / conveyed them from the western region of the Dee near Chester, / from which with downward flow it seeks the Irish Sea. / I am greatly delighted, believe me, that remote lands have nurtured [5] / a loving heart, and so faithful a head, / and because the far-off region is indebted to me for a charming comrade, / yet from which it is willing to return him in a short while upon command. / The city holds me which the Thames washes with its back-flowing surge, / but my pleasant native home does not keep me against my will. [10] / At this time neither do I care to see the reedy Cam again, / nor does love of my prohibited quarters distress me just now.[2] / Its bare fields are unwelcome, so unyielding are they of mild shadows; / how improperly that place assembles the followers of Phoebus! / It is not pleasant constantly to submit to the threats of a stern tutor [15] / and to other things which are foreign to my nature. / If this be exile, to have gone to the paternal hearth / and, this banishment being free of care, to follow agreeable leisurely pursuits, / neither do I flee that name, nor reject its lot, / and, happy, I delight in the result of exile. [20] / O would that the poet never had borne anything more burdensome, / he, the lamentable exile in the land of Tomis.[3] / Then he would have conceded nothing to Ionian Homer, / nor would the foremost renown be yours, vanquished Maro.[4] / For I am permitted to dedicate my

[1] The biography of Milton's close friend is related by Donald C. Dorian in *The English Diodatis*. Diodati visited in Chester on the River Dee (from Milton's words in or around the northwestern section of the city) in the spring of 1626. His letter to Milton is extant in the British Museum (see Yale Prose, I, 337).

[2] Milton was suspended in the Lent term of 1626 as a result of a disagreement with his tutor William Chappell. On his return (around April 19), Milton was placed under Nathaniel Tovey.

[3] Ovid, banished in A.D. 8 to Tomis on the Black Sea where the Coralli lived; see *Elegy* 6, l. 19.

[4] Virgil.

free time to the gentle Muses, [25] / and books—my life—transport me entirely away. / Here the display of the curved theater captivates me, when wearied, / and the talkative stage calls me to its applause.[5] / Sometimes is heard a sly old man, sometimes a prodigal heir, / sometimes a suitor, or a soldier appears with his helmet laid aside, [30] / or an advocate rich from a ten-year lawsuit / thunders his strange discourse at an uncultivated court. / Often a crafty slave runs to the aid of a love-sick son / and, everywhere at once, he deceives the stern father under his very nose. / Often a maiden, astonished by a strange ardor—[35] / she does not know what love is—loves even while she is ignorant. / Or raging Tragedy tosses her sceptre stained with blood / and rolls her eyes under dishevelled hair, / and it is painful; not only do I watch, but I take pleasure in having seen / suffering, and sometimes sweet bitterness lies in tears: [40] / whether an unhappy youth left his joys untasted, / and, separated from his love, dies lamentably, / or whether a fierce avenger of crimes returns from the shades beyond the Styx, / disturbing with his deadly torch hearts conscious of sin, / or whether the house of Pelops is grieving, or of noble Ilus, [45] / or the palace of Creon purges its incestuous sires. / But I am not always living in concealment indoors or in the city, / nor do the hours of spring hasten by without effect on me. / The wood strewn with close-growing elm also possesses me / as well as the celebrated shade of a suburban spot. [50] / Here you may often see bands of maidens, stars / emitting seductive flames, go dancing by. / Ah, how many times have I been stunned by the wonders of a becoming figure / which might refresh even the old age of Jove; / Ah, how many times have I seen eyes surpassing jewels [55] / and even all the flaming stars which either pole rolls round; / and necks which excel the arms of twice-living Pelops,[6] / and in which flows the vein dyed with pure nectar, / and uncommon grace of brow, and shaking hair, / by which deceitful

[5] These references from his reading which follow (note ll. 26, 47) fit the comedies of Terence and the tragedies of the Greeks. The house of Pelops is represented, for example, in Aeschylus' *Agamemnon* and Euripides' *Electra;* the house of Ilus, in Euripides' *Hecuba* and *Trojan Women;* and the palace of Creon, in Sophocles' *Oedipus the King* and *Antigone.*

[6] Pelops, dismembered and offered as food to the Gods, was restored by Hermes; but the piece of shoulder eaten by Demeter had to be replaced by ivory.

Love extends his golden nets, [60] / and seductive cheeks against which the purple of the hyacinth seems / of small account, and the blush of your flower, Adonis, as well![7] / Yield, Heroides,[8] so often praised in the past, / and every mistress who subjected capricious Jove. / Yield, Achaemenian[9] maidens with towered forehead, [65] / and all that dwell in Susa, or Memnonian Nineveh.[10] / You likewise, Greek maidens, acknowledge your inferiority, / and you women of Troy and of Rome; / nor let the Tarpeian Muse vaunt the Pompeian pillars[11] / or the theaters filled with Italian robes. [70] / The prime honor is due the young women of Britain; / be satisfied, alien womanhood, to be able to follow after. / And you, London, city built by Trojan colonists,[12] / distinguished far and wide for towered height, / exceedingly happy, you enclose with your walls [75] / whatever of beauty the pendant world possesses. / Not so many stars shine down on you from the serene sky, / the ministrant multitude of Endymion's goddess,[13] / as the maidens dazzling to you in their beauty and goldenness, / the visible throng that shine forth through the trodden ways. [80] / Lofted to this place by her twin-born doves, bountiful Venus is believed / to have come, accompanied by her quiver-bearing soldier; / for this city, she neglects Cnidos and the valleys watered by the river Simois, / for this, Paphos and rosy Cyprus.[14] / But I, while the blind boy's indulgence per-

[7] The anemone sprang from the blood of Adonis, killed by a boar while hunting.

[8] heroines of legend to whom Ovid assigns the letters making up his amatory poems of this name.

[9] Persian.

[10] Susa in southwestern Persia was founded by Memnon's father; Milton's Latin confusedly connects Memnon with the Assyrian city of Nineveh.

[11] Ovid lived near the Capitoline hill, where was located the Tarpeian Rock from which criminals met their death. He praised both the theater of Pompey in the Campus Martius and other Italian theaters.

[12] According to legend, England was settled by Brutus, grandson of the Trojan Aeneas.

[13] Endymion was beloved by Selene (the Moon), who set him in perpetual sleep, descending each night to embrace him.

[14] Temples to Venus were erected at Cnidos and at Paphos, a city of Cyprus. Paris judged Venus the fairest goddess on the banks of the river Simois. The "quiver-bearing soldier" (l. 82) and the "blind boy" (l. 85) is her son Cupid.

mits, [85] / am preparing to leave the favorable walled city
most quickly; / and to escape from afar the infamous halls of
faithless Circe, / preparing with the help of divine moly.[15] /
It is decided also that I am to return to the rush-filled fens
of the Cam / and again to submit to the noise of the raucous
school. [90] / Meanwhile accept this small tribute of a loyal
friend, / and these few words forced into alternating measures.[16]

(Apr. 1626)

IN OBITUM PROCANCELLARII MEDICI
(On the Death of the Vice-Chancellor, a Physician)[1]

Learn to submit to the laws of destiny / and now offer up
suppliant hands to the Parca,[2] / descendants of Japetus,[3]
who inhabit / the pendulous orb of the earth. / If doleful
death, wandering [5] / from abandoned Taenarus,[4] once
summon you, alas: delays / and deceptions are essayed in
vain; / through the shadows of the Styx one is certain to go. /
If the right hand were strong enough / to rout appointed
death, the untamed Hercules, [10] / poisoned by the blood
of Nessus, / would not have been cast down on Emathian
Oeta.[5] / Nor would Troy have seen Hector[6] slain / by the

---

[15] Through the aid of Hermes, Ulysses was able to resist the
charms of Circe by eating the herb moly. The enchantress had
turned half his followers into swine.

[16] the elegiac couplet, consisting of an hexameter and a pen-
tameter.

---

[1] Dr. John Gostlin, Vice-Chancellor of Cambridge since 1618
and Regius Professor of Medicine since 1623, died on Oct. 21,
1626.

[2] one of the three Fates; specifically, Morta, who controlled the
advent of death.

[3] As father of Atlas, Prometheus, and Epimetheus, he was considered mankind's common progenitor.

[4] the infernal regions.

[5] To win back Hercules' love, his wife Deianira followed the
advice of the dying Nessus to smear a robe with his blood, which
Hercules was to wear; but since Nessus' blood had been stained
with the blood of the hydra, also killed by Hercules, the robe
caused fatal poisoning. Hercules had himself placed on a pyre on
Mt. Oeta in Macedonia.

[6] Athena, disguised as Hector's brother Deiphobus, urged him
to fight with Achilles, in which battle he was slain.

shameful deceit of envious Pallas, nor / him[7] whom the ghost
of Achilles killed [15] / with Locrian sword, Jove shedding
tears. / If the incantations of Hecate[8] could put / sad fate
to flight, the parent of Telegonus[9] / would have lived in
infamy, and / the sister of Aegialeus[10] to employ her potent
wand. [20] / And if the arts of the physician and unknown
herbs / were able to deceive the triple divinity, / Machaon,
knowing so much of herbs, / would not have fallen by the
spear of Eurypylus;[11] / neither would the arrow smeared
with the hydra's blood [25] / have wounded you, son of
Philyra,[12] / nor the missiles and thunderbolt of your grandfather, you, / boy cut from your mother's womb.[13] / And
you, O greater than your pupil, Apollo, / to whom the government of our gowned society was given, [30] / and whom
now leafy Cirrha mourns / and Helicon in the midst of its
waters,[14] / now you would be the happy leader to the Palladian troop, / surviving, not without glory; / nor in Charon's
boat would you traverse [35] / the fearful recesses of hell. /
But Persephone broke your thread of life, / angered, when
she saw you by your arts / and powerful potions snatch so
many / from the black jaws of death. [40] / Reverend Chan-
cellor, I pray your limbs / find peace in the gentle soil, and
from your grave / spring roses and marigolds / and the
hyacinth with purple face. / May the judgment of Aeacus[15]
be gentle upon you, [45] / and may Sicilian[16] Prosperina

[7] Sarpedon, son of Jove, who was slain by Patroclus, wearing
Achilles' armor.

[8] goddess of enchantments.

[9] Circe.

[10] Medea, who was learned in magic.

[11] Machaon, surgeon to the Greeks at Troy, was a son of
Aesculapius.

[12] Chiron was wounded by one of Hercules' arrows poisoned
by the hydra's blood.

[13] Aesculapius, so delivered by his father Apollo, was killed by
Jove, Apollo's father, because he saved men from death.

[14] In an extravagance Milton has Apollo, god of healing, learning from Gostlin, and Cirrha (near Delphi) and Helicon (the
haunt of the Muses) equating Cambridge with its poetic mourners.

[15] a judge of the dead, appointed because of his justice in ruling Aegina.

[16] Sicilian because she was carried off from Enna in Sicily by
Pluto.

smile, / and forever among the fortunate / may you walk in the Elysian field.

(Oct.–Nov. 1626)

IN PRODITIONEM BOMBARDICAM
(On the Gunpowder Plot)[1]

When recently, at the same time against the King and the British lords, / you attempted, perfidious Fawkes, your unspeakable crime, / am I mistaken, or did you wish to seem in part kind / and to compensate for the heinous deed with wicked piety? / Certainly you would send them to the courts of high heaven [5] / in a sulphurous chariot with flaming wheels; / just as he[2] whose head was inviolable by the cruel Parcae,[3] / carried off in a whirlwind, disappeared from the plains of the Jordan.

(Nov. 1626 ?)

IN EANDEM
(On the same)

Thus did you strive to vouchsafe James to Heaven, / O Beast, who lurks on the seven hills?[1] / Unless your divine majesty can bestow better favors, / spare, I pray, your insidious gifts. / Indeed he has departed ripe in years,[2] without your help [5] / and without the employment of infernal powder, to his comrades, the stars. / Thus instead, banish to the sky your detestable cowls[3] / and all the brute gods profane Rome possesses; / for unless you aid each one firmly in this or some other way, / believe me, they will hardly mount the path to heaven successfully. [10]

(Nov. 1626 ?)

[1] a Roman Catholic conspiracy by Guy Fawkes and others to blow up James I and the House of Lords on Nov. 5, 1605.

[2] Elijah (2 Kings ii. 11).

[3] Clotho, Lachesis, and Atropos, the Fates who controlled birth and death.

---

[1] the Papacy; Rome, built on seven hills, was identified by many Protestants with the whore of Babylon, who sat on a beast with seven heads (hills) and ten horns (Rev. xvii. 3–7).

[2] James died on Mar. 27, 1625.

[3] priests.

IN EANDEM
(On the same)

James derided the Purgatorial fire[1] of the soul, / without which there is no approaching of the celestial mansions. / The Latin monster with triple crown[2] gnashed its teeth at this / and moved its ten horns with frightful menace / and, it cried, "You shall not scorn my sacred rites with impunity, Englishman; [5] / you shall suffer punishment for your contempt of religion. / And if ever you enter the starry citadels, / the only way open is the sad one through the flames." / O how close you came to a calamitous truth / and only barely were your words deprived of their consequences, [10] / for he nearly ascended to the eternal regions, / a scorched ghost, whirled on high by the Tartarean[3] fire.

(Nov. 1626 ?)

IN EANDEM
(On the same)

Whom impious Rome had just marked out for her curses[1] / and condemned to the Styx and the Taenarian gulf,[2] / him, on the contrary, she now desires to lift to the stars / and wishes to elevate even to the higher Gods.

(Nov. 1626 ?)

[1] James' denial of Purgatory is found in *A Premonition to All Most Mightie Monarches* (*Works*, p. 125).

[2] the Papacy; the Pope's tiara is a triple crown. Milton thought both of the beast in Revelation and Daniel's vision of the beast with great iron teeth and ten horns, which "shall be the fourth kingdom upon earth, . . . and shall devour the whole earth, and shall tread it down, and break it in pieces" (Dan. vii. 7, 23).

[3] Tartarus was the part of the underworld where punishment for sins was exacted.

---

[1] In addition to reimposing recusancy fines in Feb. 1605, James had banished all Roman Catholic priests in Feb. 1604.

[2] the infernal regions.

IN INVENTOREM BOMBARDÆ
(On the inventor of Gunpowder)

Antiquity in blindness praised the son of Iapetus,[1] / who brought down celestial fire from the chariot of the sun, / but to me he will be greater who is believed to have stolen / the ghastly weapons and threeforked thunderbolt from Jove.[2]

(*Nov. 1626 ?*)

IN QUINTUM NOVEMBRIS
(On the fifth of November)

Now the devout James coming from the remote north / ruled over the Troy-descended people[1] and the wide-stretching realms / of the English, and now an inviolable covenant / had joined the English kingdoms with Caledonian Scots: / and the peace-maker, happy and rich, was seated [5] / on his new throne, untroubled by secret conspiracy or foe: / when the cruel tyrant[2] reigning over Acheron, which flows with fire, / the father of the Eumenides, the wandering outcast from celestial Olympus, / by chance strayed through the vast circle of the earth, / enumerating the companions of his wickedness and his faithful slaves, [10] / future participants of his rule after their woeful deaths. / Here he stirs ominous tempests in middle air; / there he contrives hatred among harmonious friends, / and arms invincible nations against mutual cordiality, / and turns flourishing kingdoms from olive-bearing peace; [15] / and whatever lovers of pure virtue he spies, / those he seeks to add to his empire, and master of guile, / he tries to corrupt the heart inaccessible to sin / and lays silent plots and stretches unseen snares, / so that he may assault the incautious, as the Caspian tigress [20] / pur-

[1] Prometheus.

[2] Compare the description of the Son after the War in Heaven in *Pl*, VI, 763–64.

---

[1] See *El.* 1, n. 12. Albion (ll. 27–28), son of Neptune, gave his name to the island and its inhabitants.

[2] Pluto, king of hell and father of the avenging spirits. Acheron and Phlegethon (l. 74) were rivers of hell. Pluto's likeness to Satan in these lines has been noted by most editors since Warton.

sues her anxious prey through the waste wildernesses / in the moonless night and under the stars winking in their drowsiness. / With like fears does Summanus³ harass the people and the cities, / he, wreathed with a smoking tornado of blue flames. / And now the white coasts with their wave-resounding cliffs [25] / appear, and the land highly esteemed by the sea god, / to which Neptune's son gave his name so long ago, / who, having sailed across the sea, did not hesitate to challenge / fierce Hercules with furious battle / before the unmerciful times of conquered Troy.⁴ [30] /

But as soon as he beholds this land blessed with wealth / and joyful peace, and with fields rich in the gifts of Ceres, / and, what pained him more, a people revering the sacred divinity / of the true god, at length he breaks into sighs / emitting Tartarean fires and ghastly sulphur. [35] / Such sighs does grim and monstrous Typhoeus,⁵ enclosed by Jove / under Sicilian Aetna, breathe from his destructive mouth. / His eyes flash and his inflexible row of teeth / hisses like the crash of arms and the blow of spear against spear. / And then, "Throughout the travelled world I found this worthy of tears only," [40] / he said; "this nation alone is rebellious toward me, / and contemptuous of my yoke and stronger than my art. / Yet if my attempts have power over anyone, it / shall not endure thus with impunity for long; it shall not go unavenged." / No further did he speak, but floats away on pitch-black wings through [45] / the liquid air; wherever he flies adverse winds precede in a mass, / clouds are thickened, and repeated thunderbolts flash. /

And now his speed has surmounted the frosty Alps, / and he reaches the borders of Italy; on his left side / was the stormy Apennine range and the ancient Sabines; [50] / on his right Etruria with its infamous magic potions, and besides / he sees the furtive kisses which you are giving to Thetis,⁶ O Tiber; / next he stands still on the citadel of Quirinus, born of Mars.⁷ / Already had evening twilight be-

³ an ancient god of nightly storms, identified with Pluto.

⁴ Albion was killed aiding his brother Lestrygon, who was fighting in Gaul against Hercules, son of Amphitryon's wife.

⁵ a giant, whom Jove struck with a thunderbolt and buried under Sicily; his head lay beneath Mt. Etna, whose eruptions he spewed forth.

⁶ a sea-nymph. The Tiber empties into the Tyrrhene Sea through a delta.

⁷ That is, Satan arrives in Rome. The Pope, whose tiara con-

stowed uncertain light, / when the wearer of the triple crown walks around the entire city, [55] / and carries the gods made of bread, and on men's shoulders / is elevated; kings precede him on bended knee, / and a most lengthy train of mendicant brothers; / and unable to see, they bear wax candles in their hands, / those born and enduring life in Cimmerian darkness. [60] / Next they enter the temples glittering with many torches / (it was that eve sacred to St. Peter) and the noise of those singing / often fills the hollow domes and the void of those places. / How Bacchus howls, and the followers of Bacchus, / chanting their orgies on Theban Aracynthus,[8] [65] / while astonished Asopus trembles under the glassy waves, / and afar off Cithaeron itself echoes from its hollow rock. /

Then at last, these things performed in a solemn fashion, / silent Night[9] left the embraces of old Erebus, / and now drives her headlong horses with a goading whip—[70] / blind Typhlos and spirited Melanchaetes, / torpid Siope, sprung from an infernal father, / and shaggy Phrix with bristly hair. / Meanwhile the tamer of kings, the heir of hell, / enters his chambers (for the secret adulterer [75] / does not spend sterile nights without a gentle concubine); / but sleep was scarcely closing his ready eyes, / when the dark lord of the shadows, the ruler of the dead, / the plunderer of man stood before him, concealed by a false shape. / His temples flashed with the gray hairs he had assumed; [80] / a long beard covered his breast; his ash-colored attire / swept the ground with a long train; and his hood hung down / from his shaven crown; and so that none might be absent from his frauds / he bound his lustful loins with hempen rope, / thrusting his slow feet into open sandals. [85] / In like manner, as rumor has it, Francis[10] used to wander alone / in the vast, loathsome desert through the haunts of wild beasts; / he carried the pious word of salvation to the people of the wood, / himself impious, and tamed the wolves and the Libyan lions. /

---

sists of three crowns, in procession with other church dignitaries, carried the Host through the streets to St. Peter's Cathedral on the eve of St. Peter's Day, June 28.

[8] a mountain in Boeotia. Asopus is a river, and Cithaeron, a range of hills lying nearby.

[9] Night and her brother Erebus (primeval darkness) were the parents of Day. The names of her team were created by Milton.

[10] St. Francis of Assisi.

But clothed in such garb, the cunning serpent, [90] / deceitful, separated his accursed lips with these words: / "Are you sleeping, my son? Does slumber still overpower your limbs? / O negligent of faith and neglectful of your flocks! / while a barbarous nation born under the northern sky / ridicules your throne and triple diadem, O venerable one, [95] / and while the quivered English contemn your laws! / Arise, up, arise, lazy one, whom the Roman emperor adores, / and for whom the unlocked gate of arched heaven lies open; / crush their swelling pride and insolent arrogance, / and let the sacrilegious know what your curse may be capable of, [100] / and what custody of the Apostolic key may avail; / and remember to avenge the scattered armada of the Spanish / and the banners of the Iberians swallowed up by the broad deep, / and the bodies of so many saints hanged on infamous gallows / recently by the reigning Amazonian virgin.[11] [105] / But if you prefer to become indolent in your soft bed / and refuse to crush the increasing strength of the foe, / he will fill the Tyrrhene Sea with a vast army / and set his glittering standards on the Aventine hill:[12] / he will destroy and burn with flames the remains of the ancients, [110] / and with profane feet will trample upon your sacred neck, / you whose shoes kings were glad to give their kisses. / Yet you will not challenge him to wars and open conflict; / such would be useless labor; you are shrewd to use deception, / of which any kind is fitting in order to spread traps for heretics; [115] / and now the great king calls the nobles with foreign speech / to council, and those sprung from the stock of celebrated men / and old venerable sires with their robe of state and gray hairs. / You will be able to scatter them limb by limb throughout the air / and to give them up to cinders, by the fire of nitrous [120] / powder exploded beneath the last chambers where they have assembled. / Immediately therefore advise whatever faithful there are in England / of the proposed deed; will any of your followers / dare not dispatch the commands of the supreme Pope? / And instantly may the fierce Gaul and the savage Spaniard [125] / invade them, smitten with dread and stupefied by calamity. / Thus at last the Marian era[13] will return

11 Elizabeth.

12 one of Rome's seven hills.

13 meaning both a Catholic age (from Mary) and an age of civil war (from Marius, who fought Sulla in 83–82 B.C.).

to that land / and you will rule again over the warlike English. / And, so you fear nothing, accept the gods and subordinate goddesses, / as many deities as are honored on your feast days." [130] / The deceiver spoke, and laying his disguise aside, / he fled to Lethe, his abominable, gloomy kingdom. /

Now rosy dawn, throwing open the eastern gates, / dresses the gilded world with returning light; / and hitherto grieving for the sad death of her swarthy son,[14] [135] / she sprinkles the mountain tops with ambrosial tears, / then the keeper[15] of the starry court banished sleep, / repeating his nocturnal visions and delightful dreams. /

There is a place enclosed in the eternal darkness of night, / once the vast foundation of a ruined dwelling, [140] / now the den of savage Murder and double-tongued Treason, / whom fierce Discord bore at one birth. / Here among the unhewn stones and broken rock lie / the unburied bones of men and corpses pierced by steel; / here malicious Deceit sits forever with distorted eyes, [145] / and Contentions and Calumny, its jaws armed with fangs, / Fury and a thousand ways of dying are seen, / and Fear and pale Horror hasten around the place, / and nimble ghosts howl perpetually through the mute silences, / and the conscious earth stagnates with blood. [150] / Besides, Murder and Treason themselves lie hid, quaking, / in the inmost depths of the cave with no one pursuing them through it, / the rough cave, full of rocks, dark with deathly shadows. / The guilty ones disperse and run away with backward glance; / these defenders of Rome, faithful through the long ages, [155] / the Babylonian high-priest[16] summons, and thus he speaks: / "A race odious to me lives on the western limits / in the surrounding sea; prudent nature has thoroughly denied / that unworthy people to join our world. / Thither, so I command, journey with swift pace, [160] / and may the king and his nobles together, that impious race, / be blown into thin air by the Tartarean powder, / and whoever for true faith have glowed with love / invite as partners of the plot and accomplices of the deed." / He ended, and the stern twins obeyed with eagerness. [165] /

[14] Memnon, son of the goddess of dawn and Tithonus, was slain by Achilles.

[15] Jove.

[16] See n. 1. to the poem on the Gunpowder Plot, beginning "Thus did you strive . . . ."

Meanwhile turning the heavens in a spacious arc, / the Lord, who shines forth from his ethereal height, looks down / and laughs at the efforts of the evil crew, / and orders the defense of his people to be upheld. /

They say there is a section where fertile Europe is separated [170] / from Asian land, and looks toward Mareotidan waters; / here is situated the lofty tower of Titanean Fame,[17] / brazen, broad, resounding, closer to the glowing stars / than Athos or Pelion piled on Ossa.[18] / A thousand doors and entrances lie open, and as many windows, [175] / and spacious courts shine through the thin walls; / here the accumulated people raise various whispers; / how the swarms of flies make noise about the milk pails / by buzzing, or through the sheepfolds of woven reed, / when the lofty Dog Star[19] assails the summer height of the sky. [180] / Indeed Fame herself, avenger of her mother, sits in her topmost fortress; / her head, girt with innumerable ears, projects out from that place, / attracting the faintest sound and seizing the lightest / murmur from the farthest limits of the wide world. / And you, O Argus,[20] unjust guardian of the heifer [185] / Io, did not roll so many eyes in your fierce face, / eyes never faltering in silent sleep, / eyes gazing over the adjacent lands far and wide. / With them is Fame accustomed always to survey places deprived of light, / and even those impervious to the radiant sun. [190] / And with a thousand tongues the blabbing one pours out / things heard and seen to anyone who chances by, and now lying, she lessens / the truth, and now she increases it with fabricated rumors. / Nevertheless, Fame, you deserved the praises

[17] Ovid's description of Fame (*Meta.*, XII, 39–63) furnished most of the details here. She is called a Titaness by Virgil (*Aen.*, IV, 173–87) because she is the daughter of Earth, who is often abused by men (see l. 181). The Tower of Fame seems to stand in Egypt (Allan Gilbert, *MLN*, XXVIII, 1913, 30), for Lake Mareotis was in Lower Egypt near Alexandria. However, D. T. Starnes (*NQ*, 196, 1951, 515–18) suggests, probably correctly, that this is an error for "Maeotidas undas" (the waters near Lake Maeotis), which lay between Europe and Asia, at the mouth of the Tanais River (Lucan, III, 272–78).

[18] The giants Otus and Ephialtes piled Mt. Pelion on Mt. Ossa (in Thessaly) in their attempt to overthrow the gods. Mt. Athos was in Macedonia, opposite Lemnos.

[19] Sirius; see *Lycidas*, n. 30.

[20] Jealous Juno had hundred-eyed Argus guard Io after she had been changed into a heifer by Jove.

of my song, / for one good deed than which no other speaks more truly, [195] / worthy to be sung by me, nor shall I repent having commemorated you / at such length in my song. To be sure, we unharmed English / bestow on you what is just for your services, O inconstant goddess. / God who restrains the eternal fires from their agitation / with his dispatched thunderbolt, the earth trembling, exhorts you: [200] / "Fame, are you silent? or does the impious throng of Papists / hide you, conspired against me and my English, / and a new massacre designed against scepter-bearing James?" / No more said, she discerned at once the Thunderer's commands, / and swift enough before, she puts on strident wings, [205] / and clothes her slender body with variegated feathers; / in her right hand she carries a loud trumpet of Temesan[21] brass. / With no delay, she now oars on her wings through the yielding air, / and seems not content to outrun the swift clouds by her flight; / now the winds, now the horses of the sun she leaves behind her back. [210] / But first, in her usual way, through the English cities / she spreads ambiguous rumors and uncertain whispers; / directly, in clear voice, she divulges the deceits and the detestable / work of treason, and likewise deeds frightful when spoken, / and she adds the authors of the crime, nor, being garrulous, is she silent [215] / about the places prepared for secret ambush; men are stunned by the reports, / and youths as well as maidens and weak old men / tremble, and the significance of such great ruin / has penetrated quickly to every age. / But meanwhile the heavenly Father from on high has compassion [220] / on his people, and thwarts the cruel and daring attempts / of the Papists; the captives are dragged to fierce punishments; / but pious incense and grateful honors are paid to God; / all the happy streets smoke with genial bonfires; / the youthful throng moves in dancing groups: and throughout the whole year [225] / no day occurs that is more celebrated than the fifth of November.

(Nov. 1626)

[21] Temesa, a town in Italy, was famous for copper mines.

ELEGIA SECUNDA
(Elegy 2)

On the Death of the Beadle of Cambridge University[1]

You who, conspicuous with your shining mace, were accustomed / so often to assemble the Palladian band,[2] / beadle as you were, the last of beadles, fierce Death, / has seized, and does not even favor one in its own service. / Although your temples were whiter than the plumes [5] / under which we understand Jove to have been disguised,[3] / O yet were you worthy to grow young again with a Haemonian potion, / worthy to be able to live to an Aesonian age,[4] / worthy to be one whom Coronides should recall from the Stygian waves / by his curative art, at the frequent entreaty of the goddess.[5] [10] / As whenever you were bidden to fetch the gowned ranks / and to go a swift messenger from your Apollo,[6] / in such manner would wing-footed Cyllenius[7] stand in the court of Ilium, / dispatched from the heavenly vault of his father. / And in like fashion Eurybates before the face of angry Achilles [15] / conveyed the stern order of his chief, Atrides.[8] / Great queen of sepulchers, attendant of Avernus, too cruel to the Muses, too cruel to Pallas, / why do you not seize those who are useless burdens of the earth? / They are the throng that should be attacked by your darts. [20] / Therefore, mourn for him, Academe, in robes of black, / and moisten with your tears the dark bier, / and

[1] Richard Ridding, who died in Nov. (?) 1626, as senior beadle, preceded academic processions bearing the official mace.

[2] Pallas Athena was the goddess of wisdom and the arts.

[3] Jove, in love with the mortal Leda, approached her in the guise of a swan.

[4] Aeson was restored to youth by Medea, whose magic brew was concocted from herbs of the valleys of Haemonia.

[5] At the prayer of Diana, Aesculapius, god of medicine, brought Hippolytus back to life.

[6] the Vice-Chancellor of Cambridge.

[7] Hermes, messenger of the gods, born on Mt. Cyllene in Arcadia, met Priam, king of Ilium, on the plain outside Troy (*Iliad*, XXIV, 334–57).

[8] Eurybates and other heralds of Agamemnon were sent to Achilles' tent to fetch his concubine Briseis (*Iliad*, I, 320–25).

let lamenting Elegy itself pour forth its sad measures / and let all the schools resound with its sorrowful dirge.

(Nov. ? 1626)

ELEGIA TERTIA
(Elegy 3)

On the Death of the Bishop of Winchester[1]

I was full of sadness, and I was sitting silent with no companion, / and many sorrows were clinging to my spirit. / Suddenly, lo, there arose a vision of the mournful destruction / which Libitina[2] wrought on English soil; / while dire death, fearful with its sepulchral torch, [5] / entered the glittering marble palaces of the nobles, / and attacked the walls laden with gold and jasper, / nor did it hesitate to overthrow hosts of princes with its scythe. / Then I remembered that illustrious duke, and his revered brother, / their bones burned on untimely pyres.[3] [10] / And I remembered the heroes whom the land saw snatched up to the sky, / and all Belgia mourned the lost leaders. / But I lamented chiefly for you, most worthy Bishop, / and once the great glory of your Winchester; / I dissolved in weeping, and complained thus with sad words: [15] / "Savage death, goddess second to Tartarean Jove,[4] / are you not satisfied that the forest suffers your rages, / that power is given to you over the grassy fields, / and that the blooming lilies wither from your pestilence, / and the crocus, and the rose sacred to beautiful Cypris,[5] [20] / just as you do not allow the oak bordering upon the river forever / to wonder at the fall of the ebbing water? / And the bird succumbs to you, although a prophet,[6] / many a one which is

[1] Lancelot Andrewes, who died on Sept. 25, 1626.

[2] the Italian goddess of the dead. The plague was severe in London in 1625–26.

[3] often identified as Duke Christian of Brunswick-Wolfenbüttel, who died in the Low Countries (Belgia) during the Thirty Years' War on June 6, 1626, and Count Ernest of Mansfeld, who died on Nov. 29. Adherents of the Protestant cause, they were brothers in arms only.

[4] Pluto, god of hell and brother of Jove.

[5] Venus.

[6] The belief was the basis of the Roman auspices (*avis spicere*), originally signs from birds in flight or song, which were prescriptions of conduct and prayer to determine whether the gods were favorable.

lifted through the liquid air on its pinions, / and the thousand beasts that stray in the dark forests, [25] / and the dumb herd which the caves of Proteus sustain.[7] / Envious one, whenever such power is allowed you, / what delights you to stain your hands with human slaughter? / and to sharpen your unerring arrows against a noble breast, / and to drive a half-divine spirit from its residence?" [30] / While, weeping, I meditated such griefs deep in my heart, / dewy Hesperus[8] rose from the western sea, / and Phoebus sank his chariot in the Tartessian[9] sea, / after measuring his course from the eastern shore. / With no delay, I lay down in cavernous bed to refresh my limbs, [35] / and night and sleep shut my eyes; / when I seemed to be walking in a broad field. / Alas! my senses cannot relate the things seen. / There all things were shining with reddish light, / just as the mountain peaks blush with the morning sun. [40] / But as when the child of Thaumas[10] spreads her riches, / the earth luxuriated in vestment of many colors. / Chloris,[11] the goddess beloved by fleet Zephyr, did not adorn / the gardens of Alcinous with so many various flowers. / Silver rivers washed the verdant field; [45] / the sand was gilded richer than Hesperian Tagus.[12] / Through the fragrant wealth stole the light breath of Favonius,[13] / the dewy breath born under innumerable roses. / Such, on the distant shores of the land of the Ganges, / is the home of Lucifer,[14] the king, imagined to be. [50] / While I myself was marvelling at the dense shades beneath the clustering vines / and the shining regions everywhere, / behold, Winchester's bishop suddenly stood before me, / the splendor of stars shone in his bright face; / a dazzling white robe flowed down to his golden ankles, [55] / a white fillet encircled his divine head. / And while the reverend old man advanced in such fashion, / the flowery earth trembled with happy sound. / The celestial multitudes ap-

[7] Proteus, the changeable ancient of the sea, herded the seals of Neptune.

[8] the evening star.

[9] Spanish, i.e., western.

[10] Iris, goddess of the rainbow.

[11] goddess of spring and flowers, and wife of the West Wind. The garden of Alcinous is described in *Od.*, VI, 291–94.

[12] the river in Spain, noted for its golden sand in the reflected sun.

[13] Zephyr.

[14] "bearer of light," the Sun.

plaud with jewelled wings, / the pure air resounds with
triumphal trumpet. [60] / Everyone salutes the new companion with an embrace and a song, / and one among them
uttered these words from his peaceful lips: / "My son, come,
and, happy, reap the joys of your father's kingdom; / here
rest forever, my son, from harsh labor." / He spoke, and the
winged troops touched their harps, [65] / but for me golden
sleep was banished with the night. / I wept for the dreams
disturbed by the mistress of Cephalus.[15] / May such dreams
often befall me! /

(Dec. 1626 ?)

IN OBITUM PRÆSULIS ELIENSIS
(On the Death of the Bishop of Ely)[1]

As yet my cheeks were not dry with flowing tears, / and eyes
not yet dry, / still were they swollen with the rain of salt
liquid, / which lately I, respectful, poured forth, / while I
rendered sorrowful obsequies to the esteemed bier [5] / of
the bishop of Winchester;[2] / when hundred-tongued Fame
(alas always / the true messenger of evil and misfortune) /
spreads through the cities of affluent Britain / and to the people sprung from Neptune[3] [10] / that you had yielded to
death, and to the cruel sisters,[4] / you, the ornament of the
race of men, / who were the prince of saints in that island /
which retains the name of Eel.[5] / Directly at that time my
restless breast [15] / surged with fervid anger, / frequently
cursing the goddess powerful in the grave: / Ovid[6] in *Ibis*
conceived / no more ominous vows in the depth of his heart, /
and the Greek poet, more sparing, [20] / cursed the dishonorable deceit of Lycambes, / and of Neobule, his own be-
trothed.[7] / But lo! while I pour out these harsh curses /

[15] Aurora, the dawn.

---

[1] Nicholas Felton (1556–1626), Master of Pembroke College,
Cambridge, from 1617 to 1619 when he succeeded Lancelot Andrewes as Bishop of Ely. He died on Oct. 6.

[2] Lancelot Andrewes, whose death was mourned in *El.* 3.

[3] See *Nov.* 5, n. 1.

[4] the three Fates.

[5] the etymological meaning of Ely ("island of eels").

[6] whose poem attacks an unidentified enemy.

[7] Archilochus was in love with Neobule, daughter of Lycambes,
who at first allowed and then forbade their marriage; to avenge
himself he wrote such bitter satires that father and daughter
hanged themselves.

and invoke death upon death, / astonished, I seem to hear
such sounds as these, [25] / on the gentle breeze beneath
the air:[8] / "Put away your blind madness; put away your
transparent / melancholy and your ineffectual threats. / Why
do you thoughtlessly profane deities unable to be harmed /
and roused swift to wrath? [30] / Death is not, as you think,
deluded wretch, / the dark daughter of Night, / nor sprung
from her father Erebus, nor from Erinys, / nor born under
desolate Chaos.[9] / But she, sent from the starry heaven, [35]
/ gathers the harvest of God everywhere; / and souls hidden
by their fleshy bulk / calls forth into light and air, / as when
the flying Hours arouse the day, / the daughters of Themis
and Jove;[10] [40] / and she leads them into the presence of
the eternal Father, / but, just, she sweeps the impious / to
the doleful realms of gloomy Tartarus, / to the infernal
abodes. / Happy, when I heard her calling, quickly [45] / I
left my loathsome prison / and, fortunate, amid the winged
warriors / I was borne aloft to the stars, / like the venerable
prophet of old,[11] snatched up to heaven, / driver of the fiery
chariot. [50] / The wain of shining Boötes did not frighten
me, / slow from the cold, nor / the claws of fearsome Scorpion, / not even your sword, Orion.[12] / I flew past the globe
of the gleaming sun, [55] / and far below my feet I saw / the
triform goddess,[13] whilst she restrained / her dragons with

[8] The following lines, to the end, are spoken by Felton's spirit.
[9] According to Cicero (De Natura Deorum, III, xvii, 44),
Death is a child of Night by Erebus, offspring of Chaos (the lower
world). Erinys was one of the three Furies.
[10] The Hours kept watch at the gates of heaven.
[11] Elijah (2 Kings ii. 11).
[12] In flight he passes three heavenly constellations: Boötes, lying
in the north and meaning "ox herder," appears to move slowly; it
is near the Great Bear, known as the Wain (wagon). Scorpio,
lying in the south, is named for its similarity to a scorpion. Orion,
lying on the equator, is in the figure of a hunter with belt and
sword.
[13] The moon (Diana) was triform because she was the virgin
moon-goddess, the patroness of virginity, and the presider over
child-birth, the chase, and nocturnal incantations. The threefold
identification rests upon the phases of the moon: increasing, full,
and waning. As goddess of nocturnal incantations she was identified with Hecate. As Davis P. Harding shows (p. 50), the dragons
of the moon were associated with Hecate because they descended
to Medea when she invoked the goddess' help to flee from Jason's
wrath.

golden reins. / Through rows of wandering stars, / through the milky regions I was conveyed, [60] / often amazed at my strange speed, / until to the shining portals / of Olympus I was come, and the crystalline realm / and the court paved with beryl. / But here I shall be silent, for who is able to proclaim, [65] / descended from human father, / the pleasures of that place? For me / it is enough to enjoy them through eternity."

(Dec. 1626 ?)

ELEGIA QUARTA
(Elegy 4)

To Thomas Young, his tutor, discharging the duty of pastor among the English merchants in business in Hamburg[1]

Quickly, my letter, run through the boundless deep; / go, seek Teutonic lands through the smooth sea; / break off dilatory delays, and let nothing, I pray, thwart your voyage, / and let nothing obstruct the path of your hastening. / I myself Aeolus[2] bridling the winds in his Sicanian cave [5] / will exhort, and the vigorous gods, / and cerulian Doris, attended by her nymphs,[3] / to give you a peaceful journey through their realms. / But you, if you are able, arrogate for yourself the swift team, / borne by which the Colchian[4] fled from the

[1] Young (1587?–1655) was Milton's tutor in 1618–20(?). By 1620 he was in Hamburg, visiting England in Mar.–July 1621 and again sometime in Jan.–Apr. 1625 (see ll. 33–38); he returned sometime between Jan. and Mar. 1628. On Mar. 27, 1628, he became vicar of St. Peter and St. Mary in Stowmarket, Suffolk. Familiar Letter 1 was written Mar. 26, 1627, to accompany this elegy, which it mentions; a further letter (No. 4), dated July 21, 1628, also survives. Young was the "TY" of "SMECTYMNUUS," the composite name of the five divines who in 1641 attacked episcopacy with *An Answer to a Book entitled "An Humble Remonstrance,"* to which was added *A Postscript*, probably written by Milton (see Wolfe, Yale Prose, I, 961–65). Barker (*MLR*, XXXII, 1937, 517–26) suggests that Young was the friend to whom *Of Reformation* was written, and Parker (*TLS*, May 16, 1936, p. 420) believes him the unknown friend of the letter in TM.

[2] god of the winds; the land of the Sicanians was Sicily.

[3] Wife of the river-god Nereus, Doris was the mother of fifty sea-nymphs.

[4] Medea fled from Jason in a chariot drawn by dragons, after murdering their children.

face of her husband, [10] / or that by which Triptolemus[5] reached the Scythian borders, / the beloved boy sent from the Eleusinian city. / But when you see the German sands become golden, / turn your steps to the walls of affluent Hamburg, / which is said to derive its name from slain Hama,[6] [15] / who it is told was brought to violent death by a Cimbrian club. / Here, renowned for his honor of the primitive faith, lives / a minister well-versed in feeding the sheep that worship Christ; / he, truly, is more than the other half of my soul: / I am constrained to live but half of my life without him. [20] / Alas for me, how many seas, how many mountains intervening / render me cut off from the other half of myself! / Dearer to me is he than you, most learned of Greeks, / to Cliniades,[7] who was the great-grand-son of Telamon; / than the lofty Stagirite[8] to his noble pupil [25] / whom the genial daughter of Chaonia bore to Libyan Jove. / What the son of Amyntor, what the heroic son of Philyra / were to the king of the Myrmidons,[9] such is he to me. / I first surveyed the Aonian retreats through his guiding, / and the sacred lawns of the twin-peaked mountain,[10] [30] / and the Pierian water I drank, and by favor of Clio, / I thrice moistened my happy lips with pure Casta-

[5] a son of Celeus, king of Eleusis, whom Ceres sent in her dragon-drawn chariot to sow wheat throughout the earth (including far Scythia). Ovid likewise wished for the chariots of Medea and Triptolemus to return him from exile (*Tristia*, III, viii, 1–4).

[6] D. T. Starnes (*A Tribute to G. C. Taylor*, 1952, p. 39) shows that Milton could have learned this legend from entries in Charles Stephanus' *Dictionarium*. Hama was a Saxon champion reputedly killed by Starchatar, a Danish (Cimbrian) giant.

[7] Alcibiades; one of Plato's dialogues bears his name.

[8] Aristotle, born in Stagira in Macedonia. His famous pupil was Alexander the Great, son of Olympias (of Chaonia in Epirus) and, in legend, of Ammon, as Jove was known in Libya.

[9] Achilles, pupil of Phoenix (son of Amyntor) and Chiron, (son of Philyra).

[10] Mt. Parnassus, the haunt of the Muses, in Aonia. The waters that flowed in Castalia, a spring on Mt. Parnassus, afforded poetic inspiration by the bestowal of the Muses, who were born in Pieria. The Muse Clio, as Simonides tells us (Frag. 56), was the "overseer of the pure lustration-water, receiver of the prayers of many a pitcher-carrier." What Milton says is that Young introduced him to the glories of the arts, and that, while under Young's guidance and as a result of the talents given him by Clio, he had thrice been poetically inspired. These early poems are apparently not extant.

lian wine. / But thrice has fiery Aethon seen the sign of the
ram, / and overspread his woolly back with new gold, / and
twice, Chloris, have you bestrewn the old earth with new [35]
/ grass, and twice Auster removed your wealth; / and yet I
have not been allowed to feast my eyes on his countenance /
or the sweet sounds of his speech to be drunk in by my ears.[11]
/ Speed, therefore, and outrun noisy Eurus[12] by your course.
/ How great is the need of my admonitions, circumstance
shows; you yourself perceive. [40] / Perhaps you will find
him sitting with his sweet wife, / stroking their dear children
on his lap; / or perhaps meditating the copious volumes of
the old fathers, / or the Holy Bible of the true God, /
saturating the delicate souls with celestial dew, [45] / the
sublime work of health-bearing religion. / As is the custom,
be careful to deliver a hearty greeting, / to speak as would
befit your master, if only he were present. / May you be
mindful to cast your discreet eyes down a little on the ground
/ and to speak these words with modest mouth: [50] /
These verses to you, if there is time for the delicate Muses
between battles,[13] / a devoted hand sends from the English
shore. / Accept this sincere wish for your welfare, though it
be late, / and may it be the more pleasing to you for that
reason. / Late indeed, but genuine it was as that which [55] /
the chaste Penelope, daughter of Icarius, received from her
dilatory husband.[14] / But why did I consent to cancel a manifest fault / which he himself is utterly unable to discharge? /
He is justly reproved as tardy, and confesses his offence, / and

[11] Because Aethon, one of the sun's horses, has entered the
zodiacal sign of the Ram (Mar. 21–Apr. 19) three times and because Chloris, goddess of flowers here signifying spring, and Auster,
the south wind here signifying autumn, have visited the earth
twice, Milton must not have seen Young since early 1625.
[12] the east wind, named because Milton was writing to Germany at the time of year that it blows.
[13] The conflicts of the Thirty Years' War threatened Hamburg
particularly after Christian IV of Denmark (a Protestant leader)
was defeated by Tilly, general of the Catholic Holy League, in
Western Germany on Aug. 27, 1626. See also ll. 71–76, where
reference is made to Bernard, William, and Frederick, Dukes of
Saxe-Weimar, who were preparing attacks against Tilly and Wal-
lenstein. Hamburg tried to remain neutral. Enyo (l. 75), a goddess of war, was noted for destruction of cities.
[14] Ulysses, disguised, revealed himself to his wife Penelope several days after his return from the Trojan War and his ensuing
travels.

is ashamed to have forsaken his duty. [60] / Do only you grant forgiveness to him confessed, and to him begging forgiveness; / crimes which lie exposed are wont to be destroyed. / No beast separates its jaws in fearful openings, / nor does the lion tear those lying prone with his wounding claw. / Often the cruel hearts of Thracian[15] lance-bearers [65] / have melted at the melancholy pleas of a suppliant, / and extended hands avert the stroke of the thunderbolt, / and a small sacrifice pacifies the angry gods. / Now for a long while was there the impulse to write to you in that place, / and love would not endure to suffer further delays; [70] / for wandering rumor imparts—alas the truthful messager of calamities— / that in places neighboring upon you wars burst forth, / that you and your city are surrounded by fierce troops, / and that now the Saxon leaders have procured arms. / Everywhere around you Enyo is devastating the fields, [75] / and now blood soaks the land sown with the flesh of men. / And Thrace has yielded its Mars to the Germans; father Mars has driven his Odrysian horses thither. / And now the ever-crested olive fades, / and the goddess[16] detesting the brazen-sounding trumpet has fled, [80] / look, has fled the earth, and now it is believed / the just maid was not the last to fly to the mansions on high. / Nevertheless in the meanwhile the horror of war resounds around you, / and you live alone and destitute on the unfamiliar soil; / and in your foreign residence, indigent, you seek the sustenance [85] / which the hearth of your forefathers does not tender you. / Fatherland, hard parent, and more cruel than the white cliffs / which the spuming wave of your coast beats, / do you think it right thus to expose your innocent children? / To a strange soil thus do you drive them with hard-heartedness? [90] / and do you suffer them to seek livelihood in remote lands / whom provident God himself has sent to you, / and who bring joyous messages from heaven, and who / teach the way which leads beyond the grave to the stars?[17] / In-

15 Thrace (Odrysia, l. 78) was the home of Mars.

16 Astraea; see *Fair Infant,* n. 9. The olive (l. 79) is the symbol of peace; it and truth are meant as perhaps forsaking earth later than justice.

17 Lines 87–94 allude to the probable reason for Young's removal to Hamburg: the requirement that ministers subscribe not only to articles concerning faith and the sacraments in the Thirty-nine Articles, but also to those concerning rites and ceremonies. The "you" of l. 95 are those church and governmental officials responsible for Young's exile.

deed, deservedly, may you, O Fatherland, live enclosed in
Stygian darkness, [95] / and deservedly perish by the eternal
hunger of the soul! / Just as the Tishbite prophet[18] in days
gone by / walked the lonely deserts of the earth with unaccustomed step / and the harsh wastes of Arabia, when he
fled / from the hands of King Ahab and yours, Sidonian
Fury, [100] / and in such fashion, with limbs lacerated by
the dreadful-sounding whip, / was Cilician Paul[19] driven
from the Emathian city; / and the ungrateful citizen of fishy
Gergessa / bade Jesus himself depart from his coasts.[20] /
But you, my tutor, take heart; let not your anxious hope fall
from griefs, [105] / nor pale dread terrify your bones. /
Although you may be covered over by shining arms / and
a thousand spears threaten you with death, / assuredly
your unarmed side shall not be violated by any weapon / and
no lance will drink your blood. [110] / For you yourself will
be safe under the radiant aegis of God.[21] / He will be guardian to you, and he will be champion to you; / he who under
the walls of Sion's fortress / vanquished so many Assyrian sol-
diers in the silent night,[22] / and turned in flight those whom
venerable Damascus [115] / sent to the borders of Samaria
from her ancient plains,[23] / and affrighted the thronging cohorts with their terrified king / when the glorious trumpet
sounded in the empty air, / when the horny hoof scourged
the dusty plain, / when the driven chariot shook the sandy
ground, [120] / and the neighing of horses rushing into battle
was heard, / and the clanking of iron swords, and the deep
roar of men. / And you (because it still remains for the sick
at heart) remember to hope / and conquer these misfortunes
by your magnanimous heart. / And do not doubt at one time

[18] Elijah, who fled into the wilderness from the anger of Ahab's
wife Jezebel, daughter of the king of Sidon (1 Kings xix. 1–4).
[19] Paul, who came from Tarsus in Cilicia, was beaten by the
multitude of Philippi in Macedonia, or Emathia (Acts xvi. 22–23).
[20] Matt. viii. 28–34 relates how Jesus cast out the devils of two
possessed only to have the citizens seek his departure because
their swine had perished along with the devils.
[21] Though Milton refers to Young's ministry under the Christian
God, he fuses with it the pagan image of Jove's protective shield,
borne by Athena, with its Gorgon head warding off all attackers.
[22] the routing of Sennacherib and his Assyrian host at Jerusalem
by the angel of God (2 Kings xix. 35).
[23] The besieging of Samaria by the Damascans under Ben-
Hadad is told in 1 and 2 Kings; the flight here described is found
in 2 Kings vii. 6–7.

or other to enjoy more fortunate years [125] / and to be able
to see again your native home.

(Mar. ? 1627)

ON THE DEATH OF A FAIR INFANT DYING OF A COUGH[1]

I

O Fairest flower no sooner blown but blasted,
Soft silken Primrose fading timelessly,
Summers chief honour if thou hadst out-lasted
Bleak winters force that made thy blossom drie;
For he being amorous on that lovely die   5
    That did thy cheek envermeil, thought to kiss
But kill'd alas, and then bewayl'd his fatal bliss.

II

For since grim *Aquilo*[2] his charioter
By boistrous rape th' *Athenian* damsel got,
He thought it toucht his Deitie full neer,   10
If likewise he some fair one wedded not,
Thereby to wipe away th' infamous blot
    Of long-uncoupled bed, and childless eld,[3]
Which 'mongst the wanton gods a foul reproach was held.

III

So mounting up in icy-pearled carr,   15
Through middle empire of the freezing air
He wanderd long, till thee he spy'd from farr,
There ended was his quest, there ceast his care.
Down he descended from his Snow-soft chair,
    But all unwares with his cold-kind embrace   20
Unhous'd thy Virgin Soul from her fair biding place.

IV

Yet art thou not inglorious in thy fate;
For so *Apollo*, with unweeting[4] hand

---

[1] Anne, daughter of Milton's sister Anne and Edward Phillips,
was born Jan. 12, 1626, and died Jan. 22, 1628. The stanza employed here, like that of the induction to the *Nativity Ode,* is perhaps derived from Phineas Fletcher.
[2] the northeast wind who stole away the Athenian princess
Orithyia.
[3] old age.
[4] "unaware" of the consequences.

Whilom[5] did slay his dearly-loved mate
Young *Hyacinth* born on *Eurotas* strand,   25
Young *Hyacinth* the pride of *Spartan* land;
  But then transform'd him to a purple flower;[6]
Alack that so to change thee winter had no power.

V

Yet can I not perswade me thou art dead
Or that thy corse corrupts in earths dark womb,   30
Or that thy beauties lie in wormie bed,
Hid from the world in a low delved tomb;
Could Heav'n for pittie thee so strictly doom?
  Oh no! for something in thy face did shine
Above mortalitie that shew'd thou wast divine.   35

VI

Resolve me then oh Soul most surely blest
(If so it be that thou these plaints dost hear)
Tell me bright Spirit where e're thou hoverest
Whether above that high first-moving Sphear[7]
Or in th' Elisian fields (if such there were).   40
  Oh say me true if thou wert mortal wight
And why from us so quickly thou didst take thy flight.

VII

Wert thou some Starr which from the ruin'd roof
Of shak't Olympus by mischance didst fall;
Which carefull *Jove* in natures true behoof   45
Took up, and in fit place did reinstall?
Or did of late earths Sons[8] besiege the wall
  Of sheenie Heav'n, and thou some goddess fled
Amongst us here below to hide thy nectar'd head?

VIII

Or wert thou that just Maid[9] who once before   50
Forsook the hated earth, O tell me sooth
And cam'st again to visit us once more?

[5] formerly.
[6] Compare *Lycidas,* 106.
[7] The primum mobile, which lay farthest away from the earth of all other spheres of heavenly bodies, imparted motion to each succeeding inner shell.
[8] the Giants, who waged war against Jove.
[9] Astraea, goddess of justice, the last of the divinities to forsake mankind at the beginning of the Bronze Age because of its impious and wicked conduct.

Or wert thou Mercy that sweet smiling Youth?
Or that crown'd Matron sage white-robed truth?
  Or any other of that heav'nly brood   55
Let down in clowdie throne to do the world some good?

IX

Or wert thou of the golden-winged hoast,
Who having clad thy self in human weed
To earth from thy prefixed[10] seat didst poast,
And after short abode flie back with speed,   60
As if to shew what creatures Heav'n doth breed,
  Thereby to set the hearts of men on fire
To scorn the sordid world, and unto Heav'n aspire?

X

But oh why didst thou not stay here below
To bless us with thy heav'n-lov'd innocence,   65
To slake his wrath whom sin hath made our foe
To turn Swift-rushing black perdition hence,
Or drive away the slaughtering pestilence,[11]
  To stand 'twixt us and our deserved smart?
But thou canst best perform that office where thou art.   70

XI

Then thou the mother of so sweet a child
Her false imagin'd loss cease to lament,
And wisely learn to curb thy sorrows wild;
Think what a present thou to God hast sent,
And render him with patience what he lent;   75
  This if thou do he will an off-spring give,[12]
That till the worlds last-end shall make thy name to live.

(Jan.–Mar. 1628)

At a Vacation Exercise in the Colledge, part Latin, part English. The Latin speeches ended, the English thus began.[1]

[10] ordained.
[11] the plague.
[12] an allusion to the imminent birth of another child; Milton's niece Elizabeth was baptized on Apr. 9, 1628, at St. Martin's-in-the-Fields.

---

[1] The Latin speeches earlier in this exercise at Cambridge and the English prose following are missing; immediately preceding these verses was the sixth prolusion ("Sportive Exercises on occasion are not inconsistent with philosophical Studies"), in which Milton had "thither packt the worst." This poetical fragment illus-

Hail native Language, that by sinews weak
Didst move my first endeavouring tongue to speak,
And mad'st imperfect words with childish trips,
Half unpronounc't, slide through my infant-lips,
Driving dumb silence from the portal dore,   5
Where he had mutely sate two years before:
Here I salute thee and thy pardon ask
That now I use thee in my latter task:
Small loss it is that thence can come unto thee,
I know my tongue but little Grace can do thee: 10
Thou needst not be ambitious to be first,
Believe me I have thither packt the worst:
And, if it happen as I did forecast,
The daintiest dishes shall be serv'd up last.
I pray thee then deny me not thy aid   15
For this same small neglect that I have made:
But haste thee strait to do me once a Pleasure,
And from thy wardrope bring thy chiefest treasure;
Not those new fangled toys, and trimming slight
Which takes our late fantasticks with delight,   20
But cull those richest Robes, and gay'st attire
Which deepest Spirits, and choicest Wits desire:
I have some naked thoughts that rove about
And loudly knock to have their passage out;
And wearie of their place do only stay   25
Till thou hast deck't them in thy best array;
That so they may without suspect or fears
Fly swiftly to this fair Assembly's ears;
Yet I had rather, if I were to chuse,
Thy service in some graver subject use,   30
Such as may make thee search thy coffers round,
Before thou cloath my fancy in fit sound:
Such where the deep transported mind may soar
Above the wheeling poles, and at Heav'ns dore
Look in, and see each blissful Deitie   35
How he before the thunderous throne doth lie,
Listening to what unshorn *Apollo*[2] sings
To th' touch of golden wires, while *Hebe* brings

---

trates his topic well, for the basis of this humor is satire on scholastic logic. The midsummer frolic for which these verses were written
consisted of numerous skits and recitals; perhaps Milton's fellow
performers were the "late fantasticks" of l. 20.

  [2] god of music, usually represented with long hair to indicate
his youth.

Immortal Nectar to her Kingly Sire:[3]
Then passing through the Sphears of watchful fire,   40
And mistie Regions of wide air next under,
And hills of Snow and lofts of piled Thunder,
May tell at length how green-ey'd *Neptune* raves,
In Heav'ns defiance mustering all his waves;[4]
Then sing of secret things that came to pass   45
When Beldam Nature in her cradle was;
And last of Kings and Queens and Heroes old,
Such as the wise *Demodocus* once told
In solemn songs at King *Alcinous* feast,[5]
While sad *Ulisses* soul and all the rest   50
Are held with his melodious harmonie
In willing chains and sweet captivitie.
But fie my wandring Muse how thou dost stray!
Expectance calls thee now another way,
Thou know'st it must be now thy only bent   55
To keep in compass of thy Predicament:[6]
Then quick about thy purpos'd business come,
That to the next I may resign my Room.

Then Ens *is represented as Father of the Predicaments his
ten Sons, whereof the Eldest stood for* Substance *with
his Canons, which* Ens *thus speaking, explains.*[7]

Good luck befriend thee Son; for at thy birth
The Fairy Ladies daunc't upon the hearth;[8]   60
Thy drowsie Nurse hath sworn she did them spie
Come tripping to the Room where thou didst lie;

[3] Jove.
[4] Neptune defied the gods in seeking revenge on Ulysses for the blinding of his son.
[5] See *Od.*, VIII, 499–522.
[6] Though he puns on the meaning of the word in logic (see next note), Milton means both the classification of subject assigned him and the plight imposed by not writing what he would prefer.
[7] Milton appeared as Ens, the Aristotelian principle of Absolute Being, father of the ten categories (or predicaments) into which all knowledge can be reduced (*Organon*, Part 1). In addition to the eldest son Substance, these are: Quantity, Quality, Relation, Place, Time, Posture, Possession, Action, and Passion. The canons are the fundamental principles or properties which are common to Substance; e.g., Substance supports the other predicaments (or accidents) and keeps them together.
[8] Thus Substance has been imbued with good fortune.

And sweetly singing round about thy Bed
Strew all their blessings on thy sleeping Head.
She heard them give thee this, that thou should'st still   65
From eyes of mortals walk invisible;[9]
Yet there is something that doth force my fear,
For once it was my dismal hap to hear
A *Sybil* old, bow-bent with crooked age,
That far events full wisely could presage,   70
And in times long and dark Prospective Glass
Fore-saw what future dayes should bring to pass;
Your Son, said she (nor can you it prevent),
Shall subject be to many an Accident.
O're all his Brethren he shall Reign as King,[10]   75
Yet every one shall make him underling,
And those that cannot live from him asunder
Ungratefully shall strive to keep him under;
In worth and excellence he shall out-go them,
Yet being above them, he shall be below them;   80
From others he shall stand in need of nothing,
Yet on his Brothers shall depend for Cloathing.
To find a Foe it shall not be his hap,[11]
And peace shall lull him in her flowry lap;
Yet shall he live in strife, and at his dore   85
Devouring war[12] shall never cease to roar:
Yea it shall be his natural property
To harbour those that are at enmity.[13]
What power, what force, what mighty spell, if not
Your learned hands, can loose this Gordian knot?[14]   90
The next, Quantity *and* Quality, *spake in Prose, then* Rela-
        tion *was call'd by his Name.*

Rivers[15] arise; whether thou be the Son

[9] invisible because Substance cannot be perceived except through
the other nine categories (the accidents of Substance) Milton puns
on "accident" in l. 74, and the literal meaning of "Substance"
("stands under") in ll. 74–80.
[10] Perhaps Edward King, subject of *Lycidas,* enacted the role
of Substance.
[11] There is no opposite to Substance.
[12] the change of substance bitterly disputed in the Eucharist.
[13] Though the accidents make up the whole (lulling peace),
some are endlessly opposed (e.g., Action and Passion).
[14] a complicated situation, difficult to undo.
[15] Not only does Milton catalogue English rivers in the remaining lines, but he puns: George or Nizell Rivers apparently was
Relation.

Of utmost *Tweed,* or *Oose,* or gulphie *Dun,*
Or *Trent,* who like some earth-born Giant spreads
His thirty Armes along th' indented Meads,
Or sullen *Mole* that runneth underneath,   95
Or *Severn* swift, guilty of Maidens[16] death,
Or rockie *Avon,* or of sedgie *Lee,*
Or coaly *Tine,* or antient hallow'd *Dee,*[17]
Or *Humber* loud that keeps the *Scythians* Name,[18]
Or *Medway* smooth, or Royal Towred *Thame.*   100

The rest was Prose.
(July 1628)

ELEGIA QUINTA
(Elegy 5)

On the coming of spring

In his perpetual cycle Time, rolling back, / now recalls fresh zephyrs, with warming spring. / And the restored earth is covered with brief youth / and now the ground, free from frost, is becoming delightfully green. / Am I mistaken? or are powers returning to my songs, [5] / and is inspiration present in me by the favor of spring? / It is present by the favor of spring, and again begins to flourish from it / (who may suspect?) and even now demands some work for itself. / The cleft Castalian peak[1] hovers before my eyes / and dreams transport Pyrene[2] to me in the night. [10] / And my excited breast enflames me with its strange emotion, / and I am made delirious, and a divine sound agitates me from within. / Apollo himself appears—I see his locks entwined / with Daphne's laurel—Apollo himself is descended.[3] / Now my mind is snatched from me into the heights of the liquid sky, [15] / and through the wandering clouds I fly, free from my body. /

[16]Sabrina's; see *A Mask,* ll. 824–32.
[17] The Dee was considered divine since its fluctuations predicted success or failure to the early Britons.
[18] Spenser tells the story of Humber, a Scythian king driven into the river where he drowned (*FQ,* II, x, 14–16; IV, xi, 38).

[1] See *El.* 4, n. 10.
[2] a fountain at Corinth.
[3] Pursued by Apollo, Daphne was turned into a laurel at her own entreaty; thereafter, the leaves of the tree became a symbol of his patronage of poetry and music.

And through shadows and through caves, the sanctuaries of
the poets, / I am borne, and to me the secret temples of the
gods are accessible. / My spirit observes all that is done on
Olympus, / and the hidden infernal regions do not escape my
eyes. [20] / What does my soul sing so sublimely from its
full mouth? / What does this madness bring forth, what this
sacred rage? / Spring which has furnished me inspiration
shall be sung through it; / her returned gifts may have been
profitable in this way. / Already, Philomela,[4] you are beginning your modulations, hidden [25] / by the young leaves,
while all the grove is still. / I in the city, you in the wood,
let us both begin together / and together let each sing the
coming of spring. / Ho! changes of spring have returned; let
us celebrate the hours / of spring, and let the unfailing Muse
take this task upon herself. [30] / Now the sun, fleeing the
Ethiopians and the fields of Tithonus, / directs his golden reins
toward Arctos' lands.[5] / Brief is the journey of night, brief is
the delay of dark night; / that dreadful one lives in exile with
her shadows. / And now Lycaonian Boötes,[6] wearied, does
not follow [35] / in his celestial wain over the course as
before; / now even the few stars keep their accustomed watch
/ about the courts of Jove throughout the entire sky. /
For deceit and slaughter and violence retired with the
night; / neither have the gods feared the wickedness of the
giants.[7] [40] / Perhaps some shepherd, reclining on the top
of a cliff / while the dewy earth reddens with the first sun-
light, / asserts, "Then, certainly on this night were you deprived, / Apollo, of your love who would delay your swift
steeds." / Delighted, Cynthia[8] returns to her forests, and resumes her quiver, [45] / when she sees on high the wheels
of Lucifer, / and setting down her feeble beams she seems
to be happy / that her task is made short by her brother's
power. / Abandon, Apollo says, your aged wedlock, Aurora; /
What is pleasing in having lain stretched out on an impotent

[4] the nightingale, whose song in spring portends success in love.
[5] the vernal equinox. Ethiopia was considered all Africa south
of Egypt; Tithonus, loved by Aurora, the dawn, stands for the
east; and Arctos, the double constellation of the Great and Lesser
Bears, is the north.
[6] See *Ely,* n. 12. Lycaon, the son of Callisto (the Wain) and
Jove, is the Lesser Bear.
[7] See *Fair Infant,* n. 8.
[8] the moon; Lucifer is the sun.

bed?[9] [50] / Aeolides,[10] the hunter, awaits you on the green lawn. / Arise; high Hymettus[11] enjoys your fires. / With modest face the blushing goddess confesses her guilt, / and drives her morning horses more swiftly. / The reviving earth shakes off her hated old age [55] / and wishes to submit to your embraces, Apollo. / Not only does she wish them, but she is worthy of them; for what is / more beautiful than she, as, voluptuous, she bares her all-bearing breasts / and breathes the harvests of Arabia, and from her elegant mouth / pours gentle fragrances with Paphian roses? [60] / Behold, her lofty brow is crowned by a sacred wood / just as a piny tower encompasses Idaean Ops,[12] / and she twines her dewy locks with various bloom / and with her flowers she is seen able to please, / just as the Sicilian goddess, wreathed round her flowing locks with flowers, [65] / was pleasing to the Taenarian god.[13] / Look, Apollo, facile loves are calling you / and vernal winds blow honey-sweet pleas. / Odor-bearing Zephyrus gently claps his cinnamon-scented wings / and the birds seem to carry their flatteries to you. [70] / The thoughtless earth does not seek your loves without dowry, / nor does she beg desired marriage, as if in need; / bounteous, she offers you health-bearing grain for medical uses / and hence she herself supports your titles.[14] / Because if money, if glittering gifts impress you [75] / (love is often bought with gifts), / she holds out to you whatever wealth conceals / under the broad sea and under the overthrown mountains. / Ah, how often when, wearied by steep Olympus, / you would sink into the western seas, [80] / does she say, Why should the blue mother receive you, / Apollo, fainting from your daily course into her Hesperian waters? / What have you to do with Tethys?[15] with Tartessian streams? / Why do you bathe your divine face in the filthy brine? / You will entrap coolness much better in my shadow, Apollo. [85] / Come hither, moisten your glittering locks in the dew; / a gentler

[9] Jove made her beloved Tithonus immortal but not eternally youthful.

[10] While hunting, Cephalus, also beloved by Aurora, unwittingly killed his jealous wife Procis.

[11] a mountain overlooking Athens.

[12] goddess of crops, identified with Earth and Cybele, the Great Mother, who was worshipped on Mt. Ida.

[13] See *Vice-Chancellor*, n. 16.

[14] Apollo was god of healing.

[15] consort of Oceanus and mother of rivers. Hesperia was the west, and Tartessus, a maritime city of Spain.

sleep will come to you in the chill grass. / Come hither and
place your rays on my bosom; / wheresoever you lie about, a
gently murmuring breeze will soothe / our bodies spread on
humid roses. [90] / A destiny like Semele's[16] (believe me)
does not frighten me, / nor the axle smoking from Phaeton's
horse. / When you, Apollo, use your fire more wisely, / come
hither and place your rays on my bosom. / Thus wanton
Earth breathes out her loves; [95] / her remaining throng
rush to ruin by example of the mother. / For now wandering
Cupid runs through all the world, / and sustains his dying
torches by the flame of the sun. / The lethal horns of his bow
resound with new strings, / the tremulous arrows glitter severely with new iron. [100] / And now he attempts to subdue
even the invincible Diana, / whoever sits in the sacred hearth
by the chaste Vesta. / Venus herself annually refreshes her
aging form, / and is believed sprung anew from the warm
sea. / Through the marble cities the youth cry aloud, Hymen; [105] / the shore and hollow rocks echo, Io, Hymen. /
He appears more elegant and more becoming in proper dress;
/ his odorous attire diffuses the perfume of purple crocus. /
And many a girl with her virgin breasts encircled with gold /
comes forth to the inward joys of lovely spring. [110] / Each
is her own vow; one vow of all is the same, / that Cytherea
will give her the man whom she desires. / Now also the shepherd is making music on his sevenfold reed pipe / and Phyllis
has songs which she joins to his. / The sailor calms his stars
with nocturnal song [115] / and calls the swift dolphins to
the surface of the shallows.[17] / Jove sports himself on high
Olympus with his spouse / and assembles the servile gods
to his feast. / Now even the satyrs, when the evening shadows rise, / flit about through the flowery fields in a swift
dance, [120] / and Sylvanus girded with his cypress foliage,
/ and the god half-goat and the goat half-god. / The Dryads
who have lurked under the ancient trees / wander through
the mountains and the lonely fields. / Maenalian Pan revels
through the crops and the thickets; [125] / hardly mother
Cybele, hardly Ceres is safe from him; / and lustful Faunus
ravishes some Oread, / while the nymph reflects to herself on
trembling feet. / And now she lies hidden, and lurking she
wishes to be seen poorly concealed, / and she flees, and fleeing

[16] Juno, in anger, persuaded her to entreat Jove to visit her, a
mortal, as a god, for Juno knew that she would be consumed by
his lightning.
[17] alluding to the myth of Arion.

she may wish herself to be made captive. [130] / The gods
also do not hesitate to prefer the woods to heaven, / and every grove possesses its own deities. / Long may every grove
possess its own deities; / ye gods, I pray, do not go from your
arboreal home! / May the golden age restore you, Jove, to a
wretched world! [135] / Why do you come back with your
cruel weapons in the clouds? / At least drive your swift team,
Apollo, as leisurely / as you can, and may the time of spring
pass slowly; / and may foul winter bring prolonged nights tar-
dily, / and may shadow attack later within our heavens. [140]

(spring 1629)

ON THE MORNING OF CHRISTS NATIVITY[1]

I

This is the Month, and this the happy morn
Wherin the Son of Heav'ns eternal King,
Of wedded Maid, and Virgin Mother born,
Our great redemption from above did bring;
For so the holy sages once did sing,   5
  That he our deadly forfeit should release,
And with his Father work us a perpetual peace.

II

That glorious Form, that Light unsufferable,
And that far-beaming blaze of Majesty,
Wherwith he wont at Heav'ns high Councel-Table,   10
To sit the midst of Trinal Unity,

<hr>

1 The theme is the celebration of Christ's harmonizing of all life
by becoming mortal man. This gift of praise for the birthday of
Christ has been divided into a pattern of creative sun or silence
(I–VIII), the concord which is the essence of music (IX–XVIII),
and the conquest and reconciliation of discordant paganism (XIX–
XXVI). The return to silence in the last stanza rounds out the
pattern drawn by Arthur Barker in *UTQ*, X (1941), 167–81.
Don C. Allen (*The Harmonious Vision*) emphasizes the conflict
between Milton's aesthetic and intellectual daemons (p. 25), but
concludes that the timelessness, immutable Nature, and harmony
of God unify the poem (p. 29). The symbolic darkness in the
later stanzas, seen against the intermingled and identified light and
music of the earlier ones, is dispersed, as Rosemond Tuve reminds
us in *Images and Themes*, p. 71, by the heavenly love, described
in XXVII in images of brightness, which will work a perpetual
peace. The fullest annotation will be found in Albert S. Cook's
notes on the ode in *Trans. of the Connecticut Acad. of Arts and
Sciences*, XV (1909), 307–68.

He laid aside;[2] and here with us to be,
   Forsook the Courts of everlasting Day,
And chose with us a darksom House of mortal Clay.

III

Say Heav'nly Muse, shall not thy sacred vein   15
Afford a present to the Infant God?
Hast thou no vers, no hymn, or solemn strein,
To welcom him to this his new abode,
Now while the Heav'n by the Suns team untrod,
   Hath took no print of the approaching light,   20
And all the spangled host keep watch in squadrons bright?

IV

See how from far upon the Eastern rode
The Star-led Wisards[3] haste with odours sweet:
O run, prevent[4] them with thy humble ode,
And lay it lowly at his blessed feet;   25
Have thou the honour first, thy Lord to greet,
   And joyn thy voice unto the Angel Quire,
From out his secret Altar toucht with hallow'd fire.[5]

THE HYMN

I

It was the Winter wild,
While the Heav'n-born-child,   30
   All meanly wrapt in the rude manger lies;
Nature in aw to him
Had doff't her gawdy trim,
   With her great Master so to sympathize:
It was no season then for her   35
To wanton with the Sun, her lusty Paramour.

II

Onely with speeches fair
She woos the gentle Air
   To hide her guilty front with innocent Snow,

---

[2] Christ's *kenosis* or emptying himself of his godhead (Phil. ii. 6–8).
[3] the three Wise Men.
[4] anticipate.
[5] Isa. vi. 6–7: "Then flew one of the seraphims unto me, having a live coal in his hand, which he had taken with the tongs from off the altar: And he laid it upon my mouth, and said, Lo, this hath touched thy lips."

And on her naked shame,   40
Pollute[6] with sinfull blame,
    The Saintly Vail of Maiden white to throw,
Confounded, that her Makers eyes
Should look so neer upon her foul deformities.

III

But he her fears to cease,   45
Sent down the meek-ey'd Peace;
    She crown'd with Olive green,[7] came softly sliding
Down through the turning sphear[8]
His ready Harbinger,
    With Turtle wing the amorous clouds dividing,   50
And waving wide her mirtle wand,
She strikes a universall Peace through Sea and Land.

IV

No War, or Battails sound
Was heard the World around:[9]
    The idle spear and shield were high up hung;   55
The hooked Chariot stood
Unstain'd with hostile blood,
    The Trumpet spake not to the armed throng,
And Kings sate still with awfull eye,
As if they surely knew their sovran Lord was by.   60

V

But peacefull was the night
Wherin the Prince of light
    His raign of peace upon the earth began:
The Winds with wonder whist,[10]
Smoothly the waters kist,   65
    Whispering new joyes to the mild Ocean,
Who now hath quite forgot to rave,
While Birds of Calm[11] sit brooding on the charmed wave.

[6] polluted.

[7] The dove Peace (the "turtledove" of l. 50) brought an olive branch to the ark as a sign of harmony with nature; the reference suggests the descent of the dove (the Spirit of God) at Christ's baptism.

[8] the heavens.

[9] No war took place in the Roman Empire for some years before Jesus' birth.

[10] hushed.

[11] the halcyons, which were supposed to breed only when the sea is calm; the waves are thought of as under a spell.

VI

The Stars with deep amaze
Stand fixt in stedfast gaze,   70
  Bending one way their pretious influence,[12]
And will not take their flight,
For all the morning light,
  Or *Lucifer*[13] that often warn'd them thence;
But in their glimmering Orbs did glow,   75
Untill their Lord himself bespake, and bid them go.

VII

And though the shady gloom
Had given day her room,
  The Sun himself with-held his wonted speed,
And hid his head for shame,   80
As his inferiour flame,
  The new-enlight'n'd world no more should need;
He saw a greater Sun appear
Then his bright Throne, or burning Axletree[14] could bear.

VIII

The Shepherds[15] on the Lawn,   85
Or ere the point of dawn,
  Sate simply chatting in a rustick row;
Full little thought they than,
That the mighty *Pan*[16]
  Was kindly[17] com to live with them below;   90
Perhaps their loves, or els their sheep,
Was all that did their silly[18] thoughts so busie keep.

IX

When such musick sweet
Their hearts and ears did greet,
  As never was by mortall singer strook,   95
Divinely-warbled voice
Answering the stringed noise,
  As all their souls in blisfull rapture took:

[12] The stars, shining toward Bethlehem, are exerting all their power of good fortune on the Christ-child.
[13] the morning star.
[14] the axle of the sun's chariot.
[15] Compare Luke ii. 8–20.
[16] Christ, the Good Shepherd.
[17] both "in kindness" and "in kinship" as man.
[18] simple.

The Air such pleasure loth to lose,
With thousand echoes still prolongs each heav'nly   100
    close.[19]

X

Nature that heard such sound
Beneath the hollow round
    Of *Cynthia's* seat,[20] the Airy region thrilling,
Now was almost won
To think her part was don,   105
    And that her raign had here its last fulfilling;
She knew such harmony[21] alone
Could hold all Heav'n and Earth in happier union.

XI

At last surrounds their sight
A Globe of circular light,   110
    That with long beams the shame-fac't night array'd,
The helmed Cherubim
And sworded Seraphim
    Are seen in glittering ranks with wings displaid,
Harping in loud and solemn quire,   115
With unexpressive[22] notes to Heav'ns new-born Heir.

XII

Such Musick (as 'tis said)[23]
Before was never made,
    But when of old the sons of morning sung,
While the Creator Great   120
His constellations set,
    And the well-ballanc't world on hinges hung,
And cast the dark foundations deep,
And bid the weltring waves their oozy channel keep.

XIII

Ring out ye Crystall sphears,[24]   125

[19] cadence.
[20] orb of the moon.
[21] in the union both of nature and of divine and human natures in the Incarnation.
[22] inexpressible.
[23] Job xxxviii. 6–7: "Whereupon are the foundations thereof fastened? . . . When the morning stars sang together, and all the sons of God shouted for joy?"
[24] The music of the nine spheres (the ninth being the Crystalline) resulted from the harmony of single tones uttered by each

Once bless our human ears,
   (If ye have power to touch our senses so)
And let your silver chime
Move in melodious time;
   And let the Base of Heav'ns deep Organ blow,   130
And with your ninefold harmony
Make up full consort[25] to th' Angelick symphony.

XIV

For if such holy Song
Enwrap our fancy long,
   Time will run back, and fetch the age of gold,[26]   135
And speckl'd[27] vanity
Will sicken soon and die,
   And leprous sin will melt from earthly mould,
And Hell it self will pass away,
And leave her dolorous mansions to the peering day.   140

XV

Yea Truth, and Justice then
Will down return to men,
   Orb'd in a Rain-bow; and like glories wearing
Mercy will sit between,
Thron'd in Celestiall sheen,   145
   With radiant feet the tissued clouds down stearing,
And Heav'n as at som festivall,
Will open wide the Gates of her high Palace Hall.

XVI

But wisest Fate sayes no,
This must not yet be so,   150
   The Babe lies yet in smiling Infancy,
That on the bitter cross
Must redeem our loss;
   So both himself and us to glorifie:

---

of the sirens as she traveled about the earth on her allotted sphere
(*Rep.*, X, 616–17). Pythagoreans believed that only the sinless
could hear this "silver chime."

[25] concert, group.

[26] the early age when Saturn ruled the world. It was an age of
innocent happiness when men lived without strife, labor, or in-
justice.

[27] polluted, abominable. The phrase may translate Horace's
"maculosum nefas" (*Odes,* IV, v, 22) with reference to Ecclesiastes.

Yet first to those ychain'd in sleep,[28]   155
The wakefull trump of doom must thunder through the deep,

XVII

With such a horrid clang
As on mount *Sinai* rang
  While the red fire, and smouldring clouds out brake:[29]
The aged Earth agast   160
With terrour of that blast,
  Shall from the surface to the center shake,
When at the worlds last session,
The dreadfull Judge in middle Air shall spread his throne.

XVIII

And then at last our bliss   165
Full and perfect is,
  But now begins; for from this happy day
Th' old Dragon[30] under ground
In straiter limits bound,
  Not half so far casts his usurped sway,   170
And wroth to see his Kingdom fail,
Swindges[31] the scaly Horrour of his foulded tail.

XIX

The Oracles are dumm,[32]
No voice or hideous humm
  Runs through the arched roof in words deceiving.   175
Apollo from his shrine
Can no more divine,

[28] death.

[29] The giving of the ten commandments (Exod. xix. 18–19: "And mount Sinai was altogether on a smoke, because the Lord descended upon it in fire: and the smoke thereof ascended as the smoke of a furnace, and the whole mount quaked. And when the voice of the trumpet sounded long, and waxed louder and louder, Moses spoke . . .") is related to Judgment Day when "The heavens being on fire shall be dissolved, and the elements shall melt with fervent heat" (2 Peter iii. 12).

[30] Rev. xx. 2–3: "And he laid hold on the dragon, that old serpent, which is the Devil, and Satan, and bound him a thousand years, And cast him into the bottomless pit, and shut him up, ..."

[31] beats, shakes (his coiled tail).

[32] The birth of Christ begins the destruction of the pagan divinities, extending through XXV, by stilling the false oracles of the heathen.

With hollow shreik the steep of *Delphos* leaving.
No nightly trance, or breathed spell,
Inspires the pale-ey'd[33] Priest from the prophetic cell.   180

XX

The lonely mountains o're,
And the resounding shore,
    A voice of weeping heard, and loud lament;[34]
From haunted spring, and dale
Edg'd with poplar pale,   185
    The parting Genius[35] is with sighing sent;
With flowr-inwov'n tresses torn
The Nimphs in twilight shade of tangled thickets mourn.

XXI

In consecrated Earth,
And on the holy Hearth,   190
    The *Lars*, and *Lemures*[36] moan with midnight plaint;
In Urns, and Altars round,
A drear, and dying sound
    Affrights the *Flamins* at their service quaint;
And the chill Marble seems to sweat,[37]   195
While each peculiar power forgoes his wonted seat.

XXII

Peor,[38] and *Baalim*,

[33] perhaps "paled with fear," derived from the Latin usage of "palleo."

[34] Matt. ii. 18: "In Rama was there a voice heard, lamentation, and weeping, and great mourning . . . ."

[35] the spirit presiding over any particular place, such as a wood.

[36] gods presiding over the home and spirits of the dead. "*Flamins*," l. 194, were Roman priests.

[37] foreboding ill (see *Ec.*, I, 480).

[38] The pagan divinities put to rout (XXII–XXV) are: *Peor*, the Phoenician sun god; *Baalim*, local Phoenician deities concerned with flocks; the Philistine fish god *Dagon*, whose statue was cast down twice because the people of Ashdod had taken the ark of God (1 Sam. v. 3–4); *Ashtaroth*, a Phoenician female divinity, identified with Astarte and Venus; *Ammon*, the North African name for Jove, who as tender of flocks was represented as a ram; *Thammuz*, the Phoenician Adonis, who was killed by a wild boar and revered as a vegetation god (compare Ezek. viii. 14: "behold, there sat women weeping for Tammuz"); *Moloch*, a Semitic deity, represented by a hollow idol filled with fire to consume sacrificed children whose cries were drowned out by cymbals and trumpets; the Egyptian deities *Isis*, the earth goddess, with the head of a

Forsake their Temples dim,
  With that twise batter'd god of *Palestine*,
And mooned *Ashtaroth*,   200
Heav'ns Queen and Mother both,
  Now sits not girt with Tapers holy shine,
The Libyc *Hammon* shrinks his horn,
In vain the *Tyrian* Maids their wounded *Thamuz* mourn.

XXIII

And sullen *Moloch* fled,   205
Hath left in shadows dred
  His burning Idol all of blackest hue;
In vain with Cymbals ring,
They call the grisly king,
  In dismall dance about the furnace blue;   210
The brutish gods of *Nile* as fast,
Isis and *Orus*, and the Dog *Anubis* hast.

XXIV

Nor is *Osiris* seen
In *Memphian* Grove, or Green,
  Trampling th' unshowr'd[39] Grass with lowings loud: 215
Nor can he be at rest
Within his sacred chest,
  Naught but profoundest Hell can be his shroud;
In vain with Timbrel'd Anthems dark
The sable-stoled Sorcerers bear his worshipt Ark.[40]   220

XXV

He feels from *Juda*'s Land
The dredded Infants hand,
  The rayes of *Bethlehem* blind his dusky eyn;
Nor all the gods beside,
Longer dare abide,   225
  Not *Typhon* huge ending in snaky twine:
Our Babe to shew his Godhead true,

---

cow (thus "brutish"); *Horus*, the hawk-headed sun god; *Anubis*,
guide of the dead with the head of a jackal; and *Osiris*, the chief
god and judge of the dead, identified with Apis, the Sacred Bull,
which was buried in the temple of Serapis at Memphis; and
Typhon, a hundred-headed serpent who killed Osiris, scattering
truth to the four winds (*Areo.*, p. 29).

39 referring to the aridity of Egypt.

40 Osiris' "sacred chest" borne by his black-robed priests to a
temple, accompanied by the sound of tambourines.

Can in his swadling bands[41] controul the damned crew.

XXVI

So when the Sun in bed,
Curtain'd with cloudy red,   230
   Pillows his chin upon an Orient wave,
The flocking shadows pale
Troop to th' infernall jail,[42]
   Each fetter'd Ghost slips to his severall grave,
And the yellow-skirted *Fayes*   235
Fly after the Night-steeds, leaving their Moon-lov'd maze.

XXVII

But see the Virgin blest,
Hath laid her Babe to rest.
   Time is our tedious[43] Song should here have ending:
Heav'ns youngest teemed Star[44]   240
Hath fixt her polisht Car,
   Her sleeping Lord with Handmaid Lamp attending,
And all about the Courtly Stable,
Bright-harnest[45] Angels sit in order serviceable.

(Dec. 1629)

ELEGIA SEXTA
(Elegy 6)

To Charles Diodati, sojourning in the country[1]

*Who, when he wrote on the thirteenth of December and
asked that his verses be excused if they were less esti-
mable than usual, being in the midst of the splendors
with which he had been received by his friends, de-
clared himself to be able to produce by no means
sufficiently auspicious work for the Muses, thus had
this answer.*

On an empty stomach I send you a wish for health, / which
you, stuffed full, can perhaps do without. / But why does your

[41] Compare Luke ii. 7. The line glances at the legend of the
strength of the infant Hercules.

[42] Evil spirits return at morning to their graves or to hell.

[43] wearying (since lengthy).

[44] The star of Bethlehem, latest born, has taken position to
shine its light on Christ the King.

[45] wearing bright armor.

[1] For Diodati, see *El.* 1, n. 1.

Muse provoke mine, / and not permit it to be able to pursue its chosen obscurity? / You would like to know by song how I return your love and revere you; [5] / believe me, you can scarcely learn this from song, / for my love is not confined by brief measures, / nor does it itself proceed unimpaired on halting feet.[2] / How well you report the customary sumptuous feasts and jovial December / and festivals that have honored the heaven-fleeing god,[3] [10] / the sports and pleasures of winter in the country, / and the French wines consumed beside agreeable fires. / Why do you complain that poetry is a fugitive from wine and feasts? / Song loves Bacchus, Bacchus loves songs.[4] / Nor did it shame Apollo to wear the green leaves of ivy [15] / and to prefer ivy to his own laurel.[5] / On the Aonian hills the assembled ninefold band / has often evoked Euoe from the Thyonean troop.[6] / Ovid sent poor verses from the Corallian fields;[7] / in that land there were no banquets, nor had the grape been planted. [20] / What but wine and roses and Lyaeus wreathed with clusters / did the Teian poet[8] sing in his shortened measures? / And Teumasian Euan inspires Pindaric odes, / and every page is redolent of the consumed wine, / while the laden chariot clatters on its back from an upset axle, [25] / and the horseman speeds on, darkened with Elean dust; / and the Roman lyricist,[9] wet with four-year-old wine, / sang of sweet Glycera and golden-haired Chloe. / Indeed your table bathed in generous provision also / nourishes the powers of your mind and encourages your genius. [30] / The Massican[10] cups foam out productive strength, / and you decant your verses contained within the wine-flask itself. / To this we add the arts and outpouring of Apollo through your inmost / heart; Bacchus,

2 the elegiac couplet.

3 that is, becoming man on earth.

4 As god of wine, who loosens care, Bacchus inspired music and poetry.

5 See *El.* 5, n. 3.

6 See *El.* 4, n. 10. Thyoneus is Bacchus, also called Lyaeus (l. 21), meaning "deliverer from care," and Teumesian Euan (l. 23), "Euoe" being a shout heard at his festivals.

7 See *El.* 1, n. 3. Reference is to *Epistles from Pontus,* IV, viii, 80–83.

8 Anacreon.

9 Horace in his *Odes.*

10 Mt. Massicus in Campania, which was celebrated for its excellent wine.

Apollo, Ceres together are favorable.[11] / No wonder then
that it is not doubted, for the three gods [35] / through you
have created their delightful songs with combined divinity. /
Now also for you the Thracian lyre[12] with inlaid gold / is
sounding, gently plucked by a melodious hand; / and the lyre
is heard about the hanging tapestries, / which rules the
maiden feet by its rhythmic art. [40] / At the least let these
scenes detain your Muses / and recall whatever sluggish in-
toxication drives away. / Believe me, while the ivory plays
on and the lyre / regales the perfumed halls with attendant
festive dance, / you will feel silent Apollo creep through your
breast [45] / like a sudden heat that permeates to the bones;
/ and through maiden eyes and sounding finger / gliding
Thalia[13] will invade all bosoms. / For gay Elegy is the
concern of many gods / and she calls those whom she wishes
to her measures; [50] / Liber gives attention to elegiac
verse, and Erato, Ceres, and Venus, / and with his rosy mother
is delicate Love. / For such poets thereafter great banquets
are allowed / and often to become soft with old wine. / But
who records wars and heaven under mature Jove, [55] / and
pious heroes and half-divine leaders, / and now who sings the
sacred counsels of the supreme gods, / now the infernal
realms bayed by the fierce dog,[14] / let him live indeed
frugally in the fashion / of the Samian teacher,[15] and let
herbage furnish his harmless food. [60] / Let the clear water
near at hand stand in its bowl of beech wood, / and let him
drink nonintoxicating potions from the pure spring. / His
youth void of crime and chaste is joined to this / by stern
morals and without stain of hand. / With like nature, shining
with sacred vestment and lustral waters, [65] / does the priest
rise to go to the hostile gods. / By this rule it is said wise
Tiresias lived / after his eyes were put out, and Ogygian

[11] Bacchus because of the wine-filled festivals, Apollo because
Diodati was preparing for a medical career, and Ceres because of
the feasts.

[12] referring to Orpheus.

[13] Muse of comedy and bucolic poetry; Erato (l. 51) is the
Muse of lyric and amatory poetry. Liber, a god of vine-growers,
was identified with Bacchus; but he also was a spirit of creative-
ness.

[14] Cerberus, guardian of Hades.

[15] Pythagoras and his school practised asceticism, particularly
in eating.

Linus,[16] / and Calchas fugitive from his appointed house, and old / Orpheus with the vanquished beasts among the forsaken caves. [70] / Thus the one poor of feast, thus Homer, drinker of water, / carried the man of Ithaca through the vast seas / and through the monster-making palace of the daughter[17] of Perseis and Apollo, / and shallows dangerous with Siren songs, / and through your mansions, infernal king, where by dark blood [75] / he is said to have engaged the trooping shades. / For truly the poet is sacred to the gods, and priest of the gods, / and his hidden heart and lips breathe Jove. / But if you will know what I am doing (if only at least / you consider it to be important to know whether I am doing anything) [80] / I am singing the King, bringer of peace by his divine origin,[18] / and the blessed times promised in the sacred books, / and the crying of our God and his stabling under the meagre roof, / who with his Father inhabits the heavenly realms; / and the heavens insufficient of stars and the hosts singing in the air, [85] / and the gods suddenly destroyed in their temples. / I dedicate these gifts in truth to the birthday of Christ, / gifts which the first light of dawn brought to me. / For you these thoughts formed on my native pipes are also waiting; / you, when I recite them, will be the judge for me of their worth. [90]

(Dec. 1629)

THE PASSION[1]

I

Ere-while of Musick, and Ethereal mirth,
Wherwith the stage of Ayr and Earth did ring,
And joyous news of heav'nly Infants birth,

---

[16] The Theban Linus instructed Orpheus and Hercules on the lyre; Calchas (l. 69) was the Greek seer at Troy.

[17] Circe.

[18] the *Nativity Ode*, written in English ("on my native pipes," l. 89) around Christmas 1629.

---

[1] Intended as a kind of sequel to the *Nativity Ode*, which is mentioned in the first stanza, these verses seem to be only an induction to the main subject, Jesus' suffering and crucifixion. An appended note indicates why the poem was not completed: "This Subject the Author finding to be above the yeers he had, when he wrote it, and nothing satisfi'd with what was begun, left it unfinisht."

My muse with Angels did divide[2] to sing;
But headlong joy is ever on the wing, 5
   In Wintry solstice like the short'n'd light
Soon swallow'd up in dark and long out-living night.

II

For now to sorrow must I tune my song,
And set my Harp to notes of saddest wo,
Which on our dearest Lord did sease e're long 10
Dangers, and snares, and wrongs, and worse then so,
Which he for us did freely undergo:
   Most perfect *Heroe*,[3] try'd in heaviest plight
Of labours huge and hard, too hard for human wight.

III

He sov'ran Priest stooping his regall head 15
That dropt with odorous oil down his fair eyes,[4]
Poor fleshly Tabernacle entered,
His starry front low-rooft beneath the skies;
O what a Mask[5] was there, what a disguise!
   Yet more; the stroke of death he must abide, 20
Then lies him meekly down fast by his Brethrens side.

IV

These latter scenes confine my roving vers,
To this Horizon is my *Phœbus*[6] bound;
His Godlike acts, and his temptations fierce,
And former sufferings other where are found; 25
Loud o're the rest *Cremona*'s Trump[7] doth sound;
   Me softer airs befit, and softer strings
Of Lute, or Viol still, more apt for mournful things.

V

Befriend me night, best Patroness of grief,
Over the Pole thy thickest mantle throw, 30

   [2] a musical term meaning to make musical divisions (measures); but perhaps "divide into parts between them."

   [3] Here Christ is paralleled with Hercules.

   [4] "Christ being come an high priest of good things to come, by a greater and more perfect tabernacle" was by God "anointed with the oil of gladness above his fellows" (Heb. ix. 11, i. 9).

   [5] the *persona* of the drama, used for the person of the Incarnation.

   [6] Muse.

   [7] the *Christiad*, an epic on the life of Christ by Marco Girolamo Vida, native of Cremona, which Milton praises over similar religious works.

And work my flatter'd fancy to belief,
That Heav'n and Earth are colour'd with my wo;
My sorrows are too dark for day to know:
    The leaves should all be black wheron I write,
And letters where my tears have washt a wannish   35
        white.[8]

VI

See, see the Chariot, and those rushing wheels
That whirl'd the Prophet[9] up at *Chebar* flood;
My spirit som transporting Cherub feels,
To bear me where the Towers of *Salem*[10] stood,
Once glorious Towers, now sunk in guiltles blood;   40
    There doth my soul in holy vision sit
In pensive trance, and anguish, and ecstatick fit.

VII

Mine eye hath found that sad Sepulchral rock
That was the Casket of Heav'ns richest store,
And here though grief my feeble hands up-lock,   45
Yet on the soft'n'd Quarry would I score
My plaining vers as lively as before;
    For sure so well instructed are my tears,
That they would fitly fall in order'd Characters.

VIII

Or should I thence hurried on viewles wing,   50
Take up a weeping on the Mountains wild,
The gentle neighbourhood of grove and spring
Would soon unboosom all thir Echoes mild,
And I (for grief is easily beguil'd)
    Might think th' infection of my sorrows loud   55
Had got a race of mourners on som pregnant cloud.
(Unfinished, Mar. 1630)

[8] A Jacobean printing practice was the use of black title pages with white letters.

[9] Ezekiel (Ezek. i. 1–16).

[10] Jerusalem was the home of sacred poetry, for David, reputed author of the psalms, reigned there thirty-three years (2 Sam. v. 5).

ELEGIA SEPTIMA
(Elegy 7)

Not yet did I know your laws, enticing Amathusia,[1] / and my breast was free from Paphian fire. / Often Cupid's arrows, childish weapons, / and especially your divine will I contemned, O Love. / You, boy, I said, pierce peace-loving doves; [5] / gentle battles are becoming to a tender warrior, / or, over the sparrows, little one, achieve your arrogant triumphs; / these are the suitable trophies of your warfare. / Why do you aim your vain darts at mankind? / Against strong men that quiver of yours has no power. [10] / This the Cyprian boy would not bear—and indeed no god is swifter / to anger—and straightaway fierce he burned with double fire. / Spring it was, and beaming through the heights of the village roofs, / the light had brought to you your first day, O May. / But my eyes still were seeking the vanishing night, [15] / nor could they endure the morning radiance. / Love stood by my bed, Love the indefatigable with painted wings; / the moving quiver betrayed the standing god; / his face betrayed him, and his sweetly menacing little eyes, / and whatever else was fitting to youth and to Love. [20] / In like manner did the Sigean youth[2] on everlasting Olympus / mix the overflowing cups for amorous Jove, / or rather Hylas,[3] who lured the lovely nymphs to his kisses, / son of Theomadas, carried off by a Naiad. / And his anger grew, but you would have thought it to be proper [25] / and his harsh threats increased, not without gall. / "Wretch, you might more safely have learned from example," he said; / "now you shall be a witness to what my right hand can do. / And you shall be counted among the men who have experienced my powers, / and as a result of your penalty, truly, I shall achieve your faithfulness. [30] / I myself, if you do not know, overcame Apollo, / and he yielded to me, proud from subduing Python,[4] / and, as often as he remembers Daphne, he acknowledges / that my arrows harm more surely and more

1 Venus.

2 the beautiful youth Ganymede.

3 He was drawn into a spring by the water nymphs who were enamored of his beauty.

4 When he killed the dragon of Delphi, Apollo boasted his archery greater than Cupid's, and so was smitten with unrequited love for Daphne.

gravely. / The Parthian horseman who is wont to conquer behind his back[5] [35] / cannot draw his taut bow more skillfully than I. / And the Cydonian hunter[6] yields to me, and he / who was the unwitting author[7] of his wife's death. / Likewise was prodigious Orion[8] also vanquished by me, / and the powers of Hercules, and the companion of Hercules.[9] [40] / Even if Jove himself hurls his bolts at me / my darts shall hold fast to the side of Jove. / Whatever else you doubt my arrows shall more surely instruct / and your own heart will not be lightly assaulted by me. / Neither will your Muses be able to protect you, fool, [45] / nor will the serpent of Apollo's son[10] extend help to you." / He spoke, and, shaking an arrow with a golden point, / he flew to the warm bosom of Cypris. / But to me the fierce lad thundered with threatening face laughably, / and to me there was nothing to fear from the boy. [50] / And sometimes places in the city where our inhabitants walk / and sometimes the nearby fields of the villages are pleasing. / A great shining throng resembling the visages of goddesses / come and go through the trodden ways. / And with their added light the day gleams with double splendor. [55] / Am I deceived? or is it from them that Apollo also obtains his rays? / I did not austerely shun these pleasurable sights, / but was guided where the impulse of youth led me. / I sent my glances to meet their looks, / poorly cautious, nor could I have restrained my eyes. [60] / By chance I remarked one surpassing all others; / her radiance was the beginning of my misfortune. / Thus Venus herself might choose to appear to mortals, / thus was the queen of the gods[11] worthy of attention. / That wicked Cupid, remembering, cast her before me, [65] / and he alone has woven these snares in my path. / Not far off the cunning one himself was hiding with his many arrows, / and the burden of his mighty torch weighed down his back. / Without delay, he

[5] The successful Parthian method of fighting was to turn one's horse as if in flight after each arrow was discharged.

[6] Cydon in southern Crete was noted for its archers.

[7] Cephalus, who accidentally killed Procris.

[8] The hunter Orion's pursuit of the Pleiades caused them and him to be turned into constellations.

[9] perhaps his most faithful companion Iolaus, who was restored to youth by Hebe.

[10] The attribute of Aesculapius was the snake, a symbol of rejuvenescence and thus of healing.

[11] Juno.

now was fixed on the eyelids, now on the mouth of the maid. /
Then he sprang upon her lips, thereupon he lighted on her
cheek, [70] / and wherever the agile dart-thrower flits in his
office— / alas for me! he strikes my defenseless breast in a
thousand places. / Forthwith unaccustomed passions assailed
my heart; / I burned with love inwardly, and was all in flame.
/ Meanwhile she who alone now was delighting me with
misery [75] / was borne off, never to return to my eyes. /
But I went forth silently complaining, and without understanding / and uncertain I often wished to retrace my step. / I am
torn apart; part stays behind, the other follows my desire, /
and I was happy to weep for pleasures so suddenly snatched
away. [80] / Thus lamented Juno's child[12] for his lost heaven,
/ cast down among the hearths of Lemnos, / and such was
Amphiaraus,[13] carried off to Hell by his terrified horses, /
when he looked back on the vanished sun. / What should I
do, unhappy and by sorrow overcome? Incipient love [85] /
one is not permitted to dismiss or to pursue. / O if only it
were granted me once to look upon her beloved / features,
and to relate my sad words in her presence! / Perhaps she is
not made of hard adamant, / perhaps she would not be deaf
to my prayers. [90] / Believe me, no one burned so unhap-
pily with love; / I may be considered the foremost and only
example. / Spare me, I pray, since you are the winged god of
gentle love; / do not let your deeds contend with your duty. /
Now O child of the goddess, your fearful bow [95] / is assuredly to me no less powerful than fire / and your altars will
smoke with my gifts. / To me you will be the only one and
the greatest one among the supreme gods. / Take away, at
least, my passions, yet do not take them; / I do not know why,
every lover is sweetly wretched. [100] / Only grant, courteous
one, if hereafter any maiden is to be mine, / that a single
point shall transfix the two in love.

(May 1630)

[12] Vulcan.

[13] A seer, Amphiaraus foreknew his death in the conflict with
the Seven against Thebes.

SONG: ON *MAY* MORNING[1]

Now the bright morning Star, Dayes harbinger,
Comes dancing from the East, and leads with her
The Flowry *May*, who from her green lap throws
The yellow Cowslip, and the pale Primrose.
    Hail bounteous *May* that dost inspire   5
    Mirth and youth, and warm desire,
    Woods and Groves are of thy dressing,
    Hill and Dale doth boast thy blessing.
Thus we salute thee with our early Song,
And welcom thee, and wish thee long.   10

(May 1630 ?)

SONNET 1[1]

O Nightingale, that on yon bloomy Spray
    Warbl'st at eeve, when all the Woods are still,[2]
    Thou with fresh hope the Lovers heart dost fill,
    While the jolly hours lead on propitious *May;*
Thy liquid notes that close the eye of Day,   5
    First heard before the shallow Cuccoo's bill
    Portend success in love; O if *Jove's* will
    Have linkt that amorous power to thy soft lay,
Now timely sing, ere the rude Bird of Hate
    Foretell my hopeles doom in som Grove nigh: 10
    As thou from yeer to yeer hast sung too late
For my relief; yet hadst no reason why.
    Whether the Muse, or Love call thee his mate,
    Both them I serve, and of their train am I.

(May 1630 ?)

[1] The song itself, ll. 5–9, is in the meter of *Epitaph on the Marchioness, L'Allegro,* and *Il Penseroso.*

[1] In the immediate background is the lyric *The Cuckoo and the Nightingale,* probably by Thomas Clanvowe though attributed to Chaucer in Milton's day.
[2] Compare *El.* 5, 25–26.

SONNET 2[1]

Charming lady, she whose beautiful name honors / the verdant valley of Reno, and the illustrious ford,[2] / justly is he
of every worth discharged / whom your noble soul does not
inspire with love, / for it sweetly shows itself from without, [5] / in its gentle acts never sparing, / and the gifts
which are the arrows and bow of Love, / there where your
high virtue flowers. / When you so sweetly speak or gaily sing
/ that its power stirs the obdurate alpine wood, [10] / let
everyone who finds himself unworthy of you / guard the entrance to the eyes and to the ears; / grace alone from above
enables him to withstand / the amorous desire which would
lodge itself in his heart.

(1630 ?)

SONNET 3

As on a rugged mountain at the darkening of evening, / the
accustomed youthful shepherdess / goes watering the alien
and beautiful little plant / that hardly spreads forth in that
strange clime, / away from its native, nourishing spring, [5] /
so Love on my alert tongue / awakens the new flower of
foreign speech / while I sing of you, gracefully noble lady, /
by my good countrymen not understood, / and the fair
Thames change with the fair Arno.[1] [10] / Love willed it,
and I at the expense of others / know that Love never willed
anything in vain. / Oh! were my sluggish heart and hard
breast / as good soil for him who plants from heaven.

(1630 ?)

[1] The following poems (Sonnets 2–6 and Canzone) are translated from Milton's Italian.
[2] As Smart showed, the lady is one Aemilia, the name of the
Italian province through which flow the Reno and the Rubicon
with its famous ford. Her family name and relationship to Milton
remain unknown.

[1] that is, exchange English for Italian. The Arno flows through
the province of Tuscany, whose dialect had become standard
Italian.

CANZONE[1]

Scoffing, amorous maidens and young men / mill about me, so, "Why write, / why do you write in a language unknown and strange / versifying of love, and how do you dare? / Speak, if your hope is never to be vain, [5] / and of your designs the best is to come to you"; / thus they go ridiculing me, "Other rivers, / other shores await you, and other seas, / on whose green banks / is bursting forth at any hour for your crown [10] / the immortal guerdon of eternal leaves. / Why on your shoulders the excessive burden?" /

Canzone, I will tell you, and you for me will reply. / My lady says, and her word is my heart, / "This is the language of which Love boasts." [15]

(1630 ?)

SONNET 4

Diodati, and I will say it to you with wonder, / that stubborn I, who used to contemn love / and frequently scoffed at his snares, / now have fallen where upright man sometimes entangles himself. / No tresses of gold nor vermeil cheeks [5] / deceive me thus, but under a new-found fancy / foreign beauty which blesses my heart, / a look highly virtuous, and in her eyes / that tranquil brightness of amiable black, / speech adorned with more than one language, [10] / and the song that could well mislead the laboring moon / from its course in middle sky, / and from her eyes shoots such great fire / that enwaxing my ears would be little help to me.[1]

(1630 ?)

SONNET 5

In truth your fair eyes, my lady, / could not but be my sun; / they powerfully strike me as the sun him / who dispatches his way through the sands of Libya, / while a fervent steam (not felt before) [5] / from that side proceeds where is my grief, / that perhaps lovers in their words / call a sigh; I know

---

[1] a fully rhymed stanza repeated several times, followed by a shorter concluding stanza called the *commiato*; obviously, Milton has used the term loosely.

[1] Milton thought of the Sirens' singing to Ulysses, whose men's ears were sealed to avoid enticement (*Od.*, XII, 39–58).

not what it may be: / the hidden part, and turbid thus concealed, / has shaken my breast, and then a bit escaping, [10]
/ there from being enclosed has either frozen or congealed; /
but as much as reaches my eyes to find its place / makes all
the nights rainy to me alone / until my dawn returns overflowing with roses.

(1630 ?)

SONNET 6

Young, gentle, and candid lover that I am, / since to fly my
self I am in doubt, / my lady, to you the humble gift of my
heart / I shall render devotedly; I, assured by many trials, /
have found it faithful, courageous, constant, [5] / in thoughts
gracious, prudent, and good; / when the wide world roars and
the thunder strikes, / it arms itself from itself, and adamantly
from within, / safe to such a degree from the chance and
envy, / from the fears and hopes of common men [10] / as
its store of indeterminate talent and high courage / and of
the sounding lyre and the Muses: / only will you discover it
in like portion less unyielding / where Love has sent his incurable dart.

(1630 ?)

ON SHAKESPEAR[1]

What needs my *Shakespear* for his honour'd Bones,
The labour of an age in piled Stones,
Or that his hallow'd reliques should be hid
Under a Star-ypointing[2] *Pyramid?*
Dear son of memory,[3] great heir of Fame,   5
What need'st thou such weak witnes of thy name?
Thou in our wonder and astonishment
Hast built thy self a live-long Monument.[4]
For whilst to th' shame of slow-endeavouring art,
Thy easie numbers flow, and that each heart   10

[1] first printed in the Second Folio of Shakespeare's plays (1632).
[2] The archaic prefix was correctly used only for the past par-
ticiple.
[3] Aside from his constancy in our memories, Shakespeare is
made a brother of the Muses, the daughters of Mnemosyne.
[4] Compare "I have built me a monument more lasting than
bronze, / A pyramid higher than a kingly tomb" (Horace, *Odes*,
III, xxx, 1–2).

Hath from the leaves of thy unvalu'd[5] Book
Those Delphick[6] lines with deep impression took,
Then thou our fancy of it self bereaving,
Dost make us Marble with too much conceaving;[7]
And so Sepulcher'd in such pomp dost lie,   15
That Kings for such a Tomb would wish to die.

(1630)

(Lines appended to Elegy 7)[1]

I with foolish mind and heedless zeal formerly / erected these
idle monuments to my wantonness. / Undoubtedly mischievous error impelled me, thus carried off, / and my ignorant
youth was a perverse teacher, / until the shady Academy
proffered its Socratic streams [5] / and untaught the admitted yoke. / Directly, with the flames from that time extinct, / my encircled breast congealed with ice, / from which
the boy himself dreaded frigidity for his arrows, / and Venus
herself is afraid of my Diomedean[2] strength. [10]

(late 1630–1631 ?)

[5] priceless.
[6] inspired by Apollo, patron of poetry, whose abode was Delphi.
[7] Shakespeare's readers are an everlasting monument to his greatness with his lines engraved on their hearts.

---

[1] The study of Plato and his Academy moved Milton to disavow,
probably not seriously, the affectation of some of his early verse.
The "monuments to my wantonness" are therefore perhaps the
various poems in Latin and English dealing with awakening amo-
rousness, although usually only *El.* 7 is suggested.

[2] The Greek warrior Diomedes wounded Venus during the Trojan War after she tried to protect Aeneas (*Iliad*, V, 334–46).

NATURAM NON PATI SENIUM
(Nature does not suffer decay)[1]

Alas how the wandering mind of man grows weak, driven /
by persistent errors, and immersed in profound darkness / it
breathes Oedipean night beneath his breast![2] / Unsound it
dares measure the deeds of the gods / by its own, and to laws
engraved on eternal adamant [5] / compare its own, and the
forever immutable / plan of fate it binds to the passing
hours. /

Therefore shall the face of Nature wither, covered over
with the wrinkles / of ploughings, and the common mother of
things,[3] / contracted of her all-bearing womb, become sterile
from old age? [10] / And herself acknowledged old, shall she
move with erroneously / certain steps, her starry head trembling? Shall foul old age / and the endless greed of years,
and squalor and mold / plague the heavens? Or shall insatiable time / devour heaven and ravage his father's very organs? [15] / Alas, could not unforeseeing Jupiter fortify / his
citadels against this execration, and banish / such an evil of
time, and yield eternal circuits? / Therefore it shall come to
pass that at some time, collapsing with / a tremendous noise,

[1] That nature does not decay was the philosophic conclusion of
both George Hakewell in *An Apologie or Declaration of the Power
and Providence of God in the Government of the World* (1627)
and other "optimists," as Tillyard calls them (*Elizabethan World
Picture*, N.Y., 1944, p. 33). Fink (*Classical Republicans*, pp. 91–
122) sees evidence that Milton came to accept the theory of
deterioration by 1642, but Joseph A. Bryant, Jr. (*SAMLA Studies in
Milton*, pp. 1–19), argues that he maintained the position taken
here without even occasional misgiving. Though commonplace,
the concept is due to Milton's faith in God: since these things
come from God, providence is immutable, matter incorruptible,
and nature undegenerate. Hanford, in "Youth of Milton," p. 105,
calls this early position "significant in its consistency both with his
humanistic inheritance and with his later attitude in theology,
politics, and education."

The poem has frequently been identified as the verses which
were "ghost-written" for another student and alluded to as printed
in a letter to Alexander Gill, dated July 2, 1628.

[2] Man, like Sophocles' Oedipus, is blind of his own doing; he
presumes against God and his laws by seeing them in relation to
his own imperfect concepts.

[3] Earth.

the vaulted floors of heaven will crash down and even [20] / each exposed pole will rattle with the collision, and Olympian Jove / will fall from his celestial court, and fearful Athena with her Gorgon / shield revealed,[4] as for example the child of Juno[5] on Aegean Lemnos / fell, cast from the sacred threshold of heaven. / You also, Phoebus, shall copy the misfortune of your son[6] [25] / in your headlong chariot, and shall be carried in sudden ruin / downward, and Nereus[7] shall steam at your extinguished light / and issue funereal hisses from the astonished deep. / Then furthermore the destruction of the foundations of Haemus[8] / will burst from its summit asunder, and indeed, dashed to the lowest depths, [30] / the Ceraunian mountains, which he had used against the upper regions / in fraternal wars, cast down, will terrify Stygian Dis. /

But the omnipotent Father, with the stars fixed more steadfastly, / has taken care of the greatest of things, and with certainty / has transfixed in balance the scales of the fates, and even [35] / commanded each individual thing in the great order to preserve / its uninterrupted course perpetually. / Therefore the Prime Wheel[9] of the world turns in its daily flight / and hastens with kindred whirling motion the encircled heavens. / Saturn, as is his wont, is by no means impeded, and as violent as formerly, / Mars flashes red lightning from his crested helmet. [40] / Bright Phoebus gleams forever youthful, / nor does the God warm the exhausted lands throughout the sloping regions / with his down-slanting chariot; but always strong in his friendly / light he runs onward the same through the signs of the spheres. / He[10] rises equally beautiful from the fragrant Indies, [45] / who drives at dawn the heavenly flock from the sky, / calling the morning, and driving them at evening into the pastures of heaven, /

[4] Perseus beheaded the Gorgon Medusa, who turned all who looked upon her to stone. Pallas Athena placed the head in her shield as a protective figure.

[5] Vulcan.

[6] Phaeton, hurled into the river Eridanus for endangering earth when he drove the chariot of the sun.

[7] the Old Man of the sea.

[8] a mountain in Thrace. The Ceraunian Mountains (l. 31) were in Epirus.

[9] See *Fair Infant*, n. 7.

[10] Venus, known as Lucifer when the morning star and as Hesperus when the evening star.

and who divides the kingdoms of time with its twin hues. /
Delia[11] waxes and wanes by turns with alternating horn, /
and she embraces the blue flame which is the sky with constant arms. [50] / Nor do the elements vary in faithfulness,
and with accustomed crash / the lurid lightning-bolts strike
the shattered rocks. / Nor through the void does Corus[12] rage
with milder roar, / and harsh Aquilo[13] draws the armed
Gelonians[14] together / with similar chill, and breathes winter,
and blows the clouds along. [55] / And even the king of the
sea,[15] as is his custom, cleaves the depths / of Sicilian
Peloros, and the trumpeter[16] of Oceanus / clamors his grating
conch through the level sea, / nor an Aegaeon[17] of less vast
bulk / do the Balearic whales carry on their back. / On the
contrary, Earth, the ancient vigor of that former age [60] /
is not removed from you; and Narcissus[18] retains his fragrance; / that youth still possesses his beauty, and that lad /
of yours, Apollo, and yours too, Cypris,[19] nor in former times
/ did knowing Earth more abundantly conceal the golden
gift of mountains, / which leads to crime, not even the gems
beneath the seas. Thus, in short, [65] / into eternity the most
just sequence of all things shall proceed, / until the final
flame shall devastate the world, far and wide / encompassing
the poles and the summits of the deserted sky; / and the
frame of the universe shall burn up in a vast funeral pyre.[20]

(1630–31 ?)

[11] the moon.

[12] the northwest wind.

[13] the northeast wind.

[14] a tribe of Scythia.

[15] Neptune, whose waves beat upon Pelorus, the northeastern
promontory of Sicily.

[16] the merman Triton.

[17] a giant with a hundred arms. The Balearic Islands lie in the
western Mediterranean Sea off Spain.

[18] Narcissus was changed into a flower when he died for love of
his own reflection.

[19] For Hyacinthus (beloved of Apollo), see *Fair Infant*, 25–27;
for Adonis (beloved of Venus), see *El.* 1, n. 7.

[20] This was also the prediction of Hakewell. Compare 2 Peter
iii. 10: "the day of the Lord will come . . . in the which the heavens shall pass away with a great noise, and the elements shall melt
with fervent heat, the earth also and the works that are therein
shall be burned up." See *PL*, XII, 547–51.

DE IDEA PLATONICA QUEMADMODUM
ARISTOTELES INTELLEXIT
(On the Platonic Idea as Aristotle understood it)[1]

Say, goddesses, guardians of the sacred groves,[2] / and you
O Memory, most fortunate mother / of the ninefold deity, and
you Eternity, / who recline at leisure in a boundless cave far
away, / keeping watch over the records and unalterable laws
of Jove, [5] / and the calendars of heaven as well as the day-
books of the gods, / say who was that first man from whose
likeness / skillful Nature fashioned the human race, / eternal,
incorruptible, coeval with the heavens, / and unique yet universal, the image of God? [10] / Certainly he is not seated,
an internal offspring, / the twin of the virgin Athena, in the
mind of Jove;[3] / but although his nature be commonplace, /
yet he exists separate unto himself by habit, / and, strange
it is, is confined by regions in fixed space; [15] / or, the comrade of the imperishable stars, / he roams through the tenfold spheres[4] of the sky, / or inhabits the nearest to the earth,
the moon: / or perhaps he is motionless, sitting by the waters
of Lethe / among the oblivious souls waiting to enter a
body:[5] [20] / or perhaps in a far-off region of the world /
the archetype of man casually advances, a prodigious giant, /
and, terrifying creature, to the gods raises his lofty head /
higher than Atlas, the bearer of the stars.[6] / The Dircean
seer,[7] to whom blindness yielded a profound light, [25] /
did not discern him in his deep hiding-place; / the swift

---

[1] Milton satirizes Aristotle's criticism of Plato's archetypal man
in *Metaphysics* by raising unimaginative and insensible objections
such as a matter-of-fact Aristotelian might do. It is evident, however, that he favors Plato's theory of ideas (or archetypes), of
which existing things are but imperfect copies. Compare the second
prolusion, "On the Harmony of the Spheres."

[2] the nine Muses whose mother was Mnemosyne (Memory).

[3] Pallas Athena sprang full-grown from the head of Jove.

[4] in the Ptolemaic system, the ten revolving spherical transparent shells, with earth as center, in which the heavenly bodies were
set.

[5] Plato often referred to transmigration of souls (e.g., *Phaedo*,
70–72); the waters of Lethe were drunk to induce forgetfulness
before reincarnation.

[6] As punishment, Atlas held up the heavens with his head and
hands.

[7] Tiresias.

grandson of Pleione[8] in the silent night did not / behold him
in the wise company of prophets; / the Assyrian priest had no
knowledge of him, although / he was mindful of the long
ancestry of aged Ninus[9] [30] / and primitive Belus, and renowned Osiris. / Even thrice-great Hermes,[10] that one glorious for his triple name / (granting his esoteric knowledge),
/ did not bequeath the like to the worshippers of Isis. / But
you, eternal glory of the Academy of the fields[11] [35] / (if
you first introduced these marvels into schools), / now will
recall the poets, exiles of your city, / since you yourself are
the greatest fabler, / or else, creator, you shall quit that state
yourself.

(late 1630–31 ?)

On the University Carrier who sick'n'd in the time of his vacancy, being forbid to go to *London*, by reason of the Plague[1]

Here lies old *Hobson*, Death hath broke his girt,
And here alas, hath laid him in the dirt,
Or els the ways being foul, twenty to one,
He's here stuck in a slough, and overthrown.
'Twas such a shifter, that if truth were known,   5
Death was half glad when he had got him down;
For he had any time this ten yeers full,

[8] Hermes, god of dreams.

[9] Ninus was reputedly the founder of Assyria; Belus and Osiris
were principal deities of Assyria and Egypt, respectively. Isis
(l. 34) was the sister and wife of Osiris.

[10] the Egyptian god Thoth, identified with Hermes by the
Neoplatonists. Milton uses a variant of this third name, Hermes
Trismegistus. He was supposedly author of magical, astrological,
and alchemical works.

[11] Plato, whose Academy was in a grove near Athens. One of
his reflections was that poets must be exiled from the ideal state
because they corrupt men's natures by encouragement of the lower
elements of the soul at the expense of the higher (*Rep.*, III, 395–
98; X, 595–607).

[1] Thomas Hobson, a coachman whose circuit lay between Cambridge and the Bull Inn in Bishopsgate Street, London, died at
eighty-seven on Jan. 1, 1631, after being forced by the plague in
the city to discontinue his weekly trips. "Hobson's choice," a choice
without an alternative, refers to his practice of requiring a cus-
tomer seeking a horse to take the one nearest the door or none at
all.

Dodg'd with him, betwixt *Cambridge* and the Bull.
And surely, Death could never have prevail'd,
Had not his weekly cours of carriage fail'd;   10
But lately finding him so long at home,
And thinking now his journeys end was come,
And that he had tane up his latest Inn,
In the kind office of a Chamberlin[2]
Shew'd him his room where he must lodge that night,   15
Pull'd off his Boots, and took away the light:
If any ask for him, it shall be sed,
Hobson has supt, and's newly gon to bed.

(early 1631)

ANOTHER ON THE SAME

Here lieth one who did most truly prove
That he could never die while he could move,
So hung his destiny never to rot
While he might still jogg on, and keep his trot,
Made of sphear-metal,[1] never to decay   5
Untill his revolution was at stay.
Time numbers[2] motion, yet (without a crime
'Gainst old truth) motion number'd out his time;
And like an Engin mov'd with wheel and waight,
His principles being ceast, he ended strait.   10
Rest that gives all men life, gave him his death,
And too much breathing put him out of breath;
Nor were it contradiction to affirm
Too long vacation hast'n'd on his term.
Meerly to drive the time away he sick'n'd,   15
Fainted, and di'd, nor would with Ale be quick'n'd;
Nay, quoth he, on his swooning bed outstretch'd,
If I may not carry, sure Ile ne're be fetch'd,
But vow though the cross Doctors all stood hearers,
For one Carrier put down to make six bearers.   20
Ease was his chief disease, and to judge right,

---

[2] Death is represented as an attendant ushering Hobson to his room in the inn where he will perpetually sleep.

---

[1] the indestructible material of which heavenly bodies are made.
[2] measures.

He di'd for heavines that his Cart went light.
His leasure told him that his time was com,
And lack of load made his life burdensom,
That even to his last breath (ther be that say't)   25
As he were prest to death, he cry'd more waight;[3]
But had his doings lasted as they were,
He had bin an immortall Carrier.
Obedient to the Moon he spent his date
In cours reciprocal, and had his fate   30
Linkt to the mutual flowing of the Seas,
Yet (strange to think) his wain[4] was his increase:
His Letters are deliver'd all and gon,
Onely remains this superscription.

(early 1631)

HOBSONS EPITAPH[1]

Here *Hobson* lies amongst his many betters,
A man not learned, yet of many letters:[2]
The Schollers well can testify as much
That have receiv'd them from his pregnant pouch.
His carriage was well known; oft hath he gon   5
In Embassy 'twixt father and the son.[3]
In *Cambridge* few (in good time be it spoken)
But well remembreth him by som good token.
From thence to *London* rode he day by day,
Till death benighting him, he lost his way.   10
No wonder is it, that he thus is gone,

[3] that is, to hasten death and end his misery. The pun with the lightness of his cart is typical of the witty opposites on which the humor of the poem is built.

[4] Another involved pun: his "wain" (cart) was his "increase" (continued accumulation of years and of wealth); and his "wane" (diminishing as of the moon to which he was obedient, or ebbing of life) was his "increase" (waxing of the moon, or passing into another state).

---

[1] Milton's authorship of this poem is not certain; see *Textual Notes*.

[2] Hobson carried the mails, but he had no academic degrees.

[3] primarily to deliver requests for money and infrequent compliances.

Since most men knew he long was drawing on.
His Team was of the best, nor could he have
Bin mir'd in any ground, but in the grave:
And here he sticks indeed, still like to stand,   15
Until some Angell lend his helping hand.
So rest in peace thou ever-toyling swain,
And supream Waggoner, next to Charls-wain.[4]

(early 1631)

AN EPITAPH
ON THE MARCHIONESS OF WINCHESTER[1]

This rich Marble doth enterr
The honour'd Wife of *Winchester*,
A Vicounts daughter, an Earls heir,
Besides what her vertues fair
Added to her noble birth,   5
More then she could own from Earth.
Summers three times eight save one
She had told, alas too soon,
After so short time of breath,
To house with darknes, and with death,   10
Yet had the number of her days
Bin as compleat as was her praise,
Nature and fate had had no strife
In giving limit to her life.
Her high birth, and her graces sweet   15
Quickly found a lover meet;
The Virgin quire for her request
The God that sits at marriage feast;[2]
He at their invoking came
But with a scarce-well-lighted flame;   20
And in his Garland as he stood,

[4] the Big Dipper, punning on his cart and his dying and ascending to the heavens.

[1] Jane, wife of John Paulet, the Marquis of Winchester (a Roman Catholic), died in childbirth, with her child, on Apr. 15, 1631, at the age of twenty-three. Her father was Thomas, Viscount of Rock-Savage, and through her mother, she was heir of Lord Darcy, Earl of Rivers.

[2] Hymen; his "scarce-well-lighted flame" indicates brevity of marriage, and the "Cipress bud" the imminency of death. Milton knew that the Paulets had been married in 1622, as ll. 15–23 in the manuscript version show (see *Textual Notes*).

Ye might discern a Cipress bud.
Once had the early Matrons run
To greet her of a lovely son,[3]
And now with second hope she goes,   25
And calls *Lucina*[4] to her throws;
But whether by mischance or blame
Atropos[5] for *Lucina* came;
And with remorsles cruelty,
Spoil'd at once both fruit and tree: 30
The haples Babe before his birth
Had burial, yet not laid in earth,
And the languisht Mothers Womb
Was not long a living Tomb.
So have I seen som tender slip   35
Sav'd with care from Winters nip,
The pride of her carnation train,
Pluck't up by som unheedy swain,
Who onely thought to crop the flowr
New shot up from vernall showr;   40
But the fair blossom hangs the head
Side-ways as on a dying bed,
And those Pearls of dew she wears
Prove to be presaging tears
Which the sad morn had let fall   45
On her hast'ning funerall.
Gentle Lady may thy grave
Peace and quiet ever have;
After this thy travail sore
Sweet rest sease thee evermore,   50
That to give the world encrease,
Short'n'd hast thy own lives lease;
Here besides the sorrowing
That thy noble House doth bring,
Here be tears of perfect moan   55
Wept for thee in *Helicon*,[6]
And som Flowers, and som Bays,

[3] Charles, later first Duke of Bolton, was born in 1629. The matrons of Rome held a festival called the Matralia on June 11, which celebrated childbirth.

[4] goddess of childbirth.

[5] the Fate who cut the thread of life.

[6] the mountain haunt of the Muses. Poems were written by the students of Cambridge to accompany her hearse (ll. 55–58); among other tributes is one by Ben Jonson.

For thy Hears to strew the ways,
Sent thee from the banks of *Came,*[7]
Devoted to thy vertuous name;   60
Whilst thou bright Saint high sit'st in glory,
Next her much like to thee in story,
That fair *Syrian* Shepherdess,[8]
Who after yeers of barrennes
The highly favour'd *Joseph* bore   65
To him that serv'd for her before,
And at her next birth much like thee,
Through pangs fled to felicity,
Far within the boosom bright
Of blazing Majesty and Light;   70
There with thee, new welcom Saint,
Like fortunes may her soul acquaint,
With thee there clad in radiant sheen,
No Marchioness, but now a Queen.

(*Apr. 1631*)

L'ALLEGRO[1]

Hence loathed Melancholy
  Of *Cerberus,*[2] and blackest midnight born,
In *Stygian* Cave forlorn
  'Mongst horrid shapes, and shreiks, and sights unholy.
Find out som uncouth[3] cell,   5
  Wher brooding darknes spreads his jealous wings,

  [7] the river which flows by Cambridge.
  [8] Rachel, who died in childbirth of Benjamin; the story of her
husband Jacob referred to here is found in Gen. xxix–xxxvii.

---

  [1] "The joyful man" delights in the pleasures of day and light,
and in those happy activities of night which are enjoyed with
others. Its companion and structurally parallel poem, *Il Penseroso,*
"the contemplative man," presents images of pensiveness and
darkness, and thus of aloneness and primarily night. Notable is
the strong Platonic element.
  The contrasting first ten lines of each poem have been traced
to a number of literary sources for metrics and subject matter. The
antithetic subjects of the twin poems were probably conceived as
a kind of scholastic exercise such as produced the first and seventh
prolusions, "Whether Day or Night Is the More Excellent" and
"Learning Makes Men Happier than Ignorance."
  [2] the watchdog of Hell through which flowed the Styx; hence,
"Stygian," l. 3.
  [3] unfamiliar.

And the night-Raven sings;
   There under *Ebon* shades, and low-brow'd Rocks,
As ragged as thy Locks,
   In dark *Cimmerian* desert ever dwell.   10

But com thou Goddes fair and free,
In Heav'n yclept[4] *Euphrosyne*,
And by men, heart-easing Mirth,
Whom lovely *Venus* at a birth
With two sister Graces more   15
To Ivy-crowned *Bacchus* bore;
Or whether (as som Sager[5] sing)
The frolick Wind that breathes the Spring,
Zephir with *Aurora* playing,
As he met her once a-Maying,   20
There on Beds of Violets blew,
And fresh-blown Roses washt in dew,
Fill'd her with thee a daughter fair,
So bucksom, blith, and debonair.
Haste thee nymph, and bring with thee   25
Jest and youthful Jollity,
Quips and Cranks, and wanton Wiles,
Nods, and Becks, and Wreathed Smiles,
Such as hang on *Hebe's*[6] cheek,
And love to live in dimple sleek;   30
Sport that wrincled Care derides,
And Laughter holding both his sides.
Com, and trip it as ye go
On the light fantastick toe,
And in thy right hand lead with thee   35
The Mountain Nymph, sweet Liberty;
And if I give thee honour due,
Mirth, admit me of thy crew
To live with her, and live with thee,
In unreproved pleasures free;   40
To hear the Lark begin his flight,
And singing startle the dull night,
From his watch-towr in the skies,
Till the dappled dawn doth rise;
Then to com in spight of sorrow,   45
And at my window bid good morrow

[4] called. The sister Graces (l. 15) are Aglaia and Thalia.
[5] probably meaning "some who are Sager."
[6] goddess of youth.

Through the Sweet-Briar, or the Vine,
Or the twisted Eglantine.
While the Cock with lively din
Scatters the rear of darknes thin,   50
And to the stack, or the Barn dore,
Stoutly struts his Dames before,
Oft list'ning how the Hounds and horn,
Chearly rouse the slumbring morn,
From the side of som Hoar[7] Hill,   55
Through the high wood echoing shrill.
Som time walking not unseen[8]
By Hedge-row Elms, or Hillocks green,
Right against the Eastern gate,
Wher the great Sun begins his state,[9]   60
Rob'd in flames, and Amber light,
The clouds in thousand Liveries dight,
While the Plowman neer at hand
Whistles o're the Furrow'd Land,
And the Milkmaid singeth blithe,   65
And the Mower whets his sithe,
And every Shepherd tells his tale
Under the Hawthorn in the dale.
Streit mine eye hath caught new pleasures
Whilst the Lantskip round it measures   70
Russet Lawns, and Fallows gray,
Where the nibling flocks do stray,
Mountains on whose barren brest
The labouring clouds do often rest:
Meadows trim with Daisies pide,[10]   75
Shallow Brooks, and Rivers wide.
Towers, and Battlements it sees
Boosom'd high in tufted Trees,
Wher perhaps som beauty lies,
The Cynosure of neighbouring eyes.   80
Hard by, a Cottage chimney smokes,
From betwixt two aged Oaks,
Where *Corydon* and *Thyrsis*[11] met
Are at their savory dinner set

[7] light gray (at dawn).
[8] out in the open.
[9] stately progress.
[10] spotted.
[11] commonplace rustic names as are "Phillis" (l. 86) and "Thestylis" (l. 88).

Of Hearbs, and other Country Messes,   85
Which the neat-handed *Phillis* dresses;
And then in haste her Bowr she leaves,
With *Thestylis* to bind the Sheaves;
Or if the earlier season lead
To the tann'd Haycock in the Mead,   90
Som times with secure[12] delight
The up-land Hamlets will invite,
When the merry Bells ring round,
And the jocond rebecks sound
To many a youth, and many a maid,   95
Dancing in the Chequer'd shade;
And young and old com forth to play
On a Sunshine Holyday,
Till the live-long day-light fail,
Then to the Spicy Nut-brown Ale,   100
With stories told of many a feat,
How *Faery Mab* the junkets eat;
She[13] was pincht, and pull'd she sed,
And he by Friars Lanthorn[14] led
Tells how the drudging *Goblin* swet,   105
To earn his Cream-bowl duly set,
When in one night, ere glimps of morn,
His shadowy Flail hath thresh'd the Corn
That ten day-labourers could not end,
Then lies him down the Lubbar Fend,   110
And stretch'd out all the Chimney's length,
Basks at the fire his hairy strength;
And Crop-full out of dores he flings,
Ere the first Cock his Mattin rings.
Thus don the Tales, to bed they creep,   115
By whispering Winds soon lull'd asleep.
Towred Cities please us then,
And the busie humm of men,
Where throngs of Knights and Barons bold,
In weeds of Peace high triumphs[15] hold,   120
With store of Ladies, whose bright eies
Rain influence, and judge the prise

[12] free from care.
[13] one of the tellers of tales, as is "he," l. 104.
[14] *ignis fatuus*, a misleading light; probably the Friar is identical with the "Goblin," l. 105, and "Lubbar Fend," l. 110 (Robin Goodfellow).
[15] festivals.

Of Wit, or Arms, while both contend
To win her Grace, whom all commend.
There let *Hymen*[16] oft appear   125
In Saffron robe, with Taper clear,
And pomp, and feast, and revelry,
With mask, and antique Pageantry,
Such sights as youthfull Poets dream
On Summer eeves by haunted stream.   130
Then to the well-trod stage anon,
If *Jonsons* learned Sock[17] be on,
Or sweetest *Shakespear* fancies[18] child,
Warble his native Wood-notes wild,
And ever against eating Cares,   135
Lap me in soft *Lydian* Aires,
Married to immortal verse
Such as the meeting soul may pierce
In notes, with many a winding bout
Of linked sweetnes long drawn out,   140
With wanton heed, and giddy cunning,
The melting voice through mazes running;
Untwisting all the chains that tie
The hidden soul of harmony.
That *Orpheus*[19] self may heave his head   145
From golden slumber on a bed
Of heapt *Elysian* flowrs, and hear
Such streins as would have won the ear
Of *Pluto*, to have quite set free
His half-regain'd *Eurydice*.   150
These delights, if thou canst give,
Mirth with thee I mean to live.[20]

(1631 ?)

[16] god of marriage, a frequent character in court masques.

[17] low-heeled slippers worn by actors in comedy; hence, when one of Jonson's comedies is being played.

[18] imagination's.

[19] Orpheus sought to recover his wife Eurydice from Pluto's realm of death; his wondrous music gained his wish for him on the condition that he not look back as she followed. But he failed as they neared the upper world and Eurydice vanished.

[20] Compare Marlowe's: "If these delights thy mind may move, Then live with me, and be my love."

IL PENSEROSO

Hence vain deluding joyes,
   The brood of folly without father bred,
How little you bested,
   Or fill the fixed mind with all your toyes;
Dwell in som idle brain,   5
   And fancies fond[1] with gaudy shapes possess,
As thick and numberless
   As the gay motes that people the Sun Beams,
Or likest hovering dreams
   The fickle Pensioners of *Morpheus*[2] train.   10

But hail thou Goddes, sage and holy,
Hail divinest Melancholy,
Whose Saintly visage is too bright
To hit the Sense of human sight;
And therfore to our weaker view,   15
O're laid with black staid Wisdoms hue.
Black, but such as in esteem,
Prince *Memnons*[3] sister might beseem,
Or that Starr'd *Ethiope* Queen[4] that strove
To set her beauties praise above   20
The Sea Nymphs, and their powers offended.
Yet thou art higher far descended,
Thee bright-hair'd *Vesta*[5] long of yore,
To solitary *Saturn* bore;
His daughter she (in *Saturns* raign,   25
Such mixture was not held a stain)
Oft in glimmering Bowrs, and glades
He met her, and in secret shades
Of woody *Ida*'s inmost grove,
While yet there was no fear of *Jove*.[6]   30
Com pensive Nun, devout and pure,

[1] foolish.

[2] attendants upon the god of dreams.

[3] an Ethiopian prince, known for his handsomeness.

[4] Cassiopeia boasted that her daughter Andromeda was more beautiful than the Nereids, for which she was made a constellation.

[5] Goddess of the hearth, Vesta was the virgin daughter of Saturn. Although the genealogy of Melancholy was apparently made up by Milton, the relation between Saturn and the "pensive nun" may have been suggested by the supposed gravity of those born under the sign of Saturn.

[6] son of Saturn, who overthrew his father's rule of the heavens.

Sober, stedfast, and demure,
All in a robe of darkest grain,
Flowing with majestick train,
And sable stole of *Cipres* Lawn,[7]   35
Over thy decent shoulders drawn.
Com, but keep thy wonted state,
With eev'n step, and musing gate,
And looks commercing with the skies,
Thy rapt soul sitting in thine eyes: 40
There held in holy passion still,
Forget thy self to Marble, till
With a sad[8] Leaden downward cast,
Thou fix them on the earth as fast.
And joyn with thee calm Peace, and Quiet,   45
Spare Fast, that oft with gods doth diet,
And hears the Muses in a ring,
Ay round about *Joves* Altar sing.
And add to these retired leasure,
That in trim Gardens takes his pleasure;   50
But first, and chiefest, with thee bring
Him that yon soars on golden wing,
Guiding the fiery-wheeled throne,[9]
The Cherub Contemplation,[10]
And the mute Silence hist along,   55
'Less *Philomel*[11] will daign a Song,
In her sweetest, saddest plight,
Smoothing the rugged brow of night,
While *Cynthia* checks her Dragon yoke,[12]
Gently o're th' accustom'd Oak;   60
Sweet Bird that shunn'st the noise of folly,
Most musicall, most melancholy!
Thee Chauntress oft the Woods among,
I woo to hear thy eeven Song;
And missing thee, I walk unseen   65
On the dry smooth-shaven Green,
To behold the wandring Moon,

[7] a fine, black fabric.
[8] firmly established.
[9] drawn from Ezekiel's vision (Ezek. i, x) of the fiery wheels and the throne above the cherubim.
[10] The cherubim had the faculty of knowledge and contemplation of divine things.
[11] the nightingale.
[12] See *Ely*, n. 13.

Riding neer her highest noon,
Like one that had bin led astray
Through the Heav'ns wide pathles way;   70
And oft, as if her head she bow'd,
Stooping through a fleecy cloud.
Oft on a Plat of rising ground,
I hear the far-off Curfew sound,
Over som wide-water'd shoar,   75
Swinging slow with sullen roar;
Or if the Ayr will not permit,
Som still removed place will fit,
Where glowing Embers through the room
Teach light to counterfeit a gloom,   80
Far from all resort of mirth,
Save the Cricket on the hearth,
Or the Belmans[13] drousie charm,
To bless the dores from nightly harm:
Or let my Lamp at midnight hour,   85
Be seen in som high lonely Towr,
Where I may oft out-watch the *Bear*,[14]
With thrice great *Hermes,* or unsphear
The spirit of *Plato* to unfold
What Worlds, or what vast Regions hold   90
Th' immortal mind that hath forsook
Her mansion in this fleshly nook:
And of those *Dæmons*[15] that are found
In fire, air, flood, or under ground,
Whose power hath a true consent   95
With Planet, or with Element.
Som time let Gorgeous Tragedy
In Scepter'd Pall com sweeping by,
Presenting *Thebes,* or *Pelops* line,
Or the tale of *Troy* divine.[16]   100
Or what (though rare) of later age,
Ennobled hath the Buskind stage

[13] the town's night-watchman.

[14] The northern constellation of the Great Bear, since it never sets, was regarded by Hermes Trismegistus (for whom see *Idea,* n. 10) as a kind of perfection. "Il Penseroso," reading Hermes, will thus study and think through the full night.

[15] Neoplatonic deities of the four elements in the next line.

[16] He seems to contemplate such plays as those dealing with the Oedipean dynasty, the house of Atreus, and Euripedes' *Trojan Women* and *Hecuba.* Tragic actors wore high-heeled boots (buskins).

But, O sad Virgin, that thy power
Might raise *Musæus*[17] from his bower,
Or bid the soul of *Orpheus* sing   105
Such notes as warbled to the string,
Drew Iron tears down *Pluto's* cheek,
And made Hell grant what Love did seek.[18]
Or call up him[19] that left half told
The story of *Cambuscan* bold,   110
Of *Camball,* and of *Algarsife,*
And who had *Canace* to wife,
That own'd the vertuous Ring and Glass,
And of the wondrous Hors of Brass,
On which the *Tartar* King did ride;   115
And if ought els, great Bards beside,
In sage and solemn tunes have sung,
Of Turneys and of Trophies hung;
Of Forests, and inchantments drear,
Where more is meant then meets the ear.   120
Thus night oft see me in thy pale career,[20]
Till civil-suited[21] Morn appeer,
Not trickt and frounc't as she was wont,
With the Attick Boy[22] to hunt,
But Cherchef't in a comly Cloud,   125
While rocking Winds are Piping loud,
Or usher'd with a shower still,
When the gust hath blown his fill,
Ending on the russling Leaves,
With minute drops from off the Eaves.   130
And when the Sun begins to fling
His flaring beams, me Goddes bring
To arched walks of twilight groves,
And shadows brown that *Sylvan*[23] loves
Of Pine, or monumental Oak,   135
Where the rude Ax with heaved stroke,
Was never heard the Nymphs to daunt,
Or fright them from their hallow'd haunt.

[17] a legendary Greek poet praised by Plato.
[18] See *L'Allegro,* n. 19.
[19] Chaucer, whose unfinished "Squire's Tale" tells this story. The ring and glass gave special powers of achievement to their owner.
[20] course.
[21] unshowily dressed.
[22] Cephalus; see *El.* 5, n. 10.
[23] Sylvanus, god of forests.

There in close covert by som Brook,
Where no profaner eye may look,   140
Hide me from Day's garish eie,
While the Bee with Honied thigh,
That at her flowry work doth sing,
And the Waters murmuring
With such consort[24] as they keep,   145
Entice the dewy-feather'd Sleep;
And let som strange mysterious dream
Wave at his Wings in Airy stream,
Of lively protrature display'd,
Softly on my eye-lids laid.   150
And as I wake, sweet musick breath
Above, about, or underneath,
Sent by som spirit to mortals good,
Or th' unseen Genius of the Wood.
But let my due feet never fail   155
To walk the studious Cloysters pale,[25]
And love the high embowed Roof,
With antick Pillars massy proof,[26]
And storied Windows richly dight,
Casting a dimm religious light.   160
There let the pealing Organ blow
To the full voic'd Quire below,
In Service high, and Anthems cleer,
As may with sweetnes, through mine ear,
Dissolve me into extasies,   165
And bring all Heav'n before mine eyes.
And may at last my weary age
Find out the peacefull hermitage,
The Hairy Gown and Mossy Cell,
Where I may sit and rightly spell,[27]   170
Of every Star that Heav'n doth shew,
And every Herb that sips the dew;
Till old experience do attain
To somthing like Prophetic strain.
These pleasures *Melancholy* give,   175
And I with thee will choose to live.

(1631 ?)

[24] harmony.
[25] the bounds of the cloister.
[26] grotesque pillars so massive as to prevent the roof from ever
falling.
[27] ponder.

SONNET 7

How soon hath Time the suttle theef of youth,
  Stoln on his wing my three and twentith yeer!
  My hasting dayes fly on with full career,[1]
  But my late spring no bud or blossom shew'th.[2]
Perhaps my semblance might deceave the truth   5
  That I to manhood am arriv'd so neer,
  And inward ripenes doth much less appear,
  That som more timely-happy spirits[3] indu'th.[4]
Yet be it[5] less or more, or soon or slow,
  It shall be still[6] in strictest measure eev'n[7]   10
  To that same lot, however mean or high,
Toward which Time leads me, and the will of Heav'n;
  All is, if I have grace to use it so,
  As ever in my great task-maisters eye.[8]

(Dec. 1632)

[1] speed.
[2] It is unlikely that any specific vocation is referred to here, though some have interpreted the line in terms of poetry.
[3] those who have matured as one might normally expect. Milton remarks his lack of accomplishment to date, the point made in a letter to a friend, to which he attached this sonnet: "I am somtyme suspicious of my selfe, & doe take notice of a certaine belated-nesse in me" (TM, p. 6).
[4] invests.
[5] inward ripening.
[6] always.
[7] level, equivalent.
[8] "All things are, as they always have been, foreseen by God, my great taskmaster, just as long as I have the grace to use my inward ripeness as He wishes." As pointed out by Lewis Campbell (*Classical Review*, VIII, 1894, 349), the lines may owe something to Pindar (*Nemean Odes*, IV, 41–43): "Whatsoever excellence Lord Destiny assigned me, well I know that the lapse of time will bring it to its appointed perfection." Yet they are Biblical too; Exod. xxxiii. 13: "Now therefore, I pray thee, if I have found grace in thy sight, shew me now thy way, that I may know thee, that I may find grace in thy sight"; and Rom. xii. 3, 6: "For I say, through the grace given unto me, to every man that is among you, not to think of himself more highly than he ought to think; but to think soberly, according as God hath dealt to every man the measure of faith . . . . Having then gifts differing according to the grace that is given to us . . . ."

ARCADES[1]

Part of an entertainment presented to the Countess Dowager of Darby[2] *at* Harefield, *by som Noble persons of her Family, who appear on the Scene in pastoral habit, moving toward the seat of State,[3] with this Song.*

1. SONG

Look Nymphs, and Shepherds look,
What sudden blaze of majesty
Is that which we from hence descry
Too divine to be mistook:
   This this is she   5
To whom our vows[4] and wishes bend,
Heer our solemn search hath end.

Fame that her high worth to raise
Seem'd erst so lavish and profuse,
We may justly now accuse   10
Of detraction from her praise,
   Less then half we find exprest,
   Envy bid conceal the rest.

Mark what radiant state she spreds
In circle round her shining throne,   15
Shooting her beams like silver threds.
This this is she alone,
   Sitting like a Goddes bright
   In the center of her light.

Might she the wise *Latona*[5] be   20

---

1 natives of Arcadia, an area of Peloponnesus, whose rivers were Alpheus (l. 30) and Ladon (l. 97) and whose mountains were Lycaeus (l. 98), Cyllene (l. 98), Erymanthus (l. 100), and Maenalus (l. 102).

2 Alice Spencer, widow of Ferdinando Stanley, Lord Strange and fifth Earl of Derby, who married Sir Thomas Egerton in 1600. Her daughter Alice had previously married his son Sir John Egerton, later Earl of Bridgewater, whose children Alice, John, and Thomas apparently took part in the entertainment. The occasion and thus the date of the presentation are uncertain.

3 where the Countess sits on "her shining throne."

4 prayers.

5 Leto, mother of Apollo and Diana.

Or the towred *Cybele*,[6]
Mother of a hunderd gods;
Juno dares not give her odds;[7]
  Who had thought this clime had held
  A deity so unparalel'd?   25

As they com forward, the Genius of the Wood[8] appears, and
turning toward them, speaks.

Gen. Stay gentle[9] Swains, for though in this disguise,
I see bright honour sparkle through your eyes.
Of famous *Arcady* ye are, and sprung
Of that renowned flood so often sung,
Divine *Alphéus*, who by secret sluse,   30
Stole under seas to meet his *Arethuse;*[10]
And ye the breathing Roses of the Wood,
Fair silver-buskin'd Nymphs as great and good,
I know this quest of yours, and free intent[11]
Was all in honour and devotion ment   35
To the great Mistres of yon princely shrine,
Whom with low reverence I adore as mine,
And with all helpfull service will comply
To furder this nights glad solemnity;
And lead ye where ye may more neer behold   40
What shallow-searching *Fame* hath left untold;
Which I full oft amidst these shades alone
Have sate to wonder at, and gaze upon:
For know by lot[12] from *Jove* I am the powr
Of this fair Wood, and live in Oak'n bowr,   45
To nurse the Saplings tall, and curl the grove
With Ringlets quaint, and wanton windings wove.
And all my Plants I save from nightly ill

[6] the Great Mother, whose crown indicated her guidance to men in fortifying their cities (see *Aen.*, X, 252–53).

[7] "dares not wager with her" since the odds (advantage) are in her favor.

[8] See *Nativity Ode*, n. 35. Henry Lawes (see *Mask* and *Son.* 13) may have enacted this role and written music for the entertainment.

[9] of gentlemanly rank.

[10] The river-god Alpheus fell in love with the nymph Arethuse as she bathed. She fled to Ortygia (an island off Sicily) where Diana transformed her into a fountain, but Alpheus flowed beneath the sea ("by secret sluse") to be united with her.

[11] lavish intention.

[12] allotment.

Of noisom winds, or blasting vapours chill,
And from the Boughs brush off the evil dew,[13]   50
And heal the harms of thwarting[14] thunder blew
Or what the cross dire-looking Planet[15] smites,
Or hurtfull Worm[16] with canker'd venom bites.
When Eev'ning gray doth rise, I fetch[17] my round
Over the mount, and all this hallow'd ground,   55
And early ere the odorous breath of morn
Awakes the slumbring leaves, or tassel'd horn[18]
Shakes the high thicket, hast I all about,
Number my ranks,[19] and visit every sprout
With puissant words, and murmurs made to bless,[20]   60
But els in deep of night when drowsines
Hath lockt up mortal sense, then listen I
To the celestial *Sirens* harmony,
That sit upon the nine enfolded Sphears,[21]
And sing to those that hold the vital shears,[22]   65
And turn the Adamantine spindle round,
On which the fate of gods and men is wound.
Such sweet compulsion doth in musick lie,
To lull the daughters of *Necessity*
And keep unsteddy Nature to her Law,   70
And the low world in measur'd motion draw
After the heav'nly tune, which none can hear
Of human mould with gross unpurged ear;
And yet such musick worthiest were to blaze
The peerles height of her immortal praise,   75
Whose lustre leads us, and for her most fit,
If my inferior hand or voice could hit
Inimitable sounds, yet as we go,
What ere the skill of lesser gods can show,

[13] hoarfrost (frozen dew).
[14] traversing (the sky).
[15] Saturn; see *Damon*, n. 13.
[16] the injurious cankerworm.
[17] take.
[18] the huntsman's horn, adorned with tassels.
[19] count my rows (of plants).
[20] with prayers for growth.
[21] See *Nativity Ode*, n. 24.
[22] The Fates, the daughters of Necessity, were Clotho, who held the spindle of life, on which the spheres turned; Lachesis, who drew off the thread; and Atropos, who cut it short with her shears.

I will assay,[23] her worth to celebrate,   80
And so attend ye toward her glittering state;
Where ye may all that are of noble stemm
Approach, and kiss her sacred vestures hemm.

2. SONG

O're the smooth enamel'd green
Where no print of step hath been,   85
  Follow me as I sing,
  And touch the warbled string.
Under the shady roof
Of branching Elm Star-proof,
  Follow me;   90
I will bring you where she sits,
Clad in splendor as befits
  Her deity.
  Such a rural Queen
All *Arcadia* hath not seen.   95

3. SONG

Nymphs and Shepherds dance no more
By sandy *Ladons* lillied banks.
On old *Lycæus* or *Cyllene* hoar,
  Trip no more in twilight ranks,
Though *Erymanth* your loss deplore,   100
  A better soyl shall give ye thanks.
From the stony *Mænalus*
Bring your Flocks, and live with us.
  Heer ye shall have greater grace
  To serve the Lady of this place.   105
  Though *Syrinx*[24] your *Pans* Mistres were,
  Yet *Syrinx* well might wait on her.
  Such a rural Queen
All *Arcadia* hath not seen.

(1633–34 ?)

[23] attempt.
[24] a nymph, unsuccessfully wooed by Pan.

A MASK[1]

THE PERSONS

The attendant Spirit afterwards in the habit of *Thyrsis*
Comus with his crew
The Lady
1 Brother
2 Brother
Sabrina the Nymph

The first scene discovers a wild wood. The attendant Spirit
descends or enters.

Before the starry threshold of *Joves* court
My mansion is, where those immortal shapes
Of bright aëreal spirits live insphear'd
In regions mild of calm and serene air,
Above the smoak and stirr of this dim spot,   5
Which men call Earth, and with low-thoughted care
Confin'd and pester'd in this pinfold heer,
Strive to keep up a frail and feavourish beeing
Unmindfull of the crown that vertue gives

[1] Written originally in celebration of the Earl of Bridgewater's
election as Lord President of Wales, *A Mask* was presented on
Sept. 29, 1634, at Ludlow Castle, with his three children enacting
the Lady and her brothers. Thyrsis was played by Henry Lawes,
music tutor to the Bridgewater family and composer of the music
for the masque. As a masque, the work employs songs, dances,
ideal and unreal characters and powers; but its length and dra-
matic action create a play unlike most other masques. Its more
usual name of "Comus" is the result of its popularity in the eight-
eenth century as a play with music by Thomas Arne, into which
frequently were interpolated passages from *L'Allegro*. But this title
gives a false impression, for Milton's emphasis is not on evil but
on the positive virtue of Temperance, on the dynamic purity of
Chastity, as Woodhouse and others have argued. Basically the
masque is a temptation in a wilderness involving Comus' proffer of
drink, his admonition that the earth's riches and beauty must not
be hoarded, and his immobilizing the Lady in alabaster, which
nonetheless cannot immanacle her mind "while Heav'n sees good."
What overcomes Comus' glozing words is Virtue, which "may be
assail'd but never hurt."

After this mortal change to her true servants   10
Amongst the enthron'd gods on sainted seats.
Yet som there be that by due steps aspire
To lay thir just hands on that golden key
That opes the palace of Eternity:
To such my errand is, and but for such,   15
I would not soil these pure ambrosial weeds[2]
With the rank vapours of this sin-worn mould.
    But to my task. *Neptune* besides the sway
Of every salt flood and each ebbing stream
Took in by lot 'twixt high, and neather *Jove*[3]   20
Imperial rule of all the sea-girt Iles
That like to rich and various gems inlay
The unadorned bosom of the deep,
Which he to grace his tributary gods
By course commits to severall goverment   25
And gives them leave to wear thir saphire crowns
And weild thir little tridents, but this Ile
The greatest and the best of all the main
He quarters to his blu-hair'd deities,
And all this tract[4] that fronts the falling sun   30
A noble peer of mickle[5] trust and power
Has in his charge, with temper'd aw to guide
An old and haughty nation proud in Arms:
Where his fair ofspring nurs't in princely lore
Are comming to attend thir fathers state   35
And new-entrusted Scepter, but thir way
Lies through the perplext paths of this drear wood,
The nodding horror of whose shady brows
Threats the forlorn and wandring passinger.
And heer thir tender age might suffer perill,   40
But that by quick command from Soveran *Jove*
I was dispatcht for thir defence, and guard;
And listen why, for I will tell you now
What never yet was heard in tale or song
From old or modern Bard in hall, or bowr.   45
    Bacchus, that first from out the purple grape

[2] immortal garments.
[3] Pluto.
[4] Wales, whose Lord President was the Earl of Bridgewater; the celebration of his "new-entrusted Scepter" awaits the arrival of his children through "this drear wood"—the story background for the masque.
[5] great.

Crush't the sweet poyson of mis-used wine
After the *Tuscan* mariners transform'd
Coasting the *Tyrrhene* shore, as the winds listed
On *Circe*'s Iland[6] fell (who knows not *Circe*   50
The daughter of the Sun? whose charmed cup
Whoever tasted lost his upright shape
And downward fell into a groveling swine)
This nymph that gaz'd upon his clustring locks
With ivy berries wreath'd, and his blith youth   55
Had by him ere he parted thence, a son
Much like his father, but his mother more,
Whom therfore she brought up, and *Comus* nam'd,
Who ripe and frolick of his full grown age,
Roaving the *Celtick*, and *Iberian* feilds,[7]   60
At last betakes him to this ominous wood,
And in thick shelter of black shade imbowr'd,
Excells his mother at her mighty art,
Offring to every weary travailer
His orient liquor in a crystal glass   65
To quench the drouth of *Phœbus*, which as they tast
(For most do tast through fond intemperate thirst)
Soon as the potion works, thir human countnance,
Th' express resemblance of the gods, is chang'd
Into som brutish form of wolf or bear   70
Or Ounce,[8] or tiger, hog, or bearded goat,
All other parts remaining as they were,
And they, so perfect is thir misery,
Not once perceave thir foul disfigurement,
But boast themselves more comely then before   75
And all thir freinds and native home forget
To roul with pleasure in a sensual stie.
Therfore when any favour'd of high *Jove*
Chances to pass through this adventrous glade,
Swift as the sparkle of a glancing star   80
I shoot from Heav'n to give him safe convoy
As now I do: but first I must put off
These my sky robes spun out of *Iris* woof[9]
And take the weeds and likenes of a swain
That to the service of this house belongs,   85

[6] Aeaea where the enchantress transformed Ulysses' men to swine.
[7] French and Spanish lands, known for their wine.
[8] lynx.
[9] material of a rainbow.

Who with his soft pipe and smooth-dittied song
Well knows to still the wild winds when they roar,[10]
And hush the waving woods, nor of less faith,
And in this office of his mountain watch,
Likeliest and neerest to the present aid   90
Of this occasion, but I hear the tread
Of hatefull steps, I must be veiwles now.

Comus *enters with a charming rod in one hand, his glass in
the other, with him a rout of monsters headed like
sundry sorts of wild beasts, but otherwise like men
and women, their apparell glistring; they com in making a riotous and unruly noise, with torches in their
hands.*

Comus. The star that bids the shepherd fold,[11]
Now the top of Heav'n doth hold,
And the gilded car of day   95
His glowing axle doth allay[12]
In the steep *Atlantick* stream,
And the slope sun his upward beam
Shoots against the dusky pole,
Pacing toward the other goal   100
Of his chamber in the East.
Mean while welcom Joy and feast,
Midnight shout, and revelry,
Tipsie dance, and jollity.
Braid your locks with rosie twine   105
Dropping odours, dropping wine.
Rigor now is gon to bed,
And Advice with scrupulous head,
Strict age, and sowr severity
With thir grave saws in slumber lie.   110
We that are of purer fire
Imitate the starry quire,[13]
Who in thir nightly watchfull sphears
Lead in swift round the months and years.
The sounds and seas with all thir finny drove   115

[10] Milton praises Lawes (the "swain" of l. 84) by comparison
with Orpheus.
[11] The evening star, Hesperus, rising, is a sign to gather sheep
into their fold for the night.
[12] cool.
[13] those creating the music of the spheres.

Now to the moon in wavering morrice[14] move,
And on the tawny sands and shelves
Trip the pert fairies, and the dapper elves.
By dimpled brook and fountain brim,
The wood nymphs deckt with daysies trim   120
Thir merry wakes[15] and pastimes keep:
What hath night to do with sleep?
Night has better sweets to prove,
Venus now wakes, and wak'ns Love.
Com let us our rights begin,   125
'Tis only daylight that makes sin
Which these dun shades will ne're report.
Hail goddess of nocturnal sport,
Dark-vaild Cotytto,[16] t' whom the secret flame
Of midnight torches burns; mysterious Dame   130
That ne're art call'd, but when the dragon womb
Of Stygian darknes spitts her thickest gloom
And makes one blot of all the air,
Stay thy cloudy ebon chair,
Wherin thou rid'st with *Hecat'*,[17] and befreind   135
Us thy vow'd preists till utmost end
Of all thy dues be don and none left out,
Ere the blabbing eastern scout,
The nice morn on th' *Indian* steep
From her cabin'd loop hole peep,   140
And to the tell-tale sun discry
Our conceal'd solemnity.
Com, knit hands, and beat the ground,
In a light fantastick round.

The Measure.

Break off, break off, I feel the different pace   145
Of som chast footing neer about this ground,
Run to your shrouds within these brakes and trees,
Our number may affright. Som virgin sure
(For so I can distinguish by mine art)
Benighted in these woods. Now to my charms,   150
And to my wily trains;[18] I shall e're long

---

[14] a rustic dance.
[15] night revels.
[16] a Thracian goddess of nightly pleasure.
[17] goddess of the moon (her team was three dragons, l. 131)
and of witchcraft.
[18] tricks.

Be well stock't with as fair a herd as graz'd
About my mother *Circe*. Thus I hurl
My dazling spells into the spungy air,
Of power to cheat the eye with blear illusion   155
And give it false presentments, lest the place
And my quaint habits breed astonishment
And put the damsel to suspicious flight,
Which must not be, for that's against my course;
I under fair pretence of freindly ends   160
And well-plac't words of glozing [19] courtesie
Baited with reasons not unplausible
Wind me into the easie-hearted man,
And hugg him into snares. When once her eye
Hath met the vertue of this magick dust,   165
I shall appear som harmles villager
Whom thrift keeps up about his country gear,
But heer she comes, I fairly step aside
And hearken, if I may, her buisness heer.

The Lady enters.

Lady. This way the noise was, if mine ear be true,   170
My best guide now; me thought it was the sound
Of riot and ill-manag'd merriment,
Such as the jocond flute or gamesom pipe
Stirrs up amongst the loose unletter'd hinds,
When for thir teeming flocks, and granges full   175
In wanton dance they praise the bounteous *Pan*[20]
And thank the gods amiss. I should be loath
To meet the rudeness and swill'd insolence
Of such late wassailers; yet O where els
Shall I inform my unacquainted feet   180
In the blind maze of this tangl'd Wood?
My brothers when they saw me wearied out
With this long way, resolving heer to lodge
Under the spreading favour of these pines,
Stept, as they sed, to the next thicket side   185
To bring me berries, or such cooling fruit
As the kind hospitable woods provide.
They left me then, when the gray-hooded Eev'n
Like a sad votarist in palmers weeds[21]

[19] flattering.
[20] here the god of shepherds.
[21] a serious religious devotee whose dress shows that he has kept
his vow of a pilgrimage to the Holy Land.

Rose from the hindmost wheels of *Phœbus* wain. 190
But where they are and why they came not back
Is now the labour of my thoughts; 'tis likeliest
They had ingag'd thir wandring steps too far,
And envious darknes, e're they could return,
Had stoln them from me; els O theevish night 195
Why shouldst thou, but for som fellonious end,
In thy dark lantern thus close up the stars
That nature hung in Heav'n, and fill'd thir lamps
With everlasting oil, to give due light
To the misled and lonely travailer? 200
This is the place, as well as I may guess,
Whence eev'n now the tumult of loud mirth
Was rife and perfet in my list'ning ear,
Yet nought but single darknes do I find.
What might this be? A thousand fantasies 205
Begin to throng into my memory
Of calling shapes, and beckning shadows dire,
And airy tongues, that syllable mens names
On sands, and shoars, and desert wildernesses.
These thoughts may startle well, but not astound 210
The vertuous mind, that ever walks attended
By a strong siding champion conscience——
O welcm pure-ey'd Faith, white-handed Hope,
Thou flittering Angel girt with golden wings,
And thou unblemish't form of Chastity, 215
I see ye visibly, and now beleeve
That he, the supreme good, t' whom all things ill
Are but as slavish officers of vengeance,
Would send a glistring guardian if need were
To keep my life and honour unassail'd. 220
Was I deceav'd, or did a sable cloud
Turn forth her silver lining on the night?
I did not err, there does a sable cloud
Turn forth her silver lining on the night
And casts a gleam over this tufted grove. 225
I cannot hallow to my brothers, but
Such noise as I can make to be heard fardest
Ile venter, for my new-enliv'n'd spirits
Prompt me; and they perhaps are not far off.

SONG

> *Sweet Echo, sweetest nymph that liv'st unseen*   230
> *Within thy airy cell*
> *By slow Mæander's* [22] *margent green,*
> *And in the violet-imbroider'd vale*
> *Where the love-lorn nightingale*
> *Nightly to thee her sad song mourneth well.*   235
> *Canst thou not tell me of a gentle pair*
> *That likest thy* Narcissus *are?*[23]
> *O if thou have*
> *Hid them in som flowry Cave,*
> *Tell me but where*   240
> *Sweet Queen of Parly, Daughter of the Sphear,*
> *So maist thou be translated to the skies,*
> *And give resounding grace to all Heav'ns harmonies.*

Comus. Can any mortal mixture of Earths mould
Breath such divine inchanting ravishment?   245
Sure somthing holy lodges in that brest,
And with these raptures moves the vocal air
To testifie his hidd'n residence;
How sweetly did they float upon the wings
Of silence, through the empty-vaulted night,   250
At every fall[24] smoothing the raven down
Of darknes till she smil'd: I have oft heard
My Mother *Circe* with the Sirens three,
Amidst the flowry-kirtl'd *Naiades*
Culling thir potent hearbs, and balefull drugs,   255
Who as they sung, would take the prison'd soul,
And lap it in *Elysium; Scylla*[25] wept,
And chid her barking waves into attention,
And fell *Charybdis* murmur'd soft applause:
Yet they in pleasing slumber lull'd the sense,   260
And in sweet madnes rob'd it of it self,
But such a sacred, and home-felt delight,
Such sober certainty of waking bliss
I never heard till now. Ile speak to her

[22] a winding river.
[23] The Lady likens her brothers to a beautiful youth beloved by Echo.
[24] musical cadence.
[25] rocks lying opposite the whirlpool Charybdis, which Ulysses had to pass, personified as a woman with six heads that barked like dogs.

And she shall be my Queen. Hail forren wonder   265
Whom certain these rough shades did never breed
Unless the Goddes that in rurall shrine
Dwell'st heer with *Pan* or *Silvan*, by blest song
Forbidding every bleak unkindly fog
To touch the prosperous growth of this tall wood.   270
   Lady. Nay gentle shepherd, ill is lost that praise
That is addrest to unattending ears,
Not any boast of skill, but extreme shift
How to regain my sever'd company
Compell'd me to awake the courteous Echo   275
To give me answer from her mossie couch.
   Comus. What chance good Lady, hath bereft you thus?
   Lady. Dim darknes, and this leavy Labyrinth.
   Comus. Could that divide you from neer-ushering guides?
   Lady. They left me weary on a grassie terf.   280
   Comus. By falshood, or discourtesie or why?
   Lady. To seek i'th valley som cool freindly spring.
   Comus. And left your fair side all unguarded Lady?
   Lady. They were but twain, and purpos'd quick return.
   Comus. Perhaps fore-stalling night prevented them.   285
   Lady. How easie my misfortune is to hit!
   Comus. Imports thir loss, beside the present need?
   Lady. No less then if I should my brothers loose.
   Comus. Were they of manly prime, or youthfull bloom?
   Lady. As smooth as *Hebe*'s thir unrazor'd lips.   290
   Comus. Two such I saw, what time the labour'd ox
In his loose traces from the furrow came,
And the swink't[26] hedger at his supper sate;
I saw 'em under a green mantling vine
That crawls along the side of yon small hill,   295
Plucking ripe clusters from the tender shoots,
Thir port was more then human, as they stood;
I took it for a faery vision
Of som gay creatures of the element
That in the colours of the rainbow live   300
And play i'th plighted[27] clouds. I was aw-strook,
And as I past, I worshipt; if those you seek
It were a journey like the path to Heav'n,
To help you find them.
   Lady.   Gentle villager

[26] wearied.
[27] pleated.

What readiest way would bring me to that place?   305
   Comus. Due west it rises from this shrubby point.
   Lady. To find out that, good shepherd, I suppose,
In such a scant allowance of star-light,
Would overtask the best land-pilots art,
Without the sure guess of well-practiz'd feet.   310
   Comus. I know each lane, and every alley green
Dingle, or bushy dell of this wide wood,
And every bosky bourn[28] from side to side
My dayly walks and ancient neighbourhood,
And if your stray attendance be yet lodg'd,   315
Or shroud within these limits, I shall know
Ere morrow wake, or the low-roosted lark
From her thach't pallat rowse, if otherwise
I can conduct you Lady, to a low
But loyal cottage, where you may be safe   320
Till furder quest.
   Lady.   Shepherd I take thy word,
And trust thy honest offer'd courtesie,
Which oft is sooner found in lowly sheds
With smoaky rafters, then in tapstry halls
And courts of princes, where it first was nam'd,   325
And yet is most pretended: In a place
Less warranted then this, or less secure
I cannot be, that I should fear to change it;
Eye me blest providence, and square my triall
To my proportion'd strength. Shepherd lead on.—   330

The two Brothers.

   Elder Brother. Unmuffle ye faint stars, and thou fair moon
That wontst to love the travailers benizon,
Stoop thy pale visage through an amber cloud,
And disinherit *Chaos,* that raigns heer
In double night of darknes, and of shades;   335
Or if your influence be quite damm'd up
With black usurping mists, som gentle taper
Though a rush[29] candle from the wicker hole
Of som clay habitation visit us
With thy long levell'd rule of streaming light,   340
And thou shalt be our star of *Arcady,*

[28] stream lined with bushes.
[29] a reed made into a candle by dipping in tallow.

Or *Tyrian* Cynosure.[30]
 2 Brother.   Or if our eyes
Be barr'd that happines, might we but hear
The folded flocks pen'd in thir watled cotes,
Or sound of pastoral reed with oaten stops,   345
Or whistle from the lodge, or village cock
Count the night watches to his feathery Dames,
'Twould be som solace yet, som little chearing
In this close dungeon of innumerous bows.
But O that haples virgin our lost sister,   350
Where may she wander now, whether betake her
From the chill dew, amongst rude burrs and thistles?
Perhaps som cold bank is her boulster now
Or 'gainst the rugged bark of som broad Elm
Leans her unpillow'd head fraught with sad fears.   355
What if in wild amazement, and affright,
Or while we speak within the direfull grasp
Of Savage hunger, or of Savage heat?
 Elder Brother. Peace brother, be not over-exquisite[31]
To cast the fashion of uncertain evils;   360
For grant they be so, while they rest unknown,
What need a man forestall his date of grief,
And run to meet what he would most avoid?
Or if they be but false alarms of Fear,
How bitter is such self-delusion?   365
I do not think my sister so to seek,
Or so unprincipl'd in vertues book,
And the sweet peace that goodnes bosoms ever,
As that the single want of light and noise
(Not being in danger, as I trust she is not)   370
Could stir the constant mood of her calm thoughts,
And put them into misbecomming plight.
Vertue could see to do what vertue would
By her own radiant light, though sun and moon
Were in the flat sea sunk. And wisdoms self   375
Oft seeks to sweet retired solitude,
Where with her best nurse Contemplation
She plumes her feathers, and lets grow her wings
That in the various bustle of resort
Were all to[32] ruffl'd, and somtimes impair'd.   380

---

[30] the Great Bear and the pole star of the Lesser Bear, by which, respectively, Greek and Phoenician sailors set their course.
[31] over-precise.
[32] probably a prefix meaning "very."

He that has light within his own cleer brest
May sit i'th center,[33] and enjoy bright day,
But he that hides a dark soul, and foul thoughts
Benighted walks under the midday sun;
Himself is his own dungeon.   385
   2 Brother.   Tis most true
That musing meditation most affects[34]
The Pensive secrecy of desert cell,
Far from the cheerfull haunt of men, and herds,
And sits as safe as in a Senat house,
For who would rob a Hermit of his weeds,   390
His few books, or his beads, or maple dish,
Or do his gray hairs any violence?
But beauty like the fair Hesperian Tree
Laden with blooming gold, had need the guard
Of dragon watch with uninchanted[35] eye,   395
To save her blossoms and defend her fruit
From the rash hand of bold incontinence.
You may as well spred out the unsun'd heaps
Of misers treasure by an outlaws den,
And tell me it is safe, as bid me hope   400
Danger will wink on opportunity,
And let a single helpless maiden pass
Uninjur'd in this wild surrounding wast.
Of night, or lonelines it recks me not,[36]
I fear the dred events that dog them both,   405
Lest som ill greeting touch attempt the person
Of our unowned[37] sister.
   Elder Brother.   I do not, brother,
Inferr, as if I thought my sisters state
Secure without all doubt, or controversie:
Yet where an equall poise of hope and fear   410
Does arbitrate th' event, my nature is
That I encline to hope, rather then fear,
And banish gladly squint suspicion.
My sister is not so defenceless left
As you imagine, she has a hidden strength   415
Which you remember not.
   2 Brother.   What hidden strength,

[33] the earth.
[34] likes.
[35] unenchantable.
[36] does not matter to me.
[37] unaccompanied.

Unless the strength of Heav'n, if you mean that?

Elder Brother. I mean that too, but yet a hidden strength
Which if Heav'n gave it, may be term'd her own:
'Tis chastity, my brother, chastity: 420
She that has that, is clad in compleat steel,
And like a quiver'd nymph[38] with arrows keen
May trace huge forests, and unharbour'd heaths,
Infamous hills, and sandy perilous wilds,
Where through the sacred rayes of chastity,   425
No savage feirce, bandite, or mountaneer
Will dare to soyl her virgin purity;
Yea there, where very desolation dwells
By grots, and caverns shag'd with horrid shades,
She may pass on with unblench't majesty,   430
Be it not don in pride, or in presumption.
Som say no evil thing that walks by night
In fog, or fire, by lake, or moorie fen,
Blue meager hag, or stubborn unlaid ghost,
That breaks his magick chains at curfew time,   435
No goblin, or swart faery of the mine,
Has hurtfull power o're true virginity.
Do ye beleeve me yet, or shall I call
Antiquity from the old schools of *Greece*
To testifie the arms of chastity?   440
Hence had the huntress *Dian* her dred bow,
Fair silver-shafted Queen for ever chaste,
Wherwith she tam'd the brinded lioness
And spotted mountain pard, [39] but set at naught
The frivolous bolt of *Cupid;* gods and men   445
Fear'd her stern frown, and she was queen o'th woods.
What was that snaky-headed *Gorgon* sheild
That wise *Minerva* wore,[40] unconquer'd virgin,
Wherwith she freez'd her foes to congeal'd stone?
But rigid looks of chast austerity,   450
And noble grace that dash't brute violence
With sudden adoration, and blank aw.
So dear to Heav'n is saintly chastity,
That when a soul is found sincerely so,
A thousand liveried angels lackey her,   455
Driving far off each thing of sin and guilt,
And in cleer dream, and solemn vision

[38] like Diana, goddess of the hunt and of chastity.
[39] panther.
[40] See *El. 4,* n. 21.

Tell her of things that no gross ear can hear,
Till oft convers with heav'nly habitants
Begin to cast a beam on th' outward shape,   460
The unpolluted temple of the mind,
And turns it by degrees to the souls essence,
Till all be made immortal: but when lust
By unchast looks, loose gestures, and foul talk,
But most by lewd and lavish act of sin,   465
Lets in defilement to the inward parts,
The soul grows clotted by contagion,
Imbodies, and imbrutes,[41] till she quite loose
The divine property of her first being.
Such are those thick and gloomy shadows damp   470
Oft seen in charnel vaults, and sepulchers
Hovering, and sitting by a new made grave,
As loath to leave the body that it lov'd,
And link't it self by carnal sensualty
To a degenerate and degraded state.   475
    2 Brother. How charming is divine philosophy!
Not harsh, and crabbed as dull fools suppose,
But musical as is *Apollo*'s lute,
And a perpetual feast of nectar'd sweets,
Where no crude surfet raigns.   480
    Elder Brother.   List, list, I hear
Som far off hallow break the silent Air.
    2 Brother. Me thought so too; what should it be?
    Elder Brother.   For certain
Either som one like us night-founder'd[42] heer,
Or els som neighbour woodman, or at worst,
Som roaving robber calling to his fellows.   485
    2 Brother. Heav'n keep my sister! Agen, agen and neer,[43]
Best draw, and stand upon our guard.
    Elder Brother.   Ile hallow,
If he be freindly he comes well, if not,
Defence is a good cause, and Heav'n be for us.

          The attendant Spirit habited like a Shepherd.

That hallow I should know, what are you? speak;   490
Com not too neer, you fall on iron stakes[44] else.
    Spirit. What voice is that, my young Lord? speak agen.

[41] becomes sensual and brutish.
[42] led helplessly astray by night.
[43] nearer.
[44] swords.

2 Brother. O brother, 'tis my fathers shepherd sure.

Elder Brother. Thyrsis? Whose artfull strains have oft delaid

The huddling[45] brook to hear his madrigal,   495
And sweeten'd every muskrose of the dale,
How cam'st thou heer good Swain? hath any ram
Slip't from his fold, or young Kid lost his dam,
Or straggling weather the pen't flock forsook?
How couldst thou find this dark sequester'd nook?   500

Spirit. O my lov'd maisters heir, and his next joy,
I came not heer on such a trivial toy
As a stray'd ewe, or to pursue the stealth
Of pilfering wolf, not all the fleecy wealth
That doth enrich these downs, is worth a thought   505
To this my errand, and the care it brought.
But O my virgin Lady, where is she?
How chance she is not in your company?

Elder Brother. To tell thee sadly shepherd, without blame,
Or our neglect, we lost her as we came.   510

Spirit. Ay me unhappy! then my fears are true.

Elder Brother. What fears good *Thyrsis?* Prethee breifly shew.

Spirit. Ile tell you. Tis not vain, or fabulous,
(Though so esteem'd by shallow ignorance)
What the sage poets taught by th' heav'nly Muse,   515
Storied of old in high immortal vers
Of dire *Chimera's* and inchanted Iles,
And rifted rocks whose entrance leads to hell,
For such there be, but unbeleif is blind.

Within the navil[46] of this hideous wood,   520
Immur'd in cypress shades a sorcerer dwells
Of *Bacchus* and of *Circe* born, great *Comus,*
Deep skill'd in all his mothers witcheries,
And heer to every thirsty wanderer
By sly enticement gives his banefull cup,   525
With many murmurs mixt, whose pleasing poison
The visage quite transforms of him that drinks,
And the inglorious likenes of a beast
Fixes instead, unmoulding reasons mintage[47]
Character'd in the face; this have I learn't   530
Tending my flocks hard by i'th hilly crofts

[45] rushing forward in confusion.
[46] center.
[47] removing the look of reason in one's face.

That brow this bottom glade, whence night by night
He and his monstrous rout are heard to howl
Like stabl'd wolves, or tigers at thir prey,
Doing abhorred rites to *Hecate*   535
In thir obscured haunts of inmost bowrs.
Yet have they many baits, and guilefull spells
T' inveigle and invite th' unwary sense
Of them that pass unweeting[48] by the way.
This evening late by then the chewing flocks   540
Had tane thir supper on the savoury herb
Of Knot-grass dew-besprent, and were in fold,
I sate me down to watch upon a bank
With ivy canopied, and interwove
With flaunting honiesuckle, and began   545
Wrapt in a pleasing fit of melancholy[49]
To meditate my rural minstrelsie,
Till fancy had her fill, but ere a close[50]
The wonted roar was up amidst the woods,
And fill'd the air with barbarous dissonance,   550
At which I ceas't, and listen'd them a while,
Till an unusuall stop of sudden silence
Gave respit to the drowsie frighted steeds
That draw the litter of close-curtain'd sleep.
At last a soft and solemn breathing sound   555
Rose like a steam of rich distill'd perfumes
And stole upon the air, that even silence
Was took e're she was ware, and wish't she might
Deny her nature, and be never more
Still to be so displac't. I was all ear,   560
And took in strains that might create a soul
Under the ribs of Death, but O ere long
Too well I did perceave it was the voice
Of my most honour'd Lady, your dear sister.
Amaz'd I stood, harrow'd with greif and fear,   565
And O poor hapless nightingale thought I,
How sweet thou sing'st, how neer the deadly snare!
Then down the lawns I ran with headlong hast
Through paths and turnings oft'n trod by day,
Till guided by mine ear I found the place   570
Where that damn'd wisard hid in sly disguise

[48] unaware.
[49] pensiveness, which here leads to Thyrsis' playing his pipe
until his imagination has vented his thoughts.
[50] completion of the music.

(For so by certain signs I knew) had met
Already, ere my best speed could prevent,[51]
The aidless innocent Lady his wisht prey,
Who gently askt if he had seen such two,   575
Supposing him som neighbour villager;
Longer I durst not stay, but soon I guess't
Ye were the two she meant; with that I sprung
Into swift flight, till I had found you heer,
But furder know I not.   580
    2 Brother.   O night and shades,
How are ye joyn'd with hell in triple knot
Against th' unarmed weakness of one virgin
Alone, and helpless! Is this the confidence
You gave me brother?
    Elder Brother.   Yes, and keep it still,
Lean on it safely, not a period[52]   585
Shall be unsaid for me: against the threats
Of malice or of sorcery, or that power
Which erring men call chance, this I hold firm,
Vertue may be assail'd, but never hurt,
Surpris'd by unjust force, but not enthrall'd,   590
Yea even that which mischeif meant most harm
Shall in the happy trial prove most glory.
But evil on it self shall back recoyl,
And mix no more with goodness, when at last
Gather'd like scum, and setl'd to it self   595
It shall be in eternal restless change
Self-fed, and self-consum'd; if this fail,
The pillar'd firmament is rott'nness,
And earths base built on stubble. But com let's on.
Against th' opposing will and arm of Heav'n   600
May never this just sword be lifted up,
But for that damn'd magician, let him be girt
With all the greisly legions that troop
Under the sooty flag of *Acheron*,
Harpies and *Hydras*, or all the monstrous buggs[53]   605
'Twixt *Africa* and *Inde*. Ile find him out,
And force him to restore his purchase[54] back,
Or drag him by the curls and cleave his scalp
Down to the hipps.

[51] outrun (their meeting).
[52] sentence.
[53] bugbears, bogies.
[54] prey.

Spirit.   Alas good ventrous youth,
I love thy courage yet, and bold emprise,[55]   610
But heer thy sword can do thee little stead;
Farr other arms and other weapons must
Be those that quell the might of hellish charms,
He with his bare wand can unthred thy joynts,
And crumble all thy sinews.   615
    Elder Brother.   Why prethee shepherd,
How durst thou then thy self approach so neer
As to make this relation?
    Spirit.   Care and utmost shifts
How to secure the Lady from surprisal
Brought to my mind a certain shepherd lad
Of small regard to see to, yet well skill'd   620
In every vertuous[56] plant and healing herb
That spreds her verdant leaf to th' morning ray;
He lov'd me well, and oft would beg me sing,
Which when I did, he on the tender grass
Would sit and hearken ev'n to extasie,   625
And in requitall ope his leathern scrip,
And shew me simples[57] of a thousand names
Telling thir strange and vigorous faculties;
Amongst the rest a small unsightly root,
But of divine effect, he cull'd me out;   630
The leaf was darkish, and had prickles on it,
But in another country, as he said,
Bore a bright golden flowr, but not in this soyl:
Unknown, and like esteem'd, and the dull swayn
Treads on it dayly with his clouted shoon,[58]   635
And yet more med'cinal is it then that *Moly*
Which *Hermes* once to wise *Ulysses* gave;[59]
He call'd it *Hæmony,* and gave it me,
And bad me keep it as of sovran use
'Gainst all inchantments, mildew blast, or damp   640
Or gastly Furies apparition;
I purs't it up, but little reck'ning made,
Till now that this extremity compell'd,
But now I find it true; for by this means
I knew the foul inchanter though disguis'd   645

55 enterprise.
56 health-giving.
57 medicinal plants.
58 shoes heavy with nails.
59 to ward off Circe's charms.

Enter'd the very lime-twigs of his spells,
And yet came off: if you have this about you
(As I will give you when we go) you may
Boldly assault the necromancers hall;
Where if he be, with dauntless hardihood,   650
And brandish't blade rush on him, break his glass,
And shed the lushious liquor on the ground
But sease his wand; though he and his curst crew
Feirce sign of battail make, and menace high,
Or like the sons of *Vulcan* vomit smoak,[60]   655
Yet will they soon retire, if he but shrink.
    Elder Brother. Thyrsis lead on apace, Ile follow thee,
And som good angel bear a sheild before us.[61]

The scene changes to a stately Palace, set out with all man-
        ner of deliciousness: soft Musick, Tables spred with all
        dainties. Comus *appears with his rabble, and the Lady*
        set in an inchanted Chair, to whom he offers his
        Glass; which she puts by, and goes about to rise.

    Comus. Nay Lady sit; if I but wave this wand,
Your nervs are all chain'd up in alablaster   660
And you a statue; or as *Daphne* was
Root-bound, that fled *Apollo.*[62]
    Lady.   Fool do not boast,
Thou canst not touch the freedom of my mind
With all they charms, although this corporal rind
Thou hast immanacl'd, while Heav'n sees good.   665
    Comus. Why are you vext Lady? why do you frown?
Heer dwell no frowns, nor anger, from these gates
Sorrow flies farr: See here be all the pleasures
That fancy can beget on youthfull thoughts,
When the fresh blood grows lively, and returns   670
Brisk as the *April* buds in primrose season.
And first behold this cordial Julep heer
That flames, and dances in his crystal bounds
With spirits of balm, and fragrant syrops mixt.
Not that *Nepenthes*[63] which the wife of *Thone*   675
In *Egypt* gave to *Jove*-born *Helena*
Is of such power to stir up joy as this,
To life so freindly, or so cool to thirst.

[60] They were conceived as lying beneath volcanoes.
[61] The attendant spirit as Thyrsis is doing just that.
[62] See *El.* 5, n. 3.
[63] an opiate. Reference is *Od.,* IV, 221.

Why should you be so cruel to your self,
And to those dainty limms which nature lent   680
For gentle usage, and soft delicacy?
But you invert the cov'nants of her trust,
And harshly deal like an ill borrower
With that which you receav'd on other terms,
Scorning the unexempt condition   685
By which all mortal frailty must subsist,
Refreshment after toil, ease after pain,
That have bin tir'd all day without repast,
And timely rest have wanted, but fair Virgin,
This will restore all soon.   690
    Lady.   'Twill not false traitor,
'Twill not restore the truth and honesty
That thou hast banisht from thy tongue with lies;
Was this the cottage, and the safe abode
Thou toldst me of? What grim aspects are these,
These oughly-headed monsters? Mercy guard me!   695
Hence with thy brew'd inchantments, foul deceaver;
Hast thou betrai'd my credulous innocence
With visor'd falshood and base forgeries
And wouldst thou seek again to trap me heer
With lickerish[64] baits fit to ensnare a brute?   700
Were it a draft for *Juno* when she banquets,
I would not taste thy treasonous offer; none
But such as are good men can give good things,
And that which is not good is not delicious
To a well-govern'd and wise appetite.   705
    Comus. O foolishnes of men! that lend thir ears
To those budge[65] doctors of the stoick furr,
And fetch thir precepts from the cynick tub,[66]
Praising the lean and sallow abstinence.
Wherfore did nature powr her bounties forth   710
With such a full and unwithdrawing hand,
Covering the earth with odours, fruits, and flocks,
Thronging the seas with spawn innumerable,
But all to please and sate the curious taste?
And set to work millions of spinning worms   715
That in thir green shops weave the smooth-hair'd silk
To deck her sons, and that no corner might
Be vacant of her plenty, in her own loyns

[64] lustful.
[65] a fur used on scholars' gowns; hence, solemn, austere.
[66] Diogenes renounced luxury by living in a tub.

She hutch't[67] th' all-worshipt ore and precious gems
To store her children with; if all the world   720
Should in a pet of temperance feed on pulse,
Drink the clear stream, and nothing wear but freise,[68]
Th' all-giver would be unthank't, would be unprais'd,
Not half his riches known, and yet dispis'd,
And we should serve him as a grudging maister,   725
As a penurious niggard of his wealth,
And live like natures bastards, not her sons,
Who would be quite surcharg'd with her own waight
And strangl'd with her wast fertility;
Th' earth cumber'd, and the wing'd air dark't   730
        with plumes,
The herds would over-multitude thir Lords,
The sea o'refraught would swell, and th' unsought diamonds
Would so emblaze the forhead of the deep[69]
And so bestudd with stars that they below
Would grow inur'd to light, and com at last   735
To gaze upon the sun with shameless brows.
List Lady be not coy, and be not cozen'd[70]
With that same vaunted name virginity;
Beauty is natures coyn, must not be hoorded,
But must be currant, and the good therof   740
Consists in mutual and partak'n bliss,
Unsavoury in th' injoyment of it self.
If you let slip time, like a neglected rose
It withers on the stalk with languish't head.
Beauty is natures brag, and must be shown   745
In courts, at feasts, on high solemnities
Where most may wonder at the workmanship;
It is for homely features to keep home,
They had thir name thence; course complexions
And cheeks of sorry grain[71] will serve to ply   750
The sampler, or to teize[72] the huswifes wooll.
What need a vermeil-tinctur'd lip for that,
Love-darting eyes, or tresses like the morn?
There was another meaning in these guifts,
Think what, and be advis'd, you are but young yet.   755

[67] closed up.
[68] a shaggy woolen fabric.
[69] the earth.
[70] deluded.
[71] pale color.
[72] comb.

Lady. I had not thought to have unlockt my lips
In this unhallow'd air, but that this jugler
Would think to charm my judgement, as mine eyes
Obtruding false rules pranckt in reasons garb.
I hate when vice can bolt[73] her arguments,   760
And vertue has no tongue to check her pride:
Impostor, do not charge most innocent nature,
As if she would her children should be riotous
With her abundance; she good cateress,
Means her provision only to the good   765
That live according to her sober laws
And holy dictate of spare temperance:
If every just man that now pines with want
Had but a moderate and beseeming share
Of that which lewdly-pamper'd Luxury   770
Now heaps upon som few with vast excess,
Natures full blessings would be well dispens't
In unsuperfluous eev'n proportion,
And she no whit encumber'd with her store,
And then the giver would be better thankt,   775
His praise due paid, for swinish gluttony
Ne're looks to Heav'n amidst his gorgeous feast,
But with besotted base ingratitude
Cramms, and blasphemes his feeder. Shall I go on?
Or have I said anough? To him that dares   780
Arm his profane tongue with contemptuous words
Against the Sun-clad power of Chastity,
Fain would I somthing say, yet to what end?
Thou hast nor Ear, nor Soul to apprehend
The sublime notion, and high mystery[74]   785
That must be utter'd to unfold the sage
And serious doctrine of Virginity,
And thou art worthy that thou shouldst not know
More happines then this thy present lot.
Enjoy your deer Wit, and gay Rhetorick   790
That hath so well been taught her dazling fence,[75]
Thou art not fit to hear thy self convinc't;
Yet should I try, the uncontrouled worth
Of this pure cause would kindle my rapt spirits

[73] pick and choose.
[74] The word combines a meaning of something beyond Comus'
comprehension and a religious article of faith known only to the
initiated.
[75] fencing, i.e., debating.

To such a flame of sacred vehemence, 795
That dumb things would be mov'd to sympathize,
And the brute Earth would lend her nerves, and shake,
Till all thy magick structures rear'd so high,
Were shatter'd into heaps o're thy false head.
    Comus. She fables not, I feel that I do fear 800
Her words set off by som superior power;
And though not mortal, yet a cold shuddring dew
Dips me all o're, as when the wrath of *Jove*
Speaks thunder, and the chains of *Erebus*[76]
To som of *Saturns* crew. I must dissemble, 805
And try her yet more strongly. Com, no more,
This is meer moral babble, and direct
Against the canon laws of our foundation;
I must not suffer this, yet 'tis but the lees
And setlings of a melancholy blood; 810
But this will cure all streight, one sip of this
Will bath the dropping spirits in delight
Beyond the bliss of dreams. Be wise and tast.

The brothers rush in with Swords drawn, wrest his Glass out
    of his hand, and break it against the ground; his rout
    make sign of resistance, but are all driven in. The at-
    tendant Spirit comes in.

    Spirit. What, have you let the false enchanter scape?
O ye mistook, ye should have snatcht his wand 815
And bound him fast; without his rod revers't
And backward mutters of dissevering power,
We cannot free the Lady that sits heer
In stony fetters fixt and motionless;
Yet stay, be not disturb'd, now I bethink me, 820
Som other means I have which may be us'd,
Which once of *Melibæus*[77] old I learnt
The soothest shepherd that e're pip't on plains.
    There is a gentle Nymph not farr from hence
That with moist curb sways the smooth Severn stream, 825
Sabrina is her name, a virgin pure;
Whilom she was the daughter of *Locrine*,
That had the scepter from his father *Brute*.
She guiltless damsell, flying the mad pursuit
Of her enraged stepdam *Guendolen*, 830

[76] that is, when Jove dooms to hell those who during his rebellion followed his father Saturn.
    [77] Spenser; see *FQ*, II, x, 19.

Commended her fair innocence to the flood
That stay'd her flight with his cross-flowing course.[78]
The water nymphs that in the bottom plaid
Held up thir pearled wrists and took her in,
Bearing her strait to aged *Nereus*[79] hall,   835
Who piteous of her woes, rear'd her lank head,
And gave her to his daughters to imbath
In nectar'd lavers strew'd with Asphodil,[80]
And through the porch and inlet of each sense
Dropt in Ambrosial oils till she reviv'd   840
And underwent a quick immortal change,
Made goddess of the river; still she retains
Her maid'n gentlenes, and oft at eeve
Visits the herds along the twilight meadows,
Helping all urchin blasts, and ill luck signs   845
That the shrewd medling elf delights to make,
Which she with pretious viold liquors heals.
For which the shepherds at thir festivals
Carrol her goodnes loud in rustick layes,
And throw sweet garland wreaths into her stream   850
Of pancies, pinks, and gaudy daffadils.
And, as the old swain said, she can unlock
The clasping charm, and thaw the numming spell,
If she be right invok't in warbled song,
For maid'nhood she loves, and will be swift   855
To aid a virgin, such as was her self
In hard besetting need; this will I try
And add the power of som adjuring verse.

SONG

Sabrina fair
  Listen where thou art sitting   860
Under the glassie, cool, translucent wave,
  In twisted braids of Lillies knitting
The loose train of thy amber-dropping hair,
  Listen for dear honours sake,
  Goddess of the silver lake,   865
    Listen and save.

[78] Milton altered Geoffrey of Monmouth's account of the murder of Estrildis and her illegitimate daughter Sabrina by Locrine's jealous wife Gwendolen.
[79] a sea-god.
[80] a flower yielding immortality.

Listen and appear to us
In name of great *Oceanus*,[81]
By th' earth-shaking *Neptunes* mace,
And *Tethys* grave majestick pace,   870
By hoary *Nereus* wrincled look,
And the *Carpathian* wizards hook,
By scaly *Tritons* winding shell,
And old sooth-saying *Glaucus* spell,
By *Leucothea*'s lovely hands,   875
And her son that rules the strands,
By *Thetis* tinsel-slipper'd feet,
And the songs of *Sirens* sweet,
By dead *Parthenope*'s dear tomb,
And fair *Ligéa*'s golden comb,   880
Wherwith she sits on diamond rocks
Sleeking her soft alluring locks,
By all the *Nymphs* that nightly dance
Upon the streams with wily glance,
Rise, rise, and heave thy rosie head   885
From thy coral-pav'n bed,
And bridle in thy headlong wave,
Till thou our summons answer'd have.
                    Listen and save.

  Sabrina rises, attended by water-nymphs, and sings.

By the rushy-fringed bank,   890
 Where grows the willow and the osier dank,
My sliding chariot stayes,
Thick set with agat, and the azurn sheen
 Of turkis[82] *blew, and emrauld green*
  That in the channell strayes,   895
Whilst from off the waters fleet
Thus I set my printless feet
 O're the Cowslips Velvet head
 That bends not as I tread.

Gentle swain at thy request   900
I am heer.

[81] The sea deities include Tethys, wife of Oceanus and mother
of rivers; Proteus, who lived in the Carpathian Sea and was known
for changing his appearance; Triton, Neptune's herald; Glaucus,
an immortal fisherman; Leucothea (or Ino) who escaped her husband's insanity with her son Melicertes by throwing herself into
the sea; Thetis, a Nereid; and the Sirens Parthenope and Ligea.
[82] turquoise.

Spirit. Goddess dear
We implore thy powerful hand
To undoe the charmed band
Of true virgin heer distrest,   905
Through the force, and through the wile
Of unblest inchanter vile.
    Sabrina. Shepherd 'tis my office best
To help insnared chastity;
Brightest Lady look on me,   910
Thus I sprinkle on thy brest
Drops that from my fountain pure,
I have kept of pretious cure,
Thrice upon thy fingers tip,
Thrice upon thy rubied lip;   915
Next this marble venom'd seat
Smear'd with gumms of glutenous heat
I touch with chast palms moist and cold,
Now the spell hath lost his hold;
And I must hast ere morning howr   920
To wait in *Amphitrite's*[83] bowr.

    Sabrina descends, and the Lady rises out of her seat.

    Spirit. Virgin, daughter of *Locrine*
Sprung of old *Anchises* line,
May thy brimmed waves for this
Thir full tribute never miss   925
From a thousand petty rills
That tumble down the snowy hills:
Summer drouth, or singed air
Never scorch thy tresses fair,
Nor wet *Octobers* torrent flood   930
Thy molten crystal fill with mudd;
May thy billows rowl ashoar
The beryl and the golden ore,
May thy lofty head be crown'd
With many a towr and terrace round,   935
And heer and there thy banks upon
With groves of myrrhe, and cinnamon.

Com Lady while Heav'n lends us grace,
Let us fly this cursed place,
Lest the sorcerer us intice   940
With som other new device.

[83] the wife of Neptune.

Not a wast or needless sound
Till we com to holier ground,
I shall be your faithfull guide
Through this gloomy covert wide,   945
And not many furlongs thence
Is your Fathers residence,
Where this night are met in state
Many a freind to gratulate
His wish't presence, and beside   950
All the swains that there abide,
With Jiggs and rural dance resort.
We shall catch them at thir sport,
And our sudden comming there
Will double all thir mirth and chere;   955
Com let us hast, the stars grow high,
But night sits monarch yet in the mid sky.

The scene changes presenting Ludlow *Town and the Presi-*
dents Castle, then com in country-dancers, after them
the attendant Spirit, with the two brothers and the
Lady.

SONG

   Spirit. Back shepherds, back, anough your play,
Till next sunshine holiday,
Heer be without duck or nod   960
Other trippings to be trod
Of lighter toes, and such court guise
As Mercury *did first devise*
With the mincing Dryades
On the lawns, and on the leas.   965

This second Song presents them to their father and mother.

Noble Lord and Lady bright,
I have brought ye new delight,
Heer behold so goodly grown
Three fair branches of your own.
Heav'n hath timely[84] tri'd thir youth,   970
Thir faith, thir patience, and thir truth.
And sent them heer through hard assays
With a crown of deathless praise,
   To triumph in victorious dance
O're sensual folly, and intemperance.   975

[84] early.

The dances ended, the Spirit Epiloguizes.

Spirit. To the Ocean now I fly,
And those happy climes that lie
Where day never shuts his eye,
Up in the broad feilds of the sky:
There I suck the liquid air   980
All amidst the gardens fair
Of *Hesperus* and his daughters three
That sing about the golden tree:
Along the crisped[85] shades and bowrs
Revels the spruce and jocond Spring,   985
The Graces, and the rosie-boosom'd Howrs,[86]
Thither all thir bounties bring,
That there eternal Summer dwells,
And west winds, with musky wing
About the cedarn alleys fling   990
Nard, and *Cassia's* balmy smells.
Iris there with humid bow
Waters the odorous banks that blow
Flowers of more mingled hew
Then her purfl'd[87] scarf can shew,   995
And drenches with *Elysian* dew
(List mortals, if your ears be true)
Beds of hyacinth and roses
Where young *Adonis* oft reposes,
Waxing well of his deep wound   1000
In slumber soft, and on the ground
Sadly sits th' *Assyrian* Queen;[88]
But farr above in spangled sheen
Celestial *Cupid* her fam'd Son advanc't
Holds his dear *Psyche*[89] sweet intranc't   1005
After her wandring labours long,
Till free consent the gods among
Make her his eternal bride,
And from her fair unspotted side

85 quivering.
86 goddesses of the seasons.
87 embroidered along the edge.
88 Venus, whose lover Adonis had been gored by a wild boar.
89 The myth points to Milton's allegory: life and heavenly bliss
are the offspring of the legitimate union of heart and soul. The
mere appetite of Venus' love causes Adonis to languish and her to
sit sadly far below the celestial heavens.

Two blissful twins are to be born,   1010
Youth and Joy; so *Jove* hath sworn.
   But now my task is smoothly don,
I can fly, or I can run
Quickly to the green earths end,
Where the bow'd welkin slow doth bend,   1015
And from thence can soar as soon
To the corners[90] of the Moon.
   Mortals that would follow me,
Love vertue, she alone is free,
She can teach ye how to clime   1020
Higher then the spheary chime;[91]
Or if Vertue feeble were,
Heav'n it self would stoop to her.

(1634, before Sept. 29;
revised, autumn–winter 1637)

PSALM 114[1]

When the children of Israel, when the noble tribes of Jacob /
left behind the land of Egypt, hated, barbarous of speech, /
already at that time the only chosen race was the sons of
Judah. / But among the people God ruled, a mighty Lord. /
The sea saw, and turning back, made the fugitive strong, [5] /
its roaring waves folded beneath, and straightaway was / the
sacred Jordan thrust back upon its silvery sources. / The
boundless mountains rushed wildly thither, skipping / as well-
filled rams in a thriving garden. / At the same time all the
strange little crags leaped up [10] / as lambs to the shepherd's pipe about their dear mother. / Why then, dread monster sea, did you make the fugitive strong, / your roaring
waves folded beneath? Why then were you, / sacred Jordan,
thrust back upon your silvery sources? / Why did the boundless mountains rush wildly, skipping [15] / as well-filled rams
in a thriving garden? / Why then did you, strange little crags,
leap up / as lambs to the shepherd's pipe about your dear
mother? / Tremble, Earth, and fear the Lord, doer of mighty
works; / Earth, fear the Lord, the highest majesty of the seed
of Isaac, [20] / who poured forth both the roaring streams
out of the rocks / and the ever-flowing fountain down from
the weeping crags.

(Nov. 1634)

[90] horns.
[91] the music of the spheres.

---

[1] translated from Milton's rendition in Greek.

Philosophus ad regem quendam qui eum ignotum et
insontem inter reos forte captum inscius damnaverat,
τὴν ἐπὶ θανάτῳ πορευόμενος hæc subito misit.[1]
(A philosopher on his way to his death suddenly sent
this message to a certain king who had unawares
condemned him, unrecognized and innocent,
when he was seized by chance among criminals.)[1]

O king, if you make an end of me, a lawful person / and a
doer of utterly no harm to man, you easily take away / one
of the wisest of heads, but later you will perceive / just as
before; surely at last, you will grieve vainly and exceedingly /
because you have destroyed such a greatly renowned bulwark
from out of the city. [5]

(Dec. 1634 ?)

ON TIME

Fly envious Time,[1] till thou run out thy race,
Call on the lazy leaden-stepping howrs,
Whose speed is but the heavy plummets[2] pace;
And glut thy self with what thy womb devours,
Which is no more then what is false and vain,   5
And meerly mortal dross;
So little is our loss,
So little is thy gain.
For when as each thing bad thou hast entomb'd,

---

[1] Though these verses sound like a paraphrase of a classic epigram, no source has been determined. If they are the result of
encouragement from Alexander Gill to try further Greek composition, the subject may have been chosen, as Parker suggests
("Notes," p. 129), to "allude to Gill's unfortunate clash with Laud
and the Star Chamber, and his subsequent pardon by King Charles
(November 30, 1630) . . . ." Two years before, Gill had toasted
the health of John Felton, assassin of the king's minister, the Duke
of Buckingham. The lines are translated from Milton's Greek.

---

[1] Cronos was jealous of even his own children (Hesiod, *Theog-
ony*, 453 ff.).
[2] the weight which by gravity moved the wheels of the clock
and in turn its hands. The poem originally was to be "set on a
clock case."

And last of all thy greedy self consum'd,   10
Then long Eternity shall greet our bliss
With an individual[3] kiss;
And Joy shall overtake us as a flood,
When every thing that is sincerely good
And perfectly divine,   15
With Truth, and Peace, and Love shall ever shine
About the supreme Throne
Of him t' whose happy-making sight alone,
When once our heav'nly-guided soul shall clime,
Then all this Earthy grosnes quit,   20
Attir'd with Stars, we shall for ever sit,
   Triumphing over Death, and Chance, and thee O Time.

(*1633–37 ?*)

UPON THE CIRCUMCISION[1]

Ye flaming Powers,[2] and winged Warriours bright
That erst with musick, and triumphant song
First heard by happy watchfull Shepherds ear,
So sweetly sung your joy the clouds along
Through the soft silence of the list'ning night,   5
Now mourn, and if sad share with us to bear
Your fiery essence can distill no tear,[3]
Burn in your sighs, and borrow
Seas wept from our deep sorrow.
He who with all Heav'ns heraldry whilere   10
Enter'd the world, now bleeds to give us ease;
Alas, how soon our sin
   Sore doth begin

[3] usually interpreted as "undividable," that is, "everlasting";
however, O. B. Hardison, Jr. (*Texas Studies in Lit. and Lang.*,
III, 1961, 107–22) argues cogently for the simpler reading: "Eternity shall greet us individually with a kiss."

[1] This poem of two fourteen-line verses, with single original lines
13–14 and 27–28, "reproduces as closely as possible the stanza used
by Petrarch in his *canzone* to the Blessed Virgin" (Prince, p. 61).
The Feast of the Circumcision of Christ, eight days after birth in
accord with Mosaic law, is Jan. 1.
[2] The Powers were sixth in the celestial hierarchy, and the
"winged Warriours" are the "helmed Cherubim" and "sworded
Seraphim" of the *Nativity Ode*, 112–13; but Milton uses the terms
to represent all the angels whose song Luke (ii. 13–14) quotes.
[3] Besides the conceit of opposites, the line refers to the opinion
that angels were incapable of performing such bodily functions.

His infancy to sease!
  O more exceeding love or law more just?[4]   15
Just law indeed, but more exceeding love!
For we by rightfull doom remediles
Were lost in death till he that dwelt above
High-thron'd in secret bliss, for us frail dust
Emptied his glory,[5] ev'n to nakednes;   20
And that great Cov'nant[6] which we still transgress
Intirely satisfi'd,
And the full wrath beside
Of vengefull Justice bore for our excess,
And seals obedience first with wounding smart   25
This day, but O ere long
    Huge pangs and strong
Will peirce more neer his heart.

(1633–37 ?)

AT A SOLEMN MUSICK

Blest pair of *Sirens,* pledges of Heav'ns joy,
Sphear-born, harmonious sisters, Voice, and Vers,[1]
Wed your divine sounds, and mixt power employ
Dead things with inbreath'd sense able to peirce
And to our high-rais'd phantasie present   5
That undisturbed Song of pure concent[2]
Ay sung before the saphire-colour'd throne
To him that sits theron
With saintly shout, and solemn Jubily,
Where the bright Seraphim in burning row   10
Thir loud up-lifted Angel trumpets blow,
And the Cherubick hoast in thousand quires

[4] This second stanza is an early statement of the high justice of God the Father and the mercy of the Son, who became man for man's salvation (see *PL*, III, 80–344; XII, 393–419).

[5] Christ's *kenosis;* see Phil. ii. 6–8.

[6] that everlasting covenant made with Abraham when the rite of circumcision was instituted (Gen. xvii. 7, 10); it implies obedience to God's will.

[1] The nine celestial sirens assigned to the nine spheres of the universe (see *Nativity Ode,* n. 21) were identified with the Muses, here specifying Polyhymnia, the muse of sacred song, and Erato, the muse of lyric poetry. Milton fuses the harmonious music of the spheres and the song of the multitude with palms in their hands before the throne of God (Rev. vii. 9).

[2] harmony.

Touch thir immortal harps of golden wires
With those just Spirits that wear victorious Palms,
Hymns devout and holy Psalms 15
Singing everlastingly;
That we on Earth with undiscording voice
May rightly answer that melodious noise
As once we did, till disproportion'd sin
Jarr'd against natures chime, and with harsh din 20
Broke the fair musick that all creatures made
To thir great Lord, whose love thir motion sway'd
In perfect Diapason,[3] whilst they stood
In first obedience, and thir state of good.
O may we soon again renew that Song, 25
And keep in tune with Heav'n, till God e're long
To his celestial consort[4] us unite
To live with him, and sing in endles morn of light.

(1637)

LYCIDAS[1]

In this Monody the Author bewails a learned Freind,[2] unfortunatly drown'd in his passage from Chester on the Irish Seas, 1637. And by occasion foretells the ruin of our corrupted Clergy then in their height.

[3] consonance of the entire compass of tones in an octave, thus referring to the harmonious song of "all creatures" regardless of relative position in the chain of being.

[4] both fellowship and company of music makers ("concert"). There is also a hint of wordplay on the meaning "marital association" ("consortium") with Christ the Bridegroom.

[1] Built on verse paragraphs of varying lengths, the poem is irregularly rhymed (including ten unrhymed lines) with key lines linking groups of rhymes, and ends in *ottavo rima*. The two so-called digressions (ll. 64–84 and 103–31), which French sees as the core of the poem (*SP*, L, 1953, 485–90), are preceded by passages concerned with death by water and followed by a passage in which water becomes the source of new life. The vernal flowers which strew Lycidas' hearse contrast with the dying vegetation in ll. 37–49, recalling the rebirth of Orpheus and such vegetation gods. As Wayne Shumaker shows (*PMLA*, LXVI, 1951, 485–94), the apotheosis (ll. 165–85), which presents the poet-priest-shepherd as still living, gives hope and courage and reconciliation to destiny and the physical world.

[2] Edward King, who attended Christ's College, Cambridge, was drowned on Aug. 10, 1637, when his ship capsized (despite good

Yet once more, O ye Laurels, and once more
Ye Myrtles brown, with Ivy never sere,
I com to pluck your berries harsh and crude,[3]
And with forc't fingers rude
Shatter your leaves before the mellowing year.   5
Bitter constraint, and sad occasion dear
Compells me to disturb your season due:
For *Lycidas* is dead, dead ere his prime
Young *Lycidas,* and hath not left his peer:
Who would not sing for *Lycidas?* he well knew   10
Himself to sing, and build the lofty rime.
He must not flote upon his watry bear
Unwept, and welter to the parching wind
Without the meed of som melodious tear.
   Begin then, Sisters of the sacred well[4]   15
That from beneath the seat of *Jove* doth spring,
Begin, and somwhat loudly sweep the string.
Hence with denial vain, and coy excuse,
So may som gentle muse
With lucky[5] words favour my destin'd urn,   20
And as he passes, turn
And bid fair peace be to my sable shroud.
For we were nurst upon the self-same hill,
Fed the same flock by fountain, shade, and rill.
   Together both ere the high Lawns appear'd   25
Under the opening eyelids of the morn,
We drove afeild, and both together heard
What time the gray fly winds her sultry[6] horn,
Batning[7] our flocks with the fresh dews of night,
Oft till the star[8] that rose in Evning bright   30
Toward Heav'ns descent had sloapt his westring wheel.
Mean while the rurall ditties were not mute,

---

weather, according to Milton, though not according to King's brother Henry). He had planned to enter the clergy and had attempted some occasional verse. The poem appears last in a collection of less distinguished Latin, Greek, and English obsequies, *Justa Edovardo King naufrago* (1638).

   [3] unripe.
   [4] the Muses; see *El.* 4, n. 10.
   [5] propitious or, George O. Marshall suggests (*Explicator,* XVII, 1959, item 66), "having an unstudied felicity."
   [6] warm from midday heat.
   [7] feeding.
   [8] Hesperus.

Temper'd to th' oaten flute:
Rough Satyrs danc't, and Fauns with clov'n heel
From the glad sound would not be absent long,   35
And old *Damœtas*[9] lov'd to hear our song.
    But O the heavy change now thou art gone,
Now thou art gon, and never must return!
Thee shepherd, thee the woods and desert caves
With wild Thyme, and the gadding vine o'regrown,   40
And all thir echoes mourn.
The willows, and the hazel copses green
Shall now no more be seen,
Fanning thir joyous leavs to thy soft layes.
As killing as the canker to the rose,   45
Or taint-worm to the weanling herds that graze,
Or frost to flowrs that thir gay wardrope wear,
When first the white thorn blows;
Such, *Lycidas*, thy loss to shepherds ear.
    Where were ye nymphs when the remorseless deep   50
Clos'd o're the head of your lov'd *Lycidas*?
For neither were ye playing on the steep,
Where your old bards the famous Drüids lie,
Nor on the shaggy top of *Mona*[10] high,
Nor yet where *Deva*[11] spreds her wisard stream: 55
Ay me, I fondly dream!
Had ye bin there, for what could that have don?
What could the Muse[12] her self that *Orpheus* bore,
The Muse her self for her inchanting son
Whom universal nature did lament,   60
When by the rout that made the hideous roar
His goary visage down the stream was sent,
Down the swift *Hebrus* to the *Lesbian* shoar.
    Alas! What boots it[13] with incessant care
To tend the homely slighted shepherds trade   65
And strictly meditate the thankless muse?
Were it not better don as others use,
To sport with *Amaryllis* in the shade,
Or with the tangles of *Neæra's* hair?

[9] apparently a tutor at Cambridge.
[10] the isle of Anglesey.
[11] the river Dee.
[12] Calliope; Orpheus was torn to pieces by drunken followers of Bacchus, and his head floated down the Hebrus to the island of Lesbos.
[13] of what advantage is it?

Fame is the spur that the clear spirit doth raise   70
(That last infirmity of noble mind)
To scorn delights, and live laborious dayes;
But the fair guerdon[14] when we hope to find
And think to burst out into sudden blaze,
Comes the blind *Fury*[15] with th' abhorred shears   75
And slits the thin-spun life. But not the praise,
Phœbus repli'd, and touch't my trembling ears;
Fame is no plant that grows on mortal soil,
Nor in the glistering foil[16]
Set off to th' world, nor in broad rumor lies,   80
But lives and spreds aloft by those pure eyes
And perfet witness of all-judging *Jove*
As he pronounces lastly on each deed,
Of so much fame in Heav'n expect thy meed.
    O Fountain *Arethuse*[17] and thou honour'd flood,   85
Smooth-sliding *Mincius,* crown'd with vocall reeds,
That strain I heard was of a higher mood:
But now my oat[18] proceeds
And listens to the Herald of the Sea[19]
That came in *Neptunes* plea,   90
He askt the waves, and askt the fellon winds,
What hard mishap hath doom'd this gentle swain?
And question'd every gust of rugged wings
That blows from off each beaked promontory,
They knew not of his story,   95
And sage *Hippotades*[20] thir answer brings,
That not a blast was from his dungeon straid,
The air was calm, and on the levell brine
Sleek *Panope* with all her sisters[21] plaid.
It was that fatall and perfidious bark   100
Built in th' eclipse, and rigg'd with curses dark,
That sunk so low that sacred head of thine.
    Next *Camus,*[22] reverend Sire, went footing slow,
His mantle hairy, and his bonnet sedge,

[14] reward.
[15] Atropos, one of the Fates.
[16] a thin leaf of metal used as a background to enhance a gem.
[17] See *Arcades,* n. 10.
[18] pastoral song.
[19] Triton, who pleads the innocence of the sea in causing King's death.
[20] god of the winds.
[21] water-nymphs.
[22] god of the river Cam, representing Cambridge University.

Inwraught with figures dim, and on the edge   105
Like to that sanguine flowr[23] inscrib'd with woe.
Ah! who hath reft, quoth he, my dearest pledge?
Last came and last did goe
The Pilot of the *Galilean* lake,[24]
Two massy keys he bore of mettalls twain   110
(The golden opes, the iron shuts amain),
He shook his mitr'd locks and stern bespake,
How well could I have spar'd for thee, young swain,
Anow of such as for thir bellies sake
Creep and intrude, and clime into the fold?   115
Of other care they little reckning make
Then how to scramble at the shearers feast
And shove away the worthy bidden guest.
Blind mouths! that scarse themselves know how to hold
A sheephook, or have learn't ought els the least   120
That to the faithfull herdsmans art belongs!
What recks it them? What need they? They are sped;[25]
And when they list, thir lean and flashy songs
Grate on thir scrannel[26] pipes of wretched straw,
The hungry sheep look up and are not fed,   125
But swoln with wind, and the rank mist they draw,
Rot inwardly, and foul contagion spred:
Besides what the grim wolf[27] with privy paw
Dayly devours apace, and little sed,
But that two-handed engine[28] at the dore   130
Stands ready to smite once and smite no more.
    Return *Alphéus*, the dred voice is past

[23] the hyacinth, named for the youth accidentally killed by Apollo; the inscription was the Greek word for "alas."

[24] St. Peter, wearing a bishop's miter and bearing the keys of heaven.

[25] What does it matter to them? What do they need? They have fared well.

[26] feeble.

[27] perhaps the Anglican church, headed by Archbishop Laud.

[28] Whatever the specific reference, the meaning seems clear: the corrupted clergy will be punished finally and absolutely. 1 Sam. xxvi. 8: "let me smite him . . . with the spear even to the earth at once, and I will not smite him the second time." Probably intended, however, is the avenging sword of the Archangel Michael ("the great vision of the guarded mount," l. 161); see *PL*, VI, 249–53, 278.

That shrunk thy streams; return *Sicilian* Muse,[29]
And call the vales and bid them hither cast
Thir bells, and flowrets of a thousand hues.   135
Ye valleys low where the mild whispers use,
Of shades and wanton winds, and gushing brooks,
On whose fresh lap the swart star[30] sparely looks,
Throw hither all your quaint enamel'd eyes
That on the green terf suck the honied showrs   140
And purple all the ground with vernal flowrs.
Bring the rathe[31] primrose that forsaken dies,
The tufted crowtoe and pale Gessamine,
The white pink, and the pansie freakt[32] with jet,
The glowing violet,   145
The musk rose and the well-attir'd woodbine,
With cowslips wan that hang the pensive head,
And every flower that sad imbroidrie wears:
Bid *Amaranthus* all his beauties shed
And daffadillies fill thir cups with tears   150
To strew the laureat herse where *Lycid'* lies.
For so to interpose a little ease,
Let our frail thoughts dally with false surmise
Ay me! whilst thee the shoars and sounding seas
Wash far away, where ere thy bones are hurl'd,   155
Whether beyond the stormy *Hebrides*
Where thou perhaps under the whelming tide
Visit'st the bottom of the monstrous[33] world;
Or whether thou to our moist vows deni'd
Sleep'st by the fable of *Bellerus*[34] old   160
Where the great vision of the guarded mount[35]
Looks toward *Namancos*, and *Bayona's* hold;
Look homeward Angel now and melt with ruth
And O ye *Dolphins*, waft the hapless youth.[36]

Weep no more, wofull shepherds weep no more,   165
For *Lycidas* your sorrow is not dead,

[29] that of Theocritus and others who wrote pastorals.
[30] the blackening Dog Star (at its height when summer heat scorches vegetation).
[31] early.
[32] spotted.
[33] full of sea monsters.
[34] a mythical Cornish giant.
[35] Off Land's End in Cornwall, a large rock, traditionally guarded by the archangel Michael, points toward Namancos and Bayona in Spain.
[36] as they carried Arion in the legend.

Sunk though he be beneath the watry floar,
So sinks the day star[37] in the Ocean bed
And yet anon repairs his drooping head
And tricks his beams, and with newspangled ore   170
Flames in the forehead of the morning sky:
So *Lycidas* sunk low but mounted high
Through the dear might of him[38] that walkt the waves:
Where other groves and other streams along
With nectar pure his oozy locks he laves   175
And hears the unexpressive[39] nuptiall song
In the blest kingdoms meek of joy and love.
There entertain him all the Saints above
In solemn troops, and sweet societies
That sing, and singing in thir glory move   180
And wipe the tears for ever from his eyes.
Now *Lycidas*, the shepherds weep no more;
Henceforth thou art the Genius of the shoar
In thy large recompence, and shalt be good
To all that wander in that perilous flood.   185
    Thus sang the uncouth swain to th' oaks and rills,
While the still morn went out with sandals gray;
He toucht the tender stops of various quills,
With eager thought warbling his *Dorick*[40] lay:
And now the Sun had stretcht out all the hills,   190
And now was dropt into the western bay;
At last he rose and twitcht his mantle blew:
To morrow to fresh woods and pastures new.

(Nov. 1637)

AD PATREM
(To my Father)

Now I long for the Pierian[1] fountains / to whirl their watery paths through my breast and to roll / through my
mouth the entire stream released from the twin peaks / so
that my Muse, her trifling songs forgotten, might rise / on
spirited wings in courtesy of my revered father. [5] / However, this grateful song she is meditating for you, dear father, / is a poor attempt; yet I do not know myself / what

[37] the sun.
[38] Christ.
[39] inexpressible.
[40] pastoral.

---

[1] See *El.* 4, n. 10.

gifts from me could more aptly / repay your gifts, although my greatest ones could never / repay yours, for by no means can barren gratitude which is paid [10] / with empty words be equal to your gifts. / But notwithstanding, this page exhibits mine, / and I have reckoned up on this paper whatever I possess of abilities, / which to me are insignificant, save those which golden Clio[2] has given, / those which to me slumbers have begotten in the remote cave [15] / and the laurel groves of the sacred wood, Parnassian shadows. /

You should not despise the poet's task, divine song, / than which nothing commends more completely the offspring of heaven / to their ethereal origins, or the human mind to its lineage, / for song preserves a holy spark of Promethean fire. [20] / The gods love song, and song has power to stir / the trembling depths of Tartarus, and to bind the lower gods; / and it restrains the stern shades with triple adamant. / By song the priestesses of Apollo and the pale lips of the fearful Sibyl[3] / disclose the mysteries of the distant future. [25] / The sacrificial priest composes songs at altars, / both when he strews about the altar pieces of the bull which shakes its golden horns / and when, sagacious, he consults hidden destinies / in the steaming entrails and seeks out the Fate in the warm viscera. / Besides, when finally we return to our native Olympus [30] / and the everlasting ages of immutable eternity are established, / we shall walk with golden crowns through the temples of heaven, / with a sweet lyre uniting us in soft songs, / to which the stars and the vault of heaven will resound from the twin poles. / And the fiery spirit[4] that circles the swift planets [35] / even now himself is singing with heavenly verses / his immortal melody and indescribable song; / while the glittering serpent[5] checks his burning hisses / and with lowered sword fierce Orion becomes gentle, / and Mauretanian Atlas no longer suffers his burden of stars. [40] / Songs were used to embellish regal banquets, / luxury and the boundless depths of an enormous appetite / were not yet known, and the dinner table foamed forth for temperate

[2] See *El.* 4, n. 10.

[3] the Sibyls at Delphi, and the Cumaean Sibyl who prophesied Aeneas' wars in Latium and led him through the world of the dead (*Aen.*, VI).

[4] Apollo, the Sun, god of poetry and music.

[5] For the Serpent (Scorpio) and Orion, see *Ely*, n. 12; for Atlas, see *Idea*, n. 6.

Lyaeus;[6] / then according to custom a poet, sitting at festal banquets, / his unshorn tresses crowned with a garland from the oak, [45] / sang deeds of heroes and emulable achievements / and chaos and the foundations of the far-reaching earth, / the creeping gods and deities feeding on acorns,[7] / and the thunderbolt not yet sought from the cavern of Etna.[8] / And lastly what will support the melody of a petty voice, [50] / empty of words and sense, and of expressive rhythm? / Such music is suitable for forest choruses, not for Orpheus, / who restrained the rivers and gave ears to the oaks / by his song, not by his cithara, and singing stirred / the shades of the dead to tears; that fame he owes to his song. [55] /

Do not continue, I beg, to contemn the sacred Muses, / and do not deem them fruitless and contemptible, by whose favor / you yourself, skillful, compose a thousand sounds to apt numbers, / and are trained to vary the melodious voice with countless modulations, / so that you are deservedly the heir of Arion's name.[9] [60] / Now since it has fallen to me to have been born a poet, / why is it strange to you that we, so closely joined by dear blood, / should follow related arts and kindred endeavor? / Apollo,[10] wishing to disperse himself between the two, / gave to me certain gifts, to my father others, [65] / and father and son, we possess the divided god. /

Although you may maintain that you hate the similar Muses of poetry, / I believe you do not. For, father, you do not bid me go / where the way lies broad, where the field of wealth is easier / and the golden hope of amassing money glitters sure; [70] / neither do you force me to the laws and the courts of the people, / so poorly overseen, nor do you doom my ears to insipid noises. / But wishing more completely to enrich my cultivated mind, / you permit me to walk by Apollo's side, his blessed companion, / removed far from city din to high retreats, [75] / for the sake of the pleasant leisures of the Aonian stream.[11] / I do not recount

[6] See *El.* 6, n. 6.

[7] the Titans who had not yet learned agriculture.

[8] The Cyclops forged Jove's thunderbolt below Mt. Etna.

[9] the semi-legendary poet saved from drowning by a dolphin, who was charmed by his song. Milton's father had contributed music to various song collections, including settings for psalms.

[10] that is, since Apollo was god of both poetry and music.

[11] See *El.* 4, n. 10.

an esteemed father's usual kindness; / greater things demand my pen. When at your expense, most honored father, / I was exposed to the eloquence of the language of Romulus / and to the charms of Latin, and the lofty names of the magniloquent Greeks, [80] / which are fitting for the sublime lips of Jove, / you advised me to add the flowers which France boasts / and the language which the modern Italian pours from his / degenerate mouth, witness by his speech to the barbarian wars, / and the mysteries which the Palestinian prophet pronounces.[12] [85] / And finally all that heaven holds and earth, our parent, / bordering upon the sky, and the air flowing between the earth and sky, / and whatever water covers, and the surface of the restless sea, / through you I am allowed to know, through you, if I will be so disposed to know. / From a separated and observing cloud knowledge appears [90] / and, naked, she bends her conspicuous features to my kisses, / unless I should wish to flee, unless it be lamentable to taste. /

Go now, gather riches, fool, you who prefer / the ancient treasures of Austria and the Peruvian lands. / What father could bestow a greater gift, or Jove himself, [95] / with the exception of heaven, if he had given all? / He bestowed no more preferable gifts, however many might have been prudent, / who trusted to his young son the common light, / the chariot of Hyperion, the reins of day, / and the tiara waving about with radiant brightness. [100] / Therefore, now that I am a part of the learned company, however humble, / I shall sit among the ivy and the laurels of the victor. / And now I shall no longer mingle unknown with the indolent rabble / and my steps shall shun profane eyes. / Begone, sleepless cares; begone, complaints, [105] / and the twisted gaze of envy with oblique goatish leer. / And do not open your serpentine jaws, fell Calumny; / you can do nothing disagreeable to me, O most detestable band, / nor am I under your authority, and with heart secure / I shall walk, lifted high from your viperous stroke. [110] /

But to you, dear father, since it is not granted me to be able / to return gifts equal to your due or to repay for your deeds, / let it be enough to have remembered, and with a grateful mind / to enumerate your repeated offices and preserve them in a loyal heart. /

And you, O my juvenile songs and amusements, [115] /

[12] in the Old Testament.

if only you dare to hope for immortality / and to remain after your master's death, and to gaze upon the light, / and if dark oblivion does not carry you beneath dense Orcus, / perhaps you will preserve these praises and the name of the father / sung again and again, as an example to a future generation. [120]

(*Mar. 1638 ?*)

AD SALSILLUM POETAM ROMANUM ÆGROTANTEM
(To Salzilli, a Roman poet, being ill)[1]

O Muse who willingly drags along with a limping step[2] / and is pleased with a halting gait like Vulcan's,[3] / and who perceives that in its fitting place it is no less gratifying / than when the flaxen-haired Deiope[4] with well-formed calves / dances before the golden couch of Juno, come hither, [5] / if it pleases you, and carry back these few words to Salzilli, / by whom our poetry is prized so cordially, / and who preferred it, undeservedly, before that of the divine poets.[5] / These things, therefore, that same Milton, brought up in London, / speaks forth, who lately forsaking his nest [10] / and that region of the northern skies (where the worst of the winds, / with raging and violent lungs, / the one that is so brisk, lets forth his gasping blasts beneath the heavens) / came alone to the fertile soil of Italy / to see its cities known to proud fame [15] / and its men and the talents of its learned youth, / to you that same Milton, Salzilli, wishes many blessings / and a healthy constitution deep within for your weakened body; / whose reins now an excessive bile impairs / and, firmly settled, emits its poison from its seat beneath your heart. [20] / Nor has the accursed thing had

1 Giovanni Salzilli, a minor poet, contributed eleven sonnets and four other poems to *Poesie de' Signori Accademici Fantastici* (1637). The two poets met while Milton was touring Italy in 1638–39.

2 Labelled "Scazontes," these iambic verses employ a reversed final foot (a trochee or spondee), thus producing a "limping" effect.

3 Vulcan was lame from birth.

4 one of Juno's nymphs.

5 Salzilli's commendatory epigram printed in the 1645 edition asserts that Milton should be crowned with the triple laurel of poetry, for he surpasses Homer, Virgil, and Tasso.

mercy although you, / so very cultivated, fashion Lesbian melody[6] with your Roman mouth. / O sweet gift of the gods, O health, Hebe's[7] / sister! And you, Phoebus, terror of diseases / as a result of slain Python, or Paean if you more [25] / willingly give ear,[8] this man is your priest. / Oak forests of Faunus, and you hills rich / with wine-tasting dew, the seats of kindly Evander,[9] / if any healthful plant grows in your valleys, / let it eagerly speed relief to the ailing poet. [30] / Thus restored anew to his dear Muses he / will delight the neighboring meadows with his sweet song. / Numa himself will marvel among the gloomy woods / where he spends blessed, eternal leisure, / leaning backwards, gazing always at his Egeria.[10] [35] / And the swelling Tiber itself, from this time calmed, / will favor the annual hope of the farmers: / nor will it run, slackened on its left rein / in excess filled, rushing over kings in their tombs; / but it will better control the bridle of its waves [40] / even to the salt realms of curving Portumnus.[11]

(Nov. ? 1638)

MANSUS
(Manso)

John Baptista Manso, Marquis of Villa, man of genius, well-praised, already for his study of literature and also for his martial courage is renowned in the foremost ranks among Italians. A dialogue on friendship written to

[6] poetry apparently imitative of the lyrics of Alcaeus and Sappho, both of Lesbos.

[7] goddess of youth.

[8] The invocation "Ie Paion" was a part of a song of healing addressed to Apollo, who had slain the dragon Python, personification of the evils of the underworld.

[9] The woodland deity Faunus, guardian of crops and king of Latium, the Roman hills, and Evander, founder of a colony on the banks of the Tiber, are called upon since Salzilli lies ill in Rome.

[10] Numa, legendary king of Rome, attributed with having written many books on sacred law, would be amazed at a restored Salzilli. Egeria, goddess of fountains, counseled Numa by a sacred spring.

[11] The Tiber frequently inundated surrounding areas, particularly those on the lower left bank. Portumnus, the god of harbors, is perhaps called "curving" because of the location of ports at shore indentations and because of the sinuousness of the Italian coast where the Tiber empties into the Tyrrhenian Sea.

him by Torquato Tasso is extant; for he was most
friendly to Tasso; by whom likewise he is honored
among the Campanian princes, in that poem which is
titled Jerusalem Conquered, Book 20:

> *Among magnanimous and courteous cavaliers*
> *Manso is resplendent.*

He honored the author sojourning in Naples with the greatest
kindness, and granted him many courteous attentions.
To whom accordingly before he left that city, the
visitor, so that he would not show himself ungrateful,
sent this poem.

These verses also, Manso, the Pierides[1] are meditating / in
your praise; for you, Manso, well-known among the choir of
Apollo, / since indeed after the death of Gallus and of Etrus-
can Maecenas,[2] / he deems no other equally worthy in
honor. / You also, if the breath of my Muse has power to
such a degree, [5] / will sit among the victorious ivy and
laurels. / Happy friendship joined you to the great Tasso /
long ago, and has inscribed your names in everlasting scrolls. /
Soon afterwards the Muse, not without wisdom, committed to
you / the sweet-tongued Marini;[3] he was pleased to be called
your foster-son, [10] / when, prolix, he sang the Assyrian
loves of the gods; / and, gentle, he benumbed the Ausonian
nymphs with his song. / So that poet, dying, bequeathed his
indebted remains to you alone / and his last wishes to you
alone. / And your dear affection has not disappointed your
friend's shade; [15] / we have seen the poet smiling from his
artfully wrought bronze. / But this was not perceived sufficiently in each one, and your tender services / did not end
in the tomb; you wish to seize them unharmed from Orcus, /
as well as you can, and to elude the greedy laws of the
Fates: / you write the ancestry of both and each one's life,
achieved [20] / under changeable fortune, their traits, and

[1] the Muses.
[2] Cornelius Gallus (69–26 B.C.) established the elegy as a
main form of Latin poetry; Gaius Maecenas was patron of a literary circle which included Virgil, Horace, Propertius, and Varius.
[3] Giambattista Marini (1569–1625) was author of *Adone*
(1623), which recounts the love of Venus for Adonis, the sun-god
of the Assyrians (l. 11). "Ausonian," l. 12, means Italian.

their gifts from Athena;[4] / eloquent rival of that man born in high Mycale / who recounted the life of Aeolian Homer.[5] / Therefore, in the name of Clio[6] and great Apollo, / father Manso, I bid you be well through a long life, [25] / a young pilgrim sent from an Hyperborean[7] clime. / You, good man will not scorn a remote Muse, / who, hardly nourished under the frozen Bear, ignorant, / has recently ventured to fly to and fro through the Italian cities. / Furthermore I believe that in the dark shadows of night I have heard [30] / the swans singing on our river / where the silvery Thames with pure urns / widely bathes her gleaming tresses in the abyss of the ocean. / And of a truth Tityrus[8] long ago attained these shores. / But we, neither an uncultivated race nor one unserviceable to Apollo, [35] / in the region of the world which is furrowed by the sevenfold Triones, / endure in the long night wintry Boötes.[9] / We therefore worship Apollo; we have sent presents to him, / golden ears of grain, and yellow apples in baskets, / and fragrant crocus (unless antiquity bestows vain things), [40] / and choice dances from the race of the Druids. / (The ancient Druid nation, experienced in the sacred rites of the gods, / used to sing the praises of heroes and their emulable deeds.) / So often as the Greek maidens encircle with festive music / the altars in grassy Delos, according to their custom, [45] / they celebrate with happy songs Corinedian Loxo / and prophetic Upis, with flaxen-haired Hecaerge, / painted diversely to their naked breasts with Caledonian dye.[10] / Fortunate old man![11] therefore, wherever through the world / the glory and the

[4] Manso wrote a biography of Tasso, but one of Marini is unknown except for this reference. The gifts of Athena are wisdom and intellectual pursuits.

[5] Herodotus, supposedly born in Mycale, a promontory of Asia Minor.

[6] the Muse of history.

[7] northern.

[8] Chaucer, whom Spenser represented thus in Shepheardes Calendar, Feb., 92; June, 81; Dec., 4. Spenser sang of the swans on the Thames in Prothalamion, 37 ff.

[9] See Ely, n. 12. The Triones (ploughing oxen) were the seven principal stars in each of the Bears.

[10] Loxo, Upis, and Hecaerge—names for Diana, who was born on Delos—are northern (Corinedian, British) maidens in Callimachus' Hymn to Delos, 291–94.

[11] In Milton's mind was Virgil's Ec. I, 46, praising one retired to his farm.

great name of Torquato shall be celebrated [50] / and the
illustrious fame of immortal Marini shall grow anew, / you
shall also spring repeatedly into the mouths and applause of
men, / and with equal swiftness you shall tread upon the
road of immortality. / It shall be said then that Apollo
dwelled in your house of his own accord, / and that the
Muses came as attendants to your doors: [55] / and yet not
freely did that same Apollo, fugitive from heaven, / approach
the rural home of King Admetus,[12] / although he had been
host to great Hercules; / when he wished so much to escape
the noisy ploughmen, / he retired to the renowned cave of
the gentle Chiron[13] [60] / among the moist woodlands and
leafy abodes / near the river Peneus: there often under the
dark ilex, / to the sound of the cithara, won by his friend's
soft plea, / he would lighten the hard labors of exile by his
voice. / Then neither bank nor rocks fixed under the lowest
abyss [65] / would stay in place; the Trachinian cliff tot-
tered, / and no longer felt the vast weight in its accustomed
forests, / and displaced mountain-ashes hastened from their
hills, / and the spotted lynxes were soothed by the strange
song. / Old man, beloved of the gods, favorable Jove must
have been present [70] / at your birth, and Phoebus must
have purified you with his mellow light, / and the grandson
of Atlas;[14] for no one, unless favored from birth / by the
heavenly gods, could have befriended a great poet. / Therefore to you old age blooms with lasting flower, / and, vigorous, gains the spindles of Aeson,[15] [75] / preserving the
honors of brow not yet falling to you, / and esteeming your
talents and mature power of mind. / O if my lot might grant
me such a friend, / one who so well knows how to honor the
devotees of Apollo, / if ever I shall recall our native kings in
songs, [80] / and likewise Arthur waging wars under the
earth; / or proclaim the magnanimous heroes of the invincible table / with their convenant of companionship, and (O
only let the spirit be present) / shatter the Saxon phalanxes
under British Mars. / And when at last, having traversed the

[12] Apollo, exiled for vengeance on the Cyclops, served as a serf
with Admetus, king of Pherae, for a year. For the visit of Hercules,
see *Son.* 23, n. 2.

[13] the centaur, who lived in Thessaly; the Trachinian cliff
(1. 66) is Mt. Oeta.

[14] Hermes, inventor of the lyre.

[15] Aeson was restored to youth by his daughter-in-law Medea,
thus reversing the spindles of the Fates.

hours of a not silent life, [85] / and full of years, I bequeath
to the ashes their due, / he should stand by my couch with
tearful eyes, / it shall be enough if I might say to him standing there, Would I were in your care; / he would be solicitous
for my limbs, relaxed by livid death, / gently to be gathered
in a little urn. [90] / And perhaps he might fashion my
features from marble, / fastening my locks with a garland
of either Paphian myrtle / or Parnassian laurel,[16] so I should
rest in untroubled peace. / Then also, if to that degree faithful, if certain of the rewards of the good, / I myself, far
removed in the upper air of the heaven-dwelling gods, [95] /
where labor and a pure mind and fervid virtue lead, / shall
see these things from some part of the secret world / (as
many as the fates allow), and with my whole heart, / smiling,
shall be suffused with brilliant light on my serene face / and
at the same time I shall congratulate myself, full of joy, on
ethereal Olympus. [100]

(Dec. 1638)

AD LEONORAM ROMÆ CANENTEM
(To Leonora singing in Rome)[1]

Each person's own particular angel (so believe, nations) /
from the heavenly orders protects us with his wings. / What
wonder, Leonora, if a greater glory be yours? / Certainly
your voice itself pours forth the presence of God. / Either
God or certainly a third mind from the empty skies[2] [5] /
secretly winds through your throat effectively; / winds effectively and willingly teaches mortal hearts / how they may
gradually become accustomed to immortal sounds. / But if
God is all things in truth, and through all things diffused, /
in you alone he speaks, and holds all others mute. [10]

(Feb. ? 1639)

[16] from Paphos, sacred to Venus, and Mt. Parnassus, sacred to
the Muses.

---

[1] the Neapolitan singer Leonora Baroni, whom Milton heard in
the palace of Cardinal Barberini in Rome.
[2] perhaps the Holy Ghost, third person of the Trinity.

AD EANDEM
(To the same)

Another Leonora captured the poet Torquato, / from excessive love of whom he went mad.[1] / Ah, unfortunate man, how much more happily in your age / he might have been ruined, and for you, Leonora! / And he would have heard you singing with Pierian voice [5] / to set in motion the golden strings of your mother's lute.[2] / Although he had rolled his eyes more furiously than Dircean Pentheus,[3] / or raved to total immobility, / you still could have quieted his wandering senses / in their blind giddiness by your voice; [10] / and you, breathing peace beneath his suffering heart, / could have restored him to himself with your heart-moving song.

(Feb. ? 1639)

AD EANDEM
(To the same)

Why, credulous Naples, do you vaunt your clear-voiced Siren / and the famous temple of Parthenope,[1] daughter of Achelous, / and your shore-Naiad, perished on the coast, / her consecrated body to be dedicated on a Chalcidian pyre? / In truth she lives and, for the delightful surge of the Tiber, [5] / has exchanged the roaring of raucous Pausilipus.[2] /

[1] Torquato Tasso had spells of derangement for many years before his death in 1595; his love for Leonora d'Este, sister of his patron Alfonso, Duke of Ferrara, was romantically given as the cause.

[2] Adriana Baroni, an accomplished musician and lutist. Pierian refers to the Muses.

[3] a king of Thebes, who was torn to pieces by followers of Bacchus.

---

[1] a siren, who, after drowning herself because of Ulysses' escape, was washed ashore in the bay of Naples, an area settled by Greeks from Chalcis.

[2] a mountain northwest of Naples, through which a much travelled road passed. Leonora, now in Rome, has left the noise of Naples behind.

There, honored by the favorable zeal of the sons of Romulus, / she detains both men and gods with her song.

(Feb. ? 1639)

EPITAPHIUM DAMONIS
(Damon's Epitaph)[1]

ARGUMENT

Thyrsis and Damon, shepherds of the same neighborhood, were friends from childhood, since for the most part they had followed the same studies. Thyrsis received the news concerning Damon's death, travelling abroad for the sake of amusement.[2] Afterwards having returned home and upon having ascertained this to be so, he bewailed himself and his loneliness in this song. Moreover Charles Diodati is seen here in the person of Damon, descended through paternal forebears from the Etrurian city of Lucca, in other respects an Englishman; a youth distinguished while he lived by genius, learning, and the other most honorable virtues.

Nymphs of Himera[3]—for you remember Daphnis and Hylas / and the long-lamented fate of Bion— / proclaim your Sicilian song through the towns of the Thames: / what cries the mournful Thyrsis poured forth, what murmurings, / and with what incessant complaints he vexed the caves [5] / and rivers, the wandering streams and recesses of the woods, /

[1] In addition to likenesses to the pastoral elegies and idyls of Theocritus, Bion, and Moschus, *Damon* frequently echoes Virgil (e.g., the refrain from *Ec.*, VII, 44, and the similarity of form to *Ec.*, X) and Castiglione's *Alcon*; see T. P. Harrison, Jr., *PMLA*, L (1935), 480–93. But Dorian (*English Diodatis*, pp. 177–78) points out the break with tradition: *Damon* is devoid of real mourners other than Milton. "And because of this concentration on the emotional problem of his personal bereavement, it tells considerably less than do most pastoral elegies of the shepherd who is gone."

[2] Charles Diodati (Damon) was buried at St. Anne's, Blackfriars, London, on Aug. 27, 1638, while Milton (Thyrsis) was abroad. Milton was probably informed of his death (from the plague?) when he reached Venice around Apr. 1639 (see n. 4 below). See also *El.* 1, n. 1, for material about Diodati.

[3] A nymph of the Sicilian river Himera punished Daphnis for refusing her love (Theocritus, *Idyl* 1); and Bion was mourned by the Sicilian poet Moschus. For Hylas, see *El.* 7, n. 3.

when to himself he lamented Damon, prematurely borne away, nor did he / banish the deep night with his griefs, wandering through lonely places. / And now twice[4] was the stalk with its green ear rising, / and twice were the yellow harvests being counted in the barns, [10] / since the last day had swept Damon beneath the shadows, / and still Thyrsis was not present; namely, love of the sweet Muse / was keeping that shepherd in the Tuscan city. / But when his mind was full and the care of the flock / left behind[5] called him home, and as soon as he sat under the accustomed elm, [15] / then truly, then at last, he felt the loss of his friend, / and began to disburden his great sorrow thus: /

Go home unfed, your master has no time now, my lambs. / Ah me! what on earth, what divinities in heaven shall I affirm, / since they have torn you away to inexorable death, Damon? [20] / Thus do you forsake us, thus shall your virtue go below without a name, / and be joined to the troop of unknown shades? / But he[6] who divides the souls with his golden wand / would not wish this, and he would lead you into a multitude worthy of you, / and would keep at a distance the entire slothful, silent herd. [25] /

Go home unfed, your master has no time now, my lambs. / Whatever will be, assuredly, unless a wolf sees me first,[7] / you shall not crumble to dust in an unwept sepulchre; / your repute will endure and flourish long / among the shepherds. To you they shall be glad to pay their vows [30] / second after Daphnis, after Daphnis to sing praises, / while Pales, while Faunus loves the fields:[8] / if there is any worth in having cultivated the ancient faith and piety / and the arts of Pallas, and in having possessed a comrade of songs. /

Go home unfed, your master has no time now, my lambs. [35] / These certainly await you, for you these rewards will exist, Damon. / But what at length will become

[4] referring to Italian, not English, agriculture; both winter and spring wheat are harvested in the Arno valley. The imperfect tenses of ll. 9–13 imply that Milton did not learn of Diodati's death until after his second stay in Florence, the Tuscan city, in Mar. 1639.

[5] possibly Milton's nephews Edward and John Phillips, who joined his household shortly after his return.

[6] Hermes, who led the dead to the nether world.

[7] Seen by a wolf first, a man became blind.

[8] Pales was a tutelary of shepherds and flocks; Faunus, of crops and herds.

of me now? what faithful companion / will cling to my side, as you often were wont / in the hard winters and through the regions full of snows, / or under the fierce sun, with herbs dying from thirst, [40] / whether the task was to advance on great lions from a distance / or to frighten hungry wolves away from the high sheepfolds. / Who will be wont to lull my time with speaking and singing? /

Go home unfed, your master has no time now, my lambs. / To whom shall I confide my heart? Who will teach me to assuage [45] / my mordant cares, who to deceive the long night / with pleasant conversations, while the delicate pear hisses / before the grateful fire, and the hearth crackles with nuts, as the evil / southwind rattles all the doors, and whistles in the elm above. /

Go home unfed, your master has no time now, my lambs. [50] / Or in summer, when the day is turned to noon, / when Pan enjoys sleep, hidden in the shade of an oak, / and the nymphs return to their well-known haunts beneath the waters, / and the shepherds lie concealed, the farmer snores under a hedge, / who will bring back to me your flatteries, who then [55] / your laughter and Attic salt,[9] your cultured graces? /

Go home unfed, your master has no time now, my lambs. / But now alone in the fields, now alone in the pastures I roam / wherever the branching shadows are made dense by the valleys, / there I await the evening; overhead the rain and the southeast wind[10] [60] / sorrowfully resound, and in the restless twilight of the buffeted wood. /

Go home unfed, your master has no time now, my lambs. / Alas, how entangled with insolent weeds are my once cultivated / fields, and the tall grain itself is drooping with neglect, / the unmarried grape withers on its slighted vine, [65] / nor do myrtle groves delight; my sheep also offend, but they / mourn and turn their faces to their master. /

Go home unfed, your master has no time now, my lambs. / Tityrus calls to the hazels, Alphesiboeus to the mountain ashes, / Aegon to the willows, handsome Amyntas to the rivers:[11] [70] / Here are the icy springs, here the pastures

9 poignant and delicate wit.
10 The southeast wind and the rain suggest composition of *Damon* in autumn (around Oct.).
11 Tityrus, Aegon, and Amyntas are shepherds of idyllic literature; Milton may have derived the name of the fourth from Alphesiboea, daughter of the Arcadian king Phegeus.

spread with moss, / here the zephyrs, here the arbutus sounds amidst the quiet waters. / They sing to deaf ears; having stumbled on them, I vanished into the shrubs. /

Go home unfed, your master has no time now, my lambs. / Mopsus[12] came after them, for he had marked me by chance returning, [75] / and truly Mopsus did understand the songs of birds and the stars: / Thyrsis, what now? he said, what excessive bile torments you? / Either love is destroying you or a star is wickedly bewitching you. / Saturn's star[13] has often been painful to shepherds, / and it pierces the inmost heart with its slanting leaden bullet. [80] /

Go home unfed, your master has no time now, my lambs. / The nymphs are amazed, and they speak, What is to become of you, Thyrsis? / What do you wish for yourself? that brow of youth is not wont to be / melancholy, nor its eyes grim, nor its countenance severe; / these things justly desire dances and nimble sports [85] / and always love; twice miserable he who loved late. /

Go home unfed, your master has no time now, my lambs. / Hyas came, and Dryope, and Aegle, the daughter of Baucis, / well-versed in melodies and skilled with the harp, but ruined by pride; / Chloris, a neighbor of the Idumanian river, came.[14] [90] / Neither flatteries nor consoling words, / nothing moves me, if anything appears, nor any hope of the future. /

Go home unfed, your master has no time now, my lambs. / Ah me, alas! how similarly the young bullocks play through the meadows, / all comrades together under a law harmonious to themselves, [95] / and none parts a friend from one more than from another / of the herd; thus the wolves come to their food in packs, / and the shaggy asses are joined with their mates in turn; / the law of the sea is the same, on the

[12] a fusion of the Greek seer and of Virgil's shepherd (Ec., V, VIII). For the relation of birds to prophecy, see El. 3, n. 6.

[13] The planet Saturn, alchemically the name for lead, was known for its gloomy and sullen aspect.

[14] The mourners seem to be the Hyades, nymphs of rain, who were changed into stars; Dryope, who was changed into a lotus tree; Aegle, one of the Heliades, who was changed into a poplar tree; and Chloris, goddess of flowers. Baucis probably means an old woman. The Idumanian river is the Chelmer, leading into Blackwater Bay in Essex; but identification of a specific person is lacking.

deserted shore Proteus[15] / counts his hosts of seals, and least
valuable of birds, [100] / the sparrow always has someone
with whom he may be, and to all the grains / flies about
free, returning late to his own nest; / if chance has delivered
him to death, or a kite has brought him misfortune / with
its hooked beak, or a peasant has brought him down with an
arrow, / forthwith that bird seeks another for companion
flight. [105] / We men are an insensible race, and driven
on by detestable fate, / a nation hostile in our minds and
discordant in our heart, / scarcely does anybody find one
equal to himself in a thousand, / or if a destiny not unkind
were granted at last to our prayers, / an unexpected hour,
as far as you will have trusted time, [110] / steals that one,
leaving behind an eternal loss to future ages. /

Go home unfed, your master has no time now, my lambs. /
Alas! what wandering fancy carried me into unknown climes
/ to pass through airy rocks and the snow-capped Alps? /
Was it of such worth to have seen buried Rome? [115] /
although it were such as he viewed it when long ago / Tityrus[16] himself left his sheep and fields, / that I could have
been absent from you, from so dear a companion, / that I
could set between you so many deep seas, so many mountains, / so many forests, so many rocky lands and roaring
rivers? [120] / Ah, surely I would have been permitted to
touch his right hand at the last / and his calmed eyes dying
very peacefully, / and to have said, Farewell! you will go to
the stars remembering me. /

Go home unfed, your master has no time now, my lambs. /
And even though I never shall repent to remember you, [125]
/ Tuscan shepherds, youths devoted to the Muses, / here
was grace and charm; and you also Damon were a Tuscan, /
from whom you claim your descent from the ancient city of
Lucca. / O how great I was when stretched beside / the
murmurings of the cool Arno and the poplar-grove, where
was the softer grass, [130] / I could pluck now violets, now
the tallest myrtles, / and hear Menalcas contending with
Lycidas! / And even I myself dared to compete,[17] nor do I

15 See *El.* 3, n. 7.

16 Chaucer; it is unlikely that Milton would have been aware
that Rome was not on his itinerary. Spenser used this name of
Chaucer, and Milton would intend comparison only with an English poet.

17 referring to *Idyl* 7 of Theocritus and Milton's poetical per-
formances at the Svogliati Academy in Florence.

suppose that I much / displeased, for your gifts[18] are still with me, / the baskets of twigs, those of wicker, and the shepherd pipes with waxen bonds. [135] / Indeed Dati and Francini taught their beech trees my name / and both were noted for their songs / and learning, both of Lydian blood.[19] /

Go home unfed, your master has no time now, my lambs. / These things the dewy moon spoke to me, then full of joy, [140] / when alone I shut the tender kids in their wattled folds. / Ah, how often did I say, when dark ashes possessed you, / Now Damon is singing or now he is stretching out his nets for a hare, / now he is weaving osiers for himself although it be for various uses. / And then what future I was hoping for with my affable mind [145] / I snatched from my trivial desire and supposed my present circumstances. / Hark, good friend! are you doing anything? unless anything detain you by accident, / let us go and lie for a while in the clear shade, / either beside the waters of the Colne[20] or where lie the lands of Cassivelaunas. / You shall run through your medicinal potions for me, your herbs, [150] / and your hellebore, humble crocuses, and leaf of hyacinth, / and what plants that marsh holds, and the arts of the physicians. / Ah! let the plants perish, let the arts of the physicians perish, / and the herbs, since they themselves have accomplished nothing for their master. / Even I—for I do not know what my pipe was pouring forth [155] / loudly—now daylight is present after the eleventh night— / perhaps I was then directing my lips to my new pipes, / yet they have burst asunder with their binding broken, and no further / were they able to carry the grave notes; I question also that I may not be / vain, and yet I may recite; depart, you woods. [160] /

Go home unfed, your master has no time now, my lambs. / I myself shall celebrate[21] the Dardanian ships through the

[18] poems and books of verse from his Italian friends, among whom were Carlo Dati and Antonio Francini.

[19] Lydians were supposed to have founded an early colony in Italy.

[20] the river near Horton. Cassivelaunas was an early British military leader.

[21] Subjects for English epical works included the invasion of England by Brutus (son of Aeneas), and the Trojan colony; the conquests of Gaul and Rome by the British kings Brennus and Belinus; the military engagements in Rome of Arviragus, son of Cymbeline; the settlement of the Britons, fleeing the Saxons, in

Rutupian sea, / and the ancient kingdom of Inogene, daughter of Pandrasus, / the chieftains Brennus and Arviragus, and old Belinus, / and the Armorican colonists at last under the law of the Britons; [165] / then Igraine pregnant with Arthur by fatal deception, / Gorlois' counterfeit features and assumed arms, / the guile of Merlin. O then if life remain to me, / you, my pipe, will hang far off on an aged pine tree / quite forgotten by me, or changed, you shall shrill a tale of Britain [170] / to your native Muses! What then? one can not do everything, / one can not hope to do everything. For me it is sufficiently ample / reward, and to me great glory— even if I be unknown forever / and utterly inglorious to the outside world— / if blonde Ouse read me under her locks and the drinker of the Alne [175] / and the Humber well-filled with whirlpools, and every wood along the Trent, / and before all my Thames, and the Tamar blackened by mines, / and if the Orkneys in their distant seas become acquainted with me.[22] /

Go home unfed, your master has no time now, my lambs. / These things I was keeping for you in the tough bark of the laurel, [180] / these and more besides; moreover the two cups[23] which Manso / gave me, Manso, not the least glory of the Chalcidian shore,[24] / these a marvellous work of art, and he himself singular, / and he had engraved them around with a twofold theme. / In the middle are the waves of the Red Sea, and odor-bearing spring, [185] / the far-reaching shores of Arabia, and the woods exuding balsam gums; / among those woods the Phoenix, divine bird, unique on earth, / gleaming cerulean with diversely colored wings, /

Armorica (Brittany); the begetting of Arthur through Merlin's magic of making Uther Pendragon appear to Igraine as her husband Gorlois; and perhaps a further but different epic on a British theme. Dardanus was the progenitor of the royal race of Troy; Rutupiae was a part of Kent; and Inogene was Brutus' wife.

[22] The rivers Ouse, Alne, Humber, Trent, and Tamar (in a valley famous for mines) cover much of England, and the Orkneys signify Scotland; Milton's reward will be enough if the British Isles read and know his work.

[23] Michele de Filippis' suggestion that Milton is referring to books, Manso's *Erocallia* and *Poesie Nomiche* (see *PMLA*, LI, 1936, 745–56), is supported by Donald C. Dorian (*PMLA*, LIV, 1939, 612–13), since the same simile of cups for books is found in Pindar's seventh Olympian Ode.

[24] the Bay of Naples.

watches Aurora rising over the glassy waters. / In another part are the wide-extending sky and mighty Olympus. [190] / Who would imagine? here also Love,[25] his quiver painted against a cloud, / his gleaming arms, his torches and darts stained with gold-bronze; / from this place he does not smite trifling spirits or the ignoble heart / of the rabble, but, whirling around with flaming eyes, / he endlessly scatters his darts aloft through the spheres, [195] / unwearied, and never aims toward downward shots. / Hence holy minds and the images of the gods have taken fire. /

You also are among these—for no uncertain hope deceives me, Damon— / you also are among these certainly; for where else might your sweet / and holy simplicity have gone, for where else your radiant virtue? [200] / It would not be proper to have sought you in Lethean Orcus,[26] / neither do tears for you befit, nor shall I shed them more. / Away, my tears; Damon lives in the pure air, / the air he so pure possesses: he rejected the rainbow with his foot. / Among the souls of heroes and immortal gods, [205] / he consumes the heavenly draughts and drinks their joys / with his sacred mouth. But you, since having received the privilege of heaven, / are on the right hand; and peaceful, favor me, however you may be called, / whether you will be our Damon, or hearken more favorably to / Diodati, by which divine name[27] the whole [210] / of heaven will know you, and you will be called Damon in the woods. / Because blushing modesty and youth without blemish / were dear to you, because the delight of marriage was tasted not at all, / lo! likewise the rewards of virginity are reserved for you. / You, encircled around your glorious head with a shining crown [215] / and riding in happy bowers entwined with palm leaves, / shall pursue eternally the immortal marriage / where song and mingled lyre rage with blessed dances, / and festal orgies revel under the thyrsus of Sion.[28]

(autumn 1639)

[25] the Platonic Heavenly Eros.

[26] See *Idea*, n. 5.

[27] literally, "god-given."

[28] Diodati is envisioned as joining the heavenly host (Rev. vii. 9) in Bacchic dance of ecstasy under the thyrsus (a staff twined with ivy and vine shoots borne by Bacchantes) of Sion (the heavenly city of God).

SONNET 8

Captain or Colonel, or Knight in Arms,
  Whose chance on these defenceless dores may sease,[1]
  If ever deed of honour did thee please,
  Guard them, and him within protect from harms.
He can requite thee, for he knows the charms   5
  That call Fame on such gentle acts as these,
  And he can spread thy name o're lands and seas,
  What ever clime the suns bright circle warms.
Lift not thy spear against the Muses bowr:[2]
  The great *Emathian* Conqueror[3] bidd spare   10
  The house of *Pindarus*, when temple and towr
Went to the ground: and the repeated air
  Of sad *Electra's* poet[4] had the power
  To save th' *Athenian* walls from ruin bare.

(Nov. 1642)

SONNET 9

Ladie, that in the prime of earliest youth
  Wisely hast shun'd the broad way and the green[1]

[1] During the earlier days of the First Civil War the Royalist army, after a victory at Edgehill on Oct. 23, 1642, advanced toward London but retreated Nov. 12–13. Milton's home in Aldersgate Street was just beyond the London city gate; the MS title indicated (in jest) that the sonnet was to be tacked on his door.

[2] Despite the mocking tone of the thin spear raised against the undefended door, Milton is seriously comparing the far-reaching powers of poetry with the inglorious limitations of war.

[3] Alexander the Great of Macedonia (Emathia). Thebes was attacked in 335 B.C. for revolt against Macedonia; the Congress of Corinth decreed that the city was to be razed.

[4] Euripides. The first chorus of that play (ll. 167 ff.) reputedly dissuaded the Spartans from sacking Athens in 404 B.C.

[1] The unidentified lady is commended for her steadfast and virtuous life: unlike the Bride who unwisely and unsuccessfully sought her Lord "in the broad ways" (S. of Sol. iii. 2), the lady will attain the kingdom of Heaven because she has followed Jesus' admonition: "Enter ye at the strait gate: for wide is the gate, and broad is the way, that leadeth to destruction, . . . and narrow is the way, which leadeth unto life" (Matt. vii. 13, 14).

And with those few art eminently seen
That labour up the hill of heav'nly Truth,[2]
The better part with *Mary* and with *Ruth*[3]   5
Chosen thou hast, and they that overween
And at thy growing vertues fret thir spleen
No anger find in thee, but pitty and ruth.
Thy care is fixt and zealously attends
To fill thy odorous lamp with deeds of light   10
And Hope that reaps not shame. Therfore be sure[4]
Thou, when the Bridegroom with his feastfull freinds
Passes to bliss at the midd howr of night,
Hast gain'd thy entrance, Virgin wise and pure.[5]

(*1643–45*)

SONNET 10

Daughter to that good Earle,[1] once President
Of *Englands* Counsel, and her Treasury,
Who liv'd in both, unstain'd with gold or fee,
And left them both, more in himself content,

The green way of the impatient and complaining comes from Job viii. 12–13, 16: "Whilst it is yet in his greenness, and not cut down, it withereth before any other herb. So are the paths of all that forget God; and the hypocrite's hope shall perish: . . . He is green before the sun. . . ."

[2] God's holy hill is gained through perseverance of the virtuous life, for Jesus had said, "I am the way, the truth, and the life: no man cometh unto the Father, but by me" (John xiv. 6). Compare Hesiod's Hill of Virtue (*Works and Days*, 287).

[3] Mary, who steadfastly sat at Jesus' feet to hear his word, had "chosen that good part, which shall not be taken away from her" (Luke x. 42). Ruth, known to the people to be a steadfast and virtuous woman (Ruth i. 18, iii. 11), chose to follow Naomi and her advice, thus becoming a progenitor of Joseph, husband of Jesus' mother, through her marriage to Boaz.

[4] be assured.

[5] The wise virgins, who had filled their lamps in preparation for the time that the kingdom of Heaven would be at hand, were ready when at midnight the Bridegroom came (Matt. xxv. 1–13). As Brooks and Hardy note (p. 160), "it was at midnight too . . . that Boaz awakened to find Ruth at his feet, and when he lay down he had just come from a feast" (Ruth iii. 7–8).

---

[1] Sir James Ley, Earl of Marlborough, Lord Chief Justice, Lord High Treasurer, and Lord President of the Council of State under Charles I. The subject of the sonnet was Lady Margaret, wife of a Captain Hobson.

Till the sad breaking of that Parlament   5
  Broke him,[2] as that dishonest victory
  At *Chæronéa,* fatal to liberty
  Kill'd with report that Old man eloquent,[3]
Though later born then to have known the daies
  Wherin your Father flourisht, yet by you   10
  Madam, me thinks I see him living yet;
So well your words his noble Vertues praise,
  That all both judge you to relate them true
  And to possess them, Honourd *Margaret.*

(1643–45)

IN EFFIGIEI EJUS SCULPTOREM
(On the Engraver of His Likeness)[1]

This image was drawn by an untaught hand, / you might perhaps say, looking at the form of the original. / But since here you do not recognize the modelled face, friends, / laugh at a bad imitation by a worthless artist.

(1645)

SONNET 11[1]

I did but prompt the age to quit thir clogs
  By the known rules of ancient liberty,[2]

[2] Charles' Third Parliament was dissolved by him on Mar. 10, 1629, primarily because of the intractable opposition of Commons to tonnage and poundage; Marlborough died four days later. The next parliament (the Short Parliament) was not called until Apr. 13, 1640.

[3] Isocrates. Philip of Macedonia's defeat of Thebes and Athens at Chaeronea in 338 B.C., ending Greek independence, reputedly caused the well-known orator to commit suicide four days later. Like this shameful victory, Charles' thwarting of the people's will was a curtailment of liberty.

---

[1] A poorly drawn portrait served as a frontispiece in the 1645 edition of the poems; these lines in Greek appeared beneath.

---

[1] See the *Textual Notes* for numbering.

[2] The twin divorce tracts *Tetrachordon* and *Colasterion* were published Mar. 4, 1645; to Milton his work on divorce was part of his contribution to true liberty (*Defensio secunda,* pp. 90–91). In *Tetrachordon* he justified divorce through exposition of Deut. xxiv. 1, 2. Among the published detractions of *Tetrachordon* was Ephraim Pagitt's *Heresiography,* the second edition (1645), which remarks Milton's recourse to scripture to maintain his opinion (p. 142).

When strait a barbarous noise environs me
Of Owls and cuckoes, asses, apes and dogs.
As when those hinds that were transform'd to frogs   5
    Rail'd at *Latona's* twin-born progeny
    Which after held the Sun and Moon in Fee.[3]
But this is got by casting pearl to hogs;[4]
That bawl for freedom in thir senseles mood,
    And still[5] revolt when Truth would set them free.   10
    Licence they mean, when they cry liberty,
For who loves that, must first be wise, and good;
    But from that mark how farr they roav, we see
    For all this wast of wealth, and loss of blood.[6]

(*autumn 1645 ?*)

SONNET 13

Harry,[1] whose tunefull and well-measur'd song
    First taught our English Music how to span
    Words with just note and accent, not to scan
With *Midas* eares,[2] committing short and long,

[3] The twin children of Latona and Jove were Apollo, god of
the sun, and Diana, goddess of the moon. The Lycian peasants
who refused Latona and her children drink were turned into frogs
by Jove. As Parker has noted (*Explicator*, VIII, 1949, item 3) the
fact that Milton's derided pamphlets were published together re-
called this image of the twin gods.

[4] Adapted from Matt. vii. 6: "Give not that which is holy unto
the dogs, neither cast ye your pearls before swine, lest they trample them under their feet, and turn again and rend you."

[5] nevertheless.

[6] The image likens the people who think they aim at liberty
by means of Civil War to wasteful archers whose arrows (rovers)
miss their mark and merely wound their prey.

[1] Henry Lawes (1596–1662), who wrote the music for *Mask*
(and perhaps for *Arcades*), enacted the attendant spirit, and was
instrumental in having the work published. The sonnet was prefixed to *Choice Psalmes put into Musick For Three Voices* (1648);
Milton's nephews, Edward and John Phillips, contributed commendatory lyrics to Lawes' *Ayres* (1653). The standard biography
is Willa M. Evans' *Henry Lawes, Musician and Friend to Poets*
(New York, 1941).

[2] Apollo changed Midas' ears to those of an ass for his obtuse-
ness in declaring Pan a superior flutist to Apollo. Milton is praising
Lawes' faithful attention to lyrics, in distinction to some lesser
seventeenth-century composers' practice of altering them to fit
their music.

Thy worth and skill exempts thee from the throng,   5
  With praise anough for Envy to look wan;
  To after-age thou shalt be writt the man
  That with smooth air couldst humor best our tongue.
Thou honourst Vers, and Vers must lend her wing
  To honour thee, the Preist of *Phœbus* quire   10
  That tun'st thir happiest lines in hymn, or story.[3]
Dante shall give Fame leav to set thee higher
  Then his *Casella*,[4] whom he woo'd to sing
  Met in the milder shades of Purgatory.

(Feb. 1646)

SONNET 14[1]

When Faith and Love which parted from thee never,
  Had rip'n'd thy just soul to dwell with God,
  Meekly thou didst resigne this earthy load
  Of death, call'd life; which us from life doth sever.
Thy Works and Almes, and all thy good Endeavor   5
  Staid not behind, nor in the grave were trod;
  But as Faith pointed with her golden rod,
  Follow'd thee up to joy and bliss for ever.
Love led them on, and Faith who knew them best
  Thy handmaids, clad them o're with purple beames   10
  And azure wings, that up they flew so drest,
And spake the truth of thee in glorious theames[2]
  Before the Judge, who thenceforth bidd thee rest,
  And drink thy fill of pure immortal streames.

(Dec. 1646)

[3] referring to Lawes' setting of William Cartwright's *The Complaint of Ariadne*.

[4] a Florentine musician and friend of Dante. When Dante arrived in Purgatory from Hell, he spied Casella, who sang the second canzone of Dante's *Convitio* (*Purgatorio*, II, 76–123).

---

[1] Mrs. Catharine Thomason, wife of the book collector George Thomason, was buried on Dec. 12, 1646. The poem is a tissue of Biblical allusions, such as the Christian armor of Faith and Love (Eph. vi. 13–24), the just who shall live by faith (Gal. iii. 11), the meek who inherit the earth (Matt. v.5), the judgment according to one's faith and works (James ii. 22, 24), the ascent of alms to God (Acts x. 4), the river of immortality (Rev. xxii. 1).

[2] As Grierson pointed out (*TLS*, Jan. 15, 1925, p. 40), the term is musical; it is a song before the throne of God (Rev. xiv. 2–3).

SAMSON AGONISTES[1]

OF THAT SORT OF DRAMATIC POEM
WHICH IS CALL'D TRAGEDY

Tragedy, as it was antiently compos'd, hath been ever held
the gravest, moralest, and most profitable of all other Poems:
therefore said by *Aristotle* to be of power by raising pity and
fear, or terror, to purge the mind of those and such like passions, that is to temper and reduce them to just measure with
a kind of delight, stirr'd up by reading or seeing those passions well imitated.[2] Nor is Nature wanting in her own effects to make good his assertion: for so in Physic things of
melancholic hue and quality are us'd against melancholy,
sowr against sowr, salt to remove salt humours. Hence Philosophers and other gravest Writers, as *Cicero, Plutarch* and
others, frequently cite out of Tragic Poets, both to adorn and
illustrate thir discourse. The Apostle *Paul* himself thought it
not unworthy to insert a verse of *Euripides* into the Text of
Holy Scripture, 1 *Cor.* 15.33.[3] and *Paræus*[4] commenting on
the *Revelation,* divides the whole Book as a Tragedy, into

[1] Drawn from Hebraic material (Judges xiii–xvi) and Greek
tragic structure, the drama reflects both Christian traditions (see
Krouse's survey) and Hellenistic spirit (see Parker's study). In "SA
and Milton in Old Age," p. 181, Hanford remarks, "By representing a clearly marked triumph of the human will over its own
weakness, and by the substitution of Providence for blind fate as
the power which overrules the action, the play provides material
for a different understanding of catharsis from that contemplated
by Aristotle." Based on Greek tragedy, Milton's drama consists of
five episodes each followed by a chorus (stasimon) in addition to
the opening and closing passages. The regeneration of Samson, the
main "plot" of the play, is developed through these five episodes,
and thus forges the champion of truth indicated by the title.
Biographical interpretations have been commonplace because of
the element of blindness, but if the suggested earlier dating is
correct, many allusions to contemporary and marital problems
which have been inferred are invalidated.

[2] The principle of catharsis is described in *Poetics,* VI.

[3] "Evil communications corrupt good manners," attributed also
to Menander.

[4] David Pareus (1548–1622), a Calvinist theologian, in his
Operum Theologicorum.

Acts distinguisht each by a Chorus of Heavenly Harpings and Song between. Heretofore Men in highest dignity have labour'd not a little to be thought able to compose a Tragedy. Of that honour *Dionysius* the elder[5] was no less ambitious, then before of his attaining to the Tyranny. *Augustus Cæsar* also had begun his *Ajax*, but unable to please his own judgment with what he had begun, left it unfinisht.[6] *Seneca* the Philosopher is by some thought the Author of those Tragedies (at least the best of them) that go under that name. *Gregory Nazianzen* a Father of the Church, thought it not unbeseeming the sanctity of his person to write a Tragedy, which he entitl'd, *Christ suffering*.[7] This is mention'd to vindicate Tragedy from the small esteem, or rather infamy, which in the account of many it undergoes at this day with other common Interludes; hap'ning through the Poets error of intermixing Comic stuff with Tragic sadness and gravity; or introducing trivial and vulgar persons, which by all judicious hath bin counted absurd; and brought in without discretion, corruptly to gratifie the people. And though antient Tragedy use no Prologue,[8] yet using sometimes, in case of self defence, or explanation, that which *Martial* calls an Epistle; in behalf of this Tragedy coming forth after the antient manner, much different from what among us passes for best, thus much before-hand may be Epistl'd; that *Chorus* is here introduc'd after the Greek manner, not antient only but modern, and still in use among the *Italians*. In the modelling therefore of this Poem, with good reason, the Antients and *Italians* are rather follow'd, as of much more authority and fame. The measure of Verse us'd in the Chorus is of all sorts, call'd by the Greeks *Monostrophic*,[9] or rather *Apolelymenon*, without regard had to *Strophe, Antistrophe* or *Epod*, which were a kind of Stanzas fram'd only for the Music, then us'd with the Chorus that sung; not essential to the Poem, and therefore not material; or being divided into Stanzas or Pauses, they may be call'd *Allæostropha*.[10] Division into Act and Scene referring chiefly to the Stage (to which this work never was

---

[5] tyrant of Syracuse, who wrote numerous literary works.

[6] See Suetonius, II, lxxxv.

[7] This was a common ascription, though wrong.

[8] a "defense" of the writing of the play, not the passage preceding the entrance of the chorus.

[9] explained by the next phrase.

[10] strophes of varying lengths.

intended) is here omitted. It suffices if the whole Drama be found not produc't beyond the fift Act.

Of the style and uniformitie, and that commonly call'd the Plot, whether intricate or explicit, which is nothing indeed but such œconomy, or disposition of the fable as may stand best with verisimilitude and decorum, they only will best judge who are not unacquainted with *Æschulus*, *Sophocles*, and *Euripides*, the three Tragic Poets unequall'd yet by any, and the best rule to all who endeavour to write Tragedy. The circumscription of time wherein the whole Drama begins and ends, is according to antient rule, and best example, within the space of 24 hours.

THE ARGUMENT

Samson made Captive, Blind, and now in the Prison at *Gaza*,[11] there to labour as in a common work-house, on a Festival day, in the general cessation from labour, comes forth into the open Air, to a place nigh, somewhat retir'd, there to sit a while and bemoan his condition. Where he happens at length to be visited by certain friends and equals of his tribe, which make the Chorus, who seek to comfort him what they can; then by his old Father *Manoa*, who endeavours the like, and withal tells him his purpose to procure his liberty by ransom; lastly, that this Feast was proclaim'd by the *Philistins* as a day of Thanksgiving for thir deliverance from the hands of *Samson*, which yet more troubles him. *Manoa* then departs to prosecute his endeavour with the *Philistian* Lords for *Samson's* redemption; who in the mean while is visited by other persons; and lastly by a publick Officer to require his coming to the Feast before the Lords and People, to play or shew his strength in thir presence; he at first refuses, dismissing the publick Officer with absolute denyal to come; at length perswaded inwardly that this was from God, he yields to go along with him, who came now the second time with great threatnings to fetch him; the Chorus yet remaining on the place, *Manoa* returns full of joyful hope, to procure e're long his Sons deliverance: in the midst of which discourse an Ebrew comes in haste, confusedly at first; and afterward more distinctly relating the Catastrophe, what *Samson* had done to the *Philistins*, and by accident to himself; wherewith the Tragedy ends.

[11] a principal city of the Philistines, lying on the eastern Mediterranean in Palestine.

THE PERSONS

Samson
Manoa *the Father of* Samson
Dalila *his Wife*
Harapha *of* Gath
Publick Officer
Messenger
Chorus *of* Danites

The Scene before the Prison in Gaza

Samson. A little onward lend thy guiding hand
To these dark steps, a little further on;
For yonder bank hath choice of Sun or shade,
There I am wont to sit, when any chance
Relieves me from my task of servile toyl,   5
Daily in the common Prison else enjoyn'd me,
Where I a Prisoner chain'd, scarce freely draw
The air imprison'd also, close and damp,
Unwholsom draught: but here I feel amends,
The breath of Heav'n fresh-blowing, pure and sweet,   10
With day-spring born; here leave me to respire.
This day a solemn Feast the people hold
To *Dagon*[12] thir Sea-Idol, and forbid
Laborious works, unwillingly this rest
Thir Superstition yields me; hence with leave   15
Retiring from the popular noise, I seek
This unfrequented place to find some ease;
Ease to the body some, none to the mind
From restless thoughts, that like a deadly swarm
Of Hornets arm'd, no sooner found alone,   20
But rush upon me thronging, and present
Times past, what once I was, and what am now.
O wherefore was my birth from Heav'n foretold
Twice by an Angel, who at last in sight
Of both my Parents all in flames ascended   25
From off the Altar, where an Off'ring burn'd,
As in a fiery column charioting
His Godlike presence, and from some great act
Or benefit reveal'd to *Abraham's* race?
Why was my breeding order'd and prescrib'd   30
As of a person separate to God,

[12] See *Nativity Ode,* n. 38.

Design'd for great exploits; if I must dye
Betray'd, Captiv'd, and both my Eyes put out,
Made of my Enemies the scorn and gaze;
To grind in Brazen Fetters under task   35
With this Heav'n-gifted strength? O glorious strength
Put to the labour of a Beast, debas't
Lower then bondslave! Promise was that I
Should *Israel* from *Philistian* yoke deliver;
Ask for this great Deliverer now, and find him   40
Eyeless in *Gaza* at the Mill with slaves,
Himself in bonds under *Philistian* yoke;
Yet stay, let me not rashly call in doubt
Divine Prediction; what if all foretold
Had been fulfill'd but through mine own default,   45
Whom have I to complain of but my self?
Who this high gift of strength committed to me,
In what part lodg'd, how easily bereft me,
Under the Seal of silence could not keep,
But weakly to a woman must reveal it,   50
O'recome with importunity and tears.
O impotence of mind, in body strong!
But what is strength without a double share
Of wisdom? Vast, unwieldy, burdensom,
Proudly secure, yet liable to fall   55
By weakest suttleties, not made to rule,
But to subserve where wisdom bears command.
God, when he gave me strength, to shew withal
How slight the gift was, hung it in my Hair.
But peace, I must not quarrel with the will   60
Of highest dispensation, which herein
Happ'ly had ends above my reach to know:
Suffices that to me strength is my bane,
And proves the sourse of all my miseries;
So many, and so huge, that each apart   65
Would ask[13] a life to wail, but chief of all,
O loss of sight, of thee I most complain!
Blind among enemies, O worse then chains,
Dungeon, or beggery, or decrepit age!
Light the prime work of God to me is extinct,   70
And all her various objects of delight
Annull'd, which might in part my grief have eas'd,
Inferiour to the vilest now become
Of man or worm; the vilest here excel me,

---

[13] require.

They creep, yet see, I dark in light expos'd   75
To daily fraud, contempt, abuse and wrong,
Within doors, or without, still as a fool,
In power of others, never in my own;
Scarce half I seem to live, dead more then half.
O dark, dark, dark, amid the blaze of noon,   80
Irrecoverably dark, total Eclipse
Without all hope of day!
O first created Beam, and thou great Word,
Let there be light, and light was over all;
Why am I thus bereav'd thy prime decree?   85
The Sun to me is dark
And silent as the Moon,
When she deserts the night
Hid in her vacant interlunar[14] cave.
Since light so necessary is to life,   90
And almost life it self, if it be true
That light is in the Soul,
She all in every part; why was the sight
To such a tender ball as th' eye confin'd?
So obvious and so easie to be quench't,   95
And not as feeling through all parts diffus'd,
That she might look at will through every pore?
Then had I not been thus exil'd from light;
As in the land of darkness yet in light,
To live a life half dead, a living death,   100
And buried; but O yet more miserable!
My self, my Sepulcher, a moving Grave,
Buried, yet not exempt
By priviledge of death and burial
From worst of other evils, pains and wrongs,   105
But made hereby obnoxious[15] more
To all the miseries of life,
Life in captivity
Among inhuman foes.
But who are these? for with joint pace I hear   110
The tread of many feet stearing this way;
Perhaps my enemies who come to stare
At my affliction, and perhaps to insult,

[14] the interval between the old and the new moons; during this
period the moon was thought by the ancients to be "vacating" the
night in a cave. The etymologies of "cave" and "vacant" emphasize the "emptiness" of darkness.
[15] susceptible (to something harmful).

Thir daily practice to afflict me more.
 Chorus. This, this is he; softly a while,   115
Let us not break in upon him;
O change beyond report, thought, or belief!
See how he lies at random, carelesly diffus'd,[16]
With languish't head unprop,
As one past hope, abandon'd,   120
And by himself giv'n over;
In slavish habit, ill-fitted weeds
O're worn and soild;
Or do my eyes misrepresent? Can this be hee,
That Heroic, that Renown'd,   125
Irresistible[17] *Samson?* whom unarm'd
No strength of man, or fiercest wild beast could withstand;
Who tore the Lion, as the Lion tears the Kid,[18]
Ran on embattell'd Armies clad in Iron,
And weaponless himself,   130
Made Arms ridiculous, useless the forgery
Of brazen shield and spear, the hammer'd Cuirass,
Chalybean[19] temper'd steel, and frock of mail
Adamantean Proof;
But safest he who stood aloof,   135
When insupportably[20] his foot advanc't,
In scorn of thir proud arms and warlike tools,
Spurn'd them to death by Troops. The bold *Ascalonite*[21]
Fled from his Lion ramp,[22] old Warriors turn'd
Thir plated backs under his heel;   140
Or grovling soild thir crested helmets in the dust.
Then with what trivial weapon came to hand,
The Jaw of a dead Ass, his sword of bone,
A thousand fore-skins[23] fell, the flower of *Palestin*

[16] spread in all directions.
[17] too powerful to be resisted.
[18] Judges xiv. 5–6: "a young lion roared against him . . . and he rent him as he would have rent a kid, and he had nothing in his hand."
[19] referring to natives of Pontus, on the Black Sea, known for their iron work.
[20] too powerful to be resisted.
[21] Ascalon was a Philistine coastal city; Judges xiv. 19.
[22] rage.
[23] uncircumcised Philistines; Judges xv. 15–17. The following exploit is found in Judges xvi. 3; Azza is a variant of Gaza. The giants are the children of Anak who were expelled from Hebron by Caleb (Judges i. 20).

In *Ramath-lechi* famous to this day: 145
Then by main force pull'd up, and on his shoulders bore
The Gates of *Azza*, Post, and massie Bar
Up to the Hill of *Hebron*, seat of Giants old,
No journey of a Sabbath day, and loaded so;
Like whom the Gentiles feign to bear up Heav'n.[24]   150
Which shall I first bewail,
Thy Bondage or lost Sight,
Prison within Prison
Inseparably dark?
Thou art become (O worst imprisonment!)   155
The Dungeon of thy self; thy Soul
(Which Men enjoying sight oft without cause complain)
Imprison'd now indeed,
In real darkness of the body dwells,
Shut up from outward light   160
T' incorporate with gloomy night;
For inward light alas
Puts forth no visual beam.
O mirror of our fickle state,[25]
Since man on earth unparallel'd!   165
The rarer thy example stands,
By how much from the top of wondrous glory,
Strongest of mortal men,
To lowest pitch of abject fortune thou art fall'n.
For him I reckon not in high estate   170
Whom long descent of birth
Or the sphear of fortune raises;
But thee whose strength, while vertue was her mate,
Might have subdu'd the Earth,
Universally crown'd with highest praises.   175
    Samson. I hear the sound of words, thir sense the air
Dissolves unjointed e're it reach my ear.
    Chorus. Hee speaks, let us draw nigh. Matchless in might,
The glory late of *Israel*, now the grief;
We come thy friends and neighbours not unknown   180
From *Eshtaol* and *Zora's* fruitful Vale[26]
To visit or bewail thee, or if better,
Counsel or Consolation we may bring,

[24] Atlas.
[25] example of decline through chance (i.e., the spin of Fortune's wheel, l. 172).
[26] cities from which Manoah came in the coastal valley of Sorec (l. 229).

Salve to thy Sores; apt words have power to swage
The tumors[27] of a troubl'd mind, 185
And are as Balm to fester'd wounds.
    Samson. Your coming, Friends, revives me, for I learn
Now of my own experience, not by talk,
How counterfeit a coin they are who friends
Bear in their Superscription[28] (of the most 190
I would be understood): in prosperous days
They swarm, but in adverse withdraw their head
Not to be found, though sought. Yee see, O friends,
How many evils have enclos'd me round;
Yet that which was the worst now least afflicts me, 195
Blindness, for had I sight, confus'd with shame,
How could I once look up, or heave the head,
Who like a foolish Pilot have shipwrack't
My Vessel trusted to me from above,
Gloriously rigg'd; and for a word, a tear, 200
Fool, have divulg'd the secret gift of God
To a deceitful Woman: tell me Friends,
Am I not sung and proverb'd for a Fool
In every street, do they not say, how well
Are come upon him his deserts? yet why? 205
Immeasurable strength they might behold
In me, of wisdom nothing more then mean;
This with the other should, at least, have paird,
These two proportiond ill drove me transverse.[29]
    Chorus. Tax not divine disposal, wisest Men 210
Have err'd, and by bad Women been deceiv'd;
And shall again, pretend they ne're so wise.
Deject not then so overmuch thy self,
Who hast of sorrow thy full load besides;
Yet truth to say, I oft have heard men wonder 215
Why thou shouldst wed *Philistian* women rather
Then of thine own Tribe fairer, or as fair,
At least of thy own Nation, and as noble.
    Samson. The first I saw at *Timna*,[30] and she pleas'd
Mee, not my Parents, that I sought to wed, 220
The daughter of an Infidel: they knew not

[27] meaning "swellings," the word connotes the exaggeration or preoccupation arising from psychological disorder.

[28] an inscription on a coin.

[29] to thwart my intended use to God.

[30] See Judges xiv. 1–4; his marriage to Dalila is told in Judges xiv. 16–17.

That what I motion'd was of God; I knew
From intimate impulse, and therefore urg'd
The Marriage on; that by occasion hence
I might begin *Israel's* Deliverance,   225
The work to which I was divinely call'd;
She proving false, the next I took to Wife
(O that I never had! fond wish too late)
Was in the Vale of *Sorec, Dalila,*
That specious Monster, my accomplisht snare.   230
I thought it lawful from my former act,
And the same end; still watching to oppress
Israel's oppressours: of what now I suffer
She was not the prime cause, but I my self,
Who vanquisht with a peal[31] of words (O weakness!)   235
Gave up my fort of silence to a Woman.
    Chorus. In seeking just occasion to provoke
The *Philistine,* thy Countries Enemy,
Thou never wast remiss, I bear thee witness:
Yet *Israel* still serves with all his Sons.[32]   240
    Samson. That fault I take not on me, but transfer
On *Israel's* Governours, and Heads of Tribes,
Who seeing those great acts which God had done
Singly by me against their Conquerours
Acknowledg'd not, or not at all consider'd   245
Deliverance offerd: I on th' other side
Us'd no ambition to commend my deeds,[33]
The deeds themselves, though mute, spoke loud the dooer;
But they persisted deaf, and would not seem
To count them things worth notice, till at length   250
Thir Lords the *Philistines* with gather'd powers
Enterd *Judea* seeking mee, who then
Safe to the rock of *Etham* was retir'd,
Not flying, but fore-casting in what place
To set upon them, what advantag'd best;   255
Mean while the men of *Judah* to prevent
The harrass of thir Land, beset me round;
I willingly on some conditions came
Into thir hands, and they as gladly yield me
To the uncircumcis'd a welcom prey,   260
Bound with two cords; but cords to me were threds

[31] a volley (as of gunfire).
[32] The Israelites are still subjugated by the Philistines.
[33] I did not **walk about** soliciting commendation **for my deeds.**

Toucht with the flame: on thir whole Host I flew
Unarm'd, and with a trivial weapon fell'd
Their choicest youth; they only liv'd who fled.
Had *Judah* that day join'd, or one whole Tribe,   265
They had by this possess'd the Towers of *Gath*,[34]
And lorded over them whom now they serve;
But what more oft in Nations grown corrupt,
And by thir vices brought to servitude,
Then to love Bondage more then Liberty,   270
Bondage with ease then strenuous liberty;
And to despise, or envy, or suspect
Whom God hath of his special favour rais'd
As thir Deliverer; if he aught begin,
How frequent to desert him, and at last   275
To heap ingratitude on worthiest deeds?
   Chorus. Thy words to my remembrance bring
How *Succoth* and the Fort of *Penuel*
This great Deliverer contemn'd,
The matchless *Gideon* in pursuit   280
Of *Madian* and her vanquisht Kings:[35]
And how ingrateful *Ephraim*
Had dealt with *Jephtha*, who by argument,
Not worse then by his shield and spear
Defended *Israel* from the *Ammonite*,   285
Had not his prowess quell'd thir pride
In that sore battel when so many dy'd
Without Reprieve adjudg'd to death,
For want of well pronouncing *Shibboleth*.[36]
   Samson. Of such examples add mee to the roul,   290
Mee easily indeed mine[37] may neglect,
But Gods propos'd deliverance not so.
   Chorus. Just are the ways of God,
And justifiable to Men;
Unless there be who think not God at all,   295
If any be, they walk obscure;
For of such Doctrine never was there School,

---

[34] a principal city of Philistia.

[35] The cities of Succoth and Penuel refused to help the Hebrew general Gideon when he was pursuing the kings of Midian (Judges vii. 4–9).

[36] Judges xi. 12–23, xii. 1–6. The Ephraimites were detected and slain by Jephthah's Gileadites when they could not pronounce the first syllable of "Shibboleth" correctly.

[37] my nation.

But the heart of the Fool,[38]
And no man therein Doctor but himself.
   Yet more there be who doubt his ways not just,   300
As to his own edicts, found contradicting,
Then give the rains to wandring thought,
Regardless of his glories diminution;
Till by thir own perplexities involv'd
They ravel more, still less resolv'd,   305
But never find self-satisfying solution.
   As if they would confine th' interminable,
And tie him to his own prescript,
Who made our Laws to bind us, not himself,
And hath full right t' exempt   310
Whom so it pleases him by choice
From National obstriction,[39] without taint
Of sin, or legal debt;
For with his own Laws he can best dispence.
   He would not else who never wanted means,   315
Nor in respect of th' enemy just cause
To set his people free,
Have prompted this Heroic *Nazarite,*
Against his vow of strictest purity,
To seek in marriage that fallacious[40] Bride,   320
Unclean, unchaste.
   Down[41] Reason then, at least vain reasonings down,
Though Reason here aver
That moral verdit quits her of unclean:
Unchaste was subsequent, her stain not his.   325
   But see here comes thy reverend Sire
With careful[42] step, Locks white as doune,
Old *Manoah:* advise[43]
Forthwith how thou oughtst to receive him.
   Samson. Ay me, another inward grief awak't,   380
With mention of that name renews th' assault.
   Manoa. Brethren and men of *Dan,* for such ye seem,
Though in this uncouth[44] place; if old respect,

[38] Psalms xiv. 1: "The fool hath said in his heart, There is no God."
[39] the obligation of the Israelites not to marry outside their nation.
[40] deceitful.
[41] subordinate (to faith and revelation).
[42] full of concern.
[43] consider.
[44] strange.

As I suppose, towards your once gloried friend,
My Son now Captive, hither hath inform'd[45] 335
Your younger feet, while mine cast back with age
Came lagging after; say if he be here.
  Chorus. As signal now in low dejected state,
As earst in highest, behold him where he lies.
  Manoa. O miserable change! is this the man, 340
That invincible *Samson*, far renown'd,
The dread of *Israel's* foes, who with a strength
Equivalent to Angels walk'd thir streets,
None offering fight; who single combatant
Duell'd thir Armies rank't in proud array, 345
Himself an Army, now unequal match
To save himself against a coward arm'd
At one spears length. O ever failing trust
In mortal strength! and oh what not in man
Deceivable and vain! Nay what thing good 350
Pray'd for, but often proves our woe, our bane?
I pray'd for Children, and thought barrenness
In wedlock a reproach; I gain'd a Son,
And such a Son as all Men hail'd me happy;
Who would be now a Father in my stead? 355
O wherefore did God grant me my request,
And as a blessing with such pomp adorn'd?
Why are his gifts desirable, to tempt
Our earnest Prayers, then giv'n with solemn hand
As Graces, draw a Scorpions tail behind? 360
For this did th' Angel twice descend? for this
Ordain'd thy nurture holy, as of a Plant;
Select, and Sacred, Glorious for a while,
The miracle of men: then in an hour
Ensnar'd, assaulted, overcome, led bound, 365
Thy Foes derision, Captive, Poor, and Blind
Into a Dungeon thrust, to work with Slaves?
Alas methinks whom God hath chosen once
To worthiest deeds, if he through frailty err,
He should not so o'rewhelm, and as a thrall 370
Subject him to so foul indignities,
Be it but for honours sake of former deeds.
  Samson. Appoint[46] not heav'nly disposition, Father,
Nothing of all these evils hath befall'n me
But justly; I my self have brought them on, 375

[45] directed.
[46] arraign.

Sole Author I, sole cause: if aught seem vile,
As vile hath been my folly, who have profan'd[47]
The mystery of God giv'n me under pledge
Of vow, and have betray'd it to a woman,
A *Canaanite,* my faithless enemy. 380
This well I knew, nor was at all surpris'd,
But warn'd by oft experience: did not she
Of *Timna* first betray me, and reveal
The secret[48] wrested from me in her highth
Of Nuptial Love profest, carrying it strait 385
To them who had corrupted her, my Spies,
And Rivals? In this other was there found
More Faith? who also in her prime of love,
Spousal embraces, vitiated with Gold,
Though offer'd only, by the scent conceiv'd 390
Her spurious first-born; Treason against me?
Thrice she assay'd with flattering prayers and sighs,
And amorous reproaches to win from me
My capital[49] secret, in what part my strength
Lay stor'd, in what part summ'd, that she might know: 395
Thrice I deluded her, and turn'd to sport
Her importunity, each time perceiving
How openly, and with what impudence
She purpos'd to betray me, and (which was worse
Then undissembl'd hate) with what contempt 400
She sought to make me Traytor to my self;
Yet the fourth time, when mustring all her wiles,
With blandisht parlies, feminine assaults,
Tongue-batteries, she surceas'd not day nor night
To storm me over-watch't,[50] and wearied out. 405
At times when men seek most repose and rest,
I yielded, and unlock'd her all my heart,
Who with a grain of manhood well resolv'd
Might easily have shook off all her snares:
But foul effeminacy held me yok't 410
Her Bond-slave; O indignity, O blot
To Honour and Religion! servil mind
Rewarded well with servil punishment!
The base degree to which I now am fall'n,
These rags, this grinding, is not yet so base 415

[47] impiously revealed.
[48] the answer to Samson's riddle (Judges xiv. 12–18).
[49] "major," "fatal," and connected with the head.
[50] tired from being vigilant.

As was my former servitude, ignoble,
Unmanly, ignominious, infamous,
True slavery, and that blindness worse then this,
That saw not how degeneratly I serv'd.
    Manoa. I cannot praise thy Marriage choises, Son,   420
Rather approv'd them not; but thou didst plead
Divine impulsion prompting how thou might'st
Find some occasion to infest our Foes.
I state not that; this I am sure; our Foes
Found soon occasion thereby to make thee   425
Thir Captive, and thir triumph; thou the sooner
Temptation found'st, or over-potent charms
To violate the sacred trust of silence
Deposited within thee; which t' have kept
Tacit, was in thy power; true; and thou bear'st   430
Enough, and more the burden of that fault;
Bitterly hast thou paid, and still art paying
That rigid score. A worse thing yet remains,
This day the *Philistines* a popular Feast
Here celebrate in *Gaza;* and proclaim   435
Great Pomp, and Sacrifice, and Praises loud
To *Dagon,* as their God who hath deliver'd
Thee *Samson,* bound and blind into thir hands,
Them out of thine, who slew'st them many a slain.
So *Dagon* shall be magnifi'd, and God,   440
Besides whom is no God, compar'd with Idols,
Disglorifi'd, blasphem'd, and had in scorn
By th' Idolatrous rout amidst thir wine;
Which to have come to pass by means of thee,
Samson, of all thy sufferings think the heaviest,   445
Of all reproach the most with shame that ever
Could have befall'n thee and thy Fathers house.
    Samson. Father, I do acknowledge and confess
That I this honour, I this pomp have brought
To *Dagon,* and advanc'd his praises high   450
Among the Heathen round; to God have brought
Dishonour, obloquie, and op't the mouths
Of Idolists, and Atheists; have brought scandal
To *Israel,* diffidence[51] of God, and doubt
In feeble hearts, propense anough before   455
To waver, or fall off and joyn with Idols;
Which is my chief affliction, shame and sorrow,
The anguish of my Soul, that suffers not

[51] distrust.

Mine eie to harbour sleep, or thoughts to rest.
This only hope relieves me, that the strife   460
With me hath end; all the contest is now
'Twixt God and *Dagon; Dagon* hath presum'd,
Me overthrown, to enter lists with God,
His Deity comparing and preferring
Before the God of *Abraham*. He, be sure,   465
Will not connive,[52] or linger, thus provok'd,
But will arise and his great name assert:
Dagon must stoop, and shall e're long receive
Such a discomfit, as shall quite despoil him
Of all these boasted Trophies won on me,   470
And with confusion blank his Worshippers.
   Manoa. With cause this hope relieves thee, and these words
I as a Prophecy receive: for God,
Nothing more certain, will not long defer
To vindicate the glory of his name   475
Against all competition, nor will long
Endure it, doubtful whether God be Lord,
Or *Dagon*. But for thee what shall be done?
Thou must not in the mean while here forgot
Lie in this miserable loathsom plight   480
Neglected. I already have made way
To some *Philistian* Lords, with whom to treat
About thy ransom: well they may by this
Have satisfi'd thir utmost of revenge
By pains and slaveries, worse then death inflicted   485
On thee, who now no more canst do them harm.
   Samson. Spare that proposal, Father, spare the trouble
Of that sollicitation; let me here,
As I deserve, pay on my punishment;
And expiate, if possible, my crime,   490
Shameful garrulity. To have reveal'd
Secrets of men, the secrets of a friend,
How hainous had the fact been, how deserving
Contempt, and scorn of all, to be excluded
All friendship, and avoided as a blab,   495
The mark of fool set on his front![53]
But I Gods counsel have not kept, his holy secret
Presumptuously have publish'd, impiously,
Weakly at least, and shamefully: A sin
That Gentiles in thir Parables condemn   500

[52] shut his eyes.
[53] forehead.

To thir abyss and horrid pains confin'd.[54]
   Manoa. Be penitent and for thy fault contrite,
But act not in thy own affliction, Son;
Repent the sin, but if the punishment
Thou canst avoid, self-preservation bids;   505
Or th' execution leave to high disposal,
And let another hand, not thine, exact
Thy penal forfeit from thy self; perhaps
God will relent, and quit thee all his debt;
Who evermore approves and more accepts   510
(Best pleas'd with humble and filial submission)
Him who imploring mercy sues for life,
Then who self-rigorous chooses death as due;
Which argues over-just, and self-displeas'd
For self-offence, more then for God offended.   515
Reject not then what offerd means, who knows
But God hath set before us, to return thee
Home to thy countrey and his sacred house,
Where thou mayst bring thy off'rings, to avert
His further ire, with praiers and vows renew'd.   520
   Samson. His pardon I implore; but as for life,
To what end should I seek it? when in strength
All mortals I excell'd, and great in hopes
With youthful courage and magnanimous[55] thoughts
Of birth from Heav'n foretold and high exploits,   525
Full of divine instinct, after some proof
Of acts indeed heroic, far beyond
The Sons of *Anac*, famous now and blaz'd,
Fearless of danger, like a petty God
I walk'd about admir'd of all and dreaded   530
On hostile ground, none daring my affront.
Then swoll'n with pride into the snare I fell
Of fair fallacious looks, venereal trains,[56]
Soft'n'd with pleasure and voluptuous life;
At length to lay my head and hallow'd pledge   535
Of all my strength in the lascivious lap
Of a deceitful Concubine who shore me
Like a tame Weather, all my precious fleece,
Then turn'd me out ridiculous, despoil'd,
Shav'n, and disarm'd among my enemies.   540

[54] referring to Tantalus who had divulged the secrets of the gods.
[55] heroic for God's greater glory.
[56] tricks of love (from Venus).

Chorus. Desire of wine and all delicious drinks,
Which many a famous Warriour overturns,
Thou couldst repress, nor did the dancing Rubie
Sparkling, out-pow'rd, the flavor, or the smell,
Or taste that cheers the heart of Gods and men,   545
Allure thee from the cool Crystalline stream.
    Samson. Where ever fountain or fresh current flow'd
Against the Eastern ray, translucent, pure,
With touch ætherial of Heav'ns fiery rod
I drank, from the clear milkie juice[57] allaying   550
Thirst, and refresht; nor envy'd them the grape
Whose heads that turbulent liquor fills with fumes.
    Chorus. O madness, to think use of strongest wines
And strongest drinks our chief support of health,
When God with these forbid'n made choice to rear   555
His mighty Champion, strong above compare,
Whose drink was only from the liquid brook.
    Samson. But what avail'd this temperance, not compleat
Against another object more enticing?
What boots it at one gate to make defence,   560
And at another to let in the foe
Effeminatly vanquish't? by which means,
Now blind, disheart'n'd, sham'd, dishonour'd, quell'd,
To what can I be useful, wherein serve
My Nation, and the work from Heav'n impos'd,   565
But to sit idle on the houshold hearth,
A burdenous drone; to visitants a gaze,
Or pitied object, these redundant locks
Robustious to no purpose clustring down,
Vain monument of strength; till length of years   570
And sedentary numness craze[58] my limbs
To a contemptible old age obscure.
Here rather let me drudge and earn my bread,
Till vermin or the draff[59] of servil food
Consume me, and oft-invocated death   575
Hast'n the welcom end of all my pains.
    Manoa. Wilt thou then serve the *Philistines* with that gift
Which was expresly giv'n thee to annoy them?
Better at home lie bed-rid, not only idle,
Inglorious, unimploy'd, with age out-worn.   580
But God who caus'd a fountain at thy prayer

[57] fresh water.
[58] weaken.
[59] refuse or offal.

From the dry ground to spring,[60] thy thirst t' allay
After the brunt of battel, can as easie
Cause light again within thy eies to spring,
Wherewith to serve him better then thou hast;   585
And I perswade me so; why else his strength
Miraculous yet remaining in those locks?
His might continues in thee not for naught,
Nor shall his wondrous gifts be frustrate thus.
   Samson. All otherwise to me my thoughts portend,   590
That these dark orbs no more shall treat with light,
Nor th' other light of life continue long,
But yield to double darkness nigh at hand:
So much I feel my genial[61] spirits droop,
My hopes all flat, nature within me seems   595
In all her functions weary of her self;
My race of glory run, and race of shame,
And I shall shortly be with them that rest.
   Manoa. Believe not these suggestions which proceed
From anguish of the mind and humours black,   600
That mingle with thy fancy. I however
Must not omit a Fathers timely care
To prosecute the means of thy deliverance
By ransom or how else: mean while be calm,
And healing words from these thy friends admit.   605
   Samson. O that torment should not be confin'd
To the bodies wounds and sores
With maladies innumerable
In heart, head, brest, and reins;
But must secret passage find   610
To th' inmost mind,
There exercise all his fierce accidents,[62]
And on her purest spirits prey,
As on entrails, joints, and limbs,
With answerable pains, but more intense,   615
Though void of corporal sense.
   My griefs not only pain me
As a lingring disease,
But finding no redress, ferment and rage,
Nor less then wounds immedicable   620
Ranckle, and fester, and gangrene,
To black mortification.

---

[60] at Ramath-lechi (Judges xv. 18–19).
[61] natural.
[62] symptoms.

Thoughts my Tormentors arm'd with deadly stings
Mangle my apprehensive tenderest parts,[63]
Exasperate, exulcerate, and raise   625
Dire inflammation which no cooling herb
Or medcinal liquor can asswage,
Nor breath of Vernal Air from snowy *Alp.*
Sleep hath forsook and giv'n me o're
To deaths benumming Opium as my only cure.   630
Thence faintings, swounings of despair,
And sense of Heav'ns desertion.
    I was his nursling once and choice delight,
His destin'd from the womb,
Promisd by Heav'nly message twice descending.   635
Under his special eie
Abstemious I grew up and thriv'd amain;
He led me on to mightiest deeds
Above the nerve of mortal arm
Against th' uncircumcis'd, our enemies.   640
But now hath cast me off as never known,
And to those cruel enemies,
Whom I by his appointment had provok't,
Left me all helpless with th' irreparable loss
Of sight, reserv'd alive to be repeated   645
The subject of thir cruelty, or scorn.
Nor am I in the list of them that hope;
Hopeless are all my evils, all remediless;
This one prayer yet remains, might I be heard,
No long petition, speedy death,   650
The close of all my miseries, and the balm.
    Chorus. Many are the sayings of the wise
In antient and in modern books enroll'd;
Extolling Patience as the truest fortitude;
And to the bearing well of all calamities,   655
All chances incident to mans frail life
Consolatories writ
With studied argument, and much perswasion sought
Lenient of grief and anxious thought,
But with th' afflicted in his pangs thir sound   660
Little prevails, or rather seems a tune,
Harsh, and of dissonant mood from his complaint,
Unless he feel within
Some sourse of consolation from above;

[63] the mind and the senses.

Secret refreshings, that repair his strength,   665
And fainting spirits uphold.
   God of our Fathers, what is man!
That thou towards him with hand so various,
Or might I say contrarious,
Temperst thy providence through his short course,   670
Not ev'nly, as thou rul'st
Th' Angelic orders and inferiour creatures mute,
Irrational and brute.
Nor do I name of men the common rout,
That wandring loose about   675
Grow up and perish, as the summer flie,
Heads without name no more rememberd,
But such as thou hast solemnly elected,
With gifts and graces eminently adorn'd
To some great work, thy glory,   680
And peoples safety, which in part they effect:
Yet toward these thus dignifi'd, thou oft
Amidst thir highth of noon,
Changest thy countenance, and thy hand with no regard
Of highest favours past   685
From thee on them, or them to thee of service.
   Nor only dost degrade them, or remit
To life obscur'd, which were a fair dismission,
But throw'st them lower then thou didst exalt them high,
Unseemly falls in human eie,   690
Too grievous for the trespass or omission,
Oft leav'st them to the hostile sword
Of Heathen and prophane, thir carkasses
To dogs and fowls a prey, or else captiv'd:
Or to th' unjust tribunals, under change of times,   695
And condemnation of th' ingrateful multitude.
If these they scape, perhaps in poverty
With sickness and disease thou bow'st them down,
Painful diseases and deform'd,
In crude[64] old age;   700
Though not disordinate, yet causless suffring
The punishment of dissolute days, in fine,
Just or unjust, alike seem miserable,
For oft alike, both come to evil end.
   So deal not with this once thy glorious Champion, 705
The Image of thy strength, and mighty minister.
What do I beg? how hast thou dealt already?

[64] premature.

Behold him in this state calamitous, and turn
His labours, for thou canst, to peaceful end.
    But who is this, what thing of Sea or Land?   710
Femal of sex it seems,
That so bedeckt, ornate, and gay,
Comes this way sailing
Like a stately Ship
Of *Tarsus,* bound for th' Isles   715
Of *Javan* or *Gadier*[65]
With all her bravery on, and tackle trim,
Sails fill'd, and streamers waving,
Courted by all the winds that hold them play,
An Amber[66] scent of odorous perfume   720
Her harbinger, a damsel train behind;
Some rich *Philistian* Matron she may seem,
And now at nearer view, no other certain
Then *Dalila* thy wife.
    Samson. My Wife, my Traytress, let her not come
        near me.   725
    Chorus. Yet on she moves, now stands and eies thee fixt,
About t' have spoke, but now, with head declin'd
Like a fair flower surcharg'd with dew, she weeps
And words addrest seem into tears dissolv'd,
Wetting the borders of her silk'n veil: 730
But now again she makes address to speak.
    Dalila. With doubtful feet and wavering resolution
I came, still dreading thy displeasure, *Samson,*
Which to have merited, without excuse,
I cannot but acknowledge; yet if tears   735
May expiate (though the fact more evil drew
In the perverse event then I foresaw)
My penance hath not slack'n'd, though my pardon
No way assur'd. But conjugal affection
Prevailing over fear, and timerous doubt   740
Hath led me on desirous to behold
Once more thy face, and know of thy estate,
If aught in my ability may serve
To light'n what thou suffer'st, and appease
Thy mind with what amends is in my power,   745

[65] Tarsus (now an area of Turkey) is here identified with the
proud Biblical Tarshish; the isles of Noah's grandson are the isles
of Greece, and Gadier is Cadiz. The ship was frequently used as a
symbol of prostitution.
[66] ambergris.

Though late, yet in some part to recompense
My rash but more unfortunate misdeed.
   Samson. Out, out *Hyæna;* these are thy wonted arts,
And arts of every woman false like thee,
To break all faith, all vows, deceive, betray,   750
Then as repentant to submit, beseech,
And reconcilement move[67] with feign'd remorse,
Confess, and promise wonders in her change,
Not truly penitent, but chief to try
Her husband, how far urg'd his patience bears,   755
His vertue or weakness which way t' assail:
Then with more cautious and instructed skill
Again transgresses, and again submits;
That wisest and best men full oft beguil'd
With goodness principl'd not to reject   760
The penitent, but ever to forgive,
Are drawn to wear out miserable days,
Entangl'd with a poysnous bosom snake,
If not by quick destruction soon cut off
As I by thee, to Ages an example.   765
   Dalila. Yet hear me *Samson;* not that I endeavour
To lessen or extenuate my offence,
But that on th' other side if it be weigh'd
By it self, with aggravations not surcharg'd,
Or else with just allowance counterpois'd,   770
I may, if possible, thy pardon find
The easier towards me, or thy hatred less.
First granting, as I do, it was a weakness
In me, but incident to all our sex,
Curiosity, inquisitive, importune   775
Of secrets, then with like infirmity
To publish them, both common female faults:
Was it not weakness also to make known
For importunity, that is for naught,
Wherein consisted all thy strength and safety?   780
To what I did thou shewdst me first the way.
But I to enemies reveal'd, and should not.
Nor shouldst thou have trusted that to womans frailty:
E're I to thee, thou to thy self wast cruel.
Let weakness then with weakness come to parl   785
So near related, or the same of kind,
Thine forgive mine; that men may censure thine
The gentler, if severely thou exact not

[67] propose.

More strength from me, then in thy self was found.
And what if Love, which thou interpret'st hate,   790
The jealousie of Love, powerful of sway
In human hearts, nor less in mine towards thee,
Caus'd what I did? I saw thee mutable
Of fancy, feard lest one day thou wouldst leave me
As her at *Timna*, sought by all means therefore   795
How to endear, and hold thee to me firmest:
No better way I saw then by importuning
To learn thy secrets, get into my power
Thy key of strength and safety: thou wilt say,
Why then reveal'd? I was assur'd by those   800
Who tempted me, that nothing was design'd
Against thee but safe custody, and hold:
That made for me, I knew that liberty
Would draw thee forth to perilous enterprises,
While I at home sate full of cares and fears   805
Wailing thy absence in my widow'd bed;
Here I should still enjoy thee day and night
Mine and Loves prisoner, not the *Philistines*,
Whole to my self, unhazarded abroad,
Fearless at home of partners in my love.   810
These reasons in Loves law have past for good,
Though fond and reasonless to some perhaps;
And Love hath oft, well meaning, wrought much wo,
Yet always pity or pardon hath obtain'd.
Be not unlike all others, not austere   815
As thou art strong, inflexible as steel.
If thou in strength all mortals dost exceed,
In uncompassionate anger do not so.
    Samson. How cunningly the sorceress displays
Her own transgressions, to upbraid me mine!   820
That malice not repentance brought thee hither,
By this appears: I gave, thou say'st, th' example,
I led the way; bitter reproach, but true,
I to my self was false e're thou to me;
Such pardon therefore as I give my folly,   825
Take to thy wicked deed: which when thou seest
Impartial, self-severe, inexorable,
Thou wilt renounce thy seeking, and much rather
Confess it feign'd, weakness is thy excuse,
And I believe it. Weakness to resist   830
Philistian gold: if weakness may excuse,
What Murtherer, what Traytor, Parricide,

Incestuous, Sacrilegious, but may plead it?
All wickedness is weakness: that plea therefore
With God or Man will gain thee no remission.   835
But Love constrain'd thee; call it furious rage
To satisfie thy lust: Love seeks to have Love;
My love how couldst thou hope, who tookst the way
To raise in me inexpiable hate,
Knowing, as needs I must, by thee betray'd?   840
In vain thou striv'st to cover shame with shame,
Or by evasions thy crime uncoverst more.
    Dalila. Since thou determinst weakness for no plea
In man or woman, though to thy own condemning,
Hear what assaults I had, what snares besides,   845
What sieges girt me round, e're I consented;
Which might have aw'd the best resolv'd of men,
The constantest t' have yielded without blame.
It was not gold, as to my charge thou lay'st,
That wrought with me: thou know'st the Magistrates   850
And Princes of my countrey came in person,
Sollicited, commanded, threat'n'd, urg'd,
Adjur'd by all the bonds of civil Duty
And of Religion, press'd how just it was,
How honourable, how glorious to entrap   855
A common enemy, who had destroy'd
Such numbers of our Nation: and the Priest
Was not behind, but ever at my ear,
Preaching how meritorious with the gods
It would be to ensnare an irreligious   860
Dishonourer of *Dagon:* what had I
T' oppose against such powerful arguments?
Only my love of thee held long debate;
And combated in silence all these reasons
With hard contest: at length that grounded maxim   865
So rife and celebrated in the mouths
Of wisest men; that to the public good
Private respects must yield; with grave authority
Took full possession of me and prevail'd;
Vertue, as I thought, truth, duty so enjoyning.   870
    Samson. I thought where all thy circling wiles would end;
In feign'd Religion, smooth hypocrisie.
But had thy love, still odiously pretended,
Bin, as it ought, sincere, it would have taught thee
Far other reasonings, brought forth other deeds.   875
I before all the daughters of my Tribe

And of my Nation chose thee from among
My enemies, lov'd thee, as too well thou knew'st,
Too well, unbosom'd all my secrets to thee,
Not only of levity, but over-power'd   880
By thy request, who could deny thee nothing;
Yet now am judg'd an enemy. Why then
Didst thou at first receive me for thy husband?
Then, as since then, thy countries foe profest:
Being once a wife, for me thou wast to leave   885
Parents and countrey; nor was I their subject,
Nor under their protection but my own,
Thou mine, not theirs: if aught against my life
Thy countrey sought of thee, it sought unjustly,
Against the law of nature, law of nations,   890
No more thy countrey, but an impious crew
Of men conspiring to uphold thir state
By worse then hostile deeds, violating th' ends
For which our countrey is a name so dear;
Not therefore to be obey'd. But zeal mov'd thee;   895
To please thy gods thou didst it; gods unable
To acquit themselves and prosecute their foes
But by ungodly deeds, the contradiction
Of their own deity, Gods cannot be:
Less therefore to be pleas'd, obey'd, or fear'd;   900
These false pretexts and varnish'd colours failing,
Bare in thy guilt how foul must thou appear!
   Dalila. In argument with men a woman ever
Goes by the worse, whatever be her cause.
   Samson. For want of words no doubt, or lack of
      breath,   905
Witness when I was worried with thy peals.[68]
   Dalila. I was a fool, too rash, and quite mistaken
In what I thought would have succeeded best.
Let me obtain forgiveness of thee, *Samson,*
Afford me place to shew what recompence   910
Towards thee I intend for what I have misdone,
Misguided; only what remains past cure
Bear not too sensibly,[69] nor still insist
T' afflict thy self in vain: though sight be lost,
Life yet hath many solaces, enjoy'd   915
Where other senses want[70] not their delights

[68] volleys of words (as of gunfire).
[69] passionately.
[70] lack.

At home in leisure and domestic ease,
Exempt from many a care and chance to which
Eye-sight exposes daily men abroad.
I to the Lords will intercede, not doubting   920
Thir favourable ear, that I may fetch thee
From forth this loathsom prison-house, t' abide
With me, where my redoubl'd love and care
With nursing diligence, to me glad office,
May ever tend about thee to old age   925
With all things grateful chear'd, and so suppli'd,
That what by me thou hast lost thou least shalt miss.
    Samson. No, no, of my condition take no care;
It fits not; thou and I long since are twain;
Nor think me so unwary or accurst   930
To bring my feet again into the snare
Where once I have been caught; I know thy trains
Though dearly to my cost, thy ginns, and toyls;[71]
Thy fair enchanted cup, and warbling charms
No more on me have power, their force is null'd,   935
So much of Adders wisdom I have learn't[72]
To fence my ear against thy sorceries.
If in my flower of youth and strength, when all men
Lov'd, honour'd, fear'd me, thou alone could hate me
Thy Husband, slight me, sell me, and forgo me;   940
How wouldst thou use me now, blind, and thereby
Deceiveable, in most things as a child
Helpless, thence easily contemn'd, scorn'd,
And last neglected? How wouldst thou insult
When I must live uxorious to thy will   945
In perfet thraldom, how again betray me,
Bearing my words and doings to the Lords
To gloss upon, and censuring, frown or smile?
This Gaol I count the house of Liberty
To thine whose doors my feet shall never enter.   950
    Dalila. Let me approach at least, and touch thy hand.
    Samson. Not for thy life, lest fierce remembrance wake
My sudden rage to tear thee joint by joint.
At distance I forgive thee, go with that;
Bewail thy falshood, and the pious works   955
It hath brought forth to make thee memorable
Among illustrious women, faithful wives:
Cherish thy hast'n'd widowhood with the gold

[71] snares, and nets to trap game.
[72] Adders were proverbially deaf.

Of Matrimonial treason: so farewel.

    Dalila. I see thou art implacable, more deaf   960
To prayers, then winds and seas, yet winds to seas
Are reconcil'd at length, and Sea to Shore:
Thy anger, unappeasable, still rages,
Eternal tempest never to be calm'd.
Why do I humble thus my self, and suing   965
For peace, reap nothing but repulse and hate?
Bid go with evil omen and the brand
Of infamy upon my name denounc't?
To mix with thy concernments I desist
Henceforth, nor too much disapprove my own.   970
Fame if not double-fac't is double-mouth'd,
And with contrary blast proclaims most deeds,
On both his wings, one black, the other white,
Bears greatest names in his wild aerie flight.
My name perhaps among the Circumcis'd   975
In *Dan,* in *Judah,* and the bordering Tribes,
To all posterity may stand defam'd,
With malediction mention'd, and the blot
Of falshood most unconjugal traduc't.
But in my countrey where I most desire,   980
In *Ecron, Gaza, Asdod,* and in *Gath*[73]
I shall be nam'd among the famousest
Of Women, sung at solemn festivals,
Living and dead recorded, who to save
Her countrey from a fierce destroyer, chose   985
Above the faith of wedlock-bands, my tomb
With odours[74] visited and annual flowers,
Not less renown'd then in Mount *Ephraim,*
Jael, who with inhospitable guile
Smote *Sisera* sleeping through the Temples nail'd.[75]   990
Nor shall I count it hainous to enjoy
The public marks of honour and reward
Conferr'd upon me, for the piety
Which to my countrey I was judg'd t' have shewn.
At this who ever envies or repines   995
I leave him to his lot, and like my own.

    Chorus. She's gone, a manifest Serpent by her sting
Discover'd in the end, till now conceal'd.

[73] Philistine cities.

[74] spices burnt in ritual offerings.

[75] Jael struck a nail through the temples of the Canaanite leader Sisera (Judges v. 24–27).

Samson. So let her go, God sent her to debase me,
And aggravate my folly who committed   1000
To such a viper his most sacred trust
Of secresie, my safety, and my life.
   Chorus. Yet beauty, though injurious, hath strange power,
After offence returning, to regain
Love once possest, nor can be easily   1005
Repuls't, without much inward passion felt
And secret sting of amorous remorse.
   Samson. Love-quarrels oft in pleasing concord end,
Not wedlock-trechery endangering life.
   Chorus. It is not vertue, wisdom, valour, wit,   1010
Strength, comliness of shape, or amplest merit
That womans love can win or long inherit;[76]
But what it is, hard is to say,
Harder to hit,
(Which way soever men refer it)   1015
Much like thy riddle, *Samson*, in one day
Or seven, though one should musing sit;
   If any of these or all, the *Timnian* bride
Had not so soon preferr'd
Thy Paranymph,[77] worthless to thee compar'd,   1020
Successour in thy bed,
Nor both so loosly disally'd
Thir nuptials, nor this last so trecherously
Had shorn the fatal harvest of thy head.
Is it for that such outward ornament   1025
Was lavish't on thir Sex, that inward gifts
Were left for hast unfinish't, judgment scant,
Capacity not rais'd to apprehend
Or value what is best
In choice, but oftest to affect[78] the wrong?   1030
Or was too much of self-love mixt,
Of constancy no root infixt,
That either they love nothing, or not long?
   What e're it be, to wisest men and best
Seeming at first all heav'nly under virgin veil,   1035
Soft, modest, meek, demure,
Once join'd, the contrary she proves, a thorn
Intestin, far within defensive arms
A cleaving mischief, in his way to vertue

[76] possess.
[77] Best Man, at a wedding.
[78] prefer.

Adverse and turbulent, or by her charms   1040
Draws him awry enslav'd
With dotage, and his sense deprav'd
To folly and shameful deeds which ruin ends.
What Pilot so expert but needs must wreck
Embarqu'd with such a Stears-mate at the Helm?   1045
   Favour'd of Heav'n who finds
One vertuous rarely found,
That in domestic good combines:
Happy that house! his way to peace is smooth:
But vertue which breaks through all opposition,   1050
And all temptation can remove,
Most shines and most is acceptable above.
   Therefore Gods universal Law
Gave to the man despotic power
Over his female in due awe,   1055
Nor from that right to part an hour,
Smile she or lowr:
So shall he least confusion draw
On his whole life, not sway'd
By female usurpation, nor dismay'd.   1060
   But had we best retire, I see a storm?
   Samson. Fair days have oft contracted wind and rain.
   Chorus. But this another kind of tempest brings.
   Samson. Be less abstruse, my riddling days are past.
   Chorus. Look now for no inchanting voice, nor fear   1065
The bait of honied words; a rougher tongue
Draws hitherward, I know him by his stride,
The Giant *Harapha* of *Gath,* his look
Haughty as is his pile high-built and proud.
Comes he in peace? what wind hath blown him hither   1070
I less conjecture then when first I saw
The sumptuous *Dalila* floating this way:
His habit carries peace, his brow defiance.
   Samson. Or peace or not, alike to me he comes.
   Chorus. His fraught[79] we soon shall know, he now
     arrives.   1075
   Harapha. I come not *Samson,* to condole thy chance,
As these perhaps, yet wish it had not been,
Though for no friendly intent. I am of *Gath,*
Men call me *Harapha,* of stock renown'd
As *Og* or *Anak* and the *Emims* old   1080
That *Kiriathaim* held; thou knowst me now

   [79] cargo, i.e., business.

If thou at all art known. Much I have heard
Of thy prodigious might and feats perform'd
Incredible to me, in this displeas'd,
That I was never present on the place   1085
Of those encounters, where we might have tri'd
Each others force in camp or listed field:[80]
And now am come to see of whom such noise
Hath walk'd about, and each limb to survey,
If thy appearance answer loud report.   1090
    Samson. The way to know were not to see but taste.
    Harapha. Dost thou already single[81] me; I thought
Gyves and the Mill had tam'd thee? O that fortune
Had brought me to the field where thou art fam'd
T' have wrought such wonders with an Asses Jaw;   1095
I should have forc'd thee soon wish other arms,
Or left thy carkass where the Ass lay thrown:
So had the glory of Prowess been recover'd
To *Palestine,* won by a *Philistine*
From the unforeskinn'd race, of whom thou bear'st   1100
The highest name for valiant Acts; that honour
Certain t' have won by mortal duel from thee,
I lose, prevented by thy eyes put out.
    Samson. Boast not of what thou wouldst have done, but do
What then thou would'st, thou seest it in thy hand.   1105
    Harapha. To combat with a blind man I disdain,
And thou hast need much washing to be toucht.
    Samson. Such usage as your honourable Lords
Afford me assassinated[82] and betray'd,
Who durst not with thir whole united powers   1110
In fight withstand me single and unarm'd,
Nor in the house with chamber Ambushes
Close-banded durst attaque me, no not sleeping,
Till they had hir'd a woman with their gold
Breaking her Marriage Faith to circumvent me.   1115
Therefore without feign'd shifts let be assign'd
Some narrow place enclos'd, where sight may give thee,
Or rather flight, no great advantage on me;
Then put on all thy gorgeous arms, thy Helmet
And Brigandine[83] of brass, thy broad Habergeon,[84]   1120

[80] plain of battle or tournament field.
[81] challenge to single combat.
[82] treacherously attacked.
[83] plated body armor.
[84] jacket of mail.

Vant-brass and Greves, and Gauntlet,[85] add thy Spear
A Weavers beam,[86] and seven-times-folded shield,
I only with an Oak'n staff will meet thee,
And raise such out-cries on thy clatter'd Iron,
Which long shall not with-hold mee from thy head,   1125
That in a little time while breath remains thee,
Thou oft shalt wish thy self at *Gath* to boast
Again in safety what thou wouldst have done
To *Samson*, but shalt never see *Gath* more.
   Harapha. Thou durst not thus disparage glorious
     arms   1130
Which greatest Heroes have in battel worn,
Thir ornament and safety, had not spells
And black enchantments, some Magicians Art
Arm'd thee or charm'd thee strong, which thou from Heav'n
Feign'dst at thy birth was giv'n thee in thy hair,   1135
Where strength can least abide, though all thy hairs
Were bristles rang'd like those that ridge the back
Of chaf't wild Boars, or ruffl'd Porcupines.
   Samson. I know no Spells, use no forbidden Arts;
My trust is in the living God who gave me   1140
At my Nativity this strength, diffus'd
No less through all my sinews, joints and bones,
Then thine, while I preserv'd these locks unshorn,
The pledge of my unviolated vow.
For proof hereof, if *Dagon* be thy god,   1145
Go to his Temple, invocate his aid
With solemnest devotion, spread before him
How highly it concerns his glory now
To frustrate and dissolve these Magic spells,
Which I to be the power of *Israel*'s God   1150
Avow, and challenge *Dagon* to the test,
Offering to combat thee his Champion bold,
With th' utmost of his Godhead seconded:
Then thou shalt see, or rather to thy sorrow
Soon feel, whose God is strongest, thine or mine.   1155
   Harapha. Presume not on thy God, what e're he be,
Thee he regards not, owns not, hath cut off
Quite from his people, and deliver'd up
Into thy Enemies hand, permitted them
To put out both thine eyes, and fetter'd send thee   1160

---

[85] respectively, armor for the forearm, the legs, and the hand.
[86] The staff of Goliath's spear was also like a weaver's beam
(1 Sam. xvii. 7).

Into the common Prison, there to grind
Among the Slaves and Asses thy comrades,
As good for nothing else, no better service
With those thy boyst'rous[87] locks, no worthy match
For valour to assail, nor by the sword   1165
Of noble Warriour, so to stain his honour,
But by the Barbers razor best subdu'd.
    Samson. All these indignities, for such they are
From thine,[88] these evils I deserve and more,
Acknowledge them from God inflicted on me   1170
Justly, yet despair not of his final pardon
Whose ear is ever open; and his eye
Gracious to re-admit the suppliant;
In confidence whereof I once again
Defie thee to the trial of mortal fight,   1175
By combat to decide whose god is God,
Thine or whom I with *Israel's* Sons adore.
    Harapha. Fair honour that thou dost thy God, in trusting
He will accept thee to defend his cause,
A Murtherer, a Revolter, and a Robber.   1180
    Samson. Tongue-doughtie Giant, how dost thou prove me
      these?
    Harapha. Is not thy Nation subject to our Lords?
Thir Magistrates confest it, when they took thee
As a League-breaker and deliver'd bound
Into our hands: for hadst thou not committed   1185
Notorious murder on those thirty men
At *Askalon*, who never did thee harm,
Then like a Robber strip'dst them of thir robes?[89]
The *Philistines*, when thou hadst broke the league,
Went up with armed powers thee only seeking,   1190
To others did no violence nor spoil.
    Samson. Among the Daughters of the *Philistines*
I chose a Wife, which argu'd me no foe;
And in your City held my Nuptial Feast:
But your ill-meaning Politician Lords,   1195
Under pretence of Bridal friends and guests,
Appointed to await me thirty spies,
Who threatning cruel death constrain'd the bride
To wring from me and tell to them my secret,
That solv'd the riddle which I had propos'd.   1200

[87] coarse and strong.
[88] thy people.
[89] See Judges xiv. 19.

When I perceiv'd all set on enmity,
As on my enemies, where ever chanc'd,
I us'd hostility, and took thir spoil
To pay my underminers in thir coin.
My Nation was subjected to your Lords.   1205
It was the force of Conquest; force with force
Is well ejected when the Conquer'd can.
But I a private person, whom my Countrey
As a league-breaker gave up bound, presum'd
Single Rebellion and did Hostile Acts.   1210
I was no private but a person rais'd
With strength sufficient and command from Heav'n
To free my Countrey; if their servile minds
Me their Deliverer sent would not receive,
But to thir Masters gave me up for nought,   1215
Th' unworthier they; whence to this day they serve.
I was to do my part from Heav'n assign'd,
And had perform'd it if my known offence
Had not disabl'd me, not all your force:
These shifts refuted, answer thy appellant   1220
Though by his blindness maim'd for high attempts,
Who now defies thee thrice to single fight,
As a petty enterprise of small enforce.
    Harapha. With thee a Man condemn'd, a Slave enrol'd,
Due by the Law to capital punishment?   1225
To fight with thee no man of arms will deign.
    Samson. Cam'st thou for this, vain boaster, to survey me,
To descant on my strength, and give thy verdit?
Come nearer, part not hence so slight inform'd;
But take good heed my hand survey not thee.   1230
    Harapha. O _Baal-zebub!_[90] can my ears unus'd
Hear these dishonours, and not render death?
    Samson. No man with-holds thee, nothing from thy hand
Fear I incurable; bring up thy van,[91]
My heels are fetter'd, but my fist is free.   1235
    Harapha. This insolence other kind of answer fits.
    Samson. Go baffl'd[92] coward, lest I run upon thee,
Though in these chains, bulk without spirit vast,
And with one buffet lay thy structure low,
Or swing thee in the Air, then dash thee down   1240
To th' hazard of thy brains and shatter'd sides.

[90] sun god of the Philistines.
[91] front line of battle.
[92] disgraced.

Harapha. By *Astaroth*[93] e're long thou shalt lament
These braveries in Irons loaden on thee.
　Chorus. His Giantship is gone somewhat crest-fall'n,
Stalking with less unconsci'nable strides,　　　　　1245
And lower looks, but in a sultrie chafe.
　Samson. I dread him not, nor all his Giant-brood,
Though Fame divulge him Father of five Sons
All of Gigantic size, *Goliah* chief.[94]
　Chorus. He will directly to the Lords, I fear,　　1250
And with malitious counsel stir them up
Some way or other yet further to afflict thee.
　Samson. He must allege some cause, and offer'd fight
Will not dare mention, lest a question rise
Whether he durst accept the offer or not,　　　　　1255
And that he durst not plain enough appear'd.
Much more affliction then already felt
They cannot well impose, nor I sustain;
If they intend advantage of my labours
The work of many hands, which earns my keeping　1260
With no small profit daily to my owners.
But come what will, my deadliest foe will prove
My speediest friend, by death to rid me hence,
The worst that he can give, to me the best.
Yet so it may fall out, because thir end　　　　　1265
Is hate, not help to me, it may with mine
Draw thir own ruin who attempt the deed.
　Chorus. Oh how comely it is and how reviving
To the Spirits of just men long opprest!
When God into the hands of thir deliverer　　　　1270
Puts invincible might
To quell the mighty of the Earth, th' oppressour,
The brute and boist'rous force of violent men
Hardy and industrious to support
Tyrannic power, but raging to pursue　　　　　　1275
The righteous and all such as honour Truth;
He all thir Ammunition
And feats of War defeats
With plain Heroic magnitude of mind
And celestial vigour arm'd,　　　　　　　　　　1280
Thir Armories and Magazins contemns,
Renders them useless, while
With winged expedition

[93] queen of heaven.
[94] alluding to 2 Sam. xxi. 15–22.

Swift as the lightning glance he executes
His errand on the wicked, who surpris'd   1285
Lose thir defence, distracted and amaz'd.
    But patience is more oft the exercise
Of Saints, the trial of thir fortitude,
Making them each his own Deliverer,
And Victor over all   1290
That tyrannie or fortune can inflict;
Either of these is in thy lot,
Samson, with might endu'd
Above the Sons of men; but sight bereav'd
May chance to number thee with those   1295
Whom Patience finally must crown.
This Idols day hath bin to thee no day of rest,
    Labouring thy mind
More then the working day thy hands,
And yet perhaps more trouble is behind.   1300
For I descry this way
Some other tending, in his hand
A Scepter or quaint[95] staff he bears,
Comes on amain, speed in his look.
By his habit I discern him now   1305
A Public Officer, and now at hand.
His message will be short and voluble.
    Officer. **Ebrews,** the Pris'ner *Samson* here I seek.
    Chorus. His manacles remark[96] him, there he sits.
    Officer. Samson, to thee our Lords thus bid me say;   1310
This day to *Dagon* is a solemn Feast,
With Sacrifices, Triumph, Pomp, and Games;
Thy strength they know surpassing human rate,
And now some public proof thereof require
To honour this great Feast, and great Assembly;   1315
Rise therefore with all speed and come along,
Where I will see thee heart'n'd and fresh clad
T' appear as fits before th' illustrious Lords.
    Samson. Thou knowst I am an *Ebrew*, therefore tell them,
Our Law forbids at thir Religious Rites   1320
My presence; for that cause I cannot come.
    Officer. This answer, be assur'd, will not content them.
    Samson. Have they not Sword-players, and ev'ry sort
Of Gymnic Artists, Wrestlers, Riders, Runners,
Juglers and Dancers, Antics, Mummers, Mimics,   1325

[95] skillfully wrought.
[96] point him out.

But they must pick me out with shackles tir'd,
And over-labour'd at thir publick Mill,
To make them sport with blind activity?
Do they not seek occasion of new quarrels
On my refusal to distress me more, 1330
Or make a game of my calamities?
Return the way thou cam'st, I will not come.
   Officer. Regard thy self,[97] this will offend them highly.
   Samson. My self? my conscience and internal peace.
Can they think me so broken, so debas'd 1335
With corporal servitude, that my mind ever
Will condescend to such absurd commands?
Although thir drudge, to be thir fool or jester,
And in my midst of sorrow and heart-grief
To shew them feats, and play before thir god, 1340
The worst of all indignities, yet on me
Joyn'd[98] with extream contempt? I will not come.
   Officer. My message was impos'd on me with speed,
Brooks no delay: is this thy resolution?
   Samson. So take it with what speed thy message
     needs. 1345
   Officer. I am sorry what this stoutness[99] will produce.
   Samson. Perhaps thou shalt have cause to sorrow indeed.
   Chorus. Consider, *Samson*; matters now are strain'd
Up to the highth, whether to hold or break;
He's gone, and who knows how he may report 1350
Thy words by adding fuel to the flame?
Expect another message more imperious,
More Lordly thund'ring then thou well wilt bear.
   Samson. Shall I abuse this Consecrated gift
Of strength, again returning with my hair 1355
After my great transgression, so requite
Favour renew'd, and add a greater sin
By prostituting holy things to Idols;
A *Nazarite* in place abominable
Vaunting my strength in honour to thir *Dagon*? 1360
Besides, how vile, contemptible, ridiculous,
What act more execrably unclean, prophane?
   Chorus. Yet with this strength thou serv'st the *Philistines*,
Idolatrous, uncircumcis'd, unclean.
   Samson. Not in thir Idol-worship, but by labour 1365

[97] beware.
[98] imposed.
[99] courage.

Honest and lawful to deserve my food
Of those who have me in thir civil power.
    Chorus. Where the heart joins not, outward acts defile not.
    Samson. Where outward force constrains, the sentence
       holds;
But who constrains me to the Temple of *Dagon*,   1370
Not dragging? the *Philistian* Lords command.
Commands are no constraints. If I obey them,
I do it freely; venturing to displease
God for the fear of Man, and Man prefer,
Set God behind: which in his jealousie   1375
Shall never, unrepented, find forgiveness.
Yet that he may dispense with[1] me or thee
Present in Temples at Idolatrous Rites
For some important cause, thou needst not doubt.
    Chorus. How thou wilt here come off surmounts my
      reach.   1380
    Samson. Be of good courage, I begin to feel
Some rouzing motions in me which dispose
To something extraordinary my thoughts.
I with this Messenger will go along,
Nothing to do, be sure, that may dishonour   1385
Our Law, or stain my vow of *Nazarite*.
If there be aught of presage in the mind,
This day will be remarkable in my life
By some great act, or of my days the last.
    Chorus. In time thou hast resolv'd, the man returns.   1390
    Officer. Samson, this second message from our Lords
To thee I am bid say. Art thou our Slave,
Our Captive, at the public Mill our drudge,
And dar'st thou at our sending and command
Dispute thy coming? come without delay;   1395
Or we shall find such Engines to assail
And hamper thee, as thou shalt come of force,
Though thou wert firmlier fast'n'd then a rock.
    Samson. I could be well content to try thir Art,
Which to no few of them would prove pernicious.   1400
Yet knowing thir advantages too many,
Because they shall not[2] trail me through thir streets
Like a wild Beast, I am content to go.
Masters commands come with a power resistless
To such as owe them absolute subjection;   1405

[1] give a dispensation to.
[2] because I do not desire them to.

And for a life who will not change his purpose?
(So mutable are all the ways of men)
Yet this be sure, in nothing to comply
Scandalous or forbidden in our Law.
    Officer. I praise thy resolution, doff these links: 1410
By this compliance thou wilt win the Lords
To favour, and perhaps to set thee free.
    Samson. Brethren farewel, your company along
I will not wish, lest it perhaps offend them
To see me girt with Friends; and how the sight   1415
Of me as of a common Enemy,
So dreaded once, may now exasperate them
I know not. Lords are Lordliest in thir wine;
And the well-feasted Priest then soonest fir'd
With zeal, if aught Religion seem concern'd: 1420
No less the people on thir Holy-days
Impetuous, insolent, unquenchable;
Happ'n what may, of me expect to hear
Nothing dishonourable, impure, unworthy
Our God, our Law, my Nation, or my self,   1425
The last of me or no I cannot warrant.
    Chorus. Go, and the Holy One
Of *Israel* be thy guide
To what may serve his glory best, and spread his name
Great among the Heathen round: 1430
Send thee the Angel of thy Birth, to stand
Fast by thy side, who from thy Fathers field
Rode up in flames after his message told
Of thy conception, and be now a shield
Of fire; that Spirit that first rusht on thee   1435
In the Camp of *Dan*
Be efficacious in thee now at need.
For never was from Heav'n imparted
Measure of strength so great to mortal seed,
As in thy wond'rous actions hath been seen.   1440
But wherefore comes old *Manoa* in such hast
With youthful steps? much livelier then e're while
He seems: supposing here to find his Son,
Or of him bringing to us some glad news?
    Manoa. Peace with you brethren; my inducement
        hither   1445
Was not at present here to find my Son,
By order of the Lords new parted hence
To come and play before them at thir Feast.

I heard all as I came, the City rings
And numbers thither flock; I had no will,   1450
Lest I should see him forc't to things unseemly.
But that which mov'd my coming now, was chiefly
To give ye part with me what hope I have
With good success to work his liberty.
    Chorus. That hope would much rejoyce us to
           partake   1455
With thee; say reverend Sire, we thirst to hear.
    Manoa. I have attempted[3] one by one the Lords
Either at home, or through the high street passing,
With supplication prone and Fathers tears
T' accept of ransom for my Son thir pris'ner;   1460
Some much averse I found and wondrous harsh,
Contemptuous, proud, set on revenge and spite;
That part most reverenc'd *Dagon* and his Priests;
Others more moderate seeming, but thir aim
Private reward, for which both God and State   1465
They easily would set to sale; a third
More generous far and civil, who confess'd
They had anough reveng'd, having reduc't
Thir foe to misery beneath thir fears;
The rest was magnanimity to remit,[4]   1470
If some convenient ransom were propos'd.
What noise or shout was that? it tore the Skie.
    Chorus. Doubtless the people shouting to behold
Thir once great dread, captive, and blind before them,
Or at some proof of strength before them shown.   1475
    Manoa. His ransom, if my whole inheritance
May compass it, shall willingly be paid
And numberd down: much rather I shall chuse
To live the poorest in my Tribe, then richest,
And he in that calamitous prison left.   1480
No, I am fixt not to part hence without him.
For his redemption all my Patrimony,
If I need be, I am ready to forgo
And quit: not wanting him, I shall want nothing.
    Chorus. Fathers are wont to lay up for thir Sons,   1485
Thou for thy Son art bent to lay out all;
Sons wont to nurse thir Parents in old age,
Thou in old age car'st how to nurse thy Son,
Made older then thy age through eye-sight lost.

    [3] tried to persuade.
    [4] The rest of their revenge they would magnanimously remit.

Manoa. It shall be my delight to tend his eyes,   1490
And view him sitting in the house, ennobl'd
With all those high exploits by him atchiev'd,
And on his shoulders waving down those locks,
That of a Nation arm'd the strength contain'd:
And I perswade me God had not permitted   1495
His strength again to grow up with his hair
Garrison'd round about him like a Camp
Of faithful Souldiery, were not his purpose
To use him further yet in some great service,
Not to sit idle with so great a gift   1500
Useless, and thence ridiculous about him.
And since his strength with eye-sight was not lost,
God will restore him eye-sight to his strength.
  Chorus. Thy hopes are not ill founded nor seem vain
Of his delivery, and thy joy thereon   1505
Conceiv'd, agreeable to a Fathers love,
In both which we, as next[5] participate.
  Manoa. I know your friendly minds and—O what noise!
Mercy of Heav'n what hideous noise was that!
Horribly loud unlike the former shout.   1510
  Chorus. Noise call you it or universal groan
As if the whole inhabitation perish'd;
Blood, death, and deathful deeds are in that noise,
Ruin, destruction at the utmost point.
  Manoa. Of ruin indeed methought I heard the noise,   1515
Oh it continues, they have slain my Son.
  Chorus. Thy Son is rather slaying them, that outcry
From slaughter of one foe could not ascend.
  Manoa. Some dismal accident it needs must be;
What shall we do, stay here or run and see?   1520
  Chorus. Best keep together here, lest running thither
We unawares run into dangers mouth.
This evil on the *Philistines* is fall'n,
From whom could else a general cry be heard?
The sufferers then will scarce molest us here,   1525
From other hands we need not much to fear.
What if his eye-sight (for to *Israels* God
Nothing is hard) by miracle restor'd,
He now be dealing dole among his foes,
And over heaps of slaughter'd walk his way?   1530
  Manoa. That were a joy presumptuous to be thought.
  Chorus. Yet God hath wrought things as incredible

[5] as kinsmen.

For his people of old; what hinders now?
    Manoa. He can I know, but doubt to think he will;
Yet Hope would fain subscribe, and tempts Belief.   1535
A little stay will bring some notice hither.
    Chorus. Of good or bad so great, of bad the sooner;
For evil news rides post, while good news baits.[6]
And to our wish I see one hither speeding,
An *Ebrew*, as I guess, and of our Tribe.   1540
    Messenger. O whither shall I run, or which way flie
The sight of this so horrid spectacle
Which earst my eyes beheld and yet behold;
For dire imagination still persues me?
But providence or instinct of nature seems,   1545
Or reason though disturb'd, and scarse consulted
T' have guided me aright, I know not how,
To thee first reverend *Manoa*, and to these
My Countreymen, whom here I knew remaining,
As at some distance from the place of horrour,   1550
So in the sad event too much concern'd.
    Manoa. The accident was loud, and here before thee
With rueful cry, yet what it was we hear not,
No Preface needs, thou seest we long to know.
    Messenger. It would burst forth, but I recover
        breath   1555
And sense distract, to know well what I utter.
    Manoa. Tell us the sum, the circumstance defer.
    Messenger. Gaza yet stands, but all her Sons are fall'n,
All in a moment overwhelm'd and fall'n.
    Manoa. Sad, but thou knowst to *Israelites* not
        saddest   1560
The desolation of a Hostile City.
    Messenger. Feed on that first, there may in grief be surfet.
    Manoa. Relate by whom.
    Messenger.   By *Samson.*
    Manoa.   That still lessens
The sorrow, and converts it nigh to joy.
    Messenger. Ah *Manoa*, I refrain too suddenly   1565
To utter what will come at last too soon;
Lest evil tidings with too rude irruption
Hitting thy aged ear should pierce too deep.
    Manoa. Suspense in news is torture, speak them out.
    Messenger. Then take the worst in brief, *Samson* is
        dead.   1570

[6] moves slowly.

Manoa. The worst indeed, O all my hope's defeated
To free him hence! but death who sets all free
Hath paid his ransom now and full discharge.
What windy[7] joy this day had I conceiv'd
Hopeful of his Delivery, which now proves   1575
Abortive as the first-born bloom of spring
Nipt with the lagging rear of winters frost.
Yet e're I give the rains to grief, say first,
How dy'd he? death to life is crown or shame.
All by him fell thou say'st, by whom fell he,   1580
What glorious hand gave *Samson* his deaths wound?
 Messenger. Unwounded of his enemies he fell.
 Manoa. Wearied with slaughter then or how? explain.
 Messenger. By his own hands.
 Manoa.   Self-violence? what cause
Brought him so soon at variance with himself
Among his foes?   1585
 Messenger.   Inevitable cause
At once both to destroy and be destroy'd;
The Edifice where all were met to see him
Upon thir heads and on his own he pull'd.
 Manoa. O lastly over-strong against thy self!   1590
A dreadful way thou took'st to thy revenge.
More than anough we know; but while things yet
Are in confusion, give us if thou canst,
Eye-witness of what first or last was done,
Relation more particular and distinct.   1595
 Messenger. Occasions drew me early to this City,
And as the gates I enter'd with Sun-rise,
The morning Trumpets Festival proclaim'd
Through each high street: little I had dispatch't
When all abroad was rumour'd that this day   1600
Samson should be brought forth to shew the people
Proof of his mighty strength in feats and games;
I sorrow'd at his captive state, but minded[8]
Not to be absent at that spectacle.
The building was a spacious Theatre   1605
Half round on two main Pillars vaulted high,
With seats where all the Lords and each degree
Of sort,[9] might sit in order to behold,
The other side was op'n, where the throng

 [7] empty.
 [8] resolved.
 [9] quality.

On banks[10] and scaffolds under Skie might stand;   1610
I among these aloof obscurely stood.
The Feast and noon grew high, and Sacrifice
Had fill'd thir hearts with mirth, high chear, and wine,
When to thir sports they turn'd. Immediately
Was *Samson* as a public servant brought,   1615
In thir state Livery clad; before him Pipes
And Timbrels, on each side went armed guards,
Both horse and foot before him and behind,
Archers, and Slingers, Cataphracts and Spears.[11]
At sight of him the people with a shout   1620
Rifted the Air clamouring thir god with praise,
Who had made thir dreadful enemy thir thrall.
He patient but undaunted where they led him,
Came to the place, and what was set before him
Which without help of eye might be assay'd,   1625
To heave, pull, draw, or break, he still perform'd
All with incredible, stupendious force,
None daring to appear Antagonist.
At length for intermission sake they led him
Between the pillars; he his guide requested   1630
(For so from such as nearer stood we heard)
As over-tir'd to let him lean a while
With both his arms on those two massie Pillars
That to the arched roof gave main support.
He unsuspitious led him; which when *Samson*   1635
Felt in his arms, with head a while enclin'd,
And eyes fast fixt he stood, as one who pray'd,
Or some great matter in his mind revolv'd.
At last with head erect thus cry'd aloud,
Hitherto, Lords, what your commands impos'd   1640
I have perform'd, as reason was, obeying,
Not without wonder or delight beheld.
Now of my own accord such other tryal
I mean to shew you of my strength, yet greater;
As with amaze shall strike all who behold.   1645
This utter'd, straining all his nerves he bow'd;
As with the force of winds and waters pent,
When Mountains tremble, those two massie Pillars
With horrible convulsion to and fro,
He tugg'd, he shook, till down they came and drew   1650
The whole roof after them, with burst of thunder

[10] benches.
[11] men and horses clad in armor, and spearsmen.

Upon the heads of all who sate beneath,
Lords, Ladies, Captains, Councellors, or Priests,
Thir choice nobility and flower, not only
Of this but each *Philistian* City round   1655
Met from all parts to solemnize this Feast.
Samson with these immixt, inevitably
Pull'd down the same destruction on himself;
The vulgar only scap'd who stood without.
   Chorus. O dearly-bought revenge, yet glorious!   1660
Living or dying thou hast fulfill'd
The work for which thou wast foretold
To *Israel*, and now ly'st victorious
Among thy slain self-kill'd
Not willingly, but tangl'd in the fold   1665
Of dire necessity, whose law in death conjoin'd
Thee with thy slaughter'd foes in number more
Then all thy life had slain before.
   Semichorus. While thir hearts were jocund and sublime,[12]
Drunk with Idolatry, drunk with Wine,   1670
And fat regorg'd of Bulls and Goats,
Chaunting thir Idol, and preferring
Before our living Dread who dwells
In *Silo*[13] his bright Sanctuary:
Among them he a spirit of phrenzie sent,   1675
Who hurt thir minds,
And urg'd them on with mad desire
To call in hast for thir destroyer;
They only set on sport and play
Unweetingly importun'd   1680
Thir own destruction to come speedy upon them.
So fond are mortal men
Fall'n into wrath divine,
As thir own ruin on themselves t' invite,
Insensate left, or to sense reprobate,   1685
And with blindness internal struck.
   Semichorus. But he though blind of sight,
Despis'd and thought extinguish't quite,
With inward eyes illuminated
His fierie vertue rouz'd   1690
From under ashes into sudden flame,
And as an ev'ning Dragon[14] came,

[12] elated.
[13] Shiloh.
[14] serpent; but Lee S. Cox (*MLN*, LXXVI, 1961, 577–84) in-

Assailant on the perched roosts,
And nests in order rang'd
Of tame villatic[15] Fowl; but as an Eagle   1695
His cloudless thunder bolted on thir heads.
So vertue giv'n for lost,
Deprest, and overthrown, as seem'd,
Like that self-begott'n bird[16]
In th' *Arabian* woods embost,[17]   1700
That no second knows nor third,
And lay e're while a Holocaust,
From out her ashie womb now teem'd,
Revives, reflourishes, then vigorous most
When most unactive deem'd,   1705
And though her body die, her fame survives,
A secular[18] bird ages of lives.
     Manoa. Come, come, no time for lamentation now,
Nor much more cause, *Samson* hath quit himself
Like *Samson,* and heroicly hath finish'd   1710
A life Heroic, on his Enemies
Fully reveng'd, hath left them years of mourning,
And lamentation to the Sons of *Caphtor*
Through all *Philistian* bounds. To *Israel*
Honour hath left, and freedom, let but them   1715
Find courage to lay hold on this occasion,
To himself and Fathers house eternal fame;
And which is best and happiest yet, all this
With God not parted from him, as was feard,
But favouring and assisting to the end.   1720
Nothing is here for tears, nothing to wail
Or knock the breast, no weakness, no contempt,
Dispraise, or blame, nothing but well and fair,
And what may quiet us in a death so noble.
Let us go find the body where it lies   1725
Soak't in his enemies blood, and from the stream
With lavers pure and cleansing herbs wash off
The clotted gore. I with what speed the while

---

terprets the phrase as the "blind seeing one," Samson being one
whose inner powers transfix others through his eyes but one who
sees darkly, with human limitations of vision.
     [15] farmhouse.
     [16] the Phoenix.
     [17] sheltered.
     [18] living for centuries.

(*Gaza* is not in plight[19] to say us nay)
Will send for all my kindred, all my friends   1730
To fetch him hence and solemnly attend
With silent obsequie and funeral train
Home to his Fathers house: there will I build him
A Monument, and plant it round with shade
Of Laurel ever green, and branching Palm,   1735
With all his Trophies hung, and Acts enroll'd
In copious Legend, or sweet Lyric Song.
Thither shall all the valiant youth resort,
And from his memory inflame thir breasts
To matchless valour, and adventures high: 1740
The Virgins also shall on feastful days
Visit his Tomb with flowers, only bewailing
His lot unfortunate in nuptial choice,
From whence captivity and loss of eyes.
     Chorus. All is best, though we oft doubt,   1745
What th' unsearchable dispose[20]
Of highest wisdom brings about,
And ever best found in the close.
Oft he seems to hide his face,
But unexpectedly returns   1750
And to his faithful Champion hath in place
Bore witness gloriously; whence *Gaza* mourns
And all that band them to resist
His uncontroulable intent;
His servants he with new acquist[21]   1755
Of true experience from this great event
With peace and consolation hath dismist,
And calm of mind all passion spent.
        (*1646–48 ?; revised, 1653 or later ?*)[22]

19 condition.
20 ordering.
21 acquisition.
22 Traditional dating places SA last of Milton's poetic works
(c. 1670), but this has been challenged by Parker, Gilbert, and
the editor (see articles listed in the bibliography). The dates given
here are those conjectured by Parker. For a contrary view, see
Ernest Sirluck, *Journal of Eng. and Ger. Philology,* LX (1961),
749–85.

AD JOANNEM ROÜSIUM
(To John Rouse)

Librarian of Oxford University

*An Ode concerning a lost volume of poems which he re-
quested be sent to him a second time, so that it might
be put back with my others in the public library.*[1]

STROPHE 1

Two-part book rejoicing in single garb,[2] / although with
double leaf, / and glittering with no painstaking elegance, /
which a hand once / young wrought, [5] / a careful hand,
yet by no means too great a poet's, / while, unsettled, now
through the Ausonian[3] shades, / now through British lawns
he dallied, / innocent of people and out of touch with life, /
he indulged his native lute, soon afterwards in like manner [10] / with Daunian[4] lyre he resounded his foreign air /
to those around him, and barely touched the soil with his foot.

ANTISTROPHE

Who, little book, who with evil intent / withdrew you from
your remaining brothers? / when, dispatched from the
city, [15] / immediately upon request by my learned friend, /
you were travelling the distinguished road / to the birthplace
of the Thames,[5] / the blue father, / where are the limpid
fountains [20] / of the Aonides,[6] and the sacred Bacchic

---

[1] Complying with Rouse's request, Milton sent to the Bodleian
Library a second copy of his 1645 *Poems,* in which today the
manuscript of this ode is found. The eleven prose tracts published
to date (c. 1646) had been sent, with an autograph inscription,
with the first copy.

[2] The *Poems* were published with separate title pages and pagi-
nation ("gemina fronde") for the English and the Latin poems;
copies of the Latin poems without the English poems are extant.

[3] Italian.

[4] Italian.

[5] Oxford.

[6] See *El.* 4, n. 10; l. 66 is also explained by this note.

dance / known to the world through endless / ages, fallen away under the revolving heavens, / but celebrated to eternity?

Today what god or lofty creature of god, [25] / having pity on the primitive nature of my nation, / (if we have atoned sufficiently for our former offences / and the base idleness of our unmanly extravagance) / will remove forever the execrable civil wars of its citizenry,[7] / and what sainted man will call back the nourishing studies [30] / and the banished Muses without abode / now in nearly all the bounds of England; / and who will pierce with Apollo's quiver / the foul birds / with menacing talons, [35] / and drive the pest of Phineas far from Pegasus' stream?[8]

But, little book, though by the bad faith of the messenger / or his negligence, / you have wandered once from the company of your brothers, / whether some den holds you fast [40] / or some hidden recess, perhaps wherein / you are rubbed by the vile, calloused hand of a tasteless huckster, / be cheered, fortunate one; behold! again / a new hope shines to enable you / to avoid the abyss of Lethe, and be conveyed [45] / to the supreme court of Jove on oaring wing,

for Rouse selects you / for his own property, and from the rightful collection / promised, complains you to be removed, / and he requests you return to him, to whose care [50] / are the glorious monuments of men assigned: / and indeed

[7] reference primarily to the Civil Wars and a former extravagant life.

[8] Apollo was god of archery. The Harpies (as noisome, ravenous birds) were sent to steal or defile the food of Phineus. Pegasus, the winged horse, had created the fountain Hippocrene, sacred to the Muses, by the stamp of his foot, and with his aid Bellerophon had destroyed the Chimaera and attempted to fly to heaven. Oxford is thus likened to Pegasus because of its cultivation of the Muses, its dispelling of ignorance, and its attempt at high achievement. The surrender of royalist Oxford to the Parliamentarians occurred six months before Milton wrote in June 1646.

in the sacred sanctuaries / over which he himself presides he has wished you to be preserved, / a faithful custodian of immortal works / and a guardian of treasure nobler [55] / than the golden tripods, and the Delphic gifts, / which Ion protects, / the honorable grandson of Erechtheus, / in the rich temple of the god, his father,⁹ / Ion, born of Actaean Creusa. [60]

ANTISTROPHE

Therefore you shall fly to see / the delightful groves of the Muses, / and again you shall find your way to the divine home of Phoebus / in the Oxford valley, which he frequents / in preference to Delos [65] / and the cleft peak of Parnassus: / You shall go full of honor, / since you also depart possessed of / a distinguished lot, invited by the prayer of a fortunate friend. / There you shall be read among the august names [70] / of authors, the ancient lights and true glory / both of the Greek and the Latin people.

EPODE

You at last my labors have not been in vain, / whatever that sterile genius has brought forth. / Now I bid you hope for placid rest [75] / discharged from envy in a later age, in the blessed abodes / which the good Hermes¹⁰ gives / and the expert protection of Rouse, / where never shall penetrate the insolent speech of the multitude and even / the vicious throng of readers shall retire far off; [80] / but our distant descendants, / and a more prudent age / will perhaps exercise a fairer judgment / of things from its unbiassed breast. / Then with envy entombed, [85] / a rational posterity will know if I deserve any merit, / thanks to Rouse.

(The ode consists of three strophes, and the same number of antistrophes, closed at last by one epode; although all do not correspond exactly in the number of verses or in fixed parts where there are cola, nevertheless I have divided them thus in order to observe convenience in reading rather than respect to ancient rules of versifying. In other respects this type more correctly should probably have been called monostrophic. The meters are partly regularly patterned, partly free. There

⁹ Apollo's temple at Delphi.
¹⁰ god of learning.

are two Phaleucian lines which admit a spondee in the third
foot, which same practice Catullus freely employed in the
second foot.)[11]

(*Jan. 1647*)

THE FIFTH ODE OF HORACE. BOOK I.

Quis multa gracilis te puer in rosa render'd almost word for
    word without rime according to the Latin Measure,
    as near as the Language will permit.[1]

What slender Youth bedew'd with liquid odours
Courts thee on Roses in some pleasant Cave,
    Pyrrha? for whom bindst thou
    In wreaths thy golden Hair,
Plain in thy neatness? O how oft shall he   5
On Faith and changed Gods complain: and Seas
    Rough with black winds and storms
    Unwonted shall admire:
Who now enjoyes thee credulous, all Gold,
Who always vacant, always amiable   10
    Hopes thee; of flattering gales
    Unmindfull. Hapless they
To whom thou untry'd seem'st fair. Me in my vow'd
Picture the sacred wall declares t' have hung
    My dank and dropping weeds   15
    To the stern God of Sea.

(*1646–48 ?*)

[11] Milton's concern in drawing attention to his prosodic experiment should be read alongside remarks accompanying the *Fifth
Ode* and *Psalms* 80–88 and alongside the metrics of *SA*. Prefacing
the drama is the similar verse description: "call'd by the Greeks
Monostrophic, or rather *Apolelymenon,* without regard had to
Strophe, Antistrophe or *Epod.*" The Phaleucian consisted of a
spondee, a dactyl, and three trochees. Catullus is thought of here
primarily because he employed the hendecasyllabic line so frequently.

[1] Milton aimed at reproducing Horace's quantitative meters, and
so subjoined the Latin text to allow the reader to evaluate his
rendition. Perhaps this translation, along with *Ps.* 80–88, which
also emphasize the nature of the rendering, was intended as an
exercise of prosodic discipline.

SONNET 12

A book was writt of late call'd *Tetrachordon*,[1]
  And wov'n close both matter, form, and stile,
  The subject new; it walk'd the town a while,
  Numbring good intellects; now seldom por'd on.
Cries the stall-reader, bless us! what a word on   5
  A title page is this! and som in file
  Stand spelling fals, while one might walk to Mile-
  End Green.[2] Why is it harder, Sirs, then Gordon,[3]
Colkitto, or Macdonnell, or Galasp?[4]
  Those rugged names to our like mouths grow sleek   10
  That would have made *Quintilian*[5] stare and gasp.
Thy age, like ours, O Soul of Sir *John Cheek*,[6]
  Hated not learning wors then toad or Asp,
  When thou taught'st *Cambridge*, and King *Edward*
    Greek.[7]

(1647 ?)

[1] Milton's pamphlet confirming his *Doctrine and Discipline of Divorce* was published Mar. 4, 1645. The four "tones" on which Milton's tetrachord is built are Gen. i. 27–28, Deut. xxiv. 1–2, Matt. v. 31–32, and 1 Cor. vii. 10–16, "the foure chief places in Scripture, which treat of Mariage, or nullities in Mariage."

[2] the intersection of Cambridge Heath Road and Whitechapel Road, which is one measured mile along the latter thoroughfare from Aldgate.

[3] James Gordon, Lord Aboyne, influential, though vacillating, adherent of the Scots Royalist James Graham, Marquis of Montrose; at the battle of Auldearn, May 8–9, 1645, he aided Mac-Donnell in routing the Parliamentary army.

[4] The three names all refer to Alexander MacDonnell, known as MacColkitto and MacGillespie, Montrose's major-general. For his victory at Auldearn, MacDonnell is famed in Gaelic legend; he was knighted by Montrose in 1645. Milton contrasts the repute of these two enemies of the Parliamentarians in mid-1645 and the concurrent derision of advocates of true liberty like himself.

[5] the Roman rhetorician, whose *Institutio Oratoria* ("The Education of an Orator") warned of the corruptions of language from foreign sources and of the need for the study of Greek.

[6] First professor of Greek at Cambridge, Cheke introduced "Erasmian" pronunciation, rejecting the identical sounding of various vowels and diphthongs. He became tutor to Prince Edward in 1544, continuing after the accession, and was one of seven divines appointed to draw up a body of laws for church administration.

[7] The final five lines are concerned with (1) the lack of learn-

ON THE FORCERS OF CONSCIENCE[1]

Because you have thrown off your Prelate Lord
  And with stiff vows renounc'd his Liturgie[2]
  To seise the widow'd whore Plurality[3]
  From them whose sin ye envi'd, not abhorr'd,
Dare ye for this adjure the civill sword   5
  To force our Consciences that Christ set free,
  And ride us with a classic Hierarchy[4]
  Taught ye by meer A.S.[5] and *Rotherford?*[6]

---

ing and of appreciation of learning in Milton's age, which is contrasted with the humanism of Cheke's "reformative age" when Quintilian's concept that education should produce men of high character and culture prevailed; and (2) a comparison between the reception of his efforts and of the work by Cheke and other divines to enact relaxations of church laws of divorce (discussed on p. 97 of *Tetrachordon*). Only Edward VI's untimely death prevented establishment of these divorce laws by Parliament.

[1] The "new" forcers of conscience as they were called in the 1673 printing of this tailed sonnet may be those who in the last months of 1646 particularly demanded immediate legislation for the repression of heresy and error and who tried to effect Presbyterian organization throughout England. In January 1647 Clarendon commented on the intolerant measures which were provoking revolt among the Independents and the army (see *State Papers*, Nos. 2396, 2405).

[2] In Aug. 1645 the House of Commons forbade public and private use of the *Book of Common Prayer*.

[3] Although prelates who held multiple posts were "thrown off" when episcopacy was formally abolished in July 1643, the Presbyterian system supported the same kind of pluralism.

[4] Presbyterian administration was built on the classis (or synod), which was composed of all ministers and elders of a district; it thus had control over the clergy and religious affairs in that district. Provinces were to be established throughout England, according to the Westminster Assembly, which in turn were to be subdivided into classes.

[5] Adam Stewart, a Scot who, using only initials, pamphleteered for orthodox Presbyterianism; he was a member of both Assembly and Parliament.

[6] Samuel Rutherford (1600?–1661), author of *Plea for Presbytery* (1642) and Scots member of the Assembly from 1643 through 1647.

Men whose life, learning, faith and pure intent
   Would have bin held in high esteem with *Paul*   10
Must now be nam'd and printed Hereticks
By shallow *Edwards*[7] and Scotch what d'ye call;[8]
   But we doe hope to find out all your tricks,
   Your plots and packings wors then those of *Trent*,[9]
            That so the Parlament   15
May with their wholsom and preventive sheares
Clip your Phylacteries[10] though bauk your eares
            And succour our just feares
When they shall read this cleerly in your charge
New Presbyter is but old Preist writt large.[11]   20

                    (early 1647 ?)

[PSALMS 80–88]

In accord with usual practice in printing Biblical texts, Milton pointed out in the first edition of these omitted psalms
that "all but what is in a different Character (i.e., italicized)
are the very words of the text, Translated from the Original."
The nine psalms were rendered in the common measure

[7] Thomas Edwards (1599–1647), author of *Gangraena* (1646),
subtitled, "a Catalogue and Discovery of many of the Errours,
Heresies, Blasphemies and pernicious Practices of the Sectaries of
this time," and of *The Casting down of the last Stronghold of
Satan, or a Treatise against Toleration and pretended Liberty of
Conscience* (1647).

[8] Robert Baillie (1599–1662), another Scots member of the Assembly (until 1646), who directed his attacks against the Independents.

[9] The Council of Trent, opened in 1545, undertook the reform
of the Church in three separate synods through 1563, but any
hope of reconciliation with the Protestants was thwarted by dog-
matic decisions and a voting procedure which packed the Council
in the Pope's favor.

[10] square leather boxes containing scriptural passages, worn by
Jews at prayer. But they became symbols of hypocrisy since they
were worn openly by the Pharisees only to impress others (Matt.
xxiii. 5). However, such ministers as Milton indicts will not be removed from future service to the Church—the meaning of the
image of not cutting off (bauking) their ears (see Donald C.
Dorian, *MLN*, LVI, 1941, 63). William Prynne, who is referred
to in the original version of this line in the TM, had both ears cut
off in 1637 for his attack against episcopacy.

[11] "Preist" and the longer "Presbyter" both derive from the
Greek *presbyteros*.

(ballad stanza) of standard psalters (e.g., Sternhold and Hopkins), paraphrasing rather than translating, and expanding or compressing original verses as desired. Marginal notes cited the Hebrew (or a more literal translation). Written in April 1648 during the Civil Wars, the subject matter and tone of the psalms may reflect Milton's dejection from the course of events and his hope for the future under enlightened leadership. See also William B. Hunter, Jr.'s discussion in *PQ*, XL (1961), 485–94.

SONNET 15

Fairfax,[1] whose name in armes through *Europe* rings,
   Filling each mouth with envy, or with praise,
   And all her jealous monarchs with amaze,
   And rumors loud, that daunt remotest kings,
Thy firm unshak'n vertue ever brings   5
   Victory home, though new rebellions raise
   Thir Hydra heads, and the fals *North*[2] displaies
   Her brok'n league, to imp her serpent wings,
O yet a nobler task awaits thy hand;[3]
   For what can Warrs[4] but endless warr still breed,   10
   Till Truth, and Right from Violence be freed,
And Public Faith cleard from the shamefull brand
   Of Public Fraud. In vain doth Valour bleed
   While Avarice, and Rapine share the land.

(Aug. 1648)

[1] Sir Thomas Fairfax (1612–1671), commander in chief of the Parliamentarian army, who, amongst other victories, captured Colchester on August 27, 1648, after a seventy-five day siege, at the end of the Second Civil War.

[2] Scotland. After having entered into the Solemn League and Covenant with Parliament on Sept. 25, 1643, the Scots broke the League by invading England in August under James, Duke of Hamilton. Since joining the Parliamentarians had impaired her usually serpentine wings, Milton is saying, Scotland has now imped them (repaired them by inserting new feathers) through a return to treacherous action.

[3] However, Fairfax resigned his military command in June 1650 because of unwillingness to attack Scotland unless provoked by invasion.

[4] that is, specifically, the current Civil Wars.

Verse from *Pro Populo Anglicano defensio*

Who released to Salmasius[1] his "hundred"[2] / and taught the magpie to presume our words? / Master of art the belly, and the hundred / Jacobuses,[3] the inwards of the purse of the exiled king, led him. / Because if a hope of deceitful coin glistened, [5] / this fellow, who lately threatened to demolish the supremacy / of the Pope,[4] the Antichrist, with a single puff, / would gratuitously sing the song of the Cardinals.[5]

(1650)

SONNET 16

Cromwell, our cheif of men, who through a cloud
    Not of warr onely, but detractions rude,
    Guided by faith and matchless Fortitude
    To peace and truth thy glorious way hast plough'd,
And on the neck of crowned Fortune proud   5
    Hast reard Gods Trophies and his work pursu'd,
    While *Darwen* stream with blood of Scots imbru'd,
    And *Dunbarr* feild resounds thy praises loud,
And *Worcesters* laureat wreath;[1] yet much remains
    To conquer still; peace hath her victories   10

[1] Claude de Saumaise (1588–1653), who condemned the English regicides in *Defensio regia pro Carolo I ad Serenissimum Magnæ Britanniæ regem Carolum II* (1649); *Pro Populo Anglicano defensio* was written as a reply.

[2] a subdivision of an English shire. Salmasius attempted to turn English terms into Latin (here "Hundreda"); Milton is ridiculing his spurious knowledge of English law.

[3] The Jacobus, named for James I, was a gold coin worth about twenty-two shillings. Salmasius was reputed to be persuaded to write *Defensio regia* for a hundred Jacobuses; this is denied in *Claudii Salmasii Ad Johannem Miltonum Responsio* (1660), p. 270.

[4] Salmasius had attacked the supremacy of the Pope in *De primatu papæ* (1645).

[5] the ecclesiastical officers.

[1] Cromwell was victorious against the Scots at the battle near Preston on the Darwen, Aug. 17–20, 1648; at Dunbar, Scotland, Sept. 3, 1650; and at Worcester, Sept. 3, 1651.

No less renown'd then warr, new foes arise
Threatning to bind our souls with secular chains:[2]
    Help us to save free Conscience from the paw
    Of hireling wolves whose Gospell is their maw.[3]

                    (May 1652)

SONNET 17

Vane,[1] young in yeares, but in sage counsell old,
    Then whom a better Senator ne're held
    The helm of *Rome*, when gowns not armes repell'd
    The feirce *Epeirot* and th' *African* bold,[2]
Whether to settle peace or to unfold   5
    The drift of hollow states[3] hard to be spell'd,
    Then to advise how warr may best, upheld,

[2] Fifteen proposals were offered in Mar. 1652 to the Committee for the Propagation of the Gospel by some of its members, recommending that the clergy be supported by the State. Spiritual matters ("our souls") would thus be subject to "secular chains." To maintain freedom of moral action, Milton believed, no excess or undue manner of giving or taking recompense can exist in the church (*Hirelings*, p. 8). The gospel should not be used for remuneration, nor should we listen to those who are thinking only of their own stomachs and pleasures.

[3] John x. 12: "But he that is an hireling, and not the shepherd, whose own the sheep are not, seeth the wolf coming, and leaveth the sheep, and fleeth: and the wolf catcheth them, and scattereth the sheep."

[1] Sir Henry Vane the Younger (1613–1662), councillor of state, one of the commissioners who settled the union with Scotland and its civil government (Dec. 1651–Mar. 1652), and committeeman appointed to establish relations and alliances with European powers.

[2] The Roman Senate rejected peace with Pyrrhus of Epeirus despite his victories at Heraclea (280 B.C.) and Ausculam (279 B.C.), and rallied the people in 216 B.C. to stave off Hannibal, the Carthaginian leader, after his successes in 218–217.

[3] the United Provinces (the Netherlands); Milton puns on the name "Holland" with its low-lying land and on its alleged insincerity. The Navigation Act of Oct. 1651, aiming at breaking Dutch maritime supremacy, precipitated the first Anglo-Dutch War in 1652. Vane endeavored to maintain peace, but ended negotiations in June when it became evident that the Dutch did not really want peace. Like the Epeirots and the Carthaginians, the Dutch were initially successful.

Move by her two main nerves, Iron and Gold[4]
In all her equipage; besides to know
Both spirituall power and civill, what each means,   10
What severs each thou hast learnt, which few have don.
The bounds of either sword[5] to thee we ow.
Therfore on thy firm hand religion leans
In peace, and reck'ns thee her eldest son.

(June ? 1652)

PSALM 1[1]

Blest is the man who hath not walk'd astray
In counsel of the wicked, and i'th way
Of sinners hath not stood, and in the seat
Of scorners hath not sate. But in the great
Jehovahs Law is ever his delight,   5
And in his Law he studies day and night.
He shall be as a tree which planted grows
By watry streams, and in his season knows

[4] Among others Cicero (*Philippics*, V, 2) called money the nerves of war, and Machiavelli (*Discourses*, II, x) compared armed force as iron sinew. The lines allude to Vane's activities as member of the committee of defence and as treasurer of the navy.

[5] the spiritual sword and the civil sword. Vane advocated broad religious tolerance, arguing against the proposals of the committee for the propagation of faith; in this he showed awareness of the limits and the separation of these powers. His example not followed, it was necessary to counsel Richard Cromwell and Parliament further in 1659: "both commonwealth and religion will at length, if ever, flourish in Christendom, when either they who govern discern between civil and religious, or they only who so discern shall be admitted to govern" (*Treatise of Civil Power*, p. A5^r).

[1] The following eight psalms experiment with various meters, rhyme schemes, and rhythms, perhaps as exercises prefatory to renewed poetic activity. It is probably significant that their run-on lines and frequent full medial stops move close to the continuity of rhythm in the blank verse of *PL*; Hunter ("Sources," p. 143) remarks that "their syllabic nature is the same as that of *PL*." These translations were undoubtedly important in the full development of reversed feet (e.g., in No. 7) and the displaced caesura (e.g., in No. 2) which characterize Milton's mature poetry. Milton makes no attempt in these close translations to maintain the verse structure of either the Hebrew originals or standard English renditions.

Parker ("Date of *SA*," pp. 161 ff.) calls attention to the anguished entreaty and sense of God's protection in these psalms, which may reflect personal afflictions.

To yield his fruit, and his leaf shall not fall,
And what he takes in hand shall prosper all.   10
Not so the wicked, but as chaff which fann'd
The wind drives, so the wicked shall not stand
In judgment, or abide their tryal then,
Nor sinners in th' assembly of just men.
For the Lord knows th' upright way of the just,   15
And the way of bad men to ruin must.

(Aug. 7 ?, 1653)

PSALM 2[1]

Why do the Gentiles tumult, and the Nations
    Muse a vain thing, the Kings of th' earth upstand
    With power, and Princes in their Congregations
Lay deep their plots together through each Land,
    Against the Lord and his Messiah dear.   5
    Let us break off, say they, by strength of hand
Their bonds, and cast from us, no more to wear,
    Their twisted cords: he who in Heav'n doth dwell
    Shall laugh, the Lord shall scoff them, then severe
Speak to them in his wrath, and in his fell   10
    And fierce ire trouble them; but I saith hee
    Anointed have my King (though ye rebell)
On Sion my holi'hill. A firm decree
    I will declare; the Lord to me hath said
    Thou art my Son I have begotten thee   15
This day; ask of me, and the grant is made;
    As thy possession I on thee bestow
    Th' Heathen, and as thy conquest to be sway'd
Earths utmost bounds: them shalt thou bring full low
    With Iron Scepter bruis'd, and them disperse   20
    Like to a potters vessel shiver'd so.
And now be wise at length ye Kings averse
    Be taught ye Judges of the earth; with fear
    Jehovah serve, and let your joy converse
With trembling; kiss the Son least he appear   25
    In anger and ye perish in the way
    If once his wrath take fire like fuel sere.
Happy all those who have in him their stay.

(Aug. 8, 1653)

---

[1] Here Milton used Dante's *terza rima* or, as he labeled these stanzas, *terzetti,* but the lines are not end-stopped.

PSALM 3

When he fled from Absalom.

Lord how many are my foes,
       How many those
   That in arms against me rise.
       Many are they
   That of my life distrustfully thus say,   5
No help for him in God there lies.
But thou Lord art my shield my glory,
       Thee through my story
   Th' exalter of my head I count;
       Aloud I cry'd   10
Unto Jehovah, he full soon reply'd
And heard me from his holy mount.
I lay and slept, I wak'd again,
       For my sustain
   Was the Lord. Of many millions   15
       The populous rout
   I fear not though incamping round about
They pitch against me their Pavillions.
Rise Lord, save me my God for thou
       Hast smote ere now   20
   On the cheek-bone all my foes,
       Of men abhorr'd
   Hast broke the teeth. This help was from the Lord;
Thy blessing on thy people flows.

(Aug. 9, 1653)

PSALM 4

Answer me when I call
God of my righteousness;
In straits and in distress
Thou didst me disinthrall
And set at large; now spare,   5
   Now pity me, and hear my earnest praier.
Great ones how long will ye
My glory have in scorn,
How long be thus forborn
Still to love vanity,   10
To love, to seek, to prize
   Things false and vain and nothing else but lies?

Yet know the Lord hath chose,
Chose to himself apart
The good and meek of heart   15
(For whom to chuse he knows);
Jehovah from on high
   Will hear my voyce what time to him I crie.
Be aw'd, and do not sin,
Speak to your hearts alone,   20
Upon your beds, each one,
And be at peace within.
Offer the offerings just
   Of righteousness and in Jehovah trust.
Many there be that say   25
Who yet will shew us good?
Talking like this worlds brood;
But Lord, thus let me pray,
On us lift up the light,
   Lift up the favour of thy count'nance bright.   30
Into my heart more joy
And gladness thou hast put
Then when a year of glut
Their stores doth over-cloy
And from their plenteous grounds   35
   With vast increase their corn and wine abounds.
In peace at once will I
Both lay me down and sleep
For thou alone dost keep
Me safe where ere I lie: 40
As in a rocky Cell
   Thou Lord alone in safety mak'st me dwell.

       (Aug. 10, 1653)

PSALM 5

Jehovah to my words give ear
   My meditation waigh,
The voyce of my complaining hear
My King and God for unto thee I pray.
   Jehovah thou my early voyce   5
      Shalt in the morning hear,
   I'th morning I to thee with choyce
Will rank my praiers, and watch till thou appear.

For thou art not a God that takes
   In wickedness delight,   10
Evil with thee no biding makes
Fools or mad men stand not within thy sight.
   All workers of iniquity
     Thou hat'st; and them unblest
   Thou wilt destroy that speak a lie;   15
The bloodi' and guileful man God doth detest.
   But I will in thy mercies dear,
     Thy numerous mercies go
   Into thy house; I in thy fear
Will towards thy holy temple worship low.   20
   Lord lead me in thy righteousness,
     Lead me because of those
   That do observe if I transgress,
Set thy wayes right before, where my step goes.
   For in his faltring mouth unstable   25
     No word is firm or sooth;
   Their inside, troubles miserable;
An open grave their throat, their tongue they smooth.
   God, find them guilty, let them fall
     By their own counsels quell'd;   30
   Push them in their rebellions all
Still on; for against thee they have rebell'd;
   Then all who trust in thee shall bring
     Their joy, while thou from blame
   Defend'st them, they shall ever sing   35
And shall triumph in thee, who love thy name.
   For thou Jehovah wilt be found
     To bless the just man still,
   As with a shield thou will surround
Him with thy lasting favour and good will.   40

        (Aug. 12, 1653)

PSALM 6

Lord in thine anger do not reprehend me
   Nor in thy hot displeasure me correct;
Pity me Lord for I am much deject,
   Am very weak and faint; heal and amend me,
For all my bones, that even with anguish ache,   5
   Are troubled, yea my soul is troubled sore;
And thou O Lord how long? turn Lord, restore
   My soul, O save me for thy goodness sake

For in death no remembrance is of thee;
   Who in the grave can celebrate thy praise?   10
Wearied I am with sighing out my dayes,
   Nightly my Couch I make a kind of Sea;
My Bed I water with my tears; mine Eie
   Through grief consumes, is waxen old and dark
I'th midst of all mine enemies that mark.   15
   Depart all ye that work iniquitie.
Depart from me, for the voice of my weeping
   The Lord hath heard, the Lord hath heard my praier
My supplication with acceptance fair
   The Lord will own, and have me in his keeping.   20
Mine enemies shall all be blank and dash't
   With much confusion; then grow red with shame,
They shall return in hast the way they came
   And in a moment shall be quite abash't.

(Aug. 13, 1653)

PSALM 7

Upon the words of Chush *the* Benjamite *against him.*

Lord my God to thee I flie,
Save me and secure me under
Thy protection while I crie,
Least as a Lion (and no wonder)
He hast to tear my Soul asunder   5
Tearing and no rescue nigh.

Lord my God if I have thought
Or done this, if wickedness
Be in my hands, if I have wrought
Ill to him that meant me peace,   10
Or to him have render'd less,
And not freed my foe for naught;

Let th' enemy pursue my soul
And overtake it, let me tread
My life down to the earth and roul   15
In the dust my glory dead,
In the dust and there outspread
Lodge it with dishonour foul.

Rise Jehovah in thine ire
Rouze thy self amidst the rage   20
Of my foes that urge like fire;
And wake for me, their furi' asswage;
Judgment here thou didst ingage
And command which I desire.

So th' assemblies of each Nation   25
Will surround thee, seeking right,
Thence to thy glorious habitation
Return on high and in their sight.
Jehovah judgeth most upright
All people from the worlds foundation.   30

Judge me Lord, be judge in this
According to my righteousness
And the innocence which is
Upon me: cause at length to cease
Of evil men the wickedness   35
And their power that do amiss.

But the just establish fast,
Since thou art the just God that tries
Hearts and reins. On God is cast
My defence, and in him lies,   40
In him who both just and wise
Saves th' upright of heart at last.

God is a just Judge and severe,
And God is every day offended;
If th' unjust will not forbear,   45
His Sword he whets, his Bow hath bended
Already, and for him intended
The tools of death, that waits him near.

(His arrows purposely made he
For them that persecute.) Behold   50
He travels big with vanitie,
Trouble he hath conceav'd of old
As in a womb, and from that mould
Hath at length brought forth a lie.

He dig'd a pit, and delv'd it deep,   55
And fell into the pit he made;
His mischief that due course doth keep,
Turns on his head, and his ill trade
Of violence will undelay'd
Fall on his crown with ruin steep.   60

Then will I Jehovah's praise
According to his justice raise
And sing the Name and Deitie
Of Jehovah the most high.

       (Aug. 13, 1653)

PSALM 8

O Jehovah our Lord, how wondrous great
  And glorious is thy name through all the earth!
So as above the Heav'ns thy praise to set
  Out of the tender mouths of latest birth,

Out of the mouths of babes and sucklings thou   5
  Hast founded strength because of all thy foes
To stint th' enemy, and slack th' avengers brow
  That bends his rage thy providence t'oppose.

When I behold thy Heav'ns, thy Fingers art,
  The Moon and Starrs which thou so bright hast set   10
In the pure firmament, then saith my heart,
  O what is man that thou remembrest yet,

And think'st upon him; or of man begot
  That him thou visit'st and of him art found;
Scarce to be less then Gods, thou mad'st his lot,   15
  With honour and with state thou hast him crown'd.

O're the works of thy hand thou mad'st him Lord,
  Thou hast put all under his lordly feet,
All Flocks, and Herds, by thy commanding word,
  All beasts that in the field or forrest meet.   20

Fowl of the Heav'ns, and Fish that through the wet
  Sea-paths in shoals do slide. And know no dearth.
O Jehovah our Lord, how wondrous great
  And glorious is thy name through all the earth.

       (Aug. 14, 1653)

Verse from *Defensio secunda*

Rejoice, mackerel, and whosoever is of the fish in the deep, /
who may inhabit through the winter the frigid, chilling seas!
/ That good knight Salmasius[1] in pity meditates / to enwrap
your nudity; / and abounding in paper he is furnishing for
you [5] / paper garments exhibiting the arms / and name
and honor of Claudius Salmasius, / so that through all the
fish-market you may deport yourselves / the knight's followers, in cases right for papers and in little boxes, / most pleasing to men wiping their noses on their sleeve.[2] [10]

(1654 ?)

SONNET 18

Avenge O Lord thy slaughter'd Saints, whose bones
 Lie scatter'd on the *Alpine* mountains cold,[1]
 Ev'n them who kept thy truth so pure of old
 When all our Fathers worship't Stocks and Stones,[2]
Forget not: in thy book record their groans   5
 Who were thy Sheep and in their antient fold
 Slain by the bloody *Piemontese* that roll'd

[1] For Salmasius, see note to the verse from *Defensio prima*.
The likeness of his name to Latin *salmo* (the salmon) and his presentation with the indiscriminately conferred Order of St. Michael
by Louis XIII made Salmasius the target of a punning sneer.
 [2] "A cant appellation among the Romans for fishmongers," according to Thomas Warton.

---

[1] The "slaughter'd Saints" were the Vaudois (descendants of the
Waldenses) who lived in the foothills of the Alps. The Waldenses,
followers of Peter Waldo, around 1179 broke with the Papacy over
dogmas and practices which in their judgment had developed after
Apostolic times. Like them, the Vaudois believed the Bible to be
the sole guide to salvation. In an effort to stamp out rising heresies
and thus win papal favor, the Duke of Savoy ordered the Vaudois
to repudiate their dissent, thereby inspiring a fanatic army of
Savoyards, French, and Irish to an attack on them on Apr. 24,
1655. Among the Miltonic state papers are letters from Cromwell
requesting the cooperation of Sweden, the United Provinces, the
Swiss Cantons, and others in putting an end to the persecution,
which continued through October.
 [2] As David S. Berkeley pointed out (*Explicator*, XV, 1957, item
58), Milton thought of the idolaters in Jer. ii. 27, who say "to a
stock, Thou art my father; and to a stone, Thou hast brought me
forth."

Mother with Infant down the Rocks.[3] Their moans
The Vales redoubl'd to the Hills, and they
    To Heav'n. Their martyr'd blood and ashes sow[4]   10
O're all th' *Italian* fields where still doth sway
The triple Tyrant:[5] that from these may grow
    A hunderd-fold,[6] who having learnt thy way
Early may fly the *Babylonian* wo.[7]

(May ? 1655)

SONNET 19

When I consider how my light is spent,
    E're half my days[1] in this dark world and wide,
    And that one Talent which is death to hide
    Lodg'd with me useless, though my Soul more bent
To serve therewith my Maker, and present   5

[3] Sir Samuel Morland, Cromwell's representative to Savoy, detailed such charges in *The History of the Evangelical Churches of the Valleys of Piemont* (1658).

[4] "Blood of martyrs is the seed of the Church" (Tertullian, *Apologeticus*, 50). The whore of Babylon (which Milton and other Protestants identified with the Roman Catholic Church) is "drunken with the blood of the saints, and with the blood of the martyrs of Jesus" (Rev. xvii. 6).

[5] the Pope; compare the poem on the Gunpowder Plot beginning "James derided," n. 2.

[6] To the parable of the sower, whose seed "bringeth forth, some an hundredfold" (Matt. xiii. 3–23), suggests Kester Svendsen (*Shakespeare Ass'n. Bulletin*, XX, 1945, p. 155, n. 12), Milton added the legend of Cadmus, who sowed dragon's teeth from which sprang up armed warriors. It is interesting to note that this is the hundredth word in the sonnet.

[7] The fall and desolation of Babylon is described in Jer. li and Rev. xviii; in its fall will be "found the blood of prophets, and of saints, and all that were slain upon the earth" (Rev. v. 24).

[1] that is, probably before he had reached the age of fifty. If so, Milton may have thought of the Lord's words after the scourging and purifying of Israel: "There shall be no more thence an infant of days, nor an old man that hath not filled his days; for the child shall die an hundred years old but the sinner being a hundred years old shall be accursed" (Isa. lxv. 20). The phrase has frequently been interpreted in terms of normal life span and the Biblical three score and ten years, requiring an earlier date of composition. Maurice Kelley reviews the external evidence for dating in 1655 in *Seventeenth-Century News*, XI (1953), 29.

My true account, least he returning chide;[2]
Doth God exact day labour, light deny'd,[3]
I fondly[4] ask; but patience to prevent
That murmur, soon replies, God doth not need
Either man's work or his own gifts, who best   10
Bear his mild yoak,[5] they serve him best, his State
Is Kingly. Thousands at his bidding speed
And post o're Land and Ocean without rest:
They also serve who only stand[6] and wait.

(*Oct.* ? *1655*)

SONNET 20[1]

Lawrence of vertuous Father vertuous Son,[2]
Now that the Fields are dank, and ways are mire,
Where shall we sometimes meet, and by the fire

[2] The use of the parable of the talents (Matt. xxv. 14–30) emphasizes both Milton's service despite blindness and his single-purposed ability "to reason against that man" who has brought oppression to God's children (*Reason*, p. 35). In a letter to a friend in the TM, Milton also mentioned "that command in the gospel set out by the terrible seasing of him that hid the talent"; and in *Reason* (p. 35) he spoke of "those few talents which God at that present had lent me."

[3] In the letter to a friend he remarked "that the day is at hand wherin Christ commands all to labour while there is light" (John ix. 4); with this command Jesus turned to heal the blind man. Behind the play of "light" and "dark" are the further words of Jesus: "Yet a little while is the light with you. Walk while ye have the light, lest darkness come upon you" (John xii. 35).

[4] foolishly.

[5] Harry F. Robins (*RES*, VII, 1956, 360–66) first noted the pertinency of Christ's answer to those who would be righteous: "Come unto me, all ye that labour and are heavy laden . . . Take my yoke upon you, and learn of me . . . For my yoke is easy and my burden is light" (Matt. xi. 28–30).

[6] The word indicates that Milton is attentively ready to serve God; he is not sitting down.

[1] Milton's note of invitation to conversation and a "neat repast" unites the verse epistle and sonnet in a gentle admonition to those who would allow no lightness in their lives. The echoes of Horace's invitations in *Odes*, I, iv, and I, xi, for example, underline the aptness of style here and in *Son.* 21.

[2] Edward Lawrence, who died in 1657, was a member of Parliament; his father was Henry Lawrence, Lord President of Cromwell's Council of State (1653–1659). The line imitates Horace's "O matre pulchra filia pulchrior" (*Odes*, I, xvi, 1).

Help wast a sullen day; what may be won
From the hard Season gaining: time will run   5
    On smoother, till *Favonius*[3] re-inspire
    The frozen earth; and cloth in fresh attire
    The Lillie and Rose, that neither sow'd nor spun.[4]
What neat repast shall feast us, light and choice,
    Of Attick tast,[5] with wine, whence we may rise   10
    To hear the lute well toucht, or artfull voice
Warble immortal notes and *Tuskan*[6] air?
    He who of those delights can judge, and spare[7]
    To interpose them oft, is not unwise.

(Oct.–Nov. 1655)

SONNET 21

Cyriack,[1] whose Grandsire on the Royal Bench
    Of Brittish *Themis*, with no mean applause
    Pronounc't and in his volumes taught our Laws,[2]
    Which others at their Barr so often wrench;
To day deep thoughts resolve with me to drench   5
    In mirth, that after no repenting draws;
    Let *Euclid* rest and *Archimedes* pause,
    And what the *Swede* intends and what the *French*.[3]

---

[3] the west wind (Zephyr), husband of Chloris, goddess of spring.

[4] "Consider the lilies of the field, how they grow; they toil not, neither do they spin" (Matt. vi. 28).

[5] explained by "light and choice."

[6] Italian.

[7] "spare time" as Fraser Neiman (*PMLA*, LXIV, 1949, 480–83) and Elizabeth Jackson (*PMLA*, LXV, 1950, 328–29) illustrate.

---

[1] Cyriack Skinner (1627–1700), Milton's student at Aldersgate Street and probable amanuensis, was a lawyer from Lincoln's Inn. Parker (*TLS*, Sept. 13, 1957, p. 547) argues that he is the author of the so-called Anonymous Life which was written by the scribe of the copies of this sonnet and No. 22 in TM.

[2] Skinner's grandfather Sir Edward Coke (1552–1634), Chief Justice of the King's Bench, was influential in reaching decisions unfavorable to James I concerning constitutional questions. His *Reports* and *The Institutes of the Law of England* are compendia still important to modern-day jurisprudence. Themis was the Greek personification of Justice.

[3] Line 7 refers to mathematical and scientific interests. The current First Northern War against Poland aimed at Swedish annexation of southeastern Baltic areas; the Treaty of Westminster (Oct.

To measure life learn thou betimes, and know
 Toward solid good what leads the nearest way;   10
 For other things mild Heav'n a time ordains,
And disapproves that care, though wise in show,
 ·That with superfluous burden loads the day,
 And when God sends a cheerfull hour, refrains.

(Oct.–Nov. 1655)

SONNET 22

Cyriack, this three years day these eyes, though clear
 To outward view of blemish or of spot,[1]
 Bereft of light thir seeing have forgot,
 Nor to thir idle orbs doth sight appear
Of Sun or Moon or Starr throughout the year,   5
 Or man, or woman. Yet I argue not
 Against heav'ns hand or will, nor bate a jot
 Of heart or hope; but still bear up and steer
Right onward. What supports me dost thou ask?
 The conscience, Friend, t' have lost them overply'd   10
 In liberties defence,[2] my noble task,
Of which all *Europe* talks from side to side.
 This thought might lead me through the worlds vain mask
 Content though blind, had I no better guide.[3]

(Dec. 1655)

12, 1655) between England and France did not settle Mazarin's
relations with Spain as Cromwell wished.

 J. H. Finley, Jr. (*Harvard Studies in Class. Philo.*, XLVIII,
1937, 64–67), reviews the echoes of Horace (such as *Odes*, II, xi,
1–6, to which should be added *Epistles*, I, xi, 22); these lead to
Biblical admonitions of moderation (Eccl. iii. 1–9).

---

 [1] A similar description is found in *Defensio secunda*, p. 42
("from without they are unimpaired, clear and bright without a
cloud").
 [2] referring to *Pro Populo Anglicano defensio*, the writing of
which he said (*Defensio secunda*, p. 47) hastened his loss of sight.
 [3] Perhaps the line owes something to Luke i. 79: God on high
shines forth "To give light to them that sit in darkness and in
the shadow of death, to guide our feet into the way of peace."

SONNET 23

Mee thought I saw my late espoused saint[1]
   Brought to me like *Alcestis* from the grave
   Whom *Joves* great son to her glad husband gave
   Rescu'd from death by force though pale and faint.[2]
Mine as whom washt from spot of child-bed taint   5
   Purification in th' old law did save,[3]
   And such, as yet once more I trust to have
   Full sight of her in heav'n without restraint,
Came vested all in white, pure as her mind:
   Her face was vail'd, yet to my fancied sight   10
   Love, sweetness, goodness in her person shin'd
So clear, as in no face with more delight.
   But O as to imbrace me she enclin'd,
   I wak'd, she fled, and day brought back my night.

(1656–58 ?)

[1] traditionally considered to be Milton's second wife Kátherine Woodcock, whom he married Nov. 12, 1656, but W. R. Parker suggests his first wife Mary Powell (*RES*, XXI, 1945, 235–38). Argument for Mary depends upon the interpretation of ll. 5–9; argument for Katherine depends upon Milton's unsentimental references to Mary in the nuncupative will, interpretation of "late espoused" and ll. 5–9, 10–12, the lack of evidence of the scribe's employment before Jan. 14, 1658, and the etymology of "Katherine." All arguments are reviewed in *NQ*, n.s. III (1956), 202–3. T. B. Stroup (*PQ*, XXXIX, 1960, 125–26) suggests a likeness between Mary and Aeneas' vision of Creusa. Considering the real subject a heavenly vision, Leo Spitzer (*Hopkins Review*, IV, Summer 1951, 17–25) analyzes the organization of the sonnet as a tripartite crescendo drawn from the pagan, the Jewish, and the Christian traditions. Thomas Wheeler (*SP*, LVIII, 1961, 510–15) believes Milton portrays his ideal mate rather than either wife.

[2] Through Apollo's intervention, Admetus was allowed longer life when his wife, Alcestis, consented to die at his destined time. Hercules, considered Jove's son, learning of her noble death, intercepted Thanatos to restore the veiled Alcestis to her husband.

[3] Lev. xii. 5: "But if she bear a maid child, then she shall be unclean two weeks, as in her separation: and she shall continue in the blood of her purifying three score and six days." Mary died about May 5, 1652, after giving birth to Milton's daughter Deborah a few days earlier. Katherine died Feb. 3, 1658, after giving birth to a daughter Katherine on Oct. 19, 1657.

PARADISE LOST[1]

The Measure is *English* Heroic Verse without Rime, as that
of *Homer* in *Greek,* and of *Virgil* in *Latin;* Rime being no
necessary Adjunct or true Ornament of Poem or good Verse,
in longer Works especially, but the Invention of a barbarous

[1] The ten books of the epic in the 1667 edition became twelve
in the second edition (1674) by the division of VII into VII and
VIII, and of X into XI and XII. The early books (I, II, IV) emphasize the nature of the fall from grace and the nature of evil;
the means of regaining grace is expounded in III, in Raphael's
discussion of free will and the revolt of Satan in V, and in the war
in heaven in VI. At first evil seems to dominate (a strong cause
for the former criticial judgment of Satan as hero), but the victory
over Satan counsels Man against the "terrible Example . . . of
disobedience" (VI, 910–11). The later books relate the actual fall
of Adam and Eve and its consequences for Man and his history
thereafter. The poem, beginning classically in the middle of the
action, goes both forward and backward, Raphael bringing the
action up to date and Michael foretelling the future.

The "message" of the epic is that true freedom lies in obedience
—and obedience is not bondage. Man has free will to choose although his choices may be limited. Obedience requires faith in
God and God's omniscience. The fall has thus been considered
"fortunate" since it points to the need for obedience to God's will.

The universe depicted by Milton is complex and reflects the
astronomical theories of his age, including four of the most important ones (compare VIII, 12–168). Basically, however, the created
universe with earth as center consists of ten spheres: those of the
seven planets and the fixed stars, the Crystalline Sphere, and the
outermost primum mobile. Surrounding the universe is boundless
Chaos (II, 890–967), in which is found Hell (II, 570–628). The
middle layer of air (frequently referred to), which lies between
earth and the first sphere of the moon, is the region in which
clouds, winds, rains, snow, thunder, etc., are generated.

The poem, a compendium of the scientific, metaphysical, politi-
cal, moral, and theological doctrines of the times, adheres to the
theory of accommodation: because actual knowledge of God is
beyond the comprehension of man, He "accommodates" or adjusts
what He reveals to the limited, finite understanding of mankind
and to the inadequacies of human vocabulary. He conveys His
truths in words, images, parables, etc., which are accurate and

Age, to set off wretched matter and lame Meeter; grac't indeed since by the use of some famous modern Poets, carried away by Custom, but much to thir own vexation, hindrance, and constraint to express many things otherwise, and for the most part worse then else they would have exprest them. Not without cause therefore some both *Italian* and *Spanish* Poets of prime note have rejected Rime both in longer and shorter Works, as have also long since our best *English* Tragedies, as a thing of it self, to all judicious ears, triveal and of no true musical delight; which consists only in apt Numbers, fit quantity of Syllables, and the sense variously drawn out from one Verse into another, not in the jingling sound of like endings, a fault avoyded by the learned Ancients both in Poetry and all good Oratory. This neglect then of Rime so little is to be taken for a defect, though it may seem so perhaps to vulgar Readers, that it rather is to be esteem'd an example set, the first in *English*, of ancient liberty recover'd to Heroic Poem from the troublesom and modern bondage of Riming.

BOOK I

THE ARGUMENT

This first Book proposes, first in brief, the whole Subject, Mans disobedience, and the loss thereupon of Paradise wherein he was plac't: *Then touches* the prime cause of his fall, the Serpent, or rather *Satan* in the Serpent; who revolting from God, and drawing to his side many Legions of Angels, was by the command of God driven out of Heaven with all his Crew into the great Deep. *Which action past over, the Poem hasts into the midst of things, presenting* Satan with his Angels now fallen into Hell, *describ'd here,* not in the Center *(for Heaven and Earth may be suppos'd as yet not made, certainly not yet accurst)* but in a place of utter darkness, fitliest call'd *Chaos:* Here *Satan* with his Angels lying on the burning Lake, thunder-struck and astonisht, after a certain space recovers, as from confusion, calls up him who next in Order and Dignity lay by him; they confer of thir miserable fall. *Satan* awakens all his Legions, who lay till then in the

complete to the extent that human intellect is capable of grasping them. The Bible, as the foremost revelation of God, is cited throughout for its "types" or "shadows" of God, God's acts and will, and God's accommodation. References to the Bible are generally omitted in the notes because of their profusion and intricacy.

same manner confounded; they rise, thir Numbers, array of
Battel, thir chief Leaders nam'd, according to the Idols known
afterwards in *Canaan* and the Countries adjoyning. To these
Satan directs his Speech, comforts them with hope yet of
regaining Heaven, but tells them lastly of a new World and
new kind of Creature to be created, according to an ancient
Prophesie or report in Heaven; *for that Angels were long before this visible Creation, was the opinion of many ancient
Fathers.* To find out the truth of this Prophesie, and what to
determin thereon he refers to a full Councel. What his Associates thence attempt. *Pandemonium* the Palace of *Satan*
rises, suddenly built out of the Deep: The infernal Peers there
sit in Councel.

Of Mans First Disobedience, and the Fruit
Of that Forbidden Tree, whose mortal tast
Brought Death into the World, and all our woe,
With loss of *Eden,* till one greater Man[2]
Restore us, and regain the blissful Seat,   5
Sing Heav'nly Muse,[3] that on the secret top
Of *Oreb,* or of *Sinai,* didst inspire
That Shepherd,[4] who first taught the chosen Seed,
In the Beginning how the Heav'ns and Earth
Rose out of *Chaos:* Or if *Sion* Hill   10
Delight thee more, and *Siloa's* Brook that flow'd
Fast by the Oracle of God;[5] I thence
Invoke thy aid to my adventrous Song,
That with no middle flight intends to soar
Above th' *Aonian* Mount,[6] while it pursues   15
Things unattempted yet in Prose or Rime.
And chiefly Thou O Spirit, that dost prefer
Before all Temples th' upright heart and pure,
Instruct me, for Thou know'st; Thou from the first
Wast present, and with mighty wings outspread   20
Dove-like satst brooding on the vast Abyss
And mad'st it pregnant: What in me is dark
Illumin, what is low raise and support;
That to the highth of this great Argument
I may assert Eternal Providence,   25

2 Christ.
3 Urania; see also VII, 1.
4 Moses.
5 the temple in Jerusalem, the site of divine revelation.
6 Mt. Parnassus; see *El. 4,* n. 10.

And justifie the wayes of God to men.
    Say first, for Heav'n hides nothing from thy view
Nor the deep Tract of Hell, say first what cause
Mov'd our Grand Parents in that happy State,
Favour'd of Heav'n so highly, to fall off   30
From thir Creator, and transgress his Will
For one restraint, Lords of the World besides?
Who first seduc'd them to that foul revolt?
Th' infernal Serpent; he it was, whose guile
Stird up with Envy and Revenge, deceiv'd   35
The Mother of Mankind, what time his Pride
Had cast him out from Heav'n, with all his Host
Of Rebel Angels, by whose aid aspiring
To set himself in Glory above his Peers,
He trusted to have equal'd the most High,   40
If he oppos'd; and with ambitious aim
Against the Throne and Monarchy of God
Rais'd impious War in Heav'n and Battel proud
With vain attempt. Him the Almighty Power
Hurld headlong flaming from th' Ethereal Skie   45
With hideous ruin and combustion down
To bottomless perdition, there to dwell
In Adamantine Chains and penal Fire,
Who durst defie th' Omnipotent to Arms.
Nine times the Space that measures Day and Night   50
To mortal men, he with his horrid crew
Lay vanquisht, rowling in the fiery Gulf
Confounded though immortal: But his doom
Reserv'd him to more wrath; for now the thought
Both of lost happiness and lasting pain   55
Torments him; round he throws his baleful eyes
That witness'd huge affliction and dismay
Mixt with obdurate pride and stedfast hate:
At once as far as Angels kenn he views
The dismal Situation waste and wild,   60
A Dungeon horrible, on all sides round
As one great Furnace flam'd, yet from those flames
No light, but rather darkness visible
Serv'd only to discover sights of woe,
Regions of sorrow, doleful shades, where peace   65
And rest can never dwell, hope never comes
That comes to all; but torture without end
Still urges, and a fiery Deluge, fed
With ever-burning Sulphur unconsum'd:

Such place Eternal Justice had prepar'd   70
For those rebellious, here thir Prison ordain'd
In utter darkness, and thir portion set
As far remov'd from God and light of Heav'n
As from the Center thrice to th' utmost Pole.[7]
O how unlike the place from whence they fell!   75
There the companions of his fall, o'rewhelm'd
With Floods and Whirlwinds of tempestuous fire,
He soon discerns, and weltring by his side
One next himself in power, and next in crime,
Long after known in *Palestine*, and nam'd   80
Beëlzebub. To whom th' Arch-Enemy,
And thence in Heav'n call'd Satan,[8] with bold words
Breaking the horrid silence thus began.
    If thou beest he; but O how fall'n! how chang'd
From him, who in the happy Realms of Light   85
Cloth'd with transcendent brightness didst outshine
Myriads though bright: If he whom mutual league,
United thoughts and counsels, equal hope
And hazard in the Glorious Enterprize,
Joynd with me once, now misery hath joynd   90
In equal ruin: into what Pit thou seest
From what highth fall'n, so much the stronger prov'd
He with his Thunder: and till then who knew
The force of those dire Arms? yet not for those,
Nor what the Potent Victor in his rage   95
Can else inflict, do I repent or change,
Though chang'd in outward lustre; that fixt mind
And high disdain, from sence of injur'd merit,
That with the mightiest rais'd me to contend,
And to the fierce contention brought along   100
Innumerable force to Spirits arm'd
That durst dislike his reign, and me preferring,
His utmost power with adverse power oppos'd
In dubious Battel on the Plains of Heav'n,
And shook his throne. What though the field be lost?   105
All is not lost; th' unconquerable Will,
And study of revenge, immortal hate,
And courage never to submit or yield:
And what is else not to be overcome?
That Glory never shall his wrath or might   110

[7] The distance between hell and heaven is three times that between earth and the primum mobile, or outermost sphere.

[8] literally, "adversary." "Beelzebub" means "god of flies."

Extort from me. To bow and sue for grace
With suppliant knee, and deifie his power,
Who from the terrour of this Arm so late
Doubted[9] his Empire, that were low indeed,
That were an ignominy and shame beneath   115
This downfall; since by Fate the strength of Gods
And this Empyreal substance cannot fail,
Since through experience of this great event
In Arms not worse, in foresight much advanc't,
We may with more successful hope resolve   120
To wage by force or guile eternal Warr
Irreconcileable, to our grand Foe,
Who now triumphs, and in th' excess of joy
Sole reigning holds the Tyranny of Heav'n.
　So spake th' Apostate Angel, though in pain,   125
Vaunting aloud, but wrackt with deep despair:
And him thus answer'd soon his bold Compeer.
　O Prince, O Chief of many Throned Powers,[10]
That led th' imbattell'd Seraphim to Warr
Under thy conduct, and in dreadful deeds   130
Fearless, endanger'd Heav'ns perpetual King;
And put to proof his high Supremacy,
Whether upheld by strength, or Chance, or Fate,
Too well I see and rue the dire event,
That with sad overthrow and foul defeat   135
Hath lost us Heav'n, and all this mighty Host
In horrible destruction laid thus low,
As far as Gods and Heav'nly Essences
Can perish: for the mind and spirit remains
Invincible, and vigour soon returns,   140
Though all our Glory extinct, and happy state
Here swallow'd up in endless misery.
But what if he our Conquerour (whom I now
Of force believe Almighty, since no less
Then such could have orepow'rd such force as ours),   145
Have left us this our spirit and strength intire
Strongly to suffer and support our pains,
That we may so suffice his vengeful ire,
Or do him mightier service as his thralls
By right of Warr, what e're his business be   150
Here in the heart of Hell to work in Fire,

[9] feared for.
[10] one of the orders of angels, but Milton uses the names of
those orders to signify all the angels.

Or do his Errands in the gloomy Deep;
What can it then avail though yet we feel
Strength undiminisht, or eternal being
To undergo eternal punishment?   155
Whereto with speedy words th' Arch-fiend reply'd.
    Fall'n Cherub, to be weak is miserable
Doing or Suffering: but of this be sure,
To do aught good never will be our task,
But ever to do ill our sole delight,   160
As being the contrary to his high will
Whom we resist. If then his Providence
Out of our evil seek to bring forth good,
Our labour must be to pervert that end,
And out of good still to find means of evil;   165
Which oft times may succeed, so as perhaps
Shall grieve him, if I fail not, and disturb
His inmost counsels from thir destind aim.
But see the angry Victor hath recall'd
His Ministers of vengeance and pursuit   170
Back to the Gates of Heav'n: the Sulphurous Hail
Shot after us in storm, oreblown hath laid
The fiery Surge, that from the Precipice
Of Heav'n receiv'd us falling, and the Thunder,
Wing'd with red Lightning and impetuous rage,   175
Perhaps hath spent his shafts, and ceases now
To bellow through the vast and boundless Deep.
Let us not slip th' occasion, whether scorn,
Or satiate fury yield it from our Foe.
Seest thou yon dreary Plain, forlorn and wild,   180
The seat of desolation, voyd of light,
Save what the glimmering of these livid flames
Casts pale and dreadful? Thither let us tend
From off the tossing of these fiery waves,
There rest, if any rest can harbour there,   185
And reassembling our afflicted[11] Powers,
Consult how we may henceforth most offend
Our Enemy, our own loss how repair,
How overcome this dire Calamity,
What reinforcement we may gain from Hope,   190
If not what resolution from despair.
    Thus Satan talking to his neerest Mate
With Head up-lift above the wave, and Eyes
That sparkling blaz'd, his other Parts besides

[11] overthrown.

Prone on the Flood, extended long and large   195
Lay floating many a rood, in bulk as huge
As whom the Fables name of monstrous size,
Titanian,[12] or Earth-born, that warr'd on Jove,
Briareos or Typhon, whom the Den
By ancient Tarsus held, or that Sea-beast   200
Leviathan,[13] which God of all his works
Created hugest that swim th' Ocean stream:
Him haply slumbring on the Norway foam
The Pilot of some small night-founder'd Skiff,
Deeming some Island, oft, as Sea-men tell,   205
With fixed Anchor in his skaly rind
Moors by his side under the Lee, while Night
Invests the Sea, and wished Morn delayes:
So stretcht out huge in length the Arch-fiend lay
Chain'd on the burning Lake, nor ever thence   210
Had ris'n or heav'd his head, but that the will
And high permission of all-ruling Heav'n
Left him at large to his own dark designs,
That with reiterated crimes he might
Heap on himself damnation, while he sought   215
Evil to others, and enrag'd might see
How all his malice serv'd but to bring forth
Infinite goodness, grace and mercy shewn
On Man by him seduc't, but on himself
Treble confusion, wrath and vengeance pour'd.   220
Forthwith upright he rears from off the Pool
His mighty Stature; on each hand the flames
Drivn backward slope thir pointing spires, and rowl'd
In billows, leave i' th' midst a horrid Vale.
Then with expanded wings he stears his flight   225
Aloft, incumbent on the dusky Air
That felt unusual weight, till on dry Land
He lights, if it were Land that ever burn'd
With solid, as the Lake with liquid fire;
And such appear'd in hue,[14] as when the force   230
Of subterranean wind transports a Hill

[12] the goddess Earth, whose sons, including hundred-armed
Briareus, were giants. Typhon was a giant with a hundred heads.
[13] a whale-like monster, often called a serpent and identified
with Satan.
[14] form, appearance.

Torn from *Pelorus*,[15] or the shatter'd side
Of thundring *Ætna*, whose combustible
And fewel'd entrails thence conceiving Fire,
Sublim'd[16] with Mineral fury, aid the Winds,   235
And leave a singed bottom all involv'd
With stench and smoak: Such resting found the sole
Of unblest feet. Him followed his next Mate,
Both glorying to have scap't the *Stygian* flood
As Gods, and by thir own recover'd strength,   240
Not by the sufferance of supernal Power.
  Is this the Region, this the Soil, the Clime,
Said then the lost Arch-Angel, this the seat
That we must change for Heav'n, this mournful gloom
For that celestial light? Be it so, since he   245
Who now is Sovran can dispose and bid
What shall be right: fardest from him is best
Whom reason hath equald, force hath made supream
Above his equals. Farewel happy Fields
Where Joy for ever dwells: Hail horrours, hail   250
Infernal world, and thou profoundest Hell
Receive thy new Possessor: One who brings
A mind not to be chang'd by Place or Time.
The mind is its own place, and in it self
Can make a Heav'n of Hell, a Hell of Heav'n.   255
What matter where, if I be still the same,
And what I should be, all but less than he
Whom Thunder hath made greater? Here at least
We shall be free; th' Almighty hath not built
Here for his envy, will not drive us hence: 260
Here we may reign secure, and in my choyce
To reign is worth ambition though in Hell:
Better to reign in Hell, then serve in Heav'n.
But wherefore let we then our faithful friends,
Th' associates and copartners of our loss   265
Lye thus astonisht on th' oblivious Pool,[17]
And call them not to share with us their part
In this unhappy Mansion, or once more
With rallied Arms to try what may be yet
Regaind in Heav'n, or what more lost in Hell?   270
  So *Satan* spake, and him *Beëlzebub*

[15] a promontory of Sicily near Mt. Etna, whose eruption is described.
[16] refined.
[17] Lethe, infernal river of forgetfulness.

Thus answer'd. Leader of those Armies bright,
Which but th' Omnipotent none could have foyl'd,
If once they hear that voyce, thir liveliest pledge
Of hope in fears and dangers, heard so oft   275
In worst extreams, and on the perilous edge
Of battel when it rag'd, in all assaults
Thir surest signal, they will soon resume
New courage and revive, though now they lye
Groveling and prostrate on yon Lake of Fire,   280
As we erewhile, astounded and amaz'd,
No wonder, fall'n such a pernicious highth.
   He scarce had ceas't when the superiour Fiend
Was moving toward the shoar; his ponderous shield
Ethereal temper, massy, large and round,   285
Behind him cast; the broad circumference
Hung on his shoulders like the Moon, whose Orb
Through Optic Glass the *Tuscan* Artist[18] views
At Ev'ning from the top of *Fesole,*
Or in *Valdarno,* to descry new Lands,   290
Rivers or Mountains in her spotty Globe.
His Spear, to equal which the tallest Pine
Hewn on *Norwegian* hills, to be the Mast
Of some great Ammiral,[19] were but a wand,
He walkt with to support uneasie steps   295
Over the burning Marl, not like those steps
On Heavens Azure, and the torrid Clime
Smote on him sore besides, vaulted with Fire;
Nathless he so endur'd, till on the Beach
Of that inflamed Sea, he stood and call'd   300
His Legions, Angel Forms, who lay intrans't
Thick as Autumnal Leaves that strow the Brooks
In *Vallombrosa,*[20] where th' *Etrurian* shades
High overarch't imbowr; or scatterd sedge
Afloat, when with fierce Winds *Orion*[21] arm'd   305
Hath vext the Red-Sea Coast, whose waves orethrew
Busiris and his *Memphian* Chivalry,
While with perfidious hatred they pursu'd

[18] Galileo, who lived in Fiesole above the valley of the Arno.
[19] the flagship of a fleet.
[20] near Florence.
[21] the equatorial constellation associated with winter storms. Milton mistakenly identified Busiris, an Egyptian king who persecuted foreigners, with the Pharaoh who pursued the Israelites across the Red Sea (see D. C. Allen, *MLN,* LXV, 1950, 115–16).

The Sojourners of *Goshen*, who beheld
From the safe shore thir floating Carkases   310
And broken Chariot Wheels, so thick bestrown
Abject and lost lay these, covering the Flood,
Under amazement of thir hideous change.
He call'd so loud, that all the hollow Deep
Of Hell resounded. Princes, Potentates,   315
Warriers, the Flowr of Heav'n, once yours, now lost,
If such astonishment as this can sieze
Eternal spirits; or have ye chos'n this place
After the toyl of Battel to repose
Your wearied vertue, for the ease you find   320
To slumber here, as in the Vales of Heav'n?
Or in this abject posture have ye sworn
T' adore the Conquerour? who now beholds
Cherub and Seraph rowling in the Flood
With scatter'd Arms and Ensigns, till anon   325
His swift pursuers from Heav'n Gates discern
Th' advantage, and descending tread us down
Thus drooping, or with linked Thunderbolts
Transfix us to the bottom of this Gulf.
Awake, arise, or be for ever fall'n.   330
    They heard, and were abasht, and up they sprung
Upon the wing, as when men wont to watch
On duty, sleeping found by whom they dread,
Rouse and bestir themselves ere well awake.
Nor did they not perceave the evil plight   335
In which they were, or the fierce pains not feel;
Yet to thir Generals Voyce they soon obeyd
Innumerable. As when the potent Rod
Of *Amrams* Son[22] in *Egypts* evill day
Wav'd round the Coast, up call'd a pitchy cloud   340
Of *Locusts*, warping[23] on the Eastern Wind,
That ore the Realm of impious *Pharaoh* hung
Like Night, and darken'd all the Land of *Nile*:
So numberless were those bad Angels seen
Hovering on wing under the Cope of Hell   345
'Twixt upper, nether, and surrounding Fires;
Till, as a signal giv'n, th' uplifted Spear
Of thir great Sultan waving to direct
Thir course, in even ballance down they light

[22] Moses.
[23] moving forward.

On the firm brimstone, and fill all the Plain;   350
A multitude, like which the populous North
Pour'd never from her frozen loyns, to pass
Rhene or the *Danaw*,[24] when her barbarous Sons
Came like a Deluge on the South, and spread
Beneath *Gibralter* to the *Lybian* sands.[25]   355
Forthwith from every Squadron and each Band
The Heads and Leaders thither hast where stood
Thir great Commander; Godlike shapes and forms
Excelling human, Princely Dignities,
And Powers that earst in Heaven sat on Thrones;   360
Though of thir Names in heav'nly Records now
Be no memorial blotted out and raz'd
By thir Rebellion, from the Books of Life.
Nor had they yet among the Sons of *Eve*
Got them new Names, till wandring ore the Earth,   365
Through Gods high sufferance for the tryal of man,
By falsities and lyes the greatest part
Of Mankind they corrupted to forsake
God thir Creator, and th' invisible
Glory of him that made them, to transform   370
Oft to the Image of a Brute, adorn'd
With gay Religions full of Pomp and Gold,
And Devils to adore for Deities:
Then were they known to men by various Names,
And various Idols through the Heathen World.   375
Say, Muse, thir Names then known, who first, who last,
Rous'd from thir slumber, on that fiery Couch,
At thir great Emperors call, as next in worth
Came singly where he stood on the bare strand,
While the promiscuous croud stood yet aloof?   380
The chief were those who from the Pit of Hell
Roaming to seek thir prey on earth, durst fix
Thir Seats long after next the Seat of God,
Thir Altars by his Altar, Gods ador'd
Among the Nations round, and durst abide   385
Jehovah thundring out of *Sion*, thron'd
Between the Cherubim; yea, often plac'd
Within his Sanctuary it self thir Shrines,
Abominations; and with cursed things
His holy Rites, and solemn Feasts profan'd,   390

[24] Rhine or the Danube.
[25] The Vandals invaded Spain and thence North Africa.

And with thir darkness durst affront his light.
First *Moloch*,[26] horrid King besmear'd with blood
Of human sacrifice, and parents tears,
Though for the noyse of Drums and Timbrels loud
Thir childrens cries unheard, that past through fire   395
To his grim Idol. Him the *Ammonite*
Worshipt in *Rabba* and her watry Plain,
In *Argob* and in *Basan*, to the stream
Of utmost *Arnon*. Nor content with such
Audacious neighbourhood, the wisest heart   400
Of *Solomon* he led by fraud to build
His Temple right against the Temple of God
On that opprobrious Hill,[27] and made his Grove
The pleasant Vally of *Hinnom, Tophet* thence
And black *Gehenna* call'd, the Type of Hell.   405
Next *Chemos*,[28] th' obscene dread of *Moabs* Sons,
From *Aroar* to *Nebo*, and the wild
Of Southmost *Abarim;* in *Hesebon*
And *Horonaim, Seons* Realm, beyond
The flowry Dale of *Sibma* clad with Vines,   410
And *Eleale* to th' *Asphaltick* Pool.[29]
Peor his other Name, when he entic'd
Israel in *Sittim* on thir march from *Nile*
To do him wanton rites, which cost them woe.
Yet thence his lustful Orgies he enlarg'd   415
Ev'n to that Hill of scandal, by the Grove
Of *Moloch* homicide, lust hard by hate;
Till good *Josiah* drove them thence to Hell.
With these came they, who from the bordring flood
Of old *Euphrates* to the Brook[30] that parts   420
Egypt from *Syrian* ground, had general Names
Of *Baalim* and *Ashtaroth*,[31] those male,
These Feminine. For Spirits when they please
Can either Sex assume, or both; so soft
And uncompounded is thir Essence pure,   425

[26] literally, "king"; see *Nativity Ode*, n. 38. He was worshipped
by the Ammonites.
[27] the Mount of Olives (2 Kings xxiii. 13); called also "that Hill
of scandal" (l. 416).
[28] the god of the Moabites, whose lands are cited in the following lines.
[29] the Dead Sea.
[30] the Besor.
[31] plural forms of the Phoenician male and female chief gods.

Not ti'd or manacl'd with joynt or limb,
Nor founded on the brittle strength of bones,
Like cumbrous flesh; but in what shape they choose
Dilated or condens't, bright or obscure,
Can execute thir aerie purposes,   430
And works of love or enmity fulfill.
For these the Race of *Israel* oft forsook
Thir living strength, and unfrequented left
His righteous Altar, bowing lowly down
To bestial Gods; for which thir heads as low   435
Bow'd down in Battel, sunk before the Spear
Of despicable foes. With these in troop
Came *Astoreth*, whom the *Phœnicians* call'd
Astarte, Queen of Heav'n, with crescent Horns;
To whose bright Image nightly by the Moon   440
Sidonian Virgins paid thir Vows and Songs,
In *Sion* also not unsung, where stood
Her Temple on th' offensive Mountain, built
By that uxorious King,[32] whose heart though large,
Beguil'd by fair Idolatresses, fell   445
To Idols foul. *Thammuz*[33] came next behind,
Whose annual wound in *Lebanon* allur'd
The *Syrian* Damsels to lament his fate
In amorous ditties all a Summers day,
While smooth *Adonis* from his native Rock   450
Ran purple to the Sea, suppos'd with blood
Of *Thammuz* yearly wounded: the Love-tale
Infected *Sions* daughters with like heat,
Whose wanton passions in the sacred Porch
Ezekiel saw, when by the Vision led   455
His eye survay'd the dark Idolatries
Of alienated *Judah*. Next came one
Who mourn'd in earnest, when the Captive Ark
Maim'd his brute Image, head and hands lopt off
In his own Temple, on the grunsel[34] edge,   460
Where he fell flat, and sham'd his Worshipers:
Dagon[35] his Name, Sea Monster, upward Man
And downward Fish: yet had his Temple high
Rear'd in *Azotus*, dreaded through the Coast·
Of *Palestine*, in *Gath* and *Ascalon*   465

[32] Solomon.
[33] identified with Adonis; see *Nativity Ode*, n. 38.
[34] threshold.
[35] god of the Philistines, whose chief cities are listed.

And *Accaron* and *Gaza's* frontier bounds.
Him follow'd *Rimmon*, whose delightful Seat
Was fair *Damascus*, on the fertil Banks
Of *Abbana* and *Pharphar*, lucid streams.
He also against the house of God was bold: 470
A Leper[36] once he lost and gain'd a King,
Ahaz his sottish Conquerour, whom he drew
Gods Altar to disparage and displace
For one of *Syrian* mode, whereon to burn
His odious offrings, and adore the Gods   475
Whom he had vanquisht. After these appear'd
A crew who under Names of old Renown,
Osiris, Isis, Orus[37] and thir Train
With monstrous shapes and sorceries abus'd
Fanatic *Egypt* and her Priests, to seek   480
Thir wandring Gods disguis'd in brutish forms
Rather then human. Nor did *Israel* scape
Th' infection when thir borrow'd Gold compos'd
The Calf[38] in *Oreb:* and the Rebel King[39]
Doubl'd that sin in *Bethel* and in *Dan*,   485
Lik'ning his Maker to the Grazed Ox,
Jehovah, who in one Night when he pass'd
From *Egypt* marching, equal'd with one stroke
Both her first born and all her bleating Gods.[40]
Belial came last, then whom a Spirit more lewd   490
Fell not from Heaven, or more gross to love
Vice for it self: To him no Temple stood
Or Altar smoak'd; yet who more oft then hee
In Temples and at Altars, when the Priest
Turns Atheist, as did *Ely's* Sons, who fill'd   495
With lust and violence the house of God.
In Courts and Palaces he also Reigns
And in luxurious Cities, where the noyse
Of riot ascends above thir loftiest Towrs,
And injury and outrage: And when Night   500
Darkens the Streets, then wander forth the Sons
Of *Belial*, flown with insolence and wine.
Witness the Streets of *Sodom*, and that night
In *Gibeah*, when th' hospitable door

[36] Naaman; see 2 Kings v.
[37] See *Nativity Ode*, n. 38.
[38] identified with the Egyptian Apis, a sacred bull.
[39] Jeroboam; see 1 Kings xii. 25–33.
[40] Exod. xii. 29.

Expos'd a Matron to avoid worse rape.[41]   505
These were the prime in order and in might;
The rest were long to tell, though far renown'd,
Th' *Ionian* Gods, of *Javans*[42] Issue held
Gods, yet confest later then Heav'n and Earth
Thir boasted Parents; *Titan*[43] Heav'ns first born   510
With his enormous brood, and birthright seis'd
By younger *Saturn*, he from mightier *Jove*
His own and *Rhea*'s Son like measure found;
So *Jove* usurping reign'd: these first in *Creet*
And *Ida* known, thence on the Snowy top   515
Of cold *Olympus* rul'd the middle Air
Thir highest Heav'n; or on the *Delphian* Cliff,[44]
Or in *Dodona*, and through all the bounds
Of *Doric* Land; or who with *Saturn* old
Fled over *Adria*[45] to th' *Hesperian* Fields,   520
And ore the *Celtic* roam'd the utmost Isles.
All these and more came flocking; but with looks
Down cast and damp, yet such wherein appear'd
Obscure som glimps of joy, to have found thir chief
Not in despair, to have found themselves not lost   525
In loss it self; which on his count'nance cast
Like doubtful hue: but he his wonted pride
Soon recollecting, with high words, that bore
Semblance of worth, not substance, gently rais'd
Thir fainting courage, and dispel'd thir fears.   530
Then strait commands that at the warlike sound
Of Trumpets loud and Clarions be upreard
His mighty Standard; that proud honour claim'd
Azazel as his right, a Cherub tall:
Who forthwith from the glittering Staff unfurld   535
Th' Imperial Ensign, which full high advanc't
Shon like a Meteor streaming to the Wind
With Gemms and Golden lustre rich imblaz'd,
Seraphic arms and Trophies: all the while
Sonorous mettal blowing Martial sounds: 540
At which the universal Host upsent

[41] See Judges xix. 22–28.
[42] Ion, his issue being the Ionian Greeks, but identified with Japeth's son.
[43] Uranus.
[44] Mt. Parnassus.
[45] the Adriatic, then the western lands (Italy, France, the British Isles).

A shout that tore Hells Concave, and beyond
Frighted the Reign of *Chaos* and old Night.[46]
All in a moment through the gloom were seen
Ten thousand Banners rise into the Air   545
With Orient Colours waving: with them rose
A Forrest huge of Spears: and thronging Helms
Appear'd, and serried Shields in thick array
Of depth immeasurable: Anon they move
In perfect *Phalanx* to the *Dorian* mood   550
Of Flutes and soft Recorders; such as rais'd
To highth of noblest temper Hero's old
Arming to Battel, and in stead of rage
Deliberate valour breath'd, firm and unmov'd
With dread of death to flight or foul retreat,   555
Nor wanting power to mitigate and swage
With solemn touches, troubl'd thoughts, and chase
Anguish and doubt and fear and sorrow and pain
From mortal or immortal minds. Thus they
Breathing united force with fixed thought   560
Mov'd on in silence to soft Pipes that charm'd
Thir painful steps o're the burnt soyl; and now
Advanc't in view they stand, a horrid Front
Of dreadful length and dazling Arms, in guise
Of Warriers old with order'd Spear and Shield,   565
Awaiting what command thir mighty Chief
Had to impose: He through the armed Files
Darts his experienc't eye, and soon traverse
The whole Battalion views, thir order due,
Thir visages and stature as of Gods,   570
Thir number last he summs. And now his heart
Distends with pride, and hardning in his strength
Glories: For never since created man,
Met such imbodied force, as nam'd with these
Could merit more then that small infantry[47]   575
Warr'd on by Cranes: though all the Giant brood
Of *Phlegra* with th' Heroic Race were joyn'd
That fought at *Thebes* and *Ilium,* on each side
Mixt with auxiliar Gods; and what resounds
In Fable or *Romance* of *Uthers* Son[48]   580

[46] the area ruled by Chaos and Erebus.
[47] "that Pigmean Race Beyond the *Indian* Mount" (ll. 780–81);
see *Iliad,* III, 1–5, for the battle, and Pliny (VII, vii) for the pyg-
mies' abode.
[48] Arthur.

Begirt with *British* and *Armoric*[49] Knights;
And all who since, Baptiz'd or Infidel
Jousted in *Aspramont* or *Montalban*,
Damasco, or *Marocco*, or *Trebisond*,
Or whom *Biserta* sent from *Afric* shore   585
When *Charlemain* with all his Peerage fell
By *Fontarabbia*. Thus far these beyond
Compare of mortal prowess, yet observ'd
Thir dread commander: he above the rest
In shape and gesture proudly eminent   590
Stood like a Towr; his form had yet not lost
All her Original brightness, nor appear'd
Less then Arch Angel ruind, and th' excess
Of Glory obscur'd: As when the Sun new ris'n
Looks through the Horizontal misty Air   595
Shorn of his Beams, or from behind the Moon
In dim Eclips disastrous twilight sheds
On half the Nations, and with fear of change
Perplexes Monarchs. Dark'n'd so, yet shon
Above them all th' Arch Angel: but his face   600
Deep scars of Thunder had intrencht, and care
Sat on his faded cheek, but under Brows
Of dauntless courage, and considerate Pride
Waiting revenge: cruel his eye, but cast
Signs of remorse and passion to behold   605
The fellows of his crime, the followers rather
(Far other once beheld in bliss) condemn'd
For ever now to have thir lot in pain,
Millions of Spirits for his fault amerc't[50]
Of Heav'n, and from Eternal Splendors flung   610
For his revolt, yet faithfull how they stood,
Thir Glory witherd. As when Heavens Fire
Hath scath'd the Forrest Oaks, or Mountain Pines,
With singed top thir stately growth though bare
Stands on the blasted Heath. He now prepar'd   615
To speak; whereat thir doubl'd Ranks they bend
From wing to wing, and half enclose him round
With all his Peers: attention held them mute.
Thrice he assayd, and thrice in spight of scorn,
Tears such as Angels weep, burst forth: at last   620
Words interwove with sighs found out thir way.

[49] of Brittany.
[50] punished.

O Myriads of immortal Spirits, O Powers
Matchless, but with th' Almighty, and that strife
Was not inglorious, though th' event[51] was dire,
As this place testifies, and this dire change   625
Hateful to utter: but what power of mind
Foreseeing or presaging, from the Depth
Of knowledge past or present, could have fear'd,
How such united force of Gods, how such
As stood like these, could ever know repulse?   630
For who can yet beleeve, though after loss,
That all these puissant Legions, whose exile
Hath emptied Heav'n, shall fail to re-ascend
Self-rais'd, and repossess thir native seat?
For mee be witness all the Host of Heav'n,   635
If counsels different, or danger shun'd
By mee, have lost our hopes. But he who reigns
Monarch in Heav'n, till then as one secure
Sat on his Throne, upheld by old repute,
Consent or custom, and his Regal State   640
Put forth at full, but still his strength conceal'd,
Which tempted our attempt, and wrought our fall.
Henceforth his might we know, and know our own
So as not either to provoke, or dread
New warr, provok't; our better part remains   645
To work in close design, by fraud or guile
What force effected not: that he no less
At length from us may find, who overcomes
By force, hath overcome but half his foe.
Space may produce new Worlds; whereof so rife   650
There went a fame[52] in Heav'n that he ere long
Intended to create, and therein plant
A generation, whom his choice regard
Should favour equal to the Sons of Heav'n:
Thither, if but to pry, shall be perhaps   655
Our first eruption, thither or elsewhere:
For this Infernal Pit shall never hold
Cælestial Spirits in Bondage, nor th' Abyss
Long under darkness cover. But these thoughts
Full Counsel must mature: Peace is despaird,   660
For who can think Submission? Warr then, Warr
Open or understood must be resolv'd.

[51] outcome.
[52] rumor.

Illustrations

THE THIRTEEN ILLUSTRATIONS in this volume all derive from *Paradise Lost. A Poem in Twelve Books. The Authour John Milton. The Fourth Edition, Adorn'd with sculptures,* a folio which Jacob Tonson published by subscription in 1688. The portrait of Milton, by Robert White, is based on William Faithorne's engraving of his authorized portrait of the poet, at the age of 62, made from life, used as the frontispiece of Milton's *History of Britain,* 1670. The details of the face and costume were taken directly from Faithorne's print, but White added the decorative elements surrounding the picture and the tribute by John Dryden.

The twelve other "sculptures" were designed by John Baptist de Medina and engraved by M. Burgess. They constitute a significant contemporary commentary on *Paradise Lost.* See Helen Gardner, "Milton's First Illustrator," *Essays and Studies of the English Association,* n.s. IX (London, 1956), 27–38, and C. H. Collins, "Some Illustrators of Milton's *Paradise Lost* (1688–1850)," *The Library,* 5th ser., III (1948), 1–21, 101–119.

Three Poets, *in three distant* Ages *born,*
Greece, Italy, *and* England *did adorn.*
The First *in loftiness of thought Surpass'd,*
The Next *in* Majesty; *in both the* Last.
The force *of* Nature *cou'd no farther goe:*
To make a Third *she joynd the former two.*

R. White *sculp*:

JOHN MILTON

BOOK I

M.Burgesse sculp.

BOOK II

Medina inven.

MBurg. sculp.

BOOK III

BOOK IV

S. de Medina Inu.   NBurgesse sculp

BOOK V

Nedina inven.

Burg. sculp.

BOOK VI

Medina delin.

Burghers sculp.

BOOK VII

BOOK VIII

B. de Medina Inven.

NBurgesse sculp.

BOOK IX

B. de Medina Inven.   T. Burgesse sculp.

BOOK X

Medina Invent. MBurg. sculp.

BOOK XI

MBurgefse sculp.

BOOK XII

He spake: and to confirm his words, out-flew
Millions of flaming swords, drawn from the thighs
Of mighty Cherubim; the sudden blaze   665
Far round illumin'd hell: highly they rag'd
Against the Highest, and fierce with grasped Arms
Clash'd on thir sounding Shields the din of war,
Hurling defiance toward the Vault of Heav'n.
There stood a Hill not far whose griesly top   670
Belch'd fire and rowling smoak; the rest entire
Shon with a glossie scurff, undoubted sign
That in his womb was hid metallic Ore,
The work of Sulphur. Thither wing'd with speed
A numerous Brigad hasten'd. As when Bands   675
Of Pioners with Spade and Pickax arm'd
Forerun the Royal Camp, to trench a Field,
Or cast a Rampart. Mammon[53] led them on,
Mammon, the least erected Spirit that fell
From heav'n, for ev'n in heav'n his looks and thoughts   680
Were always downward bent, admiring more
The riches of Heav'ns pavement, trod'n Gold,
Then aught divine or holy else enjoy'd
In vision beatific: by him first
Men also, and by his suggestion taught,   685
Ransack'd the Center, and with impious hands
Rifl'd the bowels of thir mother Earth
For Treasures better hid. Soon had his crew
Op'nd into the Hill a spacious wound
And dig'd out ribs of Gold. Let none admire   690
That riches grow in Hell; that soyl may best
Deserve the precious bane. And here let those
Who boast in mortal things, and wondring tell
Of Babel,[54] and the works of Memphian Kings
Learn how thir greatest Monuments of Fame,   695
And Strength and Art are easily outdone
By Spirits reprobate, and in an hour
What in an age they with incessant toyl
And hands innumerable scarce perform.
Nigh on the Plain in many cells prepar'd,   700
That underneath had veins of liquid fire
Sluic'd from the Lake, a second multitude

[53] literally, "wealth."
[54] capital of the tyrant Nimrod, which is compared with the pyramids.

With wondrous Art founded the massie Ore,
Severing each kind, and scum'd the Bullion dross:
A third as soon had form'd within the ground   705
A various mould, and from the boyling cells
By strange conveyance fill'd each hollow nook,
As in an Organ from one blast of wind
To many a row of Pipes the sound-board breaths.
Anon out of the earth a Fabrick huge   710
Rose like an Exhalation, with the sound
Of Dulcet Symphonies and voices sweet,
Built like a Temple, where *Pilasters* round
Were set, and Doric pillars overlaid
With Golden Architrave; nor did there want   715
Cornice or Freeze, with bossy[55] Sculptures grav'n,
The Roof was fretted Gold. Not *Babilon,*
Nor great *Alcairo*[56] such magnificence
Equal'd in all thir glories, to inshrine
Belus or *Serapis*[57] thir Gods, or seat   720
Thir Kings, when *Ægypt* with *Assyria* strove
In wealth and luxurie. Th' ascending pile
Stood fixt her stately highth, and strait the dores
Op'ning thir brazen foulds discover wide
Within, her ample spaces, o're the smooth   725
And level pavement: from the arched roof
Pendant by suttle Magic many a row
Of Starry Lamps and blazing Cressets fed
With *Naphtha* and *Asphaltus* yeilded light
As from a sky. The hasty multitude   730
Admiring enter'd, and the work some praise
And some the Architect: his hand was known
In Heav'n by many a Towred structure high,
Where Scepter'd Angels held thir residence,
And sat as Princes, whom the supreme King   735
Exalted to such power, and gave to rule,
Each in his Hierarchie, the Orders bright.
Nor was his name unheard or unador'd
In ancient *Greece;* and in *Ausonian*[58] land
Men call'd him *Mulciber;*[59] and how he fell   740
From Heav'n, they fabl'd, thrown by angry *Jove*

55 embossed.
56 Memphis, near modern Cairo.
57 Baal or Osiris.
58 Italian.
59 Vulcan, whose fall is recounted in *Iliad,* I, 588–95.

Sheer o're the Chrystal Battlements: from Morn
To Noon he fell, from Noon to dewy Eve,
A Summers day; and with the setting Sun
Dropt from the Zenith like a falling Star,   745
On *Lemnos* th' *Ægæan* Ile: thus they relate,
Erring; for he with this rebellious rout
Fell long before; nor aught avail'd him now
To have built in Heav'n high Towrs; nor did he scape
By all his Engins, but was headlong sent   750
With his industrious crew to build in hell.
Mean while the winged Haralds by command
Of Sovran power, with awful Ceremony
And Trumpets sound throughout the Host proclaim
A solemn Councel forthwith to be held   755
At *Pandæmonium,*[60] the high Capitol
Of Satan and his Peers: thir summons call'd
From every Band and squared Regiment
By place or choice the worthiest; they anon
With hunderds and with thousands trooping came   760
Attended: all access was throng'd, the Gates
And Porches wide, but chief the spacious Hall
(Though like a cover'd field, where Champions bold
Wont ride in arm'd, and at the Soldans chair
Defi'd the best of *Paynim* chivalry   765
To mortal combat or carreer with Lance)
Thick swarm'd, both on the ground and in the air,
Brusht with the hiss of russling wings. As Bees
In spring time, when the Sun with *Taurus*[61] rides,
Pour forth thir populous youth about the Hive   770
In clusters; they among fresh dews and flowers
Flie to and fro, or on the smoothed Plank,
The suburb of thir Straw-built Cittadel,
New rub'd with Baum, expatiate[62] and confer
Thir State affairs. So thick the aerie crowd   775
Swarm'd and were strait'n'd; till the Signal giv'n.
Behold a wonder! they but now who seemd
In bigness to surpass Earths Giant Sons
Now less than smallest Dwarfs, in narrow room
Throng numberless, like that Pigmean Race   780
Beyond the *Indian* Mount, or Faerie Elves,

[60] "all the spirits," and then pejoratively "all the demons."
[61] the Zodiacal sign for Apr. 20–May 20.
[62] walk about.

Whose midnight Revels, by a Forrest side
Or Fountain some belated Peasant sees,
Or dreams he sees, while over-head the Moon
Sits Arbitress, and neerer to the Earth   785
Wheels her pale course, they on thir mirth and dance
Intent, with jocond Music charm his ear;
At once with joy and fear his heart rebounds.
Thus incorporeal Spirits to smallest forms
Reduc'd thir shapes immense, and were at large,   790
Though without number still amidst the Hall
Of that infernal Court. But far within
And in thir own dimensions like themselves
The great Seraphic Lords and Cherubim
In close recess and secret conclave sat   795
A thousand Demy-Gods on golden seats,
Frequent[63] and full. After short silence then
And summons read, the great consult began.

BOOK II

THE ARGUMENT

The Consultation begun, *Satan* debates whether another Battel
be to be hazarded for the recovery of Heaven: some advise
it, others dissuade: A third proposal is prefer'd, mention'd
before by *Satan*, to search the truth of that Prophesie or
Tradition in Heaven concerning another world, and another
kind of creature equal or not much inferiour to themselves,
about this time to be created: Thir doubt who shall be sent
on this difficult search: *Satan* thir chief undertakes alone the
voyage, is honourd and applauded. The Councel thus ended,
the rest betake them several wayes and to several imployments, as thir inclinations lead them, to entertain the time till
Satan return. He passes on his Journey to Hell Gates, finds
them shut, and who sat there to guard them, by whom at
length they are op'n'd, and discover to him the great Gulf
between Hell and Heaven; with what difficulty he passes
through, directed by *Chaos*, the Power of that place, to the
sight of this new World which he sought.

High on a Throne of Royal State, which far
Outshon the wealth of *Ormus*[1] and of *Ind*,

[63] crowded.

---

[1] Hormuz, on the Persian gulf, was famous for precious gems.

Or where the gorgeous East with richest hand
Showrs on her Kings *Barbaric* Pearl and Gold,[2]
Satan exalted sat, by merit rais'd   5
To that bad eminence; and from despair
Thus high uplifted beyond hope, aspires
Beyond thus high, insatiate to pursue
Vain Warr with Heav'n, and by success untaught
His proud imaginations thus displaid.   10
    Powers and Dominions, Deities of Heav'n,
For since no deep within her gulf can hold
Immortal vigor, though opprest and fall'n,
I give not Heav'n for lost. From this descent
Celestial vertues rising, will appear   15
More glorious and more dread then from no fall,
And trust themselves to fear no second fate:
Mee though just right, and the fixt Laws of Heav'n
Did first create your Leader, next, free choice,
With what besides, in Counsel or in Fight,   20
Hath bin achiev'd of merit, yet this loss
Thus farr at least recover'd, hath much more
Establisht in a safe unenvied Throne
Yeilded with full consent. The happier state
In Heav'n, which follows dignity, might draw   25
Envy from each inferior; but who here
Will envy whom the highest place exposes
Formost to stand against the Thunderers aim
Your bulwark, and condemns to greatest share
Of endless pain? where there is then no good   30
For which to strive, no strife can grow up there
From Faction; for none sure will claim in Hell
Precedence, none, whose portion is so small
Of present pain, that with ambitious mind
Will covet more. With this advantage then   35
To union, and firm Faith, and firm accord,
More then can be in Heav'n, we now return
To claim our just inheritance of old,
Surer to prosper then prosperity
Could have assur'd us; and by what best way,   40
Whether of open Warr or covert guile,
We now debate; who can advise, may speak.
    He ceas'd, and next him *Moloc*, Scepter'd King
Stood up, the strongest and the fiercest Spirit

[2] a custom in eastern empires.

That fought in Heav'n; now fiercer by despair: 45
His trust was with th' Eternal to be deem'd
Equal in strength, and rather then be less
Car'd not to be at all; with that care lost
Went all his fear: of God, or Hell, or worse
He reck'd not, and these words thereafter spake.   50
    My sentence is for open Warr: Of Wiles,
More unexpert, I boast not: them let those
Contrive who need, or when they need, not now.
For while they sit contriving, shall the rest,
Millions that stand in Arms, and longing wait   55
The Signal to ascend, sit lingring here
Heav'ns fugitives, and for thir dwelling place
Accept this dark opprobrious Den of shame,
The Prison of his Tyranny who Reigns
By our delay? no, let us rather choose   60
Arm'd with Hell flames and fury all at once
O're Heav'ns high Towrs to force resistless way,
Turning our Tortures into horrid Arms
Against the Torturer; when to meet the noise
Of his Almighty Engin he shall hear   65
Infernal Thunder, and for Lightning see
Black fire and horror shot with equal rage
Among his Angels; and his Throne it self
Mixt with *Tartarean* Sulphur, and strange fire,
His own invented Torments. But perhaps   70
The way seems difficult and steep to scale
With upright wing against a higher foe.
Let such bethink them, if the sleepy drench
Of that forgetful Lake benumm not still,
That in our proper motion we ascend   75
Up to our native seat: descent and fall
To us is adverse.[3] Who but felt of late
When the fierce Foe hung on our brok'n Rear
Insulting, and pursu'd us through the Deep,
With what compulsion and laborious flight   80
We sunk thus low? Th' ascent is easie then;
Th' event is fear'd; should we again provoke
Our stronger, some worse way his wrath may find
To our destruction: if there be in Hell
Fear to be worse destroy'd: what can be worse   85
Then to dwell here, driv'n out from bliss, condemn'd

[3] since angels were made of heavenly quintessence.

In this abhorred deep to utter woe;
Where pain of unextinguishable fire
Must exercise us without hope of end
The Vassals of his anger, when the Scourge   90
Inexorably, and the torturing hour
Calls us to Penance? More destroy'd then thus
We should be quite abolisht and expire.
What fear we then? what doubt we to incense
His utmost ire? which to the highth enrag'd,   95
Will either quite consume us, and reduce
To nothing this essential, happier farr
Then miserable to have eternal being:
Or if our substance be indeed Divine,
And cannot cease to be, we are at worst   100
On this side nothing; and by proof we feel
Our power sufficient to disturb his Heav'n,
And with perpetual inrodes to Allarm,
Though inaccessible, his fatal Throne:
Which if not Victory is yet Revenge.   105
      He ended frowning, and his look denounc'd
Desperate revenge, and Battel dangerous
To less then Gods. On th' other side up rose
Belial, in act more graceful and humane;
A fairer person lost not Heav'n; he seemd   110
For dignity compos'd and high exploit:
But all was false and hollow; though his Tongue
Dropt Manna, and could make the worse appear
The better reason, to perplex and dash
Maturest Counsels: for his thoughts were low;   115
To vice industrious, but to Nobler deeds
Timorous and slothful: yet he pleas'd the ear,
And with perswasive accent thus began.
      I should be much for open Warr, O Peers,
As not behind in hate; if what was urg'd   120
Main reason to perswade immediate Warr,
Did not disswade me most, and seem to cast
Ominous conjecture on the whole success:
When he who most excels in fact of Arms,
In what he counsels and in what excels   125
Mistrustful, grounds his courage on despair
And utter dissolution, as the scope
Of all his aim, after some dire revenge.
First, what Revenge? the Towrs of Heav'n are fill'd
With Armed watch, that render all access   130

Impregnable; oft on the bordering Deep
Encamp thir Legions, or with obscure wing
Scout farr and wide into the Realm of night,
Scorning surprize. Or could we break our way
By force, and at our heels all Hell should rise   135
With blackest Insurrection, to confound
Heav'ns purest Light, yet our great Enemy
All incorruptible would on his Throne
Sit unpolluted, and th' Ethereal mould
Incapable of stain would soon expel   140
Her mischief, and purge off the baser fire
Victorious. Thus repuls'd, our final hope
Is flat despair: we must exasperate
Th' Almighty Victor to spend all his rage,
And that must end us, that must be our cure,   145
To be no more; sad cure; for who would loose,
Though full of pain, this intellectual being,
Those thoughts that wander through Eternity,
To perish rather, swallowd up and lost
In the wide womb of uncreated night,   150
Devoid of sense and motion? and who knows,
Let this be good, whether our angry Foe
Can give it, or will ever? how he can
Is doubtful; that he never will is sure.
Will he, so wise, let loose at once his ire,   155
Belike through impotence, or unaware,
To give his Enemies thir wish, and end
Them in his anger, whom his anger saves
To punish endless? wherefore cease we then?
Say they who counsel Warr, we are decreed,   160
Reserv'd and destin'd to Eternal woe;
Whatever doing, what can we suffer more,
What can we suffer worse? is this then worst,
Thus sitting, thus consulting, thus in Arms?
What when we fled amain, pursu'd and strook   165
With Heav'ns afflicting Thunder, and besought
The Deep to shelter us? this Hell then seem'd
A refuge from those wounds: or when we lay
Chain'd on the burning Lake? that sure was worse.
What if the breath that kindl'd those grim fires   170
Awak'd should blow them into sevenfold rage
And plunge us in the flames? or from above
Should intermitted vengeance arm again
His red right hand to plague us? what if all

Her stores were open'd, and this Firmament   175
Of Hell should spout her Cataracts of Fire,
Impendent horrors, threatning hideous fall
One day upon our heads; while we perhaps
Designing or exhorting glorious warr,
Caught in a fierie Tempest shall be hurl'd   180
Each on his rock transfixt, the sport and prey
Of racking whirlwinds, or for ever sunk
Under yon boyling Ocean, wrapt in Chains;
There to converse with everlasting groans,
Unrespited, unpitied, unrepreev'd,   185
Ages of hopeless end; this would be worse.
Warr therefore, open or conceal'd, alike
My voice disswades; for what can force or guile
With him, or who deceive his mind, whose eye
Views all things at one view? he from heav'ns highth   190
All these our motions vain, sees and derides;
Not more Almighty to resist our might
Then wise to frustrate all our plots and wiles.
Shall we then live thus vile, the Race of Heav'n
Thus trampl'd, thus expell'd to suffer here   195
Chains and these Torments? better these then worse
By my advice; since fate inevitable
Subdues us, and Omnipotent Decree,
The Victors will. To suffer, as to doe,
Our strength is equal, nor the Law unjust   200
That so ordains: this was at first resolv'd,
If we were wise, against so great a foe
Contending, and so doubtful what might fall.
I laugh, when those who at the Spear are bold
And vent'rous, if that fail them, shrink and fear   205
What yet they know must follow, to endure
Exile, or ignominy, or bonds, or pain,
The sentence of thir Conquerour: This is now
Our doom; which if we can sustain and bear,
Our Supream Foe in time may much remit   210
His anger, and perhaps thus farr remov'd
Not mind us not offending, satisfi'd
With what is punish't; whence these raging fires
Will slack'n, if his breath stir not thir flames.
Our purer essence then will overcome   215
Thir noxious vapour, or enur'd not feel,
Or chang'd at length, and to the place conformd
In temper and in nature, will receive

Familiar the fierce heat, and void of pain;
This horror will grow mild, this darkness light, 220
Besides what hope the never-ending flight
Of future dayes may bring, what chance, what change
Worth waiting, since our present lot appeers
For happy though but ill, for ill not worst,
If we procure not to our selves more woe. 225
    Thus *Belial* with words cloath'd in reasons garb
Counsel'd ignoble ease, and peaceful sloath,
Not peace: and after him thus *Mammon* spake.
    Either to disinthrone the King of Heav'n
We warr, if warr be best, or to regain 230
Our own right lost: him to unthrone we then
May hope, when everlasting Fate shall yeild
To fickle Chance, and *Chaos* judge the strife:
The former vain to hope argues as vain
The latter: for what place can be for us 235
Within Heav'ns bound, unless Heav'ns Lord supream
We overpower? Suppose he should relent
And publish Grace to all, on promise made
Of new Subjection; with what eyes could we
Stand in his presence humble, and receive 240
Strict Laws impos'd, to celebrate his Throne
With warbl'd Hymns, and to his Godhead sing
Forc't Halleluiahs; while he Lordly sits
Our envied Sovran, and his Altar breathes
Ambrosial Odours and Ambrosial Flowers, 245
Our servile offerings. This must be our task
In Heav'n, this our delight; how wearisom
Eternity so spent in worship paid
To whom we hate. Let us not then pursue
By force impossible, by leave obtain'd 250
Unacceptable, though in Heav'n, our state
Of splendid vassalage, but rather seek
Our own good from our selves, and from our own
Live to our selves, though in this vast recess,
Free, and to none accountable, preferring 255
Hard liberty before the easie yoke
Of servile Pomp. Our greatness will appear
Then most conspicuous, when great things of small,
Useful of hurtful, prosperous of adverse
We can create, and in what place so e're 260
Thrive under evil, and work ease out of pain
Through labour and indurance. This deep world

Of darkness do we dread? How oft amidst
Thick clouds and dark doth Heav'ns all-ruling Sire
Choose to reside, his Glory unobscur'd,   265
And with the Majesty of darkness round
Covers his Throne; from whence deep thunders roar
Must'ring thir rage, and Heav'n resembles Hell?
As he our darkness, cannot we his Light
Imitate when we please? This Desart soil   270
Wants not her hidden lustre, Gemms and Gold;
Nor want we skill or Art, from whence to raise
Magnificence; and what can Heav'n shew more?
Our torments also may in length of time
Become our Elements, these piercing Fires   275
As soft as now severe, our temper chang'd
Into their temper; which must needs remove
The sensible of pain. All things invite
To peaceful Counsels, and the settl'd State
Of order, how in safety best we may   280
Compose our present evils, with regard
Of what we are and where, dismissing quite
All thoughts of warr: ye have what I advise.
    He scarce had finisht, when such murmur filld
Th' Assembly, as when hollow Rocks retain   285
The sound of blustring winds, which all night long
Had rous'd the Sea, now with hoarse cadence lull
Sea-faring men orewatcht, whose Bark by chance
Or Pinnace anchors in a craggy Bay
After the Tempest: Such applause was heard   290
As *Mammon* ended, and his Sentence pleas'd,
Advising peace: for such another Field
They dreaded worse then Hell: so much the fear
Of Thunder and the Sword of *Michael*
Wrought still within them; and no less desire   295
To found this nether Empire, which might rise
By pollicy, and long process of time,
In emulation opposite to Heav'n.
Which when *Beëlzebub* perceiv'd, then whom,
Satan except, none higher sat, with grave   300
Aspect he rose, and in his rising seem'd
A Pillar of State; deep on his Front engrav'n
Deliberation sat and public care;
And Princely counsel in his face yet shon,
Majestic though in ruin: sage he stood   305
With *Atlantean* shoulders fit to bear

The weight of mightiest Monarchies; his look
Drew audience and attention still as Night
Or Summers Noon-tide air, while thus he spake.
    Thrones and Imperial Powers, off-spring of heav'n,   310
Ethereal Vertues; or these Titles now
Must we renounce, and changing stile be call'd
Princes of Hell? for so the popular vote
Inclines, here to continue, and build up here
A growing Empire; doubtless; while we dream,   315
And know not that the King of Heav'n hath doom'd
This place our dungeon, not our safe retreat
Beyond his Potent arm, to live exempt
From Heav'ns high jurisdiction, in new League
Banded against his Throne, but to remain   320
In strictest bondage, though thus far remov'd,
Under th' inevitable curb, reserv'd
His captive multitude: For he, be sure,
In highth or depth, still first and last will Reign
Sole King, and of his Kingdom loose no part   325
By our revolt, but over Hell extend
His Empire, and with Iron Scepter rule
Us here, as with his Golden those in Heav'n.
What sit we then projecting peace and Warr?
Warr hath determin'd us, and foild with loss   330
Irreparable; tearms of peace yet none
Voutsaf't or sought; for what peace will be giv'n
To us enslav'd, but custody severe,
And stripes, and arbitrary punishment
Inflicted? and what peace can we return,   335
But to our power hostility and hate,
Untam'd reluctance,[4] and revenge though slow,
Yet ever plotting how the Conqueror least
May reap his conquest, and may least rejoyce
In doing what we most in suffering feel?   340
Nor will occasion want, nor shall we need
With dangerous expedition to invade
Heav'n, whose high walls fear no assault or Siege,
Or ambush from the Deep. What if we find
Some easier enterprize? There is a place   345
(If ancient and prophetic fame in Heav'n
Err not) another World, the happy seat
Of som new Race call'd *Man*, about this time

[4] revolt.

To be created like to us, though less
In power and excellence, but favour'd more　　350
Of him who rules above; so was his will
Pronounc'd among the Gods, and by an Oath,
That shook Heav'ns whole circumference, confirm'd.
Thither let us bend all our thoughts, to learn
What creatures there inhabit, of what mould,　　355
Or substance, how endu'd, and what thir Power,
And where thir weakness, how attempted best,
By force or suttlety: Though Heav'n be shut,
And Heav'ns high Arbitrator sit secure
In his own strength, this place may lye expos'd　　360
The utmost border of his Kingdom, left
To their defence who hold it: here perhaps
Som advantagious act may be achiev'd
By sudden onset, either with Hell fire
To waste his whole Creation, or possess　　365
All as our own, and drive as we were driv'n,
The punie habitants, or if not drive,
Seduce them to our Party, that thir God
May prove thir foe, and with repenting hand
Abolish his own works. This would surpass　　370
Common revenge, and interrupt his joy
In our Confusion, and our Joy upraise
In his disturbance; when his darling Sons
Hurl'd headlong to partake with us, shall curse
Thir frail Originals,[5] and faded bliss,　　375
Faded so soon. Advise if this be worth
Attempting, or to sit in darkness here
Hatching vain Empires. Thus *Beëlzebub*
Pleaded his devilish Counsel, first devis'd
By *Satan*, and in part propos'd: for whence,　　380
But from the Author of all ill could Spring
So deep a malice, to confound the race
Of mankind in one root, and Earth with Hell
To mingle and involve, done all to spite
The great Creatour? But thir spite still serves　　385
His glory to augment. The bold design
Pleas'd highly those infernal States, and joy
Sparkl'd in all thir eyes; with full assent
They vote: whereat his speech he thus renews.
　　Well have ye judg'd, well ended long debate,　　390

[5] Adam and Eve.

Synod of Gods, and like to what ye are,
Great things resolv'd, which from the lowest deep
Will once more lift us up, in spight of Fate,
Neerer our ancient Seat; perhaps in view
Of those bright confines, whence with neighbouring Arms   395
And opportune excursion we may chance
Re-enter Heav'n; or else in some mild Zone
Dwell not unvisited of Heav'ns fair Light
Secure, and at the brightning Orient beam
Purge off this gloom; the soft delicious Air,   400
To heal the scarr of these corrosive Fires
Shall breath her balm. But first whom shall we send
In search of this new world, whom shall we find
Sufficient? who shall tempt with wandring feet
The dark unbottom'd infinite Abyss   405
And through the palpable obscure find out
His uncouth[6] way, or spread his aerie flight
Upborn with indefatigable wings
Over the vast abrupt, ere he arrive
The happy Ile; what strength, what art can then   410
Suffice, or what evasion bear him safe
Through the strict Senteries and Stations thick
Of Angels watching round? Here he had need
All circumspection, and we now no less
Choice in our suffrage; for on whom we send,   415
The weight of all and our last hope relies.
   This said, he sat; and expectation held
His look suspence, awaiting who appeer'd
To second, or oppose, or undertake
The perilous attempt: but all sat mute,   420
Pondering the danger with deep thoughts; and each
In others count'nance read his own dismay
Astonisht: none among the choice and prime
Of those Heav'n-warring Champions could be found
So hardie as to proffer or accept   425
Alone the dreadful voyage; till at last
Satan, whom now transcendent glory rais'd
Above his fellows, with Monarchal pride
Conscious of highest worth, unmov'd thus spake.
   O Progeny of Heav'n, Empyreal Thrones,   430
With reason hath deep silence and demurr
Seis'd us, though undismaid: long is the way

[6] unknown.

And hard, that out of Hell leads up to light;
Our prison strong, this huge convex of Fire,
Outrageous to devour, immures us round   435
Ninefold, and gates of burning Adamant
Barr'd over us prohibit all egress.
These past, if any pass, the void profound
Of unessential Night receives him next
Wide gaping, and with utter loss of being   440
Threatens him, plung'd in that abortive gulf.
If thence he scape into whatever world,
Or unknown Region, what remains him less
Then unknown dangers and as hard escape.
But I should ill become this Throne, O Peers,   445
And this Imperial Sov'ranty, adorn'd
With splendor, arm'd with power, if aught propos'd
And judg'd of public moment, in the shape
Of difficulty or danger could deterr
Mee from attempting. Wherefore do I assume   450
These Royalties, and not refuse to Reign,
Refusing to accept as great a share
Of hazard as of honour, due alike
To him who Reigns, and so much to him due
Of hazard more, as he above the rest   455
High honourd sits? Go therfore mighty Powers,
Terror of Heav'n, though fall'n; intend[7] at home,
While here shall be our home, what best may ease
The present misery, and render Hell
More tollerable; if there be cure or charm   460
To respite or deceive, or slack the pain
Of this ill Mansion: intermit no watch
Against a wakeful Foe, while I abroad
Through all the coasts of dark destruction seek
Deliverance for us all: this enterprize   465
None shall partake with me. Thus saying rose
The Monarch, and prevented all reply,
Prudent, least from his resolution rais'd
Others among the chief might offer now
(Certain to be refus'd) what erst they feard;   470
And so refus'd might in opinion stand
His rivals, winning cheap the high repute
Which he through hazard huge must earn. But they
Dreaded not more th' adventure then his voice

[7] direct your thoughts to.

Forbidding; and at once with him they rose;   475
Thir rising all at once was as the sound
Of Thunder heard remote. Towards him they bend
With awful reverence prone; and as a God
Extoll him equal to the highest in Heav'n:
Nor fail'd they to express how much they prais'd,   480
That for the general safety he despis'd
His own: for neither do the Spirits damn'd
Loose all thir vertue; least bad men should boast
Thir specious deeds on earth, which glory excites,
Or close ambition varnisht o're with zeal.   485
Thus they thir doubtful consultations dark
Ended rejoycing in thir matchless Chief:
As when from mountain tops the dusky clouds
Ascending, while the North wind sleeps, o'respread
Heav'ns chearful face, the lowring Element   490
Scowls ore the dark'n'd lantskip Snow, or showr;
If chance the radiant Sun with farewell sweet
Extend his ev'ning beam, the fields revive,
The birds thir notes renew, and bleating herds
Attest thir joy, that hill and valley rings.   495
O shame to men! Devil with Devil damn'd
Firm concord holds, men onely disagree
Of Creatures rational, though under hope
Of heav'nly Grace: and God proclaiming peace,
Yet live in hatred, enmity, and strife   500
Among themselves, and levie cruel warrs,
Wasting the Earth, each other to destroy:
As if (which might induce us to accord)
Man had not hellish foes anow besides,
That day and night for his destruction wait.   505
    The *Stygian* Councel thus dissolv'd; and forth
In order came the grand infernal Peers,
Midst came thir mighty Paramount, and seemd
Alone th' Antagonist of Heav'n, nor less
Then Hells dread Emperour with pomp Supream,   510
And God-like imitated State; him round
A Globe of fierie Seraphim inclos'd
With bright imblazonrie, and horrent Arms.
Then of thir Session ended they bid cry
With Trumpets regal sound the great result: 515
Toward the four winds four speedy Cherubim

Put to thir mouths the sounding Alchymie[8]
By Haralds voice explain'd:[9] the hollow Abyss
Heard farr and wide, and all the host of Hell
With deafning shout, return'd them loud acclaim.   520
Thence more at ease thir minds and somwhat rais'd
By false presumptuous hope, the ranged powers
Disband, and wandring, each his several way
Pursues, as inclination or sad choice
Leads him perplext, where he may likeliest find   525
Truce to his restless thoughts, and entertain
The irksom hours, till his great Chief return.
Part on the Plain, or in the Air sublime
Upon the wing, or in swift race contend,
As at th' Olympian Games or *Pythian* fields;   530
Part curb thir fierie Steeds, or shun the Goal
With rapid wheels, or fronted Brigads form.
As when to warn proud Cities warr appears
Wag'd in the troubl'd Skie, and Armies rush
To Battel in the Clouds, before each Van   535
Prick forth the Aerie Knights, and couch thir spears
Till thickest Legions close; with feats of Arms
From either end of Heav'n the welkin burns.
Others with vast *Typhœan*[10] rage more fell
Rend up both Rocks and Hills, and ride the Air   540
In whirlwind; Hell scarce holds the wild uproar.
As when *Alcides*[11] from *Oechalia* Crown'd
With conquest, felt th' envenom'd robe, and tore
Through pain up by the roots *Thessalian* Pines,
And *Lichas* from the top of *Oeta* threw   545
Into th' *Euboic* Sea. Others more mild,
Retreated in a silent valley, sing
With notes Angelical to many a Harp
Thir own Heroic deeds and hapless fall
By doom of Battel; and complain that Fate   550
Free Vertue should enthrall to Force or Chance.
Thir song was partial, but the harmony
(What could it less when Spirits immortal sing?)
Suspended Hell, and took with ravishment
The thronging audience. In discourse more sweet   555

[8] the alloy (brass) of which trumpets were made.
[9] proclaimed.
[10] a hundred-headed giant.
[11] Hercules; see *Vice-Chancellor*, n. 5.

(For Eloquence the Soul, Song charms the Sense,)
Others apart sat on a Hill retir'd,
In thoughts more elevate, and reason'd high
Of Providence, Foreknowledge, Will and Fate,
Fixt Fate, free will, foreknowledge absolute,   560
And found no end, in wandring mazes lost.
Of good and evil much they argu'd then,
Of happiness and final misery,
Passion and Apathie, and glory and shame,
Vain wisdom all, and false Philosophie: 565
Yet with a pleasing sorcerie could charm
Pain for a while or anguish, and excite
Fallacious hope, or arm th' obdured brest
With stubborn patience as with triple steel.
Another part in Squadrons and gross Bands,   570
On bold adventure to discover wide
That dismal world, if any Clime perhaps
Might yeild them easier habitation, bend
Four ways thir flying March, along the Banks
Of four infernal Rivers that disgorge   575
Into the burning Lake thir baleful streams;
Abhorred *Styx* the flood of deadly hate,
Sad *Acheron* of sorrow, black and deep;
Cocytus, nam'd of lamentation loud
Heard on the ruful stream; fierce *Phlegeton*   580
Whose waves of torrent fire inflame with rage.
Farr off from these a slow and silent stream,
Lethe the River of Oblivion rouls
Her watrie Labyrinth, whereof who drinks,
Forthwith his former state and being forgets,   585
Forgets both joy and grief, pleasure and pain.
Beyond this flood a frozen Continent
Lies dark and wild, beat with perpetual storms
Of Whirlwind and dire Hail, which on firm land
Thaws not, but gathers heap, and ruin seems   590
Of ancient pile; all else deep snow and ice,
A gulf profound as that *Serbonian* Bog[12]
Betwixt *Damiata* and mount *Casius* old,
Where Armies whole have sunk: the parching Air
Burns frore, and cold performs th' effect of Fire.   595
Thither by harpy-footed Furies hail'd,
At certain revolutions all the damn'd

[12] in northern Egypt.

Are brought: and feel by turns the bitter change
Of fierce extreams, extreams by change more fierce,
From Beds of raging Fire to starve[13] in Ice   600
Thir soft Ethereal warmth, and there to pine
Immovable, infixt, and frozen round,
Periods of time, thence hurried back to fire.
They ferry over this *Lethean* Sound
Both to and fro, thir sorrow to augment,   605
And wish and struggle, as they pass, to reach
The tempting stream, with one small drop to loose
In sweet forgetfulness all pain and woe,
All in one moment, and so neer the brink;
But Fate withstands, and to oppose th' attempt   610
Medusa with *Gorgonian* terror guards
The Ford, and of it self the water flies
All taste of living wight, as once it fled
The lip of *Tantalus.*[14] Thus roving on
In confus'd march forlorn, th' adventrous Bands   615
With shuddring horror pale, and eyes agast
View'd first thir lamentable lot, and found
No rest: through many a dark and drearie Vale
They pass'd, and many a Region dolorous,
O're many a frozen, many a fierie Alp,   620
Rocks, Caves, Lakes, Fens, Bogs, Dens, and shades of death,
A Universe of death, which God by curse
Created evil, for evil only good,
Where all life dies, death lives, and nature breeds,
Perverse, all monstrous, all prodigious things,   625
Abominable, inutterable, and worse
Then Fables yet have feign'd, or fear conceiv'd,
Gorgons and *Hydra's,* and *Chimera's* dire.
  Mean while the Adversary of God and Man,
Satan with thoughts inflam'd of highest design,   630
Puts on swift wings, and towards the Gates of Hell
Explores his solitary flight; som times
He scours the right hand coast, som times the left,
Now shaves with level wing the Deep, then soars
Up to the fiery Concave touring high.   635
As when farr off at Sea a Fleet descri'd
Hangs in the Clouds, by *Æquinoctial* Winds

[13] to die.
[14] whose punishment in hell was never to clutch the grapes he
reached for or drink from the water in which he stood.

Close sailing from *Bengala,* or the Iles
Of *Ternate* and *Tidore,*[15] whence Merchants bring
Thir spicie Drugs: they on the Trading Flood   640
Through the wide *Ethiopian* to the Cape[16]
Ply stemming nightly toward the Pole. So seem'd
Farr off the flying Fiend: at last appeer
Hell bounds high reaching to the horrid Roof,
And thrice threefold the Gates; three folds were Brass,   645
Three Iron, three of Adamantine Rock,
Impenetrable, impal'd with circling fire,
Yet unconsum'd. Before the Gates there sat
On either side a formidable shape;
The one seem'd Woman to the waste, and fair,   650
But ended foul in many a scaly fould
Voluminous and vast, a Serpent arm'd
With mortal sting: about her middle round
A cry of Hell Hounds never ceasing bark'd
With wide *Cerberean* mouths full loud, and rung   655
A hideous Peal: yet, when they list, would creep,
If aught disturb'd thir noyse, into her woomb,
And kennel there, yet there still bark'd and howl'd,
Within unseen. Farr less abhorr'd then these
Vex'd *Scylla* bathing in the Sea that parts   660
Calabria from the hoarce *Trinacrian*[17] shore:
Nor uglier follow the Night-Hag,[18] when call'd
In secret, riding through the Air she comes
Lur'd with the smell of infant blood, to dance
With *Lapland* Witches, while the labouring Moon   665
Eclipses at thir charms. The other shape,
If shape it might be call'd that shape had none
Distinguishable in member, joynt, or limb,
Or substance might be call'd that shadow seem'd,
For each seem'd either; black it stood as Night,   670
Fierce as ten Furies, terrible as Hell,
And shook a dreadful Dart; what seem'd his head
The likeness of a Kingly Crown had on.
Satan was now at hand, and from his seat
The Monster moving onward came as fast   675
With horrid strides, Hell trembled as he strode.

[15] islands of the Moluccas.
[16] Through the Indian Ocean to the Cape of Good Hope.
[17] Sicilian; see *Mask,* n. 25.
[18] Hecate.

Th' undaunted Fiend what this might be admir'd,
Admir'd, not fear'd; God and his Son except,
Created thing naught valu'd he nor shun'd;
And with disdainful look thus first began.   680
   Whence and what art thou, execrable shape,
That dar'st, though grim and terrible, advance
Thy miscreated Front athwart my way
To yonder Gates? through them I mean to pass,
That be assur'd, without leave askt of thee: 685
Retire, or taste thy folly, and learn by proof,
Hell-born, not to contend with Spirits of Heav'n.
   To whom the Goblin full of wrauth reply'd,
Art thou that Traitor Angel, art thou hee,
Who first broke peace in Heav'n and Faith, till then   690
Unbrok'n, and in proud rebellious Arms
Drew after him the third part of Heav'ns Sons
Conjur'd against the highest, for which both Thou
And they outcast from God, are here condemn'd
To waste Eternal dayes in woe and pain?   695
And reck'n'st thou thy self with Spirits of Heav'n,
Hell-doom'd, and breath'st defiance here and scorn,
Where I reign King, and to enrage thee more,
Thy King and Lord? Back to thy punishment,
False fugitive, and to thy speed add wings,   700
Least with a whip of Scorpions I pursue
Thy lingring, or with one stroke of this Dart
Strange horror seise thee, and pangs unfelt before.
   So spake the grieslie terrour, and in shape,
So speaking and so threatning, grew tenfold   705
More dreadful and deform: on th' other side
Incenst with indignation *Satan* stood
Unterrifi'd, and like a Comet burn'd,
That fires the length of *Ophiucus*[19] huge
In th' Artick Sky, and from his horrid hair   710
Shakes Pestilence and Warr. Each at the Head
Level'd his deadly aim; thir fatall hands
No second stroke intend, and such a frown
Each cast at th' other, as when two black Clouds
With Heav'ns Artillery fraught, come rattling on   715
Over the *Caspian*, then stand front to front
Hov'ring a space, till Winds the signal blow

[19] a northern constellation which significantly means "serpent-
bearer" and in which a comet appeared in 1618.

To joyn their dark Encounter in mid air:
So frownd the mighty Combatants, that Hell
Grew darker at thir frown, so matcht they stood;   720
For never but once more was either like
To meet so great a foe: and now great deeds
Had been achiev'd, whereof all Hell had rung,
Had not the Snakie Sorceress that sat
Fast by Hell Gate, and kept the fatal Key,   725
Ris'n, and with hideous outcry rush'd between.
    O Father, what intends thy hand, she cry'd,
Against thy only Son? What fury O Son,
Possesses thee to bend that mortal Dart
Against thy Fathers head? and know'st for whom;   730
For him who sits above and laughs the while
At thee ordain'd his drudge, to execute
What e're his wrath, which he calls Justice, bids,
His wrath which one day will destroy ye both.
    She spake, and at her words the hellish Pest   735
Forbore, then these to her *Satan* return'd:
    So strange thy outcry, and thy words so strange
Thou interposest, that my sudden hand
Prevented spares to tell thee yet by deeds
What it intends; till first I know of thee,   740
What thing thou art, thus double-form'd, and why
In this infernal Vale first met thou call'st
Me Father, and that Fantasm call'st my Son?
I know thee not, nor ever saw till now
Sight more detestable then him and thee.   745
    T' whom thus the Portress of Hell Gate reply'd;
Hast thou forgot me then, and do I seem
Now in thine eye so foul, once deemd so fair
In Heav'n, when at th' Assembly, and in sight
Of all the Seraphim with thee combin'd   750
In bold conspiracy against Heav'ns King,
All on a sudden miserable pain
Surpris'd thee, dim thine eyes, and dizzie swumm
In darkness, while thy head flames thick and fast
Threw forth, till on the left side op'ning wide,   755
Likest to thee in shape and count'nance bright,
Then shining heav'nly fair, a Goddess arm'd
Out of thy head I sprung:[20] amazement seis'd

[20] alluding to the birth of Athena (goddess of wisdom) from
the head of Jove. Jas. i. 15 cites the procreation of sin and death,

All th' Host of Heav'n; back they recoild affraid
At first, and call'd me *Sin*, and for a Sign   760
Portentous held me; but familiar grown,
I pleas'd, and with attractive graces won
The most averse, thee chiefly, who full oft
Thy self in me thy perfect image viewing
Becam'st enamour'd, and such joy thou took'st   765
With me in secret, that my womb conceiv'd
A growing burden. Mean while Warr arose,
And fields were fought in Heav'n; wherein remaind
(For what could else) to our Almighty Foe
Cleer Victory, to our part loss and rout   770
Through all the Empyrean: down they fell
Driv'n headlong from the Pitch of Heaven, down
Into this Deep, and in the general fall
I also; at which time this powerful Key
Into my hands was giv'n, with charge to keep   775
These Gates for ever shut, which none can pass
Without my op'ning. Pensive here I sat
Alone, but long I sat not, till my womb
Pregnant by thee, and now excessive grown
Prodigious motion felt and rueful throes.   780
At last this odious offspring whom thou seest
Thine own begotten, breaking violent way
Tore through my entrails, that with fear and pain
Distorted, all my nether shape thus grew
Transform'd: but he my inbred enemie   785
Forth issu'd, brandishing his fatal Dart
Made to destroy: I fled, and cry'd out *Death;*
Hell trembl'd at the hideous Name, and sigh'd
From all her Caves, and back resounded *Death.*
I fled, but he pursu'd (though more, it seems,   790
Inflam'd with lust then rage) and swifter far,
Mee overtook his mother all dismaid,
And in embraces forcible and foul
Ingendring with me, of that rape begot
These yelling Monsters that with ceasless cry   795
Surround me, as thou sawst, hourly conceiv'd
And hourly born, with sorrow infinite
To me, for when they list into the womb
That bred them they return, and howl and gnaw
My Bowels, thir repast; then bursting forth   800

but Arlene Swidler suggests (*Explicator*, XVII, 1959, item 41) that
parody of the Trinity underlies the passage.

Afresh with conscious terrours vex me round,
That rest or intermission none I find.
Before mine eyes in opposition sits
Grim *Death* my Son and foe, who sets them on,
And me his Parent would full soon devour   805
For want of other prey, but that he knows
His end with mine involv'd; and knows that I
Should prove a bitter Morsel, and his bane,
When ever that shall be; so Fate pronounc'd.
But thou O Father, I forewarn thee, shun   810
His deadly arrow; neither vainly hope
To be invulnerable in those bright Arms,
Though temper'd heav'nly, for that mortal dint,
Save he who reigns above, none can resist.
  She finish'd, and the suttle Fiend his lore   815
Soon learnd, now milder, and thus answerd smooth.
Dear Daughter, since thou claim'st me for thy Sire,
And my fair Son here showst me, the dear pledge
Of dalliance had with thee in Heav'n, and joys
Then sweet, now sad to mention, through dire change   820
Befall'n us unforeseen, unthought of, know
I come no enemie, but to set free
From out this dark and dismal house of pain,
Both him and thee, and all the heav'nly Host
Of Spirits that in our just pretenses arm'd   825
Fell with us from on high: from them I go
This uncouth errand sole, and one for all
My self expose, with lonely steps to tread
Th' unfounded deep, and through the void immense
To search with wandring quest a place foretold   830
Should be, and, by concurring signs, ere now
Created vast and round, a place of bliss
In the Pourlieues of Heav'n, and therein plac't
A race of upstart Creatures, to supply
Perhaps our vacant room, though more remov'd,   835
Least Heav'n surcharg'd with potent multitude
Might hap to move new broils: Be this or aught
Then this more secret now design'd, I haste
To know, and this once known, shall soon return,
And bring ye to the place where Thou and Death   840
Shall dwell at ease, and up and down unseen
Wing silently the buxom[21] Air, imbalm'd

[21] pliable.

With odours; there ye shall be fed and fill'd
Immeasurably, all things shall be your prey.
He ceas'd, for both seemd highly pleas'd, and Death 845
Grinnd horrible a gastly smile, to hear
His famine should be fill'd, and blest his maw
Destin'd to that good hour: no less rejoyc'd
His mother bad, and thus bespake her Sire.
    The key of this infernal Pit by due, 850
And by command of Heav'ns all-powerful King
I keep, by him forbidden to unlock
These Adamantine Gates; against all force
Death ready stands to interpose his dart,
Fearless to be o'rematcht by living might. 855
But what ow I to his commands above
Who hates me, and hath hither thrust me down
Into this gloom of *Tartarus* profound,
To sit in hateful Office here confin'd,
Inhabitant of Heav'n, and heav'nlie-born, 860
Here in perpetual agonie and pain,
With terrors and with clamors compasst round
Of mine own brood, that on my bowels feed:
Thou art my Father, thou my Author, thou
My being gav'st me; whom should I obey 865
But thee, whom follow? thou wilt bring me soon
To that new world of light and bliss, among
The Gods who live at ease, where I shall Reign
At thy right hand voluptuous, as beseems
Thy daughter and thy darling, without end. 870
    Thus saying, from her side the fatal Key,
Sad instrument of all our woe, she took;
And towards the Gate rouling her bestial train,
Forthwith the huge Porcullis high up drew,
Which but her self not all the *Stygian* powers 875
Could once have mov'd; then in the key-hole turns
Th' intricate wards, and every Bolt and Bar
Of massie Iron or sollid Rock with ease
Unfast'ns: on a sudden op'n flie
With impetuous recoil and jarring sound 880
Th' infernal dores, and on thir hinges grate
Harsh Thunder, that the lowest bottom shook
Of *Erebus*.[22] She op'nd, but to shut
Excel'd her power; the Gates wide op'n stood,

[22] primeval darkness, thus hell.

That with extended wings a Bannerd Host   885
Under spread Ensigns marching might pass through
With Horse and Chariots rankt in loose array;
So wide they stood, and like a Furnace mouth
Cast forth redounding smoak and ruddy flame.
Before thir eyes in sudden view appear   890
The secrets of the hoarie deep, a dark
Illimitable Ocean without bound,
Without dimension, where length, breadth, and highth,
And time and place are lost; where eldest Night
And *Chaos*, Ancestors of Nature, hold   895
Eternal *Anarchie*, amidst the noise
Of endless Warrs, and by confusion stand.
For hot, cold, moist, and dry,[23] four Champions fierce
Strive here for Maistrie, and to Battel bring
Thir embryon Atoms; they around the flag   900
Of each his Faction, in thir several Clanns,
Light-arm'd or heavy, sharp, smooth, swift or slow,
Swarm populous, unnumber'd as the Sands
Of *Barca* or *Cyrene's*[24] torrid soil,
Levied to side with warring Winds, and poise[25]   905
Thir lighter wings. To whom these most adhere,
Hee[26] rules a moment; *Chaos* Umpire sits,
And by decision more imbroils the fray
By which he Reigns: next him high Arbiter
Chance governs all. Into this wild Abyss,   910
The Womb of nature and perhaps her Grave,
Of neither Sea, nor Shore, nor Air, nor Fire,
But all these in thir pregnant causes mixt
Confus'dly, and which thus must ever fight,
Unless th' Almighty Maker them ordain   915
His dark materials to create more Worlds,
Into this wild Abyss the warie fiend
Stood on the brink of Hell and look'd a while,
Pondering his Voyage; for no narrow frith
He had to cross. Nor was his ear less peal'd   920
With noises loud and ruinous (to compare

[23] the four qualities of elements and humours—fire, choler: hot
and dry; air, blood: hot and moist; water, phlegm: cold and moist;
earth, melancholy: cold and dry.

[24] desert and a city in Libya.

[25] balance.

[26] one of the champions of l. 898.

Great things with small) then when *Bellona*[27] storms,
With all her battering Engines bent to rase
Som Capital City; or less then if this frame
Of Heav'n were falling, and these Elements   925
In mutinie had from her Axle torn
The stedfast Earth. At last his Sail-broad Vans
He spreads for flight, and in the surging smoak
Uplifted spurns the ground, thence many a League
As in a cloudy Chair ascending rides   930
Audacious, but that seat soon failing, meets
A vast vacuitie: all unawares
Fluttring his pennons vain plumb down he drops
Ten thousand fadom deep, and to this hour
Down had been falling, had not by ill chance   935
The strong rebuff of som tumultuous cloud
Instinct with Fire and Nitre hurried him
As many miles aloft: that furie stay'd,
Quencht in a Boggie *Syrtis*,[28] neither Sea,
Nor good dry Land: nigh founderd on he fares,   940
Treading the crude consistence, half on foot,
Half flying; behoves him now both Oar and Sail.
As when a Gryfon through the Wilderness
With winged course ore Hill or moarie Dale,
Pursues the *Arimaspian*,[29] who by stelth   945
Had from his wakeful custody purloind
The guarded Gold: So eagerly the fiend
Ore bog or steep, through strait, rough, dense, or rare,
With head, hands, wings or feet pursues his way,
And swims or sinks, or wades, or creeps, or flyes: 950
At length a universal hubbub wild
Of stunning sounds and voices all confus'd
Born through the hollow dark assaults his ear
With loudest vehemence: thither he plyes,
Undaunted to meet there what ever power   955
Or Spirit of the nethermost Abyss
Might in that noise reside, of whom to ask
Which way the neerest coast of darkness lyes
Bordering on light; when strait behold the Throne
Of *Chaos*, and his dark Pavilion spread   960
Wide on the wasteful Deep; with him Enthron'd

[27] Roman goddess of war.
[28] an area of northern Africa.
[29] a Scythian tribe.

Sat Sable-vested *Night*, eldest of things,
The Consort of his Reign; and by them stood
Orcus and *Ades*,[30] and the dreaded name
Of *Demogorgon; Rumor* next and *Chance*,   965
And *Tumult* and *Confusion* all imbroild,
And *Discord* with a thousand various mouths.
   T' whom *Satan* turning boldly, thus. Ye Powers
And Spirits of this nethermost Abyss,
Chaos and ancient *Night*, I come no Spy,   970
With purpose to explore or to disturb
The secrets of your Realm, but by constraint
Wandring this darksome Desert, as my way
Lies through your spacious Empire up to light,
Alone, and without guide, half lost, I seek   975
What readiest path leads where your gloomie bounds
Confine with Heav'n; or if som other place
From your Dominion won, th' Ethereal King
Possesses lately, thither to arrive
I travel this profound, direct my course;   980
Directed, no mean recompence it brings
To your behoof, if I that Region lost,
All usurpation thence expell'd, reduce
To her original darkness and your sway
(Which is my present journey) and once more   985
Erect the Standard there of ancient *Night;*
Yours be th' advantage all, mine the revenge.
   Thus *Satan;* and him thus the Anarch old
With faultring speech and visage incompos'd
Answer'd. I know thee, stranger, who thou art,   990
That mighty leading Angel, who of late
Made head against Heav'ns King, though overthrown.
I saw and heard, for such a numerous Host
Fled not in silence through the frighted deep
With ruin upon ruin, rout on rout,   995
Confusion worse confounded; and Heav'n Gates
Pourd out by millions her victorious Bands
Pursuing. I upon my Frontiers here
Keep residence; if all I can will serve,
That little which is left so to defend,   1000
Encroacht on still through our intestine broils
Weakning the Scepter of old *Night:* first Hell
Your dungeon stretching far and wide beneath;

[30] Hades.

Now lately Heav'n and Earth, another World
Hung ore my Realm, link'd in a golden Chain   1005
To that side Heav'n from whence your Legions fell:
If that way be your walk, you have not farr;
So much the neerer danger; go and speed;
Havock and spoil and ruin are my gain.
    He ceas'd; and *Satan* staid not to reply,   1010
But glad that now his Sea should find a shore,
With fresh alacritie and force renew'd
Springs upward like a Pyramid of fire
Into the wild expanse, and through the shock
Of fighting Elements, on all sides round   1015
Environ'd wins his way; harder beset
And more endanger'd, then when *Argo*[31] pass'd
Through *Bosporus* betwixt the justling Rocks:
Or when *Ulysses* on the Larbord shunnd
Charybdis, and by th' other whirlpool[32] steard. 1020
So he with difficulty and labour hard
Mov'd on, with difficulty and labour hee;
But hee once past, soon after when man fell,
Strange alteration! Sin and Death amain
Following his track, such was the will of Heav'n,   1025
Pav'd after him a broad and beat'n way
Over the dark Abyss, whose boiling Gulf
Tamely endur'd a Bridge of wondrous length
From Hell continu'd reaching th' utmost Orb
Of this frail World; by which the Spirits perverse   1030
With easie intercourse pass to and fro
To tempt or punish mortals, except whom
God and good Angels guard by special grace.
But now at last the sacred influence
Of light appears, and from the walls of Heav'n   1035
Shoots farr into the bosom of dim Night
A glimmering dawn; here Nature first begins
Her fardest verge, and *Chaos* to retire
As from her outmost works a brok'n foe
With tumult less and with less hostile din,   1040
That *Satan* with less toil, and now with ease
Wafts on the calmer wave by dubious light
And like a weather-beaten Vessel holds
Gladly the Port, though Shrouds and Tackle torn;

[31] the ship of Jason and the Argonauts.
[32] Scylla, seen here to be a symbol of Sin.

Or in the emptier waste, resembling Air,   1045
Weighs his spread wings, at leasure to behold
Farr off th' Empyreal Heav'n, extended wide
In circuit, undetermind square or round,
With Opal Towrs and Battlements adorn'd
Of living Saphire, once his native Seat;   1050
And fast by hanging in a golden Chain
This pendant world,[33] in bigness as a Starr
Of smallest Magnitude close by the Moon.
Thither full fraught with mischievous revenge,
Accurst, and in a cursed hour he hies.   1055

BOOK III

THE ARGUMENT

God sitting on his Throne sees *Satan* flying towards this world,
then newly created; shews him to the Son who sat at his
right hand; foretells the success of *Satan* in perverting mankind; clears his own Justice and Wisdom from all imputation,
having created Man free and able enough to have withstood
his Tempter; yet declares his purpose of grace towards him,
in regard he fell not of his own malice, as did *Satan*, but by
him seduc't. The Son of God renders praises to his Father for
the manifestation of his gracious purpose towards Man; but
God again declares, that Grace cannot be extended towards
Man without the satisfaction of divine Justice; Man hath offended the majesty of God by aspiring to Godhead, and
therefore with all his Progeny devoted to death must dye,
unless some one can be found sufficient to answer for his offence, and undergo his Punishment. The Son of God freely
offers himself a Ransom for Man: the Father accepts him,
ordains his incarnation, pronounces his exaltation above all
Names in Heaven and Earth; commands all the Angels to
adore him; they obey, and hymning to thir Harps in full
Quire, celebrate the Father and the Son. Mean while *Satan*
alights upon the bar convex of this Worlds outer-most Orb;
where wandring he first finds a place since call'd the Lymbo
of Vanity; what persons and things fly up thither; thence
comes to the Gate of Heaven, describ'd ascending by stairs,
and the waters above the Firmament that flow about it: His
passage thence to the Orb of the Sun; he finds there *Uriel*
the Regent of that Orb, but first changes himself into the

[33] the whole universe within the Crystalline Sphere.

shape of a meaner Angel; and pretending a zealous desire to behold the new Creation and Man whom God had plac't here, inquires of him the place of his habitation, and is directed; alights first on Mount *Niphates*.

Hail holy Light, ofspring of Heav'n first-born,
Or of th' Eternal Coeternal beam
May I express thee unblam'd? since God is light,
And never but in unapproached light
Dwelt from Eternitie, dwelt then in thee,   5
Bright effluence of bright essence increate.
Or hear'st thou rather pure Ethereal stream,
Whose Fountain who shall tell? before the Sun,
Before the Heav'ns thou wert, and at the voice
Of God, as with a Mantle didst invest   10
The rising world of waters dark and deep,
Won from the void and formless infinite.
Thee I revisit now with bolder wing,
Escap't the *Stygian* Pool, though long detain'd
In that obscure sojourn, while in my flight   15
Through utter and through middle darkness borne
With other notes then to th' *Orphean* Lyre
I sung of *Chaos* and *Eternal Night*,
Taught by the heav'nly Muse to venture down
The dark descent, and up to reascend,   20
Though hard and rare: thee I revisit safe,
And feel thy sovran vital Lamp; but thou
Revisit'st not these eyes, that rowl in vain
To find thy piercing ray, and find no dawn;
So thick a drop serene[1] hath quencht thir Orbs,   25
Or dim suffusion veild. Yet not the more
Cease I to wander where the Muses haunt
Cleer Spring, or shadie Grove, or Sunnie Hill,
Smit with the love of sacred Song; but chief
Thee Sion and the flowrie Brooks beneath   30
That wash thy hallowd feet, and warbling flow,
Nightly I visit: nor somtimes forget
Those other two equal'd with me in Fate,
So were I equal'd with them in renown,

[1] total blindness (*gutta serena*); "suffusion" is partial blindness. For a reexamination of the nature of Milton's blindness, see William B. Hunter, Jr.'s article in *Journal of the History of Medicine and Allied Sciences*, XVII (1962), 333–41.

Blind *Thamyris* and blind *Mæonides*,[2]   35
And *Tiresias* and *Phineus* Prophets old.
Then feed on thoughts, that voluntarie move
Harmonious numbers; as the wakeful Bird
Sings darkling, and in shadiest Covert hid
Tunes her nocturnal Note. Thus with the Year   40
Seasons return, but not to me returns
Day, or the sweet approach of Ev'n or Morn,
Or sight of vernal bloom, or Summers Rose,
Or flocks, or heards, or human face divine;
But cloud in stead, and ever-during dark   45
Surrounds me, from the chearful wayes of men
Cut off, and for the Book of knowledge fair
Presented with a Universal blanc
Of Natures works to mee expung'd and ras'd,
And wisdom at one entrance quite shut out.   50
So much the rather thou Celestial light
Shine inward, and the mind through all her powers
Irradiate, there plant eyes, all mist from thence
Purge and disperse, that I may see and tell
Of things invisible to mortal sight.   55
   Now had th' Almighty Father from above,
From the pure Empyrean where he sits
High Thron'd above all highth, bent down his eye,
His own works and their works at once to view:
About him all the Sanctities of Heav'n   60
Stood thick as Starrs, and from his sight receiv'd
Beatitude past utterance; on his right
The radiant image of his Glory sat,
His onely Son; on Earth he first beheld
Our two first Parents, yet the onely two   65
Of mankind, in the happie Garden plac't,
Reaping immortal fruits of joy and love,
Uninterrupted joy, unrivald love
In blissful solitude; he then survey'd
Hell and the Gulf between, and *Satan* there   70
Coasting the wall of Heav'n on this side Night
In the dun Air sublime, and ready now
To stoop with wearied wings, and willing feet
On the bare outside of this World, that seem'd
Firm land imbosom'd without Firmament,   75

---

[2] Homer. Thamyris is mentioned in *Iliad*, II, 595; Phineas, blinded by the sun, was victimized by the Harpies.

Uncertain which, in Ocean or in Air.
Him God beholding from his prospect high,
Wherein past, present, future he beholds,
Thus to his onely Son foreseeing spake.
   Onely begotten Son, seest thou what rage   80
Transports our adversarie, whom no bounds
Prescrib'd, no barrs of Hell, nor all the chains
Heapt on him there, nor yet the main Abyss
Wide interrupt can hold; so bent he seems
On desperat revenge, that shall redound   85
Upon his own rebellious head. And now
Through all restraint broke loose he wings his way
Not farr off Heav'n, in the Precincts of light,
Directly towards the new created World,
And Man there plac't, with purpose to assay   90
If him by force he can destroy, or worse,
By som false guile pervert; and shall pervert;
For man will heark'n to his glozing lyes,
And easily transgress the sole Command,
Sole pledge of his obedience: So will fall   95
Hee and his faithless Progenie: whose fault?
Whose but his own? ingrate, he had of mee
All he could have; I made him just and right,
Sufficient to have stood, though free to fall.
Such I created all th' Ethereal Powers   100
And Spirits, both them who stood and them who faild;
Freely they stood who stood, and fell who fell.
Not free, what proof could they have givn sincere
Of true allegiance, constant Faith or Love,
Where onely what they needs must do, appeard,   105
Not what they would? what praise could they receive?
What pleasure I from such obedience paid,
When Will and Reason (Reason also is choice)
Useless and vain, of freedom both despoild,
Made passive both, had serv'd necessitie,   110
Not mee. They therefore as to right belong'd,
So were created, nor can justly accuse
Thir maker, or thir making, or thir Fate;
As if Predestination over-rul'd
Thir will, dispos'd by absolute Decree   115
Or high foreknowledge; they themselves decreed
Thir own revolt, not I: if I foreknew,
Foreknowledge had no influence on their fault,
Which had no less prov'd certain unforeknown.

So without least impulse or shadow of Fate,   120
Or aught by me immutablie foreseen,
They trespass, Authors to themselves in all
Both what they judge and what they choose; for so
I formd them free, and free they must remain,
Till they enthrall themselves: I else must change   125
Thir nature, and revoke the high Decree
Unchangeable, Eternal, which ordain'd
Thir freedom, they themselves ordain'd thir fall.
The first sort by thir own suggestion fell,
Self-tempted, self-deprav'd: Man falls deceiv'd   130
By the other first: Man therefore shall find grace,
The other none: in Mercy and Justice both,
Through Heav'n and Earth, so shall my glorie excel,
But Mercy first and last shall brightest shine.[3]
    Thus while God spake, ambrosial fragrance fill'd   135
All Heav'n, and in the blessed Spirits elect
Sense of new joy ineffable diffus'd:
Beyond compare the Son of God was seen
Most glorious, in him all his Father shon
Substantially[4] express'd, and in his face   140
Divine compassion visibly appeerd,
Love without end, and without measure Grace,
Which uttering thus he to his Father spake.
    O Father, gracious was that word which clos'd
Thy sovran sentence, that Man should find grace;   145
For which both Heav'n and Earth shall high extoll
Thy praises, with th' innumerable sound
Of Hymns and sacred Songs, wherewith thy Throne
Encompass'd shall resound thee ever blest.
For should Man finally be lost, should Man   150
Thy creature late so lov'd, thy youngest Son
Fall circumvented thus by fraud, though joynd
With his own folly? that be from thee farr,
That farr be from thee, Father, who art Judge
Of all things made, and judgest onely right.   155
Or shall the Adversarie thus obtain

[3] Mercy is to be granted through the love of the Son, who will atone for human disobedience and thereby pacify the wrath of the Father, guardian of Divine Justice. C. A. Patrides (*PMLA*, LXXIV, 1959, 7–13) makes clear that the atonement demanded by the Father here was accepted by both contemporary Protestant thinkers and earlier writers.

[4] in like substance.

His end, and frustrate thine, shall he fulfill
His malice, and thy goodness bring to naught,
Or proud return though to his heavier doom,
Yet with revenge accomplish't and to Hell   160
Draw after him the whole Race of mankind,
By him corrupted? or wilt thou thy self
Abolish thy Creation, and unmake,
For him, what for thy glorie thou hast made?
So should thy goodness and thy greatness both   165
Be questiond and blaspheam'd without defence.
  To whom the great Creatour thus reply'd.
O Son, in whom my Soul hath chief delight,
Son of my bosom, Son who art alone
My word, my wisdom, and effectual might,   170
All hast thou spok'n as my thoughts are, all
As my Eternal purpose hath decreed:
Man shall not quite be lost, but sav'd who will,
Yet not of will in him, but grace in me
Freely voutsaft; once more I will renew   175
His lapsed powers, though forfeit and enthrall'd
By sin to foul exorbitant desires;
Upheld by me, yet once more he shall stand
On even ground against his mortal foe,
By me upheld, that he may know how frail   180
His fall'n condition is, and to me ow
All his deliv'rance, and to none but me.
Some I have chosen of peculiar grace
Elect above the rest; so is my will:
The rest shall hear me call, and oft be warnd   185
Thir sinful state, and to appease betimes
Th' incensed Deitie, while offerd grace
Invites; for I will cleer thir senses dark,
What may suffice, and soft'n stonie hearts
To pray, repent, and bring obedience due.   190
To prayer, repentance, and obedience due,
Though but endevord with sincere intent,
Mine ear shall not be slow, mine eye not shut.
And I will place within them as a guide
My Umpire _Conscience_, whom if they will hear,   195
Light after light well us'd they shall attain,
And to the end persisting, safe arrive.
This my long sufferance and my day of grace
They who neglect and scorn, shall never taste;
But hard be hard'n'd, blind be blinded more,   200

That they may stumble on, and deeper fall;
And none but such from mercy I exclude.
But yet all is not don; Man disobeying,
Disloyal breaks his fealtie, and sinns
Against the high Supremacie of Heav'n,   205
Affecting God-head, and so loosing all,
To expiate his Treason hath naught left,
But to destruction sacred and devote,
He with his whole posteritie must die,
Die hee or Justice must; unless for him   210
Som other able, and as willing, pay
The rigid satisfaction, death for death.
Say Heav'nly Powers, where shall we find such love,
Which of ye will be mortal to redeem
Mans mortal crime, and just th' unjust to save,   215
Dwels in all Heaven charitie so dear?
     He ask'd, but all the Heav'nly Quire stood mute,
And silence was in Heav'n: on mans behalf
Patron or Intercessor none appeerd,
Much less that durst upon his own head draw   220
The deadly forfeiture, and ransom set.
And now without redemption all mankind
Must have bin lost, adjudg'd to Death and Hell
By doom severe, had not the Son of God,
In whom the fulness dwels of love divine,   225
His dearest mediation thus renewd.
     Father, thy word is past, man shall find grace;
And shall grace not find means, that finds her way,
The speediest of thy winged messengers,
To visit all thy creatures, and to all   230
Comes unprevented, unimplor'd, unsought,
Happie for man, so coming; he her aid
Can never seek, once dead in sins and lost;
Attonement for himself, or offering meet,
Indebted and undon, hath none to bring: 235
Behold mee then, mee for him, life for life
I offer, on mee let thine anger fall;
Account mee man; I for his sake will leave
Thy bosom, and this glorie next to thee
Freely put off, and for him lastly die   240
Well pleas'd, on me let Death wreck all his rage;
Under his gloomie power I shall not long
Lie vanquisht; thou hast givn me to possess
Life in my self for ever, by thee I live,

Though now to Death I yeild, and am his due   245
All that of me can die, yet that debt paid,
Thou wilt not leave me in the loathsom grave
His prey, nor suffer my unspotted Soul
For ever with corruption there to dwell;
But I shall rise Victorious, and subdue   250
My Vanquisher, spoild of his vanted spoil;
Death his deaths wound shall then receive, and stoop
Inglorious, of his mortall sting disarm'd.
I through the ample Air in Triumph high
Shall lead Hell Captive maugre[5] Hell, and show   255
The powers of darkness bound. Thou at the sight
Pleas'd, out of Heaven shalt look down and smile,
While by thee rais'd I ruin all my Foes,
Death last, and with his Carcass glut the Grave:
Then with the multitude of my redeemd   260
Shall enter Heav'n long absent, and return,
Father, to see thy face, wherein no cloud
Of anger shall remain, but peace assur'd,
And reconcilement; wrauth shall be no more
Thenceforth, but in thy presence Joy entire.   265
    His words here ended, but his meek aspect
Silent yet spake, and breath'd immortal love
To mortal men, above which only shon
Filial obedience: as a sacrifice
Glad to be offer'd, he attends the will   270
Of his great Father. Admiration seis'd
All Heav'n, what this might mean, and whither tend
Wondring; but soon th' Almighty thus reply'd:
    O thou in Heav'n and Earth the only peace
Found out for mankind under wrauth, O thou   275
My sole complacence! well thou know'st how dear,
To me are all my works, nor Man the least
Though last created, that for him I spare
Thee from my bosom and right hand, to save,
By loosing thee a while, the whole Race lost.   280
Thou therefore whom thou only canst redeem,
Thir Nature also to thy Nature joyn;
And be thy self Man among men on Earth,
Made flesh, when time shall be, of Virgin seed,
By wondrous birth: Be thou in *Adams* room   285
The Head of all mankind, though *Adams* Son.

[5] in spite of.

As in him perish all men, so in thee
As from a second root shall be restor'd,
As many as are restor'd, without thee none.
His crime makes guiltie all his Sons, thy merit   290
Imputed shall absolve them who renounce
Thir own both righteous and unrighteous deeds,
And live in thee transplanted, and from thee
Receive new life. So Man, as is most just,
Shall satisfie for Man, be judg'd and die,   295
And dying rise, and rising with him raise
His Brethren, ransomd with his own dear life.
So Heav'nly love shall outdo Hellish hate,
Giving to death, and dying to redeem,
So dearly to redeem what Hellish hate   300
So easily destroy'd, and still destroyes
In those who, when they may, accept not grace.
Nor shalt thou by descending to assume
Mans Nature, less'n or degrade thine own.
Because thou hast, though Thron'd in highest bliss   305
Equal to God, and equally enjoying
God-like fruition, quitted all to save
A World from utter loss, and hast been found
By Merit more then Birthright Son of God,
Found worthiest to be so by being Good,   310
Farr more then Great or High; because in thee
Love hath abounded more then Glory abounds,
Therefore thy Humiliation shall exalt
With thee thy Manhood also to this Throne;
Here shalt thou sit incarnate, here shalt Reign   315
Both God and Man, Son both of God and Man,
Anointed universal King; all Power
I give thee, reign for ever, and assume
Thy Merits; under thee as Head Supream
Thrones, Princedoms, Powers, Dominions I reduce: 320
All knees to thee shall bow, of them that bide
In Heav'n, or Earth, or under Earth in Hell;
When thou attended gloriously from Heav'n
Shalt in the Sky appeer, and from thee send
The summoning Arch-Angels to proclaim   325
Thy dread Tribunal: forthwith from all Winds
The living, and forthwith the cited dead
Of all past Ages to the general Doom
Shall hast'n, such a peal shall rouse thir sleep.
Then all thy Saints assembl'd, thou shalt judge   330

Bad men and Angels, they arraign'd shall sink
Beneath thy Sentence; Hell her numbers full,
Thenceforth shall be for ever shut. Mean while
The World shall burn, and from her ashes spring
New Heav'n and Earth, wherein the just shall dwell   335
And after all thir tribulations long
See golden days, fruitful of golden deeds,
With Joy and Love triumphing, and fair Truth.
Then thou thy regal Scepter shalt lay by,
For regal Scepter then no more shall need,   340
God shall be All in All. But all ye Gods,
Adore him, who to compass all this dies,
Adore the Son, and honour him as mee.
    No sooner had th' Almighty ceas't, but all
The multitude of Angels with a shout   345
Loud as from numbers without number, sweet
As from blest voices, uttering joy, Heav'n rung
With Jubilee, and loud Hosanna's filld
Th' eternal Regions: lowly reverent
Towards either Throne they bow, and to the ground   350
With solemn adoration down they cast
Thir Crowns inwove with Amarant and Gold,
Immortal Amarant, a Flowr which once
In Paradise, fast by the Tree of Life
Began to bloom, but soon for mans offence   355
To Heav'n remov'd where first it grew, there grows,
And flowrs aloft shading the Fount of Life,
And where the river of Bliss through midst of Heavn
Rowls o're *Elisian* Flowrs her Amber stream;
With these that never fade the Spirits Elect   360
Bind thir resplendent locks inwreath'd with beams,
Now in loose Garlands thick thrown off, the bright
Pavement that like a Sea of Jasper shon
Impurpl'd with Celestial Roses smil'd.
Then Crown'd again thir gold'n Harps they took,   365
Harps ever tun'd, that glittering by thir side
Like Quivers hung, and with Præamble sweet
Of charming symphonie they introduce
This sacred Song, and waken raptures high;
No voice exempt, no voice but well could join   370
Melodious part, such concord is in Heav'n.
    Thee Father first they sung Omnipotent,
Immutable, Immortal, Infinite,
Eternal King; thee Author of all being,

Fountain of Light, thy self invisible   375
Amidst the glorious brightness where thou sit'st
Thron'd inaccessible, but when thou shad'st
The full blaze of thy beams, and through a cloud
Drawn round about thee like a radiant Shrine,
Dark with excessive bright thy skirts appeer,   380
Yet dazle Heav'n, that brightest Seraphim
Approach not, but with both wings veil thir eyes.
Thee next they sang of all Creation first,
Begotten Son, Divine Similitude,
In whose conspicuous count'nance, without cloud   385
Made visible, th' Almighty Father shines,
Whom else no Creature can behold; on thee
Impress th' effulgence of his Glorie abides,
Transfus'd on thee his ample Spirit rests.
Hee Heav'n of Heav'ns and all the Powers therein   390
By thee created, and by thee threw down
Th' aspiring Dominations: thou that day
Thy Fathers dreadful Thunder didst not spare,
Nor stop thy flaming Chariot wheels, that shook
Heav'ns everlasting Frame, while o're the necks   395
Thou drov'st of warring Angels disarraid.
Back from pursuit thy Powers with loud acclaim
Thee only extoll'd, Son of thy Fathers might,
To execute fierce vengeance on his foes,
Not so on Man; him through their malice fall'n,   400
Father of Mercie and Grace, thou didst not doom
So strictly, but much more to pitie encline:
No sooner did thy dear and onely Son
Perceive thee purpos'd not to doom frail Man
So strictly, but much more to pitie enclin'd,   405
He to appease thy wrauth, and end the strife
Of Mercy and Justice in thy face discern'd,
Regardless of the Bliss wherein hee sat
Second to thee, offerd himself to die
For mans offence. O unexampl'd love,   410
Love no where to be found less then Divine!
Hail Son of God, Saviour of Men, thy Name
Shall be the copious matter of my Song
Henceforth, and never shall my Harp thy praise
Forget, nor from thy Fathers praise disjoin.   415
    Thus they in Heav'n, above the starry Sphear,
Thir happie hours enjoy and hymning spent.
Mean while upon the firm opacous Globe

Of this round World, whose first convex divides
The luminous inferior Orbs, enclos'd   420
From *Chaos* and th' inroad of Darkness old,
Satan alighted walks: a Globe farr off
It seem'd, now seems a boundless Continent
Dark, waste, and wild, under the frown of Night
Starless expos'd, and ever-threatning storms   425
Of *Chaos* blustring round, inclement skie;
Save on that side which from the wall of Heav'n
Though distant farr som small reflection gains
Of glimmering air less vext with tempest loud:
Here walk'd the Fiend at large in spacious field.   430
As when a Vultur on *Imaus*⁶ bred,
Whose snowie ridge the roving *Tartar* bounds,
Dislodging from a Region scarce of prey
To gorge the flesh of Lambs or yeanling Kids
On Hills where Flocks are fed, flies toward the Springs 435
Of *Ganges* or *Hydaspes*, *Indian* streams;
But in his way lights on the barren plains
Of *Sericana*, where *Chineses* drive
With Sails and Wind thir canie Waggons light:
So on this windie Sea of Land, the Fiend   440
Walk'd up and down alone bent on his prey,
Alone, for other Creature in this place
Living or liveless to be found was none,
None yet, but store hereafter from the earth
Up hither like Aereal vapours flew   445
Of all things transitorie and vain, when Sin
With vanity had filld the works of men:
Both all things vain, and all who in vain things
Built thir fond hopes of Glorie or lasting fame,
Or happiness in this or th' other life;   450
All who have thir reward on Earth, the fruits
Of painful Superstition and blind Zeal,
Naught seeking but the praise of men, here find
Fit retribution, emptie as thir deeds;
All th' unaccomplisht works of Natures hand,   455
Abortive, monstrous, or unkindly⁷ mixt,
Dissolv'd on Earth, fleet hither, and in vain,
Till final dissolution, wander here,

⁶ a mountain in the Himalayas.
⁷ both in the modern sense and with the meaning "unnatural."

Not in the neighbouring Moon, as some[8] have dreamd;
Those argent Fields more likely habitants,   460
Translated Saints,[9] or middle Spirits hold
Betwixt th' Angelical and Human kind:
Hither of ill-joynd Sons and Daughters born
First from the ancient World those Giants came
With many a vain exploit, though then renownd: 465
The builders next of *Babel* on the Plain
Of *Sennaar*, and still with vain designe
New *Babels*, had they wherewithall, would build:
Others came single; he who to be deemd
A God, leap'd fondly into *Ætna* flames,   470
Empedocles, and hee who to enjoy
Plato's Elysium, leap'd into the Sea,
Cleombrotus, and many more too long,
Embryo's and Idiots, Eremits and Friers
White, Black and Grey,[10] with all thir trumperie.   475
Here Pilgrims roam, that stray'd so farr to seek
In *Golgotha* him dead, who lives in Heav'n;
And they who to be sure of Paradise
Dying put on the weeds of *Dominic*,
Or in *Franciscan* think to pass disguis'd;   480
They pass the Planets seven, and pass the fixt,
And that Crystalline Sphear whose ballance weighs
The Trepidation[11] talkt, and that first mov'd;
And now Saint *Peter* at Heav'ns Wicket seems
To wait them with his Keys, and now at foot   485
Of Heav'ns ascent they lift thir Feet, when loe
A violent cross wind from either Coast
Blows them transverse ten thousand Leagues awry
Into the devious Air; then might ye see
Cowls, Hoods and Habits with thir wearers tost   490
And flutterd into Raggs, then Reliques, Beads,
Indulgences, Dispenses, Pardons, Bulls,
The sport of Winds: all these upwhirld aloft
Fly o're the backside of the World farr off
Into a *Limbo* large and broad, since calld   495

[8] e.g., Ariosto.
[9] Enoch and Elijah.
[10] Carmelites, Dominicans, and Franciscans.
[11] Two theories were advanced ("talkt"): the Ptolemaic explained trepidation as the backward motion of the fixed stars which created the equinoxes; the Copernican classified it as the wobble of the earth rotating on its axis.

The Paradise of Fools, to few unknown
Long after, now unpeopl'd, and untrod;
All this dark Globe the Fiend found as he pass'd,
And long he wanderd, till at last a gleam
Of dawning light turnd thither-ward in haste   500
His travell'd steps; farr distant he descries
Ascending by degrees magnificent
Up to the wall of Heav'n a Structure high,
At top whereof, but farr more rich appeerd
The work as of a Kingly Palace Gate   505
With Frontispice of Diamond and Gold
Imbellisht, thick with sparkling orient Gemms
The Portal shon, inimitable on Earth
By Model, or by shading Pencil drawn.
The Stairs were such as whereon *Jacob* saw   510
Angels ascending and descending, bands
Of Guardians bright, when he from *Esau* fled
To *Padan-Aram* in the field of *Luz*,
Dreaming by night under the open Skie,
And waking cri'd, *This is the Gate of Heav'n.*   515
Each Stair mysteriously[12] was meant, nor stood
There alwayes, but drawn up to Heav'n somtimes
Viewless, and underneath a bright Sea flow'd
Of Jasper, or of liquid Pearl, whereon
Who after came from Earth, sayling arriv'd,   520
Wafted by Angels, or flew o're the Lake
Rapt in a Chariot drawn by fiery Steeds.
The Stairs were then let down, whether to dare
The Fiend by easie ascent, or aggravate
His sad exclusion from the dores of Bliss.   525
Direct against which op'n'd from beneath,
Just o're the blissful seat of Paradise,
A passage down to th' Earth, a passage wide,
Wider by farr then that of after-times
Over Mount *Sion*, and, though that were large,   530
Over the *Promis'd Land* to God so dear,
By which, to visit oft those happy Tribes,
On high behests his Angels to and fro
Pass'd frequent, and his eye with choice regard
From *Paneas*[13] the fount of *Jordans* flood   535
To *Beërsaba*, where the *Holy Land*

---

[12] allegorically; the stairs are Jacob's ladder (Gen. xxviii. 12).
[13] a city of Dan. The lines survey all of the Holy Land.

Borders on *Ægypt* and th' *Arabian* shoar;
So wide the op'ning seemd, where bounds were set
To darkness, such as bound the Ocean wave.
Satan from hence now on the lower stair   540
That scal'd by steps of Gold to Heav'n Gate
Looks down with wonder at the sudden view
Of all this World at once. As when a Scout
Through dark and desart wayes with peril gone
All night; at last by break of chearful dawn   545
Obtains the brow of some high-climbing Hill,
Which to his eye discovers unaware
The goodly prospect of some forein land
First-seen, or some renown'd Metropolis
With glistering Spires and Pinnacles adornd,   550
Which now the Rising Sun guilds with his beams.
Such wonder seis'd, though after Heaven seen,
The Spirit maligne, but much more envy seis'd
At sight of all this World beheld so fair.
Round he surveys, and well might, where he stood   555
So high above the circling Canopie
Of Nights extended shade; from Eastern Point
Of *Libra* to the fleecie Starr[14] that bears
Andromeda farr off *Atlantic* Seas
Beyond th' *Horizon;* then from Pole to Pole   560
He views in bredth, and without longer pause
Down right into the Worlds first Region throws
His flight precipitant, and winds with ease
Through the pure marble Air his oblique way
Amongst innumerable Starrs, that shon   565
Stars distant, but nigh hand seemd other Worlds,
Or other Worlds they seemd, or happy Iles,
Like those *Hesperian* Gardens fam'd of old,
Fortunate Fields, and Groves and flowrie Vales,
Thrice happy Iles, but who dwelt happy there   570
He stayd not to enquire: above them all
The golden Sun in splendor likest Heav'n
Allur'd his eye: Thither his course he bends
Through the calm Firmament; but up or down
By center, or eccentric,[15] hard to tell,   575
Or Longitude, where the great Luminarie

[14] Aries, the ram.
[15] toward or away from the center (the earth), "hard to tell" because of the varying views of the universe.

Alooff the vulgar Constellations thick,
That from his Lordly eye keep distance due,
Dispenses Light from farr; they as they move
Thir Starry dance in numbers that compute   580
Days, months, and years, towards his all-chearing Lamp
Turn swift thir various motions, or are turnd
By his Magnetic beam, that gently warms
The Univers, and to each inward part
With gentle penetration, though unseen,   585
Shoots invisible vertue ev'n to the deep:
So wondrously was set his Station bright.
There lands the Fiend, a spot like which perhaps
Astronomer in the Sun's lucent Orb
Through his glaz'd Optic Tube yet never saw.[16]   590
The place he found beyond expression bright,
Compar'd with aught on Earth, Mettal or Stone;
Not all parts like, but all alike informd
With radiant light, as glowing Iron with fire;
If mettal, part seemd Gold, part Silver cleer;   595
If stone, Carbuncle most or Chrysolite,
Rubie or Topaz, to the Twelve that shon
In *Aarons* Brest-plate, and a stone[17] besides
Imagind rather oft then elsewhere seen,
That stone, or like to that which here below   600
Philosophers in vain so long have sought,
In vain, though by thir powerful Art they bind
Volatil *Hermes,* and call up unbound
In various shapes old *Proteus* from the Sea,
Draind through a Limbec to his Native form.   605
What wonder then if fields and regions here
Breathe forth *Elixir* pure, and Rivers run
Potable Gold, when with one vertuous touch

[16] Galileo had discerned sunspots in 1609.

[17] the philosopher's stone (the *"Elixir"* of l. 607) which would
turn base metal into gold. An alembic (l. 605) was a vessel in
which the "Native" (l. 605) form of a substance was distilled.
Mercury ("Volatil *Hermes,*" l. 603) was thought a component of
all minerals, and the changeable Proteus was symbolic of basic
matter. (See Edgar H. Duncan, *Osiris*, XI, 1954, 386–421.) The
sun, thought to produce gold and precious gems, was a true al-
chemist (ll. 609 ff.). Urim ("radiant") and Thummim in Aaron's
breastplate arm the Son when he ascends after the War in Heaven
with Victory at his right hand (VI. 760–63). They were considered
mediums for the revelation of God's will.

Th' Arch-chimic Sun so farr from us remote
Produces with Terrestrial Humor mixt   610
Here in the dark so many precious things
Of colour glorious and effect so rare?
Here matter new to gaze the Devil met
Undazl'd, farr and wide his eye commands,
For sight no obstacle found here, nor shade,   615
But all Sun-shine, as when his Beams at Noon
Culminate from th' Æquator, as they now
Shot upward still direct, whence no way round
Shadow from body opaque can fall, and th' Air,
No where so cleer, sharp'n'd his visual ray   620
To objects distant farr, whereby he soon
Saw within kenn a glorious Angel stand,
The same whom *John* saw also in the Sun:[18]
His back was turnd, but not his brightness hid;
Of beaming sunnie Raies, a golden tiar   625
Circl'd his Head, nor less his Locks behind
Illustrious on his Shoulders fledge with wings
Lay waving round; on som great charge imploy'd
He seemd, or fixt in cogitation deep.
Glad was the Spirit impure; as now in hope   630
To find who might direct his wandring flight
To Paradise the happie seat of Man,
His journies end and our beginning woe.
But first he casts to change his proper shape,
Which else might work him danger or delay: 635
And now a stripling Cherub he appeers,
Not of the prime, yet such as in his face
Youth smil'd Celestial, and to every Limb
Sutable grace diffus'd, so well he feign'd;
Under a Coronet his flowing hair   640
In curls on either cheek plaid, wings he wore
Of many a colour'd plume sprinkl'd with Gold,
His habit fit for speed succinct, and held
Before his decent steps a Silver wand.
He drew not nigh unheard, the Angel bright,   645
Ere he drew nigh, his radiant visage turnd,
Admonisht by his ear, and strait was known
Th' Arch-Angel *Uriel*, one of the seav'n
Who in Gods presence, neerest to his Throne

[18] See Rev. xix. 17.

Stand ready at command, and are his Eyes[19]   650
That run through all the Heav'ns, or down to th' Earth
Bear his swift errands over moist and dry,
O're Sea and Land: him *Satan* thus accosts.
    Uriel, for thou of those seav'n Spirits that stand
In sight of Gods high Throne, gloriously bright,   655
The first art wont his great authentic will
Interpreter through highest Heav'n to bring,
Where all his Sons thy Embassie attend;
And here art likeliest by supream decree
Like honour to obtain, and as his Eye   660
To visit oft this new Creation round;
Unspeakable desire to see, and know
All these his wondrous works, but chiefly Man,
His chief delight and favour, him for whom
All these his works so wondrous he ordaind,   665
Hath brought me from the Quires of Cherubim
Alone thus wandring. Brightest Seraph tell
In which of all these shining Orbs hath Man
His fixed seat, or fixed seat hath none,
But all these shining Orbs his choice to dwell;   670
That I may find him, and with secret gaze,
Or open admiration him behold
On whom the great Creator hath bestowd
Worlds, and on whom hath all these graces powrd;
That both in him and all things, as is meet,   675
The Universal Maker we may praise;
Who justly hath drivn out his Rebell Foes
To deepest Hell, and to repair that loss
Created this new happie Race of Men
To serve him better: wise are all his wayes.   680
    So spake the false dissembler unperceiv'd;
For neither Man nor Angel can discern
Hypocrisie, the only evil that walks
Invisible, except to God alone,
By his permissive will, through Heav'n and Earth: 685
And oft though wisdom wake, suspicion sleeps
At wisdoms Gate, and to simplicitie
Resigns her charge, while goodness thinks no ill
Where no ill seems: Which now for once beguil'd
Uriel, though Regent of the Sun, and held   690
The sharpest sighted Spirit of all in Heav'n;

[19] See Rev. iv. 5 and Zech. iv. 10.

Who to the fraudulent Impostor foul
In his uprightness answer thus returnd.
Fair Angel, thy desire which tends to know
The works of God, thereby to glorifie   695
The great Work-Maister, leads to no excess
That reaches blame, but rather merits praise
The more it seems excess, that led thee hither
From thy Empyreal Mansion thus alone,
To witness with thine eyes what some perhaps   700
Contented with report hear onely in heav'n:
For wonderful indeed are all his works,
Pleasant to know, and worthiest to be all
Had in remembrance always with delight;
But what created mind can comprehend   705
Thir number, or the wisdom infinite
That brought them forth, but hid thir causes deep.
I saw when at his Word the formless Mass,
This worlds material mould, came to a heap:
Confusion heard his voice, and wild uproar   710
Stood rul'd, stood vast infinitude confin'd;
Till at his second bidding darkness fled,
Light shon, and order from disorder sprung:
Swift to thir several Quarters hasted then
The cumbrous Elements, Earth, Flood, Air, Fire,   715
And this Ethereal quintessence of Heav'n
Flew upward, spirited with various forms,
That rowld orbicular, and turnd to Starrs
Numberless, as thou seest, and how they move;
Each had his place appointed, each his course,   720
The rest in circuit walls this Universe.
Look downward on that Globe whose hither side
With light from hence, though but reflected, shines;
That place is Earth the seat of Man, that light
His day, which else as th' other Hemisphere   725
Night would invade, but there the neighbouring Moon
(So call that opposite fair Starr) her aid
Timely interposes, and her monthly round
Still ending, still renewing through mid Heav'n,
With borrowd light her countenance triform[20]   730
Hence fills and empties to enlighten th' Earth,
And in her pale dominion checks the night.
That spot to which I point is *Paradise*,

[20] See *Ely*, n. 13.

Adams abode, those loftie shades his Bowr.
Thy way thou canst not miss, me mine requires.   735
   Thus said, he turnd, and *Satan* bowing low,
As to superior Spirits is wont in Heav'n,
Where honour due and reverence none neglects,
Took leave, and toward the coast of Earth beneath,
Down from th' Ecliptic, sped with hop'd success,   740
Throws his steep flight in many an Aerie wheel,
Nor staid, till on *Niphates*[21] top he lights.

BOOK IV

THE ARGUMENT

Satan now in prospect of *Eden,* and nigh the place where he
must now attempt the bold enterprize which he undertook
alone against God and Man, falls into many doubts with himself, and many passions, fear, envy, and despare; but at
length confirms himself in evil; journeys on to Paradise,
whose outward prospect and scituation is described, over-
leaps the bounds, sits in the shape of a Cormorant on the
Tree of life, as highest in the Garden to look about him. The
Garden describ'd; *Satans* first sight of *Adam* and *Eve;* his
wonder at thir excellent form and happy state, but with resolution to work thir fall; overhears thir discourse, thence
gathers that the Tree of knowledge was forbidden them to
eat of, under penalty of death; and thereon intends to found
his Temptation, by seducing them to transgress: then leaves
them a while, to know further of thir state by some other
means. Mean while *Uriel* descending on a Sun-beam warns
Gabriel, who had in charge the Gate of Paradise, that some
evil spirit had escap'd the Deep, and past at Noon by his
Sphere in the shape of a good Angel down to Paradise, discovered after by his furious gestures in the Mount. *Gabriel*
promises to find him ere morning. Night coming on, *Adam*
and *Eve* discourse of going to thir rest: thir Bower describ'd;
thir Evening worship *Gabriel* drawing forth his Bands of
Night-watch to walk the round of Paradise, appoints two
strong Angels to *Adams* Bower, least the evill spirit should
be there doing some harm to *Adam* or *Eve* sleeping; there
they find him at the ear of *Eve,* tempting her in a dream, and
bring him, though unwilling, to *Gabriel;* by whom question'd,
he scornfully answers, prepares resistance, but hinder'd by a
Sign from Heaven, flies out of Paradise.

[21] a mountain in Armenia, near Assyria; see also IV, 126.

O for that warning voice,[1] which he who saw
Th' *Apocalyps,* heard cry in Heaven aloud,
Then when the Dragon, put to second rout,
Came furious down to be reveng'd on men,
Wo to th' inhabitants on Earth! that now,   5
While time was, our first Parents had bin warnd
The coming of thir secret foe, and scap'd
Haply so scap'd his mortal snare; for now
Satan, now first inflam'd with rage, came down,
The Tempter ere th' Accuser of man-kind,   10
To wreck on innocent frail man his loss
Of that first Battel, and his flight to Hell:
Yet not rejoycing in his speed, though bold,
Far off and fearless, nor with cause to boast,
Begins his dire attempt, which nigh the birth   15
Now rowling, boils in his tumultuous brest,
And like a devillish Engine back recoils
Upon himself; horror and doubt distract
His troubl'd thoughts, and from the bottom stirr
The Hell within him, for within him Hell   20
He brings, and round about him, nor from Hell
One step no more then from himself can fly
By change of place: Now conscience wakes despair
That slumberd, wakes the bitter memorie
Of what he was, what is, and what must be   25
Worse; of worse deeds worse sufferings must ensue.
Sometimes towards *Eden* which now in his view
Lay pleasant, his griev'd look he fixes sad,
Sometimes towards Heav'n and the full-blazing Sun,
Which now sat high in his Meridian Towr: 30
Then much revolving, thus in sighs began.
    O thou that with surpassing Glory crownd,
Look'st from thy sole Dominion like the God
Of this new World; at whose sight all the Starrs
Hide thir diminisht heads; to thee I call,   35
But with no friendly voice, and add thy name
O Sun, to tell thee how I hate thy beams
That bring to my remembrance from what state
I fell, how glorious once above thy Sphear;
Till Pride and worse Ambition threw me down   40
Warring in Heav'n against Heav'ns matchless King:

[1] See Rev. xii. 7–13.

Ah wherefore! he deserv'd no such return
From me, whom he created what I was
In that bright eminence, and with his good
Upbraided none; nor was his service hard.   45
What could be less then to afford him praise,
The easiest recompence, and pay him thanks,
How due! yet all his good prov'd ill in me,
And wrought but malice; lifted up so high
I sdeind² subjection, and thought one step higher   50
Would set me highest, and in a moment quit
The debt immense of endless gratitude,
So burthensome still paying, still to ow;
Forgetful what from him I still receiv'd,
And understood not that a grateful mind   55
By owing owes not, but still pays, at once
Indebted and discharg'd; what burden then?
O had his powerful Destiny ordaind
Me some inferiour Angel, I had stood
Then happie; no unbounded hope had rais'd   60
Ambition. Yet why not? som other Power
As great might have aspir'd, and me though mean
Drawn to his part; but other Powers as great
Fell not, but stand unshak'n, from within
Or from without, to all temptations arm'd.   65
Hadst thou the same free Will and Power to stand?
Thou hadst: whom hast thou then or what t' accuse,
But Heav'ns free Love dealt equally to all?
Be then his Love accurst, since love or hate,
To me alike, it deals eternal woe.   70
Nay curs'd be thou; since against his thy will
Chose freely what it now so justly rues.
Me miserable! which way shall I flie
Infinite wrauth, and infinite despair?
Which way I flie is Hell; my self am Hell;   75
And in the lowest deep a lower deep
Still threatning to devour me opens wide,
To which the Hell I suffer seems a Heav'n.
O then at last relent: is there no place
Left for Repentance, none for Pardon left?   80
None left but by submission; and that word
Disdain forbids me, and my dread of shame

² disdained.

Among the Spirits beneath, whom I seduc'd
With other promises and other vaunts
Then to submit, boasting I could subdue   85
Th' Omnipotent. Ay me, they little know
How dearly I abide that boast so vain,
Under what torments inwardly I groan:
While they adore me on the Throne of Hell,
With Diadem and Scepter high advanc't   90
The lower still I fall, onely supream
In miserie; such joy Ambition finds.
But say I could repent and could obtain
By Act of Grace my former state; how soon
Would highth recall high thoughts, how soon unsay   95
What feign'd submission swore: ease would recant
Vows made in pain, as violent and void.
For never can true reconcilement grow
Where wounds of deadly hate have peirc'd so deep:
Which would but lead me to a worse relapse,   100
And heavier fall: so should I purchase dear
Short intermission bought with double smart.
This knows my punisher; therefore as farr
From granting hee, as I from begging peace:
All hope excluded thus, behold in stead   105
Of us out-cast, exil'd, his new delight,
Mankind created, and for him this World.
So farwell Hope, and with Hope farwell Fear,
Farwell Remorse: all Good to me is lost;
Evil be thou my Good; by thee at least   110
Divided Empire with Heav'ns King I hold
By thee, and more then half perhaps will reigne;
As Man ere long, and this new World shall know.
    Thus while he spake, each passion dimm'd his face
Thrice chang'd with pale, ire, envie and despair,   115
Which marrd his borrow'd visage, and betraid
Him counterfet, if any eye beheld.
For heav'nly minds from such distempers foul
Are ever cleer. Whereof hee soon aware,
Each perturbation smooth'd with outward calm,   120
Artificer of fraud; and was the first
That practis'd falshood under saintly shew,
Deep malice to conceal, couch't with revenge:
Yet not anough had practis'd to deceive
Uriel once warnd; whose eye pursu'd him down   125
The way he went, and on th' Assyrian mount

Saw him disfigur'd, more then could befall
Spirit of happie sort: his gestures fierce
He mark'd and mad demeanour, then alone,
As he suppos'd, all unobserv'd, unseen.   130
So on he fares, and to the border comes
Of *Eden*, where delicious Paradise,
Now nearer, Crowns with her enclosure green,
As with a rural mound the champain head[3]
Of a steep wilderness, whose hairie sides   135
With thicket overgrown, grottesque and wild,
Access deni'd; and over head up grew
Insuperable highth of loftiest shade,
Cedar, and Pine, and Firr, and branching Palm,
A Silvan Scene, and as the ranks ascend   140
Shade above shade, a woodie Theatre
Of stateliest view. Yet higher then thir tops
The verdurous wall of Paradise up sprung:
Which to our general Sire gave prospect large
Into his neather Empire neighbouring round.   145
And higher then that Wall a circling row
Of goodliest Trees loaden with fairest Fruit,
Blossoms and Fruit at once of golden hue
Appeerd, with gay enameld colours mixt:
On which the Sun more glad impress'd his beams   150
Then in fair Evening Cloud, or humid Bow,
When God hath showrd the earth; so lovely seemd
That Lantskip: And of pure now purer air
Meets his approach, and to the heart inspires
Vernal delight and joy, able to drive   155
All sadness but despair: now gentle gales
Fanning thir odoriferous wings dispense
Native perfumes, and whisper whence they stole
Those balmie spoils. As when to them who sail
Beyond the *Cape of Hope,* and now are past   160
Mozambic, off at Sea North-East winds blow
Sabean[4] Odours from the spicie shoar
Of *Arabie* the blest, with such delay
Well pleas'd they slack thir course, and many a League
Chear'd with the grateful smell old Ocean smiles.   165
So entertaind those odorous sweets the Fiend
Who came thir bane, though with them better pleas'd

[3] plateau.
[4] of Sheba, part of Arabia Felix.

Then *Asmodeus*[5] with the fishie fume,
That drove him, though enamourd, from the Spouse
Of *Tobits* Son, and with a vengeance sent   170
From *Media* post to *Ægypt*, there fast bound.
   Now to th' ascent of that steep savage[6] Hill
Satan had journied on, pensive and slow;
But further way found none, so thick entwin'd,
As one continu'd brake, the undergrowth   175
Of shrubs and tangling bushes had perplext
All path of Man or Beast that past that way:
One Gate there only was, and that look'd East
On th' other side: which when th' arch-fellon saw
Due entrance he disdaind, and in contempt,   180
At one slight bound high overleap'd all bound
Of Hill or highest Wall, and sheer within
Lights on his feet. As when a prowling Wolf,
Whom hunger drives to seek new haunt for prey,
Watching where Shepherds pen thir Flocks at eeve   185
In hurdl'd Cotes amid the field secure,
Leaps o're the fence with ease into the Fould:
Or as a Thief bent to unhoord the cash
Of some rich Burgher, whose substantial dores,
Cross-barrd and bolted fast, fear no assault,   190
In at the window climbs, or o're the tiles;
So clomb this first grand Thief into Gods Fould:
So since into his Church lewd Hirelings climb.
Thence up he flew, and on the Tree of Life,
The middle Tree and highest there that grew,   195
Sat like a Cormorant;[7] yet not true Life
Thereby regaind, but sat devising Death
To them who liv'd; nor on the vertue thought
Of that life-giving Plant, but only us'd
For prospect, what well us'd had bin the pledge   200
Of immortality. So little knows
Any, but God alone, to value right
The good before him, but perverts best things
To worst abuse, or to thir meanest use.
Beneath him with new wonder now he views   205
To all delight of human sense expos'd
In narrow room Natures whole wealth, yea more,

[5] See Tobit viii.
[6] woody.
[7] traditional symbol of greed.

A Heav'n on Earth: for blissful Paradise
Of God the Garden was, by him in th' East
Of *Eden* planted; *Eden* stretch'd her Line   210
From *Auran*[8] Eastward to the Royal Towrs
Of great *Seleucia*, built by *Grecian* Kings,
Or where the Sons of *Eden* long before
Dwelt in *Telassar:* in this pleasant soil
His farr more pleasant Garden God ordaind;   215
Out of the fertil ground he caus'd to grow
All Trees of noblest kind for sight, smell, taste;
And all amid them stood the Tree of Life,
High eminent, blooming Ambrosial Fruit
Of vegetable Gold; and next to Life   220
Our Death the Tree of Knowledge grew fast by,
Knowledge of Good bought dear by knowing ill.
Southward through *Eden* went a River[9] large,
Nor chang'd his course, but through the shaggie hill
Pass'd underneath ingulft, for God had thrown   225
That Mountain as his Garden mould high rais'd
Upon the rapid current, which through veins
Of porous Earth with kindly thirst up drawn,
Rose a fresh Fountain, and with many a rill
Waterd the Garden; thence united fell   230
Down the steep glade, and met the neather Flood,
Which from his darksom passage now appeers,
And now divided into four main Streams,[10]
Runs divers, wandring many a famous Realm
And Country whereof here needs no account,   235
But rather to tell how, if Art could tell,
How from that Saphire Fount the crisped Brooks,
Rowling on Orient Pearl and sands of Gold,
With mazie error[11] under pendant shades
Ran Nectar, visiting each plant, and fed   240
Flowrs worthy of Paradise which not nice Art
In Beds and curious Knots,[12] but Nature boon[13]
Powrd forth profuse on Hill and Dale and Plain,
Both where the morning Sun first warmly smote

[8] on the Euphrates; Seleucia, founded by one of Alexander's generals, was on the Tigris.

[9] probably the Tigris (see ll. 210–12).

[10] traditionally the Nile, Euphrates, Tigris, and Indus.

[11] wandering.

[12] elaborate flower gardens.

[13] bountiful.

The open field, and where the unpierc't shade   245
Imbrownd the noontide Bowrs: Thus was this place,
A happy rural seat of various view;
Groves whose rich Trees wept odorous Gumms and Balm,
Others whose fruit burnisht with Golden Rind
Hung amiable, *Hesperian* Fables true,   250
If true, here only, and of delicious taste:
Betwixt them Lawns, or level Downs, and Flocks
Grasing the tender herb, were interpos'd,
Or palmie hilloc, or the flowrie lap
Of som irriguous Valley spred her store,   255
Flowrs of all hue, and without Thorn the Rose:
Another side, umbrageous Grots and Caves
Of cool recess, o're which the mantling vine
Layes forth her purple Grape, and gently creeps
Luxuriant; mean while murmuring waters fall   260
Down the slope hills, disperst, or in a Lake,
That to the fringed Bank with Myrtle crownd,
Her chrystal mirror holds, unite thir streams.
The Birds thir quire apply; aires, vernal aires,
Breathing the smell of field and grove, attune   265
The trembling leaves, while Universal *Pan*
Knit with the *Graces*[14] and the *Hours* in dance
Led on th' Eternal Spring. Not that fair field
Of *Enna*, where *Proserpin* gathring flowrs
Her self a fairer Flowr by gloomie *Dis*   270
Was gatherd,[15] which cost *Ceres* all that pain
To seek her through the world; nor that sweet Grove
Of *Daphne*[16] by *Orontes*, and th' inspir'd
Castalian Spring might with this Paradise
Of *Eden* strive; nor that *Nyseian* Ile   275
Girt with the River *Triton*, where old *Cham*,[17]
Whom Gentiles *Ammon* call and *Lybian Jove*,
Hid *Amalthea* and her Florid Son
Young *Bacchus* from his Stepdame *Rhea's* eye;

[14] The Graces were Aglaia (Brilliance), Euphrosyne (Joy), and Thalia (Bloom); the Hours were the goddesses of the seasons.
[15] See *Vice-Chancellor*, n. 17. Ceres was the mother of Proserpina.
[16] The groves of Daphne on the Orontes in Syria were the site of a temple to Apollo; the spring on Mt. Parnassus inspired great poetry and foretold oracles.
[17] Ham, identified with Ammon.

Nor where *Abassin*[18] Kings thir issue Guard,   280
Mount *Amara,* though this by som suppos'd
True Paradise under the *Ethiop* Line
By *Nilus* head, enclos'd with shining Rock,
A whole dayes journey high, but wide remote
From this *Assyrian* Garden, where the Fiend   285
Saw undelighted all delight, all kind
Of living Creatures new to sight and strange:
Two of far nobler shape erect and tall,
Godlike erect, with native Honour clad
In naked Majestie seemd Lords of all,   290
And worthie seemd, for in thir looks Divine
The image of thir glorious Maker shon,
Truth, Wisdom, Sanctitude severe and pure,
Severe, but in true filial freedom plac't;
Whence true autoritie in men; though both   295
Not equal, as thir sex not equal seemd;
For contemplation hee and valour formd,
For softness shee and sweet attractive Grace,
Hee for God only, shee for God in him:
His fair large Front and Eye sublime declar'd   300
Absolute rule; and Hyacinthin Locks
Round from his parted forelock manly hung
Clustring, but not beneath his shoulders broad:
Shee as a vail down to the slender waste
Her unadorned golden tresses wore   305
Dissheveld, but in wanton ringlets wav'd
As the Vine curls her tendrils, which impli'd
Subjection, but requir'd with gentle sway,
And by her yeilded, by him best receiv'd,
Yeilded with coy submission, modest pride,   310
And sweet reluctant amorous delay.
Nor those mysterious parts were then conceald,
Then was not guiltie shame, dishonest[19] shame
Of natures works, honor dishonorable,
Sin-bred, how have ye troubl'd all mankind   315
With shews instead, meer shews of seeming pure,
And banisht from mans life his happiest life,
Simplicitie and spotless innocence.
So pass'd they naked on, nor shund the sight
Of God or Angel, for they thought no ill: 320

[18] Abyssinian.
[19] unchaste.

So hand in hand they pass'd, the loveliest pair
That ever since in loves imbraces met,
Adam the goodliest man of men since born
His Sons, the fairest of her Daughters *Eve.*
Under a tuft of shade that on a green   325
Stood whispering soft, by a fresh Fountain side
They sat them down, and after no more toil
Of thir sweet Gardning labour then suffic'd
To recommend cool *Zephyr,* and made ease
More easie, wholsom thirst and appetite   330
More grateful, to thir Supper Fruits they fell,
Nectarine Fruits which the compliant boughs
Yeilded them, side-long as they sat recline
On the soft downie Bank damaskt with flowrs:
The savourie pulp they chew, and in the rind   335
Still as they thirsted scoop the brimming stream;
Nor gentle purpose,[20] nor endearing smiles
Wanted, nor youthful dalliance as beseems
Fair couple, linkt in happie nuptial League,
Alone as they. About them frisking playd   340
All Beasts of th' Earth, since wild, and of all chase
In Wood or Wilderness, Forrest or Den;
Sporting the Lion ramp'd, and in his paw
Dandl'd the Kid; Bears, Tygers, Ounces, Pards
Gambold before them, th' unwieldy Elephant   345
To make them mirth us'd all his might, and wreath'd
His Lithe Proboscis; close the Serpent sly
Insinuating,[21] wove with Gordian twine
His breaded train, and of his fatal guile
Gave proof unheeded; others on the grass   350
Coucht, and now fild with pasture gazing sat,
Or Bedward ruminating: for the Sun
Declin'd was hasting now with prone carreer
To th' Ocean Iles,[22] and in th' ascending Scale
Of Heav'n the Starrs that usher Evening rose: 355
When *Satan* still in gaze, as first he stood,
Scarce thus at length faild speech recoverd sad.
    O Hell! what doe mine eyes with grief behold,
Into our room of bliss thus high advanc't
Creatures of other mould, earth-born perhaps,   360

[20] conversation.
[21] with the added meaning "coiling"; his wile ("train") is difficult to untangle ("Gordian").
[22] the Azores.

Not Spirits, yet to heav'nly Spirits bright
Little inferior; whom my thoughts pursue
With wonder, and could love, so lively shines
In them Divine resemblance, and such grace
The hand that formd them on thir shape hath pourd.   365
Ah gentle pair, yee little think how nigh
Your change approaches, when all these delights
Will vanish and deliver ye to woe,
More woe, the more your taste is now of joy;
Happie, but for so happie ill secur'd   370
Long to continue, and this high seat your Heav'n
Ill fenc't for Heav'n to keep out such a foe
As now is enterd; yet no purpos'd foe
To you whom I could pittie thus forlorn
Though I unpittied: League with you I seek,   375
And mutual amitie so streight, so close,
That I with you must dwell, or you with me
Henceforth; my dwelling haply may not please
Like this fair Paradise, your sense, yet such
Accept your Makers work; he gave it me,   380
Which I as freely give; Hell shall unfold,
To entertain you two, her widest Gates,
And send forth all her Kings; there will be room,
Not like these narrow limits, to receive
Your numerous ofspring; if no better place,   385
Thank him who puts me loath to this revenge
On you who wrong me not for him who wrong'd.
And should I at your harmless innocence
Melt, as I doe, yet public reason just,
Honour and Empire with revenge enlarg'd,   390
By conquering this new World, compels me now
To do what else though damnd I should abhorr.
   So spake the Fiend, and with necessitie,
The Tyrants plea, excus'd his devilish deeds.
Then from his loftie stand on that high Tree   395
Down he alights among the sportful Herd
Of those fourfooted kinds, himself now one,
Now other, as thir shape serv'd best his end
Neerer to view his prey, and unespi'd
To mark what of thir state he more might learn   400
By word or action markt: about them round
A Lion now he stalks with fierie glare,
Then as a Tiger, who by chance hath spi'd
In some Purlieu two gentle Fawns at play,

Strait couches close, then rising changes oft   405
His couchant watch, as one who chose his ground
Whence rushing he might surest seise them both
Grip't in each paw: when *Adam* first of men
To first of women *Eve* thus moving speech,
Turnd him all ear to hear new utterance flow.   410
   Sole partner and sole part of all these joyes,
Dearer thy self then all; needs must the Power
That made us, and for us this ample World
Be infinitly good, and of his good
As liberal and free as infinite,   415
That rais'd us from the dust and plac't us here
In all this happiness, who at his hand
Have nothing merited, nor can perform
Aught whereof hee hath need, hee who requires
From us no other service then to keep   420
This one, this easie charge, of all the Trees
In Paradise that bear delicious fruit
So various, not to taste that onely Tree
Of knowledge, planted by the Tree of Life,
So neer grows Death to Life, what ere Death is,   425
Som dreadful thing no doubt; for well thou knowst
God hath pronounc't it death to taste that Tree,
The only sign of our obedience left
Among so many signes of power and rule
Conferrd upon us, and Dominion giv'n   430
Over all other Creatures that possess
Earth, Air, and Sea. Then let us not think hard
One easie prohibition, who enjoy
Free leave so large to all things else, and choice
Unlimited of manifold delights: 435
But let us ever praise him, and extoll
His bountie, following our delightful task
To prune these growing Plants, and tend these Flowrs,
Which were it toilsom, yet with thee were sweet.
   To whom thus *Eve* repli'd. O thou for whom   440
And from whom I was formd flesh of thy flesh,
And without whom am to no end, my Guide
And Head, what thou hast said is just and right.
For wee to him indeed all praises owe,
And daily thanks, I chiefly who enjoy   445
So farr the happier Lot, enjoying thee
Præeminent by so much odds, while thou
Like consort to thy self canst no where find.

That day I oft remember, when from sleep
I first awak't, and found my self repos'd   450
Under a shade on flowrs, much wondring where
And what I was, whence thither brought, and how.
Not distant far from thence a murmuring sound
Of waters issu'd from a Cave and spread
Into a liquid Plain, then stood unmov'd   455
Pure as th' expanse of Heav'n; I thither went
With unexperienc't thought, and laid me down
On the green bank, to look into the cleer
Smooth Lake, that to me seemd another Skie.
As I bent down to look, just opposite,   460
A Shape within the watry gleam appeerd
Bending to look on me, I started back,
It started back, but pleas'd I soon returnd,
Pleas'd it returnd as soon with answering looks
Of sympathie and love; there I had fixt   465
Mine eyes till now, and pin'd with vain desire,
Had not a voice thus warnd me, What thou seest,
What there thou seest fair Creature is thy self,
With thee it came and goes: but follow me,
And I will bring thee where no shadow staies   470
Thy coming, and thy soft imbraces, hee
Whose image thou art, him thou shall enjoy
Inseparablie thine, to him shalt bear
Multitudes like thy self, and thence be call'd
Mother of human Race: what could I doe,   475
But follow strait, invisibly thus led?
Till I espi'd thee, fair indeed and tall,
Under a Platan, yet methought less fair,
Less winning soft, less amiablie mild,
Then that smooth watry image; back I turnd,   480
Thou following cryd'st aloud, Return fair *Eve,*
Whom fli'st thou? whom thou fli'st, of him thou art,
His flesh, his bone; to give thee being I lent
Out of my side to thee, neerest my heart
Substantial Life, to have thee by my side   485
Henceforth an individual[23] solace dear;
Part of my Soul I seek thee, and thee claim
My other half: with that thy gentle hand
Seis'd mine, I yeilded, and from that time see
How beauty is excelld by manly grace   490

[23] undividable.

And wisdom, which alone is truly fair.
   So spake our general Mother, and with eyes
Of conjugal attraction unreprov'd,
And meek surrender, half imbracing leand
On our first Father, half her swelling Breast   495
Naked met his under the flowing Gold
Of her loose tresses hid: he in delight
Both of her Beauty and submissive Charms
Smil'd with superior Love, as *Jupiter*
On *Juno*[24] smiles, when he impregns the Clouds   500
That shed *May* Flowers; and press'd her Matron lip
With kisses pure: aside the Devil turnd
For envie, yet with jealous leer maligne
Ey'd them askance, and to himself thus plaind.
   Sight hateful, sight tormenting! thus these two   505
Imparadis't in one anothers arms
The happier *Eden*, shall enjoy thir fill
Of bliss on bliss, while I to Hell am thrust,
Where neither joy nor love, but fierce desire,
Among our other torments not the least,   510
Still unfulfill'd with pain of longing pines;
Yet let me not forget what I have gain'd
From thir own mouths; all is not theirs it seems:
One fatal Tree there stands of Knowledge call'd,
Forbidden them to taste: Knowledge forbidd'n?   515
Suspicious, reasonless. Why should thir Lord
Envie them that? can it be sin to know,
Can it be death? and do they onely stand
By Ignorance, is that thir happie state,
The proof of thir obedience and thir faith?   520
O fair foundation laid whereon to build
Thir ruin! Hence I will excite thir minds
With more desire to know, and to reject
Envious commands, invented with designe
To keep them low whom knowledge might exalt   525
Equal with Gods; aspiring to be such,
They taste and die: what likelier can ensue?
But first with narrow search I must walk round
This Garden, and no corner leave unspi'd;
A chance but chance may lead where I may meet   530
Some wandring Spirit of Heav'n, by Fountain side,
Or in thick shade retir'd, from him to draw

[24] i.e., the sun on air.

What further would be learnt. Live while ye may,
Yet happie pair; enjoy, till I return,
Short pleasures, for long woes are to succeed.   535
    So saying, his proud step he scornful turn'd,
But with sly circumspection, and began
Through wood, through waste, o're hill, o're dale his roam.
Mean while in utmost Longitude, where Heav'n
With Earth and Ocean meets, the setting Sun   540
Slowly descended, and with right aspect[25]
Against the eastern Gate of Paradise
Leveld his eevning Rayes: it was a Rock
Of Alablaster, pil'd up to the Clouds,
Conspicuous farr, winding with one ascent   545
Accessible from Earth, one entrance high;
The rest was craggie cliff, that overhung
Still as it rose, impossible to climb.
Betwixt these rockie Pillars *Gabriel* sat
Chief of th' Angelic Guards, awaiting night;   550
About him exercis'd Heroic Games
Th' unarmed Youth of Heav'n, but nigh at hand
Celestial Armourie, Shields, Helms, and Speares
Hung high with Diamond flaming, and with Gold.
Thither came *Uriel*, gliding through the Eev'n   555
On a Sun beam, swift as a shooting Starr
In *Autumn* thwarts the night, when vapors fir'd
Impress the Air, and shews the Mariner
From what point of his Compass to beware
Impetuous winds: he thus began in haste.   560
    Gabriel, to thee thy cours by Lot hath giv'n
Charge and strict watch that to this happie place
No evil thing approach or enter in;
This day at highth of Noon came to my Sphear
A Spirit, zealous, as he seem'd, to know   565
More of th' Almighties works, and chiefly Man
Gods latest Image: I describ'd his way
Bent all on speed, and markt his Aerie Gate;
But in the Mount that lies from *Eden* North,
Where he first lighted, soon discernd his looks   570
Alien from Heav'n, with passions foul obscur'd:
Mine eye pursu'd him still, but under shade
Lost sight of him; one of the banisht crew
I fear, hath ventur'd from the deep, to raise

[25] direct look.

New troubles; him thy care must be to find.   575
   To whom the winged Warriour thus returnd:
Uriel, no wonder if thy perfet sight,
Amid the Suns bright circle where thou sitst,
See farr and wide: in at this Gate none pass
The vigilance here plac't, but such as come   580
Well known from Heav'n; and since Meridian hour
No Creature thence: if Spirit of other sort,
So minded, have oreleapt these earthie bounds
On purpose, hard thou knowst it to exclude
Spiritual substance with corporeal barr.   585
But if within the circuit of these walks
In whatsoever shape he lurk, of whom
Thou tellst, by morrow dawning I shall know.
   So promis'd hee, and *Uriel* to his charge
Returnd on that bright beam, whose point now rais'd   590
Bore him slope downward to the Sun now fall'n
Beneath th' *Azores;* whither the prime Orb,
Incredible how swift, had thither rowl'd
Diurnal, or this less volubil Earth
By shorter flight to th' East, had left him there   595
Arraying with reflected Purple and Gold
The Clouds that on his Western Throne attend:
Now came still Eevning on, and Twilight gray
Had in her sober Liverie all things clad;
Silence accompanied, for Beast and Bird,   600
They to thir grassie Couch, these to thir Nests
Were slunk, all but the wakeful Nightingale;
She all night long her amorous descant sung;
Silence was pleas'd: now glow'd the Firmament
With living Saphirs: *Hesperus* that led   605
The starrie Host, rode brightest, till the Moon
Rising in clouded Majestie, at length
Apparent Queen unvaild her peerless light,
And o're the dark her Silver Mantle threw.
   When *Adam* thus to *Eve:* Fair Consort, th' hour   610
Of night, and all things now retir'd to rest
 Mind us of like repose, since God hath set
Labour and rest, as day and night to men
Successive, and the timely dew of sleep
Now falling with soft slumbrous weight inclines   615
Our eye-lids; other Creatures all day long
Rove idle unimploid, and less need rest;
Man hath his daily work of body or mind

Appointed, which declares his Dignitie,
And the regard of Heav'n on all his waies; 620
While other Animals unactive range,
And of thir doings God takes no account.
To morrow ere fresh Morning streak the East
With first approach of light, we must be ris'n,
And at our pleasant labour, to reform 625
Yon flowrie Arbors, yonder Allies green,
Our walk at noon, with branches overgrown,
That mock our scant manuring, and require
More hands then ours to lop thir wanton growth:
Those Blossoms also, and those dropping Gumms, 630
That lie bestrown unsightly and unsmooth,
Ask riddance, if we mean to tread with ease;
Mean while, as Nature wills, Night bids us rest.
　　To whom thus *Eve* with perfet beauty adornd.
My Author and Disposer, what thou bidst 635
Unargu'd I obey; so God ordains,
God is thy Law, thou mine: to know no more
Is womans happiest knowledge and her praise.
With thee conversing I forget all time,
All seasons and thir change, all please alike. 640
Sweet is the breath of morn, her rising sweet,
With charm[26] of earliest Birds; pleasant the Sun
When first on this delightful Land he spreads
His orient Beams, on herb, tree, fruit, and flowr,
Glistring with dew; fragrant the fertil earth 645
After soft showers; and sweet the coming on
Of grateful Eevning mild, then silent Night
With this her solemn Bird and this fair Moon,
And these the Gemms of Heav'n, her starrie train:
But neither breath of Morn when she ascends 650
With charm of earliest Birds, nor rising Sun
On this delightful land, nor herb, fruit, flowr,
Glistring with dew, nor fragrance after showers,
Nor grateful Eevning mild, nor silent Night
With this her solemn Bird, nor walk by Moon, 655
Or glittering Starr-light without thee is sweet.
But wherfore all night long shine these, for whom
This glorious sight, when sleep hath shut all eyes?
　　To whom our general Ancestor repli'd.
Daughter of God and Man, accomplisht *Eve*, 660

[26] song.

Those have thir course to finish, round the Earth,
By morrow Eevning, and from Land to Land
In order, though to Nations yet unborn,
Ministring light prepar'd, they set and rise;
Least total darkness should by Night regain   665
Her old possession, and extinguish life
In Nature and all things, which these soft fires
Not only enlighten, but with kindly heat
Of various influence foment and warm,
Temper or nourish, or in part shed down   670
Thir stellar vertue on all kinds that grow
On Earth, made hereby apter to receive
Perfection from the Suns more potent Ray.
These then, though unbeheld in deep of night,
Shine not in vain, nor think, though men were none,   675
That heav'n would want spectators, God want praise;
Millions of spiritual Creatures walk the Earth
Unseen, both when we wake, and when we sleep:
All these with ceasless praise his works behold
Both day and night: how often from the steep   680
Of echoing Hill or Thicket have we heard
Celestial voices to the midnight air,
Sole, or responsive each to others note
Singing thir great Creator: oft in bands
While they keep watch, or nightly rounding walk   685
With Heav'nly touch of instrumental sounds
In full harmonic number joind, thir songs
Divide the night,[27] and lift our thoughts to Heav'n.
    Thus talking hand in hand alone they pass'd
On to thir blissful Bower; it was a place   690
Chos'n by the sovran Planter, when he fram'd
All things to mans delightful use; the roof
Of thickest covert was inwoven shade
Laurel and Mirtle, and what higher grew
Of firm and fragrant leaf; on either side   695
Acanthus, and each odorous bushie shrub
Fenc'd up the verdant wall; each beauteous flowr,
Iris all hues, Roses, and Gessamin
Rear'd high thir flourisht[28] heads between, and wrought
Mosaic; underfoot the Violet,   700
Crocus, and Hyacinth with rich inlay

[27] into the watches of l. 685.
[28] adorned with flowers.

Broiderd the ground, more colour'd then with stone
Of costliest Emblem:²⁹ other Creature here
Beast, Bird, Insect, or Worm durst enter none;
Such was thir awe of Man. In shadier Bower   705
More sacred and sequesterd, though but feign'd,
Pan or *Silvanus* never slept, nor Nymph,
Nor *Faunus* haunted. Here in close recess
With Flowers, Garlands, and sweet-smelling Herbs
Espoused *Eve* deckt first her Nuptial Bed,   710
And heav'nly Quires the Hymenæan³⁰ sung,
What day the genial³¹ Angel to our Sire
Brought her in naked beauty more adorn'd,
More lovely then *Pandora*,³² whom the Gods
Endowd with all thir gifts, and O too like   715
In sad event, when to th' unwiser Son
Of *Japhet* brought by *Hermes*, she ensnar'd
Mankind with her fair looks, to be aveng'd
On him who had stole *Joves* authentic fire.
    Thus at thir shadie Lodge arriv'd, both stood,   720
Both turnd, and under op'n Skie ador'd
The God that made both Skie, Air, Earth and Heav'n
Which they beheld, the Moons resplendent Globe
And starrie Pole: Thou also mad'st the Night,
Maker Omnipotent, and thou the Day,   725
Which we in our appointed work imployd
Have finisht happie in our mutual help
And mutual love, the Crown of all our bliss
Ordaind by thee, and this delicious place
For us too large, where thy abundance wants   730
Partakers, and uncropt falls to the ground.
But thou hast promis'd from us two a Race
To fill the Earth, who shall with us extoll
Thy goodness infinite, both when we wake,
And when we seek, as now, thy gift of sleep.   735
    This said unanimous, and other Rites
Observing none, but adoration pure
Which God likes best, into thir inmost bowr

²⁹ inlaid with precious gems.
³⁰ marriage song.
³¹ nuptial.
³² literally, "all-gifted"; through curiosity, she allowed the
world's evils to fly from a magic box, only hope remaining behind.
Her husband was Epimethus, brother of Prometheus, sons of
Japetus, who was identified with Noah's son Japhet.

Handed they went; and eas'd the putting off
These troublesom disguises which wee wear,   740
Strait side by side were laid, nor turnd I ween
Adam from his fair Spouse, nor *Eve* the Rites
Mysterious of connubial Love refus'd:
Whatever Hypocrites austerely talk
Of puritie and place and innocence,   745
Defaming as impure what God declares
Pure, and commands to som, leaves free to all.
Our Maker bids increase, who bids abstain
But our Destroyer, foe to God and Man?
Hail wedded Love, mysterious Law, true sourse   750
Of human ofspring, sole proprietie,
In Paradise of all things common else.
By thee adulterous lust was driv'n from men
Among the bestial herds to raunge, by thee
Founded in Reason, Loyal, Just, and Pure,   755
Relations dear, and all the Charities
Of Father, Son, and Brother first were known.
Farr be it, that I should write thee sin or blame,
Or think thee unbefitting holiest place,
Perpetual Fountain of Domestic sweets,   760
Whose bed is undefil'd and chast pronounc't,
Present, or past, as Saints and Patriarchs us'd.
Here Love his golden shafts imploies, here lights
His constant Lamp, and waves his purple wings,
Reigns here and revels; not in the bought smile   765
Of Harlots, loveless, joyless, unindeard,
Casual fruition, nor in Court Amours
Mixt Dance, or wanton Mask, or Midnight Ball,
Or Serenate, which the starv'd Lover sings
To his proud fair, best quitted with disdain.   770
These lulld by Nightingales imbracing slept,
And on thir naked limbs the flowrie roof
Showrd Roses, which the Morn repair'd. Sleep on
Blest pair; and O yet happiest if ye seek
No happier state, and know to know no more.   775
    Now had night measur'd with her shaddowie Cone
Half way up Hill this vast Sublunar Vault,
And from thir Ivorie Port the Cherubim
Forth issuing at th' accustomd hour stood armd
To thir night watches in warlike Parade,   780
When *Gabriel* to his next in power thus spake.
    Uzziel, half these draw off, and coast the South

With strictest watch; these other wheel the North,
Our circuit meets full West. As flame they part
Half wheeling to the Shield, half to the Spear.   785
From these, two strong and suttle Spirits he calld
That neer him stood, and gave them thus in charge.
   Ithuriel and *Zephon*, with wing'd speed
Search through this Garden, leav unsearcht no nook,
But chiefly where those two fair Creatures Lodge,   790
Now laid perhaps asleep secure of harm.
This Eevning from the Sun's decline arriv'd
Who tells of som infernal Spirit seen
Hitherward bent (who could have thought?) escap'd
The barrs of Hell, on errand bad no doubt: 795
Such where ye find, seise fast, and hither bring.
   So saying, on he led his radiant Files,
Daz'ling the Moon; these to the Bower direct
In search of whom they sought: him there they found
Squat like a Toad, close at the ear of *Eve;*   800
Assaying by his Devilish art to reach
The Organs of her Fancie, and with them forge
Illusions as he list, Phantasms and Dreams,
Or if, inspiring venom, he might taint
Th' animal Spirits that from pure blood arise   805
Like gentle breaths from Rivers pure, thence raise
At least distemperd, discontented thoughts,
Vain hopes, vain aimes, inordinate desires
Blown up with high conceits ingendring pride.
Him thus intent *Ithuriel* with his Spear   810
Touch'd lightly; for no falshood can endure
Touch of Celestial temper, but returns
Of force to its own likeness: up he starts
Discoverd and surpriz'd. As when a spark
Lights on a heap of nitrous Powder, laid   815
Fit for the Tun som Magazin to store
Against a rumord Warr, the Smuttie grain
With sudden blaze diffus'd, inflames the Air:
So started up in his own shape the Fiend.
Back stept those two fair Angels half amaz'd   820
So sudden to behold the grieslie King;
Yet thus, unmov'd with fear, accost him soon.
   Which of those rebell Spirits adjudg'd to Hell
Com'st thou, escap'd thy prison, and transform'd,
Why satst thou like an enemie in wait   825
Here watching at the head of these that sleep?

Know ye not then said *Satan*, fill'd with scorn,
Know ye not mee? ye knew me once no mate
For you, there sitting where ye durst not soar;
Not to know mee argues your selves unknown,   830
The lowest of your throng; or if ye know,
Why ask ye, and superfluous begin
Your message, like to end as much in vain?
To whom thus *Zephon*, answering scorn with scorn.
Think not, revolted Spirit, thy shape the same,   835
Or undiminisht brightness, to be known
As when thou stoodst in Heav'n upright and pure;
That Glorie then, when thou no more wast good,
Departed from thee, and thou resembl'st now
Thy sin and place of doom obscure and foul.   840
But come, for thou, be sure, shalt give account
To him who sent us, whose charge is to keep
This place inviolable, and these from harm.
So spake the Cherub, and his grave rebuke
Severe in youthful beautie, added grace   845
Invincible: abasht the Devil stood,
And felt how awful goodness is, and saw
Vertue in her shape how lovely, saw, and pin'd
His loss; but chiefly to find here observ'd
His lustre visibly impar'd; yet seemd   850
Undaunted. If I must contend, said he,
Best with the best, the Sender not the sent,
Or all at once; more glorie will be wonn,
Or less be lost. Thy fear, said *Zephon* bold,
Will save us trial what the least can doe   855
Single against thee wicked, and thence weak.
The Fiend repli'd not, overcome with rage;
But like a proud Steed reind, went hautie on,
Chaumping his iron curb: to strive or flie
He held it vain; awe from above had quelld   860
His heart, not else dismai'd. Now drew they nigh
The western Point, where those half-rounding guards
Just met, and closing stood in squadron joind
Awaiting next command. To whom thir Chief
Gabriel from the Front thus calld aloud.   865
O friends, I hear the tread of nimble feet
Hasting this way, and now by glimps discern
Ithuriel and *Zephon* through the shade,
And with them comes a third of Regal port,
But faded splendor wan; who by his gate   870

And fierce demeanour seems the Prince of Hell,
Not likely to part hence without contest;
Stand firm, for in his look defiance lours.
    He scarce had ended, when those two approach'd
And brief related whom they brought, wher found,   875
How busied, in what form and posture coucht.
    To whom with stern regard thus *Gabriel* spake.
Why hast thou, *Satan*, broke the bounds prescrib'd
To thy transgressions, and disturb'd the charge
Of others, who approve not to transgress   880
By thy example, but have power and right
To question thy bold entrance on this place;
Imploi'd it seems to violate sleep, and those
Whose dwelling God hath planted here in bliss?
    To whom thus *Satan*, with contemptuous brow.   885
Gabriel, thou hadst in Heav'n th' esteem of wise,
And such I held thee; but this question askt
Puts me in doubt. Lives ther who loves his pain?
Who would not, finding way, break loose from Hell,
Though thither doomd? Thou wouldst thy self, no doubt, 890
And boldly venture to whatever place
Farthest from pain, where thou mightst hope to change
Torment with ease, and soonest recompence
Dole with delight, which in this place I sought;
To thee no reason; who knowst only good,   895
But evil hast not tri'd: and wilt object
His will who bound us? let him surer barr
His Iron Gates, if he intends our stay
In that dark durance: thus much what was askt.
The rest is true, they found me where they say;   900
But that implies not violence or harm.
    Thus he in scorn. The warlike Angel mov'd,
Disdainfully half smiling thus repli'd.
O loss of one in Heav'n to judge of wise,
Since *Satan* fell, whom follie overthrew,   905
And now returns him from his prison scap't,
Gravely in doubt whether to hold them wise
Or not, who ask what boldness brought him hither
Unlicenc't from his bounds in Hell prescrib'd;
So wise he judges it to fly from pain   910
However, and to scape his punishment.
So judge thou still, presumptuous, till the wrauth,
Which thou incurr'st by flying, meet thy flight
Seavenfold, and scourge that wisdom back to Hell,

Which taught thee yet no better, that no pain   915
Can equal anger infinite provok't.
But wherefore thou alone? wherefore with thee
Came not all Hell broke loose? is pain to them
Less pain, less to be fled, or thou then they
Less hardie to endure? courageous Chief,   920
The first in flight from pain, had'st thou alledg'd
To thy deserted host this cause of flight,
Thou surely hadst not come sole fugitive.
　To which the Fiend thus answerd frowning stern.
Not that I less endure, or shrink from pain,   925
Insulting Angel, well thou knowst I stood
Thy fiercest, when in Battel to thy aid
The blasting volied Thunder made all speed
And seconded thy else not dreaded Spear.
But still thy words at random, as before,   930
Argue thy inexperience what behooves
From hard assaies and ill successes past
A faithful Leader, not to hazard all
Through wayes of danger by himself untri'd.
I therefore, I alone first undertook   935
To wing the desolate Abyss, and spie
This new created World, whereof in Hell
Fame is not silent, here in hope to find
Better abode, and my afflicted Powers
To settle here on Earth, or in mid Air;   940
Though for possession put to try once more
What thou and thy gay Legions dare against;
Whose easier business were to serve thir Lord
High up in Heav'n, with songs to hymn his Throne,
And practis'd distances to cringe, not fight.   945
　To whom the warriour Angel soon repli'd.
To say and strait unsay, pretending first
Wise to flie pain, professing next the Spie,
Argues no Leader, but a lyar trac't,
Satan, and couldst thou faithful add? O name,   950
O sacred name of faithfulness profan'd!
Faithful to whom? to thy rebellious crew?
Armie of Fiends, fit body to fit head;
Was this your discipline and faith ingag'd,
Your military obedience, to dissolve   955
Allegeance to th' acknowledg'd Power supream?
And thou sly hypocrite, who now wouldst seem
Patron of liberty, who more then thou

Once fawn'd, and cring'd, and servilly ador'd
Heav'ns awful Monarch? wherefore but in hope   960
To dispossess him, and thy self to reigne?
But mark what I arreed³³ thee now, avant;
Flie thither whence thou fledst: if from this hour
Within these hallowd limits thou appeer,
Back to th' infernal pit I drag thee chaind,   965
And Seal thee so, as henceforth not to scorn
The facil gates of hell too slightly barrd.
    So threatn'd hee, but *Satan* to no threats
Gave heed, but waxing more in rage repli'd.
    Then when I am thy captive talk of chains,   970
Proud limitarie³⁴ Cherub, but ere then
Farr heavier load thy self expect to feel
From my prevailing arm, though Heavens King
Ride on thy wings, and thou with thy Compeers,
Us'd to the yoak, draw'st his triumphant wheels   975
In progress through the rode of Heav'n Star-pav'd.
    While thus he spake, th' Angelic Squadron bright
Turnd fierie red, sharpning in mooned horns
Thir Phalanx, and began to hemm him round
With ported Spears, as thick as when a field   980
Of *Ceres* ripe for harvest waving bends
Her bearded Grove of ears, which way the wind
Swayes them; the careful Plowman doubting stands
Least on the threshing floor his hopeful sheaves
Prove chaff. On th' other side *Satan* allarm'd   985
Collecting all his might dilated stood,
Like *Teneriff* or *Atlas*³⁵ unremov'd:
His stature reacht the Skie, and on his Crest
Sat horror Plum'd; nor wanted in his grasp
What seemd both Spear and Shield: now dreadful
        deeds   990
Might have ensu'd, nor onely Paradise
In this commotion, but the Starrie Cope
Of Heav'n perhaps, or all the Elements
At least had gon to rack, disturb'd and torn
With violence of this conflict, had not soon   995
Th' Eternal to prevent such horrid fray

³³ advise.
³⁴ guarder of boundaries.
³⁵ mountains in the Canary Islands and north Africa.

Hung forth in Heav'n his golden Scales, yet seen[36]
Betwixt *Astrea* and the *Scorpion* signe,
Wherein all things created first he weigh'd,
The pendulous round Earth with ballanc't Air   1000
In counterpoise, now ponders all events,
Battels and Realms: in these he put two weights
The sequel each of parting and of fight;
The latter quick up flew, and kickt the beam;
Which *Gabriel* spying, thus bespake the Fiend.   1005
   Satan, I know thy strength, and thou knowst mine,
Neither our own but giv'n; what follie then
To boast what Arms can doe, since thine no more
Then Heav'n permits, nor mine, though doubl'd now
To trample thee as mire: for proof look up,   1010
And read thy Lot in yon celestial Sign
Where thou art weigh'd, and shown how light, how weak,
If thou resist. The Fiend lookt up and knew
His mounted scale aloft: nor more; but fled
Murmuring, and with him fled the shades of night.   1015

BOOK V

THE ARGUMENT

Morning approach't, *Eve* relates to *Adam* her troublesome
dream; he likes it not, yet comforts her: They come forth to
thir day labours: Thir Morning Hymn at the Door of thir
Bower. God to render Man inexcusable sends *Raphael* to admonish him of his obedience, of his free estate, of his enemy
near at hand; who he is, and why his enemy, and whatever
else may avail *Adam* to know. *Raphael* comes down to Paradise, his appearance describ'd, his coming discern'd by *Adam*
afar off sitting at the door of his Bower; he goes out to meet
him, brings him to his lodge, entertains him with the choycest
fruits of Paradise got together by *Eve;* thir discourse at Table:
Raphael performs his message, minds *Adam* of his state and of
his enemy; relates at *Adams* request who that enemy is, and
how he came to be so, beginning from his first revolt in
Heaven, and the occasion thereof; how he drew his Legions
after him to the parts of the North, and there incited them
to rebel with him, perswading all but only *Abdiel* a Seraph,

[36] Libra in the Zodiac lies between Virgo and Scorpio. Zeus
weighed the fate of the Greeks and the Trojans (*Iliad*, VIII, 69–
72) and of Achilles and Hector (*Iliad*, XXII, 209).

who in Argument diswades and opposes him, then forsakes
him.

Now Morn her rosie steps in th' Eastern Clime
Advancing, sow'd the Earth with Orient Pearl,
When *Adam* wak't, so customd, for his sleep
Was Aerie light, from pure digestion bred,
And temperat vapors[1] bland, which th' only sound   5
Of leaves and fuming rills, *Aurora's* fan,
Lightly dispers'd, and the shrill Matin Song
Of Birds on every bough; so much the more
His wonder was to find unwak'nd *Eve*
With Tresses discompos'd, and glowing Cheek,   10
As through unquiet rest: he on his side
Leaning half-rais'd, with looks of cordial Love
Hung over her enamour'd, and beheld
Beautie, which whether waking or asleep,
Shot forth peculiar Graces; then with voice   15
Mild, as when *Zephyrus* on *Flora* breathes,
Her hand soft touching, whisperd thus. Awake
My fairest, my espous'd, my latest found,
Heav'ns last best gift, my ever new delight,
Awake, the morning shines, and the fresh field   20
Calls us, we lose the prime, to mark how spring
Our tended Plants, how blows the Citron Grove,
What drops the Myrrh, and what the balmie Reed,[2]
How Nature paints her colours, how the Bee
Sits on the Bloom extracting liquid sweet.   25
Such whispering wak'd her, but with startl'd eye
On *Adam*, whom imbracing, thus she spake.
O Sole in whom my thoughts find all repose,
My Glorie, my Perfection, glad I see
Thy face, and Morn return'd, for I this Night,   30
Such night till this I never pass'd, have dream'd,
If dream'd, not as I oft am wont, of thee,
Works of day pass't, or morrows next designe,
But of offence and trouble, which my mind
Knew never till this irksom night; methought   35
Close at mine ear one call'd me forth to walk
With gentle voice, I thought it thine; it said,
Why sleepst thou *Eve?* now is the pleasant time,

[1] exhalations.
[2] the balsam, source of balm.

The cool, the silent, save where silence yields
To the night-warbling Bird, that now awake   40
Tunes sweetest his love-labor'd song; now reignes
Full Orb'd the Moon, and with more pleasing light
Shadowie sets off the face of things; in vain,
If none regard; Heav'n wakes with all his eyes,
Whom to behold but thee, Natures desire,   45
In whose sight all things joy, with ravishment
Attracted by thy beauty still to gaze.
I rose as at thy call, but found thee not;
To find thee I directed then my walk;
And on, methought, alone I pass'd through ways   50
That brought me on a sudden to the Tree
Of interdicted Knowledge: fair it seem'd,
Much fairer to my Fancie then by day:
And as I wondring lookt, beside it stood
One shap'd and wing'd like one of those from Heav'n   55
By us oft seen; his dewie locks distill'd
Ambrosia; on that Tree he also gaz'd;
And O fair Plant, said he, with fruit surcharg'd,
Deigns none to ease thy load and taste thy sweet,
Nor God, nor Man; is Knowledge so despis'd?   60
Or envie, or what reserve forbids to taste?
Forbid who will, none shall from me withhold
Longer thy offerd good, why else set here?
This said he paus'd not, but with ventrous Arm
He pluckt, he tasted; mee damp horror chil'd   65
At such bold words voucht with a deed so bold:
But he thus overjoy'd, O Fruit Divine,
Sweet of thy self, but much more sweet thus cropt,
Forbidd'n here, it seems, as onely fit
For Gods, yet able to make Gods of Men: 70
And why not Gods of Men, since good, the more
Communicated, more abundant grows,
The Author not impair'd, but honourd more?
Here, happie Creature, fair Angelic *Eve,*
Partake thou also; happie though thou art,   75
Happier thou mayst be, worthier canst not be:
Taste this, and be henceforth among the Gods
Thy self a Goddess, not to Earth confind,
But somtimes in the Air, as wee, somtimes
Ascend to Heav'n, by merit thine, and see   80
What life the Gods live there, and such live thou.
So saying, he drew nigh, and to me held,

Evn to my mouth of that same fruit held part
Which he had pluckt; the pleasant savourie smell
So quick'nd appetite, that I, methought,   85
Could not but taste. Forthwith up to the Clouds
With him I flew, and underneath beheld
The Earth outstretcht immense, a prospect wide
And various: wondring at my flight and change
To this high exaltation; suddenly   90
My Guide was gon, and I, me thought, sunk down,
And fell asleep; but O how glad I wak'd
To find this but a dream! Thus *Eve* her Night
Related, and thus *Adam* answerd sad.

    Best Image of my self and dearer half,   95
The trouble of thy thoughts this night in sleep
Affects me equally; nor can I like
This uncouth dream, of evil sprung I fear;
Yet evil whence? in thee can harbour none,
Created pure. But know that in the Soul   100
Are many lesser Faculties that serve
Reason as chief; among these Fansie next
Her office holds; of all external things,
Which the five watchful Senses represent,
She forms Imaginations, Aerie shapes,   105
Which Reason joyning or disjoyning, frames
All what we affirm or what deny, and call
Our knowledge or opinion; then retires
Into her private Cell when Nature rests.
Oft in her absence mimic Fansie wakes   110
To imitate her; but misjoyning shapes,
Wild work produces oft, and most in dreams,
Ill matching words and deeds long past or late.
Som such resemblances methinks I find
Of our last Eevnings talk, in this thy dream,   115
But with addition strange: yet be not sad.
Evil into the mind of God[3] or Man
May come and go, so unapprov'd, and leave
No spot or blame behind: Which gives me hope
That what in sleep thou didst abhorr to dream,   120
Waking thou never wilt consent to do.
Be not disheart'nd then, nor cloud those looks
That wont to be more chearful and serene
Then when fair Morning first smiles on the World,

[3] The omniscience of God admits of evil.

And let us to our fresh imployments rise   125
Among the Groves, the Fountains, and the Flowrs
That open now thir choicest bosom'd smells
Reserv'd from night, and kept for thee in store.
   So cheard he his fair Spouse, and she was cheard,
But silently a gentle tear let fall   130
From either eye, and wip'd them with her hair;
Two other precious drops that ready stood,
Each in thir chrystal sluce, hee ere they fell
Kiss'd as the gracious signs of sweet remorse
And pious awe, that feard to have offended.   135
   So all was cleard, and to the Field they haste.
But first from under shadie arborous roof,
Soon as they forth were come to open sight
Of day-spring, and the Sun, who scarce up ris'n
With wheels yet hov'ring o're the Ocean brim,   140
Shot paralel to th' earth his dewie ray,
Discovering in wide Lantskip all the East
Of Paradise and *Edens* happie Plains,
Lowly they bow'd adoring, and began
Thir Orisons, each Morning duly paid   145
In various style, for neither various style
Nor holy rapture wanted they to praise
Thir Maker, in fit strains pronounc't or sung
Unmeditated, such prompt eloquence
Flowd from thir lips, in Prose or numerous[4] Verse,   150
More tuneable then needed Lute or Harp
To add more sweetness, and they thus began.
   These are thy glorious works, Parent of good,
Almightie, thine this universal Frame,
Thus wondrous fair; thy self how wondrous then!   155
Unspeakable, who sitst above these Heav'ns
To us invisible or dimly seen
In these thy lowest works, yet these declare
Thy goodness beyond thought, and Power Divine:
Speak yee who best can tell, ye Sons of light,   160
Angels, for yee behold him, and with songs
And choral symphonies, Day without Night,
Circle his Throne rejoycing, yee in Heav'n,
On Earth joyn all ye Creatures to extoll
Him first, him last, him midst, and without end.   165

   [4] metrical.

Fairest of Starrs,[5] last in the train of Night,
If better thou belong not to the dawn,
Sure pledge of day, that crownst the smiling Morn
With thy bright Circlet, praise him in thy Sphear
While day arises, that sweet hour of Prime.   170
Thou Sun, of this great World both Eye and Soul,
Acknowledge him thy Greater, sound his praise
In thy eternal course, both when thou climb'st,
And when high Noon hast gaind, and when thou fallst.
Moon, that now meetst the orient Sun, now fli'st   175
With the fixt Starrs, fixt in thir Orb that flies,[6]
And yee five other wandring Fires that move
In mystic Dance not without Song, resound
His praise, who out of Darkness call'd up Light.
Air, and ye Elements the eldest birth   180
Of Natures Womb, that in quaternion[7] run
Perpetual Circle, multiform; and mix
And nourish all things, let your ceasless change
Varie to our great Maker still new praise.
Ye Mists and Exhalations that now rise   185
From Hill or steaming Lake, duskie or grey,
Till the Sun paint your fleecie skirts with Gold,
In honour to the Worlds great Author rise,
Whether to deck with Clouds th' uncolourd[8] skie,
Or wet the thirstie Earth with falling showers,   190
Rising or falling still advance his praise.
His praise ye Winds, that from four Quarters blow,
Breath soft or loud; and wave your tops, ye Pines,
With every Plant, in sign of Worship wave.
Fountains and yee, that warble, as ye flow,   195
Melodious murmurs, warbling tune his praise.
Joyn voices all ye living Souls, ye Birds,
That singing up to Heaven Gate ascend,
Bear on your wings and in your notes his praise;
Yee that in Waters glide, and yee that walk   200
The Earth, and stately tread, or lowly creep;
Witness if I be silent, Morn or Eev'n,

[5] Venus (Lucifer as the morning star, Hesperus as the evening star).

[6] the sphere of fixed stars which circle the earth once every twenty-four hours. The "wandering Fires" are the planets Mercury, Venus, Mars, Jupiter, and Saturn.

[7] the four elements variously combined.

[8] of one color.

To Hill, or Valley, Fountain, or fresh shade
Made vocal by my Song, and taught his praise.
Hail universal Lord, be bounteous still   205
To give us onely good; and if the night
Have gather'd aught of evil or conceald,
Disperse it, as now light dispels the dark.
   So pray'd they innocent, and to thir thoughts
Firm peace recoverd soon and wonted calm.   210
On to thir mornings rural work they haste
Among sweet dews and flowrs; where any row
Of Fruit-trees overwoodie reach'd too farr
Thir pamperd boughs, and needed hands to check
Fruitless imbraces: or they led the Vine   215
To wed her Elm; she spous'd about him twines
Her mariageable arms, and with her brings
Her dowr th' adopted Clusters, to adorn
His barren leaves. Them thus imploid beheld
With pittie Heav'ns high King, and to him call'd   220
Raphael, the sociable Spirit, that deign'd
To travel with *Tobias*, and secur'd
His marriage with the seaventimes-wedded Maid.[9]
   Raphael, said hee, thou hear'st what stir on Earth
Satan from Hell scap't through the darksom Gulf   225
Hath rais'd in Paradise, and how disturb'd
This night the human pair, how he designes
In them at once to ruin all mankind.
Go therefore, half this day as friend with friend
Converse with *Adam*, in what Bowr or shade   230
Thou find'st him from the heat of Noon retir'd,
To respit his day-labour with repast,
Or with repose; and such discourse bring on,
As may advise him of his happie state,
Happiness in his power left free to will,   235
Left to his own free Will, his Will though free,
Yet mutable; whence warn him to beware
He swerve not too secure: tell him withall
His danger, and from whom, what enemie
Late failn himself from Heav'n, is plotting now   240
The fall of others from like state of bliss;
By violence, no, for that shall be withstood,
But by deceit and lies; this let him know,
Least wilfully transgressing he pretend

[9] See Tobit viii.

Surprisal, unadmonisht, unforewarnd.   245
   So spake th' Eternal Father, and fulfilld
All Justice: nor delaid the winged Saint
After his charge receiv'd; but from among
Thousand Celestial Ardors,[10] where he stood
Vaild with his gorgeous wings, up springing light   250
Flew through the midst of Heav'n; th' angelic Quires
On each hand parting, to his speed gave way
Through all th' Empyreal road; till at the Gate
Of Heav'n arriv'd, the gate self-opend wide
On golden Hinges turning, as by work   255
Divine the sov'ran Architect had fram'd.
From hence, no cloud, or, to obstruct his sight,
Starr interpos'd, however small he sees,
Not unconform to other shining Globes,
Earth and the Gard'n of God, with Cedars crownd   260
Above all Hills. As when by night the Glass[11]
Of *Galileo*, less assur'd, observes
Imagind Lands and Regions in the Moon:
Or Pilot from amidst the *Cyclades*[12]
Delos or *Samos* first appeering kenns   265
A cloudy spot. Down thither prone[13] in flight
He speeds, and through the vast Ethereal Skie
Sails between worlds and worlds, with steddie wing
Now on the polar winds, then with quick Fann[14]
Winnows the buxom Air; till within soar   270
Of Towring Eagles, to all the Fowls he seems
A *Phœnix*, gaz'd by all, as that sole Bird
When to enshrine his reliques in the Sun's
Bright Temple, to *Ægyptian Thebes* he flies.[15]
At once on th' Eastern cliff of Paradise   275
He lights, and to his proper shape returns
A Seraph wing'd; six wings he wore, to shade
His lineaments Divine; the pair that clad
Each shoulder broad, came mantling o're his brest
With regal Ornament; the middle pair   280

[10] angels.
[11] telescope.
[12] Aegean islands.
[13] downward.
[14] wing.
[15] The unique and undying Phoenix rose from its own ashes in Heliopolis ("city of the sun") rather than in the neighboring Egyptian city of Thebes, according to Ovid, *Meta.*, XV, 391–407.

Girt like a Starrie Zone his waste, and round
Skirted his loins and thighs with downie Gold
And colours dipt in Heav'n; the third his feet
Shaddowd from either heel with featherd mail
Skie-tinctur'd grain.[16] Like *Maia's* son[17] he stood, 285
And shook his Plumes, that Heav'nly fragrance filld
The circuit wide. Strait knew him all the Bands
Of Angels under watch; and to his state,
And to his message high in honour rise;
For on som message high they guess'd him bound. 290
Thir glittering Tents he pass'd, and now is come
Into the blissful field, through Groves of Myrrh,
And flowring Odours, Cassia, Nard, and Balm;
A Wilderness of sweets; for Nature here
Wantond as in her prime, and plaid at will 295
Her Virgin Fancies, pouring forth more sweet,
Wild above Rule or Art; enormous bliss.
Him through the spicie Forrest onward com
Adam discernd, as in the dore he sat
Of his cool Bowr, while now the mounted Sun 300
Shot down direct his fervid Raies to warm
Earths inmost womb, more warmth then *Adam* needs;
And *Eve* within, due at her hour prepar'd
For dinner savourie fruits, of taste to please
True appetite, and not disrelish thirst 305
Of nectarous draughts between, from milkie stream,
Berrie or Grape: to whom thus *Adam* call'd.
  Haste hither *Eve,* and worth thy sight behold
Eastward among those Trees, what glorious shape
Comes this way moving; seems another Morn 310
Ris'n on mid-noon; som great behest from Heav'n
To us perhaps he brings, and will voutsafe
This day to be our Guest. But goe with speed,
And what thy stores contain, bring forth and pour
Abundance, fit to honour and receive 315
Our Heav'nly stranger; well we may afford
Our givers thir own gifts, and large bestow
From large bestowd, where Nature multiplies
Her fertil growth, and by disburd'ning grows
More fruitful, which instructs us not to spare. 320
  To whom thus *Eve. Adam,* earths hallowd mould,

[16] colored blue.
[17] Hermes.

Of God inspir'd, small store will serve, where store,
All seasons, ripe for use hangs on the stalk;
Save what by frugal storing firmness gains
To nourish, and superfluous moist consumes: 325
But I will haste and from each bough and break,
Each Plant and juiciest Gourd will pluck such choice
To entertain our Angel guest, as hee
Beholding shall confess that here on Earth
God hath dispenst his bounties as in Heav'n.   330
   So saying, with dispatchful looks in haste
She turns, on hospitable thoughts intent
What choice to chuse for delicacie best,
What order, so contriv'd as not to mix
Tastes, not well joynd, inelegant, but bring   335
Taste after taste upheld with kindliest[18] change,
Bestirs her then, and from each tender stalk
Whatever Earth all-bearing Mother yeilds
In *India* East or West,[19] or middle shoar
In *Pontus* or the *Punic* Coast,[20] or where   340
Alcinous reign'd, fruit of all kinds, in coat,
Rough, or smooth rind, or bearded husk, or shell
She gathers, Tribute large, and on the board
Heaps with unsparing hand; for drink the Grape
She crushes, inoffensive moust, and meaths[21]   345
From many a berrie, and from sweet kernels prest
She tempers dulcet creams, nor these to hold
Wants her fit vessels pure, then strews the ground
With Rose and Odours from the shrub unfum'd.[22]
Mean while our Primitive great Sire, to meet   350
His god-like Guest, walks forth, without more train
Accompani'd then with his own compleat
Perfections, in himself was all his state,
More solemn then the tedious pomp that waits
On Princes, when thir rich Retinue long   355
Of Horses led, and Grooms besmeard with Gold
Dazles the crowd, and sets them all agape.
Neerer his presence *Adam* though not awd,

[18] most natural.

[19] India and the Indies (East) and America (West).

[20] the Black Sea or the Carthaginian coast. Alcinous' gardens of perpetual spring and harvest were visited by Ulysses (*Od.*, VII, 125 ff.).

[21] unfermented liquor and meads.

[22] unburned; it is natural odor rather than that from incense.

Yet with submiss approach and reverence meek,
As to a superior Nature, bowing low,   360
Thus said. Native of Heav'n, for other place
None can then Heav'n such glorious shape contain;
Since by descending from the Thrones above,
Those happie places thou hast deign'd a while
To want, and honour these, voutsafe with us   365
Two onely, who yet by sov'ran gift possess
This spacious ground, in yonder shadie Bowr
To rest, and what the Garden choicest bears
To sit and taste, till this meridian heat
Be over, and the Sun more cool decline.   370
    Whom thus th' Angelic Vertue answerd mild.
Adam, I therefore came, nor art thou such
Created, or such place hast here to dwell,
As may not oft invite, though Spirits of Heav'n
To visit thee; lead on then where thy Bowr   375
Oreshades; for these mid-hours, till Eevning rise
I have at will. So to the Silvan Lodge
They came, that like *Pomona's*[23] Arbour smil'd
With flowrets deck't and fragrant smells; but *Eve*
Undeckt, save with her self more lovely fair   380
Then Wood-Nymph, or the fairest Goddess feign'd
Of three[24] that in Mount *Ida* naked strove,
Stood t' entertain her guest from Heav'n; no vail
Shee needed, Vertue-proof, no thought infirm
Alterd her cheek. On whom the Angel *Hail*   385
Bestowd, the holy salutation us'd
Long after to blest *Marie,* second *Eve.*
    Hail Mother of Mankind, whose fruitful Womb
Shall fill the World more numerous with thy Sons
Then with these various fruits the Trees of God   390
Have heap'd this Table. Rais'd of grassie terf
Thir Table was, and mossie seats had round,
And on her ample Square from side to side
All *Autumn* pil'd, though *Spring* and *Autumn* here
Danc'd hand in hand. A while discourse they hold;   395
No fear lest Dinner cool; when thus began
Our Authour. Heav'nly stranger, please to taste
These bounties which our Nourisher, from whom

[23] Roman goddess of fruits.
[24] Juno, Minerva, and Venus whose beauty was judged by Paris
on Mt. Ida.

All perfet good unmeasur'd out, descends,
To us for food and for delight hath caus'd   400
The Earth to yeild; unsavourie food perhaps
To spiritual Natures; only this I know,
That one Celestial Father gives to all.
    To whom the Angel. Therefore what he gives
(Whose praise be ever sung) to man in part   405
Spiritual, may of purest Spirits be found
No ingrateful food: and food alike those pure
Intelligential substances require
As doth your Rational; and both contain
Within them every lower facultie   410
Of sense, whereby they hear, see, smell, touch, taste,
Tasting concoct,[25] digest, assimilate,
And corporeal to incorporeal turn.
For know, whatever was created, needs
To be sustaind and fed; of Elements   415
The grosser feeds the purer, Earth the Sea,
Earth and the Sea feed Air, the Air those Fires
Ethereal, and as lowest first the Moon;
Whence in her visage round those spots, unpurg'd
Vapours not yet into her substance turnd.[26]   420
Nor doth the Moon no nourishment exhale
From her moist Continent to higher Orbs.
The Sun that light imparts to all, receives
From all his alimental recompence
In humid exhalations, and at Ev'n   425
Sups with the Ocean: though in Heav'n the Trees
Of life ambrosial fruitage bear, and vines
Yeild Nectar, though from off the boughs each Morn
We brush mellifluous Dews, and find the ground
Cover'd with pearly grain:[27] yet God hath here   430
Varied his bounty so with new delights,
As may compare with Heaven; and to taste
Think not I shall be nice. So down they sat,
And to thir viands fell, nor seemingly
The Angel, nor in mist, the common gloss   435
Of Theologians, but with keen dispatch
Of real hunger, and concoctive heat
To transubstantiate; what redounds,[28] transpires

[25] begin to digest.
[26] Moon spots had been thought to be exhalations from earth.
[27] manna.
[28] overflows.

Through Spirits with ease; nor wonder; if by fire
Of sooty coal th' Empiric Alchimist   440
Can turn, or holds it possible to turn
Metals of drossiest Ore to perfet Gold
As from the Mine. Mean while at Table *Eve*
Ministerd naked, and thir flowing cups
With pleasant liquors crown'd: O innocence   445
Deserving Paradise! if ever, then,
Then had the Sons of God excuse t' have bin
Enamour'd at that sight; but in those hearts
Love unlibidinous reign'd, nor jealousie
Was understood, the injur'd Lovers Hell.   450
    Thus when with meats and drinks they had suffic'd,
Not burd'nd Nature, sudden mind arose
In *Adam*, not to let th' occasion pass
Giv'n him by this great Conference to know
Of things above his World, and of thir being   455
Who dwell in Heav'n, whose excellence he saw
Transcend his own so farr, whose radiant forms
Divine effulgence, whose high Power so far
Exceeded human, and his wary speech
Thus to th' Empyreal Minister he fram'd.   460
    Inhabitant with God, now know I well
Thy favour, in this honour done to man,
Under whose lowly roof thou hast voutsaf't
To enter, and these earthly fruits to taste,
Food not of Angels, yet accepted so,   465
As that more willingly thou couldst not seem
At Heav'ns high feasts t' have fed: yet what compare?
    To whom the winged Hierarch repli'd.
O *Adam*, one Almightie is, from whom
All things proceed, and up to him return,[29]   470
If not deprav'd from good, created all
Such to perfection, one first matter all,
Indu'd with various forms, various degrees
Of substance, and in things that live, of life;
But more refin'd, more spiritous, and pure,   475
As neerer to him plac't or neerer tending

[29] referring to the chain of being which tends upward toward
its creator. Man's natural bodily spirits (ll. 483 ff.) are raised to
the vital emotional spirits and then to the intellectual (animal)
spirits. Thus man is able to reason, but his conclusions are those
which angels know intuitively.

Each in thir several active Sphears assign'd,
Till body up to spirit work, in bounds
Proportiond to each kind. So from the root
Springs lighter the green stalk, from thence the leaves   480
More aerie, last the bright consummate flowr
Spirits odorous breathes: flowrs and thir fruit
Mans nourishment, by gradual scale sublim'd
To vital Spirits aspire, to animal,
To intellectual, give both life and sense,   485
Fansie and understanding, whence the Soul
Reason receives, and reason is her being,
Discursive, or Intuitive; discourse
Is oftest yours, the latter most is ours,
Differing but in degree, of kind the same.   490
Wonder not then, what God for you saw good
If I refuse not, but convert, as you,
To proper substance; time may come when men
With Angels may participate, and find
No inconvenient Diet, nor too light Fare: 495
And from these corporal nutriments perhaps
Your bodies may at last turn all to Spirit,
Improv'd by tract of time, and wing'd ascend
Ethereal, as wee, or may at choice
Here or in Heav'nly Paradises dwell;   500
If ye be found obedient, and retain
Unalterably firm his love entire
Whose progenie you are. Mean while enjoy
Your fill what happiness this happie state
Can comprehend, incapable of more.   505
    To whom the Patriarch of mankind repli'd.
O favourable spirit, propitious guest,
Well hast thou taught the way that might direct
Our knowledge, and the scale of Nature set
From center to circumference, whereon   510
In contemplation of created things
By steps we may ascend to God. But say,
What meant that caution joind, *if ye be found
Obedient?* can we want obedience then
To him, or possibly his love desert   515
Who formd us from the dust, and plac'd us here
Full to the utmost measure of what bliss
Human desires can seek or apprehend?
    To whom the Angel. Son of Heav'n and Earth,
Attend: That thou art happie, owe to God;   520

That thou continu'st such, owe to thy self,
That is, to thy obedience; therein stand.
This was that caution giv'n thee; be advis'd.
God made thee perfet, not immutable;
And good he made thee, but to persevere   525
He left it in thy power, ordaind thy will
By nature free, not over-rul'd by Fate
Inextricable, or strict necessity;
Our voluntarie service he requires,
Not our necessitated, such with him   530
Finds no acceptance, nor can find, for how
Can hearts, not free, be tri'd whether they serve
Willing or no, who will but what they must
By Destinie, and can no other choose?
My self and all th' Angelic Host that stand   535
In sight of God enthron'd, our happie state
Hold, as you yours, while our obedience holds;
On other surety none; freely we serve,
Because wee freely love, as in our will
To love or not; in this we stand or fall: 540
And som are fall'n, to disobedience fall'n,
And so from Heav'n to deepest Hell; O fall
From what high state of bliss into what woe!
    To whom our great Progenitor. Thy words
Attentive, and with more delighted ear,   545
Divine instructer, I have heard, then when
Cherubic Songs by night from neighbouring Hills
Aereal Music send: nor knew I not
To be both will and deed created free;
Yet that we never shall forget to love   550
Our maker, and obey him whose command
Single, is yet so just, my constant thoughts
Assur'd me, and still assure: though what thou tellst
Hath past in Heav'n, som doubt within me move,
But more desire to hear, if thou consent,   555
The full relation, which must needs be strange,
Worthy of Sacred silence to be heard;
And we have yet large day, for scarce the Sun
Hath finisht half his journey, and scarce begins
His other half in the great Zone of Heav'n.   560
    Thus *Adam* made request, and *Raphael*
After short pause assenting, thus began.
    High matter thou injoinst me, O prime of men,
Sad task and hard, for how shall I relate

To human sense th' invisible exploits   565
Of warring Spirits; how without remorse
The ruin of so many glorious once
And perfet while they stood; how last unfould
The secrets of another world, perhaps
Not lawful to reveal? yet for thy good   570
This is dispenc't, and what surmounts the reach
Of human sense, I shall delineate so,
By lik'ning spiritual to corporal forms,
As may express them best, though what if Earth
Be but the shaddow of Heav'n,[30] and things therein   575
Each t' other like, more then on earth is thought?
  As yet this world was not, and *Chaos* wild
Reign'd where these Heav'ns now rowl, where Earth now
        rests
Upon her Center pois'd, when on a day
(For Time, though in Eternitie, appli'd   580
To motion, measures all things durable
By present, past, and future) on such day
As Heav'ns great Year[31] brings forth, th' Empyreal Host
Of Angels by Imperial summons call'd,
Innumerable before th' Almighties Throne   585
Forthwith from all the ends of Heav'n appeerd
Under thir Hierarchs in orders bright;
Ten thousand thousand Ensignes high advanc'd,
Standards, and Gonfalons twixt Van and Rear
Stream in the Air, and for distinction serve   590
Of Hierarchies, of Orders, and Degrees;
Or in thir glittering Tissues bear imblaz'd
Holy Memorials, acts of Zeal and Love
Recorded eminent. Thus when in Orbs
Of circuit inexpressible they stood,   595
Orb within Orb, the Father infinite,
By whom in bliss imbosom'd sat the Son,
Amidst as from a flaming Mount, whose top
Brightness had made invisible, thus spake.
  Hear all ye Angels, Progenie of Light,   600
Thrones, Dominations, Princedoms, Vertues, Powers,
Hear my Decree, which unrevok't shall stand.

[30] typologically, that is, as a foreshadowing of Heaven, according to William G. Madsen (*PMLA*, LXXV, 1960, 519–26), rather than Platonically as a simulation of Heaven.
[31] the time it would take the star to complete the equinoctial precession, around 26,000 years.

This day I have begot[32] whom I declare
My onely Son, and on this holy Hill
Him have anointed, whom ye now behold   605
At my right hand; your Head I him appoint;
And by my Self have sworn to him shall bow
All knees in Heav'n, and shall confess him Lord:
Under his great Vice-gerent Reign abide
United as one individual Soul   610
For ever happie: him who disobeys
Mee disobeys, breaks union, and that day
Cast out from God and blessed vision, falls
Into utter darkness, deep ingulft, his place
Ordaind without redemption, without end.   615
    So spake th' Omnipotent, and with his words
All seemd well pleas'd, all seem'd, but were not all.
That day, as other solemn dayes, they spent
In song and dance about the sacred Hill,
Mystical dance, which yonder starrie Sphear   620
Of Planets and of fixt in all her Wheels
Resembles nearest, mazes intricate,
Eccentric, intervolv'd, yet regular
Then most, when most irregular they seem:
And in thir motions harmonie Divine   625
So smooths her charming tones, that Gods own ear
Listens delighted. Eevning now approach'd
(For wee have also our Eevning and our Morn,
Wee ours for change delectable, not need)
Forthwith from dance to sweet repast they turn   630
Desirous; all in Circles as they stood,
Tables are set, and on a sudden pil'd
With Angels Food, and rubied Nectar flows:
In Pearl, in Diamond, and massie Gold
Fruit of delicious Vines, the growth of Heav'n.   635
On flowrs repos'd, and with fresh flowrets crownd,
They eat, they drink, and in communion sweet
Quaff immortalitie and joy, secure
Of surfet where full measure onely bounds
Excess, before th' all-bounteous King, who showrd   640
With copious hand, rejoycing in thir joy.
Now when ambrosial Night with Clouds exhal'd
From that high mount of God, whence light and shade

[32] not the creation of the Son, but his anointing as king; see
Milton's translation of *Ps.* 2 (verses 6–7).

Spring both, the face of brightest Heav'n had chang'd
To grateful Twilight (for Night comes not there   645
In darker veil) and roseat Dews dispos'd
All but th' unsleeping eyes of God to rest,
Wide over all the Plain, and wider farr
Then all this globous Earth in Plain outspred,
(Such are the Courts of God) th' Angelic throng   650
Disperst in Bands and Files thir Camp extend
By living Streams among the Trees of Life,
Pavilions numberless, and sudden reard,
Celestial Tabernacles, where they slept
Fannd with cool Winds, save those who in thir course   655
Melodious Hymns about the sovran Throne
Alternate all night long: but not so wak'd
Satan, so call him now, his former name
Is heard no more in Heav'n; he of the first,
If not the first Arch-Angel, great in Power,   660
In favour and in præeminence, yet fraught
With envie against the Son of God, that day
Honourd by his great Father, and proclaimd
Messiah King anointed, could not bear
Through pride that sight, and thought himself impaird.   665
Deep malice thence conceiving and disdain,
Soon as midnight brought on the duskie hour
Friendliest to sleep and silence, he resolv'd
With all his Legions to dislodge, and leave
Unworshipt, unobey'd the Throne supream   670
Contemptuous, and his next subordinate[33]
Awak'ning, thus to him in secret spake.
   Sleepst thou Companion dear, what sleep can close
Thy eye-lids? and remembrest what Decree
Of yesterday, so late hath past the lips   675
Of Heav'ns Almightie. Thou to me thy thoughts
Wast wont, I mine to thee was wont t' impart;
Both waking we were one; how then can now
Thy sleep dissent? new Laws thou seest impos'd;
New Laws from him who reigns, new minds may raise   680
In us who serve, new Counsels, to debate
What doubtful may ensue, more in this place
To utter is not safe. Assemble thou
Of all those Myriads which we lead the chief;
Tell them that by command, ere yet dim Night   685

[33] Beelzebub.

Her shadowie Cloud withdraws, I am to haste,
And all who under me thir Banners wave,
Homeward with flying march where we possess
The Quarters of the North, there to prepare
Fit entertainment to receive our King   690
The great *Messiah*, and his new commands,
Who speedily through all the Hierarchies
Intends to pass triumphant, and give Laws.
    So spake the false Arch-Angel, and infus'd
Bad influence into th' unwarie brest   695
Of his Associate; hee together calls,
Or several one by one, the Regent Powers,
Under him Regent, tells, as he was taught,
That the most High commanding, now ere Night,
Now ere dim Night had disincumberd Heav'n,   700
The great Hierarchal Standard was to move;
Tells the suggested cause, and casts between
Ambiguous words and jealousies, to sound
Or taint integritie; but all obey'd
The wonted signal, and superior voice   705
Of thir great Potentate; for great indeed
His name, and high was his degree in Heav'n;
His count'nance, as the Morning Starr that guides
The starrie flock, allur'd them, and with lyes
Drew after him the third part of Heav'ns Host: 710
Mean while th' Eternal eye, whose sight discerns
Abstrusest thoughts, from forth his holy Mount
And from within the golden Lamps that burn
Nightly before him, saw without thir light
Rebellion rising, saw in whom, how spred   715
Among the sons of Morn, what multitudes
Were banded to oppose his high Decree;
And smiling to his onely Son thus said.
    Son, thou in whom my glory I behold
In full resplendence, Heir of all my might,   720
Neerly it now concerns us to be sure
Of our Omnipotence, and with what Arms
We mean to hold what anciently we claim
Of Deitie or Empire, such a foe
Is rising, who intends t' erect his Throne   725
Equal to ours, throughout the spacious North;
Nor so content, hath in his thought to try
In battel, what our Power is, or our right.
Let us advise, and to this hazard draw

With speed what force is left, and all imploy   730
In our defence, lest unawares we lose
This our high place, our Sanctuarie, our Hill.
   To whom the Son with calm aspect and cleer
Light'ning Divine, ineffable, serene,
Made answer. Mightie Father, thou thy foes   735
Justly hast in derision, and secure
Laugh'st at thir vain designes and tumults vain,
Matter to mee of Glory, whom thir hate
Illustrates, when they see all Regal Power
Giv'n me to quell thir pride, and in event   740
Know whether I be dextrous to subdue
Thy Rebels, or be found the worst in Heav'n.
   So spake the Son, but *Satan* with his Powers
Farr was advanc't on winged speed, an Host
Innumerable as the Starrs of Night,   745
Or Starrs of Morning, Dew-drops, which the Sun
Impearls on every leaf and every flower.
Regions they pass'd, the mightie Regencies
Of Seraphim and Potentates and Thrones
In thir triple Degrees, Regions to which   750
All thy Dominion, *Adam,* is no more
Then what this Garden is to all the Earth,
And all the Sea, from one entire globose[34]
Stretcht into Longitude; which having pass'd
At length into the limits of the North   755
They came, and *Satan* to his Royal seat
High on a Hill, far blazing, as a Mount
Rais'd on a Mount, with Pyramids and Towrs
From Diamond Quarries hew'n, and Rocks of Gold,
The Palace of great *Lucifer* (so call   760
That Structure in the Dialect of men
Interpreted), which not long after, he
Affecting all equality with God,
In imitation of that Mount whereon
Messiah was declar'd in sight of Heav'n,   765
The Mountain of the Congregation call'd;
For thither he assembl'd all his Train,
Pretending so commanded to consult
About the great reception of thir King,
Thither to come, and with calumnious Art   770
Of counterfeted truth thus held thir ears.

[34] sphere.

Thrones, Dominations, Princedoms, Vertues, Powers,
If these magnific Titles yet remain
Not meerly titular, since by Decree
Another now hath to himself ingross't   775
All Power, and us eclipst under the name
Of King anointed, for whom all this haste
Of midnight march, and hurried meeting here,
This onely to consult how we may best
With what may be devis'd of honours new   780
Receive him coming to receive from us
Knee-tribute yet unpaid, prostration vile,
Too much to one, but double how endur'd,
To one and to his image now proclaim'd?
But what if better counsels might erect   785
Our minds and teach us to cast off this Yoke?
Will ye submit your necks, and chuse to bend
The supple knee? ye will not, if I trust
To know ye right, or if ye know your selves
Natives and Sons of Heav'n possest before   790
By none, and if not equal all, yet free,
Equally free; for Orders and Degrees
Jarr not with liberty, but well consist.
Who can in reason then or right assume
Monarchie over such as live by right   795
His equals, if in power and splendor less,
In freedom equal? or can introduce
Law and Edict on us, who without law
Err not, much less for this to be our Lord,
And look for adoration to th' abuse   800
Of those Imperial Titles which assert
Our being ordain'd to govern, not to serve?
    Thus farr his bold discourse without controul
Had audience, when among the Seraphim
Abdiel, then whom none with more zeal ador'd   805
The Deitie, and divine commands obei'd,
Stood up, and in a flame of zeal severe
The current of his fury thus oppos'd.
    O argument blasphemous, false and proud!
Words which no ear ever to hear in Heav'n   810
Expected, least of all from thee, ingrate
In place thy self so high above thy Peers.
Canst thou with impious obloquie condemn
The just Decree of God, pronounc't and sworn,
That to his only Son by right endu'd   815

With Regal Scepter, every Soul in Heav'n
Shall bend the knee, and in that honour due
Confess him rightful King? unjust thou saist
Flatly unjust, to bind with Laws the free,
And equal over equals to let Reigne,   820
One over all with unsucceeded power.
Shalt thou give Law to God, shalt thou dispute
With him the points of libertie, who made
Thee what thou art, and formd the Pow'rs of Heav'n
Such as he pleas'd, and circumscrib'd thir being?   825
Yet by experience taught we know how good,
And of our good, and of our dignitie
How provident he is, how farr from thought
To make us less, bent rather to exalt
Our happie state under one Head more neer   830
United. But to grant it thee unjust,
That equal over equals Monarch Reigne:
Thy self though great and glorious dost thou count,
Or all Angelic Nature joind in one,
Equal to him begotten Son, by whom   835
As by his Word the mighty Father made
All things, ev'n thee, and all the Spirits of Heav'n
By him created in thir bright degrees,
Crownd them with Glory, and to thir Glory nam'd
Thrones, Dominations, Princedoms, Vertues, Powers,   840
Essential Powers, nor by his Reign obscur'd,
But more illustrious made, since he the Head
One of our number thus reduc't becomes,
His Laws our Laws, all honour to him done
Returns our own. Cease then this impious rage,   845
And tempt not these; but hast'n to appease
Th' incensed Father, and th' incensed Son,
While Pardon may be found in time besought.
    So spake the fervent Angel, but his zeal
None seconded, as out of season judg'd,   850
Or singular and rash, whereat rejoic'd
Th' Apostat, and more haughty thus repli'd.
That we were formd then saist thou? and the work
Of secondarie hands, by task transferd
From Father to his Son? strange point and new!   855
Doctrin which we would know whence learnt: who saw
When this creation was? rememberst thou
Thy making, while the Maker gave thee being?
We know no time when we were not as now;

Know none before us, self-begot, self-rais'd   860
By our own quick'ning power, when fatal course
Had circl'd his full Orb, the birth mature
Of this our native Heav'n, Ethereal Sons.
Our puissance is our own, our own right hand
Shall teach us highest deeds, by proof to try   865
Who is our equal: then thou shalt behold
Whether by supplication we intend
Address, and to begirt th' Almighty Throne
Beseeching or besieging. This report,
These tidings carrie to th' anointed King;   870
And fly, ere evil intercept thy flight.
     He said, and as the sound of waters deep
Hoarce murmur echo'd to his words applause
Through the infinite Host, nor less for that
The flaming Seraph fearless, though alone   875
Encompass'd round with foes, thus answerd bold.
     O alienate from God, O spirit accurst,
Forsak'n of all good; I see thy fall
Determind, and thy hapless crew involv'd
In this perfidious fraud, contagion spred   880
Both of thy crime and punishment: henceforth
No more be troubl'd how to quit the yoke
Of Gods *Messiah;* those indulgent Laws
Will not be now voutsaf't, other Decrees
Against thee are gon forth without recall;   885
That Golden Scepter which thou didst reject
Is now an Iron Rod to bruise and break
Thy disobedience. Well thou didst advise,
Yet not for thy advise or threats I fly
These wicked Tents devoted,[35] least the wrauth   890
Impendent, raging into sudden flame
Distinguish not: for soon expect to feel
His Thunder on thy head, devouring fire.
Then who created thee lamenting learn,
When who can uncreate thee thou shalt know.   895
     So spake the Seraph *Abdiel* faithful found,
Among the faithless, faithful only hee;
Among innumerable false, unmov'd,
Unshak'n, unseduc'd, unterrifi'd
His Loyaltie he kept, his Love, his Zeal;   900
Nor number, nor example with him wrought

[35] doomed.

To swerve from truth, or change his constant mind
Though single. From amidst them forth he pass'd,
Long way through hostile scorn, which he susteind
Superior, nor of violence fear'd aught;   905
And with retorted[36] scorn his back he turn'd
On those proud Towrs to swift destruction doom'd.

BOOK VI

THE ARGUMENT

Raphael continues to relate how *Michael* and *Gabriel* were
sent forth to battel against *Satan* and his Angels. The first
Fight describ'd: *Satan* and his Powers retire under Night: He
calls a Councel, invents devilish Engines, which in the second
dayes Fight put *Michael* and his Angels to some disorder;
but they at length pulling up Mountains overwhelm'd both
the force and Machins of *Satan:* Yet the Tumult not so ending, God on the third day sends *Messiah* his Son, for whom
he had reserv'd the glory of that Victory: Hee in the Power
of his Father coming to the place, and causing all his Legions
to stand still on either side, with his Chariot and Thunder
driving into the midst of his Enemies, pursues them unable
to resist towards the wall of Heaven; which opening, they
leap down with horrour and confusion into the place of punishment prepar'd for them in the Deep: *Messiah* returns with
triumph to his Father.

All night the dreadless Angel unpursu'd
Through Heav'ns wide Champain held his way, till Morn,
Wak't by the circling Hours, with rosie hand
Unbarr'd the gates of Light. There is a Cave
Within the Mount of God, fast by his Throne,   5
Where light and darkness in perpetual round
Lodge and dislodge by turns, which makes through Heav'n
Grateful vicissitude,[1] like Day and Night;
Light issues forth, and at the other dore
Obsequious[2] darkness enters, till her hour   10
To veil the Heav'n, though darkness there might well

[36] turned back.

---

[1] "change, variety, movement, the mark of vitality and joy char-
acteristic of both the divine and the human master artist's work"
(Joseph H. Summers, *PMLA*, LXIX, 1954, 251–64).
[2] compliantly following.

Seem twilight here; and now went forth the Morn
Such as in highest Heav'n, arrayd in Gold
Empyreal, from before her vanisht Night,
Shot through with orient Beams: when all the Plain   15
Coverd with thick embatteld Squadrons bright,
Chariots and flaming Armes, and fierie Steeds
Reflecting blaze on blaze, first met his view:
Warr he perceav'd, warr in procinct,³ and found
Already known what he for news had thought   20
To have reported: gladly then he mixt
Among those friendly Powers who him receav'd
With joy and acclamations loud, that one
That of so many Myriads fall'n, yet one
Returnd not lost: On to the sacred hill   25
They led him high applauded, and present
Before the seat supream; from whence a voice
From midst a Golden Cloud thus mild was heard.
    Servant of God,⁴ well done, well hast thou fought
The better fight, who single hast maintaind   30
Against revolted multitudes the Cause
Of Truth, in word mightier then they in Armes;
And for the testimonie of Truth hast born
Universal reproach, far worse to bear
Then violence: for this was all thy care   35
To stand approv'd in sight of God, though Worlds
Judg'd thee perverse: the easier conquest now
Remains thee, aided by this host of friends,
Back on thy foes more glorious to return
Then scornd thou didst depart, and to subdue   40
By force, who reason for thir Law refuse,
Right reason for thir Law, and for thir King
Messiah, who by right of merit Reigns.
Go *Michael* of Celestial Armies Prince,
And thou in Military prowess next   45
Gabriel, lead forth to Battel these my Sons
Invincible, lead forth my armed Saints
By Thousands and by Millions rang'd for fight;
Equal in number to that Godless crew
Rebellious, them with Fire and hostile Armes   50
Fearless assault, and to the brow of Heav'n
Pursuing drive them out from God and bliss,

³ readiness.
⁴ the literal meaning of Abdiel.

Into thir place of punishment, the Gulf
Of *Tartarus*, which ready opens wide
His fiery *Chaos* to receave thir fall.   55
   So spake the Sovran voice, and Clouds began
To darken all the Hill, and smoak to rowl
In duskie wreaths, reluctant flames, the signe
Of wrauth awak't: nor with less dread the loud
Ethereal Trumpet from on high gan blow: 60
At which command the Powers Militant,
That stood for Heav'n, in mighty Quadrate[5] joyn'd
Of Union irresistible, mov'd on
In silence thir bright Legions, to the sound
Of instrumental Harmonie that breath'd   65
Heroic Ardor to advent'rous deeds
Under thir God-like Leaders, in the Cause
Of God and his *Messiah*. On they move
Indissolubly firm; nor obvious[6] Hill,
Nor streit'ning[7] Vale, nor Wood, nor Stream divides   70
Thir perfet ranks; for high above the ground
Thir march was, and the passive Air upbore
Thir nimble tread, as when the total kind
Of Birds in orderly array on wing
Came summond over *Eden* to receive   75
Thir names of thee; so over many a tract
Of Heav'n they march'd, and many a Province wide
Tenfold the length of this terrene: at last
Farr in th' Horizon to the North appeer'd
From skirt to skirt a fierie Region, stretcht   80
In battailous aspect, and neerer view
Bristl'd with upright beams innumerable
Of rigid Spears, and Helmets throng'd, and Shields
Various, with boastful Argument[8] portraid,
The banded Powers of *Satan* hasting on   85
With furious expedition; for they weend
That self-same day by fight, or by surprize
To win the Mount of God, and on his Throne
To set the envier of his State, the proud
Aspirer, but thir thoughts prov'd fond and vain   90
In the mid way: though strange to us it seemd

[5] (a maneuver in the shape of a) square.
[6] lying in the way.
[7] narrowing.
[8] inscription.

At first, that Angel should with Angel warr,
And in fierce hosting⁹ meet, who wont to meet
So oft in Festivals of joy and love
Unanimous, as sons of one great Sire   95
Hymning th' Eternal Father: but the shout
Of Battel now began, and rushing sound
Of onset ended soon each milder thought.
High in the midst exalted as a God
Th' Apostat in his Sun-bright Chariot sate   100
Idol of Majestie Divine, enclos'd
With Flaming Cherubim, and golden Shields;
Then lighted from his gorgeous Throne, for now
'Twixt Host and Host but narrow space was left,
A dreadful intervall, and Front to Front   105
Presented stood in terrible array
Of hideous length: before the cloudie Van,
On the rough edge of battel ere it joyn'd,
Satan with vast and haughtie strides advanc't,
Came towring, armd in Adamant and Gold;   110
Abdiel that sight endur'd not, where he stood
Among the mightiest, bent on highest deeds,
And thus his own undaunted heart explores.
    O Heav'n! that such resemblance of the Highest
Should yet remain, where faith and realtie¹⁰   115
Remain not; wherfore should not strength and might
There fail where Vertue fails, or weakest prove
Where boldest; though to sight unconquerable?
His puissance, trusting in th' Almightie's aid,
I mean to try, whose Reason I have tri'd¹¹   120
Unsound and false; nor is it aught but just,
That he who in debate of Truth hath won,
Should win in Arms, in both disputes alike
Victor; though brutish that contest and foul,
When Reason hath to deal with force, yet so   125
Most reason is that Reason overcome.
    So pondering, and from his armed Peers
Forth stepping opposite, half way he met
His daring foe, at this prevention more
Incens't, and thus securely him defi'd.   130
    Proud, art thou met? thy hope was to have reacht

⁹ fighting of hosts (of angels).
¹⁰ loyalty.
¹¹ tested and found.

The highth of thy aspiring unoppos'd,
The Throne of God unguarded, and his side
Abandond at the terror of thy Power
Or potent tongue; fool, not to think how vain 135
Against th' Omnipotent to rise in Arms;
Who out of smallest things could without end
Have rais'd incessant Armies to defeat
Thy folly; or with solitarie hand
Reaching beyond all limit at one blow 140
Unaided could have finisht thee, and whelmd
Thy Legions under darkness; but thou seest
All are not of thy Train; there be who Faith
Prefer, and Pietie to God, though then
To thee not visible, when I alone 145
Seemd in thy World erroneous to dissent
From all: my Sect thou seest, now learn too late
How few somtimes may know, when thousands err.
　　Whom the grand foe with scornful eye askance
Thus answerd. Ill for thee, but in wisht hour 150
Of my revenge, first sought for thou returnst
From flight, seditious Angel, to receave
Thy merited reward, the first assay[12]
Of this right hand provok't, since first that tongue
Inspir'd with contradiction durst oppose 155
A third part of the Gods, in Synod met
Thir Deities to assert, who while they feel
Vigour Divine within them, can allow
Omnipotence to none. But well thou comst
Before thy fellows, ambitious to win 160
From me som Plume, that thy success may show
Destruction to the rest: this pause between
(Unanswerd least thou boast) to let thee know;
At first I thought that Libertie and Heav'n
To heav'nly Souls had bin all one: but now 165
I see that most through sloth had rather serve,
Ministring Spirits, traind up in Feast and Song;
Such hast thou arm'd, the Minstrelsie[13] of Heav'n,
Servilitie with freedom to contend,
As both thir deeds compar'd this day shall prove. 170
　　To whom in brief thus *Abdiel* stern repli'd.

[12] trial.
[13] the angels who sing God's hymns and whom Satan calls
servile.

Apostat, still thou errst, nor end wilt find
Of erring, from the path of truth remote:
Unjustly thou deprav'st it with the name
Of *Servitude* to serve whom God ordains,   175
Or Nature; God and Nature bid the same,
When he who rules is worthiest, and excells
Them whom he governs. This is servitude,
To serve th' unwise, or him who hath rebell'd
Against his worthier, as thine now serve thee,   180
Thy self not free, but to thy self enthrall'd;
Yet leudly dar'st our ministring upbraid.
Reign thou in Hell thy Kingdom, let mee serve
In Heav'n God ever blest, and his Divine
Behests obey, worthiest to be obey'd,   185
Yet Chains in Hell, not Realms expect: mean while
From mee returnd, as erst thou saidst, from flight,
This greeting on thy impious Crest receive.
    So saying, a noble stroke he lifted high,
Which hung not, but so swift with tempest fell   190
On the proud Crest of *Satan*, that no sight,
Nor motion of swift thought, less could his Shield
Such ruin intercept: ten paces huge
He back recoild; the tenth on bended knee
His massie Spear upstaid; as if on Earth   195
Winds under ground or waters forcing way
Sidelong, had push't a Mountain from his seat
Half sunk with all his Pines. Amazement seis'd
The Rebel Thrones, but greater rage to see
Thus foil'd thir mightiest, ours joy fill'd, and shout,   200
Presage of Victorie and fierce desire
Of Battel: whereat *Michael* bid sound
Th' Arch-Angel trumpet; through the vast of Heav'n
It sounded, and the faithful Armies rung
Hosanna to the Highest: nor stood at gaze   205
The adverse Legions, nor less hideous joyn'd
The horrid shock: now storming furie rose,
And clamour such as heard in Heav'n till now
Was never, Arms on Armour clashing bray'd
Horrible discord, and the madding Wheels   210
Of brazen Chariots rag'd; dire was the noise
Of conflict; over head the dismal hiss
Of fiery Darts in flaming volies flew,
And flying vaulted either Host with fire.

So under fierie Cope[14] together rush'd   215
Both Battels main, with ruinous assault
And inextinguishable rage; all Heav'n
Resounded, and had Earth bin then, all Earth
Had to her Center shook. What wonder? when
Millions of fierce encountring Angels fought   220
On either side, the least of whom could weild
These Elements, and arm him with the force
Of all thir Regions: how much more of Power
Armie against Armie numberless to raise
Dreadful combustion warring, and disturb,   225
Though not destroy, thir happie Native seat;
Had not th' Eternal King Omnipotent
From his strong hold of Heav'n high over-rul'd
And limited thir might; though numberd such
As each divided Legion might have seemd   230
A numerous Host, in strength each armed hand
A Legion; led in fight, yet Leader seemd
Each Warriour single as in Chief, expert
When to advance, or stand, or turn the sway
Of Battel, open when, and when to close   235
The ridges[15] of grim Warr; no thought of flight,
None of retreat, no unbecoming deed
That argu'd fear; each on himself reli'd,
As onely in his arm the moment[16] lay
Of victorie; deeds of eternal fame   240
Were don, but infinite: for wide was spred
That Warr and various; somtimes on firm ground
A standing fight, then soaring on main wing
Tormented all the Air; all Air seemd then
Conflicting Fire: long time in eeven scale   245
The Battel hung; till *Satan,* who that day
Prodigious power had shewn, and met in Armes
No equal, raunging through the dire attack
Of fighting Seraphim confus'd, at length
Saw where the Sword of *Michael* smote, and fell'd   250
Squadrons at once, with huge two-handed sway
Brandisht aloft the horrid edge came down
Wide wasting; such destruction to withstand
He hasted, and oppos'd the rockie Orb

[14] canopy of the sky.
[15] lines of warriors.
[16] the mechanical tendency to move.

Of tenfold Adamant, his ample Shield   255
A vast circumference: At his approach
The great Arch-Angel from his warlike toil
Surceas'd, and glad as hoping here to end
Intestine War in Heav'n, th' arch foe subdu'd
Or Captive drag'd in Chains, with hostile frown   260
And visage all enflam'd first thus began.
    Author of evil, unknown till thy revolt,
Unnam'd in Heav'n, now plenteous, as thou seest
These Acts of hateful strife, hateful to all,
Though heaviest by just measure on thy self   265
And thy adherents: how hast thou disturb'd
Heav'ns blessed peace, and into Nature brought
Miserie, uncreated till the crime
Of thy Rebellion? how hast thou instill'd
Thy malice into thousands, once upright   270
And faithful, now prov'd false. But think not here
To trouble Holy Rest; Heav'n casts thee out
From all her Confines. Heav'n the seat of bliss
Brooks not the works of violence and Warr.
Hence then, and evil go with thee along   275
Thy ofspring, to the place of evil, Hell,
Thou and thy wicked crew; there mingle broils,
Ere this avenging Sword begin thy doom,
Or som more sudden vengeance wing'd from God
Precipitate thee with augmented pain.   280
    So spake the Prince of Angels; to whom thus
The Adversarie. Nor think thou with wind
Of airie threats to aw whom yet with deeds
Thou canst not. Hast thou turnd the least of these
To flight, or if to fall, but that they rise   285
Unvanquisht, easier to transact with mee
That thou shouldst hope, imperious, and with threats
To chase me hence? err not that so shall end
The strife which thou call'st evil, but wee style
The strife of Glorie: which we mean to win,   290
Or turn this Heav'n it self into the Hell
Thou fablest, here however to dwell free,
If not to reign: mean while thy utmost force,
And join him nam'd *Almighty* to thy aid,
I flie not, but have sought thee farr and nigh.   295
    They ended parle, and both addrest[17] for fight

[17] prepared.

Unspeakable; for who, though with the tongue
Of Angels, can relate, or to what things
Liken on Earth conspicuous, that may lift
Human imagination to such highth   300
Of Godlike Power: for likest Gods they seemd,
Stood they or mov'd, in stature, motion, arms
Fit to decide the Empire of great Heav'n.
Now wav'd thir fierie Swords, and in the Air
Made horrid Circles; two broad Suns thir Shields   305
Blaz'd opposite, while expectation stood
In horror; from each hand with speed retir'd
Where erst was thickest fight, th' Angelic throng,
And left large field, unsafe within the wind
Of such commotion, such as to set forth   310
Great things by small, if Natures concord broke,
Among the Constellations warr were sprung,
Two Planets rushing from aspect maligne
Of fiercest opposition in mid Skie,
Should combat, and thir jarring Sphears confound.   315
Together both with next t' Almightie Arm,
Uplifted imminent one stroke they aim'd
That might determine,[18] and not need repeat,
As not of power, at once; nor odds[19] appeerd
In might or swift prevention; but the sword   320
Of *Michael* from the Armorie of God
Was giv'n him temperd so, that neither keen
Nor solid might resist that edge; it met
The sword of *Satan* with steep force to smite
Descending, and in half cut sheer, nor staid,   325
But with swift wheel reverse, deep entring shar'd
All his right side; then *Satan* first knew pain,
And writh'd him to and fro convolv'd; so sore
The griding[20] sword with discontinuous wound
Pass'd through him, but th' Ethereal substance clos'd   330
Not long divisible, and from the gash
A stream of Nectarous humor issuing flow'd
Sanguin, such as Celestial Spirits may bleed,
And all his Armour staind ere while so bright.
Forthwith on all sides to his aid was run   335
By Angels many and strong, who interpos'd

[18] (the outcome).
[19] advantage; "prevention" (l. 320) means "anticipation."
[20] cutting, thus "discontinuing" or separating the flesh.

Defence, while others bore him on thir Shields
Back to his Chariot; where it stood retir'd
From off the files of warr; there they him laid
Gnashing for anguish and despite and shame   340
To find himself not matchless, and his pride
Humbl'd by such rebuke, so farr beneath
His confidence to equal God in power.
Yet soon he heal'd; for Spirits that live throughout
Vital in every part, not as frail man   345
In Entrails, Heart or Head, Liver or Reins,
Cannot but by annihilating die;
Nor in thir liquid texture mortal wound
Receive, no more then can the fluid Air:
All Heart they live, all Head, all Eye, all Ear,   350
All Intellect, all Sense, and as they please,
They Limb themselves, and colour, shape or size
Assume, as likes them best, condense or rare.
    Mean while in other parts like deeds deserv'd
Memorial, where the might of *Gabriel* fought,   355
And with fierce Ensignes pierc'd the deep array
Of *Moloc* furious King, who him defi'd,
And at his Chariot wheels to drag him bound
Threat'n'd, nor from the Holie One of Heav'n
Refrein'd his tongue blasphemous; but anon   360
Down clov'n to the waste, with shatterd Armes
And uncouth pain fled bellowing. On each wing
Uriel and *Raphael* his vaunting foe,
Though huge, and in a Rock of Diamond Armd,
Vanquish'd *Adramelec*, and *Asmadai*,   365
Two potent Thrones, that to be less then Gods
Disdain'd, but meaner thoughts learnd in thir flight,
Mangl'd with gastly wounds through Plate and Mail.
Nor stood unmindful *Abdiel* to annoy
The Atheist crew, but with redoubl'd blow   370
Ariel and *Arioc*, and the violence
Of *Ramiel* scorcht and blasted overthrew.
I might relate of thousands, and thir names
Eternize here on Earth; but those elect
Angels contented with thir fame in Heav'n   375
Seek not the praise of men: the other sort
In might though wondrous and in Acts of Warr,
Nor of Renown less eager, yet by doom
Canceld from Heav'n and sacred memorie,
Nameless in dark oblivion let them dwell.   380

For strength from Truth divided and from Just,
Illaudable, naught merits but dispraise
And ignominie, yet to glorie aspires
Vain glorious, and through infamie seeks fame:
Therfore Eternal silence be thir doom.   385
  And now thir mightiest quell'd, the battel swerv'd,
With many an inrode gor'd; deformed rout
Enter'd, and foul disorder; all the ground
With shiverd armour strown, and on a heap
Chariot and Charioter lay overturnd   390
And fierie foaming Steeds; what stood, recoyld
Orewearied, through the faint Satanic Host
Defensive scarse, or with pale fear surpris'd,
Then first with fear surpris'd and sense of pain
Fled ignominious, to such evil brought   395
By sin of disobedience, till that hour
Not liable to fear or flight or pain.
Far otherwise th' inviolable Saints
In Cubic Phalanx firm advanc't entire,
Invulnerable, impenitrably arm'd: 400
Such high advantages thir innocence
Gave them above thir foes, not to have sinn'd,
Not to have disobei'd; in fight they stood
Unwearied, unobnoxious[21] to be pain'd
By wound, though from thir place by violence mov'd.   405
  Now Night her course began, and over Heav'n
Inducing darkness, grateful truce impos'd,
And silence on the odious dinn of Warr:
Under her Cloudie covert both retir'd,
Victor and Vanquisht: on the foughten field   410
Michael and his Angels prevalent[22]
Encamping, plac'd in Guard thir Watches round,
Cherubic waving fires: on th' other part
Satan with his rebellious disappeerd,
Far in the dark dislodg'd, and void of rest,   415
His Potentates to Councel call'd by night;
And in the midst thus undismai'd began.
  O now in danger tri'd, now known in Armes
Not to be overpowerd, Companions dear,
Found worthy not of Libertie alone,   420
Too mean pretense, but what we more affect,

[21] not subject to injury.
[22] dominant, victorious.

Honour, Dominion, Glorie, and renown,
Who have sustaind one day in doubtful fight
(And if one day, why not Eternal dayes?)
What Heavens Lord had powerfullest to send   425
Against us from about his Throne, and judg'd
Sufficient to subdue us to his will,
But proves not so: then fallible, it seems,
Of future we may deem him, though till now
Omniscient thought. True is, less firmly arm'd,   430
Some disadvantage we endur'd and pain,
Till now not known, but known as soon contemn'd,
Since now we find this our Empyreal form
Incapable of mortal injurie
Imperishable, and though peirc'd with wound,   435
Soon closing, and by native vigour heal'd.
Of evil then so small as easie think
The remedie; perhaps more valid Armes,
Weapons more violent, when next we meet,
May serve to better us, and worse our foes,   440
Or equal what between us made the odds,
In Nature none: if other hidden cause
Left them Superiour, while we can preserve
Unhurt our minds, and understanding sound,
Due search and consultation will disclose.   445
     He sat; and in th' assembly next upstood
Nisroc,[23] of Principalities the prime;
As one he stood escap't from cruel fight,
Sore toild, his riv'n Armes to havoc hewn,
And cloudie in aspect thus answering spake.   450
Deliverer from new Lords, leader to free
Enjoyment of our right as Gods; yet hard
For Gods, and too unequal work we find
Against unequal armes to fight in pain,
Against unpaind, impassive;[24] from which evil   455
Ruin must needs ensue; for what avails
Valour or strength, though matchless, quell'd with pain
Which all subdues, and makes remiss the hands
Of Mightiest. Sense of pleasure we may well
Spare out of life perhaps, and not repine,   460
But live content, which is the calmest life:
But pain is perfet miserie, the worst

[23] an Assyrian deity; see 2 Kings xix. 37.
[24] incapable of feeling.

Of evils, and excessive, overturns
All patience. He who therefore can invent
With what more forcible we may offend   465
Our yet unwounded Enemies, or arm
Our selves with like defence, to me deserves
No less then for deliverance what we owe.
    Whereto with look compos'd *Satan* repli'd.
Not uninvented that, which thou aright   470
Beleivst so main to our success, I bring;
Which of us who beholds the bright surface
Of this Ethereous mould whereon we stand,
This continent of spacious Heav'n, adornd
With Plant, Fruit, Flowr Ambrosial, Gemms and Gold,   475
Whose Eye so superficially surveys
These things, as not to mind from whence they grow
Deep under ground, materials dark and crude,
Of spiritous and fierie spume,[25] till toucht
With Heav'ns ray, and temperd they shoot forth   480
So beauteous, op'ning to the ambient light.
These in thir dark Nativitie the Deep
Shall yeild us, pregnant with infernal flame,
Which into hollow Engins long and round
Thick-rammd, at th' other bore with touch of fire   485
Dilated and infuriate shall send forth
From far with thundring noise among our foes
Such implements of mischief as shall dash
To pieces, and orewhelm whatever stands
Adverse, that they shall fear we have disarmd   490
The Thunderer of his only dreaded bolt.
Nor long shall be our labour, yet ere dawn,
Effect shall end our wish. Mean while revive;
Abandon fear; to strength and counsel joind
Think nothing hard, much less to be despaird.   495
He ended, and his words thir drooping chere[26]
Enlight'n'd, and thir languisht hope reviv'd.
Th' invention all admir'd, and each, how hee
To be th' inventer miss'd, so easie it seemd
Once found, which yet unfound most would have thought 500
Impossible: yet haply of thy Race
In future dayes, if Malice should abound,
Some one intent on mischief, or inspir'd

[25] foam of air and fire (acting below the earth); see l. 512.
[26] countenance.

With dev'lish machination might devise
Like instrument to plague the Sons of men   505
For sin, on warr and mutual slaughter bent.
Forthwith from Councel to the work they flew,
None arguing stood, innumerable hands
Were ready, in a moment up they turnd
Wide the Celestial soil, and saw beneath   510
Th' originals of Nature in thir crude
Conception; Sulphurous and Nitrous Foam
They found, they mingl'd, and with suttle Art,
Concocted and adusted[27] they reduc'd
To blackest grain, and into store convey'd: 515
Part hidd'n veins digg'd up (nor hath this Earth
Entrails unlike) of Mineral and Stone,
Whereof to found thir Engins and thir Balls
Of missive ruin;[28] part incentive reed
Provide, pernicious with one touch to fire.   520
So all ere day-spring, under conscious Night
Secret they finish'd, and in order set,
With silent circumspection unespi'd.
Now when fair Morn Orient in Heav'n appeerd
Up rose the Victor Angels, and to Arms   525
The matin Trumpet Sung: in Arms they stood
Of Golden Panoplie, refulgent Host,
Soon banded; others from the dawning Hills
Look'd round, and Scouts each Coast light-armed scour,
Each quarter, to descrie the distant foe,   530
Where lodg'd, or whither fled, or if for fight,
In motion or in alt: him soon they met
Under spred Ensignes moving nigh, in slow
But firm Battalion; back with speediest Sail
Zophiel, of Cherubim the swiftest wing,   535
Came flying, and in mid Air aloud thus cri'd.
    Arm, Warriours, Arm for fight, the foe at hand,
Whom fled we thought, will save us long pursuit
This day, fear not his flight; so thick a Cloud
He comes, and settl'd in his face I see   540
Sad[29] resolution and secure:[30] let each
His Adamantine coat gird well, and each

[27] cooked together and burned.
[28] destruction from propelled matter; the "reed" is the match
which will light the fuse.
[29] firmly established.
[30] without anxiety.

Fit well his Helm, gripe fast his orbed Shield,
Born eevn or high, for this day will pour down,
If I conjecture aught, no drizling showr,   545
But ratling storm of Arrows barb'd with fire.
So warnd he them aware themselves, and soon
In order, quit of all impediment;
Instant without disturb they took Allarm,
And onward move Embattell'd; when behold   550
Not distant far with heavie pace the Foe
Approaching gross and huge; in hollow Cube
Training his devilish Enginrie, impal'd[31]
On every side with shaddowing Squadrons Deep,
To hide the fraud. At interview both stood   555
A while, but suddenly at head appeerd
Satan: And thus was heard Commanding loud.
   Vanguard, to Right and Left the Front unfould;
That all may see who hate us, how we seek
Peace and composure,[32] and with open brest   560
Stand readie to receive them, if they like
Our overture, and turn not back perverse;
But that I doubt, however witness Heav'n,
Heav'n witness thou anon, while we discharge
Freely our part; yee who appointed stand   565
Do as you have in charge, and briefly touch
What we propound, and loud that all may hear.
   So scoffing in ambiguous words he scarce
Had ended; when to Right and Left the Front
Divided, and to either Flank retir'd.   570
Which to our eyes discoverd new and strange,
A triple-mounted row of Pillars laid
On Wheels (for like to Pillars most they seem'd
Or hollow'd bodies made of Oak or Firr
With branches lopt, in Wood or Mountain fell'd)   575
Brass, Iron, Stonie mould,[33] had not thir mouths
With hideous orifice gap't on us wide,
Portending hollow truce; at each behind
A Seraph stood, and in his hand a Reed
Stood waving tipt with fire; while we suspense,   580
Collected stood within our thoughts amus'd,[34]

[31] hemmed in.
[32] agreement.
[33] material (of the earth).
[34] wondering.

Not long, for sudden all at once thir Reeds
Put forth, and to a narrow vent appli'd
With nicest touch. Immediate in a flame,
But soon obscur'd with smoak, all Heav'n appeerd,   585
From those deep-throated Engins belcht, whose roar
Emboweld[35] with outragious noise the Air,
And all her entrails tore, disgorging foul
Thir devilish glut, chaind Thunderbolts and Hail
Of Iron Globes, which on the Victor Host   590
Level'd, with such impetuous furie smote,
That whom they hit, none on thir feet might stand,
Though standing else as Rocks, but down they fell
By thousands, Angel on Arch-Angel rowl'd;
The sooner for thir Arms, unarm'd they might   595
Have easily as Spirits evaded swift
By quick contraction or remove; but now
Foul dissipation follow'd and forc't rout;
Nor serv'd it to relax thir serried files.
What should they do? if on they rusht, repulse   600
Repeated, and indecent overthrow
Doubl'd, would render them yet more despis'd,
And to thir foes a laughter; for in view
Stood rankt of Seraphim another row
In posture to displode thir second tire[36]   605
Of Thunder: back defeated to return
They worse abhorr'd. *Satan* beheld thir plight,
And to his Mates thus in derision call'd.
    O Friends, why come not on these Victors proud?
Ere while they fierce were coming, and when wee,   610
To entertain them fair with open Front
And Brest (what could we more?), propounded terms
Of composition, strait they chang'd thir minds,
Flew off, and into strange vagaries fell,
As they would dance, yet for a dance they seemd   615
Somwhat extravagant and wild, perhaps
For joy of offerd peace: but I suppose
If our proposals once again were heard
We should compel them to a quick result.
    To whom thus *Belial* in like gamesom mood.   620
Leader, the terms we sent were terms of weight,
Of hard contents, and full of force urg'd home,

[35] filled.
[36] discharge.

Such as we might perceive amus'd them all,
And stumbl'd many, who receives them right,
Had need from head to foot well understand; 625
Not understood, this gift they have besides,
They shew us when our foes walk not upright.
    So they among themselves in pleasant vein
Stood scoffing, highth'n'd in thir thoughts beyond
All doubt of Victorie, eternal might 630
To match with thir inventions they presum'd
So easie, and of his Thunder made a scorn,
And all his Host derided, while they stood
A while in trouble; but they stood not long,
Rage prompted them at length, and found them arms 635
Against such hellish mischief fit t' oppose.
Forthwith (behold the excellence, the power
Which God hath in his mighty Angels plac'd)
Thir Arms away they threw, and to the Hills
(For Earth hath this variety from Heav'n 640
Of pleasure situate in Hill and Dale)
Light as the Lightning glimps they ran, they flew,
From thir foundations loosning to and fro
They pluckt the seated Hills with all thir load,
Rocks, Waters, Woods, and by the shaggie tops 645
Up lifting bore them in thir hands:[37] Amaze,
Be sure, and terrour seis'd the rebel Host,
When coming towards them so dread they saw
The bottom of the Mountains upward turn'd,
Till on those cursed Engins triple-row 650
They saw them whelm'd, and all thir confidence
Under the weight of Mountains buried deep,
Themselves invaded next, and on thir heads
Main Promontories flung, which in the Air
Came shadowing, and opprest whole Legions arm'd, 655
Thir armor help'd thir harm, crush't in and bruis'd
Into thir substance pent, which wrought them pain
Implacable, and many a dolorous groan,
Long strugling underneath, ere they could wind
Out of such prison, though Spirits of purest light, 660
Purest at first, now gross by sinning grown.
The rest in imitation to like Armes
Betook them, and the neighbouring Hills uptore;

[37] Compare the piling of Mt. Pelion on Mt. Ossa by the Giants
of earth.

So Hills amid the Air encounterd Hills
Hurl'd to and fro with jaculation dire,   665
That under ground they fought in dismal shade;
Infernal noise; Warr seem'd a civil[38] Game
To this uproar; horrid confusion heapt
Upon confusion rose: and now all Heav'n
Had gon to wrack, with ruin overspred,   670
Had not th' Almightie Father where he sits
Shrin'd in his Sanctuarie of Heav'n secure,
Consulting on the sum of things, foreseen
This tumult, and permitted all, advis'd:[39]
That his great purpose he might so fulfill,   675
To honour his Anointed Son aveng'd
Upon his enemies, and to declare
All power on him transferr'd: whence to his Son
Th' Assessor[40] of his Throne he thus began.
    Effulgence of my Glorie, Son belov'd,   680
Son in whose face invisible is beheld
Visibly, what by Deitie I am,
And in whose hand what by Decree I doe,
Second Omnipotence, two dayes are past,
Two dayes, as we compute the dayes of Heav'n,   685
Since *Michael* and his Powers went forth to tame
These disobedient; sore hath been thir fight,
As likeliest was, when two such Foes met arm'd;
For to themselves I left them, and thou knowst,
Equal in their Creation they were form'd,   690
Save what sin hath impaird, which yet hath wrought
Insensibly, for I suspend thir doom;
Whence in perpetual fight they needs must last
Endless, and no solution will be found:
Warr wearied hath perform'd what Warr can do,   695
And to disorder'd rage let loose the reins,
With Mountains as with Weapons arm'd, which makes
Wild work in Heav'n, and dangerous to the main.
Two dayes are therefore past, the third is thine;
For thee I have ordain'd it, and thus farr   700
Have sufferd, that the Glorie may be thine
Of ending this great Warr, since none but Thou
Can end it. Into thee such Vertue and Grace

[38] both nonmilitary and civilized.
[39] after having thought it out.
[40] sharer.

Immense I have transfus'd, that all may know
In Heav'n and Hell thy Power above compare,   705
And this perverse Commotion governd thus,
To manifest thee worthiest to be Heir
Of all things, to be Heir and to be King
By Sacred Unction,[41] thy deserved right.
Go then thou Mightiest in thy Fathers might,   710
Ascend my Chariot, guide the rapid Wheels
That shake Heav'ns basis, bring forth all my Warr,
My Bow and Thunder, my Almightie Arms
Gird on, and Sword upon thy puissant Thigh;
Pursue these sons of Darkness, drive them out   715
From all Heav'ns bounds into the utter Deep:
There let them learn, as likes them, to despise
God and *Messiah* his anointed King.
    He said, and on his Son with Rayes direct
Shon full, he all his Father full exprest   720
Ineffably into his face receiv'd,
And thus the filial Godhead answering spake.
    O Father, O Supream of heav'nly Thrones,
First, Highest, Holiest, Best, thou alwayes seekst
To glorifie thy Son, I alwayes thee,   725
As is most just; this I my Glorie account,
My exaltation, and my whole delight,
That thou in me well pleas'd, declarst thy will
Fulfill'd, which to fulfil is all my bliss.
Scepter and Power, thy giving, I assume,   730
And gladlier shall resign, when in the end
Thou shalt be All in All, and I in thee
For ever, and in mee all whom thou lov'st:
But whom thou hat'st, I hate, and can put on
Thy terrors, as I put thy mildness on,   735
Image of thee in all things; and shall soon,
Armd with thy might, rid heav'n of these rebell'd,
To thir prepar'd ill Mansion driven down
To chains of darkness, and th' undying Worm,
That from thy just obedience could revolt,   740
Whom to obey is happiness entire.
Then shall thy Saints unmixt, and from th' impure
Farr separate, circling thy holy Mount
Unfained *Halleluiahs* to thee sing,
Hymns of high praise, and I among them chief.   745

[41] anointing; see *PL*, III, 317.

So said, he o're his Scepter bowing, rose
From the right hand of Glorie where he sate,
And the third sacred Morn began to shine
Dawning through Heav'n: forth rush'd with whirlwind sound
The Chariot[42] of Paternal Deitie,   750
Flashing thick flames, Wheel within Wheel undrawn,
It self instinct[43] with Spirit, but convoyd
By four Cherubic shapes, four Faces each
Had wondrous, as with Starrs thir bodies all
And Wings were set with Eyes, with Eyes the wheels   755
Of Beril, and careering Fires between;
Over thir heads a chrystal Firmament,
Whereon a Saphir Throne, inlaid with pure
Amber, and colours of the showrie Arch.
Hee in Celestial Panoplie all armd   760
Of radiant *Urim*,[44] work divinely wrought,
Ascended, at his right hand Victorie
Sate Eagle-wing'd, beside him hung his Bow
And Quiver with three-bolted Thunder stor'd,
And from about him fierce Effusion rowld   765
Of smoak and bickering[45] flame, and sparkles dire;
Attended with ten thousand thousand Saints,
He onward came, farr off his coming shon,
And twentie thousand (I thir number heard)
Chariots of God, half on each hand were seen: 770
Hee on the wings of Cherub rode sublime
On the Chrystallin Skie, in Saphir Thron'd.
Illustrious farr and wide, but by his own
First seen, them unexpected joy surpriz'd,
When the great Ensign of *Messiah* blaz'd   775
Aloft by Angels born, his Sign in Heav'n:
Under whose conduct *Michael* soon reduc'd[46]
His Armie, circumfus'd[47] on either Wing,
Under thir Head imbodied all in one.
Before him Power Divine his way prepar'd;   780

[42] See Ezek. i.
[43] imbued.
[44] the jewels on Aaron's breastplate (Exod. xxviii. 30); see n. 17
to III, 598. Undoubtedly significant is the first word of the next
line, "Ascended": it was the central word of the 1667 edition since
5,275 lines precede it and follow it.
[45] quivering.
[46] led back.
[47] diffused around.

At his command th' uprooted Hills retir'd
Each to his place, they heard his voice and went
Obsequious, Heav'n his wonted face renewd,
And with fresh Flowrets Hill and Valley smil'd.
This saw his hapless Foes but stood obdur'd,[48]   785
And to rebellious fight rallied thir Powers
Insensate, hope conceiving from despair.
In heav'nly Spirits could such perverseness dwell?
But to convince the proud what Signs avail,
Or Wonders move th' obdurate to relent?   790
They hard'n'd more by what might most reclame,
Grieving to see his Glorie, at the sight
Took envie, and aspiring to his highth,
Stood reimbattell'd fierce, by force or fraud
Weening to prosper, and at length prevail   795
Against God and *Messiah,* or to fall
In universal ruin last, and now
To final Battel drew, disdaining flight,
Or faint retreat; when the great Son of God
To all his Host on either hand thus spake.   800
    Stand still in bright array ye Saints, here stand
Ye Angels arm'd, this day from Battel rest;
Faithful hath been your warfare, and of God
Accepted, fearless in his righteous Cause,
And as ye have receiv'd, so have ye don   805
Invincibly; but of this cursed crew
The punishment to other hand belongs,
Vengeance is his, or whose he sole appoints;
Number to this dayes work is not ordain'd
Nor multitude, stand onely and behold   810
Gods indignation on these Godless pourd
By mee; not you but mee they have despis'd,
Yet envied; against mee is all thir rage,
Because the Father, t' whom in Heav'n supream
Kingdom and Power and Glorie appertains,   815
Hath honourd me according to his will.
Therefore to mee thir doom he hath assign'd;
That they may have thir wish, to trie with mee
In Battel which the stronger proves, they all,
Or I alone against them, since by strength   820
They measure all, of other excellence
Not emulous, nor care who them excells;

[48] intractable.

Nor other strife with them do I voutsafe.
   So spake the Son, and into terrour chang'd
His count'nance too severe to be beheld   825
And full of wrauth bent on his Enemies.
At once the Four spred out thir Starrie wings
With dreadful shade contiguous, and the Orbs
Of his fierce Chariot rowl'd, as with the sound
Of torrent Floods, or of a numerous Host.   830
Hee on his impious Foes right onward drove,
Gloomie as Night; under his burning Wheels
The stedfast Empyrean shook throughout,
All but the Throne it self of God. Full soon
Among them he arriv'd; in his right hand   835
Grasping ten thousand Thunders, which he sent
Before him, such as in thir Souls infix'd
Plagues;[49] they astonisht all resistance lost,
All courage; down thir idle weapons drop'd;
O're Shields and Helmes, and helmed heads he rode   840
Of Thrones and mighty Seraphim prostrate,
That wisht the Mountains now might be again
Thrown on them as a shelter from his ire.
Nor less on either side tempestuous fell
His arrows, from the fourfold-visag'd Four,   845
Distinct with eyes, and from the living Wheels,
Distinct alike with multitude of eyes,
One Spirit in them rul'd, and every eye
Glar'd lightning, and shot forth pernicious fire
Among th' accurst, that witherd all thir strength,   850
And of thir wonted vigour left them draind,
Exhausted, spiritless, afflicted, fall'n.
Yet half his strength he put not forth, but check'd
His Thunder in mid Volie, for he meant
Not to destroy, but root them out of Heav'n: 855
The overthrown he rais'd, and as a Heard
Of Goats or timerous flock together throng'd
Drove them before him Thunder-struck, pursu'd
With terrors and with furies to the bounds
And Chrystal wall of Heav'n, which op'ning wide,   860
Rowl'd inward, and a spacious Gap disclos'd
Into the wastful Deep; the monstrous sight
Strook them with horror backward, but far worse
Urg'd them behind; headlong themselvs they threw

[49] blows.

Down from the verge of Heav'n, Eternal wrauth   865
Burnt after them to the bottomless pit.
    Hell heard th' unsufferable noise, Hell saw
Heav'n ruining[50] from Heav'n and would have fled
Affrighted; but strict Fate had cast too deep
Her dark foundations, and too fast had bound.   870
Nine dayes they fell; confounded *Chaos* roard,
And felt tenfold confusion in thir fall
Through his wild Anarchie, so huge a rout
Incumberd him with ruin; Hell at last
Yawning receav'd them whole, and on them clos'd,   875
Hell thir fit habitation fraught with fire
Unquenchable, the house of woe and pain.
Disburd'n'd Heav'n rejoic'd, and soon repaird
Her mural breach, returning whence it rowl'd.
Sole Victor from th' expulsion of his Foes   880
Messiah his triumphal Chariot turnd:
To meet him all his Saints, who silent stood
Eye witnesses of his Almightie Acts,
With Jubilie advanc'd; and as they went,
Shaded with branching Palm, each order bright,   885
Sung Triumph, and him sung Victorious King,
Son, Heir, and Lord, to him Dominion giv'n,
Worthiest to Reign: he celebrated rode
Triumphant through mid Heav'n, into the Courts
And Temple of his mightie Father Thron'd   890
On high: who into Glorie him receav'd,
Where now he sits at the right hand of bliss.
    Thus measuring things in Heav'n by things on Earth
At thy request, and that thou maist beware
By what is past, to thee I have reveal'd   895
What might have else to human Race bin hid;
The discord which befell, and Warr in Heav'n
Among th' Angelic Powers, and the deep fall
Of those too high aspiring, who rebell'd
With *Satan*, hee who envies now thy state,   900
Who now is plotting how he may seduce
Thee also from obedience, that with him
Bereav'd of happiness thou maist partake
His punishment, Eternal miserie;
Which would be all his solace and revenge,   905
As a despite don against the most High,

[50] falling.

Thee once to gain Companion of his woe.
But list'n not to his Temptations, warn
Thy weaker;[51] let it profit thee t' have heard
By terrible Example the reward   910
Of disobedience; firm they might have stood,
Yet fell; remember, and fear to transgress.

BOOK VII

THE ARGUMENT

Raphael at the request of *Adam* relates how and wherefore
this world was first created; that God, after the expelling of
Satan and his Angels out of Heaven, declar'd his pleasure to
create another World and other Creatures to dwell therein;
sends his Son with Glory and attendance of Angels to perform
the work of Creation in six dayes: the Angels celebrate with
Hymns the performance thereof, and his reascention into
Heaven.

Descend from Heav'n *Urania*,[1] by that name
If rightly thou art call'd, whose Voice divine
Following, above th' *Olympian* Hill I soar,
Above the flight of *Pegasean*[2] wing.
The meaning, not the Name I call: for thou   5
Nor of the Muses nine, nor on the top
Of old *Olympus* dwell'st, but Heav'nlie born,
Before the Hills appeerd, or Fountain flow'd,
Thou with Eternal wisdom didst converse,[3]
Wisdom thy Sister, and with her didst play   10
In presence of th' Almightie Father, pleas'd
With thy Celestial Song. Up led by thee
Into the Heav'n of Heav'ns I have presum'd,
An Earthlie Guest, and drawn Empyreal Air,
Thy tempring; with like safetie guided down   15
Return me to my Native Element:
Least from this flying Steed unrein'd (as once

---

[51] Eve.

---

[1] the Muse of astronomy, the meaning of whose name ("heavenly") emphasizes Milton's invoking of divine inspiration. In Prov. viii Wisdom, from "the top of high places," tells the sons of men of the Creation, the subject of this book.

[2] For Pegasus and Bellerophon (l. 18), see *Rouse*, n. 8.

[3] associate, live.

Bellerophon, though from a lower Clime),
Dismounted, on th' *Aleian* Field I fall
Erroneous there to wander and forlorn.   20
Half yet remains unsung but narrower bound
Within the visible Diurnal Sphear;
Standing on Earth, not rapt above the Pole,[4]
More safe I sing with mortal voice, unchang'd
To hoarce or mute, though fall'n on evil dayes,   25
On evil dayes though fall'n, and evil tongues;[5]
In darkness, and with dangers compast round,
And solitude; yet not alone, while thou
Visit'st my slumbers Nightly, or when Morn
Purples the East: still govern thou my Song,   30
Urania, and fit audience find, though few.
But drive farr off the barbarous dissonance
Of *Bacchus* and his revellers, the Race
Of that wild Rout that tore the *Thracian* Bard[6]
In *Rhodope,* where Woods and Rocks had Eares   35
To rapture, till the savage clamor dround
Both Harp and Voice; nor could the Muse defend
Her Son. So fail not thou, who thee implores:
For thou art Heav'nlie, shee an empty dream.
    Say Goddess, what ensu'd when *Raphael,*   40
The affable Arch-Angel, had forewarn'd
Adam by dire example to beware
Apostasie, by what befell in Heav'n
To those Apostates, least the like befall
In Paradise to *Adam* or his Race,   45
Charg'd not to touch the interdicted Tree,
If they transgress, and slight that sole command,
So easily obeyd amid the choice
Of all tasts else to please thir appetite,
Though wandring. He with his consorted[7] *Eve*   50
The storie heard attentive, and was fill'd
With admiration, and deep Muse to hear
Of things so high and strange, things to thir thought
So unimaginable as hate in Heav'n,
And Warr so neer the Peace of God in bliss   55
With such confusion: but the evil soon

[4] not transported above the primum mobile.
[5] a temporal reference to the period of the Restoration (1660 and ff.); the "darkness" (l. 27) is his blindness.
[6] Orpheus; see *Lycidas,* n. 12.
[7] marital partner (from "consortium").

Driv'n back redounded[8] as a flood on those
From whom it sprung, impossible to mix
With Blessedness. Whence *Adam* soon repeal'd[9]
The doubts that in his heart arose: and now   60
Led on, yet sinless, with desire to know
What neerer might concern him, how this World
Of Heav'n and Earth conspicuous first began,
When, and whereof created, for what cause,
What within *Eden* or without was done   65
Before his memorie, as one whose drouth
Yet scarce allay'd still eyes the current stream,
Whose liquid murmur heard new thirst excites,
Proceeded thus to ask his Heav'nly Guest.
    Great things, and full of wonder in our eares,   70
Farr differing from this World, thou hast reveal'd
Divine interpreter, by favour sent
Down from the Empyrean to forewarn
Us timely of what might else have bin our loss,
Unknown, which human knowledge could not reach: 75
For which to th' infinitly Good we owe
Immortal thanks, and his admonishment
Receave with solemn purpose to observe
Immutably his sovran will, the end
Of what we are. But since thou hast voutsaf't   80
Gently for our instruction to impart
Things above Earthly thought, which yet concernd
Our knowing, as to highest wisdom seemd,
Deign to descend now lower, and relate
What may no less perhaps avail us known,   85
How first began this Heav'n which we behold
Distant so high, with moving Fires adornd
Innumerable, and this which yeelds or fills
All space, the ambient Air wide interfus'd
Imbracing round this florid Earth, what cause   90
Mov'd the Creator in his holy Rest
Through all Eternitie so late to build
In *Chaos*, and the work begun, how soon
Absolv'd,[10] if unforbid thou maist unfould
What wee, not to explore the secrets ask   95
Of his Eternal Empire, but the more

[8] surged back.
[9] called back.
[10] finished.

To magnifie his works, the more we know.
And the great Light of Day yet wants to run
Much of his Race though steep, suspense in Heav'n
Held by thy voice, thy potent voice he heares,   100
And longer will delay to hear thee tell
His Generation, and the rising Birth
Of Nature from the unapparent[11] Deep:
Or if the Starr of Eevning and the Moon
Haste to thy audience, Night with her will bring   105
Silence, and Sleep listning to thee will watch,[12]
Or we can bid his absence, till thy Song
End, and dismiss thee ere the Morning shine.
    Thus *Adam* his illustrious Guest besought:
    And thus the Godlike Angel answerd mild.   110
This also thy request with caution askt
Obtain: though to recount Almightie works
What words or tongue of Seraph can suffice,
Or heart of man suffice to comprehend?
Yet what thou canst attain, which best may serve   115
To glorifie the Maker, and inferr
Thee also happier, shall not be withheld
Thy hearing, such Commission from above
I have receav'd, to answer thy desire
Of knowledge within bounds; beyond abstain   120
To ask, nor let thine own inventions hope
Things not reveal'd, which th' invisible King,
Onely Omniscient, hath supprest in Night,
To none communicable in Earth or Heaven:
Anough is left besides to search and know.   125
But Knowledge is as food, and needs no less
Her Temperance over Appetite, to know
In measure what the mind may well contain,
Oppresses else with Surfet, and soon turns
Wisdom to Folly, as Nourishment to Wind.   130
    Know then, that after *Lucifer* from Heav'n
(So call him, brighter once amidst the Host
Of Angels, then that Starr[13] the Starrs among)
Fell with his flaming Legions through the Deep
Into his place, and the great Son returnd   135
Victorious with his saints, th' Omnipotent

---

[11] unseen (since it lies outside the primum mobile) and formless.
[12] keep watch.
[13] Venus, called Lucifer as the morning star.

Eternal Father from his Throne beheld
Thir multitude, and to his Son thus spake.
    At least our envious Foe hath fail'd, who thought
All like himself rebellious, by whose aid   140
This inaccessible high strength, the seat
Of Deitie supream, us dispossest,
He trusted to have seis'd, and into fraud
Drew many, whom thir place knows here no more;[14]
Yet farr the greater part have kept, I see,   145
Thir station, Heav'n yet populous retains
Number sufficient to possess her Realmes
Though wide, and this high Temple to frequent
With Ministeries due and solemn Rites:
But least his heart exalt him in the harm   150
Already done, to have dispeopl'd Heav'n,
My damage fondly[15] deem'd, I can repair
That detriment, if such it be to lose
Self-lost, and in a moment will create
Another World, out of one man a Race   155
Of men innumerable, there to dwell,
Not here, till by degrees of merit rais'd
They open to themselves at length the way
Up hither, under long obedience tri'd,
And Earth be chang'd to Heav'n, and Heav'n to Earth,   160
One Kingdom, Joy and Union without end.
Mean while inhabit lax,[16] ye Powers of Heav'n,
And thou my Word, begotten Son, by thee
This I perform, speak thou, and be it don:
My overshadowing Spirit and might with thee   165
I send along, ride forth, and bid the Deep
Within appointed bounds be Heav'n and Earth,
Boundless the Deep, because I am who fill
Infinitude, nor vacuous the space.
Though I uncircumscrib'd my self retire,[17]   170
And put not forth my goodness, which is free
To act or not, Necessitie and Chance
Approach not mee, and what I will is Fate.
    So spake th' Almightie, and to what he spake

14 Job vii. 10: "Neither shall his place know him any more."
15 foolishly.
16 scattered; "fill all those relinquished areas left uninhabited
by those who joined Satan."
17 God is not limited even though he withdraws his influence
from part of infinitude, thus leaving Chaos.

His Word, the filial Godhead, gave effect.   175
Immediate are the Acts of God, more swift
Then time or motion, but to human ears
Cannot without process of speech be told,
So told as earthly notion can receave.
Great triumph and rejoycing was in Heav'n   180
When such was heard declar'd th' Almightie's will;
Glorie they sung to the most High, good will
To future men, and in thir dwellings peace:
Glorie to him whose just avenging ire
Had driven out th' ungodly from his sight   185
And th' habitations of the just; to him
Glorie and praise, whose wisdom had ordain'd
Good out of evil to create, in stead
Of Spirits maligne a better Race to bring
Into thir vacant room, and thence diffuse   190
His good to Worlds and Ages infinite.
So sang the Hierarchies: Mean while the Son
On his great Expedition now appeer'd,
Girt with Omnipotence, with Radiance crown'd
Of Majestie Divine, Sapience and Love   195
Immense, and all his Father in him shon.
About his Chariot numberless were pour'd
Cherub and Seraph, Potentates and Thrones,
And Vertues, winged Spirits, and Chariots wing'd,
From th' Armoury of God, where stand of old   200
Myriads between two brazen Mountains lodg'd
Against a solemn day, harnest at hand,
Celestial Equipage; and now came forth
Spontaneous, for within them Spirit liv'd,
Attendant on thir Lord: Heav'n op'n'd wide   205
Her ever during[18] Gates, Harmonious sound
On golden Hinges moving, to let forth
The King of Glorie in his powerful Word
And Spirit coming to create new Worlds.
On heav'nly ground they stood, and from the shore   210
They view'd the vast immeasurable Abyss
Outrageous as a Sea, dark, wasteful, wild,
Up from the bottom turn'd by furious winds
And surging waves, as Mountains to assault
Heav'ns highth, and with the Center mix the Pole.   215
    Silence, ye troubl'd waves, and thou Deep, peace,

---

[18] everlasting.

Said then th' Omnific[19] Word, your discord end:
   Nor staid, but on the Wings of Cherubim
Uplifted, in Paternal Glorie rode
Farr into *Chaos*, and the World unborn;   220
For *Chaos* heard his voice: him all his Train
Follow'd in bright procession to behold
Creation, and the wonders of his might.
Then staid the fervid Wheels, and in his hand
He took the golden Compasses,[20] prepar'd   225
In Gods Eternal store, to circumscribe
This Universe, and all created things:
One foot he center'd, and the other turn'd
Round through the vast profunditie obscure,
And said, thus farr extend, thus farr thy bounds,   230
This be thy just Circumference, O World.
Thus God the Heav'n created, thus the Earth,
Matter unform'd and void: Darkness profound
Cover'd th' Abyss: but on the watrie calm
His brooding wings the Spirit of God outspred,   235
And vital vertue infus'd, and vital warmth
Throughout the fluid Mass, but downward purg'd
The black tartareous[21] cold infernal dregs
Adverse to life: then founded, then conglob'd
Like things to like, the rest to several place   240
Disparted, and between spun out the Air,
And Earth self ballanc't on her Center hung.
   Let ther be Light, said God, and forthwith Light
Ethereal, first of things, quintessence pure
Sprung from the Deep, and from her Native East   245
To journie through the airie gloom began,
Sphear'd in a radiant Cloud, for yet the Sun
Was not; shee in a cloudie Tabernacle
Sojourn'd the while. God saw the Light was good;
And light from darkness by the Hemisphere   250
Divided: Light the Day, and Darkness Night
He nam'd. Thus was the first Day Eev'n and Morn:
Nor past uncelebrated, nor unsung
By the Celestial Quires, when Orient Light

19 all-creating.
20 Prov. viii. 27: "When he prepared the heavens, I was there: when he set a compass upon the face of the depth."
21 both hellish (from Tartarus) and sedimentary (from the incrustation of the residue from grapes in wine-making).

Exhaling first from Darkness they beheld; 255
Birth-day of Heav'n and Earth; with joy and shout
The hollow Universal Orb they fill'd,
And touch't thir Golden Harps, and hymning prais'd
God and his works, Creatour him they sung,
Both when first Eevning was, and when first Morn. 260
    Again, God said, let ther be Firmament[22]
Amid the Waters, and let it divide
The Waters from the Waters: and God made
The Firmament, expanse of liquid, pure,
Transparent, Elemental Air, diffus'd 265
In circuit to the uttermost convex
Of this great Round: partition firm and sure,
The Waters underneath from those above
Dividing: for as Earth, so he the World
Built on circumfluous Waters calm, in wide 270
Crystallin Ocean, and the loud misrule
Of *Chaos* farr remov'd, least fierce extreams
Continguous might distemper the whole frame:
And Heav'n he nam'd the Firmament: So Eev'n
And Morning *Chorus* sung the second Day. 275
    The Earth was form'd, but in the Womb as yet
Of Waters, Embryon immature involv'd,
Appeer'd not: over all the face of Earth
Main Ocean flow'd, not idle, but with warm
Prolific humour soft'ning all her Globe, 280
Fermented the great Mother to conceave,
Satiate with genial[23] moisture, when God said
Be gather'd now ye Waters under Heav'n
Into one place, and let dry Land appeer.
Immediately the Mountains huge appeer 285
Emergent, and thir broad bare backs upheave
Into the Clouds, thir tops ascend the Skie:
So high as heav'd the tumid Hills, so low
Down sunk a hollow bottom broad and deep,
Capacious bed of Waters: thither they 290
Hasted with glad precipitance, uprowl'd
As drops on dust conglobing from the drie;
Part rise in crystal Wall, or ridge direct,

[22] the heavens stretching from the seas of the universe
("Round," l. 267) to the Crystalline (watery) Sphere ("Ocean,"
l. 271); see Gen. i. 6–7.
[23] fertilizing.

For haste; such flight the great command impress'd
On the swift flouds: as Armies at the call   295
Of Trumpet (for of Armies thou hast heard)
Troop to thir Standard, so the watrie throng,
Wave rowling after Wave, where way they found,
If steep, with torrent rapture,[24] if through Plain,
Soft-ebbing; nor withstood them Rock or Hill,   300
But they, or under ground, or circuit wide
With Serpent errour[25] wandring, found thir way,
And on the washie Oose deep Channels wore;
Easie, e're God had bid the ground be drie,
All but within those banks, where Rivers now   305
Stream, and perpetual draw thir humid train.[26]
The dry Land, Earth, and the great receptacle
Of congregated Waters he call'd Seas:
And saw that it was good, and said, Let th' Earth
Put forth the verdant Grass, Herb yeilding Seed,   310
And Fruit Tree yeilding Fruit after her kind;
Whose Seed is in her self upon the Earth.
He scarce had said, when the bare Earth, till then
Desert and bare, unsightly, unadorn'd,
Brought forth the tender Grass, whose verdure clad   315
Her Universal Face with pleasant green,
Then Herbs of every leaf, that sudden flowr'd
Op'ning thir various colours, and made gay
Her bosom smelling sweet: and these scarce blown,
Forth flourish't thick the clustring Vine, forth crept   320
The smelling Gourd, up stood the cornie Reed
Embattell'd in her field: and the humble Shrub,
And Bush with frizl'd hair implicit:[27] last
Rose as in Dance the stately Trees, and spred
Thir branches hung with copious Fruit; or gemm'd[28]   325
Thir blossoms: with high woods the hills were crownd,
With tufts[29] the vallies and each fountain side,
With borders long the Rivers. That Earth now
Seemd like to Heav'n, a seat where Gods might dwell,
Or wander with delight, and love to haunt   330
Her sacred shades: though God had yet not rain'd

[24] carried along with great haste.
[25] erratic movement (like a serpent).
[26] watery course.
[27] entwined.
[28] budded.
[29] groups of trees or shrubbery.

Upon the Earth, and man to till the ground
None was, but from the Earth a dewie Mist
Went up and waterd all the ground, and each
Plant of the field, which e're it was in th' Earth　　335
God made, and every Herb, before it grew
On the green stemm; God saw that it was good.
So Eev'n and Morn recorded the Third Day.
　Again th' Almightie spake: Let there be Lights
High in th' expanse of Heaven to divide　　340
The Day from Night; and let them be for Signes,
For Seasons, and for Dayes, and circling Years,
And let them be for Lights as I ordain
Thir Office in the Firmament of Heav'n
To give Light on the Earth; and it was so.　　345
And God made two great Lights, great for thir use
To Man, the greater to have rule by Day,
The less by Night altern: and made the Starrs,
And set them in the Firmament of Heav'n
T' illuminate the Earth, and rule the Day　　350
In thir vicissitude, and rule the Night,
And Light from Darkness to divide. God saw,
Surveying his great Work, that it was good:
For of Celestial Bodies first the Sun
A mightie Sphear he fram'd, unlightsom first,　　355
Though of Ethereal Mould: then form'd the Moon
Globose, and every magnitude of Starrs,
And sowd with Starrs the Heav'n thick as a field:
Of Light by farr the greater part he took,
Transplanted from her cloudie Shrine, and plac'd　　360
In the Suns Orb, made porous to receive
And drink the liquid Light, firm to retain
Her gather'd beams, great Palace now of Light.
Hither as to thir Fountain other Starrs
Repairing, in thir gold'n Urns draw Light,　　365
And hence the Morning Planet guilds her horns;[30]
By tincture[31] or reflection they augment
Thir small peculiar, though from human sight
So farr remote, with diminution seen.
First in his East the glorious Lamp was seen,　　370
Regent of Day, and all th' Horizon round
Invested with bright Rayes, jocond to run

[30] Galileo had discovered the phases of Venus.
[31] absorption of the sun's light.

His Longitude through Heav'ns high rode: the gray
Dawn, and the *Pleiades* before him danc'd
Shedding sweet influence: less bright the Moon,   375
But opposite in leveld West was set
His mirror, with full face borrowing her Light
From him, for other light she needed none
In that aspect, and still that distance keeps
Till night, then in the East her turn she shines,   380
Revolv'd on Heav'ns great Axle, and her Reign
With thousand lesser Lights dividual[32] holds,
With thousand thousand Starrs, that then appeer'd
Spangling the Hemisphere: then first adornd
With thir bright Luminaries that Set and Rose,   385
Glad Eevning and glad Morn crownd the fourth day.
    And God said, let the Waters generate
Reptil[33] with Spawn abundant, living Soul:
And let Fowl flie above the Earth, with wings
Displayd on th' op'n Firmament of Heav'n.   390
And God created the great Whales, and each
Soul living, each that crept, which plenteously
The waters generated by thir kinds,
And every Bird of wing after his kind;
And saw that it was good, and bless'd them, saying,   395
Be fruitful, multiply, and in the Seas
And Lakes and running Streams the waters fill;
And let the Fowl be multiply'd on th' Earth.
Forthwith the Sounds and Seas, each Creek and Bay
With Frie innumerable swarm, and Shoals   400
Of Fish that with thir Finns and shining Scales
Glide under the green Wave, in Sculls[34] that oft
Bank the mid Sea: part single or with mate
Graze the Sea weed thir pasture, and through Groves
Of Coral stray, or sporting with quick glance   405
Show to the Sun thir wav'd coats dropt[35] with Gold,
Or in thir Pearlie shells at ease, attend
Moist nutriment, or under Rocks thir food
In jointed Armour watch: on smooth[36] the Seal,
And bended Dolphins play: part huge of bulk   410

[32] divided (amongst the "thousand lesser Lights").
[33] any creeping thing (but including fish).
[34] schools of fish that make a shoal in the sea (l. 403).
[35] flecked.
[36] on the smooth sea.

Wallowing unweildie, enormous in thir Gate
Tempest the Ocean: there Leviathan
Hugest of living Creatures, on the Deep
Stretcht like a Promontorie sleeps or swims,
And seems a moving Land, and at his Gills   415
Draws in, and at his Trunck spouts out a Sea.
Mean while the tepid Caves, and Fens and shoares
Thir Brood as numerous hatch, from th' Egg that soon
Bursting with kindly[37] rupture forth disclos'd
Thir callow young, but featherd soon and fledge   420
They summ'd thir Penns,[38] and soaring th' air sublime
With clang despis'd the ground, under a cloud
In prospect;[39] there the Eagle and the Stork
On Cliffs and Cedar tops thir Eyries build:
Part loosly[40] wing the Region, part more wise   425
In common, rang'd in figure wedge thir way,
Intelligent of seasons, and set forth
Thir Aerie Caravan high over Seas
Flying, and over Lands with mutual wing
Easing thir flight; so stears the prudent Crane   430
Her annual Voiage, born on Winds; the Air
Floats, as they pass, fann'd with unnumber'd plumes:
From Branch to Branch the smaller Birds with song
Solac'd the Woods, and spred thir painted wings
Till Ev'n, nor then the solemn Nightingale   435
Ceas'd warbling, but all night tun'd her soft layes:
Others on Silver Lakes and Rivers Bath'd
Thir downie Brest; the Swan with Arched neck
Between her white wings mantling[41] proudly, Rows
Her state with Oarie feet: yet oft they quit   440
The Dank, and rising on stiff Pennons, towr
The mid Aereal Skie: Others on ground
Walk'd firm; the crested Cock whose clarion sounds
The silent hours, and th' other whose gay Train
Adorns him, colour'd with the Florid hue   445
Of Rainbows and Starrie Eyes. The Waters thus
With Fish replenisht, and the Air with Fowl,
Ev'ning and Morn solemniz'd the Fift day.

[37] natural.
[38] fully feathered their wings.
[39] Seen from afar, the birds seemed to be a cloud.
[40] separately.
[41] spreading out.

The Sixt, and of Creation last arose
With Eevning Harps and Mattin, when God said,   450
Let th' Earth bring forth Soul living in her kind,
Cattel and Creeping things, and Beast of th' Earth,
Each in their kind. The Earth obey'd, and strait
Op'ning her fertil Woomb teem'd at a Birth
Innumerous living Creatures, perfet formes,   455
Limb'd and full grown: out of the ground up rose
As from his Lair the wild Beast where he wonns[42]
In Forrest wild, in Thicket, Brake, or Den;
Among the Trees in Pairs they rose, they walk'd:
The Cattel in the Fields and Meddows green: 460
Those rare and solitarie, these in flocks
Pasturing at once, and in broad Herds upsprung.
The grassie Clods now Calv'd, now half appeer'd
The Tawnie Lion, pawing to get free
His hinder parts, then springs as broke from Bonds,   465
And Rampant shakes his Brinded[43] main; the Ounce,
The Libbard, and the Tyger, as the Moal
Rising, the crumbl'd Earth above them threw
In Hillocks; the swift Stag from under ground
Bore up his branching head: scarse from his mould   470
Behemoth[44] biggest born of Earth upheav'd
His vastness: Fleec't the Flocks and bleating rose,
As Plants: ambiguous between Sea and Land
The River Horse[45] and scalie Crocodile.
At once came forth whatever creeps the ground,   475
Insect or Worm; those wav'd thir limber fans
For wings, and smallest Lineaments exact
In all the Liveries dect of Summers pride
With spots of Gold and Purple, azure and green:
These as a line thir long dimension drew,   480
Streaking the ground with sinuous trace; not all
Minims of Nature; some of Serpent kind
Wondrous in length and corpulence[46] involv'd
Thir Snakie foulds, and added wings. First crept
The Parsimonious Emmet, provident   485
Of future, in small room large heart enclos'd,

[42] lives.
[43] streaked with darker color.
[44] See Job xl. 15–24.
[45] hippopotamus.
[46] body; "involv'd" means "concealed."

Pattern of just equalitie perhaps
Hereafter, join'd in her popular Tribes
Of Commonaltie: swarming next appeer'd
The Female Bee that feeds her Husband Drone   490
Deliciously, and builds her waxen Cells
With Honey stor'd: the rest are numberless,
And thou thir Natures know'st, and gav'st them Names,
Needless to thee repeated; nor unknown
The Serpent suttl'st Beast of all the field,   495
Of huge extent somtimes, with brazen Eyes
And hairie Main terrific, though to thee
Not noxious, but obedient at thy call.
Now Heav'n in all her Glorie shon, and rowl'd
Her motions, as the great first-Movers hand   500
First wheeld thir course; Earth in her rich attire
Consummate lovely smil'd; Air, Water, Earth,
By Fowl, Fish, Beast, was flown, was swum, was walkt
Frequent; and of the Sixt day yet remain'd;
There wanted yet the Master work, the end[47]   505
Of all yet don; a Creature who not prone
And Brute as other Creatures, but endu'd
With Sanctitie of Reason, might erect
His Stature, and upright with Front serene
Govern the rest, self-knowing, and from thence   510
Magnanimous to correspond with Heav'n,
But grateful to acknowledge whence his good
Descends, thither with heart and voice and eyes
Directed in Devotion, to adore
And worship God Supream, who made him chief   515
Of all his works: therefore th' Omnipotent
Eternal Father (for where is not hee
Present) thus to his Son audibly spake.
    Let us make now Man in our image, Man
In our similitude, and let them rule   520
Over the Fish and Fowl of Sea and Air,
Beast of the Field, and over all the Earth,
And every creeping thing that creeps the ground.
This said, he formd thee, *Adam*, thee O Man
Dust of the ground, and in thy nostrils breath'd   525
The breath of Life; in his own Image hee
Created thee, in the Image of God
Express, and thou becam'st a living Soul.

[47] the object.

Male he created thee, but thy consort
Female for Race; then bless'd Mankind, and said,   530
Be fruitful, multiplie, and fill the Earth,
Subdue it, and throughout Dominion hold
Over Fish of the Sea, and Fowl of the Air,
And every living thing that moves on th' Earth.
Wherever thus created, for no place   535
Is yet distinct by name, thence, as thou know'st
He brought thee into this delicious Grove,
This Garden, planted with the Trees of God,
Delectable both to behold and taste;
And freely all thir pleasant fruit for food   540
Gave thee, all sorts are here that all th' Earth yeelds,
Varietie without end; but of the Tree
Which tasted works knowledge of Good and Evil,
Thou mai'st not; in the day thou eat'st, thou di'st;
Death is the penaltie impos'd, beware,   545
And govern well thy appetite, least sin
Surprise thee, and her black attendant Death.
Here finish'd hee, and all that he had made
View'd, and behold all was entirely good;
So Ev'n and Morn accomplish'd the Sixt day: 550
Yet not till the Creator from his work
Desisting, though unwearied, up returnd
Up to the Heav'n of Heav'ns his high abode,
Thence to behold this new created World
Th' addition of his Empire, how it shew'd   555
In prospect from his Throne, how good, how fair,
Answering his great Idea. Up he rode
Followd with acclamation and the sound
Symphonious of ten thousand Harps that tun'd
Angelic harmonies: the Earth, the Air   560
Resounded (thou remember'st, for thou heardst),
The Heav'ns and all the Constellations rung,
The Planets in thir stations list'ning stood,
While the bright Pomp ascended jubilant.
Open, ye everlasting Gates, they sung,   565
Open, ye Heav'ns, your living dores; let in
The great Creator from his work returnd
Magnificent, his Six days work, a World;
Open, and henceforth oft; for God will deigne
To visit oft the dwellings of just Men   570
Delighted, and with frequent intercourse
Thither will send his winged Messengers

On errands of supernal Grace. So sung
The glorious Train ascending: He through Heav'n,
That open'd wide her blazing Portals, led   575
To Gods Eternal house direct the way,
A broad and ample rode, whose dust is Gold
And pavement Starrs, as Starrs to thee appeer,
Seen in the Galaxie, that Milkie way
Which nightly as a circling Zone thou seest   580
Powderd with Starrs. And now on Earth the Seventh
Eev'ning arose in *Eden,* for the Sun
Was set, and twilight from the East came on,
Forerunning Night; when at the holy mount
Of Heav'ns high-seated top, th' Impereal Throne   585
Of Godhead, fixt for ever firm and sure,
The Filial Power arriv'd, and sate him down
With his great Father, for he also went
Invisible, yet staid (such priviledge
Hath Omnipresence) and the work ordain'd,   590
Author and end of all things, and from work
Now resting, bless'd and hallowd the Seav'nth day,
As resting on that day from all his work,
But not in silence holy kept; the Harp
Had work and rested not, the solemn Pipe,   595
And Dulcimer, all Organs of sweet stop,
All sounds on Fret[48] by String or Golden Wire
Temper'd soft Tunings, intermixt with Voice
Choral or Unison: of incense Clouds
Fuming from Golden Censers hid the Mount.   600
Creation and the Six dayes acts they sung,
Great are thy works, *Jehovah,* infinite
Thy power; what thought can measure thee or tongue
Relate thee; greater now in thy return
Then from the Giant Angels; thee that day   605
Thy Thunders magnifi'd; but to create
Is greater then created to destroy.
Who can impair thee, mighty King, or bound
Thy Empire? easily the proud attempt
Of Spirits apostat and thir Counsels vain   610
Thou hast repeld, while impiously they thought
Thee to diminish, and from thee withdraw
The number of thy worshippers. Who seeks
To lessen thee, against his purpose serves

[48] a stop on a stringed instrument.

To manifest the more thy might: his evil 615
Thou usest, and from thence creat'st more good.
Witness this new-made World, another Heav'n
From Heaven Gate not farr, founded in view
On the cleer *Hyaline*, the Glassie Sea;[49]
Of amplitude almost immense,[50] with Starrs 620
Numerous, and every Starr perhaps a World
Of destind habitation; but thou know'st
Thir seasons: among these the seat of men,
Earth with her nether Ocean circumfus'd,
Thir pleasant dwelling place. Thrice happie men, 625
And sons of men, whom God hath thus advanc't,
Created in his Image, there to dwell
And worship him, and in reward to rule
Over his Works, on Earth, in Sea, or Air,
And multiply a Race of Worshippers 630
Holy and just: thrice happie if they know
Thir happiness, and persevere upright.
  So sung they, and the Empyrean rung,
With *Halleluiahs*: Thus was Sabbath kept.
And thy request think now fulfill'd, that ask'd 635
How first this World and face of things began,
And what before thy memorie was don
From the beginning, that posteritie
Informd by thee might know; if else thou seekst
Aught, not surpassing human measure, say. 640

BOOK VIII

THE ARGUMENT

Adam inquires concerning celestial Motions, is doubtfully answer'd, and exhorted to search rather things more worthy of
knowledge: *Adam* assents, and still desirous to detain *Raphael*, relates to him what he remember'd since his own Creation, his placing in Paradise, his talk with God concerning
solitude and fit society, his first meeting and Nuptials with

[49] Gordon O'Brien discusses this recurrent image (in *Renaissance Poetics and the Problem of Power*, Chicago, 1956, especially
pp. 113–15) as a correspondence between the mind of man (the
"clear spirit" of *Lycidas*, 70) and the frame of heaven; derived
from Rev. xv. 2, the figure embodies the concept of knowledge and
the concept of power which come from God and are reflected back
to Heaven.
[50] unmeasurable.

Eve, his discourse with the Angel thereupon; who after admonitions repeated departs.

   The Angel ended, and in *Adams* Ear
So Charming left his voice, that he a while
Thought him still speaking, still stood fixt to hear;
Then as new wak't thus gratefully repli'd.
What thanks sufficient, or what recompence   5
Equal have I to render thee, Divine
Hystorian, who thus largely hast allayd
The thirst I had of knowledge, and voutsaf't
This friendly condescention to relate
Things else by me unsearchable, now heard   10
With wonder, but delight, and, as is due,
With glorie attributed to the high
Creator; something yet of doubt remains,
Which onely thy solution can resolve.
When I behold this goodly Frame, this World   15
Of Heav'n and Earth consisting, and compute,
Thir magnitudes, this Earth a spot, a grain,
An Atom, with the Firmament compar'd
And all her numberd Starrs, that seem to rowl
Spaces incomprehensible (for such   20
Thir distance argues and thir swift return
Diurnal) meerly to officiate[1] light
Round this opacous[2] Earth, this punctual[3] spot,
One day and night; in all thir vast survey
Useless besides, reasoning I oft admire,[4]   25
How Nature wise and frugal could commit
Such disproportions, with superfluous hand
So many nobler Bodies to create,
Greater so manifold to this one use,
For aught appeers, and on thir Orbs impose   30
Such restless revolution day by day
Repeated, while the sedentarie Earth,
That better might with farr less compass move,
Serv'd by more noble then her self, attains
Her end without least motion, and receaves,   35
As Tribute such a sumless[5] journey brought

[1] carry out their duty (of supplying); see also "officious," l. 99.
[2] dark.
[3] small and fixed in space (like a point).
[4] regard with wonder.
[5] immeasurable.

Of incorporeal speed, her warmth and light;
Speed, to describe whose swiftness Number fails.
   So spake our Sire, and by his count'nance seemd
Entring on studious thoughts abstruse, which *Eve*   40
Perceaving where she sat retir'd in sight,
With lowliness Majestic from her seat,
And Grace that won who saw to wish her stay,
Rose, and went forth among her Fruits and Flowrs,
To visit how they prosper'd, bud and bloom,   45
Her Nurserie; they at her coming sprung
And toucht by her fair tendance gladlier grew.
Yet went she not, as not with such discourse
Delighted, or not capable her ear
Of what was high: such pleasure she reserv'd,   50
Adam relating, she sole Auditress;
Her Husband the Relater she preferr'd
Before the Angel, and of him to ask
Chose rather; hee, she knew would intermix
Grateful digressions, and solve high dispute   55
With conjugal Caresses, from his Lip
Not Words alone pleas'd her. O when meet now
Such pairs, in Love and mutual Honour joyn'd?
With Goddess-like demeanour forth she went;
Not unattended, for on her as Queen   60
A pomp[6] of winning Graces waited still,
And from about her shot Darts of desire
Into all Eyes to wish her still in sight.
And *Raphael* now to *Adam*'s doubt propos'd
Benevolent and facil[7] thus repli'd.   65
   To ask or search I blame thee not, for Heav'n
Is as the Book of God before thee set,
Wherein to read his wondrous Works, and learn
His Seasons, Hours, or Dayes, or Months, or Yeares:
This to attain, whether Heav'n move or Earth,   70
Imports not, if thou reck'n right, the rest
From Man or Angel the great Architect
Did wisely to conceal, and not divulge
His secrets to be scann'd by them who ought
Rather admire; or if they list to try   75
Conjecture, he his Fabric of the Heav'ns
Hath left to thir disputes, perhaps to move

[6] procession.
[7] mild of manner.

His laughter at thir quaint Opinions wide[8]
Hereafter, when they come to model Heav'n
And calculate the Starrs, how they will weild   80
The mightie frame, how build, unbuild, contrive
To save appeerances,[9] how gird the Sphear
With Centric and Eccentric scribl'd o're,
Cycle and Epicycle, Orb in Orb:
Alreadie by thy reasoning this I guess,   85
Who art to lead thy ofspring, and supposest
That bodies bright and greater should not serve
The less not bright, nor Heav'n such journies run,
Earth sitting still, when she alone receaves
The benefit: consider first, that Great   90
Or Bright inferrs not Excellence: the Earth
Though, in comparison of Heav'n, so small,
Nor glistering, may of solid good contain
More plenty then the Sun that barren shines,
Whose vertue on it self works no effect,   95
But in the fruitful Earth; there first receav'd
His beams, unactive else, thir vigour find.
Yet not to Earth are those bright Luminaries
Officious, but to thee Earths habitant.
And for the Heav'ns wide Circuit, let it speak   100
The Makers high magnificence, who built
So spacious, and his Line stretcht out so farr;
That Man may know he dwells not in his own;
An Edifice too large for him to fill,
Lodg'd in a small partition, and the rest   105
Ordain'd for uses to his Lord best known.
The swiftness of those Circles attribute,
Though numberless, to his Omnipotence,
That to corporeal substances could add
Speed almost Spiritual; mee thou thinkst not slow,   110
Who since the Morning hour set out from Heav'n
Where God resides, and ere mid-day arriv'd
In *Eden*, distance inexpressible
By Numbers that have name. But this I urge,
Admitting Motion in the Heav'ns, to shew   115

[8] far from the truth.
[9] invent theories to explain astronomical phenomena, such as
the rotation of a sphere with the earth as center or not as center
of the universe, moving in full orbit of itself or in a small circle
whose center lay on the circumference of a large circle (orbit
within an orbit).

Invalid that which thee to doubt it mov'd;
Not that I so affirm, though so it seem
To thee who hast thy dwelling here on Earth.
God to remove his wayes from human sense,
Plac'd Heav'n from Earth so farr, that earthly sight,   120
If it presume, might err in things too high,
And no advantage gain. What if the Sun
Be Center to the World, and other Starrs
By his attractive vertue[10] and thir own
Incited, dance about him various rounds?   125
Thir wandring course now high, now low, then hid,
Progressive, retrograde, or standing still,
In six thou seest, and what if sev'nth to these
The Planet Earth, so stedfast though she seem,
Insensibly[11] three different Motions move?   130
Which else to several Sphears thou must ascribe,
Mov'd contrarie with thwart obliquities,[12]
Or save the Sun his labour, and that swift
Nocturnal and Diurnal rhomb[13] suppos'd,
Invisible else above all Starrs, the Wheel   135
Of Day and Night; which needs not thy beleef,
If Earth industrious of her self fetch Day
Travelling East, and with her part averse
From the Suns beam meet Night, her other part
Still luminous by his ray. What if that light   140
Sent from her through the wide transpicuous air,
To the terrestrial Moon be as a Starr
Enlightning her by Day, as she by Night
This Earth? reciprocal, if Land be there,
Feilds and Inhabitants: Her spots thou seest   145
As Clouds, and Clouds may rain, and Rain produce
Fruits in her soft'n'd Soil, for some to eat
Allotted there; and other Suns perhaps
With thir attendant Moons thou wilt descrie
Communicating Male and Femal[14] Light,   150

[10] magnetic attraction.

[11] imperceptibly; the three motions are rotation, revolution around the sun, and polar rotation around the ecliptic (the apparent path of the sun).

[12] the angles between the planes of the planets' equators and their orbits; each sphere's obliquity intersects another sphere's. That is, the movements of the spheres are transverse.

[13] the primum mobile.

[14] of the sun (direct) and of the moon (reflected).

Which two great Sexes animate the World,
Stor'd in each Orb perhaps with some that live.
For such vast room in Nature unpossest
By living Soul, desert and desolate,
Onely to shine, yet scarce to contribute   155
Each Orb a glimps of Light, conveyd so farr
Down to this habitable, which returns
Light back to them, is obvious to dispute.[15]
But whether thus these things, or whether not,
Whether the Sun predominant in Heav'n   160
Rise on the Earth, or Earth rise on the Sun,
Hee from the East his flaming rode begin,
Or Shee from West her silent course advance
With inoffensive[16] pace that spinning sleeps
On her soft Axle, while she paces Eev'n,   165
And beares thee soft with the smooth Air along,
Sollicit not thy thoughts with matters hid,
Leave them to God above, him serve and fear;
Of other Creatures, as him pleases best,
Wherever plac't, let him dispose: joy thou   170
In what he gives to thee, this Paradise
And thy fair *Eve;* Heav'n is for thee too high
To know what passes there; be lowlie wise:
Think onely what concerns thee and thy being;
Dream not of other Worlds, what Creatures there   175
Live, in what state, condition or degree,
Contented that thus farr hath been reveal'd
Not of Earth onely but of highest Heav'n.
    To whom thus *Adam* cleerd of doubt, repli'd.
How fully hast thou satisfi'd mee, pure   180
Intelligence of Heav'n, Angel serene,
And freed from intricacies, taught to live,
The easiest way, nor with perplexing thoughts
To interrupt the sweet of Life, from which
God hath bid dwell farr off all anxious cares,   185
And not molest us, unless we our selves
Seek them with wandring thoughts, and notions vain.
But apt the Mind or Fancie is to roave
Uncheckt, and of her roaving is no end;
Till warn'd, or by experience taught, she learn,   190

[15] evidently disputable (since there are so many and they give
off so little light).
    [16] unimpeded.

That not to know at large of things remote
From use, obscure and suttle, but to know
That which before us lies in daily life,
Is the prime Wisdom; what is more, is fume,
Or emptiness, or fond impertinence,   195
And renders us in things that most concern
Unpractis'd, unprepar'd, and still to seek.
Therefore from this high pitch let us descend
A lower flight, and speak of things at hand
Useful, whence haply mention may arise   200
Of somthing not unseasonable to ask
By sufferance, and thy wonted favour deign'd.
Thee I have heard relating what was don
Ere my remembrance: now hear mee relate
My Storie, which perhaps thou hast not heard;   205
And Day is yet not spent; till then thou seest
How suttly to detain thee I devise,
Inviting thee to hear while I relate,
Fond, were it not in hope of thy reply:
For while I sit with thee, I seem in Heav'n,   210
And sweeter thy discourse is to my ear
Then Fruits of Palm-tree pleasantest to thirst
And hunger both, from[17] labour, at the hour
Of sweet repast; they satiate, and soon fill,
Though pleasant, but thy words with Grace Divine   215
Imbu'd, bring to thir sweetness no satietie.
    To whom thus *Raphael* answer'd heav'nly meek.
Nor are thy lips ungraceful, Sire of men,
Nor tongue ineloquent; for God on thee
Abundantly his gifts hath also pour'd   220
Inward and outward both, his image fair:
Speaking or mute all comliness and grace
Attends thee, and each word, each motion formes.
Nor less think wee in Heav'n of thee on Earth
Then of our fellow servant, and inquire   225
Gladly into the wayes of God with Man:
For God we see hath honour'd thee, and set
On Man his equal Love: say therefore on;
For I that Day was absent, as befell,
Bound on a voyage uncouth[18] and obscure,   230
Farr on excursion toward the Gates of Hell;

[17] (which come) as a result of.
[18] unknown.

Squar'd in full Legion (such command we had)
To see that none thence issu'd forth a spie,
Or enemie, while God was in his work,
Least hee incenst at such eruption bold,   235
Destruction with Creation might have mixt.
Not that they durst without his leave attempt,
But us he sends upon his high behests
For state, as Sovran King, and to enure[19]
Our prompt obedience. Fast we found, fast shut   240
The dismal Gates, and barricado'd strong;
But long ere our approaching heard within
Noise, other then the sound of Dance or Song,
Torment, and loud lament, and furious rage.
Glad we return'd up to the coasts of Light   245
Ere Sabbath Eev'ning: so we had in charge.
But thy relation now; for I attend,
Pleas'd with thy words no less then thou with mine.
  So spake the Godlike Power, and thus our Sire.
For Man to tell how human Life began   250
Is hard; for who himself beginning knew?
Desire with thee still longer to converse
Induc'd me. As new wak't from soundest sleep
Soft on the flowrie herb I found me laid
In Balmie Sweat, which with his Beames the Sun   255
Soon dri'd, and on the reaking moisture fed.
Strait toward Heav'n my wondring Eyes I turnd,
And gaz'd a while the ample Skie, till rais'd
By quick instinctive motion up I sprung,
As thitherward endevoring, and upright   260
Stood on my feet; about me round I saw
Hill, Dale, and shadie Woods, and sunnie Plains,
And liquid Lapse of murmuring Streams; by these,
Creatures that liv'd, and mov'd, and walk'd, or flew,
Birds on the branches warbling; all things smil'd,   265
With fragrance and with joy my heart oreflow'd.
My self I then perus'd, and Limb by Limb
Survey'd, and sometimes went,[20] and sometimes ran
With supple joints, as lively vigour led:
But who I was, or where, or from what cause,   270
Knew not; to speak I tri'd, and forthwith spake,
My Tongue obey'd and readily could name

[19] make (obedience) a habit.
[20] walked.

What e're I saw. Thou Sun, said I, fair Light,
And thou enlight'n'd Earth, so fresh and gay,
Ye Hills and Dales, ye Rivers, Woods, and Plains,   275
And ye that live and move, fair Creatures, tell,
Tell, if ye saw, how came I thus, how here?
Not of my self; by some great Maker then,
In goodness and in power præeminent;
Tell me, how may I know him, how adore,   280
From whom I have that thus I move and live,
And feel that I am happier then I know.
While thus I call'd, and stray'd I knew not whither,
From where I first drew Air, and first beheld
This happie Light, when answer none return'd,   285
On a green shadie Bank profuse of Flowrs
Pensive I sate me down; there gentle sleep
First found me, and with soft oppression seis'd
My droused sense, untroubl'd, though I thought
I then was passing to my former state   290
Insensible, and forthwith to dissolve:
When suddenly stood at my Head a dream,
Whose inward apparition gently mov'd
My fancy to believe I yet had being,
And liv'd: One came, methought, of shape Divine,   295
And said, thy Mansion wants thee, *Adam*, rise,
First Man, of Men innumerable ordain'd
First Father, call'd by thee I come thy Guide
To the Garden of bliss, thy seat prepar'd.
So saying, by the hand he took me rais'd,   300
And over Fields and Waters, as in Air
Smooth sliding without step, last led me up
A woodie Mountain; whose high top was plain,
A Circuit wide, enclos'd, with goodliest Trees
Planted, with Walks, and Bowers, that what I saw   305
Of Earth before scarse pleasant seemd. Each Tree
Load'n with fairest Fruit that hung to th' Eye
Tempting, stirr'd in me sudden appetite
To pluck and eat; whereat I wak'd, and found
Before mine Eyes all real, as the dream   310
Had lively shadowd:[21] Here had new begun
My wandring, had not hee who was my Guide
Up hither, from among the Trees appeer'd,
Presence Divine. Rejoycing, but with aw

[21] had shown a vision which seemed real.

In adoration at his feet I fell   315
Submiss:[22] he rear'd me, and Whom thou soughtst I am,
Said mildly, Author of all this thou seest
Above, or round about thee or beneath.
This Paradise I give thee, count it thine
To Till and keep, and of the Fruit to eat: 320
Of every Tree that in the Garden grows
Eat freely with glad heart; fear here no dearth:
But of the Tree whose operation brings
Knowledge of good and ill, which I have set
The Pledge of thy Obedience and thy Faith,   325
Amid the Garden by the Tree of Life,
Remember what I warn thee, shun to taste,
And shun the bitter consequence: for know,
The day thou eat'st thereof, my sole command
Transgrest, inevitably thou shalt dye;[23]   330
From that day mortal, and this happie State
Shalt loose, expell'd from hence into a World
Of woe and sorrow. Sternly he pronounc'd
The rigid interdiction, which resounds
Yet dreadful in mine ear, though in my choice   335
Not to incur; but soon his cleer aspect
Return'd and gracious purpose thus renew'd.
Not onely these fair bounds, but all the Earth
To thee and to thy Race I give; as Lords
Possess it, and all things that therein live,   340
Or live in Sea, or Air, Beast, Fish, and Fowl.
In signe whereof each Bird and Beast behold
After thir kinds; I bring them to receave
From thee thir Names, and pay thee fealtie
With low subjection; understand the same   345
Of Fish within thir watry residence,
Not hither summond, since they cannot change
Thir Element to draw the thinner Air.
As thus he spake, each Bird and Beast behold
Approaching two and two, these cowring low   350
With blandishment, each Bird stoop'd on his wing.
I nam'd them, as they pass'd, and understood
Thir Nature, with such knowledge God endu'd
My sudden apprehension: but in these
I found not what me thought I wanted still;   355

[22] submissive.
[23] explained by ll. 331–32.

And to the Heav'nly vision thus presum'd.
  O by what Name, for thou above all these,
Above mankind, or aught then mankind higher,
Surpassest farr my naming, how may I
Adore thee, Author of this Universe,   360
And all this good to man, for whose well being
So amply, and with hands so liberal
Thou hast provided all things: but with mee
I see not who partakes. In solitude
What happiness, who can enjoy alone,   365
Or all enjoying, what contentment find?
Thus I presumptuous; and the vision bright,
As with a smile more bright'n'd, thus repli'd.
  What call'st thou solitude, is not the Earth
With various living creatures, and the Air   370
Replenisht, and all these at thy command
To come and play before thee, know'st thou not
Thir language and thir wayes, they also know,
And reason not contemptibly; with these
Find pastime, and bear rule; thy Realm is large.   375
So spake the Universal Lord, and seem'd
So ordering. I with leave of speech implor'd,
And humble deprecation thus repli'd.
  Let not my words offend thee, Heav'nly Power,
My Maker, be propitious while I speak.   380
Hast thou not made me here thy substitute,
And these inferiour farr beneath me set?
Among unequals what societie
Can sort,[24] what harmonie or true delight?
Which must be mutual, in proportion due   385
Giv'n and receiv'd; but in disparitie
The one intense, the other still remiss[25]
Cannot well suit with either, but soon prove
Tedious alike: Of fellowship I speak
Such as I seek, fit to participate   390
All rational delight, wherein the brute
Cannot be human consort; they rejoyce
Each with thir kind, Lion with Lioness;
So fitly them in pairs thou hast combin'd;
Much less can Bird with Beast, or Fish with Fowl   395

[24] be in harmony, be suitable.
[25] the one deeply concerned (taut), the other always careless (slack).

So well converse, nor with the Ox the Ape;
Wors then can Man with Beast, and least of all.
    Whereto th' Almighty answer'd, not displeas'd.
A nice[26] and suttle happiness I see
Thou to thy self proposest, in the choice   400
Of thy Associates, *Adam,* and wilt taste
No pleasure, though in pleasure, solitarie.
What thinkst thou then of mee, and this my State,
Seem I to thee sufficiently possest
Of happiness, or not? who am alone   405
From all Eternitie, for none I know
Second to me or like, equal much less.
How have I then with whom to hold converse
Save with the Creatures which I made, and those
To me inferiour, infinite descents   410
Beneath what other Creatures are to thee?
    He ceas'd, I lowly answer'd. To attain
The highth and depth of thy Eternal wayes
All human thoughts come short, Supream of things;
Thou in thy self art perfet, and in thee   415
Is no deficience found; not so is Man,
But in degree, the cause of his desire
By conversation with his like to help,
Or solace his defects. No need that thou
Shouldst propagat, already infinite;   420
And through all numbers absolute,[27] though One;
But Man by number is to manifest
His single imperfection, and beget
Like of his like, his Image multipli'd,
In unitie defective, which requires   425
Collateral love, and deerest amitie.
Thou in thy secresie although alone,
Best with thy self accompanied, seek'st not
Social communication, yet so pleas'd,
Canst raise thy Creature to what highth thou wilt   430
Of Union or Communion, deifi'd;
I by conversing cannot these erect
From prone, nor in thir wayes complacence find.
Thus I embold'n'd spake, and freedom us'd
Permissive, and acceptance found, which gain'd   435
This answer from the gratious voice Divine.

[26] discriminating.
[27] in all things perfect.

Thus farr to try thee, *Adam*, I was pleas'd,
And find thee knowing not of Beasts alone,
Which thou hast rightly nam'd, but of thy self,
Expressing well the spirit within thee free,   440
My Image, not imparted to the Brute,
Whose fellowship therefore unmeet for thee
Good reason was thou freely shouldst dislike,
And be so minded still; I, ere thou spak'st,
Knew it not good for Man to be alone,   445
And no such companie as then thou saw'st
Intended thee, for trial onely brought,
To see how thou could'st judge of fit and meet:
What next I bring shall please thee, be assur'd,
Thy likeness, thy fit help, thy other self,   450
Thy wish exactly to thy hearts desire.
    Hee ended, or I heard no more, for now
My earthly[28] by his Heav'nly overpowerd,
Which it had long stood under, streind to th' highth
In that celestial Colloquie sublime,   455
As with an object that excels the sense,
Dazl'd and spent, sunk down, and sought repair
Of sleep, which instantly fell on me, call'd
By Nature as in aid, and clos'd mine eyes.
Mine eyes he clos'd, but op'n left the Cell   460
Of Fancie my internal sight, by which
Abstract as in a transe methought I saw,
Though sleeping, where I lay, and saw the shape
Still glorious before whom awake I stood;
Who stooping op'n'd my left side, and took   465
From thence a Rib, with cordial spirits warm,
And Life-blood streaming fresh; wide was the wound,
But suddenly with flesh fill'd up and heal'd:
The Rib he formd and fashiond with his hands;
Under his forming hands a Creature grew,   470
Manlike, but different sex, so lovely fair,
That what seemd fair in all the World, seemd now
Mean, or in her summ'd up, in her containd
And in her looks, which from that time infus'd
Sweetness into my heart, unfelt before,   475
And into all things from her Air inspir'd
The spirit of love and amorous delight.
Shee disappeerd, and left me dark, I wak'd

[28] (nature).

To find her, or for ever to deplore
Her loss, and other pleasures all abjure: 480
When out of hope, behold her, not farr off,
Such as I saw her in my dream, adornd
With what all Earth or Heaven could bestow
To make her amiable: On she came,
Led by her Heav'nly Maker, though unseen,   485
And guided by his voice, nor uninformd
Of nuptial Sanctitie and marriage Rites:
Grace was in all her steps, Heav'n in her Eye,
In every gesture dignitie and love.
I overjoyd could not forbear aloud.   490
     This turn hath made amends; thou hast fulfill'd
Thy words, Creator bounteous and benigne,
Giver of all things fair, but fairest this
Of all thy gifts, nor enviest. I now see
Bone of my Bone, Flesh of my Flesh, my Self   495
Before me; Woman is her Name, of Man
Extracted; for this cause he shall forgoe
Father and Mother, and to his Wife adhere;
And they shall be one Flesh, one Heart, one Soul.
     She heard me thus, and though divinely brought,   500
Yet Innocence and Virgin Modestie,
Her vertue and the conscience of her worth,
That would be woo'd, and not unsought be won,
Not obvious, not obtrusive, but retir'd,
The more desirable, or to say all,   505
Nature her self, though pure of sinful thought,
Wrought in her so, that seeing me, she turn'd;
I follow'd her, she what was Honour knew,
And with obsequious Majestie approv'd
My pleaded reason. To the Nuptial Bowr   510
I led her blushing like the Morn: all Heav'n,
And happie Constellations on that hour
Shed thir selectest influence; the Earth
Gave sign of gratulation, and each Hill;
Joyous the Birds; fresh Gales and gentle Aires   515
Whisper'd it to the Woods, and from thir wings
Flung Rose, flung Odours from the spicie Shrub,
Disporting, till the amorous Bird of Night[29]
Sung Spousal, and bid haste the Eevning Starr
On his Hill top, to light the bridal Lamp.   520

[29] the nightingale.

Thus I have told thee all my State, and brought
My Storie to the sum of earthly bliss
Which I enjoy, and must confess to find
In all things else delight indeed, but such
As us'd or not, works in the mind no change,   525
Nor vehement desire, these delicacies
I mean of Taste, Sight, Smell, Herbs, Fruits, and Flowrs,
Walks, and the melodie of Birds; but here
Farr otherwise, transported I behold,
Transported touch; here passion first I felt,   530
Commotion strange, in all enjoyments else
Superiour and unmov'd, here onely weak
Against the charm of Beauties powerful glance.
Or Nature faild in mee, and left some part
Not proof enough such Object to sustain,   535
Or from my side subducting, took perhaps
More then enough; at least on her bestow'd
Too much of Ornament, in outward shew
Elaborate, of inward less exact.
For well I understand in the prime end   540
Of Nature her th' inferiour, in the mind
And inward Faculties, which most excell,
In outward also her resembling less
His Image who made both, and less expressing
The character of that Dominion giv'n   545
O're other Creatures; yet when I approach
Her loveliness, so absolute[30] she seems
And in her self compleat, so well to know
Her own, that what she wills to do or say,
Seems wisest, vertuousest, discreetest, best;   550
All higher knowledge in her presence falls
Degraded, Wisdom in discourse with her
Looses discount'nanc't, and like folly shews;
Authority and Reason on her wait,
As one intended first, not after made   555
Occasionally; and to consummate all,
Greatness of mind and nobleness thir seat
Build in her loveliest, and create an awe
About her, as a guard Angelic plac't.
To whom the Angel with contracted brow.   560
   Accuse not Nature, she hath don her part;
Do thou but thine, and be not diffident

[30] perfect.

Of Wisdom, she deserts thee not, if thou
Dismiss not her, when most thou needst her nigh,
By attributing overmuch to things   565
Less excellent, as thou thy self perceav'st.
For what admir'st thou, what transports thee so,
An outside? fair no doubt, and worthy well
Thy cherishing, thy honouring, and thy love,
Not thy subjection: weigh with her thy self;   570
Then value: Oft times nothing profits more
Then self-esteem, grounded on just and right
Well manag'd; of that skill[31] the more thou know'st,
The more she will acknowledge thee her Head,
And to realities yeild all her shows: 575
Made so adorn for thy delight the more,
So awful, that with honour thou maist love
Thy mate, who sees when thou art seen least wise.
But if the sense of touch whereby mankind
Is propagated seem such dear delight   580
Beyond all other, think the same voutsaf't
To Cattel and each Beast; which would not be
To them made common and divulg'd, if aught
Therein enjoy'd were worthy to subdue
The Soul of Man, or passion in him move.   585
What higher in her societie thou findst
Attractive, human, rational, love still;
In loving thou dost well, in passion not,
Wherein true Love consists not; love refines
The thoughts, and heart enlarges, hath his seat   590
In Reason, and is judicious, is the scale
By which to heav'nly Love thou maist ascend,
Not sunk in carnal pleasure, for which cause
Among the Beasts no Mate for thee was found.
    To whom thus half abash't *Adam* repli'd.   595
Neither her out-side formd so fair, nor aught
In procreation common to all kinds
(Though higher of the genial[32] Bed by far,
And with mysterious reverence I deem)
So much delights me as those graceful acts,   600
Those thousand decencies that daily flow
From all her words and actions mixt with Love
And sweet compliance, which declare unfeign'd

[31] self-esteem.
[32] procreative.

Union of Mind, or in us both one Soul;
Harmonie to behold in wedded pair   605
More grateful then harmonious sound to th' ear.
Yet these subject not; I to thee disclose
What inward thence I feel, not therefore foild,
Who meet with various objects, from the sense
Variously representing; yet still free   610
Approve the best, and follow what I approve.
To love thou blam'st me not, for love thou saist
Leads up to Heav'n, is both the way and guide;
Bear with me then, if lawful what I ask;
Love not the heav'nly Spirits, and how thir Love   615
Express they, by looks onely, or do they mix
Irradiance, virtual or immediate touch?
    To whom the Angel with a smile that glow'd
Celestial rosie red, Loves proper hue,
Answer'd. Let it suffice thee that thou know'st   620
Us happie, and without Love no happiness.
Whatever pure thou in the body enjoy'st
(And pure thou wert created) we enjoy
In eminence, and obstacle find none
Of membrane, joynt, or limb, exclusive barrs: 625
Easier then Air with Air, if Spirits embrace,
Total they mix, Union of Pure with Pure
Desiring; nor restrain'd conveyance need
As Flesh to mix with Flesh, or Soul with Soul.
But I can now no more; the parting Sun   630
Beyond the Earths green Cape and verdant Isles[33]
Hesperean[34] sets, my Signal to depart.
Be strong, live happie, and love, but first of all
Him whom to love is to obey, and keep
His great command; take heed least Passion sway   635
Thy Judgement to do aught, which else free Will
Would not admit; thine and of all thy Sons
The weal or woe in thee is plac't; beware.
I in thy persevering shall rejoyce,
And all the Blest: stand fast; to stand or fall   640
Free in thine own Arbitrement it lies.
Perfet within, no outward aid require;
And all temptation to transgress repel.
    So saying, he arose; whom *Adam* thus

[33] Cape Verde ("green") and the island of the same name.
[34] in the West.

Follow'd with benediction. Since to part,   645
Go heav'nly Guest, Ethereal Messenger,
Sent from whose sovran goodness I adore.
Gentle to me and affable hath been
Thy condescension, and shall be honour'd ever
With grateful Memorie: thou to mankind   650
Be good and friendly still, and oft return.
   So parted they, the Angel up to Heav'n
From the thick shade, and *Adam* to his Bowr.

BOOK IX

THE ARGUMENT

Satan having compast the Earth, with meditated guile returns
as a mist by Night into Paradise, enters into the Serpent sleeping. *Adam* and *Eve* in the Morning go forth to thir labours,
which *Eve* proposes to divide in several places, each labouring
apart: *Adam* consents not, alledging the danger, lest that
Enemy, of whom they were forewarn'd, should attempt her
found alone: *Eve* loath to be thought not circumspect or firm
enough, urges her going apart, the rather desirous to make
tryal of her strength; *Adam* at last yields: The Serpent finds
her alone; his subtle approach, first gazing, then speaking,
with much flattery extolling *Eve* above all other Creatures.
Eve wondring to hear the Serpent speak, asks how he attain'd to human speech and such understanding not till now;
the Serpent answers, that by tasting of a certain Tree in the
Garden he attain'd both to Speech and Reason, till then void
of both: *Eve* requires him to bring her to that Tree, and finds
it to be the Tree of Knowledge forbidden: The Serpent now
grown bolder, with many wiles and arguments induces her at
length to eat; she pleas'd with the taste deliberates awhile
whether to impart thereof to *Adam* or not, at last brings him
of the Fruit, relates what perswaded her to eat thereof: *Adam*
at first amaz'd, but perceiving her lost, resolves through vehemence of love to perish with her; and extenuating the
trespass eats also of the Fruit: The Effects thereof in them
both; they seek to cover thir nakedness; then fall to variance
and accusation of one another.

   No more of talk where God or Angel Guest
With Man, as with his Friend, familiar us'd
To sit indulgent, and with him partake

Rural repast, permitting him the while
Venial[1] discourse unblam'd: I now must change   5
Those Notes to Tragic; foul distrust, and breach
Disloyal on the part of Man, revolt,
And disobedience: On the part of Heav'n
Now alienated, distance and distaste,
Anger and just rebuke, and judgement giv'n,   10
That brought into this World a world of woe,
Sin and her shadow Death, and Miserie
Deaths Harbinger: Sad task, yet argument
Not less but more Heroic then the wrauth
Of stern *Achilles* on his Foe pursu'd[2]   15
Thrice Fugitive about *Troy* Wall; or rage
Of *Turnus* for *Lavinia* disespous'd,
Or *Neptun's* ire or *Juno's*, that so long
Perplex'd the *Greek* and *Cytherea's* Son;
If answerable style I can obtain   20
Of my Celestial Patroness,[3] who deignes
Her nightly visitation unimplor'd,
And dictates to me slumbring, or inspires
Easie my unpremeditated Verse:
Since first this Subject for Heroic Song   25
Pleas'd me long choosing, and beginning late;
Not sedulous by Nature to indite
Warrs, hitherto the onely Argument
Heroic deem'd, chief maistrie to dissect
With long and tedious havoc fabl'd Knights   30
In Battels feign'd; the better fortitude
Of Patience and Heroic Martyrdom
Unsung; or to describe Races and Games,
Or tilting Furniture,[4] emblazon'd Shields,
Impreses[5] quaint, Caparisons and Steeds;   35
Bases[6] and tinsel Trappings, gorgious Knights
At Joust and Torneament; then marshal'd Feast

---

[1] unobjectionable.

[2] referring to *Iliad*, XXII (Achilles' fighting Hector), *Aeneid*, XII (Turnus' competing with Aeneas), *Odyssey*, I (Neptune's avenging himself on Ulysses), and *Aeneid*, I (Juno's harassing Aeneas because of her anger and jealousy against his mother Venus).

[3] Urania.

[4] furnishings.

[5] devices on shields.

[6] probably the lower parts of escutcheons.

Serv'd up in Hall with Sewers,[7] and Seneshals;
The skill of Artifice or Office mean,
Not that which justly gives Heroic name   40
To Person or to Poem. Mee of these
Nor skill'd nor studious, higher Argument
Remains, sufficient of it self to raise
That name, unless an age too late,[8] or cold
Climat,[9] or Years damp my intended wing   45
Deprest, and much they may, if all be mine,
Not Hers who brings it nightly to my Ear.
    The Sun was sunk, and after him the Starr
Of *Hesperus*, whose Office is to bring
Twilight upon the Earth, short Arbiter   50
Twixt Day and Night, and now from end to end
Nights Hemisphere had veild th' Horizon round:
When *Satan* who late fled before the threats
Of *Gabriel* out of *Eden*, now improv'd
In meditated fraud and malice, bent   55
On mans destruction, maugre what might hap
Of heavier on himself, fearless return'd.
By Night he fled, and at Midnight return'd
From compassing the Earth, cautious of day,
Since *Uriel* Regent of the Sun descri'd   60
His entrance, and forewarnd the Cherubim
That kept thir watch; thence full of anguish driv'n,
The space of seven continu'd Nights[10] he rode
With darkness, thrice the Equinoctial Line
He circl'd, four times cross'd the Carr of Night   65
From Pole to Pole, traversing each Colure;
On th' eighth return'd, and on the Coast averse
From entrance or Cherubic Watch, by stealth
Found unsuspected way. There was a place,
Now not, though Sin, not Time, first wraught the change,   70
Where *Tigris* at the foot of Paradise
Into a Gulf shot under ground, till part
Rose up a Fountain by the Tree of Life;

    [7] butlers.

    [8] referring to the decay of nature; see *Nature does not suffer decay.*

    [9] The theory of the effects of cold climate is reviewed by T. B. Stroup in *Modern Language Quarterly,* IV (1943), 185–89.

    [10] consisting of three days' flight around the equator and two days' each around two meridians of longitude at right angles with each other (each colure).

In with the River sunk, and with it rose
Satan involv'd in rising Mist, then sought   75
Where to lie hid; Sea he had searcht and Land
From *Eden* over *Pontus*,[11] and the Pool
Mæotis, up beyond the River *Ob;*
Downward as farr Antartic; and in length
West from *Orontes*[12] to the Ocean barr'd   80
At *Darien,*[13] thence to the Land where flows
Ganges and *Indus:* thus the Orb he roam'd
With narrow search; and with inspection deep
Consider'd every Creature, which of all
Most opportune might serve his Wiles, and found   85
The Serpent suttlest Beast of all the Field.
Him after long debate, irresolute
Of thoughts revolv'd,[14] his final sentence chose
Fit Vessel, fittest Imp of fraud, in whom
To enter, and his dark suggestions hide   90
From sharpest sight: for in the wilie Snake,
Whatever sleights none would suspicious mark,
As from his wit and native suttletie
Proceeding, which in other Beasts observ'd
Doubt might beget of Diabolic pow'r   95
Active within beyond the sense of brute.
Thus he resolv'd, but first from inward grief
His bursting passion into plaints thus pour'd:
　　O Earth, how like to Heav'n, if not preferr'd
More justly, Seat worthier of Gods, as built   100
With second thoughts, reforming what was old!
For what God after better worse would build?
Terrestrial Heav'n, danc't round by other Heav'ns
That shine, yet bear thir bright officious Lamps,
Light above Light, for thee alone, as seems,   105
In thee concentring all thir precious beams
Of sacred influence: As God in Heav'n
Is Center, yet extends to all, so thou
Centring receav'st from all those Orbs; in thee,
Not in themselves, all thir known vertue appeers   110

[11] the Black Sea; Lake Maeotis is the Sea of Azov, and the Ob
flows to the Arctic Sea.
[12] a river in Syria.
[13] the Isthmus of Panama on the Atlantic Ocean.
[14] wavering from mulling over thoughts; "his final sentence" is
his decision to assume serpentine form.

Productive in Herb, Plant, and nobler birth
Of Creatures animate with gradual[15] life
Of Growth, Sense, Reason, all summ'd up in Man.
With what delight could I have walkt thee round,
If I could joy in aught, sweet interchange   115
Of Hill and Vallie, Rivers, Woods and Plains,
Now Land, now Sea, and Shores with Forrest crownd,
Rocks, Dens, and Caves; but I in none of these
Find place or refuge; and the more I see
Pleasures about me, so much more I feel   120
Torment within me, as from the hateful siege
Of contraries;[16] all good to me becomes
Bane, and in Heav'n much worse would be my state.
But neither here seek I, no nor in Heav'n
To dwell, unless by maistring Heav'ns Supream;   125
Nor hope to be my self less miserable
By what I seek, but others to make such
As I, though thereby worse to me redound:
For onely in destroying I find ease
To my relentless thoughts; and him destroyd,   130
Or won to what may work his utter loss,
For whom all this was made, all this will soon
Follow, as to him linkt in weal or woe,
In wo then; that destruction wide may range:
To mee shall be the glorie sole among   135
Th' infernal Powers, in one day to have marr'd
What he *Almightie* styl'd, six Nights and Days
Continu'd making, and who knows how long
Before had bin contriving, though perhaps
Not longer then since I in one Night freed   140
From servitude inglorious welnigh half
Th' Angelic Name, and thinner left the throng
Of his adorers: hee to be aveng'd,
And to repair his numbers thus impair'd,
Whether such vertue spent of old now faild   145
More Angels to Create, if they at least
Are his Created, or to spite us more,
Determin'd to advance into our room
A Creature form'd of Earth, and him endow,
Exalted from so base original,   150
With Heav'nly spoils, our spoils: What he decreed

[15] referring to links in the chain of being, upward to man.
[16] seat of conflicting feelings.

He effected; Man he made, and for him built
Magnificent this World, and Earth his seat,
Him Lord pronounc'd, and, O indignitie!
Subjected to his service Angel wings,   155
And flaming Ministers to watch and tend
Thir earthy Charge: Of these the vigilance
I dread, and to elude, thus wrapt in mist
Of midnight vapor glide obscure, and prie
In every Bush and Brake, where hap may find   160
The Serpent sleeping, in whose mazie foulds
To hide me, and the dark intent I bring.
O foul descent! that I who erst contended
With Gods to sit the highest, am now constraind
Into a Beast, and mixt with bestial slime,   165
This essence to incarnate and imbrute,
That to the hight of Deitie aspir'd;
But what will not Ambition and Revenge
Descend to? who aspires must down as low
As high he soard, obnoxious[17] first or last   170
To basest things. Revenge, at first though sweet,
Bitter ere long back on it self recoils;
Let it; I reck not, so it light well aim'd,
Since higher I fall short, on him who next
Provokes my envie, this new Favorite   175
Of Heav'n, this Man of Clay, Son of despite,
Whom us the more to spite his Maker rais'd
From dust: spite then with spite is best repaid.
    So saying, through each Thicket Danck or Drie,
Like a black mist low creeping, he held on   180
His midnight search, where soonest he might find
The Serpent: him fast sleeping soon he found
In Labyrinth of many a round self-rowl'd,
His head the midst, well stor'd with suttle wiles:
Not yet in horrid Shade or dismal Den,   185
Nor nocent yet, but on the grassie Herb
Fearless unfeard he slept: in at his Mouth
The Devil enterd, and his brutal sense,
In heart or head, possessing soon inspir'd
With act intelligential; but his sleep   190
Disturb'd not, waiting close[18] th' approach of Morn.
Now when as sacred Light began to dawn

[17] liable.
[18] hidden.

In *Eden* on the humid Flowrs, that breath'd
Thir morning incense, when all things that breath,
From th' Earths great Altar send up silent praise   195
To the Creator, and his Nostrils fill
With grateful Smell, forth came the human pair
And joynd thir vocal Worship to the Quire
Of Creatures wanting voice, that done, partake
The season, prime for sweetest Scents and Aires: 200
Then commune how that day they best may ply
Thir growing work: for much thir work outgrew
The hands dispatch of two Gardning so wide.
And *Eve* first to her Husband thus began.

    Adam, well may we labour still to dress   205
This Garden, still to tend Plant, Herb and Flowr,
Our pleasant task enjoyn'd, but till more hands
Aid us, the work under our labour grows,
Luxurious by restraint; what we by day
Lop overgrown, or prune, or prop, or bind,   210
One night or two with wanton growth derides
Tending to wild. Thou therefore now advise
Or hear what to my mind first thoughts present,
Let us divide our labours, thou where choice
Leads thee, or where most needs, whether to wind   215
The Woodbine round this Arbour, or direct
The clasping Ivie where to climb, while I
In yonder Spring of Roses[19] intermixt
With Myrtle, find what to redress till Noon:
For while so near each other thus all day   220
Our task we choose, what wonder if so near
Looks intervene and smiles, or object new
Casual discourse draw on, which intermits
Our dayes work brought to little, though begun
Early, and th' hour of Supper comes unearn'd.   225
    To whom mild answer *Adam* thus return'd.
Sole *Eve*, Associate sole, to me beyond
Compare above all living Creatures dear,
Well hast thou motion'd, well thy thoughts imployd
How we might best fulfill the work which here   230
God hath assign'd us, nor of me shalt pass
Unprais'd: for nothing lovelier can be found
In Woman, then to studie houshold good,
And good works in her Husband to promote.

[19] cluster of new-blown roses.

Yet not so strictly hath our Lord impos'd   235
Labour, as to debarr us when we need
Refreshment, whether food, or talk between,
Food of the mind, or this sweet intercourse
Of looks and smiles, for smiles from Reason flow,
To brute deni'd, and are of Love the food,   240
Love not the lowest end of human life.
For not to irksom toil, but to delight
He made us, and delight to Reason joyn'd.
These paths and Bowers doubt not but our joynt hands
Will keep from Wilderness with ease, as wide   245
As we need walk, till younger hands ere long
Assist us: But if much converse perhaps
Thee satiate, to short absence I could yeild.
For solitude somtimes is best societie,
And short retirement urges sweet return.   250
But other doubt possesses me, least harm
Befall thee sever'd from me; for thou knowst
What hath bin warn'd us, what malicious Foe
Envying our happiness, and of his own
Despairing, seeks to work us woe and shame   255
By sly assault; and somwhere nigh at hand
Watches, no doubt, with greedy hope to find
His wish and best advantage, us asunder,
Hopeless to circumvent us joynd, where each
To other speedie aid might lend at need;   260
Whether his first design be to withdraw
Our fealtie from God, or to disturb
Conjugal Love, then which perhaps no bliss
Enjoy'd by us excites his envie more;
Or this, or worse, leave not the faithful side   265
That gave thee being, still shades thee and protects.
The Wife, where danger or dishonour lurks,
Safest and seemliest by her Husband staies,
Who guards her, or with her the worst endures.
    To whom the Virgin[20] Majestie of *Eve*,   270
As one who loves, and some unkindness meets,
With sweet austeer composure thus reply'd.
    Ofspring of Heav'n and Earth, and all Earths Lord,
That such an Enemie we have, who seeks
Our ruin, both by thee informd I learn,   275
And from the parting Angel over-heard

[20] innocent.

As in a shadie nook I stood behind,
Just then returnd at shut of Evening Flowrs.
But that thou shouldst my firmness therfore doubt
To God or thee, because we have a foe   280
May tempt it, I expected not to hear.
His violence thou fearst not, being such,
As wee, not capable of death or pain,
Can either not receave, or can repell.
His fraud is then thy fear, which plain inferrs   285
Thy equal fear that my firm Faith and Love
Can by his fraud be shak'n or seduc't;
Thoughts, which how found they harbour in thy brest,
Adam, misthought of her to thee so dear?
    To whom with healing words *Adam* reply'd.   290
Daughter of God and Man, immortal *Eve*,
For such thou art, from sin and blame entire:[21]
Not diffident of thee do I dissuade
Thy absence from my sight, but to avoid
Th' attempt it self, intended by our Foe.   295
For hee who tempts, though in vain, at least asperses
The tempted with dishonour foul, suppos'd
Not incorruptible of Faith, not prooff
Against temptation: thou thy self with scorn
And anger wouldst resent the offer'd wrong,   300
Though ineffectual found: misdeem not then,
If such affront I labour to avert
From thee alone, which on us both at once
The Enemie, though bold, will hardly dare,
Or daring, first on mee th' assault shall light.   305
Nor thou his malice and false guile contemn;
Suttle he needs must be, who could seduce
Angels, nor think superfluous others aid.
I from the influence of thy looks receave
Access[22] in every Vertue, in thy sight   310
More wise, more watchful, stronger, if need were
Of outward strength; while shame, thou looking on,
Shame to be overcome or over-reacht
Would utmost vigor raise, and rais'd unite.
Why shouldst not thou like sense within thee feel   315
When I am present, and thy trial choose
With me, best witness of thy Vertue tri'd.

[21] untouched.
[22] accession, increase by addition.

So spake domestick *Adam* in his care
And Matrimonial Love; but *Eve,* who thought
Less attributed to her Faith sincere,   320
Thus her reply with accent sweet renewd.
  If this be our condition, thus to dwell
In narrow circuit strait'n'd by a Foe,
Suttle or violent, we not endu'd
Single with like defence, wherever met,   325
How are we happie, still in fear of harm?
But harm precedes not sin: onely our Foe
Tempting affronts us with his foul esteem
Of our integritie: his foul esteem
Sticks no dishonor on our Front,[23] but turns   330
Foul on himself; then wherfore shund or feard
By us? who rather double honour gain
From his surmise prov'd false, find peace within,
Favour from Heav'n, our witness from th' event.
And what is Faith, Love, Vertue unassaid   335
Alone, without exterior help sustaind?
Let us not then suspect our happie State
Left so imperfet by the Maker wise,
As not secure to single or combin'd.
Frail is our happiness, if this be so,   340
And *Eden* were no *Eden* thus expos'd.
  To whom thus *Adam* fervently repli'd.
O Woman, best are all things as the will
Of God ordain'd them, his creating hand
Nothing imperfet or deficient left   345
Of all that he Created, much less Man,
Or aught that might his happie State secure,
Secure from outward force; within himself
The danger lies, yet lies within his power:
Against his will he can receave no harm.   350
But God left free the Will, for what obeys
Reason, is free, and Reason he made right,
But bid her well beware, and still erect,[24]
Least by some fair appeering good surpris'd
She dictate false, and misinform the Will   355
To do what God expresly hath forbid.
Not then mistrust, but tender love enjoyns,

[23] forehead.
[24] always watchful.

That I should mind[25] thee oft, and mind thou me.
Firm we subsist, yet possible to swerve,
Since Reason not impossibly may meet　　　　　　　360
Some specious object by the Foe subornd,
And fall into deception unaware,
Not keeping strictest watch, as she was warnd.
Seek not temptation then, which to avoid
Were better, and most likelie if from mee　　　　365
Thou sever not: Trial will come unsought.
Wouldst thou approve[26] thy constancie, approve
First thy obedience; th' other who can know,
Not seeing thee attempted, who attest?
But if thou think, trial unsought may find　　　　370
Us both securer[27] then thus warnd thou seemst,
Go; for thy stay, not free, absents thee more;
Go in thy native innocence, relie
On what thou hast of vertue, summon all,
For God towards thee hath done his part, do thine.　　375
　　So spake the Patriarch of Mankind, but *Eve*
Persisted, yet submiss, though last, repli'd.
　　With thy permission then, and thus forewarnd
Chiefly by what thy own last reasoning words
Touch'd onely, that our trial, when least sought,　　380
May find us both perhaps farr less prepar'd,
The willinger I goe, not much expect
A Foe so proud will first the weaker seek,
So bent, the more shall shame him his repulse.
Thus saying, from her Husbands hand her hand　　385
Soft she withdrew, and like a Wood-Nymph light
Oread or *Dryad*, or of *Delia's*[28] Train,
Betook her to the Groves, but *Delia's* self
In gate surpass'd and Goddess-like deport,
Though not as shee with Bow and Quiver armd,　　390
But with such Gardning Tools as Art yet rude,
Guiltless of fire had formd, or Angels brought.
To *Pales,* or *Pomona*[29] thus adornd,

[25] remind.
[26] prove.
[27] more confident.
[28] Diana's. An oread was a mountain nymph; a dryad, a tree nymph.
[29] goddesses of flocks and herds, and of fruit. Vertumnus was god of the changing season, and Ceres, mother of Proserpina, taught men agriculture.

Likest she seemd, *Pomona* when she fled
Vertumnus, or to *Ceres* in her Prime,   395
Yet Virgin of *Proserpina* from *Jove*.
Her long with ardent look his Eye pursu'd
Delighted, but desiring more her stay.
Oft he to her his charge of quick return
Repeated, shee to him as oft engag'd   400
To be returnd by Noon amid the Bowr,
And all things in best order to invite
Noontide repast, or Afternoons repose.
O much deceav'd, much failing, hapless *Eve*,
Of thy presum'd return! event perverse!   405
Thou never from that hour in Paradise
Foundst either sweet repast, or sound repose;
Such ambush hid among sweet Flowrs and Shades
Waited with hellish rancour imminent
To intercept thy way, or send thee back   410
Despoild of Innocence, of Faith, of Bliss.
For now, and since first break of dawn the Fiend,
Meer Serpent in appearance, forth was come,
And on his Quest, where likeliest he might find
The onely two of Mankind, but in them   415
The whole included Race, his purpos'd prey.
In Bowr and Field he sought, where any tuft
Of Grove or Garden-Plot more pleasant lay,
Thir tendance or Plantation for delight,
By Fountain or by shadie Rivulet   420
He sought them both, but wish'd his hap might find
Eve separate, he wish'd, but not with hope
Of what so seldom chanc'd, when to his wish,
Beyond his hope, *Eve* separate he spies,
Veild in a Cloud of Fragrance, where she stood,   425
Half spi'd, so thick the Roses bushing round
About her glowd, oft stooping to support
Each Flowr of slender stalk, whose head though gay
Carnation, Purple, Azure, or spect with Gold,
Hung drooping unsustaind, them she upstaies   430
Gently with Mirtle band, mindless the while,
Her self, though fairest unsupported Flowr,
From her best prop so farr, and storm so nigh.
Neerer he drew, and many a walk travers'd
Of stateliest Covert, Cedar, Pine, or Palm,   435

Then voluble[30] and bold, now hid, now seen
Among thick-wov'n Arborets and Flowrs
Imborder'd on each Bank, the hand[31] of *Eve:*
Spot more delicious then those Gardens feign'd
Or of reviv'd *Adonis,* or renownd   440
Alcinous, host of old *Lærtes* Son,[32]
Or that, not Mystic,[33] where the Sapient King
Held dalliance with his fair *Egyptian* Spouse.
Much hee the Place admir'd, the Person more.
As one who long in populous City pent,   445
Where Houses thick and Sewers annoy[34] the Air,
Forth issuing on a Summers Morn to breathe
Among the pleasant Villages and Farmes
Adjoynd, from each thing met conceaves delight,
The smell of Grain, or tedded Grass,[35] or Kine,   450
Or Dairie, each rural sight, each rural sound;
If chance with Nymphlike step fair Virgin pass,
What pleasing seemd, for her now pleases more,
She most, and in her look summs all Delight.
Such Pleasure took the Serpent to behold   455
This Flowrie Plat, the sweet recess of *Eve*
Thus earlie, thus alone; her Heav'nly form
Angelic, but more soft, and Feminine,
Her graceful Innocence, her every Air
Of gesture or lest action overawd   460
His Malice, and with rapine sweet bereav'd
His fierceness of the fierce intent it brought:
That space the Evil one abstracted stood
From his own evil, and for the time remaind
Stupidly good, of enmitie disarm'd,   465
Of guile, of hate, of envie, of revenge;
But the hot Hell that alwayes in him burns,
Though in mid Heav'n, soon ended his delight,
And tortures him now more, the more he sees
Of pleasure not for him ordain'd: then soon   470
Fierce hate he recollects, and all his thoughts

[30] easily turning in and out.
[31] handiwork.
[32] Ulysses.
[33] not mythological. The "sapient king" is Solomon, who married Pharaoh's daughter (1 Kings iii. 1).
[34] pollute.
[35] grass spread out to make hay.

Of mischief, gratulating, thus excites.
　Thoughts, whither have ye led me, with what sweet
Compulsion thus transported to forget
What hither brought us, hate, not love, nor hope   475
Of Paradise for Hell, hope here to taste
Of pleasure, but all pleasure to destroy,
Save what is in destroying, other joy
To me is lost. Then let me not let pass
Occasion which now smiles, behold alone   480
The Woman, opportune to all attempts,
Her Husband, for I view far round, not nigh,
Whose higher intellectual more I shun,
And strength, of courage hautie, and of limb
Heroic built, though of terrestrial mould,   485
Foe not informidable, exempt from wound,
I not; so much hath Hell debas'd, and pain
Infeebl'd me, to what I was in Heav'n.
Shee fair, divinely fair, fit Love for Gods,
Not terrible, though terrour be in Love   490
And beautie, not approacht by stronger hate,
Hate stronger, under shew of Love well feign'd,
The way which to her ruin now I tend.
　So spake the Enemie of Mankind, enclos'd
In Serpent, Inmate bad, and toward *Eve*   495
Address'd his way, not with indented wave,
Prone on the ground, as since, but on his rear,
Circular base of rising foulds, that tour'd
Fould above fould a surging Maze, his Head
Crested aloft, and Carbuncle his Eyes;   500
With burnisht Neck of verdant Gold, erect
Amidst his circling Spires,[36] that on the grass
Floted redundant: pleasing was his shape,
And lovely, never since of Serpent kind
Lovelier, not those that in *Illyria* chang'd[37]   505
Hermione and *Cadmus,* or the God[38]
In *Epidaurus;* nor to which transformd
Ammonian Jove, or *Capitoline* was seen,
Hee with *Olympias,* this with her who bore

[36] coils.
[37] transformed (into serpents).
[38] Aesculapius, depicted as a serpent (the caduceus being his symbol) in his temple in Epidaurus.

Scipio the highth of *Rome*.[39] With tract oblique   510
At first, as one who sought access, but feard
To interrupt, side-long he works his way.
As when a Ship by skilful Stearsman wrought
Nigh Rivers mouth or Foreland, where the Wind
Veres oft, as oft so steers, and shifts her Sail;   515
So varied hee, and of his tortuous Train
Curld many a wanton wreath in sight of *Eve*,
To lure her Eye; shee busied heard the sound
Of rusling Leaves, but minded not, as us'd
To such disport before her through the Field,   520
From every Beast, more duteous at her call,
Then at *Circean* call the Herd disguis'd.[40]
Hee boulder now, uncall'd before her stood;
But as in gaze admiring: Oft he bowd
His turret Crest, and sleek enamel'd Neck,   525
Fawning, and lick'd the ground whereon she trod.
His gentle dumb expression turnd at length
The Eye of *Eve* to mark his play; he glad
Of her attention gaind, with Serpent Tongue
Organic, or impulse of vocal Air,[41]   530
His fraudulent temptation thus began.
　　Wonder not, sovran Mistress, if perhaps
Thou canst, who art sole Wonder, much less arm
Thy looks, the Heav'n of mildness, with disdain,
Displeas'd that I approach thee thus, and gaze   535
Insatiate, I thus single, nor have feard
Thy awful brow, more awful thus retir'd.
Fairest resemblance of thy Maker fair,
Thee all things living gaze on, all things thine
By gift, and thy Celestial Beautie adore   540
With ravishment beheld, there best beheld
Where universally admir'd; but here
In this enclosure wild, these Beasts among,
Beholders rude, and shallow to discern
Half what in thee is fair, one man except,   545
Who sees thee? (and what is one?) who shouldst be seen
A Goddess among Gods, ador'd and serv'd

[39] In the guise of a serpent Jove Ammon wooed Alexander the
Great's mother Olympias, and Roman Jove (Capitoline), Scipio's
mother (Sempronia).
[40] Circe had turned Ulysses' men into swine.
[41] Satan spoke either by using the serpent's forked tongue or by
vibrating the air to create vocal sounds.

By Angels numberless, thy daily Train.
    So gloz'd the Tempter, and his Proem tun'd;
Into the Heart of *Eve* his words made way,   550
Though at the voice much marveling; at length
Not unamaz'd she thus in answer spake.
What may this mean? Language of Man pronounc't
By Tongue of Brute, and human sense exprest?
The first at lest of these I thought deni'd   555
To Beasts, whom God on thir Creation-Day
Created mute to all articulat sound;
The latter I demurr,[42] for in thir looks
Much reason, and in thir actions oft appeers.
Thee, Serpent, suttlest beast of all the field   560
I knew, but not with human voice endu'd;
Redouble then this miracle, and say,
How cam'st thou speakable of mute,[43] and how
To me so friendly grown above the rest
Of brutal kind, that daily are in sight?   565
Say, for such wonder claims attention due.
    To whom the guileful Tempter thus reply'd.
Empress of this fair World, resplendent *Eve*,
Easie to mee it is to tell thee all
What thou commandst, and right thou shouldst be obeyd:
I was at first as other Beasts that graze   571
The trodden Herb, of abject thoughts and low,
As was my food, nor aught but food discern'd
Or Sex, and apprehended nothing high:
Till on a day roaving the field, I chanc'd   575
A goodly Tree farr distant to behold
Loaden with fruit of fairest colours mixt,
Ruddie and Gold: I nearer drew to gaze;
When from the boughs a savorie odour blown,
Grateful to appetite, more pleas'd my sense   580
Then smell of sweetest Fenel, or the Teats
Of Ewe or Goat dropping with Milk at Eevn,
Unsuckt of Lamb or Kid, that tend thir play.
To satisfie the sharp desire I had
Of tasting those fair Apples, I resolv'd   585
Not to deferr; hunger and thirst at once,
Powerful perswaders, quick'n'd at the scent

[42] doubt.
[43] How cam'st thou to be able to speak though otherwise incapable of human speech.

Of that alluring fruit, urg'd me so keen.
About the mossie Trunk I wound me soon,
For high from ground the branches would require   590
Thy utmost reach or *Adams:* Round the Tree
All other Beasts that saw, with like desire
Longing and envying stood, but could not reach.
Amid the Tree now got, where plenty hung
Tempting so nigh, to pluck and eat my fill   595
I spar'd not, for such pleasure till that hour
At Feed or Fountain never had I found.
Sated at length, ere long I might perceave
Strange alteration in me, to degree
Of Reason in my inward Powers, and Speech   600
Wanted not long, though to this shape retain'd.
Thenceforth to Speculations high or deep
I turnd my thoughts, and with capacious mind
Considerd all things visible in Heav'n,
Or Earth, or Middle,[44] all things fair and good;   605
But all that fair and good in thy Divine
Semblance, and in thy Beauties heav'nly Ray
United I beheld; no Fair to thine
Equivalent or second, which compel'd
Mee thus, though importune perhaps, to come   610
And gaze, and worship thee of right declar'd
Sovran of Creatures, universal Dame.
    So talk'd the spirited[45] sly Snake; and *Eve*
Yet more amaz'd unwarie thus reply'd.
    Serpent, thy overpraising leaves in doubt   615
The vertue of that Fruit, in thee first prov'd:
But say, where grows the Tree, from hence how far?
For many are the Trees of God that grow
In Paradise, and various, yet unknown
To us, in such abundance lies our choice,   620
As leaves a greater store of Fruit untoucht,
Still hanging incorruptible, till men
Grow up to thir provision,[46] and more hands
Help to disburden Nature of her Birth.
    To whom the wilie Adder, blithe and glad.   625
Empress, the way is readie, and not long,
Beyond a row of Myrtles, on a Flat,

[44] the air.
[45] embodying a spirit.
[46] to the number of men provided for.

Fast by a Fountain, one small Thicket past
Of blowing Myrrh and Balm; if thou accept
My conduct, I can bring thee thither soon.   630
    Lead then, said *Eve*. Hee leading swiftly rowld
In tangles, and made intricate seem strait,
To mischief swift. Hope elevates, and joy
Bright'ns his Crest, as when a wandring Fire,
Compact of unctuous vapor, which the Night   635
Condenses, and the cold invirons round,
Kindl'd through agitation to a Flame,
Which oft, they say, some evil Spirit attends,
Hovering and blazing with delusive Light,
Misleads th' amaz'd Night-wanderer from his way   640
To Boggs and Mires, and oft through Pond or Pool,
There swallow'd up and lost, from succour farr.
So glister'd the dire Snake, and into fraud
Led *Eve* our credulous Mother, to the Tree
Of prohibition, root of all our woe;   645
Which when she saw, thus to her guide she spake.
    Serpent, we might have spar'd our coming hither,
Fruitless to mee, though Fruit be here to excess,
The credit of whose vertue rest with thee,
Wondrous indeed, if cause of such effects.   650
But of this Tree we may not taste nor touch;
God so commanded, and left that Command
Sole Daughter[47] of his voice; the rest, we live
Law to our selves, our Reason is our Law.
    To whom the Tempter guilefully repli'd.   655
Indeed? hath God then said that of the Fruit
Of all these Garden Trees ye shall not eat,
Yet Lords declar'd of all in Earth or Air?
    To whom thus *Eve* yet sinless. Of the Fruit
Of each Tree in the Garden we may eat,   660
But of the Fruit of this fair Tree amidst
The Garden, God hath said, Ye shall not eat
Thereof, nor shall ye touch it, least ye die.
    She scarse had said, though brief, when now more bold
The Tempter, but with shew of Zeal and Love   665
To Man, and indignation at his wrong,
New part puts on, and as to passion mov'd,
Fluctuats disturb'd, yet comely, and in act

---

[47] By this term (signifying a divine revelation) Eve makes the
command less stringent.

Rais'd, as of som great matter to begin.
As when of old som Orator renound   670
In *Athens* or free *Rome,* where Eloquence
Flourishd, since mute, to som great cause addrest,
Stood in himself collected, while each part,
Motion, each act won audience ere the tongue,
Somtimes in highth began, as no delay   675
Of Preface brooking through his Zeal of Right.
So standing, moving, or to highth upgrown
The Tempter all impassiond thus began.
    O Sacred, Wise, and Wisdom-giving Plant,
Mother of Science,[48] now I feel thy Power   680
Within me cleere, not onely to discern
Things in thir Causes, but to trace the wayes
Of highest Agents, deemd however wise.
Queen of this Universe, doe not believe
Those rigid threats of Death; ye shall not Die: 685
How should ye? by the Fruit? it gives[49] you Life
To Knowledge; by the Threatner? look on mee,
Mee who have touch'd and tasted, yet both live,
And life more perfet have attaind then Fate
Meant mee, by ventring higher then my Lot.   690
Shall that be shut to Man, which to the Beast
Is open? or will God incense his ire
For such a petty Trespass, and not praise
Rather your dauntless vertue, whom the pain
Of Death denounc't, whatever thing Death be,   695
Deterrd not from atchieving what might lead
To happier life, knowledge of Good and Evil;
Of good, how just? of evil, if what is evil
Be real, why not known, since easier shunnd?
God therefore cannot hurt ye, and be just;   700
Not just, not God; not feard then, nor obeyd:
Your fear it self of Death removes the fear.
Why then was this forbid? Why but to awe,
Why but to keep ye low and ignorant,
His worshippers; he knows that in the day   705
Ye Eat thereof, your Eyes that seem so cleer,
Yet are but dim, shall perfetly be then
Op'n'd and cleerd, and ye shall be as Gods,
Knowing both Good and Evil as they know.

[48] knowledge.
[49] adds.

That ye should be as Gods, since I as Man,   710
Internal Man, is but proportion meet,
I of brute human, yee of human Gods.
So ye shall die perhaps, by putting off
Human, to put on Gods, death to be wisht,
Though threat'n'd, which no worse then this can bring.   715
And what are Gods that Man may not become
As they, participating God-like food?
The Gods are first, and that advantage use
On our belief, that all from them proceeds;
I question it, for this fair Earth I see,   720
Warm'd by the Sun, producing every kind,
Them nothing: If they all things, who enclos'd
Knowledge of Good and Evil in this Tree,
That whoso eats thereof, forthwith attains
Wisdom without their leave? and wherein lies   725
Th' offence, that Man should thus attain to know?
What can your knowledge hurt him, or this Tree
Impart against his will if all be his?
Or is it envie, and can envie dwell
In heav'nly brests? these, these and many more   730
Causes import your need of this fair Fruit.
Goddess humane, reach then, and freely taste.
     He ended, and his words replete with guile
Into her heart too easie entrance won:
Fixt on the Fruit she gaz'd, which to behold   735
Might tempt alone, and in her ears the sound
Yet rung of his perswasive words, impregn'd
With Reason, to her seeming, and with Truth;
Mean while the hour of Noon drew on, and wak'd
An eager appetite, rais'd by the smell   740
So savorie of that Fruit, which with desire,
Inclinable now grown to touch or taste,
Sollicited her longing eye; yet first
Pausing a while, thus to her self she mus'd.
     Great are thy Vertues, doubtless, best of Fruits,   745
Though kept from Man, and worthy to be admir'd,
Whose taste, too long forborn, at first assay
Gave elocution to the mute, and taught
The Tongue not made for Speech to speak thy praise:
Thy praise hee also who forbids thy use,   750
Conceals not from us, naming thee the Tree
Of Knowledge, knowledge both of good and evil;
Forbids us then to taste, but his forbidding

Commends thee more, while it inferrs the good
By thee communicated, and our want: 755
For good unknown, sure is not had, or had
And yet unknown, is as not had at all.
In plain then, what forbids he but to know,
Forbids us good, forbids us to be wise?
Such prohibitions bind not. But if Death   760
Bind us with after-bands, what profits then
Our inward freedom? In the day we eat
Of this fair Fruit, our doom is, we shall die.
How dies the Serpent? hee hath eat'n and lives,
And knows, and speaks, and reasons, and discerns,   765
Irrational till then. For us alone
Was death invented? or to us deni'd
This intellectual food, for beasts reserv'd?
For Beasts it seems: yet that one Beast which first
Hath tasted, envies not, but brings with joy   770
The good befall'n him, Author unsuspect,[50]
Friendly to man, farr from deceit or guile.
What fear I then, rather what know to fear
Under this ignorance of Good and Evil,
Of God or Death, of Law or Penaltie?   775
Here grows the Cure of all, this Fruit Divine,
Fair to the Eye, inviting to the Taste,
Of vertue to make wise: what hinders then
To reach, and feed at once both Bodie and Mind?
    So saying, her rash hand in evil hour   780
Forth reaching to the Fruit, she pluck'd, she eat:
Earth felt the wound, and Nature from her seat
Sighing through all her Works gave signs of woe,
That all was lost. Back to the Thicket slunk
The guiltie Serpent, and well might, for *Eve*   785
Intent now wholly on her taste, naught else
Regarded, such delight till then, as seemd,
In Fruit she never tasted, whether true
Or fansied so, through expectation high
Of knowledge, nor was God-head from her thought.   790
Greedily she ingorg'd without restraint,
And knew not eating Death:[51] Satiate at length,
And hight'n'd as with Wine, jocond and boon,[52]

[50] with no suspicion of his truthfulness.
[51] knew not that she was eating Death.
[52] jovial.

Thus to her self she pleasingly began.
   O Sovran, vertuous, precious of all Trees   795
In Paradise, of operation blest
To Sapience, hitherto obscur'd, infam'd,[53]
And thy fair Fruit let hang, as to no end
Created; but henceforth my early care,
Not without Song, each Morning, and due praise   800
Shall tend thee, and the fertil burden ease
Of thy full branches offer'd free to all;
Till dieted by thee I grow mature
In knowledge, as the Gods who all things know;
Though others envie what they cannot give;   805
For had the gift bin theirs, it had not here
Thus grown. Experience, next to thee I owe,
Best guide; not following thee, I had remaind
In ignorance, thou op'nst Wisdoms way,
And giv'st access, though secret she retire.   810
And I perhaps am secret; Heav'n is high,
High and remote to see from thence distinct
Each thing on Earth; and other care perhaps
May have diverted from continual watch
Our great Forbidder, safe with all his Spies   815
About him. But to *Adam* in what sort
Shall I appeer? shall I to him make known
As yet my change, and give him to partake
Full happiness with me, or rather not,
But keep the odds of Knowledge in my power   820
Without Copartner? so to add what wants
In Femal Sex, the more to draw his Love,
And render me more equal, and perhaps,
A thing not undesirable, somtime
Superior; for inferior who is free?   825
This may be well: but what if God have seen,
And Death ensue? then I shall be no more,
And *Adam* wedded to another *Eve*,
Shall live with her enjoying, I extinct;
A death to think. Confirm'd then I resolve,   830
Adam shall share with me in bliss or woe:
So dear I love him, that with him all deaths
I could endure, without him live no life.
   So saying, from the Tree her step she turnd,
But first low Reverence don, as to the power   835

That dwelt within, whose presence had infus'd
Into the plant sciential[54] sap, deriv'd
From Nectar, drink of Gods. *Adam* the while
Waiting desirous her return, had wove
Of choicest Flowrs a Garland to adorn 840
Her Tresses, and her rural labours crown,
As Reapers oft are wont thir Harvest Queen.
Great joy he promis'd to his thoughts, and new
Solace in her return, so long delay'd;
Yet oft his heart, divine[55] of somthing ill, 845
Misgave him; hee the faultring measure felt;
And forth to meet her went, the way she took
That Morn when first they parted; by the Tree
Of Knowledge he must pass, there he her met,
Scarse from the Tree returning; in her hand 850
A bough of fairest fruit that downie smil'd,
New gatherd, and ambrosial smell diffus'd.
To him she hasted, in her face excuse
Came Prologue, and Apologie to prompt,
Which with bland words at will she thus addrest. 855
    Hast thou not wonderd, *Adam,* at my stay?
Thee I have misst, and thought it long, depriv'd
Thy presence, agonie of love till now
Not felt, nor shall be twice, for never more
Mean I to trie, what rash untri'd I sought, 860
The pain of absence from thy sight. But strange
Hath bin the cause, and wonderful to hear:
This Tree is not as we are told, a Tree
Of danger tasted, nor to evil unknown
Op'ning the way, but of Divine effect 865
To open Eyes, and make them Gods who taste;
And hath bin tasted such: the Serpent wise,
Or not restraind as wee, or not obeying,
Hath eat'n of the fruit, and is become,
Not dead, as we are threat'n'd, but thenceforth 870
Endu'd with human voice and human sense,
Reasoning to admiration, and with mee
Perswasively hath so prevaild, that I
Have also tasted, and have also found
Th' effects to correspond, opener mine Eyes, 875
Dimm erst, dilated Spirits, ampler Heart,

[54] having knowledge.
[55] portending.

And growing up to Godhead; which for thee
Chiefly I sought, without thee can despise.
For bliss, as thou hast part, to me is bliss,
Tedious, unshar'd with thee, and odious soon.   880
Thou therfore also taste, that equal Lot
May joyn us, equal Joy, as equal Love;
Least thou not tasting, different degree
Disjoyn us, and I then too late renounce
Deitie for thee, when Fate will not permit.   885
    Thus *Eve* with Countnance blithe her storie told;
But in her Cheek distemper flushing glowd.
On th' other side, *Adam*, soon as he heard
The fatal Trespass don by *Eve*, amaz'd,
Astonied stood and Blank, while horror chill   890
Ran through his veins, and all his joynts relax'd;
From his slack hand the Garland wreath'd for *Eve*
Down drop'd, and all the faded Roses shed:
Speechless he stood and pale, till thus at length
First to himself he inward silence broke.   895
    O fairest of Creation, last and best
Of all Gods works, Creature in whom excell'd
Whatever can to sight or thought be formd,
Holy, divine, good, amiable, or sweet!
How art thou lost, how on a sudden lost,   900
Defac't, deflowrd, and now to Death devote?[56]
Rather how hast thou yeelded to transgress
The strict forbiddance, how to violate
The sacred Fruit forbidd'n! som cursed fraud
Of Enemie hath beguil'd thee, yet unknown,   905
And mee with thee hath ruind, for with thee
Certain my resolution is to Die;
How can I live without thee, how forgoe
Thy sweet Converse and Love so dearly joyn'd,
To live again in these wild Woods forlorn?   910
Should God create another *Eve*, and I
Another Rib afford, yet loss of thee
Would never from my heart; no no, I feel
The Link of Nature draw me: Flesh of Flesh,
Bone of my Bone thou art, and from thy State   915
Mine never shall be parted, bliss or woe.
    So having said, as one from sad dismay
Recomforted, and after thoughts disturb'd

[56] doomed.

Submitting to what seemd remediless,
Thus in calm mood his Words to *Eve* he turnd.   920
   Bold deed thou hast presum'd, adventrous *Eve,*
And peril great provok't, who thus hast dar'd
Had it bin onely coveting to Eye
That sacred Fruit, sacred to abstinence,
Much more to taste it under bann to touch.   925
But past who can recall, or don undoe?
Not God Omnipotent, nor Fate, yet so
Perhaps thou shalt not Die, perhaps the Fact
Is not so hainous now, foretasted Fruit,
Profan'd first by the Serpent, by him first   930
Made common and unhallowd ere our taste;
Nor yet on him found deadly, he yet lives,
Lives, as thou saidst, and gains to live as Man
Higher degree of Life, inducement strong
To us, as likely tasting to attain   935
Proportional ascent, which cannot be
But to be Gods, or Angels Demi-gods.
Nor can I think that God, Creator wise,
Though threatning, will in earnest so destroy
Us his prime Creatures, dignifi'd so high,   940
Set over all his Works, which in our Fall,
For us created, needs with us must fail,
Dependent made; so God shall uncreate,
Be frustrate, do, undo, and labour loose,
Not well conceav'd of God, who though his Power   945
Creation could repeat, yet would be loath
Us to abolish, least the Adversary
Triumph and say; Fickle their State whom God
Most Favors, who can please him long; Mee first
He ruind, now Mankind; whom will he next?   950
Matter of scorn, not to be giv'n the Foe.
However I with thee have fixt my Lot,
Certain[57] to undergoe like doom, if Death
Consort with thee, Death is to mee as Life;
So forcible within my heart I feel   955
The Bond of Nature draw me to my own,
My own in thee, for what thou art is mine;
Our State cannot be severd, we are one,
One Flesh; to loose thee were to loose my self.
   So *Adam,* and thus *Eve* to him repli'd.   960

[57] resolved.

O glorious trial of exceeding Love,
Illustrious evidence, example high!
Ingaging me to emulate, but short
Of thy perfection, how shall I attain,
Adam, from whose dear side I boast me sprung,   965
And gladly of our Union hear thee speak,
One Heart, one Soul in both; whereof good prooff
This day affords, declaring thee resolv'd,
Rather then Death or aught then Death more dread
Shall separate us, linkt in Love so dear,   970
To undergoe with mee one Guilt, one Crime,
If any be, of tasting this fair Fruit,
Whose vertue, for of good still good proceeds,
Direct, or by occasion hath presented
This happie trial of thy Love, which else   975
So eminently never had bin known.
Were it I thought Death menac't would ensue
This my attempt, I would sustain alone
The worst, and not perswade thee, rather die
Deserted, then oblige thee with a fact[58]   980
Pernicious to thy Peace, chiefly assur'd
Remarkably so late of thy so true,
So faithful Love unequald; but I feel
Farr otherwise th' event, not Death, but Life
Augmented, op'n'd Eyes, new Hopes, new Joyes,   985
Taste so Divine, that what of sweet before
Hath toucht my sense, flat seems to this, and harsh.
On my experience, Adam, freely taste,
And fear of Death deliver to the Winds.
    So saying, she embrac'd him, and for joy   990
Tenderly wept, much won that he his Love
Had so enobl'd, as of choice t' incurr
Divine displeasure for her sake, or Death.
In recompence (for such compliance bad
Such recompence best merits) from the bough   995
She gave him of that fair enticing Fruit
With liberal hand: he scrupl'd not to eat
Against his better knowledge, not deceav'd,
But fondly overcome with Femal charm.
Earth trembl'd from her entrails, as again   1000
In pangs, and Nature gave a second groan,
Skie lowr'd, and muttering Thunder, som sad drops

[58] bind thee with a deed.

Wept at compleating of the mortal Sin
Original; while *Adam* took no thought,
Eating his fill, nor *Eve* to iterate   1005
Her former trespass fear'd, the more to soothe
Him with her lov'd societie, that now
As with new Wine intoxicated both
They swim in mirth, and fansie that they feel
Divinitie within them breeding wings   1010
Wherewith to scorn the Earth: but that false Fruit
Farr other operation first displaid,
Carnal desire enflaming, hee on *Eve*
Began to cast lascivious Eyes, she him
As wantonly repaid; in Lust they burn: 1015
Till *Adam* thus 'gan *Eve* to dalliance move.
    Eve, now I see thou art exact of taste,[59]
And elegant, of Sapience no small part,
Since to each meaning savour we apply,
And Palate call judicious; I the praise   1020
Yeild thee, so well this day thou hast purvey'd.
Much pleasure we have lost, while we abstain'd
From this delightful Fruit, nor known till now
True relish, tasting; if such pleasure be
In things to us forbidden, it might be wish'd,   1025
For this one Tree had bin forbidden ten.
But come, so well refresh't, now let us play,
As meet is, after such delicious Fare;
For never did thy Beautie since the day
I saw thee first and wedded thee, adorn'd   1030
With all perfections, so enflame my sense
With ardor to enjoy thee, fairer now
Then ever, bountie of this vertuous Tree.
    So said he, and forbore not glance or toy
Of amorous intent, well understood   1035
Of *Eve*, whose Eye darted contagious Fire.
Her hand he seis'd, and to a shadie bank,
Thick overhead with verdant roof imbowr'd
He led her nothing loath; Flowrs were the Couch,
Pansies, and Violets, and Asphodel,   1040
And Hyacinth, Earths freshest softest lap.
There they thir fill of Love and Loves disport
Took largely, of thir mutual guilt the Seal,

[59] Since the word "savor" ("taste") derives from "Sapience," a
pun is intended referring to the act of their disobedience.

The solace of thir sin, till dewie sleep
Oppress'd them, wearied with thir amorous play.   1045
Soon as the force of that fallacious Fruit,
That with exhilerating vapour bland
About thir spirits had plaid, and inmost powers
Made err, was now exhal'd, and grosser sleep
Bred of unkindly fumes, with conscious dreams   1050
Encumberd, now had left them, up they rose
As from unrest, and each the other viewing,
Soon found thir Eyes how op'n'd, and thir minds
How dark'n'd; innocence, that as a veil
Had shadow'd them from knowing ill, was gon,   1055
Just confidence, and native righteousness,
And honour from about them, naked left
To guiltie shame: hee cover'd, but his Robe
Uncover'd more. So rose the *Danite* strong
Herculean Samson from the Harlot-lap   1060
Of *Philistean Dalilah*, and wak'd
Shorn of his strength. They destitute and bare
Of all thir vertue: silent, and in face
Confounded long they sate, as struck'n mute,
Till *Adam*, though not less then *Eve* abash't,   1065
At length gave utterance to these words constraind.
    O *Eve*, in evil hour thou didst give ear
To that false Worm, of whomsoever taught
To counterfet Mans voice, true in our Fall,
False in our promis'd Rising; since our Eyes   1070
Op'n'd we find indeed, and find we know
Both Good and Evil, Good lost, and Evil got,
Bad Fruit of Knowledge, if this be to know,
Which leaves us naked thus, of Honour void,
Of Innocence, of Faith, of Puritie,   1075
Our wonted Ornaments now soild and staind,
And in our Faces evident the signes
Of foul concupiscence; whence evil store;
Ev'n shame, the last[60] of evils; of the first
Be sure then. How shall I behold the face   1080
Henceforth of God or Angel, earst with joy
And rapture so oft beheld? those heav'nly shapes
Will dazle now this earthly, with thir blaze
Insufferably bright. O might I here
In solitude live savage, in some glade   1085

[60] worst.

Obscur'd, where highest Woods impenetrable
To Starr or Sun-light, spread thir umbrage broad
And brown[61] as Evening: Cover me ye Pines,
Ye Cedars, with innumerable boughs
Hide me, where I may never see them more.   1090
But let us now, as in bad plight, devise
What best may for the present serve to hide
The Parts of each from other, that seem most
To shame obnoxious, and unseemliest seen,
Some Tree whose broad smooth Leaves together sowd,   1095
And girded on our loyns, may cover round
Those middle parts, that this new commer, Shame,
There sit not, and reproach us as unclean.
     So counsel'd hee, and both together went
Into the thickest Wood, there soon they chose   1100
The Figtree,[62] not that kind for Fruit renown'd,
But such as at this day to *Indians* known
In *Malabar* or *Decan* spreds her Armes
Braunching so broad and long, that in the ground
The bended Twigs take root, and Daughters grow   1105
About the Mother Tree, a Pillard shade
High overarch't, and echoing Walks between;
There oft the *Indian* Herdsman shunning heat
Shelters in cool, and tends his pasturing Herds
At Loopholes cut through thickest shade: Those
     Leaves   1110
They gatherd, broad as *Amazonian* Targe,[63]
And with what skill they had, together sowd,
To gird thir waste, vain Covering if to hide
Thir guilt and dreaded shame; O how unlike
To that first naked Glorie. Such of late   1115
Columbus found th' *American* so girt
With featherd Cincture, naked else and wild
Among the Trees on Iles and woodie Shores.
Thus fenc't, and as they thought, thir shame in part
Coverd, but not at rest or ease of Mind,   1120
They sate them down to weep, nor onely Teares
Raind at thir Eyes, but high Winds worse within
Began to rise, high Passions, Anger, Hate,

[61] dark.
[62] the banyan; its leaves are not broad (l. 1111), an error deriving from Pliny.
[63] shield.

Mistrust, Suspicion, Discord, and shook sore
Thir inward State of Mind, calm Region once   1125
And full of Peace, now tost and turbulent:
For Understanding rul'd not, and the Will
Heard not her lore, both in subjection now
To sensual Appetite, who from beneath
Usurping over sovran Reason claimd   1130
Superior sway: from thus distemperd brest,
Adam, estrang'd in look and alterd stile,
Speech intermitted thus to *Eve* renewd.
    Would thou hadst heark'n'd to my words, and stai'd
With me, as I besought thee, when that strange   1135
Desire of wandring this unhappie Morn,
I know not whence possess'd thee; we had then
Remaind still happie, not as now, despoild
Of all our good, sham'd, naked, miserable.
Let none henceforth seek needless cause t' approve   1140
The Faith they owe;[64] when earnestly they seek
Such proof, conclude, they then begin to fail.
    To whom soon mov'd with touch of blame thus *Eve*.
What words have past thy Lips, *Adam* severe,
Imput'st thou that to my default, or will   1145
Of wandring, as thou call'st it, which who knows
But might as ill have happ'n'd thou being by,
Or to thy self perhaps: hadst thou bin there,
Or here th' attempt, thou couldst not have discernd
Fraud in the Serpent, speaking as he spake;   1150
No ground of enmitie between us known,
Why hee should mean me ill, or seek to harm.
Was I t' have never parted from thy side?
As good have grown there still a liveless Rib.
Being as I am, why didst not thou the Head   1155
Command me absolutely not to go,
Going into such danger as thou saidst?
Too facil then thou didst not much gainsay,
Nay, didst permit, approve, and fair dismiss.
Hadst thou bin firm and fixt in thy dissent,   1160
Neither had I transgress'd, nor thou with mee.
    To whom then first incenst *Adam* repli'd.
Is this the Love, is this the recompence
Of mine to thee, ingrateful *Eve*, exprest

[64] have.

Immutable[65] when thou wert lost, not I,   1165
Who might have liv'd and joyd immortal bliss,
Yet willingly chose rather Death with thee:
And am I now upbraided, as the cause
Of thy transgressing? not enough severe,
It seems, in thy restraint: what could I more?   1170
I warn'd thee, I admonish'd thee, foretold
The danger, and the lurking Enemie
That lay in wait; beyond this had bin force,
And force upon free will hath here no place.
But confidence then bore thee on, secure   1175
Either to meet no danger, or to find
Matter of glorious trial; and perhaps
I also err'd in overmuch admiring
What seemd in thee so perfet, that I thought
No evil durst attempt thee, but I rue   1180
That errour now, which is become my crime,
And thou th' accuser. Thus it shall befall
Him who to worth in Woman overtrusting
Lets her will rule; restraint she will not brook,
And left t' her self, if evil thence ensue,   1185
Shee first his weak indulgence will accuse.
    Thus they in mutual accusation spent
The fruitless hours, but neither self-condemning,
And of thir vain contest appeer'd no end.

BOOK X

THE ARGUMENT

Mans transgression known, the Guardian Angels forsake Paradise, and return up to Heaven to approve thir vigilance, and
are approv'd, God declaring that the entrance of *Satan* could
not be by them prevented. He sends his Son to judge the
Transgressors, who descends and gives Sentence accordingly;
then in pity cloaths them both, and reascends. *Sin* and *Death*
sitting till then at the Gates of Hell, by wondrous sympathie
feeling the success of *Satan* in this new World, and the sin
by Man there committed, resolve to sit no longer confin'd in
Hell, but to follow *Satan* thir Sire up to the place of Man:
To make the way easier from Hell to this World to and fro,
they pave a broad Highway or Bridge over *Chaos*, according to the Track that *Satan* first made; then preparing for

[65] shown to be unchangeable.

Earth, they meet him proud of his success returning to Hell;
thir mutual gratulation. *Satan* arrives at *Pandemonium,* in
full assembly relates with boasting his success against Man;
instead of applause is entertained with a general hiss by all his
audience, transform'd with himself also suddenly into Serpents, according to his doom giv'n in Paradise; then deluded
with a shew of the forbidden Tree springing up before them,
they greedily reaching to taste of the Fruit, chew dust and
bitter ashes. The proceedings of *Sin* and *Death;* God foretells
the final Victory of his Son over them, and the renewing of
all things; but for the present commands his Angels to make
several alterations in the Heavens and Elements. *Adam* more
and more perceiving his fall'n condition heavily bewails, re-
jects the condolement of *Eve;* she persists and at length ap-
peases him: then to evade the Curse likely to fall on thir
Ofspring, proposes to *Adam* violent wayes which he approves
not, but conceiving better hope, puts her in mind of the late
Promise made them, that her Seed should be reveng'd on
the Serpent, and exhorts her with him to seek Peace of the
offended Deity, by repentance and supplication.

Meanwhile the hainous and despightfull act
Of *Satan* done in Paradise, and how
Hee in the Serpent had perverted *Eve,*
Her Husband shee, to taste the fatall fruit,
Was known in Heav'n; for what can scape the Eye   5
Of God All-seeing, or deceave his Heart
Omniscient, who in all things wise and just,
Hinder'd not *Satan* to attempt the mind
Of Man, with strength entire, and free will arm'd,
Complete[1] to have discover'd and repulst   10
Whatever wiles of Foe or seeming Friend.
For still they knew, and ought t' have still remember'd
The high Injunction not to taste that Fruit,
Whoever tempted; which they not obeying,
Incurr'd, what could they less, the penaltie,   15
And manifold in sin, deserv'd to fall.
Up into Heav'n from Paradise in hast
Th' Angelic Guards ascended, mute and sad
For Man, for of his state by this they knew,
Much wondring how the suttle Fiend had stoln   20
Entrance unseen. Soon as th' unwelcome news

---

[1] perfectly equipped.

From Earth arriv'd at Heaven Gate, displeas'd
All were who heard, dim sadness did not spare
That time Celestial visages, yet mixt
With pitie, violated not thir bliss. 25
About the new-arriv'd, in multitudes
Th' ethereal People ran, to hear and know
How all befell: they towards the Throne Supream
Accountable made haste to make appear
With righteous plea, thir utmost vigilance, 30
And easily approv'd; when the most High
Eternal Father from his secret Cloud,
Amidst in Thunder utter'd thus his voice.
    Assembl'd Angels, and ye Powers return'd
From unsuccessful charge, be not dismaid, 35
Nor troubl'd at these tidings from the Earth,
Which your sincerest care could not prevent,
Foretold so lately what would come to pass,
When first this Tempter cross'd the Gulf from Hell.
I told ye then he should prevail and speed[2] 40
On his bad Errand, Man should be seduc't
And flatter'd out of all, believing lies
Against his Maker; no Decree of mine
Concurring to necessitate his Fall,
Or touch with lightest moment[3] of impulse 45
His free Will, to her own inclining left
In eevn scale. But fall'n he is, and now
What rests,[4] but that the mortal Sentence pass
On his transgression, Death denounc't that day,
Which he presumes already vain and void, 50
Because not yet inflicted, as he fear'd,
By some immediate stroak; but soon shall find
Forbearance no acquittance ere day end.
Justice shall not return as bountie scorn'd.
But whom send I to judge them? whom but thee 55
Vicegerent Son, to thee I have transferr'd
All Judgement, whether in Heav'n, or Earth, or Hell.
Easie it may be seen that I intend
Mercie collegue with Justice, sending thee
Mans Friend, his Mediator, his design'd 60
Both Ransom and Redeemer voluntarie,

[2] succeed.
[3] the force which tends to produce motion.
[4] remains.

And destin'd Man himself to judge Man fall'n.
So spake the Father, and unfoulding bright
Toward the right hand his Glorie, on the Son
Blaz'd forth unclouded Deitie; he full   65
Resplendent all his Father manifest
Express'd, and thus divinely answer'd mild.
Father Eternal, thine is to decree,
Mine both in Heav'n and Earth to do thy will
Supream, that thou in mee thy Son belov'd   70
Mayst ever rest well pleas'd. I go to judge
On Earth these thy transgressors, but thou knowst,
Whoever judg'd, the worst on mee must light,
When time shall be, for so I undertook
Before thee; and not repenting, this obtain   75
Of right, that I may mitigate thir doom
On me deriv'd,[5] yet I shall temper so
Justice with Mercie, as may illustrate[6] most
Them fully satisfied, and thee appease.
Attendance none shall need, nor Train, where none   80
Are to behold the Judgement, but the judg'd,
Those two; the third best absent is condemn'd,
Convict by flight, and Rebel to all Law
Conviction to the Serpent none belongs.
Thus saying, from his radiant Seat he rose   85
Of high collateral glorie: him Thrones and Powers,
Princedoms, and Dominations ministrant
Accompanied to Heaven Gate, from whence
Eden and all the Coast[7] in prospect lay.
Down he descended strait; the speed of Gods   90
Time counts not, though with swiftest minutes wing'd.
Now was the Sun in Western cadence[8] low
From Noon, and gentle Aires due at thir hour
To fan the Earth now wak'd, and usher in
The Eevning cool when he from wrauth more cool   95
Came the mild Judge and Intercessor both
To sentence Man: the voice of God they heard
Now walking in the Garden, by soft winds
Brought to thir Ears, while day declin'd, they heard,
And from his presence hid themselves among   100

[5] transferred.
[6] illuminate.
[7] border, surrounding area.
[8] descent.

The thickest Trees, both Man and Wife, till God
Approaching, thus to *Adam* call'd aloud.
    Where art thou *Adam,* wont with joy to meet
My coming seen far off? I miss thee here,
Not pleas'd, thus entertaind with solitude,   105
Where obvious dutie[9] erewhile appear'd unsaught:
Or come I less conspicuous, or what change
Absents thee, or what chance detains? Come forth.
He came, and with him *Eve,* more loth, though first
T' offend, discount'nanc't both, and discompos'd;   110
Love was not in thir looks, either to God
Or to each other, but apparent[10] guilt,
And shame, and perturbation, and despair,
Anger, and obstinacie, and hate, and guile.
Whence *Adam* faultring long, thus answer'd brief.   115
    I heard thee in the Garden, and of thy voice
Affraid, being naked, hid my self. To whom
The gracious Judge without revile repli'd.
    My voice thou oft hast heard, and hast not fear'd,
But still rejoyc't, how is it now become   120
So dreadful to thee? that thou art naked, who
Hath told thee? hast thou eaten of the Tree
Whereof I gave thee charge thou shouldst not eat?
    To whom thus *Adam* sore beset repli'd.
O Heav'n! in evil strait this day I stand   125
Before my Judge, either to undergoe
My self the total Crime, or to accuse
My other self, the partner of my life;
Whose failing, while her Faith to me remains,
I should conceal, and not expose to blame   130
By my complaint; but strict necessitie
Subdues me, and calamitous constraint,
Least on my head both sin and punishment,
However insupportable, be all
Devolv'd; though should I hold my peace, yet thou   135
Wouldst easily detect what I conceal.
This Woman whom thou mad'st to be my help,
And gav'st me as thy perfet gift, so good,
So fit, so acceptable, so Divine,
That from her hand I could suspect no ill,   140
And what she did, whatever in it self,

  [9] duty to meet me.
  [10] easily seen.

Her doing seem'd to justifie the deed;
Shee gave me of the Tree, and I did eat.
    To whom the sovran Presence thus repli'd.
Was shee thy God, that her thou didst obey   145
Before his voice, or was shee made thy guide,
Superior, or but equal, that to her
Thou did'st resigne thy Manhood, and the Place
Wherein God set thee above her made of thee,
And for thee, whose perfection farr excell'd   150
Hers in all real dignitie: Adornd
Shee was indeed, and lovely to attract
Thy Love, not thy Subjection, and her Gifts
Were such as under Government well seem'd,
Unseemly to bear rule, which was thy part   155
And person,[11] had'st thou known thy self aright.
    So having said, he thus to *Eve* in few:
Say Woman, what is this which thou hast done?
    To whom sad *Eve* with shame nigh overwhelm'd,
Confessing soon, yet not before her Judge   160
Bold or loquacious, thus abasht repli'd.
    The Serpent me beguil'd and I did eat.
    Which when the Lord God heard, without delay
To Judgement he proceeded on th' accus'd
Serpent though brute, unable to transferr   165
The Guilt on him who made him instrument
Of mischief, and polluted from the end
Of his Creation; justly then accurst,
As vitiated in Nature: more to know
Concern'd not Man (since he no further knew)   170
Nor alter'd his offence; yet God at last
To Satan first in sin his doom apply'd,
Though in mysterious terms, judg'd as then best:
And on the Serpent thus his curse let fall.
    Because thou hast done this, thou art accurst   175
Above all Cattel, each Beast of the Field;
Upon thy Belly groveling thou shalt goe,
And dust shalt eat all the dayes of thy Life.
Between Thee and the Woman I will put
Enmitie, and between thine and her Seed;   180
Her Seed shall bruise thy head, thou bruise his heel.
    So spake this Oracle, then verifi'd
When *Jesus* son of *Mary* second *Eve*,

[11] role.

Saw Satan fall like Lightning down from Heav'n,
Prince of the Air; then rising from his Grave   185
Spoild Principalities and Powers, triumpht
In open shew, and with ascension bright
Captivity led captive through the Air,
The Realm it self of Satan long usurpt,
Whom he shall tread at last under our feet;   190
Eevn hee who now foretold his fatal bruise,
And to the Woman thus his Sentence turn'd.   .
    Thy sorrow I will greatly multiplie
By thy Conception; Childern thou shalt bring
In sorrow forth, and to thy Husbands will   195
Thine shall submit, hee over thee shall rule.
    On *Adam* last thus judgement he pronounc'd.
Because thou hast heark'n'd to the voice of thy Wife,
And eaten of the Tree concerning which
I charg'd thee, saying: Thou shalt not eat thereof,   200
Curs'd is the ground for thy sake, thou in sorrow
Shalt eat thereof all the days of thy Life;
Thorns also and Thistles it shall bring thee forth
Unbid, and thou shalt eat th' Herb of the Field,
In the sweat of thy Face shalt thou eat Bread,   205
Till thou return unto the ground, for thou
Out of the ground wast taken, know thy Birth,
For dust thou art, and shalt to dust return.
    So judg'd he Man, both Judge and Saviour sent,
And th' instant stroke of Death denounc't that day   210
Remov'd farr off; then pittying how they stood
Before him naked to the air, that now
Must suffer change, disdain'd not to begin
Thenceforth the form of servant to assume,
As when he wash'd his servants feet, so now   215
As Father of his Familie he clad
Thir nakedness with Skins of Beasts, or slain,
Or as the Snake with youthful Coat repaid;[12]
And thought not much[13] to cloath his Enemies:
Nor hee thir outward onely with the Skins   220
Of Beasts, but inward nakedness, much more
Opprobrious, with his Robe of righteousness,
Arraying cover'd from his Fathers sight.

[12] The skins come from beasts slain for that purpose or those
recovered by new skins after shedding the old, like the snake.
[13] did not object to.

To him with swift ascent he up returnd,
Into his blissful bosom reassum'd   225
In glory as of old, to him appeas'd
All, though all-knowing, what had past with Man
Recounted, mixing intercession sweet.
Meanwhile ere thus was sin'd and judg'd on Earth,
Within the Gates of Hell sate Sin and Death,   230
In counterview within the Gates, that now
Stood open wide, belching outrageous flame
Farr into *Chaos*, since the Fiend pass'd through,
Sin opening, who thus now to Death began.
    O Son, why sit we here each other viewing   235
Idlely, while Satan our great Author thrives
In other Worlds, and happier Seat provides
For us his ofspring dear? It cannot be
But that success attends him; if mishap,
Ere this he had return'd, with fury driv'n   240
By his Avengers, since no place like this
Can fit his punishment, or their revenge.
Methinks I feel new strength within me rise,
Wings growing, and Dominion giv'n me large
Beyond this Deep; whatever draws me on,   245
Or sympathie,14 or som connatural force
Powerful at greatest distance to unite
With secret amity things of like kind
By secretest conveyance. Thou my Shade
Inseparable must with mee along: 250
For Death from Sin no power can separate.
But least the difficultie of passing back
Stay his return perhaps over this Gulf
Impassable, impervious, let us try
Adventrous work, yet to thy power and mine   255
Not unagreeable, to found a path
Over this Main from Hell to that new World
Where Satan now prevails, a Monument
Of merit high to all th' infernal Host,
Easing thir passage hence, for intercourse,15   260
Or transmigration, as thir lot shall lead.
Nor can I miss the way, so strongly drawn
By this new felt attraction and instinct.

    14 attractive power.
    15 movement back and forth between, as opposed to "transmi-
gration" (passage to one place only).

Whom thus the meager Shadow answerd soon.
Goe whither Fate and inclination strong   265
Leads thee, I shall not lag behind, nor err
The way, thou leading, such a scent I draw
Of carnage, prey innumerable, and taste
The savour of Death from all things there that live:
Nor shall I to the work thou enterprisest   270
Be wanting, but afford thee equal aid.
    So saying, with delight he snuff'd the smell
Of mortal change on Earth. As when a flock
Of ravenous Fowl, though many a League remote,
Against the day of Battel, to a Field,   275
Where Armies lie encampt, come flying, lur'd
With scent of living Carcasses design'd
For death, the following day, in bloodie fight.
So scented the grim Feature, and upturn'd
His Nostril wide into the murkie Air,   280
Sagacious of his Quarry from so farr.
Then Both from out Hell Gates into the waste
Wide Anarchie of *Chaos* damp and dark
Flew divers, and with Power (thir Power was great)
Hovering upon the Waters; what they met   285
Solid or slimie, as in raging Sea
Tost up and down, together crowded drove
From each side shoaling[16] towards the mouth of Hell.
As when two Polar Winds blowing adverse
Upon the *Cronian* Sea,[17] together drive   290
Mountains of Ice, that stop th' imagin'd way[18]
Beyond *Petsora* Eastward, to the rich
Cathaian Coast. The aggregated Soyl
Death with his Mace petrific, cold and dry,
As with a Trident smote, and fix't as firm   295
As *Delos*[19] floating once; the rest his look
Bound with *Gorgonian*[20] rigor not to move,
And with *Asphaltic* slime; broad as the Gate,
Deep to the Roots of Hell the gather'd beach
They fasten'd, and the Mole immense wraught on   300

[16] making into a shoal.
[17] the Arctic Ocean.
[18] the supposed passage to the east (Cathay) along the Siberian shore where flows the Pechora.
[19] one of the Cyclades in the Aegean Sea created by Neptune with his trident and firmly fixed in place by Zeus.
[20] petrifying.

Over the foaming deep high Archt, a Bridge
Of length prodigious joyning to the Wall[21]
Immovable of this now fenceless[22] world
Forfeit to Death; from hence a passage broad,
Smooth, easie, inoffensive[23] down to Hell.   305
So, if great things to small may be compar'd,
Xerxes, the Libertie of *Greece* to yoke,
From *Susa*[24] his *Memnonian* Palace high
Came to the Sea, and over *Hellespont*
Bridging his way, *Europe* with *Asia* joyn'd,   310
And scourg'd with many a stroak th' indignant waves.
Now had they brought the work by wondrous Art
Pontifical,[25] a ridge of pendent Rock
Over the vext Abyss, following the track
Of *Satan*, to the self-same place where hee   315
First lighted from his Wing, and landed safe
From out of *Chaos* to the outside bare
Of this round World: with Pinns of Adamant
And Chains they made all fast, too fast they made
And durable; and now in little space   320
The confines met[26] of Empyrean Heav'n
And of this World, and on the left hand Hell
With long reach interpos'd; three sev'ral wayes
In sight, to each of these three places led.
And now thir way to Earth they had descri'd,   325
To Paradise first tending, when behold
Satan in likeness of an Angel bright
Betwixt the *Centaur* and the *Scorpion* stearing
His *Zenith*, while the Sun in *Aries* rose:[27]
Disguis'd he came, but those his Childern dear   330
Thir Parent soon discern'd, though in disguise.
Hee, after *Eve* seduc't, unminded slunk
Into the Wood fast by, and changing shape
T' observe the sequel, saw his guileful act

[21] the primum mobile.
[22] both unenclosed (wide-extending) and defenseless.
[23] without impediments.
[24] the Biblical Shushan, founded by Memnon's father Tithonus.
[25] pertaining to building bridges.
[26] The bridge to hell joins the passage between heaven and earth (III, 510).
[27] Aries, under whose sign the Sun (Uriel) rises, lies opposite to Scorpio, near which is Centaurus; that is, earth is placed between Satan and Uriel.

By *Eve,* though all unweeting,[28] seconded   335
Upon her Husband, saw thir shame that sought
Vain covertures;[29] but when he saw descend
The Son of God to judge them, terrifi'd
Hee fled, not hoping to escape, but shun
The present, fearing guiltie what his wrauth   340
Might suddenly inflict; that past, return'd
By Night, and listning where the hapless Pair
Sate in thir sad discourse, and various plaint,
Thence gatherd his own doom, which understood
Not instant, but of future time. With joy   345
And tidings fraught, to Hell he now return'd,
And at the brink of *Chaos,* neer the foot
Of this new wondrous Pontifice,[30] unhop't
Met who to meet him came, his Ofspring dear.
Great joy was at thir meeting, and at sight   350
Of that stupendious Bridge his joy encreas'd.
Long hee admiring stood, till Sin, his fair
Inchanting Daughter, thus the silence broke.
    O Parent, these are thy magnific deeds,
Thy Trophies, which thou view'st as not thine own,   355
Thou art thir Author and prime Architect:
For I no sooner in my Heart divin'd,
My Heart, which by a secret harmonie
Still moves with thine, joyn'd in connexion sweet,
That thou on Earth hadst prosper'd, which thy looks   360
Now also evidence, but straight I felt
Though distant from thee Worlds between, yet felt
That I must after thee with this thy Son;
Such fatal consequence[31] unites us three:
Hell could no longer hold us in her bounds,   365
Nor this unvoyageable Gulf obscure
Detain from following thy illustrious track.
Thou hast atchiev'd our libertie, confin'd
Within Hell Gates till now, thou us impow'rd
To fortifie thus farr, and overlay   370
With this portentous Bridge the dark Abyss.
Thine now is all this World, thy vertue hath won
What thy hands builded not, thy Wisdom gain'd

[28] unawares.
[29] the coverings of fig leaves.
[30] the bridge from hell.
[31] mutual dependence.

With odds what Warr hath lost, and fully aveng'd
Our foil in Heav'n; here thou shalt Monarch reign,   375
There didst not; there let him still Victor sway,
As Battel hath adjudg'd, from this new World
Retiring, by his own doom alienated,
And henceforth Monarchie with thee divide
Of all things, parted by th' Empyreal bounds,   380
His Quadrature, from thy Orbicular World,
Or trie thee now more dang'rous to his Throne.
    Whom thus the Prince of Darkness answerd glad.
Fair Daughter, and thou Son and Grandchild both,
High proof ye now have giv'n to be the Race   385
Of *Satan* (for I glorie in the name,
Antagonist of Heav'ns Almightie King)
Amply have merited of me, of all
Th' Infernal Empire, that so neer Heav'ns dore
Triumphal with triumphal act have met,   390
Mine with this glorious Work, and made one Realm
Hell and this World, one Realm, one Continent
Of easie thorough-fare. Therefore while I
Descend through Darkness, on your Rode with ease
To my associate Powers, them to acquaint   395
With these successes, and with them rejoyce,
You two this way, among those numerous Orbs
All yours, right down to Paradise descend;
There dwell and Reign in bliss, thence on the Earth
Dominion exercise and in the Air,   400
Chiefly on Man, sole Lord of all declar'd,
Him first make sure your thrall, and lastly kill.
My Substitutes I send ye, and Create
Plenipotent on Earth, of matchless might
Issuing from mee: on your joynt vigor now   405
My hold of this new Kingdom all depends,
Through Sin to Death expos'd by my exploit.
If your joynt power prevail, th' affaires of Hell
No detriment need fear, goe and be strong.
    So saying he dismiss'd them, they with speed   410
Thir course through thickest Constellations held
Spreading thir bane; the blasted Starrs lookt wan,
And Planets, Planet-strook,[32] real Eclips
Then sufferd. Th' other way *Satan* went down

[32] unfavorably affected (as the planets themselves were considered to influence men).

The Causey[33] to Hell Gate; on either side   415
Disparted *Chaos* over built exclaimd,
And with rebounding surge the barrs assaild,
That scorn'd his indignation: through the Gate,
Wide open and unguarded, *Satan* pass'd,
And all about found desolate; for those   420
Appointed to sit there, had left thir charge,
Flown to the upper World; the rest were all
Farr to the inland retir'd, about the walls
Of *Pandæmonium*, Citie and proud seat
Of *Lucifer*, so by allusion calld,   425
Of that bright Starr to *Satan* paragond.[34]
There kept thir Watch the Legions, while the Grand
In Council sate, sollicitous what chance
Might intercept thir Emperour sent, so hee
Departing gave command, and they observ'd.[35]   430
As when the *Tartar* from his *Russian* Foe
By *Astracan*[36] over the Snowie Plains
Retires, or *Bactrian* Sophi[37] from the horns
Of *Turkish* Crescent, leaves all waste beyond
The Realm of *Aladule,* in his retreat   435
To *Tauris* or *Casbeen.*[38] So these the late
Heav'n-banisht Host, left desert utmost Hell
Many a dark League, reduc't[39] in careful Watch
Round thir Metropolis, and now expecting
Each hour their great adventurer from the search   440
Of Forrein Worlds: he through the midst unmarkt,
In shew plebeian Angel militant
Of lowest order, past; and from the dore
Of that *Plutonian* Hall, invisible
Ascended his high Throne, which under state[40]   445
Of richest texture spred, at th' upper end
Was plac't in regal lustre. Down a while
He sate, and round about him saw unseen:
At last as from a Cloud his fulgent head

[33] causeway.
[34] compared.
[35] (his command).
[36] an outpost on the Volga.
[37] king of Persia.
[38] Casbeen and Tauris (Tabriz) were Persian cities ruled by Aladule.
[39] led back.
[40] canopy.

And shape Starr bright appeer'd, or brighter, clad   450
With what permissive glory since his fall
Was left him, or false glitter: All amaz'd
At that so sudden blaze the *Stygian* throng
Bent thir aspect, and whom they wish'd beheld,
Thir mighty Chief returnd: loud was th' acclaim: 455
Forth rush'd in haste the great consulting Peers,
Rais'd from thir dark *Divan*,[41] and with like joy
Congratulant approach'd him, who with hand
Silence, and with these words attention won.
    Thrones, Dominations, Princedoms, Vertues, Powers,   460
For in possession such, not onely of right,
I call ye and declare ye now, returnd
Successful beyond hope, to lead ye forth
Triumphant out of this infernal Pit
Abominable, accurst, the house of woe,   465
And Dungeon of our Tyrant: Now possess,
As Lords, a spacious World, t' our native Heav'n
Little inferiour, by my adventure hard
With peril great atchiev'd. Long were to tell
What I have don, what sufferd, with what pain   470
Voyag'd th' unreal, vast, unbounded deep
Of horrible confusion, over which
By Sin and Death a broad way now is pav'd
To expedite your glorious march; but I
Toild out my uncouth passage, forc't to ride   475
Th' untractable Abyss, plung'd in the womb
Of unoriginal[42] *Night* and *Chaos* wild,
That jealous of thir secrets fiercely oppos'd
My journey strange, with clamorous uproar
Protesting Fate supream; thence how I found   480
The new created World, which fame in Heav'n
Long had foretold, a Fabrick wonderful
Of absolute perfection, therein Man
Plac't in a Paradise, by our exile
Made happie: Him by fraud I have seduc'd   485
From his Creator, and the more to increase
Your wonder, with an Apple; he thereat
Offended, worth your laughter, hath giv'n up
Both his beloved Man and all his World,
To Sin and Death a prey, and so to us,   490

[41] council.
[42] "unoriginated," since nothing existed before it.

Without our hazard, labour, or allarm,
To range in, and to dwell, and over Man
To rule, as over all he should have rul'd.
True is, mee also he hath judg'd, or rather
Mee not, but the brute Serpent in whose shape   495
Man I deceav'd: that which to mee belongs,
Is enmity, which he will put between
Mee and Mankind; I am to bruise his heel;
His Seed, when is not set, shall bruise my head:
A World who would not purchase with a bruise,   500
Or much more grievous pain? Ye have th' account
Of my performance: What remains, ye Gods,
But up and enter now into full bliss.
   So having said, a while he stood, expecting
Thir universal shout and high applause   505
To fill his ear, when contrary he hears
On all sides, from innumerable tongues
A dismal universal hiss, the sound
Of public scorn; he wonderd, but not long
Had leasure, wondring at himself now more;   510
His Visage drawn he felt to sharp and spare,
His Armes clung to his Ribs, his Leggs entwining
Each other, till supplanted[43] down he fell
A monstrous Serpent on his Belly prone,
Reluctant, but in vain, a greater power   515
Now rul'd him, punisht in the shape he sin'd,
According to his doom: he would have spoke,
But hiss for hiss returnd with forked tongue
To forked tongue, for now were all transform'd
Alike, to Serpents all as accessories   520
To his bold Riot:[44] dreadful was the din
Of hissing through the Hall, thick swarming now
With complicated[45] monsters, head and tail,
Scorpion and Asp, and *Amphisbæna* dire,
Cerastes hornd, *Hydrus,* and *Ellops* drear,   525
And *Dipsas* (not so thick swarm'd once the Soil

[43] tripped.
[44] revolt.
[45] twisted together. Among the fabulous serpents which follow
are the amphisbaena, which had a head at both ends, the hydrus
(a watersnake), the ellops (probably a swordfish), and the dipsas,
whose bite provoked thirst. Serpents sprang from the blood of Medusa, and Ophiusa ("full of snakes") is one of the Balearic islands. Python was killed by Apollo at Delphi.

Bedropt with blood of *Gorgon,* or the Isle
Ophiusa) but still greatest hee the midst,
Now Dragon grown, larger then whom the Sun
Ingenderd in the *Pythian* Vale on slime,   530
Huge *Python,* and his Power no less he seem'd
Above the rest still to retain; they all
Him follow'd issuing forth to th' open Field,
Where all yet left of that revolted Rout
Heav'n-fall'n, in station stood or just array,   535
Sublime[46] with expectation when to see
In Triumph issuing forth thir glorious Chief;
They saw, but other sight instead, a crowd
Of ugly Serpents; horror on them fell,
And horrid sympathie; for what they saw,   540
They felt themselvs now changing; down thir arms,
Down fell both Spear and Shield, down they as fast,
And the dire hiss renew'd, and the dire form
Catcht by Contagion, like in punishment,
As in thir crime. Thus was th' applause they meant,   545
Turnd to exploding hiss, triumph to shame
Cast on themselves from thir own mouths. There stood
A Grove hard by, sprung up with this thir change,
His will who reigns above, to aggravate
Thir penance, laden with fair Fruit like that   550
Which grew in Paradise, the bait of *Eve*
Us'd by the Tempter: on that prospect strange
Thir earnest eyes they fix'd, imagining
For one forbidden Tree a multitude
Now ris'n, to work them furder woe or shame;   555
Yet parcht with scalding thurst and hunger fierce,
Though to delude them sent, could not abstain,
But on they rould in heaps, and up the Trees
Climbing, sat thicker then the snakie locks
That curld *Megæra:*[47] greedily they pluck'd   560
The Fruitage fair to sight, like that which grew
Neer that bituminous Lake[48] where *Sodom* flam'd;
This more delusive, not the touch, but taste
Deceav'd; they fondly thinking to allay
Thir appetite with gust,[49] instead of Fruit   565

[46] upraised.
[47] one of the Furies.
[48] the Dead Sea. The fair apples of Sodom were but ashes inside.
[49] gusto, great relish.

Chewd bitter Ashes, which th' offended taste
With spattering noise rejected: oft they assayd,
Hunger and thirst constraining, drug'd[50] as oft,
With hatefullest disrelish writh'd thir jaws
With soot and cinders fill'd; so oft they fell   570
Into the same illusion, not as Man
Whom they triumph'd once lapst. Thus were they plagu'd
And worn with Famin, long and ceasless hiss,
Till thir lost shape, permitted, they resum'd,
Yearly enjoynd, some say, to undergo   575
This annual humbling certain number'd days,
To dash thir pride, and joy for Man seduc't.
However some tradition they dispers'd
Among the Heathen of thir purchase got,
And Fabl'd how the Serpent, whom they calld   580
Ophion[51] with *Eurynome,* the wide-
Encroaching *Eve* perhaps, had first the rule
Of high *Olympus,* thence by *Saturn* driv'n
And *Ops,* ere yet *Dictæan Jove* was born.
Mean while in Paradise the hellish pair   585
Too soon arriv'd, *Sin* there in power before,
Once actual, now in body, and to dwell
Habitual habitant; behind her *Death*
Close following pace for pace, not mounted yet
On his pale Horse:[52] to whom *Sin* thus began.   590
    Second of *Satan* sprung, all conquering *Death,*
What thinkst thou of our Empire now, though earnd
With travail difficult, not better farr
Then still at Hells dark threshold to have sate watch,
Unnam'd, undreaded, and thy self half starv'd?   595
    Whom thus the Sin-born Monster answerd soon.
To mee, who with eternal Famin pine,
Alike is Hell, or Paradise, or Heaven,
There best, where most with ravin I may meet;
Which here, though plenteous, all too little seems   600
To stuff this Maw, this vast unhide-bound[53] Corps.
    To whom th' incestuous Mother thus repli'd.
Thou therefore on these Herbs, and Fruits, and Flowrs

[50] sickened.

[51] a Titan whose name means "serpent"; his wife was Eurynome, whose name means "wide-encroaching." Jove, son of Saturn and Ceres, had a shrine at Mount Dicte in Crete.

[52] from Rev. vi. 8.

[53] not bound by his hide.

Feed first, on each Beast next, and Fish, and Fowl,
No homely morsels, and whatever thing   605
The Sithe of Time mows down, devour unspar'd,
Till I in Man residing through the Race,
His thoughts, his looks, words, actions all infect,
And season him thy last and sweetest prey.
    This said, they both betook them several wayes,   610
Both to destroy, or unimmortal make
All kinds, and for destruction to mature
Sooner or later; which th' Almightie seeing,
From his transcendent Seat the Saints among,
To those bright Orders utterd thus his voice.   615
    See with what heat these Dogs of Hell advance
To waste and havoc yonder World, which I
So fair and good created, and had still
Kept in that state, had not the folly of Man
Let in these wastful Furies, who impute   620
Folly to mee, so doth the Prince of Hell
And his Adherents, that with so much ease
I suffer them to enter and possess
A place so heav'nly, and conniving[54] seem
To gratifie my scornful Enemies,   625
That laugh, as if transported with some fit
Of Passion, I to them had quitted all,
At random yeilded up to their misrule;
And know not that I call'd and drew them thither
My Hell-hounds, to lick up the draff and filth   630
Which mans polluting Sin with taint hath shed
On what was pure, till cramm'd and gorg'd, nigh burst
With suckt and glutted offal, at one sling
Of thy victorious Arm, well-pleasing Son,
Both *Sin*, and *Death*, and yawning *Grave* at last   635
Through *Chaos* hurld, obstruct the mouth of Hell
For ever, and seal up his ravenous Jaws.
Then Heav'n and Earth renewd shall be made pure
To sanctitie that shall receive no stain:
Till then the Curse pronounc't on both precedes.   640
    He ended, and the heav'nly Audience loud
Sung *Halleluia*, as the sound of Seas,
Through multitude that sung: Just are thy ways,
Righteous are thy Decrees on all thy Works;

[54] shutting the eyes.

Who can extenuate[55] thee? Next, to the Son,   645
Destin'd restorer of Mankind, by whom
New Heav'n and Earth shall to the Ages rise,
Or down from Heav'n descend. Such was thir song,
While the Creator calling forth by name
His mightie Angels gave them several charge,   650
As sorted[56] best with present things. The Sun
Had first his precept so to move, so shine,
As might affect the Earth with cold and heat
Scarce tollerable, and from the North to call
Decrepit Winter, from the South to bring   655
Solstitial summers heat. To the blanc Moon
Her office they prescrib'd, to th' other five[57]
Thir planetarie motions and aspects
In *Sextile*, *Square*, and *Trine*, and *Opposite*,[58]
Of noxious efficacie, and when to joyn   660
In Synod unbenigne, and taught the fixt
Thir influence malignant when to showr,
Which of them rising with the Sun, or falling,
Should prove tempestuous: To the Winds they set
Thir corners, when with bluster to confound   665
Sea, Air, and Shoar, the Thunder when to rowl
With terror through the dark Aereal Hall.
Some say he bid his Angels turn ascanse
The Poles of Earth twice ten degrees and more
From the Suns Axle;[59] they with labour push'd   670
Oblique the Centric Globe: Som say the Sun
Was bid turn Reins from th' Equinoctial Rode
Like distant breadth to *Taurus* with the Seav'n
Atlantick Sisters, and the *Spartan* Twins
Up to the *Tropic* Crab; thence down amain   675
By *Leo* and the *Virgin* and the *Scales*,

[55] disparage.
[56] harmonized.
[57] (planets).
[58] The planets are unbenign when their conjunction ("synod,"
l. 661) is at angles of 60 degrees, 90 degrees, 120 degrees, and
180 degrees.
[59] The tilting of the earth 23.5 degrees from the sun's course,
which was the same as the celestial equator (Copernicus), or the
alteration of the sun's course a like amount (l. 673; Ptolemy)
created winter. The sun moves upward to the Tropic of Cancer
(through the Bull and the Pleiades and then through Gemini) in
Jan.–June, and southward to the Tropic of Capricorn (through
Leo, Virgo, and Libra) in July–Dec.

As deep as *Capricorn,* to bring in change
Of Seasons to each Clime; else had the Spring
Perpetual smil'd on Earth with vernant Flowrs,
Equal in Days and Nights, except to those   680
Beyond the Polar Circles; to them Day
Had unbenighted shon, while the low Sun
To recompence his distance, in thir sight
Had rounded still th' *Horizon,* and not known
Or East or West, which had forbid the Snow   685
From cold *Estotiland,*[60] and South as farr
Beneath *Magellan.* At that tasted Fruit
The Sun, as from *Thyestean* Banquet,[61] turn'd
His course intended; else how had the World
Inhabited, though sinless, more then now,   690
Avoided pinching cold and scorching heat?
These changes in the Heav'ns, though slow, produc'd
Like change on Sea and Land, sideral blast,[62]
Vapour, and Mist, and Exhalation hot,
Corrupt and Pestilent: Now from the North   695
Of *Norumbega,*[63] and the *Samoed* shoar
Bursting thir brazen Dungeon, armd with ice
And snow and hail and stormie gust and flaw,[64]
Boreas[65] and *Cæcias* and *Argestes* loud
And *Thrascias* rend the Woods and Seas upturn;   700
With adverse blast up-turns them from the South
Notus and *Afer* black with thundrous Clouds
From *Serraliona;* thwart of these as fierce
Forth rush the *Levant* and the *Ponent* Winds
Eurus and *Zephir* with thir lateral noise,   705
Sirocco, and *Libecchio.* Thus began
Outrage from liveless things; but Discord first
Daughter of Sin, among th' irrational,
Death introduc'd through fierce antipathie:

[60] Labrador. "Magellan" means the Straits of Magellan.
[61] Atreus served his brother Thyestes his sons as food at a banquet of revenge.
[62] malign influence from the stars.
[63] New England. The "*Samoed* shore" is Siberia.
[64] burst of wind.
[65] Boreas, Caecias, Argestes, and Thrascias were winds from the north; Notus and Afer (l. 702) from the south; Euras (l. 705) from the east ("Levant"), and Zephyr from the west ("Ponent"); Sirocco (l. 706) from the southeast and Libecchio from the southwest.

Beast now with Beast gan war, and Fowl with Fowl,   710
And Fish with Fish; to graze the Herb all leaving,
Devourd each other; nor stood much in awe
Of Man, but fled him, or with count'nance grim
Glar'd on him passing: these were from without
The growing miseries, which *Adam* saw   715
Alreadie in part, though hid in gloomiest shade,
To sorrow abandond, but worse felt within,
And in a troubl'd Sea of passion tost,
Thus to disburd'n sought with sad complaint.
     O miserable of happie! is this the end   720
Of this new glorious World, and mee so late
The Glory of that Glory, who now becom
Accurst of blessed, hide me from the face
Of God, whom to behold was then my highth
Of happiness: yet well, if here would end   725
The miserie, I deserv'd it, and would bear
My own deservings; but this will not serve;
All that I eat or drink, or shall beget,
Is propagated curse. O voice once heard
Delightfully, *Encrease and multiply,*   730
Now death to hear! for what can I encrease
Or multiplie, but curses on my head?
Who of all Ages to succeed, but feeling
The evil on him brought by me, will curse
My Head, Ill fare our Ancestor impure,   735
For this we may thank *Adam;* but his thanks
Shall be the execration; so besides
Mine own that bide upon me, all from mee
Shall with a fierce reflux on mee redound,[66]
On mee as on thir natural center light   740
Heavie, though in thir place. O fleeting joyes
Of Paradise, dear bought with lasting woes!
Did I request thee, Maker, from my Clay
To mould me Man, did I sollicite thee
From darkness to promote me, or here place   745
In this delicious Garden? as my Will
Concurd not to my being, it were but right
And equal to reduce me to my dust,
Desirous to resigne, and render back
All I receav'd, unable to perform   750
Thy terms too hard, by which I was to hold

[66] flow back.

The good I sought not. To the loss of that,
Sufficient penaltie, why hast thou added
The sense of endless woes? inexplicable
Thy Justice seems; yet to say truth, too late,   755
I thus contest; then should have been refus'd
Those terms whatever, when they were propos'd:
Thou didst accept them; wilt thou enjoy the good,
Then cavil the conditions? and though God
Made thee without thy leave, what if thy Son   760
Prove disobedient, and reprov'd, retort,
Wherefore didst thou beget me? I sought it not:
Wouldst thou admit for his contempt of thee
That proud excuse? yet him not thy election,
But Natural necessity begot.   765
God made thee of choice his own, and of his own
To serve him, thy reward was of his grace,
Thy punishment then justly is at his Will.
Be it so, for I submit, his doom is fair,
That dust I am, and shall to dust return: 770
O welcom hour whenever! why delayes
His hand to execute what his Decree
Fix'd on this day? why do I overlive,
Why am I mockt with death, and length'n'd out
To deathless pain? how gladly would I meet   775
Mortalitie my sentence, and be Earth
Insensible, how glad would lay me down
As in my Mothers lap? there I should rest
And sleep secure; his dreadful voice no more
Would Thunder in my ears, no fear of worse   780
To mee and to my ofspring would torment me
With cruel expectation. Yet one doubt
Pursues me still, least all I cannot die,
Least that pure breath of Life, the Spirit of Man
Which God inspir'd, cannot together perish   785
With this corporeal Clod; then in the Grave,
Or in some other dismal place, who knows
But I shall die a living Death? O thought
Horrid, if true! yet why? it was but breath
Of Life that sinn'd; what dies but what had life   790
And sin? the Bodie properly hath neither.
All of me then shall die: let this appease
The doubt, since human reach no further knows.
For though the Lord of all be infinite,
Is his wrauth also? be it, man is not so,   795

But mortal doom'd. How can he exercise
Wrath without end on Man whom Death must end?
Can he make deathless Death? that were to make
Strange contradiction, which to God himself
Impossible is held, as Argument   800
Of weakness, not of Power. Will he draw out,
For angers sake, finite to infinite
In punisht man, to satisfie his rigour
Satisfi'd never; that were to extend
His Sentence beyond dust and Natures Law,   805
By which all Causes else according still
To the reception[67] of thir matter act,
Not to th' extent of thir own Sphear. But say
That Death be not one stroak, as I suppos'd,
Bereaving sense, but endless miserie   810
From this day onward, which I feel begun
Both in me, and without me, and so last
To perpetuitie; Ay me, that fear
Comes thundring back with dreadful revolution
On my defensless head; both Death and I   815
Am found Eternal, and incorporate both,
Nor I on my part single, in mee all
Posteritie stands curst: Fair Patrimonie
That I must leave ye, Sons; O were I able
To waste it all my self, and leave ye none!   820
So disinherited how would ye bless
Me now your curse! Ah, why should all mankind
For one mans fault thus guiltless be condemn'd,
If guiltless? But from me what can proceed,
But all corrupt, both Mind and Will deprav'd,   825
Not to do onely, but to will the same
With me? how can they then acquitted stand
In sight of God? Him after all Disputes
Forc't I absolve: all my evasions vain,
And reasonings, though through Mazes, lead me still   830
But to my own conviction: first and last
On mee, mee onely, as the sourse and spring
Of all corruption, all the blame lights due;
So might the wrauth. Fond wish! couldst thou support
That burden heavier then the Earth to bear,   835

[67] The potentiality of matter is limited by that to which it is
united; that is, God will not make man's punishment infinite
though he himself is infinite.

Then all the World much heavier, though divided
With that bad Woman? Thus what thou desir'st
And what thou fearst, alike destroyes all hope
Of refuge, and concludes thee miserable
Beyond all past example and future,   840
To *Satan* only like both crime and doom.
O Conscience, into what Abyss of fears
And horrors hast thou driv'n me; out of which
I find no way, from deep to deeper plung'd!
   Thus *Adam* to himself lamented loud   845
Through the still Night, not now, as ere man fell,
Wholsom and cool, and mild, but with black Air
Accompanied, with damps and dreadful gloom,
Which to his evil Conscience represented
All things with double terror: On the ground   850
Outstretcht he lay, on the cold ground, and oft
Curs'd his Creation, Death as oft accus'd
Of tardie execution, since denounc't
The day of his offence. Why comes not Death,
Said hee, with one thrice acceptable stroke   855
To end me? Shall Truth fail to keep her word,
Justice Divine not hast'n to be just?
But Death comes not at call, Justice Divine
Mends not her slowest pace for prayers or cries.
O Woods, O Fountains, Hillocks, Dales and Bowrs,   860
With other echo late I taught your Shades
To answer, and resound farr other Song.
Whom thus afflicted when sad *Eve* beheld,
Desolate where she sate, approaching nigh,
Soft words to his fierce passion she assay'd: 865
But her with stern regard he thus repell'd.
   Out of my sight, thou Serpent, that name best
Befits thee with him leagu'd, thy self as false
And hateful; nothing wants, but that thy shape,
Like his, and colour Serpentine may shew   870
Thy inward fraud, to warn all Creatures from thee
Henceforth; least that too heav'nly form, pretended[68]
To hellish falshood, snare them. But for thee
I had persisted happie, had not thy pride
And wandring vanitie, when lest was safe,   875
Rejected my forewarning, and disdain'd
Not to be trusted, longing to be seen

[68] held before as a disguise.

Though by the Devil himself, him overweening
To over-reach, but with the Serpent meeting
Fool'd and beguil'd, by him thou, I by thee,   880
To trust thee from my side, imagin'd wise,
Constant, mature, proof against all assaults,
And understood not all was but a shew
Rather then solid vertu, all but a Rib
Crooked by nature, bent, as now appears,   885
More to the part sinister[69] from me drawn,
Well if thrown out, as supernumerarie
To my just number found. O why did God,
Creator wise, that peopl'd highest Heav'n
With Spirits Masculine, create at last   890
This noveltie on Earth, this fair defect
Of Nature, and not fill the World at once
With Men as Angels without Feminine,
Or find some other way to generate
Mankind? this mischief had not then befall'n,   895
And more that shall befall, innumerable
Disturbances on Earth through Femal snares,
And straight conjunction with this Sex: for either
He never shall find out fit Mate, but such
As some misfortune brings him, or mistake,   900
Or whom he wishes most shall seldom gain
Through her perversness, but shall see her gaind
By a farr worse, or if she love, withheld
By Parents, or his happiest choice too late
Shall meet, alreadie linkt and Wedlock-bound   905
To a fell Adversarie, his hate or shame:
Which infinite calamitie shall cause
To Human life, and houshold peace confound.
    He added not, and from her turn'd, but *Eve*
Not so repulst, with Tears that ceas'd not flowing,   910
And tresses all disorderd, at his feet
Fell humble, and imbracing them, besaught
His peace, and thus proceeded in her plaint.
    Forsake me not thus, *Adam*, witness Heav'n
What love sincere, and reverence in my heart   915
I bear thee, and unweeting have offended,
Unhappilie deceav'd; thy suppliant
I beg, and clasp thy knees; bereave me not,
Whereon I live, thy gentle looks, thy aid,

[69] a pun of "left" side and "evil."

Thy counsel in this uttermost distress,   920
My onely strength and stay: forlorn of thee,
Whither shall I betake me, where subsist?
While yet we live, scarse one short hour perhaps,
Between us two let there be peace, both joyning,
As joyn'd in injuries, one enmitie   925
Against a Foe by doom express assign'd us,
That cruel Serpent: On me exercise not
Thy hatred for this miserie befall'n,
On me already lost, mee then thy self
More miserable; both have sin'd, but thou   930
Against God onely, I against God and thee,
And to the place of judgment will return,
There with my cries importune Heav'n, that all
The sentence from thy head remov'd may light
On me, sole cause to thee of all this woe,   935
Mee mee onely just object of his ire.
    She ended weeping, and her lowlie plight,
Immoveable till peace obtain'd from fault
Acknowledg'd and deplor'd, in *Adam* wraught
Commiseration; soon his heart relented   940
Towards her, his life so late and sole delight,
Now at his feet submissive in distress,
Creature so fair his reconcilement seeking,
His counsel whom she had displeas'd, his aid;
As one disarm'd, his anger all he lost,   945
And thus with peaceful words uprais'd her soon.
    Unwarie, and too desirous, as before,
So now of what thou knowst not, who desir'st
The punishment all on thy self; alas,
Bear thine own first, ill able to sustain   950
His full wrauth whose thou feelst as yet lest part,
And my displeasure bearst so ill. If Prayers
Could alter high Decrees, I to that place
Would speed before thee, and be louder heard,
That on my head all might be visited,   955
Thy frailtie and infirmer Sex forgiv'n,
To me committed and by me expos'd.
But rise, let us no more contend, nor blame
Each other, blam'd enough elsewhere, but strive
In offices of Love, how we may light'n   960
Each others burden in our share of woe;
Since this days Death denounc't, if ought I see,
Will prove no sudden, but a slow-pac't evill,

A long days dying to augment our pain,
And to our Seed (O hapless Seed!) deriv'd.   965
    To whom thus *Eve*, recovering heart, repli'd.
Adam, by sad experiment I know
How little weight my words with thee can find,
Found so erroneous, thence by just event
Found so unfortunate; nevertheless,   970
Restor'd by thee, vile as I am, to place
Of new acceptance, hopeful to regain
Thy Love, the sole contentment of my heart,
Living or dying, from thee I will not hide
What thoughts in my unquiet brest are ris'n,   975
Tending to som relief of our extremes,
Or end, though sharp and sad, yet tolerable,
As in our evils,[70] and of easier choice.
If care of our descent perplex us most,
Which must be born to certain woe, devourd   980
By Death at last, and miserable it is
To be to others cause of misery,
Our own begotten, and of our Loins to bring
Into this cursed World a woful Race,
That after wretched Life must be at last   985
Food for so foul a Monster, in thy power
It lies, yet ere Conception to prevent
The Race unblest, to being yet unbegot.
Childless thou art, Childless remain: so Death
Shall be deceav'd his glut, and with us two   990
Be forc'd to satisfie his Rav'nous Maw.
But if thou judge it hard and difficult,
Conversing, looking, loving, to abstain
From Loves due Rites, Nuptial imbraces sweet,
And with desire to languish without hope,   995
Before the present object[71] languishing
With like desire, which would be miserie
And torment less then none of what we dread,
Then both our selves and Seed at once to free
From what we fear for both, let us make short,   1000
Let us seek Death, or he not found, supply
With our own hands his Office on our selves;
Why stand we longer shivering under feares,
That shew no end but Death, and have the power,

[70] in evils such as ours.
[71] Eve.

Of many ways to die the shortest choosing,   1005
Destruction with destruction to destroy.
    She ended heer, or vehement despair
Broke off the rest; so much of Death her thoughts
Had entertaind, as di'd her Cheeks with pale.
But *Adam* with such counsel nothing sway'd,   1010
To better hopes his more attentive mind
Labouring had rais'd, and thus to *Eve* repli'd.
    Eve, thy contempt of life and pleasure seems
To argue in thee somthing more sublime
And excellent then what thy mind contemns;   1015
But self-destruction therefore saught, refutes
That excellence thought in thee, and implies,
Not thy contempt, but anguish and regret
For loss of life and pleasure overlov'd.
Or if thou covet death, as utmost end   1020
Of miserie, so thinking to evade
The penaltie pronounc't, doubt not but God
Hath wiselier arm'd his vengeful ire then so
To be forestall'd; much more I fear least Death
So snatcht will not exempt us from the pain   1025
We are by doom to pay; rather such acts
Of contumacie will provoke the highest
To make death in us live: Then let us seek
Som safer resolution, which methinks
I have in view, calling to mind with heed   1030
Part of our Sentence, that thy Seed shall bruise
The Serpents head; piteous amends, unless
Be meant, whom I conjecture, our grand Foe
Satan, who in the Serpent hath contriv'd
Against us this deceit: to crush his head   1035
Would be revenge indeed; which will be lost
By death brought on our selves, or childless days
Resolv'd, as thou proposest; so our Foe
Shall scape his punishment ordain'd, and wee
Instead shall double ours upon our heads.   1040
No more be mention'd then of violence
Against our selves, and wilful barrenness,
That cuts us off from hope, and savours onely
Rancor and pride, impatience and despite,
Reluctance[72] against God and his just yoke   1045
Laid on our Necks. Remember with what mild

[72] struggle.

And gracious temper he both heard and judg'd
Without wrauth or reviling; wee expected
Immediate dissolution, which we thought
Was meant by Death that day, when lo, to thee   1050
Pains onely in Child-bearing were foretold,
And bringing forth, soon recompenc't with joy,
Fruit of thy Womb: On mee the Curse aslope
Glanc'd on the ground, with labour I must earn
My bread; what harm? Idleness had bin worse;   1055
My labour will sustain me; and least Cold
Or Heat should injure us, his timely care
Hath unbesaught provided, and his hands
Cloath'd us unworthie, pitying while he judg'd;
How much more, if we pray him, will his ear   1060
Be open, and his heart to pitie incline,
And teach us further by what means to shun
Th' inclement Seasons, Rain, Ice, Hail and Snow,
Which now the Skie with various Face begins
To shew us in this Mountain, while the Winds   1065
Blow moist and keen, shattering the graceful locks
Of these fair spreading Trees; which bids us seek
Som better shroud, som better warmth to cherish
Our Limbs benumm'd, ere this diurnal Starr
Leave cold the Night, how we his gather'd beams   1070
Reflected, may with matter sere foment,
Or by collision of two bodies grind
The Air attrite[73] to Fire, as late the Clouds
Justling or pusht with Winds rude in thir shock
Tine[74] the slant Lightning, whose thwart flame driv'n down
Kindles the gummie bark of Firr or Pine,   1076
And sends a comfortable heat from farr,
Which might supplie the Sun: such Fire to use,
And what may else be remedie or cure
To evils which our own misdeeds have wrought,   1080
Hee will instruct us praying, and of Grace
Beseeching him, so as we need not fear
To pass commodiously this life, sustain'd
By him with many comforts, till we end
In dust, our final rest and native home.   1085
What better can we do, then to the place

[73] The air is thought of as being "rubbed" by the collision, causing fire from friction.
[74] kindle.

Repairing where he judg'd us, prostrate fall
Before him reverent, and there confess
Humbly our faults, and pardon beg, with tears
Watering the ground, and with our sighs the Air   1090
Frequenting, sent from hearts contrite, in sign
Of sorrow unfeign'd, and humiliation meek.
Undoubtedly he will relent and turn
From his displeasure; in whose look serene,
When angry most he seem'd and most severe,   1095
What else but favor, grace, and mercie shon?
    So spake our Father penitent, nor *Eve*
Felt less remorse: they forthwith to the place
Repairing where he judg'd them prostrate fell
Before him reverent, and both confess'd   1100
Humbly thir faults, and pardon beg'd, with tears
Watering the ground, and with thir sighs the Air
Frequenting, sent from hearts contrite, in sign
Of sorrow unfeign'd, and humiliation meek.

BOOK XI

THE ARGUMENT

The Son of God presents to his Father the Prayers of our first
Parents now repenting, and intercedes for them: God accepts
them, but declares that they must no longer abide in Paradise;
sends *Michael* with a Band of Cherubim to dispossess them;
but first to reveal to *Adam* future things: *Michaels* coming
down. *Adam* shews to *Eve* certain ominous signs; he discerns
Michaels approach, goes out to meet him: the Angel de-
nounces thir departure. *Eve's* Lamentation. *Adam* pleads, but
submits: The Angel leads him up to a high Hill, sets before
him in vision what shall happ'n till the Flood.

Thus they in lowliest plight repentant stood
Praying, for from the Mercie-seat[1] above
Prevenient Grace[2] descending had remov'd
The stonie[3] from thir hearts, and made new flesh
Regenerat grow instead, that sighs now breath'd   5

    [1] a plate on which was sprinkled the blood of sacrificed animals;
thus, the throne of God.
    [2] grace which precedes (repentance).
    [3] Ezek. xi. 19: "and I will take the stony heart out of their flesh,
and will give them an heart of flesh."

Unutterable, which the Spirit of prayer
Inspir'd, and wing'd for Heav'n with speedier flight
Then loudest Oratorie: yet thir port
Not of mean suiters, nor important less
Seem'd thir Petition, then when th' ancient Pair   10
In Fables old, less ancient yet then these,
Deucalion and chaste *Pyrrha* to restore
The Race of Mankind drownd, before the Shrine
Of *Themis*[4] stood devout. To Heav'n thir prayers
Flew up, nor miss'd the way, by envious winds   15
Blow'n vagabond or frustrate: in they pass'd
Dimentionless through Heav'nly dores; then clad
With incense, where the Golden Altar fum'd,
By thir great Intercessor, came in sight
Before the Fathers Throne: Them the glad Son   20
Presenting, thus to intercede began.
    See Father, what first fruits on Earth are sprung
From thy implanted Grace in Man, these Sighs
And Prayers, which in this Golden Censer, mixt
With Incense, I thy Priest before thee bring,   25
Fruits of more pleasing savour from thy seed
Sow'n with contrition in his heart, then those
Which his own hand manuring[5] all the Trees
Of Paradise could have produc't, ere fall'n
From innocence. Now therefore bend thine ear   30
To supplication, hear his sighs though mute;
Unskilful with what words to pray, let mee
Interpret for him, mee his Advocate
And propitiation, all his works on mee
Good or not good ingraft, my Merit those   35
Shall perfet, and for these my Death shall pay.
Accept me, and in mee from these receave
The smell of peace toward Mankind, let him live
Before thee reconcil'd, at least his days
Numberd, though sad, till Death, his doom (which I   40
To mitigate thus plead, not to reverse)
To better life shall yeeld him, where with mee
All my redeemd may dwell in joy and bliss,
Made one with me as I with thee am one.

[4] goddess of justice. Deucalion and Pyrrha, surviving from the flood, cast stones to earth (compare l. 4) from which humans then sprang up.
    [5] cultivating.

To whom the Father, without Cloud, serene.   45
All thy request for Man, accepted Son,
Obtain, all thy request was my Decree:
But longer in that Paradise to dwell,
The Law I gave to Nature him forbids:
Those pure immortal Elements that know   50
No gross, no unharmoneous mixture foul,
Eject him tainted now, and purge him off
As a distemper, gross to air as gross,
And mortal food, as may dispose him best
For dissolution wrought by Sin, that first   55
Distemperd all things, and of incorrupt
Corrupted. I at first with two fair gifts
Created him endowd, with Happiness
And Immortalitie: that fondly lost,
This other serv'd but to eternize woe;   60
Till I provided Death; so Death becomes
His final remedie, and after Life
Tri'd in sharp tribulation, and refin'd
By Faith and faithful works, to second Life,
Wak't in the renovation of the just,   65
Resignes him up with Heav'n and Earth renewd.
But let us call to Synod all the Blest
Through Heav'ns wide bounds; from them I will not hide
My judgments, how with Mankind I proceed,
As how with peccant Angels late they saw;   70
And in thir state, though firm, stood more confirmd.
    He ended, and the Son gave signal high
To the bright Minister that watch'd, hee blew
His Trumpet, heard in *Oreb*[6] since perhaps
When God descended, and perhaps once more   75
To sound at general Doom.[7] Th' Angelic blast
Fill'd all the Regions: from thir blissful Bowrs
Of *Amarantin* Shade, Fountain or Spring,
By the waters of Life, where ere they sate
In fellowships of joy: the Sons of Light   80
Hasted, resorting to the Summons high,
And took thir Seats; till from his Throne supream
Th' Almighty thus pronounc'd his sovran Will.
    O Sons, like one of us Man is become

[6] Horeb or Mt. Sinai when Moses was given the Ten Commandments.
[7] Judgment Day.

To know both Good and Evil, since his taste   85
Of that defended[8] Fruit; but let him boast
His knowledge of Good lost, and Evil got,
Happier, had it suffic'd him to have known
Good by it self, and Evil not at all.
He sorrows now, repents, and prayes contrite,   90
My motions in him, longer then they move,
His heart I know, how variable and vain
Self-left.[9] Least therefore his now bolder hand
Reach also of the Tree of Life, and eat,
And live for ever, dream at least to live   95
For ever, to remove him I decree,
And send him from the Garden forth to Till
The Ground whence he was taken, fitter soil.
     Michael, this my behest have thou in charge,
Take to thee from among the Cherubim   100
Thy choice of flaming Warriours, least the Fiend
Or in behalf of[10] Man, or to invade
Vacant possession som new trouble raise:
Hast thee, and from the Paradise of God
Without remorse[11] drive out the sinful Pair,   105
From hallowd ground th' unholie, and denounce
To them and to thir Progenie from thence
Perpetual banishment. Yet least they faint
At the sad Sentence rigorously urg'd,
For I behold them soft'n'd and with tears   110
Bewailing thir excess, all terror hide.
If patiently thy bidding they obey,
Dismiss them not disconsolate; reveal
To *Adam* what shall come in future dayes,
As I shall thee enlighten, intermix   115
My Cov'nant in the womans seed renewd;
So send them forth, though sorrowing, yet in peace:
And on the East side of the Garden place,
Where entrance up from *Eden* easiest climbs,
Cherubic watch, and of a Sword the flame   120
Wide waving, all approach farr off to fright,
And guard all passage to the Tree of Life:
Least Paradise a receptacle prove

[8] forbidden.
[9] left to itself.
[10] in regard to.
[11] pity.

To Spirits foul, and all my Trees thir prey,
With whose stol'n Fruit Man once more to delude.   125
    He ceas'd; and th' Archangelic Power prepar'd
For swift descent, with him the Cohort bright
Of watchful Cherubim; four faces each
Had, like a double *Janus*, all thir shape
Spangl'd with eyes more numerous then those   130
Of *Argus*, and more wakeful then to drouze,
Charm'd with *Arcadian* Pipe, the Pastoral Reed
Of *Hermes*, or his opiate Rod.[12] Mean while
To resalute the World with sacred Light
Leucothea[13] wak'd, and with fresh dews imbalmd   135
The Earth, when *Adam* and first Matron *Eve*
Had ended now thir Orisons, and found
Strength added from above, new hope to spring
Out of despair, joy, but with fear yet linkt;
Which thus to *Eve* his welcome words renewd.   140
    Eve, easily may Faith admit, that all
The good which we enjoy, from Heav'n descends;
But that from us ought should ascend to Heav'n
So prevalent as to concern the mind
Of God high-blest, or to incline his will,   145
Hard to belief may seem; yet this will Prayer,
Or one short sigh of human breath, up-borne
Ev'n to the Seat of God. For since I saught
By Prayer th' offended Deitie to appease,
Kneel'd and before him humbl'd all my heart,   150
Methought I saw him placable and mild,
Bending his ear; perswasion in me grew
That I was heard with favour; peace returnd
Home to my brest, and to my memorie
His promise, that thy Seed shall bruise our Foe;   155
Which then not minded in dismay, yet now
Assures me that the bitterness of death
Is past, and we shall live. Whence Hail to thee,
Eve rightly call'd, Mother of all Mankind,[14]

[12] The four faces of the cherubim, "full of eyes" (Ezek. i. 15, 18), command the four quarters of the earth. Janus was the two-faced god of gates; Argus was a monster with a hundred eyes, who guarded Io and who was put to sleep by Hermes' reed and his caduceus.

[13] goddess of the dawn.

[14] Gen. iii. 20: "And Adam called his wife's name Eve; because she was the mother of all living."

Mother of all things living, since by thee   160
Man is to live, and all things live for Man.
   To whom thus *Eve* with sad[15] demeanour meek.
Ill worthie I such title should belong
To me transgressour, who for thee ordaind
A help, became thy snare; to mee reproach   165
Rather belongs, distrust and all dispraise:
But infinite in pardon was my Judge,
That I who first brought Death on all, am grac't
The sourse of life; next favourable thou,
Who highly thus to entitle me voutsaf'st,   170
Farr other name deserving. But the Field
To labour calls us now with sweat impos'd,
Though after sleepless Night; for see the Morn,
All unconcern'd with our unrest, begins
Her rosie progress smiling; let us forth,   175
I never from thy side henceforth to stray,
Wherere our days work lies, though now enjoind
Laborious, till day droop; while here we dwell,
What can be toilsom in these pleasant Walks?
Here let us live, though in fall'n state, content.   180
   So spake, so wish'd much-humbl'd *Eve*, but Fate
Subscrib'd not; Nature first gave Signs, imprest
On Bird, Beast, Air, Air suddenly eclips'd[16]
After short blush of Morn; nigh in her sight
The Bird of *Jove*,[17] stoopt from his aerie tour,   185
Two Birds of gayest plume before him drove:
Down from a Hill the Beast that reigns in Woods,[18]
First hunter then, pursu'd a gentle brace,
Goodliest of all the Forrest, Hart and Hind;
Direct to th' Eastern Gate was bent thir flight.   190
Adam observ'd, and with his Eye the chase
Pursuing, not unmov'd to *Eve* thus spake.
   O *Eve*, some furder change awaits us nigh,
Which Heav'n by these mute signs in Nature shews
Forerunners of his purpose, or to warn   195
Us haply too secure of our discharge
From penaltie, because from death releast
Some days; how long, and what till then our life,

[15] grave.
[16] darkened.
[17] the eagle, which swooped down ("stoopt") from its high
nest.
[18] the lion.

Who knows, or more then this, that we are dust,
And thither must return and be no more.   200
Why else this double object in our sight
Of flight pursu'd in th' Air and ore the ground
One way the self-same hour? why in the East
Darkness ere Dayes mid-course, and Morning light
More orient in yon Western Cloud that draws   205
O're the blew Firmament a radiant white,
And slow descends, with somthing heav'nly fraught.
    He err'd not, for by this the heav'nly Bands
Down from a Skie of Jasper lighted now
In Paradise, and on a Hill made alt,   210
A glorious Apparition, had not doubt
And carnal fear that day dimm'd *Adams* eye.
Not that more glorious, when the Angels met
Jacob in *Mahanaim,* where he saw
The field Pavilion'd with his Guardians bright;   215
Nor that which on the flaming Mount appeerd
In *Dothan,* cover'd with a Camp of Fire,
Against the *Syrian* King, who to surprize
One man, Assassin-like had levied Warr,
Warr unproclam'd.[19] The Princely Hierarch   220
In thir bright stand, there left his Powers to seise
Possession of the Garden; hee alone,
To find where *Adam* shelterd, took his way,
Not unperceav'd of *Adam,* who to *Eve,*
While the great Visitant approach'd, thus spake.   225
    Eve, now expect great tidings, which perhaps
Of us will soon determin, or impose
New Laws to be observ'd; for I descrie
From yonder blazing Cloud that veils the Hill
One of the heav'nly Host, and by his Gate   230
None of the meanest, some great Potentate
Or of the Thrones above, such Majestie
Invests him coming; yet not terrible,
That I should fear, nor sociably mild,
As *Raphael,* that I should much confide,   235
But solemn and sublime, whom not t' offend,
With reverence I must meet, and thou retire.
He ended; and th' Arch-Angel soon drew nigh,

---

[19] The servant of Elisha saw a mountain full of horses and
chariots, which had been sent by the king of Syria to seize Elisha,
besieged by fire (2 Kings vi. 13–17).

Not in his shape Celestial, but as Man
Clad to meet Man; over his lucid Armes   240
A militarie Vest of purple flowd
Livelier then *Meliboean*,[20] or the grain
Of *Sarra,* worn by Kings and Heroes old
In time of Truce; *Iris* had dipt the wooff;
His starrie Helm unbuckl'd shew'd him prime   245
In Manhood where Youth ended; by his side
As in a glistering *Zodiac*[21] hung the Sword,
Satans dire dread, and in his hand the Spear.
Adam bowd low, hee Kingly from his State
Inclin'd not, but his coming thus declar'd.   250
    Adam, Heav'ns high behest no Preface needs:
Sufficient that thy Prayers are heard, and Death,
Then due by sentence when thou didst transgress,
Defeated of his seisure many dayes
Giv'n thee of Grace, wherein thou may'st repent,   255
And one bad act with many deeds well done
Mayst cover: well may then thy Lord appeas'd
Redeem thee quite from Deaths rapacious claim;
But longer in this Paradise to dwell
Permits not; to remove thee I am come,   260
And send thee from the Garden forth to till
The ground whence thou wast tak'n, fitter Soil.
    He added not, for *Adam* at the news
Heart-strook with chilling gripe of sorrow stood,
That all his senses bound; *Eve,* who unseen   265
Yet all had heard, with audible lament
Discover'd soon the place of her retire.
    O unexpected stroke, worse then of Death!
Must I thus leave thee Paradise? thus leave
Thee Native Soil, these happie Walks and Shades,   270
Fit haunt of Gods? where I had hope to spend,
Quiet though sad, the respit of that day
That must be mortal to us both. O flowrs,
That never will in other Climate grow,
My early visitation, and my last   275
At Eev'n, which I bred up with tender hand
From the first op'ning bud, and gave ye Names,
Who now shall rear ye to the Sun, or rank
Your Tribes, and water from th' ambrosial Fount?

[20] of a town in Thessaly. Sarra is Tyre, famous for dyes.
[21] belt.

Thee lastly nuptial Bowr, by mee adornd   280
With what to sight or smell was sweet; from thee
How shall I part, and whither wander down
Into a lower World, to this obscure
And wild, how shall we breath in other Air
Less pure, accustomd to immortal Fruits?   285
    Whom thus the Angel interrupted mild.
Lament not *Eve,* but patiently resigne
What justly thou hast lost; nor set thy heart,
Thus over-fond, on that which is not thine;
Thy going is not lonely, with thee goes   290
Thy Husband, him to follow thou art bound;
Where he abides, think there thy native soil.
    Adam by this from the cold sudden damp
Recovering, and his scatterd spirits returnd,
To *Michael* thus his humble words address'd.   295
    Celestial, whether among the Thrones, or nam'd
Of them the Highest, for such of shape may seem
Prince above Princes, gently hast thou tould
Thy message, which might else in telling wound,
And in performing end us; what besides   300
Of sorrow and dejection and despair
Our frailtie can sustain, thy tidings bring,
Departure from this happy place, our sweet
Recess, and onely consolation left
Familiar to our eyes, all places else   305
Inhospitable appeer and desolate,
Nor knowing us nor known: and if by prayer
Incessant I could hope to change the will
Of him who all things can, I would not cease
To wearie him with my assiduous cries: 310
But prayer against his absolute Decree
No more avails then breath against the wind,
Blown stifling back on him that breaths it forth:
Therefore to his great bidding I submit.
This most afflicts me, that departing hence,   315
As from his face I shall be hid, depriv'd
His blessed count'nance; here I could frequent,
With worship, place by place where he voutsaf'd
Presence Divine, and to my Sons relate;
On this Mount he appeerd, under this Tree   320
Stood visible, among these Pines his voice
I heard, here with him at this Fountain talk'd:
So many grateful Altars I would rear

Of grassie Terf, and pile up every Stone
Of lustre from the brook, in memorie,   325
Or monument to Ages, and thereon
Offer sweet smelling Gumms and Fruits and Flowrs:
In yonder nether World where shall I seek
His bright appearances, or footstep trace?
For though I fled him angrie, yet recall'd   330
To life prolong'd and promis'd Race, I now
Gladly behold though but his utmost skirts
Of glory, and farr off his steps adore.
    To whom thus *Michael* with regard benigne.
Adam, thou know'st Heav'n his, and all the Earth,   335
Not this Rock onely; his Omnipresence fills
Land, Sea, and Air, and every kind that lives,
Fomented[22] by his virtual[23] power and warmd:
All th' Earth he gave thee to possess and rule,
No despicable gift; surmise not then   340
His presence to these narrow bounds confin'd
Of Paradise or *Eden:* this had been
Perhaps thy Capital Seat, from whence had spred
All generations, and had hither come
From all the ends of th' Earth, to celebrate   345
And reverence thee thir great Progenitor.
But this præeminence thou hast lost, brought down
To dwell on eeven ground now with thy Sons:
Yet doubt not but in Vallie and Plain
God is as here, and will be found alike   350
Present, and of his presence many a signe
Still following thee, still compassing thee round
With goodness and paternal Love, his Face
Express, and of his steps the track Divine.
Which that thou mayst beleeve, and be confirmd   355
Ere thou from hence depart, know I am sent
To shew thee what shall come in future dayes
To thee and to thy Ofspring; good with bad
Expect to hear, supernal Grace contending
With sinfulness of Men; thereby to learn   360
True patience, and to temper joy with fear
And pious sorrow, equally enur'd
By moderation either state to bear,
Prosperous or adverse: so shalt thou lead

[22] bathed (with warmth).
[23] efficacious.

Safest thy life, and best prepar'd endure   365
Thy mortal passage when it comes. Ascend
This Hill; let *Eve* (for I have drencht her eyes)
Here sleep below while thou to foresight wak'st,
As once thou slepst, while Shee to life was formd.
    To whom thus *Adam* gratefully repli'd.   370
Ascend, I follow thee, safe Guide, the path
Thou lead'st me, and to th' hand of Heav'n submit,
However chast'ning, to the evil turn
My obvious breast, arming to overcom
By suffering, and earn rest from labour won,   375
If so I may attain. So both ascend
In the Visions of God: It was a Hill
Of Paradise the highest, from whose top
The Hemisphere of Earth in cleerest Ken
Stretcht out to amplest reach of prospect lay.   380
Not higher that Hill nor wider looking round,
Whereon for different cause the Tempter set
Our second *Adam*[24] in the Wilderness,
To shew him all Earths Kingdoms and thir Glory.
His Eye might there command wherever stood   385
City of old or modern Fame, the Seat
Of mightiest Empire, from the destind Walls
Of *Cambalu*, seat of *Cathaian Can*[25]
And *Samarchand* by *Oxus, Temirs* Throne,[26]
To *Paquin* of *Sinæan* Kings,[27] and thence   390
To *Agra* and *Lahor* of great *Mogul*
Down to the golden *Chersonese*,[28] or where
The *Persian* in *Ecbatan* sate, or since
In *Hispahan*, or where the *Russian Ksar*
In *Mosco*, or the Sultan in *Bizance*,   395
Turchestan-born; nor could his eye not ken
Th' Empire of *Negus* to his utmost Port

[24] Christ.
[25] the Khan of China (Mongolia).
[26] the Mongolian conqueror Tamerlane's throne on the river
Oxus.
[27] Peking of Chinese Kings.
[28] the Malay peninsula. The following geographic references include Persian cities (Ecbatan, Hispahan), Turkish Byzantium
(Bizance), Abyssinia (the empire of the negus or king), coastal
towns in eastern Africa (Ercoco, Mombaza, Quiloa, Melind, Sofala), and areas of northwestern Africa (ll. 403–4). For rich
Ophir, see 1 Kings ix. 28; Sofala trafficked in gold.

Ercoco and the less Maritime Kings
Mombaza, and *Quiloa,* and *Melind,*
And *Sofala* thought *Ophir,* to the Realm   400
Of *Congo,* and *Angola* fardest South;
Or thence from *Niger* Flood to *Atlas* Mount
The Kingdoms of *Almansor, Fez* and *Sus,*
Marocco and *Algiers,* and *Tremisen;*
On *Europe* thence, and where *Rome* was to sway   405
The World: in Spirit perhaps he also saw
Rich *Mexico* the seat of *Motezume,*
And *Cusco* in *Peru,* the richer seat
Of *Atabalipa,*[29] and yet unspoil'd
Guiana, whose great Citie *Geryons* Sons[30]   410
Call *El Dorado:* but to nobler sights
Michael from *Adams* eyes the Film remov'd
Which that false Fruit that promis'd clearer sight
Had bred; then purg'd with Euphrasie and Rue[31]
The visual Nerve, for he had much to see;   415
And from the Well of Life three drops instill'd.
So deep the power of these Ingredients pierc'd,
Eevn to the inmost seat of mental sight,
That *Adam* now enforc't to close his eyes,
Sunk down and all his Spirits became intranst: 420
But him the gentle Angel by the hand
Soon rais'd, and his attention thus recall'd.
     Adam, now ope thine eyes, and first behold
Th' effects which thy original crime hath wrought
In some to spring from thee, who never touch'd   425
Th' excepted Tree, nor with the Snake conspir'd,
Nor sinn'd thy sin, yet from that sin derive
Corruption to bring forth more violent deeds.
     His eyes he op'n'd, and beheld a field,
Part arable and tilth, whereon were Sheaves   430
New reapt, the other part sheep-walks and foulds;
Ith' midst an Altar as the Land-mark stood
Rustic, of grassie sord;[32] thither anon
A sweatie Reaper[33] from his Tillage brought
First Fruits, the green Ear, and the yellow Sheaf,   435

[29] Atahualpa, the Inca king conquered by Pizarro.
[30] the Spaniards. El Dorado (the Gilded One) was a legendary king of South America, but here, a city of fabulous richness.
[31] herbs beneficial to eyesight.
[32] sward, turf.
[33] Cain, who envied his meek brother Abel (l. 436).

Uncull'd,[34] as came to hand; a Shepherd next
More meek came with the Firstlings of his Flock
Choicest and best; then sacrificing, laid
The Inwards and thir Fat, with Incense strew'd,
On the cleft Wood, and all due Rites perform'd.   440
His Offring soon propitious Fire from Heav'n
Consum'd with nimble glance, and grateful steam;
The others not, for his was not sincere;
Whereat hee inlie rag'd, and as they talk'd,
Smote him into the Midriff with a stone   445
That beat out life; he fell, and deadly pale
Groand out his Soul with gushing bloud effus'd.
Much at that sight was *Adam* in his heart
Dismai'd, and thus in haste to th' Angel cri'd.
      O Teacher, some great mischief hath befall'n   450
To that meek man, who well had sacrific'd;
Is Pietie thus and pure Devotion paid?
      T' whom *Michael* thus, hee also mov'd, repli'd.
These two are Brethren, *Adam*, and to come
Out of thy loyns; th' unjust the just hath slain,   455
For envie that his Brothers Offering found
From Heav'n acceptance; but the bloodie Fact
Will be aveng'd, and th' others Faith approv'd
Loose no reward, though here thou see him die,
Rowling in dust and gore. To which our Sire.   460
      Alas, both for the deed and for the cause!
But have I now seen Death? Is this the way
I must return to native dust? O sight
Of terrour, foul and ugly to behold,
Horrid to think, how horrible to feel!   465
      To whom thus *Michael*. Death thou hast seen
In his first shape on man; but many shapes
Of Death, and many are the wayes that lead
To his grim Cave, all dismal; yet to sense
More terrible at th' entrance then within.   470
Some, as thou saw'st, by violent stroke shall die,
By Fire, Flood, Famin, by Intemperance more
In Meats and Drinks, which on the Earth shall bring
Diseases dire, of which a monstrous crew
Before thee shall appear; that thou mayst know   475
What miserie th' inabstinence of *Eve*
Shall bring on men. Immediately a place

[34] unselected (to choose only the best).

Before his eyes appeard, sad, noysom, dark,
A Lazar-house it seemd, wherein were laid
Numbers of all diseas'd, all maladies   480
Of gastly Spasm, or racking torture, qualmes
Of heart-sick Agonie, all feavourous kinds,
Convulsions, Epilepsies, fierce Catarrhs,
Intestin Stone and Ulcer, Colic pangs,
Dæmoniac Phrenzie, moaping Melancholie   485
And Moon-struck madness, pining Atrophie,
Marasmus,[35] and wide-wasting Pestilence,
Dropsies, and Asthmas, and Joint-racking Rheums.
Dire was the tossing, deep the groans, despair
Tended the sick busiest from Couch to Couch;   490
And over them triumphant Death his Dart
Shook, but delaid to strike, though oft invok't
With vows, as thir chief good, and final hope.
Sight so deform what heart of Rock could long
Drie-ey'd behold? *Adam* could not, but wept,   495
Though not of Woman born; compassion quell'd
His best of Man, and gave him up to tears
A space, till firmer thoughts restraind excess,
And scarce recovering words his plaint renew'd.

    O miserable Mankind, to what fall   500
Degraded, to what wretched state reserv'd!
Better end heer unborn. Why is life giv'n
To be thus wrested from us? rather why
Obtruded on us thus? who if we knew
What we receive, would either not accept   505
Life offer'd, or soon beg to lay it down,
Glad to be so dismist in peace. Can thus
Th' Image of God in man created once
So goodly and erect, though faultie since,
To such unsightly sufferings be debas't   510
Under inhuman pains? Why should not Man,
Retaining still Divine similitude
In part, from such deformities be free,
And for his Makers Image sake exempt?

    Thir Makers Image, answerd *Michael*, then   515
Forsook them, when themselves they villifi'd
To serve ungovern'd appetite, and took
His Image[36] whom they serv'd, a brutish vice,

---

[35] consumption.

[36] Appetite (the image of Satan as Covetousness, Lust, and Gluttony); compare Phil. iii. 19: "whose God is their belly."

Inductive mainly to the sin of *Eve*.
Therefore so abject is thir punishment,   520
Disfiguring not Gods likeness, but thir own,
Or if his likeness, by themselves defac't
While they pervert pure Natures healthful rules
To loathsom sickness, worthily, since they
Gods Image did not reverence in themselves.   525
      I yeild it just, said *Adam*, and submit.
But is there yet no other way, besides
These painful passages, how we may come
To Death, and mix with our connatural dust?
      There is, said *Michael*, if thou well observe   530
The rule of not too much, by temperance taught
In what thou eatst and drinkst, seeking from thence
Due nourishment, not gluttonous delight,
Till many years over thy head return:
So maist thou live, till like ripe Fruit thou drop   535
Into thy Mothers lap, or be with ease
Gatherd, not harshly pluckt, for death mature:
This is old age; but then thou must outlive
Thy youth, thy strength, thy beauty, which will change
To witherd weak and gray; thy Senses then   540
Obtuse, all taste of pleasure must forgoe,
To what thou hast, and for the Air of youth
Hopeful and cheerful, in thy blood will reigne
A melancholly damp of cold and dry[37]
To waigh thy spirits down, and last consume   545
The Balm of Life. To whom our Ancestor.
      Henceforth I flie not Death, nor would prolong
Life much, bent rather how I may be quit
Fairest and easiest of this combrous charge,
Which I must keep till my appointed day   550
Of rendring up, and patiently attend
My dissolution. *Michael* repli'd,
      Nor love thy Life, nor hate; but what thou liv'st
Live well, how long or short permit to Heav'n:
And now prepare thee for another sight.   555
      He look'd and saw a spacious Plain,[38] whereon
Were Tents of various hue; by some were herds
Of Cattel grazing: others, whence the sound
Of Instruments that made melodious chime

[37] See Book II, n. 23.
[38] See Gen. iv. 16 ff. for Cain's descendants.

Was heard, of Harp and Organ; and who moov'd   560
Thir stops and chords was seen: his volant touch
Instinct[39] through all proportions low and high
Fled and pursu'd transverse the resonant fugue.
In other part stood one who at the Forge
Labouring, two massie clods of Iron and Brass   565
Had melted (whether found where casual fire
Had wasted woods on Mountain or in Vale,
Down to the veins of Earth, thence gliding hot
To som Caves mouth, or whether washt by stream
From underground) the liquid Ore he dreind   570
Into fit moulds prepar'd; from which he formd
First his own Tools; then, what might else be wrought
Fusil[40] or grav'n in mettle. After these,
But on the hether side a different sort[41]
From the high neighbouring Hills, which was thir Seat,   575
Down to the Plain descended: by thir guise
Just men they seemd, and all thir study bent
To worship God aright, and know his works
Not hid, nor those things last which might preserve
Freedom and Peace to men: they on the Plain   580
Long had not walkt, when from the Tents behold
A Beavie of fair Women, richly gay
In Gems and wanton dress; to th' Harp they sung
Soft amorous Ditties, and in dance came on:
The Men though grave, ey'd them, and let thir eyes   585
Rove without rein, till in the amorous Net
Fast caught, they lik'd, and each his liking chose;
And now of love they treat till th' Eevning Star[42]
Loves Harbinger appeerd; then all in heat
They light the Nuptial Torch, and bid invoke   590
Hymen, then first to marriage Rites invok't;
With Feast and Musick all the Tents resound.
Such happy interview and fair event
Of love and youth not lost, Songs, Garlands, Flowrs,
And charming Symphonies attach'd the heart   595
Of *Adam,* soon enclin'd t' admit delight,
The bent of Nature; which he thus express'd.
   True opener of mine eyes, prime Angel blest,

[39] imbued (by the music of the spheres).
[40] fused or cast.
[41] See Gen. vi. 1–4 for Seth's descendants ("sons of God,"
l. 622).
[42] Venus.

Much better seems this Vision, and more hope
Of peaceful dayes portends, then those two past;   600
Those were of hate and death, or pain much worse,
Here Nature seems fulfill'd in all her ends.
    To whom thus *Michael.* Judge not what is best
By pleasure, though to Nature seeming meet,
Created, as thou art, to nobler end   605
Holie and pure, conformitie divine.
Those Tents thou sawst so pleasant, were the Tents
Of wickedness, wherein shall dwell his Race
Who slew his Brother; studious they appear
Of Arts that polish Life, Inventers rare,   610
Unmindful of thir Maker, though his Spirit
Taught them, but they his gifts acknowledg'd none.
Yet they a beauteous ofspring shall beget;
For that fair femal Troop thou sawst, that seemd
Of Goddesses, so blithe, so smooth, so gay,   615
Yet empty of all good wherein consists
Womans domestic honour and chief praise;
Bred onely and completed to the taste
Of lustful appetence, to sing, to dance,
To dress, and troul[43] the Tongue, and roul the Eye.   620
To these that sober Race of Men, whose lives
Religious titl'd them the Sons of God,
Shall yeild up all thir vertue, all thir fame
Ignobly, to the trains[44] and to the smiles
Of these fair Atheists, and now swim in joy,   625
(Erelong to swim at large) and laugh; for which
The world erelong a world of tears must weep.
    To whom thus *Adam* of short joy bereft.
O pittie and shame, that they who to live well
Enterd so fair, should turn aside to tread   630
Paths indirect, or in the mid way faint!
But still I see the tenor of Mans woe
Holds on the same, from Woman to begin.
    From Mans effeminate slackness it begins,
Said th' Angel, who should better hold his place   635
By wisdom, and superiour gifts receav'd.
But now prepare thee for another Scene.
    He look'd and saw wide Territorie spred

[43] wag.
[44] tricks.

Before him,[45] Towns, and rural works between,
Cities of Men with lofty Gates and Towrs,   640
Concours in Arms, fierce Faces threatning Warr,
Giants of mightie Bone, and bould emprise;
Part wield thir Arms, part courb the foaming Steed,
Single or in Array of Battel rang'd
Both Horse and Foot, nor idlely mustring stood;   645
One way a Band select from forage drives
A herd of Beeves, fair Oxen and fair Kine
From a fat Meddow ground; or fleecy Flock,
Ewes and thir bleating Lambs over the Plain,
Thir Bootie; scarce with Life the Shepherds flye,   650
But call in aid, which tacks[46] a bloody Fray;
With cruel Tournament the Squadrons join;
Where Cattel pastur'd late, now scattered lies
With Carcasses and Arms th' ensanguind Field
Deserted: Others to a Citie strong   655
Lay Seige, encampt; by Batterie, Scale, and Mine,
Assaulting; others from the wall defend
With Dart and Jav'lin, Stones and sulfurous Fire;
On each hand slaughter and gigantic deeds.
In other part the scepter'd Haralds call   660
To Council in the Citie Gates: anon
Grey-headed men and grave, with Warriours mixt,
Assemble, and Harangues are heard, but soon
In factious opposition, till at last
Of middle Age one[47] rising, eminent   665
In wise deport, spake much of Right and Wrong,
Of Justice, of Religion, Truth and Peace,
And Judgement from above: him old and young
Exploded[48] and had seiz'd with violent hands,
Had not a Cloud descending snatch'd him thence   670
Unseen amid the throng: so violence
Proceeded, and Oppression, and Sword-Law
Through all the Plain, and refuge none was found.
Adam was all in tears, and to his guide
Lamenting turnd full sad; O what are these,   675
Deaths Ministers, not Men, who thus deal Death
Inhumanly to men, and multiply

[45] What he sees owes much to the description of Achilles' shield
in *Iliad*, XVIII, 478 ff.
[46] rapidly diverges into.
[47] Enoch.
[48] assailed with contempt.

Ten thousandfould the sin of him who slew
His Brother; for of whom such massacher
Make they but of thir Brethren, men of men?   680
But who was that Just Man, whom had not Heav'n
Rescu'd, had in his Righteousness bin lost?
    To whom thus *Michael*. These are the product
Of those ill-mated Marriages thou saw'st:
Where good with bad were matcht, who of themselves 685
Abhor to joyn; and by imprudence mixt,
Produce prodigious Births of bodie or mind.
Such were these Giants, men of high renown;[49]
For in those dayes Might onely shall be admir'd,
And Valour and Heroic Vertu call'd;   690
To overcome in Battel, and subdue
Nations, and bring home spoils with infinite
Man-slaughter, shall be held the highest pitch
Of human Glorie, and for Glorie done
Of triumph, to be styl'd great Conquerours,   695
Patrons of Mankind, Gods, and Sons of Gods,
Destroyers rightlier call'd and Plagues of men.
Thus Fame shall be atchiev'd, renown on Earth,
And what most merits fame in silence hid.
But hee the seventh from thee,[50] whom thou beheldst 700
The onely righteous in a World perverse,
And therefore hated, therefore so beset
With Foes for daring single to be just,
And utter odious Truth, that God would come
To judge them with his Saints: Him the most High   705
Rapt in a balmie Cloud with winged Steeds
Did, as thou sawst, receave, to walk with God
High in Salvation and the Climes of bliss,
Exempt from Death; to shew thee what reward
Awaits the good, the rest what punishment;   710
Which now direct thine eyes and soon behold.
    He look'd, and saw the face of things quite chang'd;
The brazen Throat of Warr had ceast to roar,
All now was turn'd to jollitie and game,
To luxurie and riot, feast and dance,   715
Marrying or prostituting, as befell,

[49] As John M. Steadman has pointed out (*PQ*, XL, 1961, 580–86), Milton's characterization of giants and the terminology of heroic virtue derives from the giants of Genesis; "might" is equated with "heroism."
[50] Enoch.

Rape or Adulterie, where passing fair
Allurd them; thence from Cups to civil Broils.
At length a Reverend Sire[51] among them came,
And of thir doings great dislike declar'd,   720
And testifi'd against thir wayes; hee oft
Frequented thir Assemblies, whereso met,
Triumphs[52] or Festivals, and to them preach'd
Conversion and Repentance, as to Souls
In Prison under Judgements imminent: 725
But all in vain: which when he saw, he ceas'd
Contending, and remov'd his Tents farr off;
Then from the Mountain hewing Timber tall,
Began to build a Vessel of huge bulk,
Measur'd by Cubit, length, and breadth, and highth,   730
Smeard round with Pitch, and in the side a dore
Contriv'd, and of provisions laid in large
For Man and Beast: when loe a wonder strange!
Of every Beast, and Bird, and Insect small
Came seavens, and pairs,[53] and enterd in, as taught   735
Thir order; last the Sire, and his three Sons
With thir four Wives; and God made fast the dore.
Meanwhile the Southwind rose, and with black wings
Wide hovering, all the Clouds together drove
From under Heav'n; the Hills to their supplie   740
Vapour, and Exhalation dusk and moist,
Sent up amain; and now the thick'n'd Skie
Like a dark Ceeling stood; down rush'd the Rain
Impetuous, and continu'd till the Earth
No more was seen; the floating Vessel swum   745
Uplifted; and secure with beaked prow
Rode tilting o're the Waves, all dwellings else
Flood overwhelmd, and them with all thir pomp
Deep under water rould; Sea cover'd Sea,
Sea without shoar; and in thir Palaces   750
Where luxurie late reign'd, Sea-monsters whelp'd
And stabl'd; of Mankind, so numerous late,
All left, in one small bottom swum imbark't.
How didst thou grieve then, *Adam,* to behold

[51] Noah.
[52] processions.
[53] Gen. vii. 2: "Of every clean beast thou shalt take to thee by
sevens, the male and his female: and of beasts that are not clean
by two, the male and his female."

The end of all thy Ofspring, end so sad,   755
Depopulation; thee another Floud,
Of tears and sorrow a Floud thee also drown'd,
And sunk thee as thy Sons; till gently reard
By th' Angel, on thy feet thou stoodst at last,
Though comfortless, as when a Father mourns   760
His Childern, all in view destroyd at once;
And scarce to th' Angel utterdst thus thy plaint.
    O Visions ill foreseen! better had I
Liv'd ignorant of future, so had borne
My part of evil onely, each dayes lot   765
Anough to bear; those now, that were dispenst⁵⁴
The burd'n of many Ages, on me light
At once, by my foreknowledge gaining Birth
Abortive, to torment me ere thir being,
With thought that they must be. Let no man seek   770
Henceforth to be foretold what shall befall
Him or his Childern, evil he may be sure,
Which neither his foreknowing can prevent,
And hee the future evil shall no less
In apprehension then in substance feel   775
Grievous to bear: but that care now is past,
Man is not whom to warn: those few escap't
Famin and anguish will at last consume
Wandring that watrie Desert: I had hope
When violence was ceas't, and Warr on Earth,   780
All would have then gon well, peace would have crownd
With length of happy dayes the race of man;
But I was farr deceav'd; for now I see
Peace to corrupt no less then Warr to waste.
How comes it thus? unfould, Celestial Guide,   785
And whether here the Race of man will end.
    To whom thus *Michael.* Those whom last thou sawst
In triumph and luxurious wealth, are they
First seen in acts of prowess eminent
And great exploits, but of true vertu void;   790
Who having spilt much blood, and don much waste
Subduing Nations, and achiev'd thereby
Fame in the World, high titles, and rich prey,
Shall change thir course to pleasure, ease, and sloth,
Surfet, and lust, till wantonness and pride   795
Raise out of friendship hostil deeds in Peace.

⁵⁴ given.

The conquerd also, and enslav'd by Warr
Shall with thir freedom lost all vertu loose
And fear of God, from whom thir pietie feign'd
In sharp contest of Battel found no aid 800
Against invaders; therefore coold in zeal
Thenceforth shall practice how to live secure,
Worldlie or dissolute, on what thir Lords
Shall leave them to enjoy; for th' Earth shall bear
More then anough, that temperance may be tri'd: 805
So all shall turn degenerate, all deprav'd,
Justice and Temperance, Truth and Faith forgot;
One Man except, the onely Son of light
In a dark Age, against example good,
Against allurement, custom, and a World 810
Offended; fearless of reproach and scorn,
Or violence, hee of thir wicked wayes
Shall them admonish, and before them set
The paths of righteousness, how much more safe,
And full of peace, denouncing wrauth to come 815
On thir impenitence; and shall return
Of them derided, but of God observ'd
The one just Man alive; by his command
Shall build a wondrous Ark, as thou beheldst,
To save himself and houshold from amidst 820
A World devote to universal rack.
No sooner hee with them of Man and Beast
Select for life shall in the Ark be lodg'd,
And shelterd round, but all the Cataracts
Of Heav'n set open on the Earth shall powr 825
Rain day and night, all fountains of the Deep
Broke up, shall heave the Ocean to usurp
Beyond all bounds, till inundation rise
Above the highest Hills: then shall this Mount
Of Paradise by might of Waves be moov'd 830
Out of his place, pushd by the horned⁵⁵ floud,
With all his verdure spoil'd, and Trees adrift
Down the great River⁵⁶ to the op'ning Gulf,
And there take root an Iland salt and bare,
The haunt of Seals and Orcs,⁵⁷ and Sea-mews clang. 835
To teach thee that God attributes to place

⁵⁵ divided into branches.
⁵⁶ the Euphrates, which flows into the Persian Gulf.
⁵⁷ whales; "mews" are the stables of the sea monsters.

No sanctitie, if none be thither brought
By Men who there frequent, or therein dwell.
And now what further shall ensue, behold.
He look'd, and saw the Ark hull[58] on the floud,   840
Which now abated, for the Clouds were fled,
Drivn by a keen North-wind, that blowing drie
Wrinkl'd the face of Deluge, as decai'd;
And the cleer Sun on his wide watrie Glass
Gaz'd hot, and of the fresh Wave largely drew,   845
As after thirst, which made thir flowing shrink
From standing lake to tripping ebb, that stole
With soft foot towards the deep, who now had stopt
His Sluces, as the Heav'n his windows shut.
The Ark no more now flotes, but seems on ground   850
Fast on the top of som high mountain fixt.
And now the tops of Hills as Rocks appeer;
With clamor thence the rapid Currents drive
Towards the retreating Sea thir furious tyde.
Forthwith from out the Ark a Raven flies,   855
And after him, the surer messenger,
A Dove sent forth once and agen to spie
Green Tree or ground whereon his foot may light;
The second time returning, in his Bill
An Olive leaf he brings, pacific signe: 860
Anon drie ground appeers, and from his Ark
The ancient Sire descends with all his Train;
Then with uplifted hands, and eyes devout,
Grateful to Heav'n, over his head beholds
A dewie Cloud, and in the Cloud a Bow   865
Conspicuous with three listed[59] colours gay,
Betok'ning peace from God, and Cov'nant new.
Whereat the heart of *Adam* erst so sad
Greatly rejoyc'd, and thus his joy broke forth.
O thou who future things canst represent   870
As present, Heav'nly instructer, I revive
At this last sight, assur'd that Man shall live
With all the Creatures, and thir seed preserve.
Farr less I now lament for one whole World
Of wicked Sons destroyd, then I rejoyce   875
For one Man found so perfet and so just,
That God voutsafes to raise another World

[58] a verb, "loom up" and "float."
[59] striped.

From him, and all his anger to forget.
But say, what mean those colourd streaks in Heavn,
Distended as the Brow of God appeas'd,   880
Or serve they as a flowrie verge to bind
The fluid skirts of that same watrie Cloud,
Least it again dissolve and showr the Earth?
    To whom th' Archangel. Dextrously thou aim'st;
So willingly doth God remit his Ire,   885
Though late repenting him of Man deprav'd,
Griev'd at his heart, when looking down he saw
The whole Earth fill'd with violence, and all flesh
Corrupting each thir way; yet those remoov'd,
Such grace shall one just Man find in his sight,   890
That he relents, not to blot out mankind,
And makes a Covenant never to destroy
The Earth again by flood, nor let the Sea
Surpass his bounds, nor Rain to drown the World
With Man therein or Beast; but when he brings   895
Over the Earth a Cloud, will therein set
His triple-colour'd Bow, whereon to look
And call to mind his Cov'nant: Day and Night,
Seed time and Harvest, Heat and hoary Frost
Shall hold thir course, till fire purge all things new, 900
Both Heav'n and Earth, wherein the just shall dwell.

BOOK XII

THE ARGUMENT

The Angel *Michael* continues from the Flood to relate what
shall succeed; then, in the mention of *Abraham*, comes by
degrees to explain, who that Seed of the Woman shall be,
which was promised *Adam* and *Eve* in the Fall; his Incarnation, Death, Resurrection, and Ascention; the state of the
Church till his second Coming. *Adam* greatly satisfied and recomforted by these Relations and Promises descends the Hill
with *Michael;* wakens *Eve,* who all this while had slept, but
with gentle dreams compos'd to quietness of mind and submission. *Michael* in either hand leads them out of Paradise,
the fiery Sword waving behind them, and the Cherubim taking thir Stations to guard the Place.

    As one who in his journey bates[1] at Noon,
Though bent on speed, so heer th' Archangel paus'd

---

[1] pauses (to eat).

Betwixt the world destroy'd and world restor'd,
If *Adam* aught perhaps might interpose;
Then with transition sweet new Speech resumes.   5
    Thus thou hast seen one World begin and end;
And Man as from a second stock proceed.
Much thou hast yet to see, but I perceave
Thy mortal sight to fail; objects divine
Must needs impair and wearie human sense: 10
Henceforth what is to com I will relate,
Thou therefore give due audience, and attend.
This second sours of Men, while yet but few;
And while the dread of judgement past remains
Fresh in thir minds, fearing the Deitie,   15
With some regard to what is just and right
Shall lead thir lives, and multiplie apace,
Labouring the soil, and reaping plenteous crop,
Corn wine and oyl; and from the herd or flock,
Oft sacrificing Bullock, Lamb, or Kid,   20
With large Wine-offerings pour'd, and sacred Feast,
Shall spend thir dayes in joy unblam'd, and dwell
Long time in peace by Families and Tribes
Under paternal rule; till one[2] shall rise
Of proud ambitious heart, who not content   25
With fair equalitie, fraternal state,
Will arrogate Dominion undeserv'd
Over his brethren, and quite dispossess
Concord and law of Nature from the Earth,
Hunting (and Men not Beasts shall be his game)   30
With Warr and hostile snare such as refuse
Subjection to his Empire tyrannous:
A mightie Hunter thence he shall be styl'd
Before the Lord, as in despite of Heav'n,
Or from Heav'n claming second Sovrantie;   35
And from Rebellion shall derive his name,
Though of Rebellion others he accuse.
Hee with a crew, whom like Ambition joyns
With him or under him to tyrannize,
Marching from *Eden* towards the West, shall find   40
The Plain,[3] wherein a black bituminous gurge

[2] Nimrod ("rebel," l. 36), the mighty hunter (l. 33) who is fabled as the founder of Babylon (Babel).
[3] Shinar; a "gurge" is a whirlpool.

Boils out from under ground, the mouth of Hell;
Of Brick, and of that stuff they cast to build
A Citie and Towr, whose top may reach to Heav'n;
And get themselves a name, least far disperst   45
In foraign Lands thir memorie be lost,
Regardless whether good or evil fame.
But God who oft descends to visit men
Unseen, and through thir habitations walks
To mark thir doings, them beholding soon,   50
Comes down to see thir Citie, ere the Tower
Obstruct Heav'n Towrs, and in derision sets
Upon thir Tongues a various⁴ Spirit to rase
Quite out thir Native Language, and instead
To sow a jangling noise of words unknown: 55
Forthwith a hideous gabble rises loud
Among the Builders; each to other calls
Not understood, till hoarse, and all in rage,
As mockt they storm; great laughter was in Heav'n
And looking down, to see the hubbub strange   60
And hear the din; thus was the building left
Ridiculous, and the work Confusion nam'd.⁵
   Whereto thus *Adam* fatherly displeas'd.
O execrable Son so to aspire
Above his Brethren, to himself assuming   65
Authoritie usurpt, from God not giv'n:
He gave us onely over Beast, Fish, Fowl
Dominion absolute; that right we hold
By his donation; but Man over men
He made not Lord; such title to himself   70
Reserving, human left from human free.
But this Usurper his encroachment proud
Stayes not on Man; to God his Tower intends
Siege and defiance: Wretched man! what food
Will he convey up thither to sustain   75
Himself and his rash Armie, where thin Air
Above the Clouds will pine his entrails gross,
And famish him of Breath, if not of Bread?
   To whom thus *Michael.* Justly thou abhorr'st
That Son, who on the quiet state of men   80
Such trouble brought, affecting to subdue
Rational Libertie; yet know withall,

⁴ quarrelsome, putting at variance.
⁵ that is, Babel.

Since thy original lapse, true Libertie
Is lost, which alwayes with right Reason dwells
Twinn'd, and from her hath no dividual being: 85
Reason in man obscur'd, or not obeyd,
Immediately inordinate desires
And upstart Passions catch the Government
From Reason, and to servitude reduce
Man till then free. Therefore since hee permits 90
Within himself unworthie Powers to reign
Over free Reason, God in Judgement just
Subjects him from without to violent Lords;
Who oft as undeservedly enthrall
His outward freedom: Tyrannie must be, 95
Though to the Tyrant thereby no excuse.
Yet somtimes Nations will decline so low
From vertue, which is reason, that no wrong,
But Justice, and some fatal curse annext
Deprives them of thir outward libertie, 100
Thir inward lost: Witness th' irreverent Son[6]
Of him who built the Ark, who for the shame
Don to his Father, heard this heavie curse,
Servant of Servants, on his vitious Race.
Thus will this latter, as the former World, 105
Still tend from bad to worse, till God at last
Wearied with their iniquities, withdraw
His presence from among them, and avert
His holy Eyes; resolving from thenceforth
To leave them to thir own polluted wayes; 110
And one peculiar Nation to select
From all the rest, of whom to be invok'd,
A Nation from one faithful man[7] to spring:
Him on this side *Euphrates* yet residing,
Bred up in Idol-worship; O that men 115
(Canst thou believe?) should be so stupid grown,
While yet the Patriark liv'd, who scap'd the Flood,
As to forsake the living God, and fall
To worship thir own work in Wood and Stone
For Gods! yet him God the most High voutsafes 120
To call by Vision from his Fathers house,
His kindred and false Gods, into a Land
Which he will shew him, and from him will raise

[6] Ham, father of Canaan.
[7] Abraham.

A mightie Nation, and upon him showr
His benediction so, that in his Seed   125
All Nations shall be blest; he straight obeys,
Not knowing to what Land, yet firm believes:
I see him, but thou canst not, with what Faith
He leaves his Gods, his Friends, and native Soil[8]
Ur of *Chaldæa,* passing now the Ford   130
To *Haran,* after him a cumbrous Train
Of Herds and Flocks, and numerous servitude;
Not wandring poor, but trusting all his wealth
With God, who call'd him, in a land unknown.
Canaan he now attains, I see his Tents   135
Pitcht about *Sechem,* and the neighbouring Plain
Of *Moreh;* there by promise he receaves
Gift to his Progenie of all that Land;
From *Hamath* Northward to the Desert South
(Things by thir names I call, though yet unnam'd)   140
From *Hermon* East to the great Western Sea,
Mount *Hermon,* yonder Sea, each place behold
In prospect, as I point them; on the shoar
Mount *Carmel;* here the double-founted stream
Jordan, true limit Eastward; but his Sons   145
Shall dwell to *Senir,* that long ridge of Hills.
This ponder, that all Nations of the Earth
Shall in his Seed be blessed; by that Seed
Is meant thy great deliverer, who shall bruise
The Serpents head; whereof to thee anon   150
Plainlier shall be reveald. This Patriarch blest,
Whom *faithful Abraham* due time shall call,
A Son,[9] and of his Son a Grand-child leaves,
Like him in faith, in wisdom, and renown;
The Grandchild with twelve Sons increast, departs   155
From *Canaan,* to a Land hereafter call'd
Egypt, divided by the River *Nile;*
See where it flows, disgorging at seaven mouths

[8] Ur was west and Haran east of the Euphrates. After travelling northwest, Abraham moves southwest into Canaan, then north to Hamath on the Orontes in Syria, to the west of which was the Great Desert. Mt. Hermon (and Senir in the same range) or more correctly (l. 145) the Jordan was considered the eastern boundary of Canaan, and the Mediterranean Sea bounded it on the west. Mt. Carmel was a promontory on the sea.

[9] Isaac, whose son was Jacob (later Israel, ll. 267–69), progenitor of the twelve tribes of Israel.

Into the Sea: to sojourn in that Land
He comes invited by a yonger Son   160
In time of dearth, a Son whose worthy deeds
Raise him to be the second in that Realm
Of *Pharao:* there he dies, and leaves his Race
Growing into a Nation, and now grown
Suspected to a sequent King, who seeks   165
To stop thir overgrowth, as inmate guests
Too numerous; whence of guests he makes them slaves
Inhospitably, and kills thir infant Males:
Till by two brethren (those two brethren call
Moses and *Aaron*) sent from God to claim   170
His people from enthralment, they return
With glory and spoil back to thir promis'd Land.
But first the lawless Tyrant, who denies
To know thir God, or message to regard,
Must be compell'd by Signes and Judgements dire;   175
To blood unshed the Rivers must be turnd,
Frogs, Lice and Flies must all his Palace fill
With loath'd intrusion, and fill all the land;
His Cattel must of Rot and Murren die,
Botches and blains must all his flesh imboss,[10]   180
And all his people; Thunder mixt with Hail,
Hail mixt with fire must rend th' *Egyptian* Skie
And wheel on th' Earth, devouring where it rouls;
What it devours not, Herb, or Fruit, or Grain,
A darksom Cloud of Locusts swarming down   185
Must eat, and on the ground leave nothing green:
Darkness must overshadow all his bounds,
Palpable darkness, and blot out three dayes;
Last with one midnight stroke all the first-born
Of *Egypt* must lie dead. Thus with ten wounds   190
The River-dragon[11] tam'd at length submits
To let his sojourners depart, and oft
Humbles his stubborn heart, but still as Ice
More hard'n'd after thaw, till in his rage
Pursuing whom he late dismiss'd, the Sea   195
Swallows him with his Host, but them lets pass
As on drie land between two christal walls,
Aw'd by the rod of *Moses* so to stand
Divided, till his rescu'd gain thir shoar:

[10] raise with swellings.
[11] Pharaoh; see Ezek. xxix. 3.

Such wondrous power God to his Saint will lend,   200
Though present in his Angel, who shall goe
Before them in a Cloud, and Pillar of Fire,
By day a Cloud, by night a Pillar of Fire,
To guide them in thir journey, and remove
Behind them, while th' obdurat King pursues: 205
All night he will pursue, but his approach
Darkness defends[12] between till morning Watch;
Then through the Firey Pillar and the Cloud
God looking forth will trouble all his Host
And craze[13] thir Chariot wheels: when by command   210
Moses once more his potent Rod extends
Over the Sea; the Sea his Rod obeys;
On thir imbattell'd ranks the Waves return,
And overwhelm thir Warr: the Race elect
Safe towards *Canaan* from the shoar advance   215
Through the wild Desert, not the readiest way,
Least entring on the *Canaanite* allarmd
Warr terrifie them inexpert, and fear
Return them back to *Egypt,* choosing rather
Inglorious life with servitude; for life   220
To noble and ignoble is more sweet
Untraind in Armes, where rashness leads not on.
This also shall they gain by thir delay
In the wide Wilderness, there they shall found
Thir government, and thir great Senate[14] choose   225
Through the twelve Tribes, to rule by Laws ordaind:
God from the Mount of *Sinai,* whose gray top
Shall tremble, he descending, will himself
In Thunder Lightning and loud Trumpets sound
Ordain them Laws; part such as appertain   230
To civil Justice, part religious Rites
Of sacrifice, informing them, by types
And shadows, of that destind Seed to bruise
The Serpent, by what means he shall achieve
Mankinds deliverance. But the voice of God   235
To mortal ear is dreadful; they beseech
That *Moses* might report to them his will,
And terror cease; he grants what they besaught
Instructed that to God is no access

[12] prohibits (by lying between the Egyptians and the Israelites).
[13] shatter.
[14] the council of seventy elders chosen by Moses (Exod. xxiv. 1–9).

Without Mediator, whose high Office now   240
Moses in figure[15] beares, to introduce
One greater, of whose day he shall foretell,
And all the Prophets in thir Age the times
Of great *Messiah* shall sing. Thus Laws and Rites
Establisht, such delight hath God in Men   245
Obedient to his will, that he voutsafes
Among them to set up his Tabernacle,
The holy One with mortal Men to dwell:
By his prescript a Sanctuary is fram'd
Of Cedar, overlaid with Gold, therein   250
An Ark, and in the Ark his Testimony,
The Records of his Cov'nant, over these
A Mercie-seat[16] of Gold between the wings
Of two bright Cherubim, before him burn
Seaven Lamps[17] as in a Zodiac representing   255
The Heav'nly fires; over the Tent a Cloud
Shall rest by Day, a fiery gleam by Night,
Save when they journie, and at length they come,
Conducted by his Angel to the Land
Promis'd to *Abraham* and his Seed: the rest   260
Were long to tell, how many Battels fought,
How many Kings destroyd, and Kingdoms won,
Or how the Sun shall in mid Heav'n stand still
A day entire, and Nights due course adjourn,
Mans voice commanding,[18] Sun in *Gibeon* stand,   265
And thou Moon in the vale of *Aialon*,
Till *Israel* overcome; so call the third
From *Abraham*, Son of *Isaac*, and from him
His whole descent, who thus shall *Canaan* win.
    Here *Adam* interpos'd. O sent from Heav'n,   270
Enlightner of my darkness, gracious things
Thou hast reveald, those chiefly which concern
Just *Abraham* and his Seed: now first I find
Mine eyes true op'ning, and my heart much eas'd,
Erwhile perplext with thoughts what would becom   275
Of mee and all Mankind; but now I see
His day, in whom all Nations shall be blest,
Favour unmerited by me, who sought

[15] as a type.
[16] See Book XI, n. 1.
[17] The candelabrum is likened to the seven planets shining throughout the universe.
[18] from Josh. x. 12.

Forbidd'n knowledge by forbidd'n means.
This yet I apprehend not, why to those   280
Among whom God will deigne to dwell on Earth
So many and so various Laws are giv'n;
So many Laws argue so many sins
Among them; how can God with such reside?
    To whom thus *Michael*. Doubt not but that sin   285
Will reign among them, as of thee begot;
And therefore was Law giv'n them to evince
Thir natural pravitie,[19] by stirring up
Sin against Law to fight; that when they see
Law can discover sin, but not remove,   290
Save by those shadowie[20] expiations weak,
The bloud of Bulls and Goats, they may conclude
Some bloud more precious must be paid for Man,
Just for unjust, that in such righteousness
To them by Faith imputed, they may find   295
Justification towards God, and peace
Of Conscience, which the Law by Ceremonies
Cannot appease, nor Man the moral part
Perform, and not performing cannot live.
So Law appears imperfet, and but giv'n   300
With purpose to resign them in full time
Up to a better Cov'nant, disciplin'd
From shadowie Types to Truth, from Flesh to Spirit,
From imposition of strict Laws, to free
Acceptance of large Grace, from servil fear   305
To filial, works of Law to works of Faith.
And therefore shall not *Moses*, though of God
Highly belov'd, being but the Minister
Of Law, his people into *Canaan* lead;
But *Joshua* whom the Gentiles *Jesus* call,[21]   310
His Name and Office bearing, who shall quell
The adversarie Serpent, and bring back
Through the worlds wilderness long wanderd man
Safe to eternal Paradise of rest.
Meanwhile they in thir earthly *Canaan* plac't   315
Long time shall dwell and prosper, but when sins
National interrupt thir public peace,
Provoking God to raise them enemies:

[19] depravity.
[20] The expiations are shadows (types) of Christ's expiation.
[21] Joshua is not only a type of Jesus; both words mean "savior."

From whom as oft he saves them penitent
By Judges first, then under Kings; of whom   320
The second,[22] both for pietie renownd
And puissant deeds, a promise shall receive
Irrevocable, that his Regal Throne
For ever shall endure; the like shall sing
All Prophecie, that of the Royal Stock   325
Of *David* (so I name this King) shall rise
A Son, the Womans Seed to thee foretold,
Foretold to *Abraham*, as in whom shall trust
All Nations, and to Kings foretold, of Kings
The last, for of his Reign shall be no end.   330
But first a long succession must ensue,
And his next Son[23] for Wealth and Wisdom fam'd,
The clouded Ark of God till then in Tents
Wandring, shall in a glorious Temple enshrine.
Such follow him, as shall be registerd   335
Part good, part bad, of bad the longer scrowl,
Whose foul Idolatries, and other faults
Heapt to the popular sum, will so incense
God, as to leave them, and expose thir Land,
Thir Citie, his Temple, and his holy Ark   340
With all his sacred things, a scorn and prey
To that proud Citie, whose high Walls thou saw'st
Left in confusion, *Babylon* thence call'd.
There in captivitie he lets them dwell
The space of seventie years, then brings them back, 345
Remembring mercie, and his Cov'nant sworn
To *David*, stablisht as the dayes of Heav'n
Returnd from *Babylon* by leave of Kings[24]
Thir Lords, whom God dispos'd, the house of God
They first re-edifie, and for a while   350
In mean estate live moderate, till grown
In wealth and multitude, factious they grow;
But first among the Priests dissension springs,
Men who attend the Altar, and should most
Endeavour Peace: thir strife pollution brings   355
Upon the Temple it self: at last they[25] seise

[22] David.
[23] Solomon.
[24] of Persia; that is, Cyrus, Cambyses, Darius, Xerxes, Artaxerxes.
[25] the Asmonean priest-princes, whose domination began with Jonathan in 153 B.C.

The Scepter, and regard not *Davids* Sons,
Then loose it to a stranger,[26] that the true
Anointed King *Messiah* might be born
Barr'd of his right; yet at his Birth a Starr   360
Unseen before in Heav'n proclaims him com,
And guides the Eastern Sages, who enquire
His place, to offer Incense, Myrrh, and Gold;
His place of birth a solemn Angel tells
To simple Shepherds, keeping watch by night;   365
They gladly thither[27] haste, and by a Quire
Of squadrond Angels hear his Carol sung.
A Virgin is his Mother, but his Sire
The Power of the most High; he shall ascend
The Throne hereditarie, and bound his Reign   370
With earths wide bounds, his glory with the Heav'ns.
    He ceas'd, discerning *Adam* with such joy
Surcharg'd, as had like grief bin dew'd in tears,
Without the vent of words, which these he breath'd.
    O Prophet of glad tidings, finisher   375
Of utmost hope! now clear I understand
What oft my steddiest thoughts have searcht in vain,
Why our great expectation should be call'd
The seed of Woman: Virgin Mother, Hail,
High in the love of Heav'n, yet from my Loyns   380
Thou shalt proceed, and from thy Womb the Son
Of God most High; so God with man unites.
Needs must the Serpent now his capital[28] bruise
Expect with mortal pain: say where and when
Thir fight, what stroke shall bruise the Victors heel.   385
    To whom thus *Michael.* Dream not of thir fight,
As of a Duel, or the local wounds
Of head or heel: not therefore joyns the Son
Manhood to God-head, with more strength to foil
Thy enemie; nor so is overcome   390
Satan, whose fall from Heav'n, a deadlier bruise,
Disabl'd not to give thee thy deaths wound:
Which hee, who comes thy Saviour, shall recure,
Not by destroying *Satan,* but his works
In thee and in thy Seed: nor can this be,   395
But by fulfilling that which thou didst want,

---

[26] Antipater, whose son Herod was ruling when Jesus was born.
[27] to Bethlehem.
[28] both "of the head" as prophesied and "fatal."

Obedience to the Law of God, impos'd
On penaltie of death, and suffering death,
The penaltie to thy transgression due,
And due to theirs which out of thine will grow: 400
So onely can high Justice rest appaid.[29]
The Law of God exact he shall fulfill
Both by obedience and by love, though love
Alone fulfill the Law; thy punishment
He shall endure by coming in the Flesh   405
To a reproachful life and cursed death,
Proclaiming Life to all who shall believe
In his redemption, and that his obedience
Imputed becomes theirs by Faith, his merits
To save them, not thir own, though legal works.   410
For this he shall live hated, be blasphem'd,
Seis'd on by force, judg'd, and to death condemnd
A shameful and accurst, naild to the Cross
By his own Nation, slain for bringing Life;
But to the Cross he nails thy Enemies,   415
The Law that is against thee, and the sins
Of all mankind, with him there crucifi'd,
Never to hurt them more who rightly trust
In this his satisfaction; so he dies,
But soon revives, Death over him no power   420
Shall long usurp; ere the third dawning light
Return, the Starrs of Morn shall see him rise
Out of his grave, fresh as the dawning light,
Thy ransom paid, which Man from death redeems,
His death for Man, as many as offerd Life   425
Neglect not, and the benefit imbrace
By Faith not void of works: this God-like act
Annuls thy doom, the death thou shouldst have dy'd,
In sin for ever lost from life; this act
Shall bruise the head of *Satan*, crush his strength   430
Defeating Sin and Death, his two main armes,
And fix farr deeper in his head thir stings
Then temporal death shall bruise the Victors heel,
Or theirs whom he redeems, a death like sleep,
A gentle wafting to immortal Life.   435
Nor after resurrection shall he stay
Longer on Earth then certain times to appeer
To his Disciples, Men who in his Life

[29] satisfied.

Still follow'd him; to them shall leave in charge
To teach all nations what of him they learn'd   440
And his Salvation, them who shall beleeve
Baptizing in the profluent[30] stream, the signe
Of washing them from guilt of sin to Life
Pure, and in mind prepar'd, if so befall,
For death, like that which the redeemer dy'd.   445
All Nations they shall teach; for from that day
Not onely to the Sons of *Abrahams* Loins
Salvation shall be Preacht, but to the Sons
Of *Abrahams* Faith wherever through the world;
So in his seed all Nations shall be blest.   450
Then to the Heav'n of Heav'ns he shall ascend
With victory, triumphing through the air
Over his foes and thine; there shall surprise
The Serpent, Prince of air, and drag in Chains
Through all his Realm, and there confounded leave;   455
Then enter into glory, and resume
His Seat at Gods right hand, exalted high
Above all names in Heav'n; and thence shall come,
When this worlds dissolution shall be ripe,
With glory and power to judge both quick[31] and dead,   460
To judge th' unfaithful dead, but to reward
His faithful, and receave them into bliss,
Whether in Heav'n or Earth, for then the Earth
Shall all be Paradise, far happier place
Then this of *Eden*, and far happier daies.   465
    So spake th' Archangel *Michael*, then paus'd,
As at the Worlds great period; and our Sire
Replete with joy and wonder thus repli'd.
    O goodness infinite, goodness immense!
That all this good of evil shall produce,   470
And evil turn to good; more wonderful
Then that which by creation first brought forth
Light out of darkness! full of doubt I stand,
Whether I should repent me now of sin
By mee done and occasiond, or rejoyce   475
Much more, that much more good thereof shall spring,
To God more glory, more good will to Men
From God, and over wrauth grace shall abound.
But say, if our deliverer up to Heav'n

   [30] smoothly flowing.
   [31] living.

Must reascend, what will betide the few   480
His faithful, left among th' unfaithful herd,
The enemies of truth; who then shall guide
His people, who defend? will they not deal
Wors with his followers then with him they dealt?
    Be sure they will, said th' Angel; but from Heav'n   485
Hee to his own a Comforter will send,
The promise of the Father, who shall dwell
His Spirit within them, and the Law of Faith
Working through love, upon thir hearts shall write,
To guide them in all truth, and also arm   490
With spiritual Armour, able to resist
Satans assaults, and quench his fierie darts,
What man can do against them, not affraid,
Though to the death, against such cruelties
With inward consolations recompenc't,   495
And oft supported so as shall amaze
Thir proudest persecuters: for the Spirit
Powrd first on his Apostles, whom he sends
T' evangelize the Nations, then on all
Baptiz'd, shall them with wondrous gifts endue   500
To speak all Tongues, and do all Miracles,
As did thir Lord before them. Thus they win
Great numbers of each Nation to receave
With joy the tidings brought from Heav'n: at length
Thir Ministry perform'd, and race well run,   505
Thir doctrine and thir story written left,
They die; but in thir room, as they forewarn,
Wolves shall succeed for teachers, grievous Wolves,
Who all the sacred mysteries of Heav'n
To thir own vile advantages shall turn   510
Of lucre and ambition, and the truth
With superstitions and traditions taint,
Left onely in those written Records pure,
Though not but by the Spirit understood.
Then shall they seek to avail themselves of names,   515
Places and titles, and with these to join
Secular power, though feigning still to act
By spiritual, to themselves appropriating
The Spirit of God, promis'd alike and giv'n
To all Beleevers; and from that pretense,   520
Spiritual Laws by carnal power shall force
On every conscience; Laws which none shall find
Left them inrould, or what the Spirit within

Shall on the heart engrave. What will they then
But force the Spirit of Grace it self, and bind   525
His consort Libertie; what, but unbuild
His living Temples, built by Faith to stand,
Thir own Faith not anothers: for on Earth
Who against Faith and Conscience can be heard
Infallible? yet many will presume: 530
Whence heavie persecution shall arise
On all who in the worship persevere
Of Spirit and Truth; the rest, farr greater part,
Will deem in outward Rites and specious formes
Religion satisfi'd; Truth shall retire   535
Bestuck with slandrous darts, and works of Faith
Rarely be found: so shall the World goe on,
To good malignant, to bad men benigne,
Under her own waight groaning, till the day
Appeer of respiration to the just,   540
And vengeance to the wicked, at return
Of him so lately promis'd to thy aid,
The Womans seed, obscurely then foretold,
Now amplier known thy Saviour and thy Lord,
Last in the Clouds from Heav'n to be reveald   545
In glory of the Father, to dissolve
Satan with his perverted World, then raise
From the conflagrant mass, purg'd and refin'd,
New Heav'ns, new Earth, Ages of endless date
Founded in righteousness and peace and love,   550
To bring forth fruits Joy and eternal Bliss.
    He ended; and thus *Adam* last reply'd.
How soon hath thy prediction, Seer blest,
Measur'd this transient World, the Race of time,
Till time stand fixt: beyond is all abyss,   555
Eternitie, whose end no eye can reach.
Greatly instructed I shall hence depart,
Greatly in peace of thought, and have my fill
Of knowledge, what this Vessel can contain;
Beyond which was my folly to aspire.   560
Henceforth I learn, that to obey is best,
And love with fear the onely God, to walk
As in his presence, ever to observe
His providence, and on him sole depend,
Mercifull over all his works, with good   565
Still overcoming evil, and by small
Accomplishing great things, by things deemd weak

Subverting worldly strong, and worldly wise
By simply meek; that suffering for Truths sake
Is fortitude to highest victorie,   570
And to the faithful Death the Gate of Life;
Taught this by his example whom I now
Acknowledge my Redeemer ever blest.
　　To whom thus also th' Angel last repli'd:
This having learnt, thou hast attaind the sum   575
Of wisdom; hope no higher, though all the Starrs
Thou knewst by name, and all th' ethereal Powers,
All secrets of the deep, all Natures works,
Or works of God in Heav'n, Air, Earth, or Sea,
And all the riches of this World enjoydst,   580
And all the rule, one Empire; onely add
Deeds to thy knowledge answerable, add Faith,
Add Vertue, Patience, Temperance, add Love,
By name to come call'd Charitie, the soul
Of all the rest: then wilt thou not be loath   585
To leave this Paradise, but shalt possess
A Paradise within thee, happier farr.
Let us descend now therefore from this top
Of Speculation; for the hour precise
Exacts our parting hence; and see the Guards,   590
By mee encampt on yonder Hill, expect[32]
Thir motion, at whose Front a flaming Sword,
In signal of remove, waves fiercely round;
We may no longer stay: go, waken *Eve;*
Her also I with gentle Dreams have calm'd   595
Portending good, and all her spirits compos'd
To meek submission: thou at season fit
Let her with thee partake what thou hast heard,
Chiefly what may concern her Faith to know,
The great deliverance by her Seed to come   600
(For by the Womans Seed) on all Mankind.
That ye may live, which will be many dayes,
Both in one Faith unanimous though sad,
With cause for evils past, yet much more cheer'd
With meditation on the happie end.   605
　　He ended, and they both descend the Hill;
Descended, *Adam* to the Bowr where *Eve*
Lay sleeping ran before, but found her wak't;
And thus with words not sad she him receav'd.

---

[32] await (their signal to move on).

Whence thou returnst, and whither wentst, I know;   610
For God is also in sleep, and Dreams advise,
Which he hath sent propitious, some great good
Presaging, since with sorrow and hearts distress
Wearied I fell asleep: but now lead on;
In mee is no delay; with thee to goe,   615
Is to stay here; without thee here to stay,
Is to go hence unwilling; thou to mee
Art all things under Heav'n, all places thou,
Who for my wilful crime art banisht hence.
This further consolation yet secure   620
I carry hence; though all by mee is lost,
Such favour I unworthie am voutsaft,
By mee the Promis'd Seed shall all restore.
    So spake our Mother *Eve*, and *Adam* heard
Well pleas'd, but answer'd not; for now too nigh   625
Th' Archangel stood, and from the other Hill
To thir fixt Station, all in bright array
The Cherubim descended; on the ground
Gliding meteorous, as Ev'ning Mist
Ris'n from a River o're the marish glides,   630
And gathers ground fast at the Labourers heel
Homeward returning. High in Front advanc't,
The brandisht Sword of God before them blaz'd
Fierce as a Comet; which with torrid heat,
And vapour as the *Libyan* Air adust,[33]   635
Began to parch that temperate Clime; whereat
In either hand the hastning Angel caught
Our lingring Parents, and to th' Eastern Gate
Led them direct, and down the Cliff as fast
To the subjected[34] Plain; then disappeer'd.   640
They looking back, all th' Eastern side beheld
Of Paradise, so late thir happie seat,
Wav'd over by that flaming Brand, the Gate
With dreadful Faces throng'd and fierie Armes:
Som natural tears they drop'd, but wip'd them soon;   645
The World was all before them, where to choose
Thir place of rest, and Providence thir guide:
They hand in hand with wandring steps and slow,
Through *Eden* took thir solitarie way.

(1642?–1665?)

[33] dried by heat.
[34] lying under (the cliff).

PARADISE REGAIN'D[1]

BOOK I

I who e're while the happy Garden sung,
By one mans disobedience lost, now sing
Recover'd Paradise to all mankind,
By one mans firm obedience fully tri'd
Through all temptation, and the Tempter foil'd   5
In all his wiles, defeated and repuls't,
And *Eden* rais'd in the wast Wilderness.
    Thou Spirit who ledst this glorious Eremite
Into the Desert, his Victorious Field
Against the Spiritual Foe, and broughtst him thence   10
By proof th' undoubted Son of God, inspire,
As thou art wont, my prompted Song else mute,
And bear through highth or depth of natures bounds

[1] Drawn from Luke iv. 1–13 and Matt. iv. 1–11, the brief epic
elaborates the three temptations in the wilderness: As Barbara
Lewalski (*SP*, LVII, 1960, 186–220) views the poem, the first
temptation (*concupiscentia carnis* or that of the flesh—hunger) explores Christ's role as prophet in I, 294–502; it is concerned with
the opposition of truth and falsehood. The second temptation (*concupiscentia oculorum* or that of the world—kingdoms) explores
Christ's role as king in II, 302–IV, 393; this extended assault on
the virtues of temperance, contentment, magnanimity, and modesty is concerned with *voluptaria* (lures of sex, II, 153–234, and
hunger, II, 302–405), *activa* (wealth, II, 406–86; glory, III, 108–
44; and kingdom, III, 150–IV, 211) and *contemplativa* (poetry
and philosophy, IV, 212–364). The third temptation (*superbia
vitae* or that of the devil—the tower) explores Christ's role as priest
in IV, 397–580; it involves imagery of the passion, sustained by
patience and fortitude, leading to full identity as Son of God.
Christ is conceived as an example of Aristotelian magnanimity, as
Merritt Y. Hughes illustrates in *SP*, XXXV (1938), 258–72; that
is, a hero who whether accepting or refusing riches, advantages, or
honors is actuated by a proper regard for his own dignity. Satan,
on the other hand, is an antitype of Christ: selfish, ambitious,
devious, quibbling, and envious. As allegory, the poem points the
way to achieve the kingdom of heaven: through virtuous obedience
to God.

With prosperous wing full summ'd[2] to tell of deeds
Above Heroic, though in secret done,   15
And unrecorded left through many an Age,
Worthy t' have not remain'd so long unsung.
   Now had the great Proclaimer[3] with a voice
More awful then the sound of Trumpet, cri'd
Repentance, and Heav'ns Kingdom nigh at hand   20
To all Baptiz'd: to his great Baptism flock'd
With aw the Regions round, and with them came
From *Nazareth* the Son of *Joseph* deem'd
To the flood *Jordan*, came as then obscure,
Unmarkt, unknown; but him the Baptist soon   25
Descri'd, divinely warn'd, and witness bore
As to his worthier, and would have resign'd
To him his Heav'nly Office, nor was long
His witness unconfirm'd: on him baptiz'd
Heav'n open'd, and in likeness of a Dove   30
The Spirit descended, while the Fathers voice
From Heav'n pronounc'd him his beloved Son.
That heard the Adversary,[4] who roving still
About the world, at that assembly fam'd
Would not be last, and with the voice divine   35
Nigh Thunder-struck, th' exalted man, to whom
Such high attest was giv'n, a while survey'd
With wonder, then with envy fraught and rage
Flies to his place, nor rests, but in mid air
To Councel summons all high mighty Peers,   40
Within thick Clouds and dark ten-fold involv'd,
A gloomy Consistory; and them amidst
With looks agast and sad he thus bespake.
   O ancient Powers of Air and this wide world,
For much more willingly I mention Air,   45
This our old Conquest, then remember Hell
Our hated habitation; well ye know
How many Ages, as the years of men,
This Universe we have possest, and rul'd
In manner at our will th' affairs of Earth,   50
Since *Adam* and his facil consort *Eve*
Lost Paradise deceiv'd by me, though since
With dread attending when that fatal wound

---

[2] with fully grown feathers; i.e., with mature poetic powers.
[3] John the Baptist.
[4] Satan.

Shall be inflicted by the Seed of *Eve*
Upon my head.[5] Long the decrees of Heav'n   55
Delay, for longest time to him is short;
And now too soon for us the circling hours
This dreaded time have compast, wherein we
Must bide the stroak of that long threat'n'd wound,
At least if so we can, and by the head   60
Broken be not intended all our power
To be infring'd, our freedom and our being
In this fair Empire won of Earth and Air;
For this ill news I bring, the Womans seed
Destin'd to this, is late of woman born: 65
His birth to our just fear gave no small cause,
But his growth now to youths full flowr, displaying
All vertue, grace and wisdom to atchieve
Things highest, greatest, multiplies my fear.
Before him a great Prophet, to proclaim   70
His coming, is sent Harbinger, who all
Invites, and in the Consecrated stream
Pretends to wash off sin, and fit them so
Purified to receive him pure, or rather
To do him honour as their King; all come,   75
And he himself among them was baptiz'd,
Not thence to be more pure, but to receive
The testimony of Heav'n, that who he is
Thenceforth the Nations may not doubt; I saw
The Prophet do him reverence, on him rising   80
Out of the water, Heav'n above the Clouds
Unfold her Crystal Dores, thence on his head
A perfect Dove descend, what e're it meant,
And out of Heav'n the Sov'raign voice I heard,
This is my Son belov'd, in him am pleas'd.   85
His Mother then is mortal, but his Sire,
He who obtains the Monarchy of Heav'n,
And what will he not do t' advance his Son?
His first-begot we know, and sore have felt,
When his fierce thunder drove us to the deep;   90
Who this is we must learn, for man he seems
In all his lineaments, though in his face
The glimpses of his Fathers glory shine.

---

[5] Gen. iii. 15: "And I will put enmity between thee [the serpent]
and the woman, and between thy seed and her seed; it shall bruise
thy head . . . ."

Ye see our danger on the utmost edge
Of hazard, which admits no long debate,   95
But must with something sudden be oppos'd,
Not force, but well couch't fraud, well woven snares,
E're in the head of Nations he appear
Their King, their Leader, and Supream on Earth.
I, when no other durst, sole undertook   100
The dismal expedition to find out
And ruin *Adam*, and th' exploit perform'd
Successfully; a calmer voyage now
Will waft me; and the way found prosperous once
Induces best to hope of like success.   105
    He ended, and his words impression left
Of much amazement to th' infernal Crew,
Distracted and surpriz'd with deep dismay
At these sad tidings; but no time was then
For long indulgence to their fears or grief: 110
Unanimous they all commit the care
And management of this main enterprize
To him their great Dictator, whose attempt
At first against mankind so well had thriv'd
In *Adam*'s overthrow, and led thir march   115
From Hell's deep-vaulted Den to dwell in light,
Regents and Potentates, and Kings, yea gods
Of many a pleasant Realm and Province wide.
So to the Coast of *Jordan* he directs
His easie steps, girded with snaky wiles,   120
Where he might likeliest find this new-declar'd,
This man of men, attested Son of God,
Temptation and all guile on him to try;
So to subvert whom he suspected rais'd
To end his Raign on Earth so long enjoy'd: 125
But contrary unweeting[6] he fulfill'd
The purpos'd Counsel pre-ordain'd and fixt
Of the most High, who in full frequence[7] bright
Of Angels, thus to *Gabriel* smiling spake.
    Gabriel this day by proof thou shalt behold,   130
Thou and all Angels conversant on Earth
With man or mens affairs, how I begin
To verifie that solemn message late,
On which I sent thee to the Virgin pure

[6] unknowing.
[7] attendance.

In *Galilee*, that she should bear a Son   135
Great in Renown, and call'd the Son of God;
Then toldst her doubting how these things could be
To her a Virgin, that on her should come
The Holy Ghost, and the power of the highest
O're-shadow her: this man born and now up-grown,   140
To shew him worthy of his birth divine
And high prediction, henceforth I expose
To Satan; let him tempt and now assay
His utmost subtilty, because he boasts
And vaunts of his great cunning to the throng   145
Of his Apostasie; he might have learnt
Less over-weening, since he fail'd in *Job*,
Whose constant perseverance overcame
Whate're his cruel malice could invent.
He now shall know I can produce a man   150
Of female Seed, far abler to resist
All his sollicitations, and at length
All his vast force, and drive him back to Hell,
Winning by Conquest what the first man lost
By fallacy surpriz'd. But first I mean   155
To exercise him in the Wilderness;
There he shall first lay down the rudiments
Of his great warfare, e're I send him forth
To conquer Sin and Death the two grand foes,
By Humiliation and strong Sufferance: 160
His weakness shall o'recome Satanic strength
And all the world, and mass of sinful flesh;
That all the Angels and Ætherial Powers,
They now, and men hereafter may discern,
From what consummate vertue I have chose   165
This perfect Man, by merit call'd my Son,
To earn Salvation for the Sons of men.
   So spake th' Eternal Father, and all Heav'n
Admiring stood a space, then into Hymns
Burst forth, and in Celestial measures mov'd,   170
Circling the Throne and Singing, while the hand
Sung with the voice, and this the argument.
   Victory and Triumph to the Son of God
Now entring his great duel, not of arms,
But to vanquish by wisdom hellish wiles.   175
The Father knows the Son; therefore secure
Ventures his filial Vertue, though untri'd,
Against whate're may tempt, whate're seduce,

Allure, or terrifie, or undermine.
Be frustrate all ye stratagems of Hell,   180
And devilish machinations come to nought.
    So they in Heav'n their Odes and Vigils tun'd:
Mean while the Son of God, who yet some days
Lodg'd in *Bethabara* where *John* baptiz'd,
Musing and much revolving in his brest,   185
How best the mighty work he might begin
Of Saviour to mankind, and which way first
Publish his God-like office now mature,
One day forth walk'd alone, the Spirit leading;
And his deep thoughts, the better to converse   190
With solitude, till far from track of men,
Thought following thought, and step by step led on,
He enter'd now the bordering Desert wild,
And with dark shades and rocks environ'd round,
His holy Meditations thus persu'd.   195
    O what a multitude of thoughts at once
Awak'n'd in me swarm, while I consider
What from within I feel my self, and hear
What from without comes often to my ears,
Ill sorting with my present state compar'd.   200
When I was yet a child, no childish play
To me was pleasing, all my mind was set
Serious to learn and know, and thence to do
What might be publick good; my self I thought
Born to that end, born to promote all truth,   205
All righteous things: therefore above my years,
The Law of God I read, and found it sweet,
Made it my whole delight, and in it grew
To such perfection, that e're yet my age
Had measur'd twice six years, at our great Feast   210
I went into the Temple, there to hear
The Teachers of our Law, and to propose
What might improve my knowledge or their own;
And was admir'd[8] by all, yet this not all
To which my Spirit aspir'd, victorious deeds   215
Flam'd in my heart, heroic acts, one while
To rescue *Israel* from the *Roman* yoke,
Then to subdue and quell o're all the earth
Brute violence and proud Tyrannick pow'r,
Till truth were freed, and equity restor'd: 220

[8] regarded with wonder.

Yet held it more humane, more heav'nly first
By winning words to conquer willing hearts,
And make perswasion do the work of fear;
At least to try, and teach the erring Soul
Not wilfully mis-doing, but unware   225
Misled; the stubborn only to subdue.
These growing thoughts my Mother soon perceiving
By words at times cast forth inly rejoyc'd,
And said to me apart, high are thy thoughts
O Son, but nourish them and let them soar   230
To what highth sacred vertue and true worth
Can raise them, though above example high;
By matchless Deeds express thy matchless Sire.
For know, thou art no Son of mortal man,
Though men esteem thee low of Parentage,   235
Thy Father is th' Eternal King, who rules
All Heav'n and Earth, Angels and Sons of men.
A messenger from God fore-told thy birth
Conceiv'd in me a Virgin, he fore-told
Thou shouldst be great and sit on *David's* Throne,   240
And of thy Kingdom there should be no end.
At thy Nativity a glorious Quire
Of Angels in the fields of *Bethlehem* sung
To Shepherds watching at their folds by night,
And told them the Messiah now was born,   245
Where they might see him, and to thee they came;
Directed to the Manger where thou lais't,
For in the Inn was left no better room:
A Star, not seen before in Heav'n appearing
Guided the Wise Men thither from the East,   250
To honour thee with Incense, Myrrh, and Gold,
By whose bright course led on they found the place,
Affirming it thy Star new grav'n in Heav'n,
By which they knew thee King of *Israel* born.
Just *Simeon* and Prophetic *Anna,* warn'd   255
By Vision,[9] found thee in the Temple, and spake
Before the Altar and the vested Priest,
Like things of thee to all that present stood.
This having heard, strait I again revolv'd
The Law and Prophets, searching what was writ   260
Concerning the Messiah, to our Scribes
Known partly, and soon found of whom they spake

[9] See Luke ii. 25–38.

I am; this chiefly, that my way must lie
Through many a hard assay ev'n to the death,
E're I the promis'd Kingdom can attain,   265
Or work Redemption for mankind, whose sins
Full weight must be transferr'd upon my head.
Yet neither thus disheart'n'd or dismay'd,
The time prefixt I waited, when behold
The Baptist (of whose birth I oft had heard,   270
Not knew by sight) now come, who was to come
Before Messiah and his way prepare.
I as all others to his Baptism came,
Which I believ'd was from above; but he
Strait knew me, and with loudest voice proclaim'd   275
Me him (for it was shew'n him so from Heav'n)
Me him whose Harbinger he was; and first
Refus'd on me his Baptism to confer,
As much his greater, and was hardly won;
But as I rose out of the laving stream,   280
Heav'n open'd her eternal doors, from whence
The Spirit descended on me like a Dove,
And last the sum of all, my Father's voice,
Audibly heard from Heav'n, pronounc'd me his,
Me his beloved Son, in whom alone   285
He was well pleas'd; by which I knew the time
Now full, that I no more should live obscure,
But openly begin, as best becomes
Th' Authority which I deriv'd from Heav'n.
And now by some strong motion I am led   290
Into this Wilderness, to what intent
I learn not yet, perhaps I need not know;
For what concerns my knowledge God reveals.
  So spake our Morning Star then in his rise,
And looking round on every side beheld   295
A pathless Desert, dusk with horrid shades;
The way he came not having mark'd, return
Was difficult, by human steps untrod;
And he still on was led, but with such thoughts
Accompanied of things past and to come   300
Lodg'd in his brest, as well might recommend
Such Solitude before choicest Society.
Full forty days he pass'd, whether on hill
Sometimes, anon in shady vale, each night
Under the covert of some ancient Oak,   305
Or Cedar, to defend him from the dew,

Or harbour'd in one Cave, is not reveal'd;
Nor tasted human food, nor hunger felt
Till those days ended, hunger'd then at last
Among wild Beasts: they at his sight grew mild,   310
Nor sleeping him nor waking harm'd, his walk
The fiery Serpent fled, and noxious Worm,[10]
The Lion and fierce Tiger glar'd aloof.
But now an aged man in Rural weeds,
Following, as seem'd, the quest of some stray Ewe,   315
Or wither'd sticks to gather; which might serve
Against a Winters day when winds blow keen,
To warm him wet return'd from field at Eve,
He saw approach, who first with curious eye
Perus'd him, then with words thus utter'd spake.   320
    Sir, what ill chance hath brought thee to this place
So far from path or road of men, who pass
In Troop or Caravan, for single none
Durst ever, who return'd, and dropt not here
His Carcass, pin'd with hunger and with droughth?   325
I ask the rather, and the more admire,
For that to me thou seem'st the man, whom late
Our new baptizing Prophet at the Ford
Of *Jordan* honour'd so, and call'd thee Son
Of God; I saw and heard, for we sometimes   330
Who dwell this wild, constrain'd by want, come forth
To Town or Village nigh (nighest is far)
Where aught we hear, and curious are to hear,
What happ'ns new; Fame also finds us out.
    To whom the Son of God. Who brought me hither   335
Will bring me hence, no other Guide I seek.
    By Miracle he may, reply'd the Swain,
What other way I see not, for we here
Live on tough roots and stubs, to thirst inur'd
More then the Camel, and to drink go far,   340
Men to much misery and hardship born;
But if thou be the Son of God, command
That out of these hard stones be made thee bread;
So shalt thou save thy self and us relieve
With Food, whereof we wretched seldom taste.   345
    He ended, and the Son of God reply'd.
Think'st thou such force in Bread? is it not written
(For I discern thee other then thou seem'st)

    [10] snake.

Man lives not by Bread only, but each Word
Proceeding from the mouth of God; who fed   350
Our Fathers here with Manna; in the Mount
Moses was forty days,[11] nor eat nor drank,
And forty days *Eliah* without food
Wander'd this barren waste,[12] the same I now:
Why dost thou then suggest to me distrust,   355
Knowing who I am, as I know who thou art?
　　Whom thus answer'd th' Arch Fiend now undisguis'd.
'Tis true, I am that Spirit unfortunate,
Who leagu'd with millions more in rash revolt
Kept not my happy Station, but was driv'n   360
With them from bliss to the bottomless deep,
Yet to that hideous place not so confin'd
By rigour unconniving,[13] but that oft
Leaving my dolorous Prison I enjoy
Large liberty to round this Globe of Earth,   365
Or range in th' Air, nor from the Heav'n of Heav'ns
Hath he excluded my resort sometimes.
I came among the Sons of God, when he
Gave up into my hands *Uzzean Job*
To prove him, and illustrate his high worth;   370
And when to all his Angels he propos'd
To draw the proud King *Ahab* into fraud
That he might fall in *Ramoth*, they demurring,
I undertook that office, and the tongues
Of all his flattering Prophets glibb'd with lies   375
To his destruction, as I had in charge.
For what he bids I do; though I have lost
Much lustre of my native brightness, lost
To be belov'd of God, I have not lost
To love, at least contemplate and admire   380
What I see excellent in good, or fair,
Or vertuous, I should so have lost all sense.
What can be then less in me then desire
To see thee and approach thee, whom I know
Declar'd the Son of God, to hear attent[14]   385
Thy wisdom, and behold thy God-like deeds?
Men generally think me much a foe

[11] Exod. xxiv. 18.
[12] 1 Kings xix. 8.
[13] always alert (literally, "not closing its eyes").
[14] attentive.

To all mankind: why should I? they to me
Never did wrong or violence, by them
I lost not what I lost, rather by them   390
I gain'd what I have gain'd, and with them dwell
Copartner in these Regions of the World,
If not disposer; lend them oft my aid,
Oft my advice by presages and signs,
And answers, oracles, portents and dreams,   395
Whereby they may direct their future life.
Envy they say excites me, thus to gain
Companions of my misery and wo.
At first it may be; but long since with wo
Nearer acquainted, now I feel by proof,   400
That fellowship in pain divides not smart,
Nor lightens aught each mans peculiar load.
Small consolation then, were Man adjoyn'd:
This wounds me most (what can it less) that Man,
Man fall'n shall be restor'd, I never more.   405
    To whom our Saviour sternly thus reply'd.
Deservedly thou griev'st, compos'd of lies
From the beginning, and in lies wilt end;
Who boast'st release from Hell, and leave to come
Into the Heav'n of Heav'ns; thou com'st indeed,   410
As a poor miserable captive thrall
Comes to the place where he before had sat
Among the Prime in Splendour, now depos'd,
Ejected, emptied, gaz'd, unpitied, shun'd,
A spectacle of ruin or of scorn   415
To all the Host of Heav'n; the happy place
Imparts to thee no happiness, no joy,
Rather inflames thy torment, representing
Lost bliss, to thee no more communicable,
So never more in Hell then when in Heav'n.   420
But thou art serviceable to Heav'ns King.
Wilt thou impute t' obedience what thy fear
Extorts, or pleasure to do ill excites?
What but thy malice mov'd thee to misdeem
Of righteous *Job*, then cruelly to afflict him   425
With all inflictions, but his patience won?
The other service was thy chosen task,
To be a liar in four hundred mouths;
For lying is thy sustenance, thy food.[15]

[15] In "Food-Word Imagery in *PR*," *English Literary History,*

Yet thou pretend'st to truth; all Oracles   430
By thee are giv'n, and what confest more true
Among the Nations? that hath been thy craft,
By mixing somewhat true to vent more lies.
But what have been thy answers, what but dark,
Ambiguous and with double sense deluding,   435
Which they who ask'd have seldom understood,
And not well understood as good not known?
Who ever by consulting at thy shrine
Return'd the wiser, or the more instruct
To fly or follow what concern'd him most,   440
And run not sooner to his fatal snare?
For God hath justly giv'n the Nations up
To thy Delusions; justly, since they fell
Idolatrous, but when his purpose is
Among them to declare his Providence   445
To thee not known, whence hast thou then thy truth,
But from him or his Angels President
In every Province, who themselves disdaining
T' approach thy Temples, give thee in command
What to the smallest tittle thou shalt say   450
To thy Adorers; thou with trembling fear,
Or like a Fawning Parasite obey'st;
Then to thy self ascrib'st the truth fore-told.
But this thy glory shall be soon retrench'd;
No more shalt thou by oracling abuse   455
The Gentiles; henceforth Oracles are ceast,
And thou no more with Pomp and Sacrifice
Shalt be enquir'd at *Delphos* or elsewhere,
At least in vain, for they shall find thee mute.
God hath now sent his living Oracle   460
Into the World, to teach his final will,
And sends his Spirit of Truth henceforth to dwell
In pious Hearts, an inward Oracle
To all truth requisite for men to know.
    So spake our Saviour; but the subtle Fiend,   465
Though inly stung with anger and disdain,
Dissembl'd, and this Answer smooth return'd.
    Sharply thou hast insisted on rebuke,

XXVIII (1961), 225–43, Lee S. Cox shows that this metaphoric
development marks a new stage of temptation in each book. The
poem defines the nature of the Word Incarnate and, as here, the
nature of Satan's word.

And urg'd me hard with doings, which not will
But misery hath wrested from me; where   470
Easily canst thou find one miserable,
And not inforc'd oft-times to part from truth;
If it may stand him more in stead to lie,
Say and unsay, feign, flatter, or abjure?
But thou art plac't above me, thou art Lord;   475
From thee I can and must submiss[16] endure
Check or reproof, and glad to scape so quit.
Hard are the ways of truth, and rough to walk,
Smooth on the tongue discourst, pleasing to th' ear,
And tuneable as Silvan Pipe or Song;   480
What wonder then if I delight to hear
Her dictates from thy mouth? most men admire
Vertue, who follow not her lore: permit me
To hear thee when I come (since no man comes)
And talk at least, though I despair t' attain.   485
Thy Father, who is holy, wise and pure,
Suffers the Hypocrite or Atheous Priest
To tread his Sacred Courts, and minister
About his Altar, handling holy things,
Praying or vowing, and vouchsaf'd his voice   490
To *Balaam*[17] Reprobate, a Prophet yet
Inspir'd; disdain not such access to me.
      To whom our Saviour with unalter'd brow.
Thy coming hither, though I know thy scope,
I bid not or forbid; do as thou find'st   495
Permission from above; thou canst not more.
      He added not; and Satan bowing low
His gray dissimulation, disappear'd
Into thin Air diffus'd: for now began
Night with her sullen wing to double-shade   500
The Desert, Fowls in thir clay nests were couch't;
And now wild Beasts came forth the woods to roam.

[16] submissive.
[17] Though pressed by the king of Moab, Balaam could not curse
the Israelites, for the Lord had imposed on him the words to speak
(Num. xxiii).

BOOK II

Mean while the new-baptiz'd, who yet remain'd
At *Jordan* with the Baptist, and had seen
Him whom they heard so late expresly call'd
Jesus Messiah, Son of God declar'd,
And on that high Authority had believ'd, 5
And with him talkt, and with him lodg'd, I mean
Andrew and *Simon*, famous after known
With others though in Holy Writ not nam'd,
Now missing him thir joy so lately found,
So lately found, and so abruptly gone, 10
Began to doubt, and doubted many days,
And as the days increas'd, increas'd thir doubt:
Sometimes they thought he might be only shewn,
And for a time caught up to God, as once
Moses was in the Mount, and missing long; 15
And the great *Thisbite*[1] who on fiery wheels
Rode up to Heav'n, yet once again to come.
Therefore as those young Prophets then with care
Sought lost *Eliah*, so in each place these
Nigh to *Bethabara*; in *Jerico* 20
The City of Palms, *Ænon*, and *Salem* Old,
Machærus and each Town or City wall'd
On this side the broad lake *Genezaret*,
Or in *Perea*, but return'd in vain.
Then on the bank of *Jordan*, by a Creek: 25
Where winds with Reeds, and Osiers whisp'ring play
Plain Fishermen, no greater men them call,
Close in a Cottage low together got
Thir unexpected loss and plaints out breath'd.
Alas, from what high hope to what relapse 30
Unlook'd for are we fall'n, our eyes beheld
Messiah certainly now come, so long
Expected of our Fathers; we have heard
His words, his wisdom full of grace and truth,
Now, now, for sure, deliverance is at hand, 35
The Kingdom shall to *Israel* be restor'd:
Thus we rejoyc'd, but soon our joy is turn'd

[1] Elijah; see 2 Kings ii.

Into perplexity and new amaze:
For whither is he gone, what accident
Hath rapt him from us? will he now retire   40
After appearance, and again prolong
Our expectation? God of *Israel*,
Send thy Messiah forth, the time is come;
Behold the Kings of th' Earth how they oppress
Thy chosen, to what highth thir pow'r unjust   45
They have exalted, and behind them cast
All fear of thee, arise and vindicate
Thy Glory, free thy people from thir yoke,
But let us wait; thus far he hath perform'd,
Sent his Anointed, and to us reveal'd him,   50
By his great Prophet, pointed at and shown,
In publick, and with him we have convers'd;
Let us be glad of this, and all our fears
Lay on his Providence; he will not fail
Nor will withdraw him now, nor will recall,   55
Mock us with his blest sight, then snatch him hence,
Soon we shall see our hope, our joy return.
    Thus they out of their plaints new hope resume
To find whom at the first they found unsought:
But to his Mother *Mary*, when she saw   60
Others return'd from Baptism, not her Son,
Nor left at *Jordan*, tidings of him none;
Within her brest, though calm; her brest though pure,
Motherly cares and fears got head, and rais'd
Some troubl'd thoughts, which she in sighs thus clad.   65
    O what avails me now that honour high
To have conceiv'd of God, or that salute,[2]
Hail highly favour'd, among women blest;
While I to sorrows am no less advanc't,
And fears as eminent, above the lot   70
Of other women, by the birth I bore,
In such a season born when scarce a Shed
Could be obtain'd to shelter him or me
From the bleak air; a Stable was our warmth,
A Manger his, yet soon enforc't to fly   75
Thence into *Egypt*, till the Murd'rous King[3]
Were dead, who sought his life, and missing fill'd
With Infant blood the streets of *Bethlehem;*

[2] Gabriel's announcement to Mary that she would bear a son.
[3] Herod.

From *Egypt* home return'd, in *Nazareth*
Hath been our dwelling many years, his life   80
Private, unactive, calm, contemplative,
Little suspicious t' any King; but now
Full grown to Man, acknowledg'd, as I hear,
By *John* the Baptist, and in publick shown,
Son own'd from Heav'n by his Father's voice;   85
I look't for some great change; to Honour? no,
But trouble, as old *Simeon* plain fore-told,
That to the fall and rising he should be
Of many in *Israel,* and to a sign
Spoken against, that through my very Soul   90
A sword shall pierce, this is my favour'd lot,
My Exaltation to Afflictions high;
Afflicted I may be, it seems, and blest;
I will not argue that, nor will repine.
But where delays he now? some great intent   95
Conceals him: when twelve years he scarce had seen,
I lost him, but so found, as well I saw
He could not lose himself; but went about
His Father's business;[4] what he meant I mus'd,
Since understand; much more his absence now   100
Thus long to some great purpose he obscures.
But I to wait with patience am inur'd;
My heart hath been a store-house long of things
And sayings laid up, portending strange events.
    Thus *Mary* pondering oft, and oft to mind   105
Recalling what remarkably had pass'd
Since first her Salutation heard, with thoughts
Meekly compos'd awaited the fulfilling:
The while her Son tracing the Desert wild,
Sole but with holiest Meditations fed,   110
Into himself descended, and at once
All his great work to come before him set;
How to begin, how to accomplish best
His end of being on Earth, and mission high:
For Satan with sly preface to return   115
Had left him vacant, and with speed was gon
Up to the middle Region of thick Air,
Where all his Potentates in Council sate;
There without sign of boast, or sign of joy,

[4] Luke ii. 42–49.

Sollicitous and blank[5] he thus began.   120
   Princes, Heav'ns antient Sons, Æthereal Thrones,
Demonian Spirits now, from the Element
Each of his reign allotted, rightlier call'd,
Powers of Fire, Air, Water, and Earth beneath,
So may we hold our place and these mild seats   125
Without new trouble; such an Enemy
Is ris'n to invade us, who no less
Threat'ns then our expulsion down to Hell;
I, as I undertook, and with the vote
Consenting in full frequence was impower'd,   130
Have found him, view'd him, tasted[6] him, but find
Far other labour to be undergon
Then when I dealt with *Adam* first of Men,
Though *Adam* by his Wives allurement fell,
However to this Man inferior far,   135
If he be Man by Mothers side at least,
With more then human gifts from Heav'n adorn'd,
Perfections absolute, Graces divine,
And amplitude of mind to greatest Deeds.
Therefore I am return'd, lest confidence   140
Of my success with *Eve* in Paradise
Deceive ye to perswasion over-sure
Of like succeeding here; I summon all
Rather to be in readiness, with hand
Or counsel to assist; lest I who erst   145
Thought none my equal, now be over-match'd.
   So spake th' old Serpent doubting, and from all
With clamour was assur'd thir utmost aid
At his command; when from amidst them rose
Belial the dissolutest Spirit that fell,   150
The sensuallest, and after *Asmodai*
The fleshliest Incubus,[7] and thus advis'd.
   Set women in his eye and in his walk,
Among daughters of men the fairest found;
Many are in each Region passing fair   155
As the noon Skie; more like to Goddesses
Then Mortal Creatures, graceful and discreet,
Expert in amorous Arts, enchanting tongues
Perswasive, Virgin majesty with mild

[5] nonplused.
[6] tested.
[7] demonic seducer.

And sweet allay'd, yet terrible to approach, 160
Skill'd to retire, and in retiring draw
Hearts after them tangl'd in Amorous Nets.
Such object hath the power to soft'n and tame
Severest temper,[8] smooth the rugged'st brow,
Enerve, and with voluptuous hope dissolve, 165
Draw out with credulous desire, and lead
At will the manliest, resolutest brest,
As the Magnetic[9] hardest Iron draws.
Women, when nothing else, beguil'd the heart
Of wisest *Solomon*, and made him build, 170
And made him bow to the Gods of his Wives.[10]
    To whom quick answer Satan thus return'd.
Belial, in much uneven scale thou weigh'st
All others by thy self; because of old
Thou thy self doat'st on womankind, admiring 175
Thir shape, thir colour, and attractive grace,
None are, thou think'st, but taken with such toys.
Before the Flood thou with thy lusty Crew,
False titl'd Sons of God, roaming the Earth
Cast wanton eyes on the daughters of men, 180
And coupl'd with them, and begot a race.
Have we not seen, or by relation heard,
In Courts and Regal Chambers how thou lurk'st,
In Wood or Grove by mossie Fountain side,
In Valley or Green Meadow to way-lay 185
Some beauty rare, *Calisto, Clymene,*
Daphne, or *Semele, Antiopa,*
Or *Amymone, Syrinx,* many more
Too long, then lay'st thy scapes on names ador'd,
Apollo, Neptune, Jupiter, or *Pan,* 190
Satyr, or Faun, or Silvan? But these haunts
Delight not all; among the Sons of Men,
How many have with a smile made small account
Of beauty and her lures, easily scorn'd
All her assaults, on worthier things intent? 195
Remember that *Pellean* Conquerour,[11]
A youth, how all the Beauties of the East
He slightly view'd, and slightly over-pass'd;

[8] temperament.
[9] magnet.
[10] See 1 Kings xi. 1–8.
[11] Alexander the Great.

How hee sirnam'd of *Africa*[12] dismiss'd
In his prime youth the fair *Iberian* maid.   200
For *Solomon* he liv'd at ease, and full
Of honour, wealth, high fare, aim'd not beyond
Higher design then to enjoy his State;
Thence to the bait of Women lay expos'd;
But he whom we attempt is wiser far   205
Then *Solomon*, of more exalted mind,
Made and set wholly on th' accomplishment
Of greatest things; what woman will you find,
Though of this Age the wonder and the fame,
On whom his leisure will vouchsafe an eye   210
Of fond desire? or should she confident,
As sitting Queen ador'd on Beauties Throne,
Descend with all her winning charms begirt
T' enamour, as the Zone[13] of *Venus* once
Wrought that effect on *Jove*, so Fables tell;   215
How would one look from his Majestick brow
Seated as on the top of Vertues hill,[14]
Discount'nance her despis'd, and put to rout
All her array; her female pride deject,
Or turn to reverent awe? for Beauty stands   220
In th' admiration only of weak minds
Led captive; cease t' admire, and all her Plumes
Fall flat and shrink into a trivial toy,
At every sudden slighting quite abasht:
Therefore with manlier objects we must try   225
His constancy, with such as have more shew
Of worth, of honour, glory, and popular praise;
Rocks whereon greatest men have oftest wreck'd;
Or that which only seems to satisfie
Lawful desires of Nature, not beyond;   230
And now I know he hungers where no food
Is to be found, in the wide Wilderness;
The rest commit to me, I shall let pass
No advantage, and his strength as oft assay.
    He ceas'd, and heard thir grant in loud acclaim;   235
Then forthwith to him takes a chosen band
Of Spirits likest to himself in guile

[12] Scipio Africanus.
[13] Venus' ornamented girdle which Juno wore to charm Jove
(*Iliad*, XIV, 214–18).
[14] See *Son.* 9, n. 2.

To be at hand, and at his beck appear,
If cause were to unfold some active Scene
Of various persons each to know his part;   240
Then to the Desert takes with these his flight;
Where still from shade to shade the Son of God
After forty days fasting had remain'd,
Now hungring first, and to himself thus said.
    Where will this end? four times ten days I have
        pass'd   245
Wandring this woody maze, and human food
Nor tasted, nor had appetite; that Fast
To Vertue I impute not, or count part
Of what I suffer here; if Nature need not,
Or God support Nature without repast   250
Though needing, what praise is it to endure?
But now I feel I hunger, which declares,
Nature hath need of what she asks; yet God
Can satisfie that need some other way,
Though hunger still remain: so it remain   255
Without this bodies wasting, I content me,
And from the sting of Famine fear no harm,
Nor mind it, fed with better thoughts that feed
Mee hungring more to do my Fathers will.
    It was the hour of night, when thus the Son   260
Commun'd in silent walk, then laid him down
Under the hospitable covert nigh
Of Trees thick interwoven; there he slept,
And dream'd, as appetite is wont to dream,
Of meats and drinks, Natures refreshment sweet;   265
Him thought,[15] he by the Brook of *Cherith* stood
And saw the Ravens with their horny beaks
Food to *Elijah* bringing Even and Morn,
Though ravenous, taught t' abstain from what they brought:
He saw the Prophet also how he fled   270
Into the Desert, and how there he slept
Under a Juniper; then how awak't,
He found his Supper on the coals prepar'd,
And by the Angel was bid rise and eat,
And eat the second time after repose,   275
The strength whereof suffic'd him forty days;
Sometimes that with *Elijah* he partook,

[15] The accounts of Elijah here are found in 1 Kings xvii. 3–7, xix. 4–8.

Or as a guest with *Daniel* at his pulse.[16]
Thus wore out night, and now the Herald Lark
Left his ground-nest, high towring to descry   280
The morns approach, and greet her with his Song:
As lightly from his grassy Couch up rose
Our Saviour, and found all was but a dream,
Fasting he went to sleep, and fasting wak'd.
Up to a hill anon his steps he rear'd,   285
From whose high top to ken the prospect round,
If Cottage were in view, Sheep-cote or Herd;
But Cottage, Herd or Sheep-cote none he saw,
Only in a bottom saw a pleasant Grove,
With chaunt of tuneful Birds resounding loud;   290
Thither he bent his way, determin'd there
To rest at noon, and enter'd soon the shade
High rooft and walks beneath, and alleys brown
That open'd in the midst a woody Scene,
Natures own work it seem'd (Nature taught Art)   295
And to a Superstitious eye the haunt
Of Wood-Gods and Wood-Nymphs; he view'd it round,
When suddenly a man before him stood,
Not rustic as before, but seemlier clad,
As one in City, or Court, or Palace bred,   300
And with fair speech these words to him address'd.
    With granted leave officious I return,
But much more wonder that the Son of God
In this wild solitude so long should bide
Of all things destitute, and well I know,   305
Not without hunger. Others of some note,
As story tells, have trod this Wilderness;
The Fugitive Bond-woman[17] with her Son
Out cast *Nebaioth,* yet found he relief
By a providing Angel; all the race   310
Of *Israel* here had famish'd, had not God
Rain'd from Heav'n Manna,[18] and that Prophet[19] bold
Native of *Thebez* wandring here was fed
Twice by a voice inviting him to eat.
Of thee these forty days none hath regard,   315

[16] peas, lentils, or beans; Dan. i. 8–16.
[17] Hagar (Gen. xxi. 14–19). Milton errs: her son was Ishmael; his son was Nebaioth.
[18] See Exod. xvi.
[19] Elijah.

Forty and more deserted here indeed.
   To whom thus Jesus; what conclud'st thou hence?
They all had need, I as thou seest have none.
   How hast thou hunger then? Satan reply'd,
Tell me if Food were now before thee set,   320
Would'st thou not eat? Thereafter as I like
The giver, answer'd Jesus. Why should that
Cause thy refusal, said the subtle Fiend,
Hast thou not right to all Created things,
Owe not all Creatures by just right to thee   325
Duty and Service, nor to stay till bid,
But tender all their power? nor mention I
Meats by the Law unclean, or offer'd first
To Idols, those young *Daniel* could refuse;
Nor proffer'd by an Enemy, though who   330
Would scruple that, with want opprest? behold
Nature asham'd, or better to express,
Troubl'd that thou shouldst hunger, hath purvey'd
From all the Elements her choicest store
To treat thee as beseems, and as her Lord   335
With honour, only deign to sit and eat.
   He spake no dream, for as his words had end,
Our Saviour lifting up his eyes beheld
In ample space under the broadest shade
A Table richly spred, in regal mode,   340
With dishes pil'd, and meats of noblest sort
And savour, Beasts of chase, or Fowl of game,
In pastry built, or from the spit, or boyl'd,
Gris-amber-steam'd; all Fish from Sea or Shore,
Freshet, or purling Brook, of shell or fin,   345
And exquisitest name, for which was drain'd
Pontus and *Lucrine* Bay,[20] and *Afric* Coast.
Alas how simple, to these Cates compar'd,
Was that crude Apple that diverted *Eve!*
And at a stately side-board by the wine   350
That fragrant smell diffus'd, in order stood
Tall stripling youths rich clad, of fairer hew
Then *Ganymed* or *Hylas*,[21] distant more
Under the Trees now trip'd, now solemn stood
Nymphs of *Diana's* train, and *Naiades*   355

[20] the Black Sea and the bay near Naples.
[21] See *El.* 7, n. 2, 3.

With fruits and flowers from *Amalthea*'s horn,[22]
And Ladies of th' *Hesperides*,[23] that seem'd
Fairer then feign'd of old, or fabl'd since
Of Fairy Damsels met in Forest wide
By Knights of *Logres*, or of *Lyones*,   360
Lancelot or *Pelleas*, or *Pellenore*,[24]
And all the while Harmonious Airs were heard
Of chiming strings, or charming pipes and winds
Of gentlest gale *Arabian* odors fann'd
From their soft wings, and *Flora*'s[25] earliest smells.   365
Such was the Splendour, and the Tempter now
His invitation earnestly renew'd.
    What doubts the Son of God to sit and eat?
These are not Fruits forbidd'n, no interdict
Defends[26] the touching of these viands pure,   370
Thir taste no knowledge works, at least of evil,
But life preserves, destroys life's enemy,
Hunger, with sweet restorative delight.
All these are Spirits of Air, and Woods, and Springs,
Thy gentle Ministers, who come to pay   375
Thee homage, and acknowledge thee thir Lord:
What doubt'st thou Son of God? sit down and eat.
    To whom thus Jesus temperately reply'd:
Said'st thou not that to all things I had right?
And who withholds my pow'r that right to use?   380
Shall I receive by gift what of my own,
When and where likes me best, I can command?
I can at will, doubt not, as soon as thou,
Command a Table in this Wilderness,
And call swift flights of Angels ministrant   385
Array'd in Glory on my cup t' attend:
Why shouldst thou then obtrude this diligence,
In vain, where no acceptance it can find,
And with my hunger what hast thou to do?
Thy pompous Delicacies I contemn,   390
And count thy specious gifts no gifts but guiles.

[22] horn of plenty.
[23] the guardians of the golden tree; see *Mask*, ll. 981–83.
[24] English geographic areas or knights, all connected with King Arthur.
[25] goddess of flowers.
[26] forbids. Satan dissembles, as Michael Fixler pointed out (*MLN*, LXX, 1955, 573–77), for certain meats and shellfish (ll. 342–45) were proscribed.

To whom thus answer'd Satan malecontent:
That I have also power to give thou seest,
If of that pow'r I bring thee voluntary
What I might have bestow'd on whom I pleas'd,   395
And rather opportunely in this place
Chose to impart to thy apparent need,
Why shouldst thou not accept it? but I see
What I can do or offer is suspect;
Of these things others quickly will dispose   400
Whose pains have earn'd the far-fet[27] spoil. With that
Both Table and Provision vanish'd quite
With sound of Harpies wings, and Talons heard;
Only the importune Tempter still remain'd,
And with these words his temptation pursu'd.   405
    By hunger, that each other Creature tames,
Thou art not to be harm'd, therefore not mov'd;
Thy temperance invincible besides,
For no allurement yields to appetite,
And all thy heart is set on high designs,   410
High actions; but wherewith to be atchiev'd?
Great acts require great means of enterprise,
Thou art unknown, unfriended, low of birth,
A Carpenter thy Father known, thy self
Bred up in poverty and streights at home;   415
Lost in a Desert here and hunger-bit:
Which way or from what hope dost thou aspire
To greatness? whence Authority deriv'st,
What Followers, what Retinue canst thou gain,
Or at thy heels the dizzy Multitude,   420
Longer then thou canst feed them on thy cost?
Money brings Honour, Friends, Conquest, and Realms;
What rais'd *Antipater* the *Edomite*,
And his Son *Herod* plac'd on *Juda*'s Throne;
(Thy throne) but gold that got him puissant friends?   425
Therefore, if at great things thou wouldst arrive,
Get Riches first, get Wealth, and Treasure heap,
Not difficult, if thou hearken to me,
Riches are mine, Fortune is in my hand;
They whom I favour thrive in wealth amain,   430
While Virtue, Valour, Wisdom sit in want.
    To whom thus Jesus patiently reply'd;
Yet Wealth without these three is impotent,

[27] far-fetched.

To gain dominion or to keep it gain'd.
Witness those antient Empires of the Earth,   435
In highth of all thir flowing wealth dissolv'd:
But men endu'd with these have oft attain'd
In lowest poverty to highest deeds;
Gideon and *Jephtha*, and the Shepherd lad,[28]
Whose off-spring on the Throne of *Juda* sat   440
So many Ages, and shall yet regain
That seat, and reign in *Israel* without end.
Among the Heathen (for throughout the World
To me is not unknown what hath been done
Worthy of Memorial) canst thou not remember   445
Quintius, Fabricius, Curius, Regulus?[29]
For I esteem those names of men so poor
Who could do mighty things, and could contemn
Riches though offer'd from the hand of Kings.
And what in me seems wanting, but that I   450
May also in this poverty as soon
Accomplish what they did, perhaps and more?
Extol not Riches then, the toyl[30] of Fools,
The wise mans cumbrance if not snare, more apt
To slacken Virtue, and abate her edge,   455
Then prompt her to do aught may merit praise.
What if with like aversion I reject
Riches and Realms; yet not for that a Crown,
Golden in shew, is but a wreath of thorns,
Brings dangers, troubles, cares, and sleepless nights   460
To him who wears the Regal Diadem,
When on his shoulders each mans burden lies;
For therein stands the office of a King,
His Honour, Vertue, Merit and chief Praise,
That for the Publick all this weight he bears.   465
Yet he who reigns within himself, and rules
Passions, Desires, and Fears, is more a King;
Which every wise and vertuous man attains:
And who attains not, ill aspire to rule
Cities of men, or head-strong Multitudes,   470
Subject himself to Anarchy within,
Or lawless passions in him which he serves.
But to guide Nations in the way of truth

28 David; see Judges vi–viii, xi–xii, and 1 Sam. xvi–xvii.
29 important early military leaders of Rome.
30 snare.

By saving Doctrine, and from errour lead
To know, and knowing worship God aright,   475
Is yet more Kingly, this attracts the Soul,
Governs the inner man, the nobler part,
That other o're the body only reigns,
And oft by force, which to a generous mind
So reigning can be no sincere delight.   480
Besides to give a Kingdom hath been thought
Greater and nobler done, and to lay down
Far more magnanimous, then to assume.
Riches are needless then, both for themselves,
And for thy reason why they should be sought,   485
To gain a Scepter, oftest better miss't.

BOOK III

So spake the Son of God, and Satan stood
A while as mute confounded what to say,
What to reply, confuted and convinc't
Of his weak arguing, and fallacious drift;
At length collecting all his Serpent wiles,   5
With soothing words renew'd, him thus accosts.
I see thou know'st what is of use to know,
What best to say canst say, to do canst do;
Thy actions to thy words accord, thy words
To thy large heart give utterance due, thy heart   10
Conteins of good, wise, just, the perfect shape.
Should Kings and Nations from thy mouth consult,
Thy Counsel would be as the Oracle
Urim and *Thummim*,[1] those oraculous gems
On *Aaron's* breast: or tongue of Seers old   15
Infallible; or wert thou sought to deeds
That might require th' array of war, thy skill
Of conduct would be such, that all the world
Could not sustain thy Prowess, or subsist
In battel, though against thy few in arms.   20
These God-like Vertues wherefore dost thou hide?
Affecting private life, or more obscure
In savage Wilderness, wherefore deprive
All Earth her wonder at thy acts, thy self
The fame and glory, glory the reward   25

[1] See Lev. viii. 8.

That sole excites to high attempts the flame
Of most erected Spirits, most temper'd pure
Ætherial, who all pleasures else despise,
All treasures and all gain esteem as dross,
And dignities and powers all but the highest?   30
Thy years are ripe, and over-ripe, the Son
Of *Macedonian Philip* had e're these
Won *Asia* and the Throne of *Cyrus*[2] held
At his dispose, young *Scipio* had brought down
The *Carthaginian* pride, young *Pompey* quell'd   35
The *Pontic* King[3] and in triumph had rode.
Yet years, and to ripe years judgment mature,
Quench not the thirst of glory, but augment.
Great *Julius*, whom now all the world admires
The more he grew in years, the more inflam'd   40
With glory, wept that he had liv'd so long
Inglorious: but thou yet art not too late.
   To whom our Saviour calmly thus reply'd.
Thou neither dost perswade me to seek wealth
For Empires sake, nor Empire to affect   45
For glories sake by all thy argument.
For what is glory but the blaze of fame,
The peoples praise, if always praise unmixt?
And what the people but a herd confus'd,
A miscellaneous rabble, who extol   50
Things vulgar, and well weigh'd, scarce worth the praise,
They praise and they admire they know not what;
And know not whom, but as one leads the other;
And what delight to be by such extoll'd,
To live upon thir tongues and be thir talk,   55
Of whom to be disprais'd were no small praise?
His lot who dares be singularly good.
Th' intelligent among them and the wise
Are few, and glory scarce of few is rais'd.
This is true glory and renown, when God   60
Looking on th' Earth, with approbation marks
The just man, and divulges him through Heav'n
To all his Angels, who with true applause
Recount his praises; thus he did to *Job*,
When to extend his fame through Heav'n and Earth,   65
As thou to thy reproach mayst well remember,

---

[2] king of Persia, defeated by Alexander the Great.
[3] Mithridates; Pompey was then (66 B.C.) forty years old.

He ask'd thee, hast thou seen my servant *Job?*
Famous he was in Heav'n, on Earth less known;
Where glory is false glory, attributed
To things not glorious, men not worthy of fame.   70
They err who count it glorious to subdue
By Conquest far and wide, to over-run
Large Countries, and in field great Battels win,
Great Cities by assault: what do these Worthies,
But rob and spoil, burn, slaughter, and enslave   75
Peaceable Nations, neighbouring, or remote,
Made Captive, yet deserving freedom more
Then those thir Conquerours, who leave behind
Nothing but ruin wheresoe're they rove,
And all the flourishing works of peace destroy,   80
Then swell with pride, and must be titl'd Gods,
Great Benefactors of mankind, Deliverers,
Worship't with Temple, Priest and Sacrifice;
One is the Son of *Jove,* of *Mars* the other,[4]
Till Conquerour Death discover them scarce men,   85
Rowling in brutish vices, and deform'd,
Violent or shameful death thir due reward.
But if there be in glory aught of good,
It may by means far different be attain'd
Without ambition, war, or violence;   90
By deeds of peace, by wisdom eminent,
By patience, temperance; I mention still
Him whom thy wrongs with Saintly patience born,
Made famous in a Land and times obscure;
Who names not now with honour patient *Job?*   95
Poor *Socrates* (who next more memorable?)
By what he taught and suffer'd for so doing,
For truths sake suffering death unjust, lives now
Equal in fame to proudest Conquerours.
Yet if for fame and glory aught be done,   100
Aught suffer'd; if young *African*[5] for fame
His wasted Country freed from *Punic* rage,
The deed becomes unprais'd, the man at least,
And loses, though but verbal, his reward.
Shall I seek glory then, as vain men seek   105
Oft not deserv'd? I seek not mine, but his

[4] Alexander was known as the son of Jove Ammon; Romulus, the son of Mars.
[5] Scipio.

Who sent me, and thereby witness whence I am.
    To whom the Tempter murmuring thus reply'd.
Think not so slight of glory; therein least
Resembling thy great Father: he seeks glory,   110
And for his glory all things made, all things
Orders and governs, nor content in Heav'n
By all his Angels glorifi'd, requires
Glory from men, from all men good or bad,
Wise or unwise, no difference, no exemption;   115
Above all Sacrifice, or hallow'd gift
Glory he requires, and glory he receives
Promiscuous from all Nations, Jew, or Greek,
Or Barbarous, nor exception hath declar'd;
From us his foes pronounc't glory he exacts.   120
    To whom our Saviour fervently reply'd.
And reason; since his word all things produc'd,
Though chiefly not for glory as prime end,
But to shew forth his goodness, and impart
His good communicable to every soul   125
Freely; of whom what could he less expect
Then glory and benediction, that is thanks,
The slightest, easiest, readiest recompence
From them who could return him nothing else,
And not returning that would likeliest render   130
Contempt instead, dishonour, obloquy?
Hard recompence, unsutable return
For so much good, so much beneficence.
But why should man seek glory? who of his own
Hath nothing, and to whom nothing belongs   135
But condemnation, ignominy, and shame?
Who for so many benefits receiv'd
Turn'd recreant[6] to God, ingrate and false,
And so of all true good himself despoil'd,
Yet, sacrilegious, to himself would take   140
That which to God alone of right belongs;
Yet so much bounty is in God, such grace,
That who advance his glory, not thir own,
Them he himself to glory will advance.
    So spake the Son of God; and here again   145
Satan had not to answer, but stood struck
With guilt of his own sin, for he himself
Insatiable of glory had lost all,

[6] unfaithful.

Yet of another Plea bethought him soon.

   Of glory as thou wilt, said he, so deem,   150
Worth or not worth the seeking, let it pass:
But to a Kingdom thou art born, ordain'd
To sit upon thy Father *David*'s Throne;
By Mothers side thy Father, though thy right
Be now in powerful hands, that will not part   155
Easily from possession won with arms;
Judæa now and all the promis'd land
Reduc't a Province under *Roman* yoke,
Obeys *Tiberius;* nor is always rul'd
With temperate sway; oft have they violated   160
The Temple,[7] oft the Law with foul affronts,
Abominations rather, as did once
Antiochus:[8] and think'st thou to regain
Thy right by sitting still or thus retiring?
So did not *Machabeus:*[9] he indeed   165
Retir'd unto the Desert, but with arms;
And o're a mighty King so oft prevail'd,
That by strong hand his Family obtain'd,
Though Priests, the Crown, and *David*'s Throne usurp'd,
With *Modin* and her Suburbs once content.   170
If Kingdom move thee not, let move thee Zeal,
And Duty; Zeal and Duty are not slow;
But on Occasions forelock watchful wait.
They themselves rather are occasion best,
Zeal of thy Fathers house, Duty to free   175
Thy Country from her Heathen servitude;
So shalt thou best fullfil, best verifie
The Prophets old, who sung thy endless raign,
The happier raign the sooner it begins,
Raign then; what canst thou better do the while?   180
   To whom our Saviour answer thus return'd.
All things are best fullfil'd in their due time,
And time there is for all things, Truth hath said: [10]
If of my raign Prophetic Writ hath told,
That it shall never end, so when begin   185
The Father in his purpose hath decreed,

[7] violation of the Holy of Holies by Pompey.
[8] See 1 Macc. i.
[9] Judas Maccabeus, born in Modin, won the throne of David after a long struggle with Antiochus.
[10] referring to Eccl. iii.

He in whose hand all times and seasons roul.
What if he hath decreed that I shall first
Be try'd in humble state, and things adverse,
By tribulations, injuries, insults,   190
Contempts, and scorns, and snares, and violence,
Suffering, abstaining, quietly expecting
Without distrust or doubt, that he may know
What I can suffer, how obey? who best
Can suffer, best can do; best reign, who first   195
Well hath obey'd; just tryal e're I merit
My exaltation without change or end.
But what concerns it thee when I begin
My everlasting Kingdom, why art thou
Sollicitous, what moves thy inquisition?   200
Know'st thou not that my rising is thy fall,
And my promotion will be thy destruction?
   To whom the Tempter inly rackt reply'd.
Let that come when it comes; all hope is lost
Of my reception into grace; what worse?   205
For where no hope is left, is left no fear;
If there be worse, the expectation more
Of worse torments me then the feeling can.
I would be at the worst; worst is my Port,
My harbour and my ultimate repose,   210
The end I would attain, my final good.
My error was my error, and my crime
My crime; whatever for it self condemn'd,
And will alike be punish'd; whether thou
Raign or raign not; though to that gentle brow   215
Willingly I could fly, and hope thy raign,
From that placid aspect and meek regard,
Rather then aggravate my evil state,
Would stand between me and thy Fathers ire
(Whose ire I dread more then the fire of Hell),   220
A shelter and a kind of shading cool
Interposition, as a summers cloud.
If I then to the worst that can be hast,
Why move thy feet so slow to what is best,
Happiest both to thy self and all the world,   225
That thou who worthiest art should'st be thir King?
Perhaps thou linger'st in deep thoughts detain'd
Of the enterprise so hazardous and high;
No wonder, for though in thee be united

What of perfection can in man be found,   230
Or human nature can receive, consider
Thy life hath yet been private, most part spent
At home, scarce view'd the *Gallilean* Towns,
And once a year *Jerusalem*, few days
Short sojourn; and what thence could'st thou observe?   235
The world thou hast not seen, much less her glory,
Empires, and Monarchs, and thir radiant Courts,
Best school of best experience, quickest insight
In all things that to greatest actions lead.
The wisest, unexperienc't, will be ever   240
Timorous and loth, with novice modesty
(As he[11] who seeking Asses found a Kingdom),
Irresolute, unhardy, unadventrous:
But I will bring thee where thou soon shalt quit
Those rudiments, and see before thine eyes   245
The Monarchies of th' Earth, thir pomp and state,
Sufficient introduction to inform
Thee, of thy self so apt, in regal Arts,
And regal Mysteries; that thou may'st know
How best their opposition to withstand.   250
    With that (such power was giv'n him then) he took
The Son of God up to a Mountain high.
It was a Mountain at whose verdant feet
A spatious plain out stretch't in circuit wide
Lay pleasant; from his side two rivers[12] flow'd,   255
Th' one winding, th' other strait and left between
Fair Champain with less rivers interveind,
Then meeting joyn'd thir tribute to the Sea:
Fertil of corn the glebe,[13] of oyl and wine,
With herds the pastures throng'd, with flocks the hills, 260
Huge Cities and high towr'd, that well might seem
The seats of mightiest Monarchs, and so large
The Prospect was, that here and there was room
For barren desert fountainless and dry.
To this high mountain top the Tempter brought   265
Our Saviour, and new train of words began.
    Well have we speeded, and o're hill and dale,
Forest and field, and flood, Temples and Towers
Cut shorter many a league; here thou behold'st

[11] Saul; see 1 Sam. ix–x.
[12] the Tigris and Euphrates.
[13] soil.

Assyria and her Empires antient bounds,   270
Araxes[14] and the *Caspian* lake, thence on
As far as *Indus* East, *Euphrates* West,
And oft beyond; to South the *Persian* Bay,
And inaccessible th' *Arabian* drouth:[15]
Here *Ninevee*, of length within her wall   275
Several days journey, built by *Ninus* old,
Of that first golden Monarchy the seat,
And seat of *Salmanassar*,[16] whose success
Israel in long captivity still mourns;
There *Babylon* the wonder of all tongues,   280
As antient, but rebuilt by him[17] who twice
Judah and all thy Father *David*'s house
Led captive, and *Jerusalem* laid waste,
Till *Cyrus*[18] set them free; *Persepolis*
His City there thou seest, and *Bactra* there;   285
Ecbatana her structure vast there shews,
And *Hecatompylos* her hunderd gates,
There *Susa* by *Choaspes*, amber stream,
The drink of none but Kings; of later fame
Built by *Emathian*,[19] or by *Parthian*[20] hands,   290
The great *Seleucia, Nisibis*, and there
Artaxata, Teredon, Ctesiphon,
Turning with easie eye thou may'st behold.
All these the *Parthian*, now some Ages past,
By great *Arsaces* led, who founded first   295
That Empire, under his dominion holds
From the luxurious Kings of *Antioch*[21] won.
And just in time thou com'st to have a view
Of his great power; for now the *Parthian* King
In *Ctesiphon* hath gather'd all his Host   300

[14] an Armenian river flowing into the Caspian. Satan surveys cities and provinces in the Persian, Mesopotamian, and Armenian complex.

[15] desert.

[16] Shalmaneser IV of Assyria captured the Israelites in 726 B.C. (see 2 Kings xvii. 3–4).

[17] Nebuchadnezzar; see Dan. i.

[18] king of Persia; see 2 Chron. xxxvi. 22–23.

[19] referring to Seleucus, general to Alexander the Great.

[20] Parthia formed an empire from conquests of Assyria, Persia, and later Seleucia. The Parthian method of fighting (ll. 305 ff.) was to turn one's horse swiftly upon discharging an arrow.

[21] seat of the Seleucid empire in Syria.

Against the *Scythian*,[22] whose incursions wild
Have wasted *Sogdiana;* to her aid
He marches now in hast; see, though from far,
His thousands, in what martial equipage
They issue forth, Steel Bows, and Shafts their arms   305
Of equal dread in flight, or in pursuit;
All Horsemen, in which fight they most excel;
See how in warlike muster they appear,
In Rhombs and wedges, and half moons, and wings.
   He look't and saw what numbers numberless   310
The City gates out powr'd, light armed Troops
In coats of Mail and military pride;
In Mail thir horses clad, yet fleet and strong,
Prauncing their riders bore, the flower and choice
Of many Provinces from bound to bound;   315
From *Arachosia*, from *Candaor* East,
And *Margiana* to the *Hyrcanian* cliffs
Of *Caucasus*, and dark *Iberian*[23] dales,
From *Atropatia* and the neighbouring plains
Of *Adiabene, Media,* and the South   320
Of *Susiana* to *Balsara's* hav'n.
He saw them in thir forms of battell rang'd,
How quick they wheel'd, and flying behind them shot
Sharp fleet of arrowie showers against the face
Of thir pursuers, and overcame by flight;   325
The field all iron cast a gleaming brown,
Not wanted clouds of foot, nor on each horn,
Cuirassiers all in steel for standing fight;
Chariots or Elephants endorst[24] with Towers
Of Archers, nor of labouring Pioners   330
A multitude with Spades and Axes arm'd
To lay hills plain, fell woods, or valleys fill,
Or where plain was raise hill, or over-lay
With bridges rivers proud, as with a yoke;
Mules after these, Camels and Dromedaries,   335
And Waggons fraught with Utensils of war.
Such forces met not, nor so wide a camp,

[22] an ancient people situated around the Black Sea, famed for savagery in battle; Sogdiana was a province of Persia.
[23] an area in the Caucasus, not Spain.
[24] punning on the Latin word for "back" and referring to howdahs.

When *Agrican*[25] with all his Northern powers
Besieg'd *Albracca,* as Romances tell;
The City of *Gallaphrone,* from thence to win   340
The fairest of her Sex *Angelica*
His daughter, sought by many Prowest[26] Knights,
Both *Paynim,* and the Peers of *Charlemane.*
Such and so numerous was thir Chivalrie;
At sight whereof the Fiend yet more presum'd,   345
And to our Saviour thus his words renew'd.
     That thou may'st know I seek not to engage
Thy Vertue, and not every way secure
On no slight grounds thy safety; hear, and mark
To what end I have brought thee hither and shewn   350
All this fair sight; thy Kingdom though foretold
By Prophet or by Angel, unless thou
Endeavour, as thy Father *David* did,
Thou never shalt obtain; prediction still
In all things, and all men, supposes means,   355
Without means us'd, what it predicts revokes.
But say thou wert possess'd of *David's* Throne
By free consent of all, none opposite,
Samaritan or *Jew;*[27] how could'st thou hope
Long to enjoy it quiet and secure,   360
Between two such enclosing enemies
Roman and *Parthian?* therefore one of these
Thou must make sure thy own, the *Parthian* first
By my advice, as nearer and of late
Found able by invasion to annoy   365
Thy country, and captive lead away her Kings
Antigonus, and old *Hyrcanus* bound,
Maugre the *Roman:*[28] it shall be my task
To render thee the *Parthian* at dispose;
Chuse which thou wilt by conquest or by league.   370
By him thou shalt regain, without him not,
That which alone can truly reinstall thee

[25] king of Tartary and lover of Angelica, for whom he besieged
Albracca, fortress of her father Gallophrone, king of Cathay. At
the court of Charlemagne, she had won the hearts of Orlando,
Rinaldo, and others, both Christians and pagans ("paynim"). (See
Boiardo, *Orlando Innamorato,* I, x.)
[26] gallantest.
[27] who were generally opposed.
[28] The Parthians helped Antigonus gain Judaea from Hyrcanus
II, who had Roman aid, in 40 B.C.

In *David*'s royal seat, his true Successour,
Deliverance of thy brethren, those ten Tribes[29]
Whose off-spring in his Territory yet serve   375
In *Habor*, and among the *Medes* dispers't,
Ten Sons of *Jacob*, two of *Joseph* lost
Thus long from *Israel*; serving as of old
Thir Fathers in the land of *Egypt* serv'd,
This offer sets before thee to deliver.   380
These if from servitude thou shalt restore
To thir inheritance, then, nor till then,
Thou on the Throne of *David* in full glory,
From *Egypt* to *Euphrates* and beyond
Shalt raign, and *Rome* or *Caesar* not need fear.   385
    To whom our Saviour answer'd thus unmov'd.
Much ostentation vain of fleshly arm,
And fragile arms, much instrument of war
Long in preparing, soon to nothing brought,
Before mine eyes thou hast set; and in my ear   390
Vented much policy,[30] and projects deep
Of enemies, of aids, battels and leagues,
Plausible to the world, to me worth naught.
Means I must use thou say'st, prediction else
Will unpredict and fail me of the Throne: 395
My time I told thee (and that time for thee
Were better farthest off) is not yet come;
When that comes think not thou to find me slack
On my part aught endeavouring, or to need
Thy politic maxims, or that cumbersome   400
Luggage of war there shewn me, argument
Of human weakness rather then of strength.
My brethren, as thou call'st them, those Ten Tribes
I must deliver, if I mean to raign
David's true heir, and his full Scepter sway   405
To just extent over all *Israel*'s Sons;
But whence to thee this zeal, where was it then
For *Israel*, or for *David*, or his Throne,
When thou stood'st up his Tempter[31] to the pride
Of numbring *Israel*, which cost the lives   410
Of threescore and ten thousand *Israelites*

---

[29] See 2 Kings xvii. 6; the "two of Joseph" (l. 377) were the tribes of Ephraim and Manasseh.
[30] governmental shrewdness.
[31] See 1 Chron. xxi.

By three days Pestilence? such was thy zeal
To *Israel* then, the same that now to me.
As for those captive Tribes, themselves were they
Who wrought their own captivity, fell off   415
From God to worship Calves, the Deities
Of *Egypt*, *Baal* next and *Ashtaroth*,[32]
And all th' Idolatries of Heathen round,
Besides thir other worse then heathenish crimes;
Nor in the land of their captivity   420
Humbled themselves, or penitent besought
The God of their fore-fathers; but so dy'd
Impenitent, and left a race behind
Like to themselves, distinguishable scarce
From Gentils, but by Circumcision vain,   425
And God with Idols in their worship joyn'd.
Should I of these the liberty regard,
Who freed, as to their antient Patrimony,
Unhumbl'd, unrepentant, unreform'd,
Headlong would follow; and to thir Gods perhaps   430
Of *Bethel* and of *Dan*? no, let them serve
Thir enemies, who serve Idols with God.
Yet he at length, time to himself best known,
Remembring *Abraham* by some wond'rous call
May bring them back repentant and sincere,   435
And at their passing cleave th' *Assyrian* flood,
While to their native land with joy they hast,
As the Red Sea and *Jordan* once he cleft,
When to the promis'd land thir Fathers pass'd;
To his due time and providence I leave them.   440
    So spake *Israel*'s true King, and to the Fiend
Made answer meet, that made void all his wiles.
So fares it when with truth falshood contends.

BOOK IV

    Perplex'd and troubl'd at his bad success
The Tempter stood, nor had what to reply,
Discover'd in his fraud, thrown from his hope,
So oft, and the perswasive Rhetoric
That sleek't his tongue, and won so much on *Eve*,   5
So little here, nay lost; but *Eve* was *Eve*,
This far his over-match, who self deceiv'd

[32] deities of the Phoenicians.

And rash, before-hand had no better weigh'd
The strength he was to cope with, or his own:
But as a man who had been matchless held   10
In cunning, over-reach't where least he thought,
To salve his credit, and for very spight
Still will be tempting him who foyls him still,
And never cease, though to his shame the more;
Or as a swarm of flies in vintage time,   15
About the wine-press where sweet moust is powr'd,
Beat off, returns as oft with humming sound;
Or surging waves against a solid rock,
Though all to shivers dash't, th' assault renew,
Vain battry, and in froth or bubbles end;   20
So Satan, whom repulse upon repulse
Met ever; and to shameful silence brought,
Yet gives not o're though desperate of success,
And his vain importunity pursues.
He brought our Saviour to the western side   25
Of that high mountain, whence he might behold
Another plain,[1] long but in bredth not wide;
Wash'd by the Southern Sea, and on the North
To equal length back'd with a ridge of hills
That screen'd the fruits of th' earth and seats of men   30
From cold *Septentrion*[2] blasts, thence in the midst
Divided by a river, of whose banks
On each side an Imperial City stood,
With Towers and Temples proudly elevate
On seven small Hills, with Palaces adorn'd,   35
Porches and Theatres, Baths, Aqueducts,
Statues and Trophees, and Triumphal Arcs,
Gardens and Groves presented to his eyes,
Above the highth of Mountains interpos'd.
By what strange Parallax[3] or Optic skill   40
Of vision multiply'd through air, or glass
Of Telescope, were curious to enquire:
And now the Tempter thus his silence broke.
    The City which thou seest no other deem

[1] The central Italian plain, with the Tyrrhene Sea to the south
and the Apennines to the northwest, is divided by the Tiber, on
which lies Rome.
[2] northern.
[3] the apparent displacement of an object seen from two different
positions.

Then great and glorious *Rome*, Queen of the Earth   45
So far renown'd, and with the spoils enricht
Of Nations; there the Capitol thou seest
Above the rest lifting his stately head
On the *Tarpeian* rock,[4] her Cittadel
Impregnable, and there Mount *Palatine*   50
Th' Imperial Palace, compass huge, and high
The Structure, skill of noblest Architects,
With gilded battlements, conspicuous far,
Turrets and Terrases, and glittering Spires.
Many a fair Edifice besides, more like   55
Houses of Gods (so well I have dispos'd
My Aerie Microscope) thou may'st behold
Outside and inside both, pillars and roofs
Carv'd work, the hand of fam'd Artificers
In Cedar, Marble, Ivory or Gold.   60
Thence to the gates cast round thine eye, and see
What conflux issuing forth, or entring in,
Pretors,[5] Proconsuls[6] to thir Provinces
Hasting or on return, in robes of State;
Lictors[7] and rods the ensigns of thir power,   65
Legions and Cohorts,[8] turmes of horse and wings:
Or Embassies from Regions far remote
In various habits on the *Appian* road,[9]
Or on th' *Æmilian*,[10] some from farthest South,
Syene,[11] and where the shadow both way falls,   70
Meroe Nilotic Isle, and more to West,
The Realm of *Bocchus* to the Black-moor Sea;
From th' *Asian* Kings and *Parthian* among these,
From *India* and the golden *Chersoness*,[12]

[4] See *El.* 1, n. 11.
[5] chiefly judicial magistrates, next in rank to consuls.
[6] provincial governors.
[7] officers, carrying fasces (a bundle of rods), who cleared the way for magistrates in public.
[8] tenth parts of a legion; a turme was a tenth part of a wing, a flank of the cavalry.
[9] lying between Rome and Brindisi.
[10] lying between Rome and the Adriatic Sea.
[11] a city on the Upper Nile. Bocchus was in northern Africa, and the Blackmoor Sea means the Mediterranean along the northwestern African coast.
[12] the Malay peninsula.

And utmost *Indian* Isle *Taprobane*,[13]   75
Dusk faces with white silken Turbants wreath'd:
From *Gallia, Gades*,[14] and the *Brittish* West,
Germans and *Scythians,* and *Sarmatians*[15] North
Beyond *Danubius* to the *Tauric* Pool.[16]
All Nations now to *Rome* obedience pay,   80
To *Rome's* great Emperour, whose wide domain
In ample Territory, wealth and power,
Civility of Manners, Arts, and Arms,
And long Renown thou justly may'st prefer
Before the *Parthian;* these two Thrones except,   85
The rest are barbarous, and scarce worth the sight,
Shar'd among petty Kings too far remov'd;
These having shewn thee, I have shewn thee all
The Kingdoms of the world, and all thir glory.
This Emperour[17] hath no Son, and now is old,   90
Old, and lascivious, and from *Rome* retir'd
To *Capreæ* an Island small but strong
On the *Campanian* shore, with purpose there
His horrid lusts in private to enjoy,
Committing to a wicked Favourite[18]   95
All publick cares, and yet of him suspicious,
Hated of all, and hating; with what ease
Indu'd with Regal Vertues as thou art,
Appearing, and beginning noble deeds,
Might'st thou expel this monster from his Throne   100
Now made a sty, and in his place ascending
A victor, people free from servile yoke!
And with my help thou may'st; to me the power
Is giv'n, and by that right I give it thee.
Aim therefore at no less then all the world,   105
Aim at the highest, without the highest attain'd
Will be for thee no sitting, or not long
On *David's* Throne, be propheci'd what will.
    To whom the Son of God unmov'd reply'd.
Nor doth this grandeur and majestic show   110
Of luxury, though call'd magnificence,

[13] Ceylon.
[14] Cadiz.
[15] people of a region between the Vistula and Volga rivers.
[16] the Sea of Azof.
[17] Tiberius.
[18] Sejanus.

More then of arms before, allure mine eye,
Much less my mind; though thou should'st add to tell
Thir sumptuous gluttonies, and gorgeous feasts
On *Cittron* tables or *Atlantic* stone;[19]   115
(For I have also heard, perhaps have read)
Their wines of *Setia, Cales,* and *Falerne,*
Chios and *Creet,*[20] and how they quaff in Gold,
Crystal and Myrrhine[21] cups imboss'd with Gems
And studs of Pearl, to me should'st tell who thirst   120
And hunger still: then Embassies thou shew'st
From Nations far and nigh; what honour that,
But tedious wast of time to sit and hear
So many hollow compliments and lies,
Outlandish flatteries? then proceed'st to talk   125
Of the Emperour, how easily subdu'd,
How gloriously; I shall, thou say'st, expel
A brutish monster: what if I withal
Expel a Devil who first made him such?
Let his tormentor Conscience find him out,   130
For him I was not sent, nor yet to free
That people victor once, now vile and base,
Deservedly made vassal, who once just,
Frugal, and mild, and temperate, conquer'd well,
But govern ill the Nations under yoke,   135
Peeling[22] thir Provinces, exhausted all
By lust and rapine; first ambitious grown
Of triumph that insulting vanity;
Then cruel, by thir sports to blood enur'd
Of fighting beasts, and men to beasts expos'd,   140
Luxurious by thir wealth, and greedier still,
And from the daily Scene effeminate.
What wise and valiant man would seek to free
These thus degenerate, by themselves enslav'd,
Or could of inward slaves make outward free?   145
Know therefore when my season comes to sit
On *David's* Throne, it shall be like a tree
Spreading and over-shadowing all the Earth,

19 tables of fine wood from citrus trees or of marble.

20 The first three are Italian areas and the last two Greek islands all famous for wines.

21 made of a semiprecious stone; the glassware was transparent, showing pieces of embedded colored glass (perhaps with gems).

22 stripping.

Or as a stone that shall to pieces dash
All Monarchies besides throughout the world,   150
And of my Kingdom there shall be no end:
Means there shall be to this, but what the means,
Is not for thee to know, nor me to tell.
   To whom the Tempter impudent repli'd.
I see all offers made by me how slight   155
Thou valu'st, because offer'd, and reject'st:
Nothing will please the difficult and nice,[23]
Or nothing more then still to contradict:
On th' other side know also thou, that I
On what I offer set as high esteem,   160
Nor what I part with mean to give for naught;
All these which in a moment thou behold'st,
The Kingdoms of the world to thee I give;
For giv'n to me, I give to whom I please,
No trifle; yet with this reserve, not else,   165
On this condition, if thou wilt fall down,
And worship me as thy superior Lord,
Easily done, and hold them all of me;
For what can less so great a gift deserve?
   Whom thus our Saviour answer'd with disdain.   170
I never lik'd thy talk, thy offers less,
Now both abhor, since thou hast dar'd to utter
Th' abominable terms, impious condition;
But I endure the time, till which expir'd,
Thou hast permission on me. It is written   175
The first of all Commandments, Thou shalt worship
The Lord thy God, and only him shalt serve;[24]
And dar'st thou to the Son of God propound
To worship thee accurst, now more accurst
For this attempt bolder then that on *Eve*,   180
And more blasphemous? which expect to rue.
The Kingdoms of the world to thee were giv'n,
Permitted rather, and by thee usurp't,
Other donation none thou canst produce:
If given, by whom but by the King of Kings,   185
God over all supreme? if giv'n to thee,
By thee how fairly is the Giver now
Repaid? But gratitude in thee is lost
Long since. Wert thou so void of fear or shame,

[23] fastidious.
[24] Matt. iv. 10.

As offer them to me the Son of God,   190
To me my own, on such abhorred pact,
That I fall down and worship thee as God?
Get thee behind me; plain thou now appear'st
That Evil one, Satan for ever damn'd.
   To whom the Fiend with fear abasht reply'd.   195
Be not so sore offended, Son of God;
Though Sons of God both Angels are and Men,
If I to try whether in higher sort
Then these thou bear'st that title, have propos'd
What both from Men and Angels I receive,   200
Tetrarchs[25] of fire, air, flood, and on the earth
Nations besides from all the quarter'd winds,
God of this world invok't and world beneath;
Who then thou art, whose coming is foretold
To me so fatal, met it most concerns.   205
The tryal hath indamag'd thee no way,
Rather more honour left and more esteem;
Me naught advantag'd, missing what I aim'd.
Therefore let pass, as they are transitory,
The Kingdoms of this world; I shall no more   210
Advise thee, gain them as thou canst, or not.
And thou thy self seem'st otherwise inclin'd
Then to a worldly Crown, addicted more
To contemplation and profound dispute,
As by that early action may be judg'd,   215
When slipping from thy Mothers eye thou went'st
Alone into the Temple;[26] there wast found
Among the gravest Rabbies disputant
On points and questions fitting *Moses* Chair,
Teaching not taught; the childhood shews the man,   220
As morning shews the day. Be famous then
By wisdom; as thy Empire must extend,
So let extend thy mind o're all the world,
In knowledge, all things in it comprehend,
All knowledge is not couch't in *Moses* Law,   225
The *Pentateuch*[27] or what the Prophets wrote,
The *Gentiles* also know, and write, and teach

[25] rulers of a quarter of the world (l. 202), but referring too
to the four enumerated elements.
[26] See Luke ii. 42–47.
[27] the first five books of the Old Testament.

To admiration, led by Natures light;
And with the *Gentiles* much thou must converse,
Ruling them by perswasion as thou mean'st,　　　230
Without thir learning how wilt thou with them,
Or they with thee hold conversation meet?
How wilt thou reason with them, how refute
Thir Idolisms, Traditions, Paradoxes?
Error by his own arms is best evinc't.　　　235
Look once more e're we leave this specular Mount
Westward, much nearer by Southwest, behold
Where on th' *Ægean* shore a City stands
Built nobly, pure the air, and light the soil,
Athens the eye of *Greece*, Mother of Arts　　　240
And Eloquence, native to famous wits
Or hospitable, in her sweet recess,
City or Suburban, studious walks and shades;
See there the Olive Grove of *Academe*,
Plato's retirement, where the *Attic* Bird[28]　　　245
Trills her thick-warbl'd notes the summer long,
There flowrie hill *Hymettus* with the sound
Of Bees industrious murmur oft invites
To studious musing; there *Ilissus* rouls
His whispering stream; within the walls then view　　　250
The schools of antient Sages; his[29] who bred
Great *Alexander* to subdue the world,
Lyceum there, and painted *Stoa*[30] next:
There thou shalt hear and learn the secret power
Of harmony in tones and numbers hit　　　255
By voice or hand, and various-measur'd verse,
Æolian charms and *Dorian Lyric* Odes,[31]
And his who gave them breath, but higher sung,
Blind *Melesigenes* thence *Homer* call'd,
Whose Poem *Phœbus* challeng'd for his own.　　　260
Thence what the lofty grave Tragœdians taught
In *Chorus* or *Iambic*, teachers best
Of moral prudence, with delight receiv'd
In brief sententious precepts, while they treat
Of fate, and chance, and change in human life;　　　265

[28] the nightingale.
[29] Aristotle.
[30] the "porch" in the marketplace of Athens where Zeno taught his Stoic philosophy.
[31] referring primarily to Sappho and Pindar.

High actions, and high passions best describing:
Thence to the famous Orators repair,
Those antient, whose resistless eloquence
Wielded at will that fierce Democratie,
Shook the Arsenal and fulmin'd over *Greece,*   270
To *Macedon,* and *Artaxerxes*[32] Throne;
To sage Philosophy next lend thine ear,
From Heav'n descended to the low-rooft house
Of *Socrates,* see there his Tenement,
Whom well inspir'd the Oracle pronounc'd   275
Wisest of men; from whose mouth issu'd forth
Mellifluous streams that water'd all the schools
Of Academics old and new, with those
Sirnam'd *Peripatetics,*[33] and the Sect
Epicurean, and the *Stoic* severe;   280
These here revolve, or, as thou lik'st, at home,
Till time mature thee to a Kingdom's waight;
These rules will render thee a King compleat
Within thy self, much more with Empire joyn'd.
    To whom our Saviour sagely thus repli'd.   285
Think not but that I know these things, or think
I know them not; not therefore am I short
Of knowing what I ought: he who receives
Light from above, from the fountain of light,
No other doctrine needs, though granted true;   290
But these are false, or little else but dreams,
Conjectures, fancies, built on nothing firm.
The first and wisest of them[34] all profess'd
To know this only, that he nothing knew;
The next[35] to fabling fell and smooth conceits,   295
A third sort[36] doubted all things, though plain sence;
Others in vertue plac'd felicity,
But vertue joyn'd with riches and long life,
In corporal pleasure he,[37] and careless ease,
The Stoic last in Philosophic pride,   300
By him call'd vertue; and his vertuous man,
Wise, perfect in himself, and all possessing

[32] king of Persia, who sided with Sparta against Athens. The orators were Demosthenes and Pericles, respectively.
[33] followers of Aristotle.
[34] Socrates.
[35] Plato.
[36] Pyrrho, founder of the Sceptics.
[37] Epicurus.

Equal to God, oft shames not to prefer,
As fearing God nor man, contemning all
Wealth, pleasure, pain or torment, death and life,   305
Which when he lists, he leaves, or boasts he can,
For all his tedious talk is but vain boast,
Or subtle shifts conviction to evade.
Alas what can they teach, and not mislead;
Ignorant of themselves, of God much more,   310
And how the world began, and how man fell
Degraded by himself, on grace depending?
Much of the Soul they talk, but all awrie,
And in themselves seek vertue, and to themselves
All glory arrogate, to God give none,   315
Rather accuse him under usual names,
Fortune and Fate, as one regardless quite
Of mortal things. Who therefore seeks in these
True wisdom, finds her not, or by delusion
Far worse, her false resemblance only meets,   320
An empty cloud. However many books
Wise men have said are wearisom; who reads
Incessantly, and to his reading brings not
A spirit and judgment equal or superior,
(And what he brings, what needs he elsewhere seek)   325
Uncertain and unsettl'd still remains,
Deep verst in books and shallow in himself,
Crude or intoxicate, collecting toys,
And trifles for choice matters, worth a spunge;
As Children gathering pibles on the shore.   330
Or if I would delight my private hours
With Music or with Poem, where so soon
As in our native Language can I find
That solace? All our Law and Story strew'd
With Hymns, our Psalms with artful terms inscrib'd,   335
Our Hebrew Songs and Harps in *Babylon*,
That pleas'd so well our Victors ear, declare
That rather *Greece* from us these Arts deriv'd;
Ill imitated, while they loudest sing
The vices of thir Deities, and thir own   340
In Fable, Hymn, or Song, so personating
Thir Gods ridiculous, and themselves past shame.
Remove their swelling Epithetes thick laid
As varnish on a Harlots cheek, the rest,
Thin sown with aught of profit or delight,   345
Will far be found unworthy to compare

With *Sion*'s songs, to all true tasts excelling,
Where God is prais'd aright, and Godlike men,
The Holiest of Holies, and his Saints;
Such are from God inspir'd, not such from thee;   350
Unless where moral vertue is express't
By light of Nature not in all quite lost.
Thir Orators thou then extoll'st, as those
The top of Eloquence, Statists[38] indeed,
And lovers of thir Country, as may seem;   355
But herein to our Prophets far beneath,
As men divinely taught, and better teaching
The solid rules of Civil Government
In thir majestic unaffected stile
Then all the Oratory of *Greece* and *Rome*.   360
In them is plainest taught, and easiest learnt,
What makes a Nation happy, and keeps it so,
What ruins Kingdoms, and lays Cities flat;
These only with our Law best form a King.
    So spake the Son of God; but Satan now   365
Quite at a loss, for all his darts were spent,
Thus to our Saviour with stern brow reply'd.
    Since neither wealth, nor honour, arms nor arts,
Kingdom nor Empire pleases thee, nor aught
By me propos'd in life contemplative,   370
Or active, tended on by glory, or fame,
What dost thou in this World? the Wilderness
For thee is fittest place, I found thee there,
And thither will return thee, yet remember
What I foretell thee, soon thou shalt have cause   375
To wish thou never hadst rejected thus
Nicely or cautiously my offer'd aid,
Which would have set thee in short time with ease
On *David*'s Throne; or Throne of all the world,
Now at full age, fulness of time, thy season,   380
When Prophesies of thee are best fullfill'd.
Now contrary, if I read aught in Heav'n,
Or Heav'n write aught of Fate, by what the Stars
Voluminous, or single characters,
In their conjunction met, give me to spell,   385
Sorrows, and labours, opposition, hate,
Attends thee, scorns, reproaches, injuries,
Violence and stripes, and lastly cruel death.

[38] statesmen.

A Kingdom they portend thee, but what Kingdom,
Real or Allegoric I discern not,   390
Now when, eternal sure, as without end,
Without beginning; for no date prefixt
Directs me in the Starry Rubric set.
   So saying he took (for still he knew his power
Not yet expir'd) and to the Wilderness   395
Brought back the Son of God, and left him there,
Feigning to disappear. Darkness now rose,
As day-light sunk, and brought in lowring night
Her shadowy off-spring unsubstantial both,
Privation meer of light and absent day.   400
Our Saviour meek and with untroubl'd mind
After his aerie jaunt, though hurried sore,
Hungry and cold betook him to his rest,
Wherever, under some concourse of shades
Whose branching arms thick intertwin'd might shield   405
From dews and damps of night his shelter'd head,
But shelter'd slept in vain, for at his head
The Tempter watch'd, and soon with ugly dreams
Disturb'd his sleep; and either Tropic now
'Gan thunder, and both ends of Heav'n, the Clouds   410
From many a horrid rift abortive pour'd
Fierce rain with lightning mixt, water with fire
In ruin reconcil'd: nor slept the winds
Within thir stony caves, but rush'd abroad
From the four hinges of the world, and fell   415
On the vext Wilderness, whose tallest Pines,
Though rooted deep as high, and sturdiest Oaks
Bow'd their Stiff necks, loaden with stormy blasts,
Or torn up sheer: ill wast thou shrouded then,
O patient Son of God, yet only stoodst   420
Unshaken; nor yet staid the terror there,
Infernal Ghosts, and Hellish Furies, round
Environ'd thee, some howl'd, some yell'd, some shriek'd,
Some bent at thee thir fiery darts, while thou
Sat'st unappall'd in calm and sinless peace.   425
Thus pass'd the night so foul till morning fair
Came forth with Pilgrim steps in amice[39] gray;
Who with her radiant finger still'd the roar
Of thunder, chas'd the clouds, and laid the winds,
And grisly Spectres, which the Fiend had rais'd   430

[39] a hood worn by the clergy.

To tempt the Son of God with terrors dire.
And now the Sun with more effectual beams
Had chear'd the face of Earth, and dry'd the wet
From drooping plant, or dropping tree; the birds
Who all things now behold more fresh and green,   435
After a night of storm so ruinous,
Clear'd up their choicest notes in bush and spray
To gratulate the sweet return of morn;
Nor yet amidst this joy and brightest morn
Was absent, after all his mischief done,   440
The Prince of darkness, glad would also seem
Of this fair change, and to our Saviour came,
Yet with no new device, they all were spent,
Rather by this his last affront resolv'd,
Desperate of better course, to vent his rage,   445
And mad despight to be so oft repell'd.
Him walking on a Sunny hill he found,
Back'd on the North and West by a thick wood,
Out of the wood he starts in wonted shape;
And in a careless mood thus to him said.   450
    Fair morning yet betides thee Son of God,
After a dismal night; I heard the rack
As Earth and Skie would mingle; but my self
Was distant; and these flaws, though mortals fear them
As dangerous to the pillard frame of Heav'n,   455
Or to the Earths dark basis underneath,
Are to the main[40] as inconsiderable,
And harmless, if not wholsom, as a sneeze[41]
To mans less universe, and soon are gone;
Yet as being oft times noxious where they light   460
On man, beast, plant, wastful and turbulent,
Like turbulencies in th' affairs of men,
Over whose heads they roar, and seem to point,
They oft fore-signifie and threaten ill:
This Tempest at this Desert most was bent;   465
Of men at thee, for only thou here dwell'st.
Did I not tell thee, if thou didst reject
The perfet season offer'd with my aid
To win thy destin'd seat, but wilt prolong

[40] the universe.
[41] Svendsen (p. 39) points out that a sneeze was thought a
benefit to health because it purged the brain ("mans less universe").

All to the push of Fate, persue thy way   470
Of gaining *David's* Throne no man knows when,
For both the when and how is no where told,
Thou shalt be what thou art ordain'd, no doubt;
For Angels have proclaim'd it, but concealing
The time and means: each act is rightliest done,   475
Not when it must, but when it may be best.
If thou observe not this, be sure to find,
What I foretold thee, many a hard assay
Of dangers, and adversities and pains,
E're thou of *Israel's* Scepter get fast hold;   480
Whereof this ominous night that clos'd thee round,
So many terrors, voices, prodigies
May warn thee, as a sure fore-going sign.
     So talk'd he, while the Son of God went on
And staid not, but in brief him answer'd thus.   485
     Mee worse then wet thou find'st not; other harm
Those terrors which thou speak'st of, did me none;
I never fear'd they could, though noising loud
And threatning nigh; what they can do as signs
Betok'ning, or ill boding, I contemn   490
As false portents, not sent from God, but thee;
Who knowing I shall raign past thy preventing,
Obtrud'st thy offer'd aid, that I accepting
At least might seem to hold all power of thee,
Ambitious spirit, and wouldst be thought my God,   495
And storm'st refus'd, thinking to terrifie
Mee to thy will; desist, thou art discern'd
And toil'st in vain, nor me in vain molest.
     To whom the Fiend now swoln with rage reply'd:
Then hear, O Son of *David*, Virgin-born;   500
For Son of God to me is yet in doubt,
Of the Messiah I have heard foretold
By all the Prophets; of thy birth at length
Announc't by *Gabriel* with the first I knew,
And of th' Angelic Song in *Bethlehem* field,   505
On thy birth-night, that sung thee Saviour born.
From that time seldom have I ceas'd to eye
Thy infancy, thy childhood, and thy youth,
Thy manhood last, though yet in private bred;
Till at the Ford of *Jordan* wither all   510
Flock'd to the Baptist, I among the rest,
Though not to be Baptiz'd, by voice from Heav'n
Heard thee pronounc'd the Son of God belov'd.

Thenceforth I thought thee worth my nearer view
And narrower Scrutiny, that I might learn   515
In what degree or meaning thou art call'd
The Son of God, which bears no single sence;
The Son of God I also am, or was,
And if I was, I am; relation stands;
All men are Sons of God; yet thee I thought   520
In some respect far higher so declar'd.
Therefore I watch'd thy footsteps from that hour,
And follow'd thee still on to this wast wild;
Where by all best conjectures I collect
Thou art to be my fatal enemy.   525
Good reason then, if I before-hand seek
To understand my Adversary, who
And what he is; his wisdom, power, intent,
By parl, or composition, truce, or league
To win him, or win from him what I can.   530
And opportunity I here have had
To try thee, sift thee, and confess have found thee
Proof against all temptation as a rock
Of Adamant, and as a Center, firm;
To th' utmost of meer man both wise and good,   535
Not more; for Honours, Riches, Kingdoms, Glory
Have been before contemn'd, and may agen:
Therefore to know what more thou art then man,
Worth naming Son of God by voice from Heav'n,
Another method I must now begin.   540
    So saying he caught him up, and without wing
Of *Hippogrif*[42] bore through the Air sublime
Over the Wilderness and o're the Plain;
Till underneath them fair *Jerusalem*,
The holy City lifted high her Towers,   545
And higher yet the glorious Temple[43] rear'd
Her pile, far off appearing like a Mount
Of Alabaster, top't with Golden Spires:
There on the highest Pinacle he set
The Son of God; and added thus in scorn: 550
    There stand, if thou wilt stand; to stand upright
Will ask thee skill; I to thy Fathers house
Have brought thee, and highest plac't, highest is best,
Now shew thy Progeny; if not to stand,

[42] a winged animal, half horse and half griffin.
[43] that built by Herod.

Cast thy self down; safely if Son of God: 555
For it is written,[44] He will give command
Concerning thee to his Angels, in thir hands
They shall up lift thee, lest at any time
Thou chance to dash thy foot against a stone.
   To whom thus Jesus: also it is written,   560
Tempt not the Lord thy God, he said and stood.
But Satan smitten with amazement fell
As when Earths Son *Antæus* (to compare
Small things with greatest) in *Irassa* strove
With *Joves Alcides*,[45] and oft foil'd still rose,   565
Receiving from his mother Earth new strength,
Fresh from his fall, and fiercer grapple joyn'd,
Throttl'd at length in th' Air, expir'd and fell;
So after many a foil the Tempter proud,
Renewing fresh assaults, amidst his pride   570
Fell whence he stood to see his Victor fall.
And as that *Theban* Monster[46] that propos'd
Her riddle, and him, who solv'd it not, devour'd;
That once found out and solv'd, for grief and spight
Cast her self headlong from th' *Ismenian* steep,   575
So strook with dread and anguish fell the Fiend,
And to his crew, that sat consulting, brought
Joyless triumphals of his hop't success,
Ruin, and desperation, and dismay,
Who durst so proudly tempt the Son of God.   580
So Satan fell and strait a fiery Globe
Of Angels on full sail of wing flew nigh,
Who on their plumy Vans[47] receiv'd him soft
From his uneasie station, and upbore
As on a floating couch through the blithe Air,   585
Then in a flowry valley set him down
On a green bank, and set before him spred
A table of Celestial Food, Divine,
Ambrosial, Fruits fetcht from the tree of life,
And from the fount of life Ambrosial drink,   590
That soon refresh'd him wearied, and repair'd

[44] Matt. iv. 6–7.
[45] Hercules, who reasoned how to subdue the giant Antaeus.
[46] the Sphinx, who devoured those unable to solve her riddle; when Oedipus gave the correct answer, she flung herself from the acropolis into the river Ismenus.
[47] wings.

What hunger, if aught hunger had impair'd,
Or thirst, and as he fed, Angelic Quires
Sung Heavenly Anthems of his victory
Over temptation, and the Tempter proud.   595
    True Image of the Father whether thron'd
In the bosom of bliss, and light of light
Conceiving, or remote from Heav'n, enshrin'd
In fleshly Tabernacle, and human form,
Wandring the Wilderness, whatever place,   600
Habit, or state, or motion, still expressing
The Son of God, with Godlike force indu'd
Against th' Attempter of thy Fathers Throne,
And Thief of Paradise; him long of old
Thou didst debel,[48] and down from Heav'n cast   605
With all his Army, now thou hast aveng'd
Supplanted *Adam,* and by vanquishing
Temptation, hast regain'd lost Paradise,
And frustrated the conquest fraudulent:
He never more henceforth will dare set foot   610
In Paradise to tempt; his snares are broke:
For though that seat of earthly bliss be fail'd,
A fairer Paradise is founded now
For *Adam* and his chosen Sons, whom thou
A Saviour art come down to re-install,   615
Where they shall dwell secure, when time shall be
Of Tempter and Temptation without fear.
But thou, Infernal Serpent, shalt not long
Rule in the Clouds; like an Autumnal Star
Or Lightning thou shalt fall from Heav'n trod down   620
Under his feet: for proof, e're this thou feel'st
Thy wound, yet not thy last and deadliest wound
By this repulse receiv'd, and hold'st in Hell
No triumph; in all her gates *Abaddon*[49] rues
Thy bold attempt; hereafter learn with awe   625
To dread the Son of God: he all unarm'd
Shall chase thee with the terror of his voice
From thy Demoniac holds, possession foul,
Thee and thy Legions, yelling they shall fly,
And beg to hide them in a herd of Swine,   630
Lest he command them down into the deep

[48] subdue.
[49] Hell.

Bound, and to torment sent before thir time.[50]
Hail Son of the most High, heir of both worlds,
Queller of Satan, on thy glorious work
Now enter, and begin to save mankind.   635
    Thus they the Son of God our Saviour meek
Sung Victor, and from Heav'nly Feast refresht
Brought on his way with joy; hee unobserv'd
Home to his Mothers house private return'd.

    (*1646–48 ?; revised or, according to some critics,
    written after 1665*)[51]

[50] See *El. 4*, n. 20.
[51] The traditional dating of the entire epic after 1665 and before *SA* has been challenged by the editor in "Chronology of Milton's Major Poems" where these dates are conjectured.

TEXTUAL NOTES

Collations of all known significant texts have been prepared for all poems. For brevity, however, only verbal variants in all texts and similar important differences are reported here. Manuscript readings which are not final are omitted, and abbreviations are generally expanded.

The basic text from which the present version of a poem is derived is marked by an asterisk. Milton's holograph copies best represent his intentions, though they contain some errors, lack full punctuation, and evidence spelling practices which were later abandoned. A basic manuscript text is altered in the direction of a basic printed text. Scribal copies and printed versions, however, are filled with idiosyncracies in mechanics. A text given in this edition follows the copy available which seems to have been closest to Milton; alterations are made when authority is found in another text, when (as with punctuation) they are necessary for easy understanding of a line, when an error seems certain, and when meter dictates. In addition a few spellings are changed to more standard (and Milton's later) forms: these include the dropping of most redundant final "e's." The result of these principles is, unfortunately, inconsistency; but it represents the kind of text offered the seventeenth-century reader without being an uncritical duplication of an original printing.

There were two collected editions of the minor poems during Milton's lifetime, one in 1645 and one in 1673; some poems appeared in separate publications or in other collected volumes, noted where pertinent. SA and PR were issued together in 1671, the only authoritative source; PL was first published in 1667 (reissued with introductory material in 1668 and 1669) and then revised for a second edition in 1674. Publication is referred to by date in the notes. Original copies in the New York Public Library are reported, compared with the facsimiles in Harris F. Fletcher's four-volume edition.

Aside from brief or incidental materials (corrections in presentation volumes, etc.) and copies with, apparently, no direct Miltonic connection, manuscript sources are the Trinity College MS (facsimile by William Aldis Wright, London,

1899), the Bridgewater MS of *A Mask*, the MS of the *Ode to Rouse*, and the MS of Book I of *PL*. These four important MSS are published in facsimile by Fletcher.

Evidence for the date of composition of each poem is cited as briefly as possible, since the researches of such men as Hanford, Parker, Tillyard, and Woodhouse have made it possible to record rather definite dates for most of the poems. For purposes of dating, the order of entry in the *TM* is obviously significant, but the arrangement within groups in the early editions is also informative, although errors or printing exigencies may have altered Milton's arrangement.

A PARAPHRASE ON PSALM 114
Date: 1624; composed, according to headnote, when Milton was fifteen.
Texts: 1645*, 1673.

PSALM 136
Date: 1624; composed, according to headnote for *Ps.* 114, when Milton was fifteen.
Texts: 1645*, 1673. A manuscript copy from the 1645 printing occurs in a poetic collection by William Sancroft (Bodleian Library, Tanner MS 466, pp. 34–35, ff. 20ᵛ–21); there are no verbal variants.
(7–8) *et al.* For &c. / For, &c. *and* For his, &c. *1645 and 1673 vacillate slightly differently between these two abbreviations.* (10, 13, 17, 21, 25) That / Who *1673.*

APOLOGUS DE RUSTICO ET HERO
Date: 1624–25; apparently written as a grammar school exercise.
Text: 1673*.

CARMINA ELEGIACA
Date: 1624–25; apparently a late grammar school exercise.
Text: MS in Netherby Hall, Longtown, Cumberland (autotype facsimile in PRO, catalogued: Autotypes / Milton &c. / Fac. 6 / Library / Shelf 156a; photograph* of autotype in British Museum, MS Add. 41063 I, f. 85; printed by A. J. Horwood, Camden Society, n.s. XVI (1876), xvi–xix, 62–63).
3 prænuncius ales. / p(   )le (   ) *reading given is that recorded by Horwood.*

"IGNAVUS SATRAPAM DEDECET . . ."
Date: 1624–25; apparently a late grammar school exercise.
Text: photograph* of autotype of MS (see note to *Carmina Elegiaca*).
4 Stratus purpureo procubuit thoro / str(   )tus purp(   )eo p(   )buit (   ) *Horwood printed the first two words; Garrod (II.371) and Columbia Milton (XVIII.643) suggest last word.*

ELEGIA PRIMA

Date: early Apr. 1626; written during the spring vacation after his rustication which occurred in the Lent term of 1626 (see ll. 9–12, 85–90). The Easter term began on Apr. 19.

Texts: 1645*, 1673.

(13) molles, / *1645 shows three states: as given,* molles *without a comma, and* molle *without* s *or a comma.* (29) auditur / *1673 is found in two states:* auditor *as given.* (40) Interdum / *1673 is found in two states:* Intredum *as given.*

IN OBITUM PROCANCELLARII MEDICI

Date: Oct.–Nov. 1626; Gostlin died Oct. 21, 1626. Milton's Latin note that the poem was written when he was sixteen is in error. It precedes *Nov. 5* in 1645.

Texts: 1645*, 1673.

IN PRODITIONEM BOMBARDICAM

Date: Nov. 1626 ?; probably composed around the same time as *Nov. 5.*

Texts: 1645*, 1673.

IN EANDEM: "Thus did you strive . . ."

Date: Nov. 1626 ?; probably composed around the same time as *Nov. 5.*

Texts: 1645*, 1673.

IN EANDEM: "James derided . . ."

Date: Nov. 1626 ?; probably composed around the same time as *Nov. 5.*

Texts: 1645*, 1673.

(4) cornua / corona *1673.* (12) *not indented 1673.*

IN EANDEM: "Whom impious Rome . . ."

Date: Nov. 1626 ?; probably composed around the same time as *Nov. 5.*

Texts: 1645*, 1673.

IN INVENTOREM BOMBARDÆ

Date: Nov. 1626 ?; probably composed around the same time as *Nov. 5.*

Texts: 1645*, 1673.

IN QUINTUM NOVEMBRIS

Date: Nov. 1626; composed, according to Latin note, when Milton was seventeen.

Texts: 1645*, 1673.

(20) ceu / seu *1645, 1673.* (45) natat / notat *1673; erratum corrects.* (75) *indented 1673.* (125) casúmque *1673* / casúque *1645.* (143) præruptaque *1673* / semifractaque *1645.*

ELEGIA SECUNDA

Date: Nov. ? 1626; composed, according to Latin note, when Milton was seventeen. Ridding's death occurred apparently in Nov.

Texts: 1645*, 1673.

ELEGIA TERTIA

Date: Dec. 1626 ?; although a Latin note says that this elegy was written when Milton was seventeen, the apparent reference (ll. 9–12) to the death of Count Ernest of Mansfeld, who was killed on Nov. 29, makes Dec. the earliest time for composition.

Texts: 1645*, 1673.

IN OBITUM PRÆSULIS ELIENSIS

Date: Dec. 1626 ?; composed after *El.* 3 (see ll. 4–6). Felton died on Oct. 6, and a Latin note places composition when Milton was seventeen, though there may be a slight error here.

Texts: 1645*, 1673.

ELEGIA QUARTA

Date: late Mar. 1627; Latin note states that it was written when Milton was eighteen, from ll. 33–34 we know that it was written after Mar. 21, and it seems to be the verse epistle referred to in his letter of Mar. 26, 1627(?). (See Parker, *MLN*, LIII [1938], 399–407, for dating of the letter.) References to the war surrounding Hamburg are in agreement with this dating, and suggest no time later than the end of April. The elegy may have been composed before or after the letter, which apparently was written the day after Easter.

Texts: 1645*, 1673.

(89) fœtus; / fætus; *1645, 1673.*

ON THE DEATH OF A FAIR INFANT DYING OF A COUGH

Date: Jan.–Mar. 1628; Milton's niece died Jan. 22 and his second niece was born Apr. 9 (see last stanza). He notes in Latin that the poem was composed when he was seventeen. But since Milton was seventeen between Dec. 1625 and Dec. 1626, the printer or scribe may have simply misread "19" as "17."

Text: 1673*.

(53) Mercy *added to defective line.* (54) crown'd / cown'd *1673.*

AT A VACATION EXERCISE

Date: July 1628; Latin note that it was delivered when Milton was nineteen.

Text: 1673*.

Printed between the *Fifth Ode* and *Forcers of Conscience,* but an *erratum* repositions immediately after *Fair Infant.* (98) hallow'd / hollowed *1673.*

ELEGIA QUINTA

Date: spring 1629; written when Milton was twenty according to Latin note.

Texts: 1645*, 1673.

(30) perennis *1673* / quotannis *1645.* (115) Navita / Natvia *1673.*

ON THE MORNING OF CHRISTS NATIVITY

Date: Dec. 1629; year given in *1645.*

Texts: 1645*, 1673. A manuscript copy from the 1645 printing occurs in a poetic collection by William Sancroft (Bodleian Library MS, Tanner 466, pp. 60–66, ff. 33ᵛ–36ᵛ); four verbal variants are noted: (52) Peace / Peace>Calme (53) or / nor (86) dawn / Day (171) wrath / wroth.
(143–44) Th' enameld *Arras* of the Rainbow wearing, | And Mercy set between, *1645*. (171) wroth *1673* / wrath *1645*.

ELEGIA SEXTA
Date: Dec. 1629; reference to Diodati's letter of Dec. 13 (headnote) and to *Nativity Ode* (ll. 79–90).
Texts: 1645*, 1673.

THE PASSION
Date: Mar. 1630; written, apparently, around Easter following the composition of the *Nativity Ode.*
Texts: 1645*, 1673.
(22) latter / latest *1673.*

ELEGIA SEPTIMA
Date: May 1630; number of elegy and position after *El.* 6 in 1645. The printed note "Anno ætatis undevigesimo" (at the age of nineteen) may have resulted, as Parker has argued ("Notes," pp. 120–21), from a scribe's misreading of Milton's "uno et vigesimo" (twenty-one).
Texts: 1645*, 1673. A correction in Milton's hand is found in the Bodleian Library copy of 1645 (catalogued 8° M168 Art, but kept as Arch G.f.17): l. 21, "ærerno" is changed to "æterno". Garrod. (II.367) has misread the letters remaining in the cropped marginal rewriting.
(2) fuit. / suit. *1645, 1673*. (21) æterno *1673* / ærerno *1645*.

SONG: ON MAY MORNING
Date: May 1630 ?; conjectural. Perhaps after Dec. 1629 (when Milton became 21) since, as Parker points out ("Notes," p. 115), he dated most of the poems which we know were written prior to that time in terms of his age; *El.* 1, *El.* 6 (month but not the year), and the five epigrams on the Gunpowder Plot do not carry notes concerning their compositional dates. The only poem which was composed apparently later and which has a date in terms of age is *El.* 7 (May 1630); of later poems only *Shakespear, Lycidas,* and *Mask* carry year dates in 1645. It may be significant that *Song* precedes *Shakespear;* however, it follows *Epitaph on the Marchioness,* which is clearly out of chronological order. Others have dated the poem from 1628 through 1632.
Texts: 1645*, 1673.

SONNET 1
Date: May 1630 ?; conjectural, but perhaps close to the Italian poems. See also textual note to *Song.* It may be significant that Milton purchased his copy of Giovanni della Casa's influential *Rime et prose* in Dec. 1629.
Texts: 1645*, 1673.

SONNET 2
Date: 1630 ?; uncertain, but perhaps sonnet group is dated by correspondences with *El.* 7 (May 1630). Compare *Son.* 2 with the elegy; ll. 1–4 of *Son.* 4 with ll. 1–4 of the elegy; and ll. 8–14 of *Son.* 6 with ll. 89–90 of the elegy. The purchase of della Casa's *Rime et Prose* in Dec. 1629 likewise suggests composition after that date. *Son.* 5, addressed to Diodati, points to—but does not require—composition before mid-April when Diodati enrolled in the Academy of Geneva.
Texts: 1645*, 1673.
(5) mostrasi / mostra si *1645, 1673.*

SONNET 3
Date: 1630 ?; see textual note for *Son.* 2.
Texts: 1645*, 1673.

CANZONE
Date: 1630 ?; see textual note for *Son.* 2.
Texts: 1645*, 1673.

SONNET 4
Date: 1630 ?; see textual note for *Son.* 2.
Texts: 1645*, 1673.

SONNET 5
Date: 1630 ?; see textual note for *Son.* 2.
Texts: 1645*, 1673.
(2) sian / fian *1673.* (10) Scossomi / Scosso mi *1645, 1673.*
(12) a trovar / e trovar *1673.*

SONNET 6
Date: 1630 ?; see textual note for *Son.* 2.
Texts: 1645*, 1673.
(6) Di / De *1645, 1673.* (8) e d'intero / d'intero *1673.*

ON SHAKESPEAR
Date: 1630; date given in 1645, in which it precedes the Hobson poems.
Texts: Shakespeare Second Folio (1632) in three states (Effigies A, B, and C); Shakespeare, *Poems* (1640); 1645*; Shakespeare Third Folio (1664); 1673.
Title An Epitaph on the admirable Dramaticke Poet W. SHAKE-SPEARE. A, B, C, William *1640, 1664.* (4) Star-ypointing / starre-ypointed *A.* (6) weak / dull *A, B, C, 1664.* (8) live-long / lasting *A, B, C, 1664.* (10) heart / part, *A, B, C, 1664.* (13) it / her *A, B, C, 1664,* our *1640.* (15) dost / doth *1640.*

LINES APPENDED TO Elegy 7
Date: late 1630–31 ? Most editors place this "renunciation" with *El.* 7, from which it is separated by a thin line in 1645, 1673. However, it obviously postdates the elegy and is separated in time

from it ("formerly," l. 2); see also ll. 7–8. F. W. Bateson (*English Poetry: a Critical Introduction* [New York, 1950], p. 161) thinks 1635 the earliest possible date, though his basis is unsound; and others have postulated the addition of the lines when the 1645 collection was being conceived. Under the influence of Plato, Milton renounces devotion to inferior love, categorically including the first six sonnets. The lines reflect the thought that produced both *Idea* and Platonic references in other poems dated here in 1631. *Texts:* 1645*, 1673.

NATURAM NON PATI SENIUM
Date: 1630–31 ?; precedes *Idea* (which see) in the editions, but was probably written at the same general time. Frequently dated June 1628 (as, therefore, is *Idea*) by those who suggest these as the verses mentioned in a letter to Alexander Gill, July 2, 1628. *Texts:* 1645*, 1673.

DE IDEA PLATONICA
Date: late 1630–31 ? Since the poem is undated by Milton, it may lie after Dec. 1629 (see textual note to *Song*). Probably it was composed after the amatory work of spring 1630, but certainly before Milton's graduation in July 1632. *Texts:* 1645*, 1673.
(19) sedens *1673* / fedens *1645*. (23) diis / iis *1673*. (36) induxti / induxit *1673*.

ON THE UNIVERSITY CARRIER
Date: early 1631; Hobson died Jan. 1, 1631.
Texts: 1645*, *Wit Restor'd* (1658), 1673, MS. 1.21, ff. 79ᵛ–80ʳ (Folger Library). A correction in Milton's hand is found in the Bodleian Library copy of 1645 (catalogued 8⁰ M168 Art, but kept as Arch G.f.17): l. 2, "A" changed to "And".
Title *Another*. 1658, On Hobson who dyed in the vacancy of his Carrage by reason of the Sicknes att Cambridge. 1630. MS. (1) broke his girt, / his desire, *1658*. (2) And *1673* / A *1645;* laid / left *1658;* dirt, / mire; *1658.* (6) when / that *1658.* (7) had / hath *1658;* this / those MS. (8) Dodg'd / Dog'dd *1658;* with him, / him *1658;* betwixt / 'twixt *1658,* MS; Bull. / *London-Bull. 1658.* (14) In the kind office / Death in the likenesse *1658,* In craftie likenes MS. (18) and's / and *1658.*

ANOTHER ON THE SAME
Date: early 1631; Hobson died Jan. 1, 1631.
Texts: Banquet of Jests (1640, 1657), 1645*, *Wit Restor'd* (1658), 1673; Huntington Library MS, H.M. 116, pp. 100–101; Bodleian MS, Malone 21, f. 69ᵛ.
Title *Upon old* Hobson *the Carrier of* Cambridge. *1640, 1657,* Vpon old Hobson Cambridge Carrier who dyed 1630 in yᵉ Vacation by reason of yᵉ Sicknesse yⁿ hot at Camb: *HMS,* On Hobson yᵉ Cambridge carrier who died 1630 in yᵉ vacancy of his carriage by reason of yᵉ sicknesse then hott at Cambridge *BMS.* (1) lieth

one / Hobson lyes, *1640, 1657, HMS, BMS*. (2) while / whilst *1640, 1657, 1658, HMS, BMS;* could / did *1640, 1657, HMS*. (3) hung / sung *1640, 1657*. (4) While / Whilst *1640, 1657, 1658,* So *HMS, BMS;* might / could *1658;* still / but *1658*. (5) sphear-metal, / spheares mettall, *1640, 1657*. (6) revolution / resolution *1640, 1658, HMS;* was at / made of *1658*. (7) a / all *1640, 1657*. (8) old truth) / truth, 'twas *1640, 1657,* old truths *HMS*. (9) an / some *1640, 1657, 1658, HMS, BMS;* wheel / wheeles *1658*. (10) being / once *1658;* ceast, / seasd, *1640*. (11) men / us *1640, 1657;* gave / giu's *HMS*. (13–26, 29–34) *omitted* *1658;* (15–20, 25–26) *omitted* 1640, 1657, HMS, BMS. (13) Nor / No *HMS*. (14) hast'n'd / hasted *BMS*. (21) chief / *omitted* HMS, BMS; right, / aright *HMS, BMS*. (22) Cart / Carts *1640, 1657;* went / were *1640, 1657,* was *HMS, BMS*. (23) him / *omitted* BMS. (27) But / For *1640, 1657, 1658, HMS, BMS;* doings / doing *HMS*. (28) an / so sure an *HMS*. (30) had / *omitted* HMS, in *BMS*. (31) Linkt / Like *BMS;* flowing / flow-ings *BMS*. (32) increase: / disease. *1640, 1657*. (33) *indented* 1640, 1657; and / are *HMS*. (34) *indented* 1640, 1657.

HOBSONS EPITAPH
Date: early 1631; Hobson died on Jan. 1, 1631.

Texts:

Banquet of Jests (1640*)	A	Additional 6400, f. 67ᵛ	J
Witts Recreation (1640)	B	Folger Library MSS	
Banquet of Jests (1657)	C	1.27, f. 68ᵛ	K
Wit Restor'd (1658)	D	452.1, p. 50	L
British Museum MSS		Bodleian Library MS	
Additional 15,227, f. 74ʳ	E	Tanner 465, pp. 235–36	M
Sloane 542, f. 52ʳ	F	Harvard Univ. Library MS	
Harleian 791, f. 45ʳ	G	Eng. 686, f. 78ʳ	N
Harleian 6931, f. 24ᵛ	H	Huntington Library MS	
Additional 30,982, f. 65	I	H.M. 116, p. 103	O

This third poem on Hobson is included with qualification. Never published by Milton, it has similarities to his acknowledged verses, which it follows in *Banquet of Jests* and precedes in *Wit Restor'd*. William R. Parker, who first propos'd Milton's authorship (Columbia Milton, XVIII, 590–92), suggests that it may have been omitted from 1645 because two poems in this vein may have been considered sufficient. *N* gives alternate indentations of lines.
Title *On Hobson the Carrier. B, On the death of* Hobson, *the* Cambridge-*Carrier* D, In Hobsonum Architabellarium Cantabrigiensem. 1631. *E,* An Epitaph on Hobson the Carrier of Cambridge *F,* An Other: *G,* on hobson the Cambridge Carrier. *I, missing* J, On Hobson died 1 Jan 1630 *K,* Vpon Mr. Hobson, carryer of Cambridge. *L,* Upon Hobson the Carrier. *M,* Hobsons Epitaph the Carrier of Cambredge *N,* Vpon Hobson yᵉ Cambridge Carrier. *O.* (1) Here *Hobson* lies amongst his many / Here lies Hobson moungst his many *I,*

Here lies Hobson amongst his many *J*, Heere lies old Hobson among his *M*, Hobson lies heare amongst his many *N;* betters, *D* / debters, *A, C, O*. (2) A man / who though *K;* not learned, *D* / unlearned, *A, B, C, E, H, J;* yet of many / yet a man of *B, G, H, I, L, M*, and yet a man of *E*, and yet of many *J*, yet was a man of *K*, but yet of many *N*. (3–4) *omitted* B, E, G, I, K, L, M. (3) The / Yee *O;* well / all *H;* testify / justifie *D*. (4) That have / Who have *D*, But he *J*, That oft *N;* from / in *J*. (5–6) *reversed* K. (5) it was well known hee many times had gone *K;* was well / is well *D, J, M*, well was *N;* hath he gon *D* / t'have begun *A, C*, haue he gon *I*. (6) In Embassy / An Embassie *D, J*, In an embassage *E*, On Embassies *F, G*, On embassage *H, L*, an Embassage *I*, On an embassage *M*, On Embassi *N*, His Embassy *O;* the / *omitted* E, M, a *J*. (7) There's few in Cambridge, to his praise be it spoken *B;* (in good time / to his praise *E, G, H, I, K, L, M*. (8) well remembreth / will remember *D, E, I, J, L, O*, may remember *B, F, G, M*, do remember *H*, well remember *K, N;* good / *missing* I. (9) thence / whence *B*, hence *M;* to *London* rode he / he rid to London *B*. (10) benighting *D* / benighted *A, C, I*. (11–12) *missing* H. (11–18) *printed:* 13–14, 11–12, 17–18 *B*. (11) Then marueile not, though he soe soune is gone, *N;* No / Nor *B, D;* wonder is it, / is't a wonder, *B*, wonder thinke yee *E*, wonder thinke it *I*, wonder thinks it *L*. (12) Since most men / Since all men *B, F, M*, For most *E*, For most men *I, L*, For all men *N;* knew / know *D, G, I, J, K, M*, know, that *E*. (13) Team / Terme *O;* of the best / very gu'd *H;* could / would *B, K, M*. (14) Bin mir'd in any ground, / Bin mir'd in any way *B, K, M*, Them mir'd in any ground *D*, In any way beene mir'd *E*, Bin mir'd in any place, *G, L*, Stucke fast in any ground *H*, beene mired any where *I;* the *D* / his *A, C, H, J*, a *L*. (15–16) *omitted* B. (15) here *F* / there *A, C, D, E, L;* indeed, still / & still is *E*, indeed, and *H*, still *M;* like to *D* / at a *A, C*. (16) Until / Except *H*, Unles *N;* some / an *H;* lend / lens *H;* his *D* / a *A, C, G, I, O*, some *F*. (17) So / Thus *B, E, G, I, K, L, M;* rest / rests *D;* thou / the *D;* ever-toyling / everlasting *B*, dusty toyling *E*. (18) to Charls-wain / Charls his Waine *B, D, F, G, H, N, O*, Charles waine *I*, Charle-maine *K*, to Charles his wayne *L*.

An Epitaph on the Marchioness of Winchester
Date: Apr. 1631; the Marchioness died on Apr. 15, 1631.
Texts: 1645*, 1673; British Museum MS, Sloane 1446, ff. 37b–38. The manuscript has a note of authorship: "Jo Milton of Chr: Coll Cambr."
Title On the Marchionesse of Winchester whoe died in Child bedd. Ap: 15. 1631 *MS*. (15–23) *MS has:* Seauen times had the yeerlie starre | in euerie signe sett vpp his carr | Since for her they did request | the god that sitts at marriage feast | (when first the earlie Matrons runne |. (24) a / her *MS*. (27) whether / whither *MS*. (40) vernall / a vernall *MS*. (42) on / one *MS*. (43) she / it *MS*.

(46) hast'ning / hastinge MS. (47) *indented* MS; thy / the MS. (49) thy / they MS. (50) sease / ceaze MS. (52) thy / thine MS. (53) *indented* MS. (61) Whilst / While MS. (64) Who / wch MS. (70) Light; / might MS.

L'ALLEGRO

Date: 1631 ?; conjectural, but later than the Hobson poems which it follows in 1645. Ants Oras indicates (*NQ*, 198, 1953, 332–33) that the prosody of *L'Allegro* and *Penseroso* is later than that of the *Epitaph on the Marchioness*. The twin poems may have been written during the summer vacation.

Texts: 1645*, 1673.

(33) ye / you *1673*. (104) he by / by the *1673*.

IL PENSEROSO

Date: 1631 ?; conjectural, but later than the Hobson poems which it follows in 1645. See note to *L'Allegro*.

Texts: 1645*, 1673. A correction in Milton's hand is found in the Bodleian Library copy of 1645 (catalogued 8° M168 Art, but kept as Arch G.f.17): l. 57, "Id" changed to "In".

(57) In *1673* / Id *1645*.

SONNET 7

Date: Dec. 1632; l. 2 places the poem after his twenty-third year had entirely passed.

Texts: 1645*, 1673, TM*.

(2) twentith / twentieth *1673*.

ARCADES

Date: 1633–34 ?; probably revised in 1637 ('see Shawcross, "Speculations"). Date is very uncertain, but composition undoubtedly lies before that of *Mask*.

Texts: 1645*, 1673, TM*. A number of lines of TM have been damaged by tearing. TM has early title "Part of a maske" which is replaced by "Part of an Entertainment at . . . ." The first song is not labelled; therefore, the second song is simply "Song" in TM, and the third, "2 Song".

(28) ye / you *TM*. (40) ye . . . ye / you . . . you *TM*. (47) With / in *TM*, *deleted*. (49) or *TM* / and *1645, 1673*. (81) ye / you *TM;* toward / towards *TM*. (91) you / yee *TM*. (94) *aligned with lines 84, 85, etc. 1645, 1673*. (96) *not indented 1645, 1673*. (101) ye / you *TM*. (104) *not indented 1645, 1673*. (105) *not indented 1645, 1673*.

A MASK

Date: before Sept. 29, 1634, date of first performance; revised and enlarged c. Sept.–Dec. 1637.

Texts: 1637, 1645*, 1673; TM*, Bridgewater MS. Two mss of five songs written by Henry Lawes are extant: British Museum Add. MS 11,518 (in an unknown hand) and the Lawes MS (in Lawes' hand). The songs are: ll. 976–83, 992–95, 998–99 (Song 1); 230–43 (Song 2); 859–66 (Song 3); 958–75 (Song 4 in two

parts); 1012–23 (Song 5). There are a number of musical differences between the two manuscripts. Verbal variants from the present text are as follows: (976) To the Ocean / From the Heav'ns *BMS, LMS.* (981) gardens / Garden *BMS, LMS.* (999) young *Adonis* soft / many'a Cherub oft *BMS, LMS.* (231) cell / shell *BMS, LMS.* (233) the / thy *BMS, LMS.* (241) Parly / Pity *BMS.* (242) translated / Transplanted *BMS, LMS.* (243) And give resounding grace / & hold a Counterpoint *BMS, LMS.* (859) Sabrina / Sabrina Sabrina *BMS, LMS.* (866) Listen / Listen Listen *BMS, LMS.* (965) On . . . on / o're . . . o're *BMS, LMS.* (967) ye / you *BMS, LMS.* (1012) But now / Now *BMS, LMS.* (1014) green earths / Earths green *BMS, LMS.* Lines 1021–22 also appear in Milton's hand in the album of Camillus Cardoyn, June 10, 1639. The Bridgewater presentation volume of 1637, in the Carl Pforzheimer Library, contains the following manuscript corrections in Milton's hand: (20) my / by; (49) comma after "Coasting" deleted; (73) in / is; (131) at / art; (223) sables / sable; (417) "you" inserted; (443) we / she; (474) sensualitie / sensualtie; (781) reproachfull / contemptuous
List of *dramatis personae* given only in 1645. Instead of *Spirit,* the MSS use *Dæmon;* the *Elder Brother* is frequently called *1 Bro.* (dir.) *The . . . enters.* / A Guardian Spirit, or Dæmon. *TM,* then a guardian spiritt or demon descendes or enters. *BM.* (Lines 975–82, 987–94, 994A, 995, 997–98) *given as prologue before l. 1 in BM.* (2) shapes / shape *1673.* (6) with / w^ch *BM.* (12) by / with *BM.* (18) *not indented* TM, BM. (20) by / my *1637.* (26) gives / give *TM.* (43) you *TM* / ye *1637, 1645.* (46) *not indented* TM; grape / Grapes *BM.* (58) Whom / w^ch *BM.* (62) shade *TM* / shades *1637, 1645, 1673.* (73) is / in *1637.* (83) robes / webs *BM.* (90) Likeliest and neerest / neerest & likliest *TM.* (dir., 92–93) Comus enters wth a charming rod & glasse of liquor with his rout all headed like some wild beasts thire garments some like mens & some like womens they come on in a wild & antick fashion *TM; his glass* / & a glass of liquor *BM; headed . . . women,* / like men & women but headed like wild beasts *BM.* (99) dusky / Northerne *BM.* (123) has *TM* / hath *1637, 1645, 1673.* (131) art / at *1637.* (132) spitts *TM* / spets *1637, 1645, 1673, BM.* (dir., 144–45) *The Measure.* / the measure (in a wild rude & wanton antick) *TM, BM.* (167) *omitted 1673;* thrift / thirst *TM, in scribe's hand.* (168) *reversed with l. 169 1673.* (169) *reversed with l. 168 1673;* heer. / hear *erratum for 1673.* (170) *Lady.* / *omitted 1637, 1645, 1673,* TM; mine / my *TM, BM.* (174) amongst *TM* / among *1637, 1645, 1673, BM.* (188–90) *omitted BM.* (189) weeds *TM* / weed *1645, 1673.* (195) stoln / stole *1645, 1673;* els . . . night / *omitted BM.* (196–225) *omitted BM.* (201) the / *missing* TM. (214) flittering *TM* / hovering *1645, 1673, TM in scribe's hand.* (223) sable / sables *1637.* (226) hallow / hollowe *BM.* (229) off. / hence *TM, BM.* (231)

cell *TM* / shell *1637, 1645, 1673, BM.* (241) *of* / to *BM.* (243)
And give resounding grace / & hold a Counterpoint *BM.* (dir., 243–
44) Comus looks in and speaks *TM, BM.* (252) she *TM* / it *1645,
1673.* (270) prosperous / prosperinge *BM.* (291) Two such /
Such tow *TM.* (294) 'em *TM* / them *1637, 1645, 1673.* (300)
colours / cooleness *BM.* (304) To / *omitted, but given as catch-
word BM.* (312) wide *TM* / wilde *1645, 1673,* wild *TM in
scribe's hand, 1637.* (317) roosted / rooster *BM.* (dir., 330–31)
the tow Brothers enter *TM.* (349) this close / lone *BM.* (356)
What if / or els *BM.* (357–65) *missing* TM, BM; *three other lines
are found:* so fares as did forsaken Proserpine | when the big rowl-
ing flakes of pitchie clowds | & darknesse wound her in. 1 bro.
Peace, brother peace |. (370) trust / hope *BM.* (384) walks in
black vapours, though the noone tyde brand *BM.* (385) blaze in
the summer solstice *BM.* (390) a / an *1637, BM.* (399) treasure
/ treasures *BM.* (401) on / at *BM.* (402) let / she *BM.* (403)
wild / wide *TM, BM.* (409) controversie: / question, no *TM, BM.*
(409 ff.) *TM, BM give five additional undeleted lines:* I could be
willing though now i'th darke to trie | a tough encounter wth the
shaggiest ruffian | that lurks by hedge or lane of this dead circuit |
to have her by my side, though I were sure | she might be free
from perill were she is |. (410) Yet / but *TM, BM.* (413) banish
gladly *TM* / gladly banish *1637, 1645, 1673, BM.* (415) imagine, / imagine brother *TM, BM.* (417) if you mean / if meane
1637. (428) there, / even *TM, BM.* (432) Som say / naye more
BM. (433) moorie *TM* / moorish *1637, 1645, 1673, BM.* (437)
Has *TM* / Hath *1645, 1673.* (438) ye / you *BM.* (443) she / we
1637. (444) naught *TM* / nought *1637, 1645, 1673.* (448)
That / the *BM.* (460) Begin / begins *BM.* (465) But / and *TM,
BM;* lewd and lavish / lewde lascivious *BM.* (472) Hovering,
TM / Lingering, *1645, 1673.* (474) sensualty / sensuality *1637,
1673, BM.* (481) off / of *1673, BM;* hallow / hollowe *BM.* (dir.,
488–89) he hallows the guardian Dæmon hallows agen & enters
in the habit of shepheard *TM,* he hallowes and is answered, the
guardian dæmon comes in habited like a shepheard. *BM.* (493)
fathers *TM* / father *1637, 1645, 1673.* (497) thou / *omitted
BM;* Swain? / shepheard, *TM, BM.* (498) his *TM* / the *1637,
1645, 1673, BM.* (513) you. *TM* / ye, *1645, 1673.* (520) *not
indented 1645.* (547) meditate / meditate upon *1673.* (553)
frighted / flighted *TM.* (555) soft / sweete, *BM.* (556) a / the
softe *BM;* steam / stream *1673;* rich / *omitted BM.* (563) did /
might *TM, BM.* (572) knew) / knowe) *BM.* (605) bugs *TM* /
forms *1645, 1673.* (608) and cleave his scalp *TM* / to a foul
death, *1645, 1673.* (609) Down to the hipps. *TM* / Curs'd as his
life. *1645, 1673.* (610) Thy / The *BM.* (616) thy self / *omitted
BM.* (626) ope / open *BM.* (632–37) *missing BM.* (637) Which
TM / That *1637, 1645, 1673, BM.* (657) Ile / I *TM, BM.* (dir.,
657–58) *State 1 of l. 1 found in British Museum copy* (C.34.d.46)
of 1637; soft Musick, / *missing* TM, BM; *appears* / is discover'd

TM; to whom . . . rise. / she offers to rise *TM.* (678A) poore ladie thou hast neede of some refreshinge *BM.* (688) have / hast *BM.* (689) have / hast *BM;* but / heere *BM.* (697–700) *missing* BM. (698) forgeries *TM* / forgery, *1637, 1645, 1673.* (731) multitude / inultitude *1637.* (733, 734) *combined into one line in BM:* would soe emblaze with starrs, that they belowe (737–55) *missing* BM. (743) a / an *TM.* (746) on *TM* / and *1637, 1645, 1673.* (751) or *TM* / and *1637, 1645, 1673.* (779, 806) *combined into one line in TM, BM:* cramms & blasphems his feeder. Come no more (779–806) *missing* TM, BM. (780) anough? / anow? *1673.* (781) contemptuous / reproachfull *1637.* (dir., 813–14) *with Swords . . . ground; /* strike his glasse downe *TM,* with swords . . . glasse of liquor out . . . ground *BM; his rout . . . resistance, /* the shapes make as though they would resist *TM; The attendant . . . in. /* Dæmon enter wth them *TM,* the Demon is to come in with the brothers. *BM.* (814) you / yee *BM;* let / left *BM.* (821) which / that *TM, BM.* (824) *not indented* TM. (828) That / whoe *BM.* (829) She / The *1673.* (834) pearled / peackled *BM.* (846A) *undeleted line in TM:* and often takes our cattell wth strange pinches. (847) *omitted* BM. (857) besetting / distressed *TM.* (dir., 866–67) The verse to singe or not. *BM.* (871–72) *assigned to* El bro: *BM.* (873–74) *assigned to* 2 bro: *BM.* (875–76) *assigned to* 2 bro: *BM.* (877–78) *assigned to* El br: *BM.* (879–82) *assigned to* El br: *BM.* (883) *song from this line onward assigned to* De: *BM.* (dir., 889–90) *by* / w^th *TM; water /* the water *TM, BM; and sings. /* Sings *TM.* (889–900) *indentations are inconsistent in texts; TM is followed in present version.* (897) *set* / rest *BM; velvet* / *omitted* BM. (900–01) *given as part of song 1637, 1645, 1673, BM.* (911) thy / this *BM.* (dir., 921–22) and / *missing* TM. (927) tumble / tumbled *1673.* (dir., 937–38) song ends *TM, BM; no line space* 1673. (951) there / neere *TM, BM.* (953) thir / this *BM.* (956) *assigned to* el br: *BM;* grow / are *1637, BM.* (dir., 957–58) Exeunt. *TM; presenting* / and then is præsented *TM, BM; com in* / enter *TM; country-dancers, /* countrie dances & such like gambols &c. *TM,* Countrie daunces, and the like &c., *BM; after them* / at these sports *TM,* towards the end of these sports *BM; Lady. /* Ladie enter *TM,* ladye come in. *BM; Song* / the Dæmon sings *TM,* the spiritt singes. *BM.* (dir., 965–66) 2 song. *TM,* 2 songe prsents . . . mother. *BM.* (972) *assays* / assaye Morgan copy of *1637.* (dir., 975–76) they dance. the dances all ended the Dæmon sings. or sayes *TM, BM.* (975–82, 987–94, 994A, 995, 997–98) *given at beginning of BM.* (976) To the Ocean / ffrom the heavens *BM.* (983–86) *missing* BM. (988) that *deleted by 1673 erratum.* (995A) yellow, watchet, greene & blew *BM.* (996) with / oft with *BM; Elysian* / Manna *BM.* (997) *missing* BM. (999) young Adonis / many a Cherub *BM;* oft / soft *BM.* (1000–1011) *missing* BM. (1012) *not indented* TM; But now / Now *BM.* (1014)

green earths / earths greene *BM*. (1018) *not indented* TM, BM.
(1020) ye / you *BM*.

PSALM 114
Date: end of Nov. 1634; from reference, apparently to this paraphrase, in a letter to Alexander Gill, dated Dec. 4.
Texts: 1645*, 1673.
15 σκαρθμοῖσιν/σκαφμοῖσιν 1673.
16 σφριγόωντες/σφριγόωντης 1673.
18 μητέρι/μητήρι 1673.

PHILOSOPHUS AD REGEM . . .
Date: Dec. 1634 ?; perhaps close to *Ps.* 114 which it follows in
1645.
Texts: 1645*, 1673.
Title insontem / in tem 1673, *two lines,* son *apparently cut off by
right margin during printing.*
1 τὸν/'τ' 1673.
4 Μὰψ αὔτως/Μαψιδίως 1673
χρόνῳ μάλα πολλὸν/τεὸν πρὸς θυμόν 1673.
5 τοιόνδ'/τοιόν δ' 1645, 1673
πόλεως/πόλιος 1673.

ON TIME
Date: 1633–1637 ?; see textual note for *Solemn Musick.*
Texts: 1645, 1673, TM*; Bodleian MS, Ashmole 36, 37, f. 22ʳ.
Title (To be) set on a clock case *TM, deleted, replaced by present
title,* Vpon a Clocke Case, or Dyall *BMS.* (2) stepping / sleepeinge
BMS. (17) the / your *BMS.* (18) t'whose / whose *BMS.* (19–
22) Shall heape our days with everlastinge store | When death
and Chance, and thou O tyme shalbee noe more. *BMS.*

UPON THE CIRCUMCISION
Date: 1633–37 ?; see textual note for *Solemn Musick.*
Texts: 1645, 1673, TM*.
(1) *not indented* 1645, 1673, TM. (14) *double indentation*
1645, 1673. (15) *not indented* 1645, 1673. (27) *not indented*
1673. (28) *double indentation* 1645, 1673.

AT A SOLEMN MUSICK
Date: 1637. Date depends on when TM was begun, since the ode
was worked out in it shortly afterward. Recent argument has suggested its first use in autumn 1637 (see Shawcross, "Speculations"). All previously dated in the early 1630's, *On Time* and
Upon the Circumcision precede *Solemn Musick* in composition but
lie apparently close to it. Unlike the early sonnets, the three odes
evidence Italian prosody drawn directly from Tuscan poetry, as
Prince shows (pp. 59–65); here Milton developed the "disciplined
improvisation" which is basic to *Lycidas.*
Texts: 1645, 1673, TM 4*. There are two preliminary drafts of
the full poem (TM 1, TM 2) and an additional revision (TM 3)
of ll. 17–28; since they are superseded by TM 4, they are not

collated. A correction in Milton's hand is found in the Bodleian Library copy of 1645 (catalogued 8⁰ M168 Art, but kept as Arch G.f.17): l. 6, "content" changed to "concent".

(6) concent / content, *1645*. (28) *not indented* 1645, 1673; *with him, and sing* / *and sing with him TM 4*.

LYCIDAS

Date: Nov. 1637; date given in TM.

Texts: Justa Edovardo King naufrago (1638), 1645*, 1673, TM*. Corrections in Milton's hand occur in the Cambridge University copy of 1638 and in British Museum copy C.21.c.42: (10) he knew / he well knew *CM, BM*. (51) lord / lov'd *CM, BM*. (53) the old / your old *CM*. (67) do, / use *CM, BM*. (157) humming / whelming *CM, BM*. (175) oazie / oozie *CM;* oosie *also in margin of CM*. (177) in the blest kingdom[s meeke] of Joy, and Love. *added CM without comma and period, BM with bracketed section torn off*. A scrap of proof for p. 21 of 1638, ll. 23–35, is found pasted on the inner side of the back cover of *De Literis & Lingua Getarum*, 1597, in the Cambridge University Library (facsimile in Fletcher, I). Corrections, etc., are: (25, 27, 28, 29, 31) *corrections of letters*. (26) eye-lids *hyphen inserted*. (27) a-field, *hyphen inserted*. (31) wheel. *period inserted*. (32) *realignment of type*. Alterations made to the TM after 1640 are not, of course, found in 1638.

Headnote *missing* 1638 And . . . height. / *missing* TM. (10) he well knew / he knew *1638, 1645, 1673*. (15) *not indented* British Museum copy 1077.d.51 of 1638. (25) *not indented* 1638. (26) opening / glimmering *1638*. (30) Oft till the ev'n-starre bright *1638;* in / at *1645, 1673*. (31) westring / burnisht *1638*. (50) *not indented* 1638. (51) lov'd / lord *1638*. (53) your / the *1638*. (56) Ay / Ah *1638*. (64) *not indented* 1638; incessant / uncessant *1638, 1645, 1673*. (65) ter̄d / end *1673*. (66) strictly / stridly *1638*. (67) use, / do, *1638*. (69) Or with / Hid in *1638*. (73) when / where *1638*. (85) *not indented* 1638. (103) *not indented* 1638. (105) Inwraught / Inwrought *1638, 1645, 1673*. (114) Anow / Enough *1638,* anough *TM*. (129) little / nothing *1645, 1673, not reinstated in TM*. (131) smite / smites *1638*. (149) beauties / beauty *1638, 1645, 1673*. (157) whelming / humming *1638, TM*. (177) *omitted* 1638.

AD PATREM

Date: Mar. 1638 ?; probably written about the time of publication of *Mask* (c. Feb.–Mar. 1638 ?), perhaps to accompany a gift copy. The poem may have been provoked by opposition to Milton's travelling abroad in preparation for a literary career. H. A. Barnett (*MLN*, LXXIII [1958], 82–83) has shown that the time of year of composition may be around Mar.

Texts: 1645*, 1673.

(8) possint / possunt *1673*.

Ad Salsillum
Date: Nov. ? 1638; during first visit to Rome since it precedes
Mansus in 1645.
Texts: 1645*, 1673.

Mansus
Date: Dec. 1638; written and sent to Manso when Milton was in
Naples.
Texts: 1645*, 1673.
(62) Peneium / Peceium *1645 Fletcher.* (82) Aut / Ant *1673.*
(83) adsit) / ad sit) *1645, 1673.*

Ad Leonoram Romæ canentem
Date: Feb. ? 1639; composed apparently during second visit to
Rome.
Texts: 1645*, 1673.

Ad eandem: "Another Leonora captured . . ."
Date: Feb. ? 1639; composed apparently during second visit to
Rome.
Texts: 1645*, 1673.
(5) canentem / canentam *1673, erratum corrects.* (8) desipuisset
/ desipuiiset *1645,* desipulisset *1673, erratum corrects.*

Ad eandem: "Why, credulous Naples, . . ."
Date: Feb. ? 1639; composed apparently during second visit to
Rome.
Texts: 1645*, 1673.

Epitaphium Damonis
Date: autumn 1639; see headnote and ll. 58–61, 64, the notably
rainy season of England being Oct.–Nov. and the poem being
written around harvest time.
Texts: 1640 (?), 1645*, 1673. At conclusion 1640 has: "Londini".
Headnote oriundus, / onundus, *1640.* (82) quid te, / *H. W. Garrod's "correction"* to quid de te (*II.370*) *can not be accepted because of prosody; the grammar is not incorrect.*

Sonnet 8
Date: before Nov. 13, 1642, the date on which the Royalist army
would have reached London.
Texts: 1645, 1673, TM* (scribe).
Title On his dore when yᵉ Citty expected an assault *TM, scribe,
deleted,* When the assault was intended to yᵉ Citty 1642 *TM, Milton, date deleted.* (3) If deed of honour did thee ever please, *1673.*

Sonnet 9
Date: 1643–45; position in TM.
Texts: 1645, 1673, TM*.
(5) with *Ruth* / the *Ruth,* 1645. (13) of night, / ( ) night *TM.*

Sonnet 10
Date: 1643–45; position in TM.

Texts: 1645, 1673, TM*.
Title To yᵉ Lady Margaret Ley *TM.*

IN EFFIGIEI EJUS SCULPTOREM
Date: 1645; written to accompany portrait, drawn in 1645 for the
first collected edition, though apparently based also on the Onslow
portrait of 1629. In *Pro se defensio* (p. 84) Milton indicates the
execution of the portrait for the edition of the poems.
Texts: 1645*, 1673. Given under portrait (frontispiece) in 1645,
without title.
2 βλέπων. / βλόπων *1673.*

SONNET 11
Date: autumn 1645 ?; traditional dating is 1646 ? since the poem
follows *Son.* 13 in TM; however, its numbering and l. 3 suggest an
earlier date of composition.
Texts: 1673, TM* 1 (Milton), TM 2 (scribe).
Numbered eleven by Milton and scribe, but transposed with *Son.*
12 by 1673 printer and erroneously titled to achieve topic reference.
Title *On the same.* 1673, On the detraction wᶜʰ follow'd upon
my writing certain treatises *TM 1, deleted; TM 2.* (4) cuckoes,
TM 2 / buzzards, *TM 1.*

SONNET 13
Date: c. Feb. 9, 1646; from TM.
Texts: Choice Psalmes put into Musick For Three Voices (1648),
1673, TM 2* (Milton), TM 3 (scribe). A first draft (TM 1) in
Milton's hand, being superseded by TM 2, is not collated except
for its title, source of the 1648 title. Present lines 6 and 8 are not
found in TM 1.
Title To my Friend Mʳ. *Henry Lawes.* 1648, To Mr. H. Lawes, *on
his Aires.* 1673, TM 3 (as result of deletions), To my freind Mʳ
Hen. Laws Feb. 9. 1645 *TM 1,* To Mʳ: Hen: Laws on the publish-
ing of his Aires *TM 2 (scribe, in reference to 1653 publication),
TM 3 (deleted to 1673 form with alteration to* Lawes). (9) lend
/ send *1673.* (11) story. / *story. *1648, which has four lines in
left margin:* "The story of Ariadne set by him in Music."

SONNET 14
Date: Dec. 1646; from TM.
Texts: 1673, TM 2* (Milton), TM 3 (scribe). A first draft (TM 1)
in Milton's hand, being superseded by TM 2, is not collated except
for its unique title.
Title On yᵉ religious memorie of Mʳˢ Catharine Thomason my
christian freind deceas'd 16 Decem. 1646 *TM 1, deleted (16, separately deleted, apparently was a false start of year).* (1) thee /
the *TM 3.* (12) in / on *1673, TM 3.*

opment (see Shawcross, "Chronology"); dates are those conjectured by Parker.

Text: 1671*.

All variants are from 1671. *Verse: paragraphed at "It suffices . . ." with no sentence break after "fift Act". Drama:* (157) complain) / complain'd) *changed by erratum.* (222) motion'd / mention'd *changed by erratum.* (306) indented State 1. (354) And such / Such *first word added by erratum.* (390) scent / sent (660) with / to *changed by erratum.* (720) scent / sent (1248) divulge / divulg'd *changed by erratum.* (1313) rate, / race, *changed by erratum.* (1527–35, 1537) *added as* Omissa. (1552) here / heard *changed by erratum.*

AD JOANNEM ROÜSIUM

Date: Jan. 1647; printed date, perhaps of delivery, is Jan. 23.

Texts: 1673; Bodleian Library MS, Lat. misc. d. 77* (scribe, with a one-word correction by Milton).

Title *Ode.* / Ode. Joannis Miltonj *MS.*

THE FIFTH ODE OF HORACE. BOOK 1.

Date: 1646–48 ?; conjectural; appears before *Forcers of Conscience* in 1673, except for incorrectly placed *Vacation Exercise.* Dated by others from 1626 to 1655, but specific Latin text may not have been published before 1636.

Text: 1673*. All variants from 1673.

English Text: Title Book / Lib.

Latin Text: Three differences from modern versions are found: "munditie" and "quoties" in l. 5, and "Intentata" in l. 13. The text published by Milton, including these variants and not evidencing differences, is found in *Quinti Horatii Flacci poëmata scholiis siva annotationibus a I. Bond illustrata* (Amsterodami: G. J. Blaeuw, 1636).

SONNET 12

Date: 1647; from position in TM.

Texts: 1673, TM 1* (Milton with revisions by scribe), TM 2 (scribe).

Numbered twelve by Milton and scribe, but transposed with *Son.* 11 by 1673 printer. (8) is it harder, / is harder *1673, erratum adds* it. (9) Colkitto, / Coliktto, *1673, corrected by erratum.*

ON THE FORCERS OF CONSCIENCE

Date: early 1647 ?; conjectured from intended position in TM. Two notes—one by Milton, one by a scribe—both place the poem between *Son.* 12 and *Son.* 15.

Texts: 1673, TM* (scribe, revisions by second scribe).

Title *On the new forcers of Conscience under the Long PARLIA-MENT. 1673.* (1) off / of *1673.* (17) bauk / bank *1673, changed by erratum.*

PSALMS 80–88

Date: Apr. 1648; published note.

Text: 1673*. All variants from 1673.
Ps. 80: (77) *verse number omitted.*

SONNET 15
Date: Aug. 1648; on basis of TM title, before news of capture of
Colchester (Aug. 27) reached London.
Texts: Letters of State (1694), TM*.
No lines are indented in 1694. In l. 8 TM reads "their" but the
editor believes Milton's "her" was altered by an unknown hand;
see note to ll. 7–8. "Warrs" in l. 10 has been mistranscribed as
"Warr," in other editions.
Title To my Lord FAIRFAX. *1694,* On yᵉ Lord Gen. Fairfax at yᵉ
seige of Colchester *TM, deleted.* (2) Filling each mouth / And fills
all Mouths *1694.* (4) that / which *1694.* (5) vertue / Valour *1694.*
(6) though / while *1694.* (8) her / their *TM.* (10) Warrs / War,
1694; endless / Acts of *1694.* (11) Truth, and Right / injur'd Truth
1694. (12) cleard from the shamefull brand / be rescu'd from the
Brand *1694.* (14) share / shares *1694.*

VERSE FROM PRO POPULO ANGLICANO DEFENSIO
Date: 1650; ordered to answer Salmasius, Jan. 8, 1650, and *Defensio prima* published in Feb. 1651.
Texts: Madan #1 (1651)*, p. 154; Madan #2 (1651), p. 202;
Madan #9 (1651), p. 249; Madan #13 (1652), p. 212; Madan
#14 (1658), p. 127. See F. F. Madan, *The Library,* Ser. 4, IV
(1923–24), 119–45, and Ser. 5, IX (1954), 112–21. The poem
appears in Chapter 8.

SONNET 16
Date: May 1652; from TM.
Texts: Letters of State (1694), TM* (scribe, revisions by second
scribe). No lines are indented in 1694.
Title To Oliver Cromwell. *1694,* To the Lord Generall Cromwell
May 1652 On the proposalls of certaine ministers at yᵉ Commtee
for Propagation of the Gospell *TM, deleted.* (1) who / that *1694;*
cloud / Croud, *1694.* (2) detractions / distractions *1694.* (5)
omitted 1694. (6) Hast reard Gods Trophies / And Fought God's
Battels, *1694.* (7) stream / Streams *1694.* (8) resounds / resound *1694.* (11) renown'd then / than those of *1694.* (12) with
/ in *1694.*

SONNET 17
Date: June ? 1652; according to a statement in 1662 (p. 93), the
sonnet was sent to Vane on July 3.
Texts: Life and Death of Sir Henry Vane (1662), *Letters of State*
(1694), TM* (scribe).
Only l. 9 is indented in 1694. *Title* To Sir HENRY VANE. *1694,*
To Sʳ Henry Vane the younger *TM, deleted.* (7) best, / best be
1694. (8) Move / Mann'd *1694.* (10) power / *omitted 1694.*
(11) severs / serves *1694.* (13) firm / Right *1694.* (14) And
reckons thee in chief her Eldest Son. *1694.*

PSALMS 1–8
Dates: Aug. 7–14, 1653; published note.
Text: 1673*.

VERSE FROM DEFENSIO SECUNDA
Date: 1654 ?; *Defensio secunda* was published in May 1654.
Texts: Ed. 1* (London, 1654), pp. 38–39; Ed. 2 (Hague, 1654),
p. 28; Ed. 3 (Hague, 1654), p. 28.
(2) algentes / algentis *Edd.* 2, 3. (4) amicire / amiciri *Ed.* 3.

SONNET 18
Date: May ? 1655; date of state letters.
Text: 1673*.
Title *On the late Massacher in* Piemont. *1673.* (10) sow / so *1673,
erratum corrects.*

SONNET 19
Date: Oct. ? 1655; position in 1673 edition. Date of composition is
frequently given as 1652 because of l. 2 and the date of Milton's
blindness; however, see n. to that line.
Text: 1673*.
(12) *indented* 1673.

SONNET 20
Date: Oct.–Nov. 1655; position in 1673 and ll. 2–5.
Text: 1673*.

SONNET 21
Date: Oct.–Nov. 1655; position in TM and 1673.
Texts: 1673*, TM*, ll. 5–14 (scribe). Lines 1–4 are missing in TM.
(2) with / with with *1673.* (8) intends / intend, *1673.*

SONNET 22
Date: Dec. 1655; position in TM and reference in l. 1 to total
blindness (around beginning of 1652).
Texts: Letters of State (1694), TM* (scribe).
No lines are indented in 1694. *Title* To Mr. *Cyriac Skinner* Upon
his Blindness. *1694.* (3) light / Sight, *1694.* (4) sight / day
1694. (5) Of / Or *1694.* (7) a / one *1694.* (12) talks / rings
1694. (13) the / this *1694.* (14) better / other *1694.*

SONNET 23
Date: 1656–58 ?; date of composition may depend on the wife intended; however, the scribe is not known to have been employed
by Milton before Jan. 1658.
Texts: 1673, TM* (scribe).

PARADISE LOST
Date: 1642 ?–1665 ?; early drafts probably date c. 1640, and Edward Phillips (Darbishire, pp. 72–73) read IV, 32–41, c. 1642.
Texts: 1667 (arguments, verse discussion, and errata added in re-
issues of 1668, 1669), 1674*; MS of I in Morgan Library (scribe,
with corrections by various hands). Two different title pages exist

for each issue of the first edition, the preliminary material being added with the second title page of 1668. There are two states of the first page of the first printing of this material: "The Printer to the Reader" appears in a four-line form and a six-line form. A second printing of the preliminary material, of sig. Z (VII.1–238), and of sig. Vv (X.1424–1541) was made at the time that the second title page of 1669 was produced. Two or three states exist in a number of signatures of 1667, two in the second printing of the verse, and three in the second printing of sig. Vv. The second edition of 1674 shows two states in sigs. A–D (Books I–II), alterations of three page numbers in later signatures, and a change of one word in the argument to X. A copy of this edition with a 1675 title page is found in the Univ. of Illinois Library; the copy shows a State 2 printing except for the recto of the B sig. in State 1. The MS apparently was the copy text for the first edition.

VERSE

and of *Virgil* / and *Virgil* 1669 printing.

BOOK I

(Argument) This / The *MS.* (25) Eternal / th' Eternal *1667, corrected by erratum.* (159) aught *MS* / ought *1667, 1674.* (173) The / This *MS.* (377) thir / the *1667, 1674, MS.* (432) these *MS* / those *1667, 1674.* (504) th' hospitable dore / hospitable Dores *1667, MS.* (505) Expos'd a Matron to avoid / Yielded thir Matrons to prevent *1667, MS.* (530) fainting / fainted *1667, MS.* (603) courage, / valour, *MS.* (703) founded *MS, 1667* / found out *1674.* (756) Capitol *MS, changed* / Capital *1667, 1674, MS.* (758) Band and / and Band *1667, reversed by erratum.*

BOOK II

(Argument) shall / should *1669 printing.* (282) where, *1667* / were, *1674.* (483) thir *1667* / her *1674.* (527) his *1667* / this *1674.* (881) grate / great *1667, corrected by erratum.*

BOOK III

(Argument) his right hand / the right hand *1669 printing;* plac't there, / plac't here, *1668 printing.* (592) Mettal / Medal *1667, 1674.* (594) With / Which *1667.* (741) in / with *1667, State 1, corrected by erratum.*

BOOK IV

(Argument) find him / find him out *1668, 1669.* (451) on *1667* / of *1674.* (627) walk / walks *1667.* (705) shadier *1667* / shadie *1674.* (928) the *1667* / thy *1674.*

BOOK V

(Argument) appearance / appearing *1669 printing.* (257) *indented* 1667, States 1, 2. (616) *not indented* 1667, State 1. (627) now / *missing* 1667. (636–40) *text revised in 1674.* (636) *missing* 1667. (637) in communion / with refection *1667.* (638–39) *missing* 1667. (640) Excess, / Are fill'd, *1667.* (659) in / *missing* 1667, added by erratum. (830) one / our *1667, State 1.*

BOOK VII

(25) dayes, / tongues; *1669 printing*. (126) as / a *1669 printing*. (224) the / his *1669 printing*. (366) her / his *1667*. (451) Soul / Fowle *1667*, Foul *1674*.

BOOK VIII

Continued as VII.641–1290 in 1667; Argument is the last half of the Argument of VII. (Argument) *Adam* inquires / *Adam* then inquires *1668, 1669;* search / seek *1669 printing*. (1–3) *added 1674*. (4) To whom thus *Adam* gratefully repli'd. *1667*. (269) as *1667* / and *1674*. (398) *not indented 1674*.

BOOK IX

This is Book VIII in 1667. (92) sleights / fleights *1667*. (186) Nor / Not *1667*. (213) hear *1667* / bear *1674*. (347) aught / ought *1667*. (394) Likest *1667* / Likeliest *1674*. (632) made / make *1667*. (922) hast *1667* / hath *1674*. (1019) we *1667* / me *1674*. (1092) for *1667* / from *1674*. (1093) from *1667* / for *1674*. (1183) Woman / Women *1667, 1674*.

BOOK X

This is Book IX in 1667. (Argument) Son / Angels *1669 printing;* meet / met *1674, State* 1; full assembly *1668, 1669* / full of assembly *1674;* taste *1668, 1669* / take *1674*. (58) may *1667* / might *1674*. (241) Avengers, / Avenger, *1667*. (397) those *1667* / these *1674*. (408) prevail, *1667* / prevailes, *1674*. (550) fair *1667* / omitted *1674*. (827) then / omitted *1667*. (989–90) So Death *printed in l. 990 in 1667, 1674*.

BOOK XI

First half of Book X (ll. 1–897) and of Argument in 1667, 1668. (Argument) but declares / and declares *1669 printing;* Cherubim / Cherubims *1669 printing*. (380) to amplest *1667* / to the amplest *1674*. (427) sin derive *1667* / derive *1674*. (485–87) *added 1674*. (551–52) Of rendring up. *Michael* to him repli'd. *1667*. (579) last / lost *1667, corrected by erratum*. (651) tacks *1667* / makes *1674*. (870) who / that *1667*.

BOOK XII

Last half of Book X (ll. 898–1541) and of Argument in 1667, 1668. (Argument) The Angel . . . Fall; / thence from the Flood relates, and by degrees explains, who that Seed of the Woman shall be; *1668, 1669*. (1–5) *added 1674*. (6) *not indented 1667*. (191) The / This *1667*. (238) what they besaught / them thir desire, *1667*. (534) Will *1667* / Well *1674*.

PARADISE REGAIN'D

Date: c. 1646–48 ?; revised or, according to some critics, written after 1665; based on evidence of prosodic development (see Shawcross, "Chronology").

Text: 1671*.

All variants are from 1671. BOOK I (226) subdue. / destroy. *erratum replaces*. (333) aught / ought (400) Nearer / Never *erratum corrects*. (417) Imparts / Imports *erratum corrects*. (470)

wrested / rested *BOOK II* (128) threat'ns then our / threat'ns our *erratum adds.* (341) pil'd, / pill'd, *erratum corrects. BOOK III* (238) insight / in sight (324) showers / shower *erratum corrects. BOOK IV* (124) compliments / complements (217) wast / was (288) ought / aught

BIBLIOGRAPHY

WORKS

Cleanth Brooks and John E. Hardy, edd., *Poems of Mr. John Milton* (New York, 1951).

Helen Darbishire, ed., *Poetical Works of John Milton*, Vols. 1–2 (Oxford, 1952–1955). Latin poems, vol. 2, ed. by H. W. Garrod.

Harris F. Fletcher, ed., *John Milton's Complete Poetical Works, Reproduced in Photographic Facsimile*, Vols. 1–4 (Univ. of Illinois Press, 1943–48).

Alfred Horwood, ed., *A Common-Place Book of John Milton* (Camden Society, 1876). In facsimile.

Walter MacKellar, *Latin Poems of John Milton* (Yale Univ. Press, 1930).

Frank A. Patterson, gen. ed., *The Works of John Milton*, 18 Vols. in 21 (Columbia Univ. Press, 1931–38).

Don M. Wolfe, gen. ed., *Complete Prose Works of John Milton*, Vols. 1–2 of 7 (Yale Univ. Press, 1953–   ).

BIBLIOGRAPHY

David H. Stevens, *Reference Guide to Milton from 1800 to the Present Day* (Univ. of Chicago Press, 1930). Through 1928.

Harris F. Fletcher, *Contributions to a Milton Bibliography, 1800–1930* (Univ. of Illinois Studies, 1931). Addenda to Stevens.

Calvin Huckabay, *John Milton: A Bibliographical Supplement, 1929–1957* (Duquesne Univ. Press, 1960).

BIOGRAPHY

Donald L. Clark, *John Milton at St. Paul's School* (Columbia Univ. Press, 1948).

Helen Darbishire, ed., *The Early Lives of Milton* (London, 1932).

Godfrey Davies, "Milton in 1660," *HLQ*, XVIII (1955), 351–63.

Donald C. Dorian, *The English Diodatis* (Rutgers Univ. Press, 1950).

Harris F. Fletcher, *The Intellectual Development of John Milton*, Vol. 1–2 (Univ. of Illinois Press, 1956–1962).

J. Milton French, *The Life Records of John Milton*, Vols. 1–5 (Rutgers Univ. Press, 1949–58).

James Holly Hanford, *John Milton, Englishman* (New York, 1949).

————, "The Youth of Milton" and "SA and Milton in Old Age," *Studies in Shakespeare, Milton, and Donne* (New York 1925).

David Masson, *The Life of Milton*, Vols. 1–7 (London, 1881–94).

William R. Parker, *Milton's Contemporary Reputation* (Ohio State Univ. Press, 1940).
E. M. W. Tillyard, *Milton* (London, 1930).
B. A. Wright, "The Alleged Falsehoods in Milton's Account of His Continental Tour," *MLR*, XXVIII (1933), 308–14.

GENERAL

Robert M. Adams, *Ikon: John Milton and the Modern Critics* (Cornell Univ. Press, 1955).
Don Cameron Allen, *The Harmonious Vision: Studies in Milton's Poetry* (Johns Hopkins Univ. Press, 1954).
Arthur Barker, *Milton and the Puritan Dilemma, 1641–1660* (Univ. of Toronto Press, 1942).
Walter C. Curry, *Milton's Ontology, Cosmogony, and Physics* (Univ. of Kentucky, 1957).
Zera S. Fink, *The Classical Republicans* (Northwestern Univ. Press, 1945; second ed., 1962).
H. J. C. Grierson, *Cross Currents in English Literature of the Seventeenth Century* (London, 1929).
William Haller, *The Rise of Puritanism* (Columbia Univ. Press, 1938).
James Holly Hanford, *A Milton Handbook,* fourth ed. (New York, 1946).
Raymond D. Havens. *The Influence of Milton on English Poetry* (Harvard Univ. Press, 1922; reprinted, New York, 1961).
William B. Hunter, Jr., "Milton's Arianism Reconsidered," *Harvard Theological Review*, LII (1959), 9–35.
————, "The Sources of Milton's Prosody," *PQ*, XXVIII (1949), 125–44.
Burton O. Kurth, *Milton and Christian Heroism* (Univ. of California Press, 1959).
William G. Madsen, "The Idea of Nature in Milton's Poetry," *Three Studies in the Renaissance* (Yale Univ. Press, 1958).
M. M. Mahood, *Poetry and Humanism* (Yale Univ. Press, 1950).
Marjorie Hope Nicolson, *The Breaking of the Circle*, Revised ed. (Columbia Univ. Press, 1960).
J. Max Patrick, ed., *SAMLA Studies in Milton* (Univ. of Florida Press, 1953).
F. T. Prince, *The Italian Element in Milton's Verse* (Oxford, 1954).
Malcolm M. Ross, *Milton's Royalism: A Study of the Conflict of Symbol and Idea in the Poems* (Cornell Univ. Press, 1943).
Irene Samuel, *Plato and Milton* (Cornell Univ. Press, 1947).
Denis Saurat, *Milton: Man and Thinker,* Revised ed. (New York, 1944; reprinted, London, 1946).
S. Ernest Sprott, *Milton's Art of Prosody* (Oxford, 1953).
Kester Svendsen, *Milton and Science* (Harvard Univ. Press, 1956).
E. M. W. Tillyard, *The Miltonic Setting: Past and Present* (Cambridge Univ. Press, 1938).

Rosemond Tuve, *Images and Themes in Five Poems by Milton* (Harvard Univ. Press, 1957).

Walter B. C. Watkins, *An Anatomy of Milton's Verse* (Louisiana Univ. Press, 1955).

James Whaler, *Counterpoint and Symbol. An Inquiry into the Rhythm of Milton's Epic Style* (Copenhagen, 1956).

George Whiting, *Milton's Literary Milieu* (Univ. of North Carolina Press, 1939).

————, *Milton and This Pendant World* (Univ. of Texas Press, 1958).

Don M. Wolfe, *Milton in the Puritan Revolution* (New York, 1941).

MINOR POEMS

Arthur Barker, "The Pattern of Milton's *Nativity Ode*," UTQ, X (1941), 167–81.

William R. Parker, "Notes on the Chronology of Milton's Latin Poems," *A Tribute to G. C. Taylor* (Univ. of North Carolina Press, 1952), pp. 113–31.

————, "Some Problems in the Chronology of Milton's Early Poems," RES, XI (1935), 276–83.

C. A. Patrides, ed., *Milton's Lycidas: The Tradition and the Poem* (New York, 1961).

John T. Shawcross, "Speculations on the Dating of the Trinity MS of Milton's Poems," MLN, LXXV (1960), 11–17.

John S. Smart, ed., *The Sonnets of John Milton* (Glasgow, 1921).

A. S. P. Woodhouse, "The Argument of Milton's *Comus*," UTQ, XI (1941), 46–71.

————, "*Comus* Once More," UTQ, XIX (1950), 218–23.

MAJOR POEMS

Douglas Bush, *Paradise Lost in Our Time* (Cornell Univ. Press, 1945).

Jackson I. Cope, *The Metaphoric Structure of "PL"* (Johns Hopkins Univ. Press, 1962).

John Diekhoff, *Milton's Paradise Lost, a Commentary on the Argument* (Columbia Univ. Press, 1946; reprinted, New York, 1958).

Joseph E. Duncan, "Milton's Four-in-One Hell," HLQ, XX (1957), 127–36.

Allan H. Gilbert, "Is *Samson Agonistes* Unfinished?" PQ, XXVIII (1949), 98–106.

————, *On the Composition of Paradise Lost* (Univ. of North Carolina Press, 1947).

James Holly Hanford, "The Temptation Motive in Milton," SP, XV (1918), 176–94.

Merritt Y. Hughes, "The Christ of *Paradise Regained* and the Renaissance Heroic Tradition," SP, XXXV (1938), 254–77.

Maurice Kelley, *This Great Argument: a Study of Milton's De*

Doctrina Christiana as a Gloss upon Paradise Lost (Princeton Univ. Press, 1941).

Watson Kirkconnell, *The Celestial Cycle: the Theme of Paradise Lost in World Literature, with Translations of the Major Analogues* (Univ. of Toronto Press, 1952).

F. Michael Krouse, *Milton's Samson and the Christian Tradition* (Princeton Univ. Press, 1949).

Barbara Kiefer Lewalski, "Theme and Structure in *Paradise Regained*," *SP*, LVII (1960), 186–220.

C. S. Lewis, *A Preface to Paradise Lost,* Revised ed. (Oxford Univ. Press, 1960).

Isabel Gamble MacCaffery, *Paradise Lost as 'Myth'* (Harvard Univ. Press, 1959).

E. L. Marilla, *The Central Problem of Paradise Lost: The Fall of Man* (Harvard Univ. Press, 1953).

Louis L. Martz, "*Paradise Regained:* The Meditative Combat," *English Literary History,* XXVII (1960), 223–47.

Ruth Mohl, *Studies in Spenser, Milton and the Theory of Monarchy* (Columbia Univ. Press, 1949; reprinted, 1962).

William R. Parker, "The Date of *Samson Agonistes*," *PQ*, XXVIII (1949), 145–66.

————, *Milton's Debt to Greek Tragedy in Samson Agonistes* (Johns Hopkins Univ. Press, 1937).

Elizabeth M. Pope, *Paradise Regained: the Tradition and the Poem* (Johns Hopkins Univ. Press, 1947).

John T. Shawcross, "The Chronology of Milton's Major Poems," *PMLA*, LXXVI (1961), 345–58.

Arnold Stein, *Answerable Style: Essays on Paradise Lost* (Univ. of Minnesota Press, 1953).

————, *Heroic Knowledge: An Interpretation of Paradise Regained and Samson Agonistes* (Univ. of Minnesota Press, 1957).

Robert H. West, *Milton and the Angels* (Univ. of Georgia Press, 1955).

Arnold Williams, *The Common Expositor: An Account of the Commentaries on Genesis, 1527–1633* (Univ. of North Carolina Press, 1948).

A. S. P. Woodhouse, "Pattern in *Paradise Lost*," *UTQ*, XXII (1953), 109–27.

INDEX OF TITLES AND FIRST LINES

Italicized page numbers refer to Textual Notes.